EXECUTIVE COMPENSATION DISCLOSURE RULES

MARK A. BORGES

update of *SEC Executive Compensation Disclosure Rules*

Business Law Section

Cover design by Tamara Kowalski/ABA Publishing.

Page layout by Quadrum Solutions.

Printed in the United States of America.

16 15 14 13 12 5 4 3 2 1

Library of Congress Cataloging-in-Publication Data

Borges, Mark A.
    Executive compensation disclosure rules / By Mark Borges.
        p. cm.
    Includes index.
    ISBN 978-1-61438-571-4 (alk. paper)
    1. Executives—Salaries, etc.—Law and legislation—United States. 2. Disclosure of information—Law and legislation—United States. I. Title.
    KF1424.B675 2012
    344.7301'281658—dc23

                    2012022532

Contents

3 | Compensation Discussion and Analysis   65

7 | Supplemental Narrative Disclosure 205

8 | Outstanding Equity Awards at Fiscal Year-End Table 217

9 | Option Exercises and Stock Vested Table 231

10 | Pension Benefits Table 241

11 | Nonqualified Deferred Compensation Table   255

12 | Potential Payments upon Termination or Change-in-Control Disclosure   269

Acknowledgments

When I was first approached with the idea of writing a book on the Securities and Exchange Commission's executive and director compensation disclosure rules in the fall of 2006, it seemed like a good idea—and a fairly straightforward task. Little did I appreciate the time involved in bringing the idea to fruition and my difficulty in sticking to a drafting schedule. Fortunately, a seemingly never-ending sequence of developments (starting with the Commission's December 2006 rule changes) gave me a series of plausible excuses as to why my delays would actually make the book better.

As is typically the case with sweeping regulatory changes, the years immediately following the adoption of the new rules resulted in numerous interpretive questions as the disclosure requirements were applied to ever-evolving executive compensation arrangements. In addition, in a surprising—and unprecedented—move, the Commission reversed its 2006 rule change in later 2009, creating a compliance challenge requiring a fair amount of explanation, both to companies complying with the disclosure requirements and investors attempting to understand the information provided. Finally, Congress, responding to the global economic crisis of 2008 and 2009, enacted a number of pay disclosure-related measures, including the landmark shareholder advisory vote on executive compensation, which have—and, over the next several years, will—dramatically change the executive compensation landscape.

These developments, some of which are ongoing, have necessitated this second edition of *SEC Executive Compensation Disclosure Rules*.

As with the original manuscript, this update would not have been possible without the tireless efforts of Susana Darwin, the Executive Editor for the Business Law Section at ABA Publishing. Understanding when needed, firm when required, and always helpful, I continue to be enormously grateful to Susana for her dedication, professionalism, and guidance. In many ways, this book is as much hers as it is mine.

I have also benefited from the assistance of many colleagues who have generously given of their time and expertise in the publication of this book. First and foremost is Alan Kailer, who willingly—and with limited recompense—took time to read my original manuscript and made numerous helpful comments and suggestions. I thank Alan for his observations and assistance, as well as for his friendship. Several other colleagues have contributed, and continue to contribute, to my understanding of the subject matter and the various issues and solutions that are discussed in this edition. These include Janet Den-Uyl, Alan Dye, Susan Eichen, Doug Frederick, Mike Kesner, Amy Knieriem, David Lynn, Sue Morgan, Ron Mueller, Polly Plimpton, Carol Silverman, and Scott Spector. I am also indebted to Keith Higgins, who not only continues to answer my questions and shape my thinking about disclosure-related issues, but also produced some of the very helpful written materials that were invaluable to my research. Notwithstanding this help and advice, the entire responsibility for the content of this book rests with me.

I would also like to thank my colleagues at Compensia, particularly Mark Edwards and Tim Sparks, for their encouragement and support, as well as for their flexibility in allowing me the time to work on this book among my other responsibilities. I owe a special debt to Broc Romanek and Jesse Brill who first gave me the opportunity to blog on executive and director compensation disclosure on their CompensationStandards.com website. Without that experience and exposure, I doubt that I would have been in a position to take on this project. Finally, I would like to acknowledge Harry Conaway, who brought me to Mercer and always indulged my ideas—no matter how overly ambitious and optimistic they may have been.

Above all, I would like to thank my family: my wife, Lynne, and my children, Grace, Elizabeth, and Christopher, for their love and support throughout this experience. You have my love and gratitude. I am forever indebted to you for creating the warm environment in which I live and work.

Mark A. Borges
June 2012

Introduction

While almost everyone who works with registrants on their executive and director compensation disclosure recognized the significance of the Securities and Exchange Commission's new rules when they were adopted in 2006, few would have predicted their central role in the aftermath of the global economic crisis of 2008 and 2009. Following the devastation on both Wall Street and Main Street, executive compensation and the relationship between pay and performance took on even greater significance as we investigated the causes of the crisis, implemented appropriate remedies, and sought to fashion responsible safeguards against a repeat experience. Executive pay also foreshadowed the larger question of income inequality in the United States, which has emerged as one of the central issues of the 2012 presidential election.

Thus, the executive and director compensation disclosure rules have taken on added importance in this environment, as they provide a window into how the senior leaders of corporate America are compensated, along with the rationale for those compensation decisions. They have also altered the way boards of directors and board compensation committees approach compensation decisions, as it is now wellunderstood that the absence of a clear explanation for a specific compensation action may not only put them on the defensive but also erode their support from shareholders.

That registrants have been able to shape their disclosures in response to changes in the environment and expectations is largely the result of the SEC's decision to adopt a "principles-based," rather than a prescriptive, disclosure system. Under this approach, registrants are required to tailor the general disclosure requirements to their own specific situations. While the transition was not always easy, generally registrants have been able to structure their disclosure not only to set forth, in a comprehensive and clear manner, their key compensation actions and decisions, but also to adjust the disclosure as needed to address the key concerns of investors and regulators at any given point in time; whether it involve equity award grant practices or the potential effect of compensation-related risk on the overall viability of the business.

This principles-based system lays out the key reporting objectives (instead of prescribing exactly what must be disclosed) and then provides guidance explaining the purpose of the objectives and demonstrating how they are to be applied using several common examples. From these objectives and examples, registrants must disclose the material aspects of their executive compensation program so that investors understand how the program works and how the amounts reported in the various compensation tables were determined.

This approach has served two important purposes. First, it ensures that a registrant's disclosure will address all of the compensation earned by and paid to its named executives, thereby eliminating the temptation for some registrants to disclose only those items that fall within the "four corners" of the rules. Second, and perhaps more notably, it establishes a system that effectively encompasses new compensation techniques as they emerge, thereby avoiding the persistent lag between compensation practices and their eventual disclosure.

Even with a half dozen years of complying with the rules under their belts, many registrants continue to face challenges in drafting their disclosure as they introduce increasingly more sophisticated and complex arrangements into their executive compensation programs. Further, although the rules are certainly more flexible, they are still complex and, at times, highly technical in nature, perhaps a reflection of the dynamic nature of executive compensation, a subject that has become a key facet of the ongoing debate about our nation's economic policies and objectives. Thus, even within the parameters of a principles-based disclosure system, most registrants have encountered questions about whether particular compensation items have to be disclosed and, if so, how to disclose them.

This book has been written as an aid to practitioners and other individuals who are responsible for compliance with these requirements. It is intended to provide an in-depth analysis of the executive and director compensation disclosure rules, their interpretation and application to various common situations, and developing trends. It describes and explains the requirements of the rules, drawing from both the language of the rules themselves as well as the related SEC releases, which contain significant commentary on how the rules are to be construed and applied. It also integrates into the discussion the supplemental guidance that has been issued by the SEC's Division of Corporation Finance since the rules were adopted, as well as the commentary and observations of experienced securities practitioners who regularly advise registrants on their disclosure obligations. Hopefully, it can serve as a single reference source for an understanding of the rules and how they are to be applied.

Chapter 1 discusses the history of executive and director compensation disclosure under the federal securities laws, as well as the evolution of the 2006 rules and their progeny. Subsequent chapters address the rules themselves. Chapter 2 explains concepts of general applicability—the registrants that are subject to the rules, the executives and directors whose compensation must be disclosed, the compensation that must be reported, and the SEC's overarching mandate that the disclosure be drafted in conformity with its plain English principles.

Chapter 3 covers the Compensation Discussion and Analysis, as well as the Compensation Committee Report that must accompany it. Chapter 4 examines the Summary Compensation Table and the various compensation components that must be reported therein. Chapter 5 is devoted to executive perquisites and other personal benefits, a subcategory of the information that must be reported in the Summary Compensation Table, but an item of special interest to investors, regulators, and the media. Chapter 6 addresses the Grants of Plan-Based Awards Table, which contains information supplementing the disclosure in the Summary Compensation Table, while Chapter 7 discusses the narrative disclosure that is to accompany these two required tables. Chapter 8 looks at the Outstanding Equity Awards at Fiscal Year-End Table, and Chapter 9 covers the Options Exercised and Stock Vested Table. These two tables track the life cycle of equity-based awards following their grant until they ultimately result in a compensatory benefit to a named executive.

Chapters 10 through 12 review the disclosure requirements for post-employment compensation arrangements. Chapter 10 covers retirement plans and other defined benefit and actuarial arrangements. Chapter 11 looks at nonqualified deferred compensation plans and arrangements, as well as nonqualified defined contribution plans. Chapter 12 addresses severance and other payments and benefits that are to be provided to the named executives upon a termination of employment or in connection with a change in control of the registrant.

Chapter 13 explains the Director Compensation Table, which, in most respects, parallels the Summary Compensation Table. Chapter 14 looks ate several other compensation-related disclosure requirements under the federal securities laws, including the performance graph, equity compensation plan disclosure, compensation plan disclosure under Schedule 14A of the Securities Exchange Act of 1934, the proxy disclosure rules, the corporate governance disclosure requirements for board compensation committees, compensation-related risk disclosure, and the related person transaction disclosure rules. Finally, Chapter 15 discusses the provisions that have so dramatically affected the area of executive compensation disclosure—the various shareholder advisory votes on executive compensation required by the Dodd-Frank Wall Street Reform and Consumer Protection Act.

To round out the materials, appendices are provided that contain the current version of the executive and director compensation disclosure rules as set forth in Item 402 of Regulation S-K, various speeches by officials of the SEC's Division of Corporation Finance on the rules and various compliance matters, and the most recent guidance from the Division of Corporation Finance on the application of the rules.

While this book reflects all of the guidance that has been published and interpretations that have been issued by the SEC up to the date of publication, it does not purport to address every issue that may arise (or has already arisen) in applying the rules to current executive and director compensation practices and decisions. It is my hope that the framework that I have established here, which largely follows the outline of the rules themselves as set forth in Item 402 of Regulation S-K, will continue to be updated and expanded to incorporate the additional guidance, interpretations, and practical responses to these issues as they emerge. In addition, I expect that future additions will continue to reflect the practical advice that is developed to address investor expectations and many of the more common disclosure questions that confront registrants.

Unlike other SEC rulemaking projects, which have been adopted and implemented at a satisfactory level within a single reporting cycle, compliance with the executive and director compensation disclosure rules is an evolving and continually changing endeavor. The initial compliance efforts during the 2007 proxy season were subject to extensive review by the Staff of the SEC's Division of Corporation Finance, resulting in a Staff Report in October 2007 that was intended to guide the preparation of registrant disclosures going forward. While the SEC Staff has not issued any subsequent reports on the quality of registrant compliance, the review of executive compensation disclosures has been incorporated into the Staff's triennial review of registrants' periodic reports under the Securities Exchange Act of 1934 and, as reflected by Staff comments on these filings, continues to be an area of significant attention. Moreover, as disclosure practices evolve in response to the mandatory shareholder advisory vote on executive compensation, which was first required during the 2011 proxy season, it is expected that the form and content of this principles-based disclosure will similarly evolve. Additionally, as the SEC completes its required rulemaking to implement the remaining compensation-related disclosure provisions of the Dodd-Frank Act, the resulting disclosures may prompt a further response from Congress, or the SEC itself, as investors and the general public react to current compensation policies and practices. Consequently, executive and director compensation disclosure is likely to remain an important topic for the foreseeable future. Hopefully, this book will serve as a useful tool to aid registrants and their advisors as we meet these challenges.

1

The Executive Compensation Disclosure Rules

How They Came About

Since the inception of the federal securities laws in the 1930s, a registrant's executive and director compensation practices and decisions have been considered an integral part of the mix of information that is to be made available to the marketplace. Investors rely on this information for critical insights into how a registrant manages its assets and deploys capital. Compensation consultants and human resources professionals use this data to monitor compensation trends and formulate effective pay strategies. The media routinely scrutinize compensation program details to better understand the behind-the-scenes machinations in executive suites and corporate boardrooms. Proxy advisory firms analyze the information to develop voting recommendations and gauge corporate governance compliance. Elected officials use the data to bolster fiscal and public policy initiatives. And, perhaps most importantly, the populace at large forms its perception of corporate ethics and behavior from this information.

Thus, the Securities and Exchange Commission's (SEC's) decision in 2006 to substantially rewrite its executive and director compensation disclosure rules was one of the seminal legal developments of the decade.

In the post-Sarbanes-Oxley environment of increased shareholder activism and at a time when executive compensation was perceived to be spiraling out of control, the SEC proposals drew the attention and input of each of these constituencies, resulting in a revised set of rules that corrected the deficiencies of the former requirements, addressed the exigencies of current pay practices, and established a foundation to ensure full and meaningful disclosure into the future. A scant four years later, this foundation was used as the vehicle for implementing several significant corporate governance reforms under the Dodd-Frank Wall Street Reform and Consumer Protection Act,[1] including the potentially far-reaching shareholder advisory vote on executive compensation.[2]

The basic framework of the rules contemplates that a registrant's disclosure is to begin with a narrative discussion analyzing its executive compensation program, explaining its pay decisions for the last completed fiscal year, and providing context for the information presented in the compensation tables. The remaining disclosure is divided into three broad categories:

- a table presenting all compensation earned and paid to the registrant's senior executive officers over a three-year period, accompanied by a table supplementing this information;
- a set of tables reporting holdings of equity-based awards and amounts realized from those holdings; and
- a set of tables and narrative disclosures reporting accumulated retirement benefits and potential post-employment payments, including amounts payable upon a change-in-control of the registrant.

Underlying the rules is the fundamental precept that the requirements are "principles based." Moving away from prior disclosure approaches, which were largely prescriptive in nature and, consequently, led to highly rigid and formalistic disclosure, the line-item requirements of the rules are simply the starting point for the disclosure. When necessary, a registrant must go beyond the literal provisions of the rules to ensure the full and fair disclosure of the details of its executive compensation program. At times, this will require a thorough understanding of the objectives of the disclosure requirements. At other times, it will require

---

1. Pub. L. No. 111-203, 123 Stat. 1376 (July 21, 2010).
2. *See* Chapter 15.

sensitivity to investor needs and expectations. In all instances, it will require a registrant to be creative and flexible. Ultimately, the goal is a full and transparent presentation of a registrant's executive compensation program and decision-making process.

The Regulatory Framework

The SEC's integrated disclosure system[3] provides a single comprehensive reporting and disclosure system for registration statements, periodic reports, and other documents that must be filed under the Securities Act of 1933, as amended (Securities Act),[4] and the Securities Exchange Act of 1934, as amended (Exchange Act).[5] This system includes a uniform set of rules found in Regulation S-K that contain the specific items of information that must be included in SEC filings.[6]

While there are a number of compensation-related provisions in the SEC's rules,[7] the bulk of the disclosure requirements for executive and director compensation are found in Item 402 of Regulation S-K.[8] Thus, where a registration statement, periodic report, or other document calls for compensation information, Item 402 prescribes the information that must be provided.

---

3. The various rulemaking projects that created the integrated disclosure system were first adopted in 1980. This system replaced the two separate sets of disclosure requirements that had developed over the years under the Securities Act of 1933 and the Securities Exchange Act of 1934.

4. 15 U.S.C. § 77a et seq. (2004).

5. 15 U.S.C. § 78a et seq. (2004).

6. *See* Regulation S-K (17 C.F.R. 229.10 et seq.). In November 2007, the separate set of rules for small business issuers contained in Regulation S-B (17 C.F.R. 228.10 et seq.) was repealed and replaced by a new set of provisions incorporated into Regulation S-K. *See* Smaller Reporting Company Regulatory Relief and Simplification, Release Nos. 33-8876, 34-56994, 39-2451 (Dec. 19, 2007), 73 Fed. Reg. 934 (Jan. 4, 2008), *available at* http://www.sec.gov/rules/final/2007/33-8876.pdf. Companies that have less than $75 million in public equity float and companies without a calculable public equity float but with revenues of less than $50 million in the previous year qualify for this scaled disclosure system. The rule changes also combined for most purposes the "small business issuer" and "nonaccelerated filer" categories of smaller companies into a new category of "smaller reporting companies."

7. *See, e.g.*, Item 201(d) of Regulation S-K (17 C.F.R. 229.201(d)) (equity compensation plan disclosure), Item 404(a) of Regulation S-K (17 C.F.R. 229.404) (related person transactions disclosure), Item 407(e) of Regulation S-K (17 C.F.R. 229.407(e)) (compensation committee disclosure), and Item 10 of Schedule 14A (17 C.F.R. 240.14a-101) (compensation plans).

8. 17 C.F.R. 229.402. Analogous requirements for smaller reporting companies are contained in Item 402(l) of Regulation S-K.

In the case of Securities Act filings, executive and director compensation information must be included in registration statements on Form S-1,[9] S-3,[10] S-4,[11] and S-11.[12] In the case of Exchange Act filings, executive and director compensation information must be included in registration statements on Form 10,[13] annual reports on Form 10-K,[14] and proxy and information statements.[15] Under the SEC's rules, the information required in Part III of an annual report on Form 10-K may be incorporated by reference from the registrant's proxy or information statement pertaining to the election of directors if this document has been or will be filed within 120 days of the end of the fiscal year.[16] Since annual reports must be filed within a fixed period of time following the end of the fiscal year, while the delivery of proxy and information statements is tied to the date of the registrant's annual meeting of shareholders, typically executive and director compensation information is physically presented in the proxy or information statement and not the annual report.

History of Compensation Disclosure Requirements

The requirements for the disclosure of executive and director compensation information are set forth in Schedule A to the Securities Act and Section 12(b) of the Exchange Act. Schedule A lists the types of information that are to be included in Securities Act registration statements.[17] Item 14 of Schedule A requires disclosure of the

---

9. *See* Item 11(l) of Form S-1 (17 C.F.R. 239.11).

10. *See* Item I.B.4(c) of Form S-3 (17 C.F.R. 239.13). Typically, the information is incorporated by reference from the registrant's annual report on Form 10-K.

11. *See* Items 18(a)(7)(ii) and 19(a)(7)(ii) of Form S-4 (17 C.F.R. 239.25). The information is required in the prospectus if the registrant is a Form S-1 issuer and may be incorporated by reference into the prospectus if the registrant is a Form S-3-eligible issuer.

12. *See* Item 22 of Form S-11 (17 C.F.R. 239.18). This form is used to register the securities of certain real estate companies.

13. *See* Item 6 of Form 10 (17 C.F.R. 249.210).

14. *See* Item 11 of Part III of Form 10-K (17 C.F.R. 249.310).

15. *See* Item 8 of Schedule 14A (17 C.F.R. 240.14a-101) and Item 1 of Schedule 14C (17 C.F.R. 240.14c-101).

16. *See* General Instruction G(3) of Form 10-K. If this 120-day deadline will not be met, the information must be physically included in the annual report.

17. *See* Section 7(a) of the Securities Act (15 U.S.C. § 77g(a)) and Schedule A (15 U.S.C. § 77aa).

remuneration, paid or estimated to be paid, by the issuer or its predecessor, directly or indirectly, during the past year and ensuing year to (a) the directors or persons performing similar functions, and (b) its officers and other persons, naming them wherever such remuneration exceeded $25,000 during any such year.

Similarly, Section 12(b) of the Exchange Act[18] requires disclosure of

(D) the directors, officers, and underwriters, and each security holder of record holding more than 10 per centum of any class of any equity security of the issuer (other than an exempted security), their remuneration and their interests in the securities of, and their material contracts with, the issuers and any person directly or indirectly controlling or controlled by, or under direct or indirect common control with the issuer; [and]

(E) remuneration to others than directors and officers exceeding $20,000 per annum.[19]

In 1938, the SEC adopted its first executive and director compensation disclosure requirements for proxy statements.[20] Since then, the SEC has periodically revised and updated these rules, alternating between narrative, tabular, and combinations of narrative and tabular disclosure to present the required information.[21] While these revisions occurred as the SEC deemed them to be necessary and appropriate, typically they took place about once a decade, reflecting the ongoing challenge in ensuring that this information was clear and useful to investors in an environment where compensation strategies and techniques were constantly evolving and changing.

---

18. 15 U.S.C. § 78*l*(b).

19. The SEC's rules substantially implement these requirements.

20. *See* Release No. 33-1823 (Aug. 11, 1938).

21. *See, e.g.,* Release No. 34-3347 (Dec. 18, 1942), 7 Fed. Reg. 10,653 (introducing the first required tabular disclosure); Release No. 34-4775 (Dec. 11, 1952), 17 Fed. Reg. 11,431 (introducing a separate table for pensions and deferred remuneration); Uniform and Integrated Reporting Requirements: Management Remuneration, Release No. 33-6003 (Dec. 4, 1978), 43 Fed. Reg. 58,151 (expanding the required tabular disclosure to cover all forms of compensation); and Disclosure of Executive Compensation, Release No. 33-6486 (Sept. 23, 1983), 48 Fed. Reg. 44,467 (limiting the required tabular disclosure to cash remuneration).

1992 Rules

Prior to 2006, the SEC had last undertaken a major review and update of the executive and director compensation disclosure rules in 1992.[22] This initiative was prompted by a then-growing clamor over excess executive pay and the lack of transparency in the compensation-setting process. In less than eight months, the SEC proposed and adopted what was considered at the time to be a drastic and sweeping set of changes to the then-existing disclosure rules. These changes established the basic disclosure framework on which the 2006 changes were built.

Eliminating most of the previously required narrative disclosure and plan descriptions, the 1992 changes adopted a tabular approach to promote comparability from year to year and from registrant to registrant.[23] They introduced the Summary Compensation Table, a tabular presentation of the individual compensation elements for a registrant's chief executive officer and four most highly compensated executive officers (other than the CEO) at fiscal year-end for the most recent fiscal year and the immediately preceding two fiscal years.[24] Several additional disclosure tables were required to be provided to supplement the information in the Summary Compensation Table, including

- a table to report specific information about stock options, stock appreciation rights, and other similar instruments granted during the last completed fiscal year;[25]
- a table to report the amount realized during the last completed fiscal year from the exercise of stock options, stock appreciation rights, and other similar instruments and the amount of

---

22. *See* Executive Compensation Disclosure, Release Nos. 33-6962, 34-31327, IC-19032 (Oct. 16, 1992), 57 Fed. Reg. 48,126 (Oct. 21, 1992), *as modified,* Executive Compensation Disclosure: Correction, Release Nos. 33-6966, 34-31420, IC-19085 (Nov. 9, 1992), 57 Fed. Reg. 53,985 (Nov. 9, 1992). The 1992 changes were part of a package of reforms adopted by the SEC to give shareholders a greater voice in executive compensation matters. These reforms included a change to an interpretive position permitting nonbinding shareholder proposals on executive and director compensation in proxy statements and the commission of a study as to the adequacy of the then-current accounting rules for the grant of stock options. *See* SEC Press Release 1992-12, Statement by Richard C. Breeden on Executive Compensation Issues (Feb. 13, 1992).

23. *See* Executive Compensation and Related Person Disclosure, Release Nos. 33-8732A, 34-54302A, IC-27444A (Aug. 29, 2006), 71 Fed. Reg. 53,158 (Sept. 8, 2006) [hereinafter Adopting Release], *available at* http://www.sec.gov/rules/final/2006/33-8732a.pdf, at Section II.

24. *See* former Item 402(b).

25. The Option/SAR Grants in Last Fiscal Year Table. *See* former Item 402(c).

unrealized appreciation in such instruments as of the end of the last fiscal year;[26]

- a table to report long-term incentive plan awards granted during the last completed fiscal year;[27] and
- a table to report historical information about the repricing of stock options and stock appreciation rights held by senior executive officers at any time during the past ten years.[28]

Under the 1992 changes, registrants were required to include in their disclosure a Board Compensation Committee Report describing their policies for compensating their executive officers, as well as discussion of the specific decisions relating to their chief executive officer's compensation for the last completed fiscal year.[29] To emphasize the significance of this report, it was to be presented over the names of the directors who made the decisions.[30] Also, registrants had to provide a graph comparing their cumulative total shareholder return against both a broad equity market index and a group of peer companies.[31]

Additional disclosure was required about potential retirement benefits under defined benefit or actuarial plans,[32] employment agreements and change-in-control arrangements,[33] and the compensation of directors.[34]

These rules became effective in the fall of 1992 and, consequently, were in place during the 1993 proxy season. Following the 1993 proxy season, the staff of the SEC's Division of Corporation Finance (SEC Staff) reviewed the executive and director compensation disclosure of nearly 20 percent of the registrants filing proxy statements during the

---

26. The Aggregated Option/SAR Exercises in Last Fiscal Year and Fiscal Year-End Option/SAR Values Table. *See* former Item 402(d).

27. The Long-Term Incentive Plans—Awards in Last Fiscal Year Table. *See* former Item 402(e).

28. The Ten-Year Option/SAR Repricings Table. *See* former Item 402(i)(3). This table was required only if a registrant had adjusted or amended the exercise price of an outstanding stock option or stock appreciation right held by a senior executive officer during the last completed fiscal year. *See* former Item 402(i)(1).

29. *See* former Item 402(k).

30. *See* former Item 402(k)(3).

31. *See* former Item 402(l).

32. *See* former Item 402(f). This disclosure included both narrative and tabular information through the presentation of a Pension Plan Table. *See* former Item 402(f)(1).

33. *See* former Item 402(h).

34. *See* former Item 402(g).

1993 proxy season (approximately 1,000 registrants). Subsequently, the SEC issued a release summarizing the results of the Staff's review and proposing a series of technical corrections to the rules to address problems that had been identified.[35] These revisions were adopted substantially as proposed.[36] Before moving on to other matters, the Staff undertook one final review of proxy statements during the 1994 proxy season to monitor the quality of compliance.

Proposed 1995 Revisions

Shortly after registrants had completed their second proxy season under the 1992 disclosure requirements, the SEC, in an attempt to build on that effort, proposed several refinements to these rules.[37] Among other things, these refinements would have required registrants to present information regarding director compensation in tabular form and permitted them to shift some of the disclosure items then required in proxy and information statements to their annual reports on Form 10-K.[38] Although the SEC solicited and received public comments on the proposals, they were never adopted.

The Current Rules

The 2006 changes to the executive compensation disclosure rules were an outgrowth of the SEC's desire to update and improve the 1992 disclosure requirements to reflect the experiences of registrants in complying with these requirements and of investors in understanding and analyzing the resulting compensation information. In addition, as

---

35. *See* Executive Compensation Disclosure; Securityholder Lists and Mailing Requests, Release Nos. 33-7009, 34-32723 (Aug. 6, 1993), 58 Fed. Reg. 42,882 (Aug. 12, 1993).

36. *See* Executive Compensation Disclosure; Securityholder Lists and Mailing Requests, Release Nos. 33-7032, 34-33229 (Nov. 22, 1993), 58 Fed. Reg. 63,010 (Nov. 29, 1993).

37. *See* Streamlining and Consolidation of Executive and Director Compensation Disclosure, Release Nos. 33-7184, 34-35894 (June 27, 1995), 60 Fed. Reg. 35,633 (July 10, 1995), *available at* http://www.sec.gov/rules/proposed/33-7184.txt.

38. Under this latter proposal, registrants would have been permitted to include the Aggregated Option/SAR Exercises in Last Fiscal Year and Fiscal Year-End Option/SAR Value Table, the Long-Term Incentive Plans Awards in Last Fiscal Years Table, the defined benefit or actuarial plan disclosure, the employment contracts and termination of employment and change-in-control arrangements disclosure, and the Report on Repricing of Options/SARs to their annual reports on Form 10-K.

the SEC noted, during the intervening years compensation programs had become increasing more sophisticated, varied, and complex, essentially outpacing the reach of the 1992 requirements. Compensation elements that had barely existed a decade earlier, such as nonqualified deferred compensation arrangements, now comprised a significant, and sometimes predominant, portion of an executive compensation package. Thus, to reinvigorate the disclosure process, as well as to provide investors with a "clearer and more complete picture of [a registrant's] compensation,"[39] the SEC began to consider possible rule changes.

Proposed Rules

On January 27, 2006, the SEC proposed amendments to Item 402 and several related rules.[40] The proposed revisions were both comprehensive and extensive, reflecting the considerable time and effort that the SEC had devoted to this subject over the preceding years. Pronouncing the tabular disclosure approach to be sound, the SEC sought to build on the strengths of the existing disclosure requirements.

Among other things, the proposals included

- requiring disclosure of the compensation of a registrant's chief financial officer;
- replacing the Board Compensation Committee Report with a new Compensation Discussion and Analysis (CD&A);
- adding a total compensation column to the Summary Compensation Table;
- revamping the supplemental compensation tables and the pension benefits table;
- adding a new table covering nonqualified deferred compensation;
- requiring an estimate of the payments and benefits potentially receivable upon a termination of employment or a change-in-control of a registrant; and

---

39. *See* John W. White, Director, Division of Corporation Finance, U.S. Securities & Exchange Comm'n, *Where's the Analysis?*, Remarks Before the Second Annual Proxy Disclosure Conference: Tackling Your 2008 Compensation Disclosures (Oct. 9, 2007) [hereinafter White Analysis Speech], *available at* http://www.sec.gov/news/speech/2007/spch100907jww.htm.

40. These included rules governing related party transactions, director independence and other corporate governance matters, the current reporting of compensation matters, and beneficial ownership. *See* Executive Compensation and Related Party Disclosure, Release Nos. 33-8655, 34-53185, IC-27218 (Jan. 27, 2006), 71 Fed. Reg. 6542 (Feb. 8, 2006), *available at* http://www.sec.gov/rules/proposed/33-8655.pdf.

- requiring that the disclosure be presented in plain English.

The SEC solicited public comment on the proposals until April 10, 2006, and, reflecting the widespread interest in the subject, received over 20,000 comments,[41] at the time the most of any proposed rulemaking project in the SEC's 75-year history. The comments came from across the spectrum of preparers and users of executive and director compensation information and included, among others, registrants, institutional investors, retail investors, attorneys, accountants, compensation consultants, actuaries, academics, members of the media, proxy advisory firms, trade associations, and elected officials. While virtually all of the commenters supported the SEC's objectives of updating the executive and director compensation disclosure requirements, they split on how the rules should be revised. As a result, the SEC received an almost overwhelming number of suggestions, criticisms, aspirations, and alternate proposals that it was required to sift through and consider.

The SEC's deliberations on the proposals were further influenced by the stock option backdating scandal that erupted during the spring of 2006. As highlighted in several prominent media reports,[42] academic studies of historical stock option grant practices revealed an unusual correlation between stock price movement and option grants. In numerous instances, a registrant's stock options, particularly options held by executives, had been granted at the lowest price of a registrant's stock for the reporting period or, in some instances, for the entire fiscal year. The frequency of these incidents strongly suggested that the timing of the awards had not been coincidental. Moreover, investigations of some registrants with suspicious option grant practices had uncovered instances where the exercise price of options had been backdated (that is, the exercise price had been based on a stock price other than the price on the option's date of grant). The large number of such discoveries, combined with the gravity of their consequences, prompted the SEC to

---

41. Ultimately, the SEC received approximately 30,000 comments (Comment file No. S7-03-06) on the rules (as proposed and adopted), including over 28,800 communications in a standard form asking the SEC to adopt new disclosure rules, require the compensation of chief executive officers be set by independent directors, and require registrants to disclose pay-for-performance data. These comment letters are available on the SEC's Web site at http://www.sec.gov/rules/proposed/s70306.shtml.

42. See, e.g., Charles Forelle and James Bandler, The Perfect Payday: Some CEOs Reap Millions by Including Stock Options When They Are Most Valuable: Luck—or Something Else? The Wall Street Journal, A1 (March 18, 2006).

address the disclosure of equity award grant practices when it adopted the proposed compensation rules changes.

Final Rules

On July 26, 2006, just six months after its proposal, the SEC adopted the current rules by a 5-0 vote.[43] Reflecting their scope and complexity, the release containing the text of the rules was not published until August 29, 2006.[44] At the same time, the SEC published an additional release soliciting additional public comment on its proposal to require the disclosure of compensation information for up to three highly compensated nonexecutive employees.[45] To date, this latter proposal had not been adopted.

The current rules became effective for Annual Reports on Form 10-K (and former Form 10-KSB) filed for fiscal years ending on or after December 15, 2006.[46] They also became effective for Securities Act registration statements and Exchange Act registration statements (including preeffective and posteffective amendments), and for any proxy or information statements filed on or after December 15, 2006, that were required to include Item 402 and 404 disclosure for fiscal years ending on or after December 15, 2006.[47] To assist registrants in transitioning to the rules, the SEC Staff issued a series of nine questions and answers concerning their application to a variety of scenarios.[48]

Following the adoption of the rules, John W. White, then the director of the SEC's Division of Corporation Finance, delivered a series of speeches elaborating on the objectives of the new rules and offering

---

43. *See* SEC Press Release 2006-123, SEC Votes to Adopt Changes to Disclosure Requirements Concerning Executive Compensation and Related Matters (July 26, 2006), *available at* http://www.sec.gov/news/press/2006/2006-123.htm.

44. *See* the Adopting Release, *supra* note 23. The Adopting Release reflects revisions to Release No. 33-8732 to conform with the publication of two releases in the Federal Register: Release No. 33-8732A and Release No. 8735, and reflects the addition of cross-references to Release No. 33-8735.

45. *See* Executive Compensation Disclosure, Release Nos. 33-8735, 34-54380, IC-27470 (Aug. 29, 2006), 71 Fed. Reg. 53,267 (Sept. 8, 2006), *available at* http://www.sec.gov/rules/proposed/2006/33-8735.pdf. Technically, this provision was not reproposed; the SEC merely solicited additional public comments.

46. *See* the Adopting Release, *supra* note 23, at Section VII.

47. *Id.*

48. This guidance is available on the SEC's Web site at http://www.sec.gov/divisions/corpfin/faqs/execcompqa.pdf.

guidance for registrants to consider in preparing their initial executive and director compensation disclosure.[49]

December 2006 Revisions

On December 22, 2006, in a surprise move, the SEC amended the rules to change the reporting of stock options and other equity awards in the Summary Compensation Table and Director Compensation Table.[50] As revised, the rules took the approach of requiring the disclosure of the compensation cost of an equity award over its requisite service period, as provided in Statement of Financial Accounting Standards (SFAS) 123(R), the predecessor to Financial Accounting Standards Board Accounting Standards Codification Topic 718, *Compensation – Stock Compensation* (FASB ASC Topic 718), rather than the award's full grant-date fair value, in these tables.[51] The amendments were adopted as interim final rules— making them immediately effective[52]—so that they could be applied to registrants' initial executive and director compensation disclosure, thereby avoiding the use of different disclosure methodologies during the transition to the rules.

The amendments had a profound effect on registrants' disclosure, requiring registrants to carefully explain the amounts reported in the Stock Awards and Option Awards columns of the Summary

49. *See* the following speeches of John W. White, Director, Division of Corporation Finance, U.S. Securities & Exchange Comm'n: *Principles Matter,* Remarks Before the Practising Law Institute Conference (Sept. 6, 2006); *The Principles Matter: Options Disclosure,* Remarks Before the Corporate Counsel Conference (Sept. 11, 2006); *An Expansive View of Teamwork: Directors, Management and the SEC,* Remarks Before the Practising Law Institute Fourth Annual Directors' Institute on Corporate Governance (Sept. 25, 2006); *Executive Compensation Disclosure and the Important Role of CFOs,* Remarks Before the CFO Executive Board (Oct. 3, 2006); and *Principles Matter: Related Person Transactions Disclosure and Disclosure Controls and Procedures,* Remarks Before the Society of Corporate Secretaries and Governance Professionals, New York Chapter (Oct. 12, 2006). These speeches are available on the SEC's Web site at http://www.sec.gov/news/speech/speecharchive/2006speech.shtml#staff.

50. *See* Executive Compensation Disclosure, Release Nos. 33-8765, 34-55009 (Dec. 22, 2006), 71 Fed. Reg. 78,338 (Dec. 29, 2006), *available at* http://www.sec.gov/rules/final/2006/33-8765.pdf.

51. For a discussion of these requirements, see Chapter 4.

52. The interim final rules were effective on Dec. 29, 2007. *See* Division of Corporation Finance, Item 402 of Regulation S-K—Executive Compensation (Aug. 8, 2007) [hereinafter Initial Staff Guidance], *available at* http://www.sec.gov/divisions/corpfin/guidance/execcomp402interp.htm, at Q&A 1.01. Compliance was required for proxy statements, information statements, and registration statements filed on or after Dec. 15, 2006, that were required to include Item 402 disclosure for fiscal years ending on or after Dec. 15, 2006, and for annual reports on Form 10-K (and former Form 10-KSB) for fiscal years ending on or after Dec. 15, 2006.

Compensation Table and Director Compensation Table and their impact on the total compensation figures reported for their executive and directors, respectively. In addition, some registrants included alternative tables to supplement the required disclosure, with the alternative table either replacing the reported equity award figures with the full grant date fair value amount or reconfiguring compensation elements to reflect their own version of total compensation, as part of their disclosure. Registrant and investor complaints about the amendments eventually led to their repeal in 2009, as discussed in the next section.

December 2009 Revisions

On July 10, 2009, the SEC proposed several amendments to its disclosure requirements, including the executive compensation disclosure rules.[53] Coming in the wake of the global economic crisis and crisis in confidence in the United States financial sector, the proposed amendments were intended to improve corporate accountability and provide additional information to enhance the ability of investors to make informed voting and investment decisions. With only minimal debate,[54] the proposed amendments, with some modifications, were adopted by the SEC on December 16, 2009.[55]

In the area of executive compensation disclosure, the amendments made two significant changes:

- They required a discussion of a registrant's compensation policies and practices as they relate to risk management and risk-taking incentives that can affect the registrant's risk and management of that risk, to the extent that risks arising from the registrant's compensation policies and practices for employees

---

53. *See* Proxy Disclosure and Solicitation Enhancements, Release Nos. 33-9052, 34-60280, IC-28817 (July 10, 2009), 74 Fed. Reg. 35,076 (July 17, 2009), *available at* http://www.sec.gov/rules/proposed/2009/33-9052.pdf.

54. The SEC received approximately 130 comment letters in response to the proposed amendments. These comment letters are available on the SEC's Web site at http://www.sec.gov/comments/s7-1309/s71309.shtml.

55. *See* Proxy Disclosure Enhancements, Release Nos. 33-9089, 34-61175, IC-29092 (December 16, 2009), 74 Fed. Reg. 68,334 (December 23, 2009) [hereinafter 2009 Adopting Release], *available at* http://www.sec.gov/rules/final/33-9089.pdf. In addition to the two items discussed in the text, the amendments also included new disclosure requirements about the fees paid to compensation consultants and their affiliates under certain circumstances. For a discussion of this requirement, see Chapter 14.

are reasonably likely to have a material adverse effect on the
registrant.[56]

- They reversed the reporting treatment of stock options and
  other equity awards in the Summary Compensation Table and
  Director Compensation Table adopted in December 2006,
  reverting back to the reporting of the aggregate grant date
  fair value of stock awards and option awards granted in the
  fiscal year as computed in accordance with FASB ASC Topic
  718,[19] rather than the dollar amount recognized for financial
  statement purposes for the fiscal year, with a special instruction
  for awards subject to performance conditions.[57]

The amendments were first applicable to proxy and information
statements, annual reports and registration statements under the
Exchange Act, registration statements under the Securities Act and
under the Investment Company Act of 1940 filed on or after February
28, 2010.[58]

Staff Interpretive Guidance

On January 24, 2007, the SEC Staff issued interpretive guidance to
assist registrants in preparing their initial executive and director
compensation disclosure under the then-new rules.[59] Consisting of a set
of 28 questions and answers of general applicability and 18 interpretive
responses regarding particular situations, the guidance updated and
replaced previous informal interpretations that had been collected and
disseminated through the Staff's Telephone Interpretations Manual.
The guidance was presented in outline form, corresponding to each of
the principal subsections of Item 402. This guidance was supplemented

---

56. *See* Item 402(s) of Regulation S-K (17 C.F.R. 229.402(s). For a discussion of this
requirement, see Chapter 14.

57. For a discussion of this amendment and its impact on the reporting of equity awards,
see Chapter 4.

58. At the same time, the SEC transferred from quarterly reports on Forms 10-Q and
annual reports on Form 10-K to the current report on Form 8-K the requirement to disclose
shareholder voting results. *See* the 2009 Adopting Release at Section II.E.

59. *See* the Initial Staff Guidance, *supra* note 52. As noted in the introduction to this
guidance, these interpretations reflected the views of the SEC Staff, and were not rules,
regulations, or statements of the SEC. Further, the SEC had neither approved nor disapproved
these interpretations. The positions taken did not necessarily contain a discussion of all material
considerations necessary to reach the conclusions stated, and they were not binding on the SEC
due to their highly informal nature. Accordingly, they were intended as general guidance and
not to be relied on as definitive.

on February 12, 2007, to add a question and answer concerning the information to be included in a preliminary proxy statement,[60] and significantly updated on August 8, 2007, to revise aspects of the original guidance and to add several additional questions and answers and interpretive responses to address to issues raised at a meeting on May 8, 2007, between the Staff and the American Bar Association's Joint Committee on Employee Benefits[61] and by registrants.[62] This update revised three questions and answers of general applicability and added 11 new questions and answers. It also updated one of the interpretive responses regarding particular situations and added nine new Staff interpretive positions.

In July 2008, the SEC Staff consolidated all of its interpretive guidance under Regulation S-K, employing a new format and numbering system.[63] This revised guidance not only incorporated all of the then-existing guidance under Item 402 of Regulation S-K, but also revised two questions and answers of general applicability and added ten new questions and answers.[64] It also revised one of the interpretive responses regarding particular situations and added one new Staff interpretive position.[65] Finally, it deleted two questions and answers which dealt with transition matters. Much of the new guidance addressed issues raised at a meeting on May 6, 2008, between the Staff and the American Bar Association's Joint Committee on Employee Benefits.[66]

---

60. *See* the Initial Staff Guidance, *supra* note 52 at Q&A 1.04.

61. *See* Questions and Answers, Technical Session between the SEC Staff and the Joint Committee on Employee Benefits (May 8, 2007), *available at* http://www.abanet.org/jceb/2007/SEC07Final.pdf. Additional helpful questions and answers on the then-new rules were published in early 2007 by Cleary Gottlieb Steen & Hamilton LLP, *Common Questions: Navigating the SEC's New Compensation Rules* (Jan. 19, 2007).

62. This update revised three of the original questions and answers and one of the interpretive positions, and added ten new questions and answers and nine interpretive positions.

63. *See* Division of Corporation Finance, Compliance and Disclosure Interpretations – Regulation S-K (July 8, 2011) [hereinafter Current Staff Guidance], *available at* http://www.sec.gov/divisions/corpfin/guidance/regs-kinterp.htm.

64. The revised questions and answers of general applicability were Q&As 118.04 and 119.07. The new questions and answers of general applicability were Q&As 118.05, 118.06, 119.12, 119.14, 119.15, 119.16, 119.17, 122.02, 125.03, and 125.04.

65. The revised interpretive response regarding a particular situation was Interpretation 217.08 and the new interpretive response was Interpretation 217.09.

66. *See* Questions and Answers, Technical Session Between the SEC Staff and the Joint Committee on Employee Benefits (May 6, 2008), *available at* http://www.americanbar.org/content/dam/aba/migrated/2011_build/employee_benefits/sec_2008.authcheckdam.pdf.

This new approach to issuing interpretive guidance greatly simplified the SEC Staff's ability to communicate its positions on questions of general applicability to registrants and their advisors, and has been used frequently in recent years. Following its July 2008 launch of the Regulation S-K interpretive guidance, the Staff has updated the guidance involving the 2006 rules ten times: May 29, 2009,[67] August 14, 2009,[68] January 20, 2010,[69] February 16, 2010,[70] March 1, 2010,[71] March 12, 2010,[72] June 4, 2010,[73] February 11, 2011,[74] March 4, 2011,[75] and July 8, 2011.[76]

Additional, albeit informal, guidance from the SEC Staff on the 2006 rules is also generally available from the American Bar Association each

---

67. This update added six new questions and answers of general applicability (Q&As 119.18, 119.19, 120.05, 120.06, 120.07, and 122.03) and one new interpretive response (Interpretation 217.14). Much of the new guidance addressed issues raised at a meeting on May 5, 2009, Between the SEC Staff and the American Bar Association's Joint Committee on Employee Benefits. See Questions and Answers, Technical Session Between the SEC Staff and the Joint Committee on Employee Benefits (May 5, 2009), available at http://www.americanbar.org/content/dam/aba/migrated/2011_build/employee_benefits/sec_2009.authcheckdam.pdf.

68. This update added two new questions and answers of general applicability (Q&As 117.03 and 125.05).

69. This update added three new questions and answers of general applicability (Q&As 117.04, 119.20, and 128A.01).

70. This updated added four new questions and answers of general applicability (Q&As 117.05, 119.21, 119.22, and 119.23).

71. This update took account of the February 29, 2010 effective date of the proxy disclosure enhancements adopted by the SEC in December 2009 and consisted of one new question and answer of general applicability (Q&A 119.24), one revised question and answer of general applicability (Q&A 119.16), one revised interpretive response regarding a particular situation (Interpretation 220.01), and the withdrawal of six questions and answers of general applicability (Q&As 119.04, 119.05, 119.11, 119.12, 119.15, and 120.05).

72. This update added three new questions and answers of general applicability (Q&As 119.25, 119.26, and 133.12).

73. This update added two new questions and answers of general applicability (Q&As 117.06 and 110.27).

74. This update involved the shareholder advisory votes on executive compensation required by new Section 14A of the Exchange Act (15 U.S.C. § 78n-1) and consisted of seven questions and answers of general applicability (Q&As 169.01. 169.02, 169.03, 169.04, 169.05, 169.06, and 128B.01).

75. This update added one new question and answer of general applicability (Q&A 118.07).

76. This update added four new questions and answers of general applicability (Q&As 108.01, 117.07, 118.08, and 119.28). It also added two questions and answers of general applicability involving Item 5.07 of Form 8-K (Q&As 121A.03 and 121A.04) that address the reporting of the vote results from the required shareholder advisory votes on executive compensation.

year following the annual meeting between the Staff and the American Bar Association's Joint Committee on Employee Benefits.[77]

The Current Staff Guidance can be found at Appendix H.

Staff Review and Comment

Following the close of the 2007 proxy season, the SEC Staff announced its intentions to conduct a focused review of the executive and director compensation disclosure prepared under the then-new rules of a selected sample of large and midsize registrants.[78] On or around August 21, 2007, the Staff sent comment letters to approximately 250 registrants. One month later, on or around September 26, 2007, comment letters were sent to approximately 100 additional registrants. Unlike a typical Staff review, these registrants were given 30 days in which to respond to the Staff comments, or to notify the Staff when a response would be forthcoming.

Based on an unscientific review of selected comment letters, it appears that the average comment letter contained seven to 12 comments. Most comments were directed to the form and content of the CD&A. Comments on the required tabular disclosure were intermittent and tended to focus on technical compliance issues. The vast majority of the comments were so-called "futures" comments, requesting that a registrant indicate that it would comply with the comment in all future filings, rather than requiring retroactive amendment of the registrant's proxy statement and/or annual report on Form 10-K.

---

77. For a summary of the questions submitted to and answers received from the meeting on May 4, 2010 with the SEC Staff, *see* Questions and Answers, Technical Session Between the SEC Staff and the Joint Committee on Employee Benefits (May 4, 2010), *available at* http://www.americanbar.org/content/dam/aba/events/employee_benefits/2010_sec_qa.authcheckdam.pdf. For a summary of the questions submitted to and answers received from the meeting on May 3, 2011 with the SEC Staff, *see* Questions and Answers, Technical Session Between the SEC Staff and the Joint Committee on Employee Benefits (May 3, 2011), *available at* http://www.americanbar.org/content/dam/aba/events/employee_benefits/2010_sec_qas.final.110811.authcheckdam.pdf. Another useful source of information about the interpretation and operation of the rules has been published, and is periodically updated, by W. Alan Kailer of Hunton & Williams, *The Securities and Exchange Commission's Executive Compensation Rules—Preparing the Executive Compensation Tables* (Jan. 2012).

78. *See* John W. White, Director, Division of Corporation Finance, U.S. Securities & Exchange Comm'n, *Corporation Finance in 2007—An Interim Report,* Remarks Before the American Bar Association Section of Business Law, Committee on Federal Regulation of Securities (Aug. 14, 2007), *available at* http://www.sec.gov/news/speech/2007/spch081407jww.htm.

Staff Report

On October 9, 2007, the SEC Staff issued a report summarizing its observations from the focused review project.[79] The report, which largely distills the comments sent to the individually reviewed companies, emphasizes two principal themes:

- The CD&A must address how and why a registrant implemented its executive compensation program and reached its specific pay decisions for the covered fiscal year.
- The disclosure is to be presented in a manner that makes it accessible to both the professional and the lay reader; thus, the CD&A and the compensation tables should be well organized, easy to follow, and written in plain English.

Like the comment letters themselves, the report focuses primarily on improving the CD&A. While the report touches on the required compensation tables, given the rigidly formatted nature of this disclosure it offers little guidance beyond a general reminder to pay close attention to the highly detailed and technical instructions that govern the tables.[80] The Staff Report was augmented by a speech by John W. White, then the director of the SEC's Division of Corporation Finance, reminding registrants of the importance of providing a thorough analysis of their executive compensation programs in their CD&A.[81]

The Staff Report can be found at Appendix I.

Staff 2009 Remarks on the Executive Compensation Disclosure Rules

In November 2009, Shelley Parratt, the Deputy Director of the SEC's Division of Corporation Finance, delivered a speech at the 4th Annual Proxy Disclosure Conference summarizing the SEC Staff's observations on the quality of the executive compensation disclosure during the

---

79. *See* Division of Corporation Finance, *Staff Observations in the Review of Executive Compensation Disclosure* (Oct. 9, 2007) [hereinafter Staff Report], *available at* http://www.sec.gov/divisions/corpfin/guidance/execcompdisclosure.htm. *See also* SEC Press Release 2007-214, Commission Staff Publishes Its Observations in the Review of Executive Compensation Disclosure (Oct. 9, 2007), *available at* http://www.sec.gov/news/press/2007/2007-214.htm.

80. The specific findings and recommendations of the Staff Report, *id.*, are discussed throughout this book, particularly in conjunction with the Compensation Discussion and Analysis. See Chapter 3.

81. *See* the White Analysis Speech, *supra* note 39.

2009 proxy season and its expectations for 2010.[82] While her remarks emphasized the need for registrants to pay particular attention to the preparation of the required analysis in the CD&A and reviewed the Staff's expectations with respect to the disclosure of the performance criteria and related target levels used in incentive compensation arrangements, they also disclosed a significant shift in the Staff's approach to reviewing the disclosure in 2010 and thereafter.

Specifically, after three year's of issuing so-called "futures" comments, the SEC Staff announced that, entering the fourth year of compliance, its expectations for quality disclosure had been heightened and that this would now be reflected in its comments. Not only has this resulted in increased scrutiny of registrants' executive compensation disclosure, it has also led to the expectation that registrants will stay abreast of the latest developments and interpretations in the disclosure area and reflect these developments and interpretations in their disclosures. In other words, registrants may no longer wait until they are individually reviewed to bring their disclosure current with the latest understanding and application of the rules. Consequently, registrants that have been determined to not be in material compliance with the rules have been required to amend their filings to bring them into compliance.

The Dodd-Frank Act

On July 21, 2010, President Barack Obama signed into law the Dodd-Frank Wall Street Reform and Consumer Protection Act (Dodd-Frank Act).[83] Although primarily devoted to reforming the financial services sector, the Dodd-Frank Act also contained several significant provisions related to executive compensation matters.[84]

---

82. *See* Shelley Parratt, Deputy Director, Division of Corporation Finance, U.S. Securities & Exchange Comm'n, *Executive Compensation Disclosure: Observations on the 2009 Proxy Season and Expectations for 2010,* Remarks Before the 4th Annual Proxy Disclosure Conference: Tackling Your 2010 Compensation Disclosures (Nov. 9, 2009), *available at* http://www.sec.gov/news/speech/2009/spch110909sp.htm

83. Pub. L. No. 111-203, 123 Stat. 1376 (July 21, 2010).

84. Two of these provisions, Sections 951 and 952, trace their origin to H.R. 4173, the "Wall Street Reform and Consumer Protection Act," which was introduced in the 111th Congress by Representative Barney Frank (D-MA). Five of the provisions, Sections 953(a), 954, 955, 956, and 957, were first introduced in the 111th Congress by Senator Christopher J. Dodd (D-CT) as part of his amendment to H.R. 4173, the "Restoring American Financial Stability Act of 2010." The remaining provision, Section 953(b), was contained in S. 3049, the "Corporate Executive Accountability Act of 2010," which was introduced in the 111th Congress by Senator Robert Menendez (D-NJ) in response to his concerns about excessive executive compensation.

Reflecting their diverse origin and varied effective dates, the implementation of the executive compensation provisions of the Dodd-Frank Act is taking place in a deliberate manner. The provisions requiring shareholder advisory votes on executive compensation and "golden parachute" compensation matters became effective during the 2011 proxy season. The remaining provisions will be effective upon the completion of SEC (and, in some instances, national securities exchange and national securities association) rulemaking, which, as of the date of this publication, had not yet been completed. Thus, these provisions may not take effect until the 2013 proxy season (or, possibly, even later).[85]

Given the potential scope and impact of these provisions, however, some registrants already have begun to comply with the spirit, if not the letter, of the provisions, in recognition of Congressional – and public – interest in the substantive topics covered.

Shareholder Approval of Executive Compensation

The central executive compensation provision of the Dodd-Frank Act is the shareholder advisory vote on executive compensation. Section 951 of the Dodd-Frank Act added Section 14A(a)(1) to the Exchange Act, which, generally, requires registrants to include a resolution in the proxy materials for their annual meetings of shareholders asking shareholders to approve, in a non-binding vote, the compensation of their executive officers, as disclosed under Item 402 of Regulation S-K (Say-on-Pay Vote). This must be done at least once every three years.[86] As the provision makes clear, the Say-on-Pay Vote is non-binding on a registrant and its board of directors, and specifically may not be construed as:

- overruling a decision by the registrant or its board of directors;
- creating or implying any change in or additional fiduciary duty for the registrant or the board; or

---

85. Section 952, which addresses compensation committee and committee advisor independence matters, provides that, no later than July 16, 2011, the SEC must, by rule, direct the national securities exchanges and national securities associations to prohibit the listing of any security of an issuer that is not in compliance with the requirements of this section. *See* Section 10C(f) of the Exchange Act (15 U.S.C. § 78j-3(f)). Each of the remaining executive compensation-related provisions is effective only upon the completion of SEC rulemaking.

86. *See* Exchange Act Rule 14a-21(a) (17 C.F.R. 240.14a-21(a)), which specifies that the Say-on-Pay Vote is required only when proxies are being solicited for an annual meeting of security holders at which directors will be elected, or a special meeting in lieu of such annual meeting, which is when disclosure of executive compensation pursuant to Item 402 is required.

- restricting or limiting the ability of shareholders to make proposals for inclusion in proxy materials relating to executive compensation.[87]

In addition, Section 14A(a)(2) of the Exchange Act requires that, not less frequently than once every six years, registrants are required to include a resolution in their proxy materials for their annual meetings of shareholders asking shareholders whether the Say-on-Pay Vote should take place every one, two, or three years (Frequency Vote).[88] Like the Say-on-Pay Vote, the results of the Frequency Vote are non-binding on a registrant or its board of directors and, among other things, is not to be construed as overruling a decision of the registrant or the board of directors.

Finally, Section 14A addresses the use of "golden parachutes" or similar compensation arrangements in connection with a merger, consolidation, or other extraordinary corporate transaction. Specifically, Section 14A(b)(1) of the Exchange Act imposes a new mandatory disclosure requirement for all proxy or consent solicitation materials pursuant to which shareholders are being asked to approve a merger or other extraordinary corporate transaction. Under this requirement, any person making a proxy or consent solicitation seeking shareholder approval of an acquisition, merger, consolidation, or proposed sale or other disposition of all or substantially all of the assets of a registrant must disclose in a clear and simple form in accordance with the SEC's rules:

- any agreements or understandings that such person has with any named executive officer (NEO) of the registrant (or that it has with the NEOs of the acquiring issuer) concerning any type of compensation (whether present, deferred, or contingent) that is based on or otherwise relates to the merger or other extraordinary corporate transaction; and

---

87. *See* Section 14A(c) of the Exchange Act (15 U.S.C. § 78n-1(c)). *See also* Item 24 to Schedule 14A (17 C.F.R. 240.14a-101), which requires disclosure in a registrant's proxy statement for an annual meeting (or other meeting of shareholders for which executive compensation disclosure pursuant to Item 402 is required) of the fact that a separate shareholder vote on executive compensation and a brief explanation of the general effect of the vote, such as whether the vote is non-binding.

88. *See also* Exchange Act Rule 14a-21(b) (17 C.F.R. 240.14a-21(b)), which specifies that the Frequency Vote is required only when proxies are solicited for an annual meeting of security holders at which directors will be elected, or a special meeting in lieu of such annual meeting, which is when disclosure of executive compensation pursuant to Item 402 is required.

- the aggregate total of all such compensation that may (and the conditions upon which it may) be paid or become payable to or on behalf of such executive officer.[89]

In addition, Section 14A(b)(2) of the Exchange Act requires that these disclosed agreements or understandings with the registrant's NEOs must be approved by shareholders pursuant to a separate non-binding vote at the meeting where shareholders are asked to approve the merger or other extraordinary corporate transaction that would trigger the payment of the compensation, unless such agreements or understandings have previously been subject to a Say-on-Pay Vote (Say-on-Golden-Parachutes Vote).[90]

As with the other advisory votes set forth in Section 14A, the Say-on-Golden-Parachutes Vote is non-binding on a registrant or its board of directors, and specifically may not be construed as overruling a decision by the registrant or its board of directors, creating or implying any change in or additional fiduciary duty for the registrant or the board of directors, or restricting or limiting the ability of shareholders to make proposals for inclusion in proxy materials relating to executive compensation.[91]

Each of the Say-on-Pay Vote and the Frequency Vote was effective for the first relevant meeting of shareholders occurring on or after January 21, 2011.[92] Consequently, in 2011, companies holding an annual

---

89. In addition, similar disclosure is required by an acquiring registrant of any agreements or understandings that it has with its NEOs and that it has with the NEOs of the target company in transactions in which the acquiring registrant is seeking shareholder approval of a merger or other transaction. *See* Items 5(a)(5) and 5(b)(3) of Schedule 14A (17 C.F.R. 240.14a-101).

90. See also Exchange Act Rule 14a-21(c) (17 C.F.R. 240.14a-21(c)), which specifies that the Say-on-Golden-Parachutes Vote is required in proxy statements for meetings at which shareholders are asked to approve an acquisition, merger, consolidation, or proposed sale or other disposition of all or substantially all of a company's assets.

91. *See* Section 14A(c) of the Exchange Act (15 U.S.C. § 78n-1(c)).

92. Notwithstanding the statutory language, the SEC took the position that, because the statute required the disclosure prescribed by Section 14A(b)(1) of the Exchange Act (15 U.S.C. § 78n-1(b)(1)) to be made "in accordance with regulations to be promulgated by the Commission," the Say-on-Golden-Parachutes Vote and related disclosure would not be required for merger proxy statements relating to a meeting of shareholders until the final rules were adopted. Final rules were adopted by the SEC on January 25, 2011 and became effective on April 4, 2011. The Say-on-Golden-Parachutes Vote provision became effective on April 25, 2011. *See* Shareholder Approval of Executive Compensation and Golden Parachute Compensation, Release Nos. 33-9178, 34-63768 (Jan. 25, 2011), 76 Fed. Reg. 6010 (Feb. 2, 2011), *available at* http://www.sec.gov/rules/final/2011/33-9178.pdf.

meeting of shareholders were required to conduct both a Say-on-Pay Vote and a Frequency Vote.

For an extensive discussion of the new shareholder advisory votes on executive compensation as enacted pursuant to the Dodd-Frank Act, see Chapter 15.

Compensation Committee Independence

Section 952 of the Dodd-Frank Act added Section 10C to the Exchange Act[93] which, generally, requires the SEC, by rule, to direct the national securities exchanges and national securities associations to prohibit the listing of any equity security of a registrant that does not require that:

- the members of its compensation committee meet enhanced independence standards; and
- the compensation committee select compensation consultants, legal counsel, or other advisers after taking into consideration independence standards established by the SEC.[94]

In addition, listed registrants are required to disclose in the proxy materials for an annual meeting of shareholders whether the compensation committee retained or obtained the advice of a compensation consultant and whether the consultant's work raised any conflicts of interest, the nature of any such conflict, and how it was addressed.[95]

Specifically, Section 10C(a) of the Exchange Act requires the SEC, by rule, to direct the national securities exchanges and national securities associations to prohibit the listing of any equity security of a registrant that does not require each member of the compensation committee of a listed registrant to be a member of the board of directors and "independent."[96] For purposes of determining an individual's

---

93. 15 U.S.C. § 78j-3.

94. *See* Sections 10C(a) and (b) of the Exchange Act (15 U.S.C. §§ 78j-3(a) and (b)).

95. See Section 10C(c)(2) of the Exchange Act (15 U.S.C. § 78j-3(c)(2)).

96. This prohibition does not apply to a controlled company, limited partnership, company in bankruptcy proceedings, open-ended management investment company that is registered under the Investment Company Act of 1940, or a foreign private issuer that provides annual disclosure to shareholders of the reasons that the foreign private issuer does not have an independent compensation committee. *See* Section 10C(a)(1) of the Exchange Act (15 U.S.C. § 78j-3(a)(1)). For this purpose, a "controlled company" is an issuer that is listed on a national securities exchange or by a national securities association and that holds an election for the board of directors of the issuer in which more than 50% of the voting power is held by an individual, a group, or another issuer. *See* Section 10C(g)(2) of the Exchange Act (15 U.S.C. § 78j-3(g)(2)). In addition, the SEC's rules are to give the national securities exchanges and

independence, these rules are to require the national securities exchanges and national securities associations to consider relevant factors, including (but apparently not limited to):

- the source of compensation of a member of the board of directors, including any consulting, advisory, or other compensatory fee paid by the registrant to such individual; and
- whether a member of the board of directors is affiliated with the listed registrant, a subsidiary of the registrant, or an affiliate of a subsidiary of the registrant.[97]

On March 30, 2011, the SEC proposed rules to implement the requirements of Section 952 of the Dodd-Frank Act and Section 10C of the Exchange Act.[98]

Independence of Compensation Consultants and Other Compensation Committee Advisers

Section 10C(b) of the Exchange Act[99] requires the SEC, by rule, to direct the national securities exchanges and national securities associations to prohibit the listing of any equity security of a registrant that does not agree that the compensation committee of a listed registrant may only select an adviser to the compensation committee after taking into consideration factors that affect the independence of such adviser as identified by the SEC.[100]

---

national securities associations the authority to exempt certain categories of issuers, including smaller reporting companies, from this requirement. See Section 10C(f)(3) of the Exchange Act (15 U.S.C. § 78j-3(f)(3)). The SEC's rules are also to provide for appropriate procedures for an issuer to have a reasonable opportunity to cure any defects that would be the basis for a de-listing for failure to satisfy the requirements of the prohibition. See Section 10C(f)(2) of the Exchange Act (15 U.S.C. § 78j-3(f)(2)).

97. See Sections 10C(a)(3)(A) and (B) of the Exchange Act (15 U.S.C. §§ 78j-3(a)(3)(A) and (B)).

98. See Listing Standards for Compensation Committees, Release Nos. 33-9199, 34-64149 (Mar. 30, 2011), 76 Fed. Reg. 18,966 (April 6, 2011), available at http://www.sec.gov/rules/proposed/2011/33-9199.pdf. In April 2011, the comment period for these proposed rules was extended until May 19, 2011. See Listing Standards for Compensation Committees, Release Nos. 33-9203, 34-64366 (April 29, 2011), 76 Fed. Reg. 25,273 (May 4, 2011), available at http://www.sec.gov/rules/proposed/2011/33-9203.pdf.

99. 15 U.S.C. § 78j-3(b).

100. See Sections 10C(b)(1) and (f) of the Exchange Act (15 U.S.C. §§ 78j-3(b)(1) and (f)). This prohibition does not apply to controlled or exempt companies, and registrants are to have a reasonable opportunity to cure any defects.

For this purpose, these factors, which are to be competitively neutral among categories of advisers and preserve the ability of compensation committees to retain the services of members of any such category, must include:

- the provision of other services to the registrant by the person that employs the adviser;
- the amount of fees received from the registrant by the person that employs the adviser as a percentage of that person's total revenue;
- the policies and procedures of the person that employs the adviser that are designed to prevent conflicts of interest;
- any business or personal relationship of the adviser with a member of the compensation committee; and
- any stock of the registrant owned by the adviser.[101]

Significantly, this provision does not require compensation committees to engage only independent advisers, but simply to determine whether any such adviser is, in fact, independent under the standards established by the SEC. Accordingly, while, as a practical matter, most compensation committees are likely to only use independent advisers, there will be situations where other considerations may outweigh these criteria in the selection process.

Section 10C also delineates the ability of the compensation committees of listed registrants to retain advisers, expressly stating that the compensation committee, in its capacity as a committee of the board of directors, may, in its sole discretion, retain and obtain the input of advisers.[102] Further, it expressly states that the compensation committee is directly responsible for the appointment and compensation of the advisers[103] and the oversight of their work.[104] Interestingly, the provision makes clear that the compensation committee is not required to follow

---

101. See Sections 10C(b)(2)(A) – (E) of the Exchange Act (15 U.S.C. §§ 78j-3(b)(2)(A) – (E)).

102. See Sections 10C(c)(1)(A) and (d)(1) of the Exchange Act (15 U.S.C. §§ 78j-3(c)(1)(A) and (d)(1)).

103. See Sections 10C(c)(1)(B) and (d)(2) of the Exchange Act (15 U.S.C. §§ 78j-3(c)(1)(B) and (d)(2)).

104. Each registrant is to provide for appropriate funding, as determined by the compensation committee, in its capacity as a committee of the board of directors, for reasonable compensation of advisers to the committee. See Section 10C(e) of the Exchange Act (15 U.S.C. § 78j-3(c)).

the advice or recommendations of its adviser or advisers,[105] and the input of advisers does not affect the ability or obligation of the committee to exercise its own judgment in discharging its responsibilities.[106]

Finally, the proxy materials for an annual meeting of the shareholders of a listed registrant must disclose whether the compensation committee retained or obtained the advice of a compensation consultant, whether the consultant's work has raised any conflict of interest, and, if so, the nature of the conflict and how it is being addressed.[107]

On March 30, 2011, the SEC proposed rules to implement the requirements of Section 952 of the Dodd-Frank Act and Section 10C of the Exchange Act.[108]

Executive Compensation Disclosures

There are two explicit disclosure provisions in the Dodd-Frank Act that relate to executive compensation: one calling for enhanced disclosure of the relationship between executive compensation and corporate financial performance and the other calling for disclosure of the relationship between senior executive compensation and median employee compensation.

Pay Versus Performance Disclosure

Section 953(a) of the Dodd-Frank Act added Section 14(i) to the Exchange Act[109] which, generally, requires the SEC to adopt rules mandating that registrants disclose in the proxy materials for an annual meeting of shareholders a clear description of the compensation required to be disclosed under Item 402 of Regulation S-K. This includes information showing the relationship between the compensation actually paid to the

---

105. *See* Sections 10C(c)(1)(C)(i) and (d)(3)(A) of the Exchange Act (15 U.S.C. §§ 78j-3(c) (1)(C)(i) and (d)(3)(A)).

106. *See* Sections 10C(c)(1)(C)(ii) and (d)(3)(B) of the Exchange Act (15 U.S.C. §§ 78j-3(c)(1)(C)(ii) and (d)(3)(B)).

107. *See* Section 10C(c)(2) of the Exchange Act (15 U.S.C. § 78j-3(c)(2)). Note that, in the case of this requirement, Section 10C(c)(2) stipulates that the required information is to be included in the proxy materials for annual meetings of shareholders occurring on or after July 21, 2011. In view of the fact that, as of the date of this publication, the SEC had not yet completed its rulemaking under Section 952 of the Dodd-Frank Act, this requirement has not yet become effective.

108. *See* Note 98, *supra.*

109. 15 U.S.C. § 78n(i).

executive officers and corporate financial performance. This disclosure may be presented graphically or in narrative form.

While the statute directs the SEC to implement this disclosure requirement by rule, it was not given a deadline for doing so. As of the date of this publication, the SEC was indicating that it intended to propose rules with respect to this provision during the January – June 2012 timeframe and adopt final rules during the July – December 2012 timeframe.[110]

Pay Ratio Disclosure

Section 953(b) of the Dodd-Frank Act requires the SEC to amend Item 402 of Regulation S-K to mandate disclosure in a registrant's Securities Act and Exchange Act filings of:

- the median annual total compensation of all employees (except the chief executive officer);
- the annual total compensation of the chief executive officer; and
- the ratio of the median employee annual total compensation to the chief executive officer's annual total compensation. [111]

For this purpose, "total compensation" is to be based on Item 402 as in effect on July 20, 2010, the day before the day the Dodd-Frank Act was signed into law.[112]

While the statute directs the SEC to implement this disclosure requirement by rule, it was not given a deadline for doing so. As of the date of this publication, the SEC was indicating that it intended to propose rules with respect to this provision during the January – June

---

110. *See* Implementing the Dodd-Frank Wall Street Reform and Consumer Protection Act – Upcoming Activity, *available at* http://www.sec.gov/spotlight/dodd-frank.shtml.

111. This disclosure is to be included in any filing described in Item 10(a) of Regulation S-K (17 C.F.R. 229.10(a)), including registration statements under the Securities Act, registration statements under Section 12 of the Exchange Act (15 U.S.C. § 78*l*), annual or other reports under Sections 13 and 15(d) of the Exchange Act (15 U.S.C. §§ 78m and 78(o)(d)), going-private transaction statements under Section 13 of the Exchange Act (15 U.S.C. § 78m), tender offer statements under Sections 13 and 14 of the Exchange Act (15 U.S.C. §§ 78m and 78n), annual reports to security holders and proxy and information statements under Section 14 of the Exchange Act (15 U.S.C. § 78n), and any other documents required to be filed under the Exchange Act.

112. See Section 953(b) of the Dodd-Frank Act.

2012 timeframe and adopt final rules during the July – December 2012 timeframe.[113]

Recovery of Erroneously Awarded Compensation

Section 954 of the Dodd-Frank Act added Section 10D to the Exchange Act[114] concerning the recovery of erroneously-awarded compensation (a so-called "clawback" policy). Generally, Section 10D requires the SEC, by rule, to direct the national securities exchanges and national securities associations to prohibit the listing of any security of a registrant that does not have a policy that:

- discloses its policy on incentive-based compensation that is based on financial information required to be reported under the securities laws; and
- provides for compensation recovery:
  - in the event the registrant is required to restate its financial statements due to material noncompliance with any financial reporting requirement;
  - covers any current or former executive officer who received incentive-based compensation (including stock options) during the three-year period preceding the date when the registrant is required to prepare the restatement; and
  - recovers the amounts in excess of what would have been paid to the executive officer under the restatement.[115]

While the statute directs the SEC to implement this disclosure requirement by rule, it was not given a deadline for doing so. As of the date of this publication, the SEC was indicating that it intended to propose rules with respect to this provision during the January – June 2012 timeframe and adopt final rules during the July – December 2012 timeframe.[116]

---

113. *See* Implementing the Dodd-Frank Wall Street Reform and Consumer Protection Act – Upcoming Activity, *available at* http://www.sec.gov/spotlight/dodd-frank.shtml.

114. 15 U.S.C. § 78j-4.

115. *See* Section 10D(b) of the Exchange Act (15 U.S.C. § 78j-4(b)).

116. *See* Implementing the Dodd-Frank Wall Street Reform and Consumer Protection Act – Upcoming Activity, *available at* http://www.sec.gov/spotlight/dodd-frank.shtml.

Disclosure Regarding Employee and Director Hedging

Section 955 of the Dodd-Frank Act added Section 14(j) to the Exchange Act[117] which, generally, requires the SEC to adopt rules mandating disclosure in the proxy materials for any annual meeting of shareholders of whether any employee or member of the board of directors of a registrant, or designee of such persons, is permitted to purchase financial instruments, including prepaid variable forwards, equity swaps, collars, and exchange funds, that are designed to hedge or offset any decrease in the market value of equity securities granted as compensation or held, directly or indirectly, by the employee or director.

Significantly, Section 14(j) does not require registrants to have a hedging policy, but simply to disclose whether they have a policy that conforms to the description in the provision.[118] Nonetheless, while couched as a disclosure, rather than a substantive, requirement, this provision appears to be designed to promote the adoption of a comprehensive hedging policy by registrants. In addition, even where a registrant already has a policy, it will now be measured against the standard established by Section 14(j).

While the statute directs the SEC to implement this disclosure requirement by rule, it was not given a deadline for doing so. As of the date of this publication, the SEC was indicating that it intended to propose rules with respect to this provision during the January – June 2012 timeframe and adopt final rules during the July – December 2012 timeframe.[119]

Voting by Brokers

Section 957 of the Dodd-Frank Act amended Section 6(b) of the Exchange Act, which sets forth the requirements for registration of a national securities exchanges, to prohibit any member that is not the beneficial owner of a security registered under Section 12 of the Exchange Act from granting a proxy to vote the security in connection with a shareholder vote with respect to the election of a member of the board of directors of an issuer, executive compensation, or any other significant matter, as

---

117. 15 U.S.C. § 78n(j).

118. It is also important to note that Section 14(j) does not require disclosure of actual hedging transactions. In the case of executive officers and directors, however, such transactions may be disclosable under Section 16(a) of the Exchange Act (15 U.S.C. § 78p(a)).

119. See Implementing the Dodd-Frank Wall Street Reform and Consumer Protection Act – Upcoming Activity, *available at* http://www.sec.gov/spotlight/dodd-frank.shtml.

determined by the SEC, unless the beneficial owner of the security has instructed the member to vote the proxy in accordance with the voting instructions of the beneficial owner.[120]

This provision both codifies the New York Stock Exchange's 2009 change to NYSE Rule 452 prohibiting exchange members from voting uninstructed shares in uncontested director elections,[121] and extends this prohibition to cover executive compensation matters, including the various advisory votes on executive compensation under Section 951 of the Dodd-Frank Act.[122] As it also applies to any shareholder vote involving "executive compensation," it appears that it could extend to numerous compensation-related matters, such as to satisfy the conditions of the "performance-based compensation" exception of Section 162(m) of the Internal Revenue Code[123] and the approval of severance agreements.

The amendment to Section 6(b) became effective on July 21, 2010. Since then, to maintain their Exchange Act registrations, the New York Stock Exchange[124] and the NASDAQ Stock Market[125] have amended their rules to add executive compensation to the list of matters upon which brokers are no longer permitted to vote uninstructed shares.

---

120. *See* Sections 6(b)(10)(A) and (B) of the Exchange Act (15 U.S.C. §§ 78f(b)(10)(A) and (B)). As set forth in the text, the prohibition on discretionary vesting of shares that are not beneficially owned for the election of directors was separable, approved in 2009, and became effective on January 1, 2010. Section 957 extended this prohibition to executive compensation and other significant matters as determined by the SEC.

121. *See* Order Approving Proposed Rule Change, as Modified by Amendment No. 4, to Amend NYSE Rule 452 and Corresponding Listed Company Manual Section 402.08 to Eliminate Broker Discretionary Voting for the Election of Directors, Except for Companies under the Investment Company Act of 1940, and to Codify Two Previously Published Interpretations That Do Not Permit Broker Discretionary Voting for Material Amendments to Investment Advisory Contracts with an Investment Company, Release No. 34-60215 (July 1, 2009).

122. This includes the Say-on-Pay Vote, the Frequency Vote, and the Say-on-Golden-Parachutes Vote.

123. 26 U.S.C. §162(m).

124. *See* Notice of Filing and Order Granting Accelerated Approval of a Proposed Rule Change to Amend NYSE Rule 452 and Listed Company Manual Section 402.08 to Eliminate Broker Discretionary Voting on Executive Compensation Matters, Release No. 34-62874 (Sept. 9, 2010).

125. *See* Notice of Filing and Order Granting Accelerated Approval of Proposed Rule Change to Prohibit Members from Voting Uninstructed Shares on Certain Matters, Release No. 34-62992 (Sept. 24, 2010).

The Jumpstart Our Business Startups (JOBS) Act

On April 5, 2012, President Barack Obama signed into law the Jumpstart Our Business Startups (JOBS) Act.[126] The primary purpose of the new law is to stimulate capital formation in a variety of ways, including, among other things, by streamlining the registration process under the Securities Act and relaxing the regulatory burden under the Exchange Act for a new category of issuer, the so-called "emerging growth company."[127]

Consistent with this objective, Section 102 of the JOBS Act amends Section 14A of the Exchange Act to exempt emerging growth companies from all of the shareholder advisory vote requirements of the statute (the Say-on-Pay Vote, the Frequency Vote, and the Say-on-Golden-Parachutes Vote) until the registrant is no longer an emerging growth company. Specifically, a registrant that is no longer an emerging growth company must include a separate resolution providing for a Say-on-Pay Vote in its proxy materials not later than the end of:

- in the case of a registrant that was an emerging growth company for less than two years after the date of the effectiveness of its initial public offering of common equity securities under the Securities Act, the three-year period beginning on such date; and
- in the case of any other registrant, the one-year period beginning on the date the registrant is no longer an emerging growth company.[128]

---

126. Pub. L. No. 112-206, 126 Stat. 306 (April 5, 2012).

127. See Section 101 of the JOBS Act, which amends Section 2(a) of the Securities Act (15 U.S.C. § 77b(a)) and Section 3(a) of the Exchange Act (15 U.S.C. § 78c(a)). As adopted, an "emerging growth company" means an issuer that had total annual gross revenues of less than $1 billion (indexed for inflation every five years by the SEC) during its most recently completed fiscal year.

128. A registrant that is an emerging growth company as of the first day of a fiscal year continues to qualify as an emerging growth company until the earliest of: (a) the last day of the fiscal year in which its annual gross revenues exceed $1 billion; (b) the last day of the fiscal year following the fifth anniversary of its initial public offering of common equity securities; (c) the date on which it has issued more than $1 billion in nonconvertible debt during the previous three-year period; or (d) the date on which it is considered to be a "large accelerated filer" for purposes of the federal securities laws. See Section 2(a)(19) of the Securities Act (15 U.S.C. § 77b(a)(19)) and Section 3(a)(80) of the Exchange Act (15 U.S.C. § 78c(a)(80)).

In addition, an emerging growth company is exempt from the disclosure requirements of Section 953(a) of the Dodd-Frank Act (the pay versus performance disclosure)[129] and the disclosure requirements of Section 953(b) of the Dodd-Frank Act (the pay ratio disclosure).[130]

Finally, an emerging growth company is permitted to comply with the executive compensation disclosure rules applicable to smaller reporting companies,[131] rather than the general disclosure requirements otherwise applicable to registrants.[132] Thus, an eligible registrant taking advantage of this scaled disclosure requirement need only provide the following information about its executive compensation program:

- a Summary Compensation Table (but covering only three (rather than five) named executive officers (including the Chief Executive Officer, but not necessarily the Chief Financial Officer) and limited to two (rather than three) fiscal years' information;[133]
- an Outstanding Equity Awards at Fiscal Year-End Table;[134] and
- a Director Compensation Table.[135]

An emerging growth company is not required to prepare a CD&A, nor is it required to provide four of the six tabular disclosures otherwise required of registrants. In addition, it need not prepare the disclosure about potential payments upon a termination of employment or a change in control of the registrant.[136]

---

129. *See* Section 102(a)(2) of the JOBS Act. *See also* Section 14(i) of the Exchange Act (15 U.S.C. § 78n(i)).

130. *See* Section 102(a)(3) of the JOBS Act. *See also* Section 953(b)(1) of the Investor Protection and Securities Reform Act of 2010 (Public Law 111-203, 124 Stat.1904 (2010)).

131. See Item 402(l) of Regulation S-K (17 CFR 229.402(l)).

132. *See* Section 102(c) of the JOBS Act.

133. *See* Item 402(n). In addition, the emerging growth company would also be required provide certain narrative discussion to the Summary Compensation Table (see Item 402(o)) and the additional narrative disclosure specified in Item 402(q).

134. *See* Item 402(p).

135. *See* Item 402(r).

136. *See* Item 402(j).

2

The Disclosure Framework

General

The executive compensation disclosure rules enhance and refine the disclosure framework first introduced in 1992, using a combination of narrative and tabular disclosure to present information about a registrant's compensation policies and practices for its senior executives and directors. The narrative disclosure consists of a Compensation Discussion and Analysis (CD&A),[1] the related Compensation Committee Report, and the narrative discussions that are to accompany the required compensation tables. This disclosure largely replaces the narrative disclosure required under the former rules. The tabular disclosure,

---

1. The CD&A replaces the former Board Compensation Committee Report. *See* Executive Compensation and Related Person Disclosure, Release Nos. 33-8732A, 34-54302A, IC-27444A (Aug. 29, 2006), 71 Fed. Reg. 53,158 (Sept. 8, 2006) [hereinafter Adopting Release], *available at* http://www.sec.gov/rules/final/2006/33-8732a.pdf, at Section II.A.4. The Board Compensation Committee Report consisted of a narrative discussion of the compensation of a registrant's chief executive officer and the policies with respect of the compensation of the registrant's executive officers generally.

which essentially reorganizes and streamlines the former compensation tables, covers three broad categories of information:

- compensation paid or earned for the last completed fiscal year (as well as the two preceding fiscal years), as presented in a revised Summary Compensation Table[2] that reports compensation paid currently or deferred (including equity compensation) and other plan-based compensation, which is supplemented by a table providing supporting information for some of the data in the Summary Compensation Table;[3]
- equity-based holdings that are compensatory or potential sources of future compensation, focusing primarily on compensatory equity-based interests that were awarded in the last completed fiscal year and in prior years,[4] as well any compensation realized from these interests during the last completed fiscal year;[5] and
- postemployment-related compensation, including retirement plans and deferred compensation arrangements, and other postemployment payments and benefits, including amounts payable in the event of a change in control of the registrant.[6]

As reconstituted, the tabular disclosure consists of seven required tables: the six previously enumerated tables and a Director Compensation Table. This reorganization is intended to make it easier for investors to understand how different compensation elements relate to each other. At the same time, the emphasis on tabular presentations enables investors to compare the compensation paid by a registrant to its senior executives from year to year and from registrant to registrant.

Unlike most of the required pay information, disclosure of a registrant's potential payments to its senior executives upon a termination of employment or a change of control may be in either narrative or tabular form. Since 2006, most registrants have used a combination of narrative discussion and accompanying tables to present this information.

---

2. See the discussion of the Summary Compensation Table in Chapter 4.

3. See the discussion of the Grants of Plan-Based Awards Table in Chapter 6.

4. See the discussion of the Outstanding Equity Awards at Fiscal Year-End Table in Chapter 8.

5. See the discussion of the Option Exercises and Stock Vested Table in Chapter 9.

6. See the discussion of the Pension Benefits Table in Chapter 10 and the Nonqualified Deferred Compensation Table in Chapter 11. See also the discussion about postemployment payments and benefits in Chapter 12.

The rules focus on the individual and total compensation of a registrant's most senior executive officers and directors. This information is intended to provide investors with an understanding of a registrant's overall compensation philosophy and the objectives and outcomes of its executive compensation program.

Unlike the former rules, which only required registrants to address a few specific topics in their narrative disclosure and emphasized strict compliance with the prescribed tabular formats, the rules take a "principles-based" approach. This approach emphasizes comprehensive and clear disclosure, requiring registrants to tailor the general disclosure requirements to their specific situations.[7]

This principles-based approach is most apparent in registrants' decisions about the content of their CD&A and where to report specific compensation items in the compensation tables. It also is evidenced in the large number of additional tables, graphs, and charts that registrants used to supplement the required disclosure.[8] While the staff of the Securities and Exchange Commission's (SEC's) Division of Corporation Finance (SEC Staff) continues to closely monitor filings for faithful compliance with the rules,[9] it takes a more relaxed stance on innovative presentations, typically commenting only where the additional disclosure is likely to confuse investors or obscure the presentation of the required information.[10]

During the initial proxy season under the rules, the SEC Staff permitted registrants that were complying with the rules for the first time to file a preliminary proxy statement under Exchange Act Rule

---

7. *See* Executive Compensation and Related Party Disclosure, Release Nos. 33-8655, 34-53185, IC-27218 (Jan. 27, 2006), 71 Fed. Reg. 6542 (Feb. 8, 2006), *available at* http://www.sec.gov/rules/proposed/33-8655.pdf, at Section II.A.1. *See also* John W. White, Director, Division of Corporation Finance, U.S. Securities Exchange Comm'n, *Principles Matter*, Remarks Before the Practicing Law Institute Conference (Sept. 6, 2006), *available at* http://www.sec.gov/news/speech/2006/spch090606jww.htm.

8. The SEC encourages registrants to use additional tables wherever tabular presentation facilitates clearer, more concise disclosure. *See* the Adopting Release, *supra* note 1, at Section VI.

9. The compensation tables must be included in the disclosure and cannot be modified except as specifically permitted by the rules. *See* Item 402(a)(5).

10. The SEC's plain-English principles specifically provide that, in designing the presentation of the information, registrants may include tables or other design elements so long as the design is not misleading and the required information is clear, understandable, consistent with applicable disclosure requirements, consistent with any other included information, and not misleading. *See* Exchange Act Rules 13a-20(c)(10) and 15d-20(c)(10) (17 C.F.R. 240.13-20(a)(10) and 240.15d-20(c)(10).

14a-6[11] omitting executive and director compensation disclosure to avoid having to file a revised preliminary proxy statement and to commence a new ten-calendar-day waiting period before disseminating definitive proxy materials so long as (a) the omitted executive and director compensation disclosure was included in the definitive proxy statement, (b) the omitted disclosure did not relate to the matter or matters that caused the registrant to file preliminary proxy materials, and (c) the omitted disclosure was not otherwise made available to the public prior to the filing of the definitive proxy statement.[12] Going forward, however, a preliminary proxy statement that omits the required executive and director compensation disclosure will necessitate a revised preliminary proxy statement and toll the ten-calendar-day waiting period specified until the required information is filed.[13]

The rules permit registrants to omit a table or column if there has been no compensation awarded to, earned by, or paid to any of the named executive officers (NEOs) or directors required to be reported in that table or column in any fiscal year covered by that table.[14] In addition, it is possible to add a column to any table as long as it does not make the requested disclosure misleading or unclear.[15]

The operation of the disclosure rules is subject to the following overarching framework.

---

11. 17 C.F.R. 240.14a-6.

12. *See* Division of Corporation Finance, Item 402 of Regulation S-K—Executive Compensation (Aug. 8, 2007), *available at* http://www.sec.gov/divisions/corpfin/guidance/execcomp402interp.htm, at Q&A 1.04.

13. *See* Division of Corporation Finance, Compliance and Disclosure Interpretations – Regulation S-K (July 8, 2011) [hereinafter Current Staff Guidance], *available at* http://www.sec.gov/divisions/corpfin/guidance/regs-kinterp.htm, at Q&A 117.02. While the SEC Staff guidance references a "situation where a company . . . is complying with the 2006 rules for the first time" as being eligible to rely on the exception to including the executive and director compensation disclosure in its preliminary proxy statement, it is unclear whether this reference is intended to cover a registrant that is subject to the proxy rules for the first time as an Exchange Act reporting company or just the transition to the then-new rules during the 2007 proxy season. The better reading is that the exception was intended to simply provide relief during the transition to the then-new rules in 2007.

14. *See* Instruction 5 to Item 402(a)(3). In the case of a table, a registrant may find it advisable to include an express statement indicating that the table has been intentionally omitted to avoid investor confusion.

15. *See* Questions and Answers, Technical Session Between the SEC Staff and the Joint Committee on Employee Benefits (May 8, 2007) [hereinafter 2007 JCEB Questions], *available at* http://www.abanet.org/jceb/2007/SEC07Final.pdf, at Question No. 8.

Companies Covered

Exchange Act Reporting Issuers

The rules apply to any SEC filing that requires executive and director compensation information. Typically, this will include registration statements filed under the Securities Act and registration statements, and periodic reports and proxy information statements filed under the Exchange Act.

As a practical matter, registrants will most frequently encounter the rules when preparing their proxy materials in connection with their annual meeting of shareholders.[16] Under the Exchange Act, any registrant with a class of securities registered under Section 12[17] must file with the SEC and transmit to its security holders a proxy or information statement prior to any annual or special meeting of its security holders.[18] In addition, under Section 13(a),[19] every issuer of a security registered pursuant to Section 12 must file with the SEC periodic reports concerning its business and financial condition, including an annual report containing executive and director compensation information.[20]

---

16. *See* Item 7 of Schedule 14A (17 C.F.R. 240.14a-101) and Item 1 of Schedule 14C (17 C.F.R. 240.14c-101).

17. Section 12 of the Exchange Act (15 U.S.C. § 78*l*). Section 12(b) requires an issuer to register a class of securities (equity or debt) before listing that class of securities on a national securities exchange. Section 12(g) requires an issuer to register a class of equity securities if, on the last day of its fiscal year, it has total assets of more than $10 million and the class of equity securities is held by more than 500 record holders. *See also* Exchange Act Rule 12g-1 (17 C.F.R. 240.12g-1). In addition, an issuer may voluntarily register a class of equity securities under Section 12(g).

18. *See* Section 14(a) and (c) of the Exchange Act (15 U.S.C. § 78n(a) and (c)). These rules require an issuer to provide a proxy or information statement to its security holders, together with a proxy card when soliciting proxies.

19. Section 13(a) of the Exchange Act (15 U.S.C. § 78m(a)). *See also* Section 15(d) of the Exchange Act (15 U.S.C. § 78o(d)). Under Section 15(d), once an issuer has a registration statement declared effective under the Securities Act, it becomes an Exchange Act reporting company and must file all reports required to be filed under Section 13.

20. *See* Item 11 of Part III of Form 10-K (17 C.F.R. 249.310).

Notwithstanding these general requirements, the SEC has established alternate reporting systems for small businesses[21] and certain foreign issuers[22] that vary many of the standard reporting requirements.

Smaller Reporting Companies

Consistent with the SEC's long-standing policy of minimizing the compliance burden for smaller registrants, the new rules differentiate between smaller reporting companies[23] and other registrants. In recognition of the fact that the executive compensation arrangements of small registrants are generally not as complex as those of other registrants, as well as the time and cost associated with complying with a disclosure framework designed for more complicated compensation programs,[24] smaller reporting companies may provide scaled rather than

---

21. *See* Item 402(l) of Regulation S-K. These rules, which were adopted on Nov. 15, 2007 (*see* Smaller Reporting Company Regulatory Relief and Simplification, Release Nos. 33-8876, 34-56994, 39-2451 (Dec. 19, 2007), 73 Fed. Reg. 934 (Jan. 4, 2008) [hereinafter Small Company Release], *available at* http://www.sec.gov/rules/final/2007/33-8876.pdf) replace Regulation SB, which was originally adopted in 1992 (*see* Small Business Initiatives Releases Nos. 33-6949, 34-30968, 39-2287 (July 30, 1992), 57 Fed. Reg. 36,442 (Aug. 1992)) to make it easier for small businesses to raise capital. Compliance with these rules, which simplify the process of selling securities to the public and reduce the cost of small businesses' reporting obligations, is optional. A smaller reporting company may elect to use either this scaled reporting system or the standard reporting system to register and report under the Exchange Act. *See* Item 10(f) of Regulation S-K (17 C.F.R. 229.10(f)).

22. *See* Form 20-F (17 C.F.R. 240.220f).

23. A "smaller reporting company" is an issuer that is not an investment company, an asset-backed issuer, or a majority-owned subsidiary of a parent that is not a smaller reporting company and that (1) had a "public float" of less than $75 million as of the last business day of its most recently completed second fiscal quarter, or (2) in the case of an initial registration statement under the Securities Act or the Exchange Act for shares of its common equity, had a "public float" of less than $75 million as of a date within 30 days of the date of the filing of the registration statement, or (3) in the case of an issuer whose "public float" (as calculated for purposes of (1) or (2) above) was zero, had annual revenues of less than $50 million during the most recently completed fiscal year for which audited financial statements are available. *See* Item 10(f)(1) of Regulation S-K (17 C.F.R. 229.10(f)(1)). In the case of alternative (1), the issuer's public float is computed by multiplying the aggregate worldwide number of shares of its voting and nonvoting common equity held by nonaffiliates by the price at which the common equity was last sold, or the average of the bid and asked prices of common equity, in the principal market for the common equity. *See* Item 10(f)(1)(i). In the case of alternative (2), the issuer's public float is computed by multiplying the aggregate worldwide number of such shares held by nonaffiliates before the registration plus, in the case of a Securities Act registration statement, the number of such shares included in the registration statement by the estimated public offering price of the shares. *See* Item 10(f)(1)(ii). The determination of whether an issuer is a smaller reporting company is to be made on an annual basis. *See* Item 10(f)(2).

24. Under the former rules, small business issuers (as these registrants were then known) were not required to provide the Board Compensation Committee Report, the Performance

full disclosure, which consists of, along with related narrative disclosure, only three tables:

- the Summary Compensation Table;[25]
- the Outstanding Equity Awards at Fiscal Year-End Table;[26] and
- the Director Compensation Table.[27]

While a number of investors sought to have small registrants provide a basic form of CD&A as part of their disclosure, the Commission, balancing the benefits of such a report with the associated compliance burden, declined to impose such a requirement.[28] It remains to be seen whether the SEC will revisit this decision in the future as CD&As evolve to become the centerpiece of the disclosure that the SEC envisions and once the shareholder advisory votes on executive compensation become applicable to smaller reporting companies.

In addition to omitting the CD&A and reducing the number of required compensation tables, the NEO group for a smaller reporting company consists of a smaller group of executive officers and includes only

- all individuals serving as the company's chief executive officer or acting in a similar capacity during the last completed fiscal year, regardless of compensation level;[29]
- the company's two most highly compensated executive officers other than the chief executive officer who were serving as

Graph, the Compensation Committee Interlocks disclosure, the Ten-Year Option/SAR Repricings Table, the Pension Plan Table, and the columns in the Option/SAR Grants in Last Fiscal Year Table disclosing potential realizable value or grant date value. *See* Executive Compensation Disclosure, Release Nos. 33-6962, 34-31327, IC-19032 (Oct. 16, 1992), 57 Fed. Reg. 48,126 (Oct. 21, 1992), *as modified*, Executive Compensation Disclosure: Correction, Release Nos. 33-6966, 34-31420, IC-19085 (Nov. 9, 1992), 57 Fed. Reg. 53,985 (Nov. 9, 1992), at Section II.A.1.a.

25. Item 402(n). *See* Chapter 4.

26. Item 402(p). *See* Chapter 8.

27. Item 402(r). *See* Chapter 13. Nor is a smaller reporting company required to provide a Performance Graph. *See* Instruction 6 to Item 201(e) of Regulation S-K (17 C.F.R. 229.201(e)).

28. *See* the Adopting Release, *supra* note 1, at n.356 and accompanying text, and the Small Company Release, *supra* note 21, at Section III.C.1. Nor are smaller reporting companies required to provide a Compensation Committee Report as part of their executive compensation disclosure. *See* Item Section 407(g)(2) of Regulation S-K (17 C.F.R 240.407(g)(2)).

29. Item 402(m)(2)(i). *See* "Persons Covered—Named Executive Officers—Chief Executive Officer," *infra*.

executive officers at the end of the last completed fiscal year;[30] and

- up to two additional individuals for whom disclosure would have been provided but for the fact that the individual was not serving as an executive officer of the company at the end of the last completed fiscal year.[31]

Thus, a smaller reporting company does not need to provide compensation information about its chief financial officer (unless he or she happens to be one of the company's two most highly compensated executive officers at the end of the last completed fiscal year). In addition, a smaller reporting company need only provide information about two, rather than three, of its most highly compensated executive officers other than its chief executive officer.

Finally, the Summary Compensation Table of a smaller reporting company has been modified from the general table required of other registrants in two significant respects. First, smaller reporting companies are required to provide information in the Summary Compensation Table only for the last two fiscal years, rather than the three fiscal years required for other registrants.[32] In addition, because the pension plan information required in the Summary Compensation Table is directly tied to the disclosure in the Pension Benefits Table, which is not required for smaller reporting companies, the table does not need to include pension plan disclosure.[33] Nonetheless, to ensure that investors are able to fully understand the information disclosed in the Summary Compensation Table (particularly in view of the single supplemental compensation table required), the accompanying narrative description must include a number of material items that essentially replace the tabular or footnote disclosure that is required of other registrants.[34]

In spite of the considerable relief afforded to small businesses, many small and midsize registrants are not eligible to use these scaled

---

30. Item 402(m)(2)(ii). *See* "Persons Covered—Named Executive Officers—Most Highly Compensated Executive Officers," *infra.*

31. Item 402(m)(2)(iii). *See* "Persons Covered—Named Executive Officers—Former Executive Officers," *infra.*

32. Item 402(n)(1). *See* Chapter 4.

33. *See* the Adopting Release, *supra* note 1, at Section II.D.1, and the Small Company Release, *supra* note 21, at Section III.C.1.

34. Item 402(q). For example, a smaller reporting company is expected to provide a description of any postemployment payments and other benefits to the extent material to an investor's understanding of its executive compensation program. *See* Item 402(q)(2). See also Chapter 7.

disclosure requirements because they exceed either the public float or revenue thresholds.[35] While during the rulemaking process, a number of commenters requested that the group of small public companies that would qualify for this disclosure framework be expanded, the SEC chose to defer consideration of this matter until 2007, when it adopted recommendations of the Advisory Committee on Smaller Public Companies to increase the number of companies eligible for the SEC's scaled disclosure and reporting requirements for smaller reporting companies.[36]

Foreign Private Issuers

As under the former rules, a foreign private issuer[37] will be deemed to comply with the rules if it satisfies the compensation disclosure requirements of Form 20-F.[38] This involves providing the information required by Items 6.B. and 6.E.2. of Form 20-F, subject to one exception. If a foreign private issuer otherwise makes more detailed information publicly available, or is required by its home jurisdiction or a market in which its securities are listed or traded to provide more detailed information, it will be deemed to comply with the new rules as long as its disclosure contains the more detailed information.[39] Further, a foreign private issuer need not file employment agreements or compensation plans as an exhibit to Form 20-F, even where it provides compensation information on an individual basis, unless the filing of these documents is required by its home jurisdiction or is otherwise publicly disclosed by the issuer.[40]

---

35. Under the former rules, a small business issuer that had not elected to use the small business forms and schedule still was permitted to use Regulation S-B for purposes of preparing its executive compensation disclosure. *See* former Item 402(a)(1). This provision was eliminated under the current rules. *See* the Adopting Release, *supra* note 1, at n.364.

36. *See* the Small Company Release, *supra* note 21.

37. For these purposes, the term "foreign private issuer" means any foreign issuer other than a foreign government (generally, any issuer that is a national of any foreign country or a corporation or other organization incorporated or organized under the laws of any foreign country), unless the issuer meets the following conditions: (1) More than 50 percent of the issuer's outstanding voting securities are directly or indirectly held of record by residents of the United States, and (2) either (a) the majority of the executive officers or directors are U.S. citizens or residents, (b) more than 50 percent of the assets of the issuer are located in the United States, or (c) the business of the issuer is administered principally in the United States. *See* Exchange Act Rule 3b-4(c) (17 C.F.R. 240.3b-4(c)).

38. *See* Item 402(a)(1). These requirements are set out in Items 6.B and 6.E.2 of Form 20-F (17 C.F.R. 240.220f).

39. *Id.*

40. *See* Instruction 4(c)(v) of the Instructions to the Exhibits to Form 20-F.

Persons Covered

The rules retain the former rule's principle of requiring compensation disclosure of a registrant's five most senior executive officers and all of the members of the registrant's board of directors but make two subtle, but significant, revisions to this framework. First, along with a registrant's chief executive officer, its chief financial officer is always included in the disclosure. Second, the determination of a registrant's most highly compensated executive officer is only based on total compensation, rather than just total annual salary and bonus as under the former rules.

Named Executive Officers

Compensation disclosure (that is, the discussion in the CD&A and tabular disclosure) is required about a registrant's chief executive officer, chief financial officer, and the three most highly compensated executive officers (other than the CEO and CFO) who were serving as executive officers at the end of the registrant's last completed fiscal year (the "named executive officers" (NEOs).[41] NEO status is based on whether an individual is an "executive officer" as defined under the Exchange Act[42] and whether he or she is employed in that capacity by the registrant at the end of the fiscal year. In addition, an executive officer of a subsidiary of a registrant may be deemed an executive officer of the registrant if he or she performs a policy-making function for the registrant.[43]

Chief Executive Officer

The NEO group includes the individual serving as the registrant's chief executive officer at the end of the last completed fiscal year, as well as any other individual who served in that capacity at any time during

---

41. *See* Item 402(a)(3) and, in the case of smaller reporting companies, Item 402(m)(2).

42. *See* Exchange Act Rule 3b-7 (17 C.F.R. 240.3b-7). As defined, the term "executive officer," when used with reference to a registrant, means its president; any vice president of the registrant in charge of a principal business unit, division, or function (such as sales, administration, or finance); any other officer who performs a policy-making function; or any other person who performs similar policy-making functions for the registrant. In addition, executive officers or other employees of subsidiaries may be deemed executive officers of the registrant if they perform such policy-making functions for the registrant. *See also* Securities Act Rule 405 (17 C.F.R. 230.405).

43. *See* Instruction 2 to Item 402(a)(3) and, in the case of smaller reporting companies, Instruction 2 to Item 402(m)(2). *See also* the Adopting Release, *supra* note 1, at n.327.

the last fiscal year.[44] In other words, all individuals who served as chief executive officer or in a similar capacity during the last completed fiscal year must be considered named executive officers of the registrant.[45] Consequently, a registrant may have more than one chief executive officer in its disclosure for the last completed fiscal year.

Under the rules, this individual (or individuals) is referred to as the "principal executive officer," or PEO.[46] The chief executive officer is to be included in the disclosure without regard to his or her actual compensation level.[47]

The rules make clear that an individual's title is not dispositive in determining whether he or she is or was the registrant's chief executive officer. Thus, all individuals who performed the duties and responsibilities of the chief executive officer or acted in a similar capacity during the last completed fiscal year are subject to disclosure.[48] This would include a "contract executive" who is hired to serve as a registrant's chief executive officer for either a specified or indefinite period.

Even though an individual may not have served as the registrant's chief executive officer for the entire covered fiscal year, all compensation paid to, or earned by, that individual during the full fiscal year for services to the registrant must be reported.[49] In addition, in the case of the Summary Compensation Table, the full year's compensation information must be provided for any prior fiscal year in which the chief executive officer served in that capacity, either for the full year or any

44. *See* Item 402(a)(3)(i) and, in the case of smaller reporting companies, Item 402(m)(2)(i).

45. On the other hand, unless an individual has served as chief executive officer or in a similar capacity for some portion of the last completed fiscal year, he or she will not be part of the NEO group simply because he or she served as chief executive officer (or in a similar capacity) during the two prior fiscal years of the three-year period covered by the Summary Compensation Table.

46. As explained in the Adopting Release, this nomenclature was selected to conform to the terms used in Item 5.02 of Form 8-K (17 C.F.R. 249.308). *See* the Adopting Release, *supra* note 1, at n.326.

47. *See* Item 402(a)(3)(i) and, in the case of smaller reporting companies, Item 402(m)(2)(i).

48. *Id.* While it is not likely to arise very often, if an executive officer or other employee of a subsidiary of the registrant performs a policy-making function for the registrant that is akin to that of a chief executive officer, his or her compensation will need to be reported. *See* Instruction 2 to Item 402(a)(3) and, in the case of smaller reporting companies, Instruction 2 to Item 402(m)(2). *See also* Exchange Act Rule 3b-7 (17 C.F.R. 240.3b-7).

49. *See* Item 402(a)(4) and, in the case of smaller reporting companies, Item 402(m)(3). Even though the text of the Item uses the word "should" rather than "shall," this provision should be interpreted as mandatory.

part of the year.[50] It is not necessary to report the chief executive officer's compensation for any other fiscal year covered by the table in which he or she served in a different capacity, even if he or she was an executive officer.

Chief Financial Officer

The NEO group includes the individual serving as the registrant's chief financial officer at the end of the last completed fiscal year, as well as any other individual who served in that capacity at any time during the last fiscal year.[51] In other words, all individuals who served as a chief financial officer or in a similar capacity during the last completed fiscal year must be considered NEOs of the registrant. Consequently, a registrant may have more than one chief financial officer in its disclosure for the last completed fiscal year.

Under the rules, this individual (or individuals) is referred to as the "principal financial officer," or PFO.[52] The chief financial officer is to be included in the disclosure without regard to his or her actual compensation level.[53]

The SEC's decision to include the chief financial officer in the NEO group is a reflection of the enhanced prominence of this position in the eyes of investors since the enactment of the Sarbanes-Oxley Act of 2002. Along with a registrant's chief executive officer, the chief financial officer must certify the registrant's Exchange Act periodic reports[54] and has overall responsibility for the fair presentation of the registrant's financial statements and other financial information.

As a practical matter, however, the express designation of the chief financial officer as a NEO means that, for some registrants, the NEO group may not reflect the registrant's five most highly compensated executive officers. In the case of registrants whose chief financial officer is not highly compensated, that individual will replace a more senior or

---

50. *Id.* Consequently, if a chief executive officer served as the president of the registrant in fiscal year one, was promoted to the chief executive officer position in fiscal year two, and served as chief executive officer for all of the last completed fiscal year, the Summary Compensation Table would include his or her compensation for the last completed fiscal year and fiscal year two, but not fiscal year one.

51. *See* Item 402(a)(3)(ii).

52. *See supra* note 46.

53. *See* Item 402(a)(3)(ii).

54. *See* Exchange Act Rules 13a-14 and 15d-14 (17 C.F.R. 240.13a-14 and 240.15d-14).

more highly compensated executive who, under the former rules, would have been subject to disclosure.

The rules make clear that an individual's title is not dispositive in determining whether he or she is or was the registrant's chief financial officer. Thus, all individuals who performed the duties and responsibilities of the chief financial officer or acted in a similar capacity during the last completed fiscal year are subject to disclosure.[55] This would include a "contract executive" who is hired to serve as a registrant's chief financial officer for either a specified or indefinite period.

Even though an individual may not have served as the registrant's chief financial officer for the entire covered fiscal year, all compensation paid to, or earned by, that individual during the full fiscal year for services to the registrant must be reported.[56] In addition, in the case of the Summary Compensation Table, the full year's compensation information must be provided for any prior fiscal year in which the chief financial officer served in that capacity, either for the full year or any part of the year.[57] It is not necessary to report the chief financial officer's compensation for any other fiscal year covered by the table in which he or she served in a different capacity, even if he or she was an executive officer.

The SEC Staff has indicated that, where an individual who was a registrant's chief financial officer for part of the last completed fiscal year then serves the registrant as an executive officer in a different capacity at the end of that fiscal year, and is among the registrant's three most highly compensated executive officers at fiscal year end, this executive officer should be included in the NEO group as an individual "serving as the registrant's principal financial officer . . . during the last completed fiscal year"[58] rather than as one of the registrant's three most highly compensated executive officers . . . who were serving as executive officers at the end of the last completed fiscal year."[59]

If an executive officer or other employee of a subsidiary of the registrant performs a policy-making function for the registrant that is

55. *See* Item 402(a)(3)(4).
56. *See* Item 402(a)(4).
57. *Id.*
58. *See* Item 402(a)(3)(ii).
59. *See* the Current Staff Guidance, *supra* note 13, at Q&A 117.06.

akin to that of a chief financial officer, is or her compensation will need to be reported.[60]

Most Highly Compensated Executive Officers

The NEO group is completed with a registrant's three most highly compensated executive officers (other than its chief executive officer and chief financial officer)[61] who were serving as executive officers[62] at the end of the last completed fiscal year[63] and whose total compensation for the fiscal year (adjusted as explained in the following paragraph[64]) exceeds $100,000.[65] A registrant should identify its three most highly compensated executive officers from among the individuals serving as executive officers at the end of the last completed fiscal year who did not serve as its principal executive officer or principal financial officer at any time during that fiscal year.[66]

---

60. *See supra* note 48.

61. That is, the individuals who are serving as chief executive officer and chief financial officer at the end of the last completed fiscal year.

62. *See supra* note 42. Generally, the determination of a registrant's executive officers will track its executive officers for purposes of Section 16 of the Exchange Act. (15 U.S.C. § 78p).

63. *See* Item 402(a)(3)(iii) and, in the case of smaller reporting companies, Item 402(m)(2)(ii) (although limited to the registrant's two most highly compensated executive officers). An individual's status as an executive officer at the end of the last completed fiscal year is dispositive. The fact that the individual terminated employment with the registrant or relinquishes his or her executive position before the relevant filings are made does not relieve the registrant of its obligation to include the individual in the NEO group.

64. As required to be disclosed pursuant to Item 402(c)(2)(x), but reduced by the amount required to be disclosed pursuant to Item 402(c)(2)(viii).

65. *See* Instruction 1 to Item 402(a)(3) and, in the case of smaller reporting companies, Instruction 1 to Item 402(m)(2). In the case of a registrant that had recently changed its fiscal year-end from December 31 to June 30 and was preparing its transition report for the six-month period ended June 30 (having previously filed its annual report on Form 10-K for the fiscal year ended on the previous December 31), and where the registrant generally had a group of executive officers that earned in excess of $100,000 each year and, in addition, during the six-month period the registrant had made an acquisition that resulted in new executive officers who, on an annual basis, would earn more than $100,000, but during the six-month period none of these existing or new officers earned more than $100,000 in total compensation, the SEC Staff advised that no disclosure was needed with respect to the executive officers who started employment during the six-month period and did not, during that period, earn more than $100,000, and that, with respect to the executive officers who were employed both during and before the six-month period, Item 402 disclosure would have to be provided for those who earned in excess of $100,000 during the one-year period ending June 30 (the same ending date as the six-month period, but extending back over six months of the preceding fiscal year). *See* the Current Staff Guidance, *supra* note 13, at Interpretation 217.04.

66. *See* the Current Staff Guidance, *supra* note 13, at Q&A 117.06.

For purposes of determining a registrant's most highly compensated executive officers, an executive officer's compensation is his or her actual compensation for the last completed fiscal year.[67] In the rare situation where two or more executive officers have the same amount of total compensation for the last completed fiscal year and, thus, tie for the third most highly compensated executive officer position, then all of these individuals would be included in the NEO group.[68]

For purposes of determining a registrant's most highly compensated executive officers, a registrant is to measure its executive officers' total compensation[69] for the last completed fiscal year as reported in the Summary Compensation Table,[70] but reduced by the amount reported in the Change in Pension Value and Nonqualified Deferred Compensation Earnings column[71] of that table. This approach, which differs from the former rules (which looked solely at total annual salary and bonus), is a response to the proliferation of alternative forms of compensation, other than salary and bonus, used to compensate executives and, in the SEC's view, a more accurate gauge of which executives are, in fact, the most highly compensated. It also reduces the ability to recharacterize or shift compensation from cash to a noncash form to avoid disclosure of an executive's pay.[72]

Accordingly, to offset concerns about the impact of compensation elements that principally reflect executives' decisions to defer compensation and wealth accumulation through pension plans, these elements have been excluded from total compensation, although the exclusion applies *solely* for purposes of determining the registrant's most highly compensated executive officers. This change also was intended to

---

67. The compensation of an incoming executive officer should not be annualized. *See* the Current Staff Guidance, *supra* note 13, at Interpretation 217.06.

68. See W. Alan Kailer, Hunton & Williams, The Securities and Exchange Commission's Executive Compensation Rules—Preparing the Executive Compensation Tables (Jan. 2012) [hereinafter Kailer], at 3.

69. Presumably, this would include compensation for services as a director (*see* Instruction 3 to Item 402(c)), as well as consulting fees.

70. *See* "Total Compensation" in Chapter 4.

71. *See* Item 402(c)(2)(viii). This provision does not apply in the case of a smaller reporting company, which is not required to include a Change in Pension Value and Nonqualified Deferred Compensation Earnings column in its Summary Compensation Table. *See* Item 402(n)(2)(viii).

72. Further, the SEC's decision to eliminate the distinction between "annual" and "long-term" compensation in the Summary Compensation Table made the use of annual salary and bonus moot.

address commenters' concerns that, because these compensation elements are outside the compensation committee's control, their inclusion would minimize the committee's pay decisions for the most recent fiscal year. Though the inclusion of equity awards in total compensation may lead to frequent changes to the NEO group, on balance, the SEC decided that this approach would provide investors a clearer picture of a registrant's most highly compensated executives.

The shift from total annual salary and bonus under the former rules[73] to total compensation under the current rules for purposes of determining a registrant's most highly compensated executive officers means that there may be less consistency in the NEO group from year to year. It also means that an extraordinary or unusual one-time payment to an executive officer may catapult that executive into the NEO group for a single year, with him or her exiting the group the following year when his or her total compensation drops back to prior levels.

The rules retain the exclusion of payments of cash compensation relating to overseas assignments that are attributable predominantly to such assignment from the calculation of an executive officer's total compensation, which have the potential to skew the determination of the individuals who were actually a registrant's most highly compensated executives.[74] This exclusion is not automatic but is to be based on the registrant's judgment that the compensation was payable primarily to offset the costs and expenses incurred by the executive officer as a result of the overseas assignment. Compensation items that may qualify for this exclusion include, among other things, base salary adjustments, exchange rate differentials, and tax equalization payments.[75] Since NEO status is not limited to U.S.-based executives, the exclusion is equally

---

73. *See* Instruction 1 to former Item 402(a)(3). Under the former rules, the determination of a registrant's most highly compensated executive officers was based solely on total annual salary and bonus for the last fiscal year, subject to a $100,000 disclosure threshold.

74. *See* Instruction 3 to Item 402(a)(3) and, in the case of smaller reporting companies, Instruction 3 to Item 402(m)(2). Under the former rules, registrants also were permitted to exclude an usually large amount of cash compensation that was not part of a recurring arrangement and was unlikely to continue. *See* Instruction 3 to former Item 402(a)(3). This exclusion has not been retained in the current rules due to concerns about the inconsistent interpretation of the exclusion's standard and its susceptibility to manipulation, particularly when applied to payments that could otherwise be characterized as bonuses (such as signing, integration, or retention bonuses). *See* the Adopting Release, *supra* note 1, at nn.336 & 337 and accompanying text.

75. Note that a housing allowance may be considered a perquisite or other personal benefit, thereby disqualifying it from this exclusion. *See* "Other Issues—Relocation Expenses" in Chapter 5.

available to foreign executive officers who are posted to an overseas assignment in the United States. Note, however, that although the compensation attributable to an overseas assignment may be excluded in determining whether an executive officer is a NEO, it must be disclosed in the Summary Compensation Table if the executive is nonetheless found to be a NEO. In other words, the exclusion applies only for purposes of determining which executive officers are a registrant's most highly compensated, and not to permit these amounts to be omitted from the Summary Compensation Table for all purposes.[76]

Occasionally, a parent company's executive officers will divide their time between the parent and a subsidiary corporation and receive a portion of their compensation from the subsidiary as well as the parent. Where both entities are Exchange Act reporting companies, the SEC Staff has advised that if an executive officer spends 100 percent (or near 100 percent) of his or her time for the subsidiary but is paid by the parent, then the compensation paid by the parent has to be reported in the compensation tables of the subsidiary.[77] If an allocation of the monies paid by the parent would be necessary because the executive officer splits time between the parent and the subsidiary, the payments made by the parent need not be included in the subsidiary's compensation tables.[78] In addition, in the event that the subsidiary pays a management fee to the parent for use of the executives, disclosure of the structure of the management agreement and fees would have to be reported under Item 404.[79] Compensation paid by the subsidiary to executive officers of the parent must be included in the parent's compensation tables if such payments are paid directly by the subsidiary.[80] Once again, if the payments are part of a management contract, disclosure of the structure of the management agreement and fees would have to be reported under Item 404.[81]

---

76. Further, the reference in the instruction to "cash" compensation probably should not be read literally. Under the former rules, which used the same phrasing as Instruction 3 to Item 402(a)(3) and Instruction 3 to Item 402(m)(2), the SEC Staff had previously informally indicated that the reference to "cash" was intended to be illustrative only, and wasn't intended to exclude stock or other forms of noncash compensation.

77. *See* the Current Staff Guidance, *supra* note 13, at Interpretation 217.08.

78. *Id.*

79. *Id. See* Item 404(a) of Regulation S-K (17 C.F.R. 229.404(a)).

80. *Id.*

81. *Id.*

In a variation from the previous situation, the SEC Staff was asked to clarify the proper reporting treatment where an executive was the chief executive officer of a parent company, an Exchange Act reporting company for all of its last completed fiscal year and, in addition, served as the chief executive officer of its consolidated subsidiary, a separate Exchange Act reporting company, for a portion of the same fiscal year. In addition, a different executive was an executive officer of the parent company for all of its last completed fiscal year and, in addition, served as the chief financial officer of the subsidiary for all of the same fiscal year. Even though the parent company made all of the salary and bonus payments to the two executives, pursuant to intercompany accounting: 60% of the chief executive officer's salary and bonus for the last completed fiscal year was allocated to the subsidiary; and 85% of the chief financial officer's salary and bonus for the last completed fiscal year was also allocated to the subsidiary. If all of the chief financial officer's salary and bonus are included, he would be one of the parent company's three most highly compensated executive officers for thr last completed fiscal year, but if the 85% allocable to the subsidiary is excluded, he would not qualify as a NEO of the parent company.

On these facts, the SEC Staff took the position that 100% of the salary and bonus of each of the two executives was to be counted in determining the three most highly compensated executive officers of the parent company and disclosed in the parent company's Summary Compensation Table.[82] In reaching this conclusion, the Staff noted that the NEO determinations and compensation disclosures of the parent company should not be affected by whether its subsidiary is a public or private entity.[83] The Staff also took the position that the Summary Compensation Table of the subsidiary should report the respective percentages (60% for the chief executive officer and 85% for the chief financial officer) of salary and bonus allocated to the subsidiary's books.[84] Finally, each Summary Compensation Table should include footnote disclosure noting the extent to which the same compensation is being reported in both tables.

Even though an individual may not have served as an executive officer for the entire covered fiscal year, or may have served in multiple executive officer positions, all compensation paid to, or earned by, that

---

82. *See* the Current Staff Guidance, *supra* note 13, at Interpretation 217.09.

83. *Id.*

84. *Id.*

individual during the full fiscal year must be considered for purposes of determining whether he or she is a NEO[85] and, if a NEO, reported.[86] Under the rules, in the case of the Summary Compensation Table, if a NEO (other than the chief executive officer or the chief financial officer) served as an executive officer of the registrant (whether or not in the same position) during any part of a fiscal year with respect to which compensation information is required, this information is to be provided as to all compensation of that individual for the full fiscal year.[87]

Note that during the transition to the full three-year Summary Compensation Table, the SEC Staff took the position that, to the extent that an individual was not a NEO in one or more of the prior fiscal years covered by the Summary Compensation Table, only compensation information for the last completed fiscal year needed to be provided.[88] Subsequently, the Staff has indicated that, where an individual is a NEO for the first time and in one or more of the prior fiscal years covered by the Summary Compensation Table was an executive officer of the registrant, the registrant must provide the disclosure required by Item 402(c)(2) in the Summary Compensation Table for the last completed fiscal year as well as each of the other fiscal years covered by the table.[89]

From time to time, the chief executive officer or chief financial officer of a registrant may step down from that position but still be serving as an executive officer at the end of the last completed fiscal year. The question has arisen as to whether this individual is to be included

85. *See* the Current Staff Guidance, *supra* note 13, at Interpretation 217.07. *See also* Kailer, *supra* note 68, at B-1.

86. *See* Item 402(a)(4) and, in the case of smaller reporting companies, Item 402(m)(3).

87. *Id.* Notably, the treatment of a registrant's chief executive officer and chief financial officer is different. Compensation information for these individuals must be reported only for the fiscal year or years in which they served in those capacities. It does not have to be reported for any fiscal year in which they served in any other capacity. *See supra* note 50.

88. *See* the Current Staff Guidance, *supra* note 13, at Q&A 119.01. *See also* the 2007 JCEB Questions, *supra* note 15, at Question No. 3. In view of the fact that the transition to the full three-year Summary Compensation Table has been completed, the SEC Staff has indicated that it is re-evaluating the need for Q&A 119.01. *See* Questions and Answers, Technical Session Between the SEC Staff and the Joint Committee on Employee Benefits (May 4, 2010) [hereinafter 2010 JCEB Questions], *available at* http://www.americanbar.org/content/dam/aba/events/employee_benefits/2010_sec_qa.authcheckdam.pdf, at Question No. 3.

89. *See* the 2010 JCEB Questions, *supra* note 88, at Question No. 3. Similarly, the SEC Staff has taken the position that, in a situation where an executive officer was a NEO in fiscal year one and also a NEO in the last completed fiscal year, but not in fiscal year two (the middle year), the registrant must provide the disclosure required by Item 402(c)(2) in the Summary Compensation Table for all three fiscal years. *See* the Current Staff Guidance, *supra* note 13, at Q&A 119.18.

in the disclosure in his or her capacity as a chief executive officer or chief financial officer, as the case may be, or as one of the registrant's other three most highly compensated executive officers. The SEC Staff has indicated that, in this situation, this individual should be included in the disclosure as a former chief executive officer or chief financial officer during the last completed fiscal year.[90] In other words, he or she would not replace another individual who was among the three most highly compensated executive officers for the fiscal year even if his or her total compensation exceeds that of these individuals.

If an executive officer or other employee of a subsidiary of the registrant performs a policy-making function for the registrant that establishes him or her as an executive officer of the registrant, his or her compensation will need to be reported.[91]

Former Executive Officers

The rules' focus on an executive officer's status as such at the end of the last completed fiscal year means that a highly compensated executive officer who has left the registrant or is no longer serving as an executive officer at fiscal year-end could potentially avoid disclosure. To foreclose this possibility, the NEO group includes up to two additional individuals for whom disclosure would have been required (as one of the three most highly compensated executive officers other than the chief executive officer or chief financial officer) but for the fact that the individual was not serving as an executive officer of the registrant at the end of the last completed fiscal year.[92]

This provision applies both to an executive officer who has terminated his or her employment with the registrant during the last completed fiscal year and to an executive officer who became a nonexecutive employee during the last completed fiscal year and did not depart from the registrant.[93] In these situations, a registrant must

---

90. *See* the Current Staff Guidance, *supra* note 13, at Q&A 117.06.

91. *See* Instruction 2 to Item 402(a)(3) and, in the case of smaller reporting companies, Instruction 2 to Item 402(m)(2). *See also* Exchange Act Rule 3b-7 (17 C.F.R. 240.3b-7).

92. *See* Item 402(a)(3)(iv) and, in the case of smaller reporting companies, Item 402(m)(2)(iii). This requirement was initially added to the former rules to prevent the manipulation of the NEO group by having an otherwise highly compensated executive officer relinquish his or her position to avoid disclosure. *See* Executive Compensation Disclosure; Securityholder Lists and Mailing Requests, Release Nos. 33-7032, 34-33229 (Nov. 22, 1993), 58 Fed. Reg. 63,010 (Nov. 29, 1993).

93. *See* the Current Staff Guidance, *supra* note 13, at Interpretation 217.07.

consider the compensation the former executive officer received during the entire fiscal year for purposes of determining whether that individual is a NEO under this provision for the last completed fiscal year.[94] If a former executive officer thus would qualify as a NEO, the registrant must disclose all of the individual's compensation for the full fiscal year (that is, the compensation for the period the individual was an executive officer and for the period the individual was a non-executive employee).[95]

The shift from total annual salary and bonus under the former rules[96] to total compensation under the current rules for purposes of determining a registrant's most highly compensated executive officers increases the likelihood that, in any given fiscal year, the NEO group will consist of more than five individuals. This is primarily due to the inclusion of amounts paid to or accrued on behalf of an executive officer in connection with a termination of employment or a change in control of the registrant in that executive's total compensation.[97] Consequently, if a former executive officer receives a significant severance payment, this may cause his or her total compensation to exceed that of one or more of the registrant's most highly compensated executive officers at the end of the last completed fiscal year even though his or her other compensation for the year (for example, base salary and/or bonus) reflects only a partial year's employment. On the other hand, the SEC Staff has indicated that, if an executive officer dies during the last completed fiscal year, the proceeds of a life insurance policy funded by the registrant and paid to the deceased executive officer's estate need not be taken into consideration in determining whether the executive officer is a member of the group of up to two additional individuals for whom disclosure is required under this provision.[98]

---

94. In the case of a NEO who became a non-executive officer employee, this would include his or her compensation both as an executive officer and as a non-executive officer employee. *Id.* The compensation of a departing executive officer should not be annualized. *See* the Current Staff Guidance, *supra* note 13, at Interpretation 217.06.

95. *Id.*

96. *See* Instruction 1 to former Item 402(a)(3).

97. *See* Item 402(c)(2)(ix)(D) and, in the case of smaller reporting companies, Item 402(n)(2)(ix)(D).

98. *See* the Current Staff Guidance, *supra* note, 13, at Interpretation 217.14.

Directors

Compensation disclosure (that is, the Director Compensation Table and accompanying narrative disclosure) is required about each member of a registrant's board of directors.[99] This includes directors who are serving on the board of directors at the end of the registrant's last completed fiscal year as well as any individual who served as a director during any part of the last completed fiscal year, even if that individual was no longer a director at fiscal year-end.[100] Disclosure also is required for an individual who served as a director during the last completed fiscal year even if he or she will not stand for reelection in the current fiscal year.[101]

Honorary or Emeritus Directors

Where a registrant's board of directors includes one or more honorary or "emeritus" directors, disclosure of the compensation paid to these individuals would appear to be based on considerations similar to those used to determine whether the individual is a reporting person for purposes of Section 16(a) of the Exchange Act.[102] Thus, if the director takes part in formulating and deciding policy issues for the registrant, it may be appropriate to treat him or her as a director subject to disclosure under the rules. Similarly, an advisory director who attends board meetings and has access to material nonpublic information of the registrant should be evaluated to determine whether the compensation paid to him or her needs to be disclosed.

Compensation Covered

The rules require clear, concise, and understandable disclosure of all compensation[103] awarded to, earned by, or paid to a registrant's NEOs, and to its directors, by any person for all services rendered in all

---

99. *See* Item 402(k)(1) and, in the case of smaller reporting companies, Item 402(r)(1).

100. *See* the Current Staff Guidance, *supra* note 13, at Q&A 127.01.

101. *See id.* at Q&A 127.02.

102. 15 U.S.C. § 78p(a). *See also* Interpretive Release on Rules Applicable to Insider Trading and Reporting, Release No. 34-18114 (Sept. 24, 1981), 46 Fed. Reg. 48,147 (Oct. 1, 1981), at Question 2.

103. While the rules speak in terms of plan and nonplan compensation, in view of the definition indicating that a plan may be applicable to one person, which effectively sweeps any compensation arrangement into the definition, it is not clear that this distinction is necessary.

capacities to the registrant and its subsidiaries.[104] This requirement is all encompassing; unless a compensation item is specifically excluded from disclosure,[105] it must be reported.[106] In addition, all compensation must be reported, even if also called for by another requirement, including transactions between a registrant and a third party where a purpose of the transaction is to furnish compensation to any of the registrant's NEOs.[107] Generally, compensation is calculated in a manner that reflects the cost of the compensation to the registrant and its security holders.[108]

In recent years, the SEC has been particularly direct in explicitly reminding registrants that the executive and director compensation disclosure rules require disclosure of "all" compensation. Moreover, this basic requirement to disclose all compensation takes precedence over the detailed requirements of the various tables in which disclosure is to be presented.[109] Consequently, unless a registrant has disclosed all plan and nonplan compensation for all services rendered that is awarded to, earned by, or paid to its executive officers and directors, whether these amounts are paid currently or deferred, it is not in compliance, literal or otherwise, with the SEC's rules.[110]

Overall, the rules retain the SEC's directive of single-year disclosure of compensation. Accordingly, no amount reported as compensation for one fiscal year need be reported in the same manner as compensation for a subsequent fiscal year.[111] Given the potential overlap of the rules in some compensation areas, this principle is likely to come into play

---

104. *See* Item 402(a)(2) and, in the case of smaller reporting companies, Item 402(m)(1).

105. *See, e.g.*, Item 402(a)(6)(ii) and, in the case of smaller reporting companies, Item 402(m)(5)(ii), which permit the exclusion of registrant payments regarding broad-based, nondiscriminatory group life, health, hospitalization, and medical reimbursement plans, and Item 402(c)(2)(ix)(A) and, in the case of smaller reporting companies, Item 402(n)(2)(ix)(A), which permit the exclusion of perquisites and other personal benefits if they total less than $10,000 for an individual NEO.

106. *See* Item 402(a)(2) and, in the case of smaller reporting companies, Item 402(m)(1).

107. *Id.* Thus compensation paid to a NEO by a parent or subsidiary of a registrant must be reported. *See also* the Current Staff Guidance, *supra* note 13, at Interpretations 217.08 and 217.13.

108. *See* the Adopting Release, *supra* note 1, at n.132.

109. *See* Alan L. Beller, Director, Division of Corporation Finance, U.S. Securities & Exchange Comm'n, Remarks Before the Conference of the NASPP, The Corporate Counsel and The Corporate Executive (Oct. 20, 2004) (often referred to as the "All Means All" speech), *available at* http://www.sec.gov/news/speech/spch102004alb.htm.

110. *See* Item 402(a)(2) and, in the case of smaller reporting companies, Item 402(m)(1).

111. *Id.* For example, a stock option reported in the Summary Compensation Table at grant does not need to be included in that table again when the option is exercised.

under the current rules more frequently than under the former rules. Because the rules envision following numerous compensation elements from their inception until final realization, however, this principle is not unlimited. For example, in the case of employee stock options, these awards will be reported first in the year of grant, each year that they remain outstanding at fiscal year-end, and then when they are eventually exercised. Similarly, a multiyear cash-based incentive award will be reported both in the year that the compensation is awarded and then again at the end of the performance period when the amount actually payable is determined. The rules reflect this approach by acknowledging that amounts reported as compensation for one fiscal year may be required to be reported in a different manner pursuant to the rules, typically in a subsequent fiscal year.[112]

This principle essentially tracks the comparable provision of the former rules,[113] and, reflecting the SEC's intention of ensuring that the disclosure is comprehensive, is, if anything, even more expansive. For example, under the former rules, transactions between a registrant and a third party that involved furnishing compensation to a NEO were reportable only if the provision of compensation was the primary purpose of the transaction.[114] Under the current rules, such compensation is reportable where compensating a NEO was merely *a* purpose of the transaction.[115] In addition, the exclusion for compensation that has been reported in a prior fiscal year has been clarified to ensure that, given the rules' tracking of certain compensation items over their entire life cycle (for example, stock options), these items are not inadvertently omitted from disclosure.

The rules also are intended to pick up compensatory transactions that previously did not need to be disclosed because they were otherwise disclosable under the related person transaction disclosure requirement of Item 404.[116] In a reversal from the former rules, Item 404 now

---

112. *Id.* Again, for example, a stock option is reported in the Summary Compensation Table in connection with its grant and in the Option Exercises and Stock Vested Table when it is exercised.

113. *See* former Item 402(a)(2).

114. *Id. See also* former Item 402(a)(5).

115. *See* Item 402(a)(2) and, in the case of smaller reporting companies, Item 402(m)(1).

116. *See* former Items 402(a)(2) and (a)(5). Former Item 402(a)(5), which provided that no response was required under Item 402 as to any third-party transaction if the transaction had been reported under Item 404, was deleted outright and former Item 402(a)(2) was amended to eliminate the controlling cross-reference.

provides that compensatory transactions with executive officers and directors need not be disclosed thereunder to the extent that they are reported under the current rules.[117] As a result, in some situations, the disclosure of some compensatory transactions may be bifurcated, with the compensation information disclosed under the current rules, while the related person transaction giving rise to that compensation will also be disclosed under Item 404.

Timing of Reporting

Generally, all compensation must be reported in the fiscal year in which it is earned, regardless of when it is actually paid to a NEO.[118] Thus, even though a registrant may not make specific compensation decisions and pay compensation amounts until after fiscal year-end, if the compensation items being decided (and paid) relate to the prior fiscal year, they should be addressed in the CD&A[119] and reported in the compensation tables for the last completed fiscal year. For example, it is common for registrants to wait until after fiscal year-end (when corporate and individual performance results have been compiled and evaluated) to make decisions with respect to the prior year's annual bonuses or incentive award payouts. Even though these decisions (and payouts) occur after fiscal year-end, because they are closely tied to the last completed fiscal year, they should be discussed in the CD&A and reported in the compensation tables for that year.

The application of the rules to equity awards, however, will result in different reporting treatment from that just described. Under the current rules, equity awards are to be reported in the Summary Compensation Table, as well as the related compensation tables, in the fiscal year in which the registrant calculates and begins to recognize compensation expense for the award for financial reporting purposes (essentially, the year in which the award is granted). Consequently, a registrant that makes compensation decisions about equity awards after fiscal year-end will typically report these awards in the fiscal year in which they are

---

117. *See* Instruction 5 to Item 404(a) of Regulation S-K (17 C.F.R. 229.404(a), Instruction 5).

118. *See, e.g.,* Item 402(a)(2) and Item 402(c)(2)(iii) and (iv).

119. *See* Instruction 2 to Item 402(b), which states that "the Compensation Discussion and Analysis should . . . cover actions regarding executive compensation that were taken after the registrant's last fiscal year end . . . that could affect a fair understanding of the NEO's compensation for the last fiscal year."

granted even though their size (or even the decision to make the award) may be closely tied to the prior fiscal year's service or performance. Nonetheless, the registrant should still consider discussing these awards in its CD&A for the last completed fiscal year if necessary to present a fair understanding of the NEOs' compensation for such fiscal year.[120] Thus, the reporting of equity awards under the rules will require the exercise of judgment by a registrant as to how to best balance the technical disclosure requirements with the objective of providing investors with a clear understanding of its executive compensation program.

Definitions

While many of the general definitions under the Exchange Act and the related rules are applicable for purpose of providing the required executive and director compensation information,[121] the rules also provide several specific definitions that apply to the disclosure. These definitions are more numerous than under the former rules, reflecting the expanded coverage of the rules.[122] Generally, the definitions are the same for both regular registrants and registrants that qualify as smaller reporting companies.

Equity

For purposes of the rules, the term "equity" is used to refer generally to stock and/or options.[123]

Stock

For purposes of the rules, the term "stock" means instruments such as common stock, restricted stock, restricted stock units, phantom stock,

---

120. Thus, it may be necessary or appropriate for a registrant to address in its CD&A equity awards made during a prior fiscal year that are reported in the compensation tables for the last completed fiscal year, or equity awards made in the last completed fiscal year that will not be reported in the compensation tables until the subsequent fiscal year. *See* Kailer, *supra* note 68, at 6.

121. *See* Exchange Act Rules 3b-1 et seq. (17 C.F.R. 240.3b-1 et seq.).

122. Under the former rules, only the terms "stock appreciation rights," "plan," and "long term incentive plan" were defined.

123. *See* Item 402(a)(6)(i) and, in the case of smaller reporting companies, Item 402(m) (5)(i).

phantom stock units, common stock equivalent units, or any similar instruments that do not have option-like features.[124]

Options

For purposes of the rules, the term "option" means instruments such as stock options, stock appreciation rights, and similar instruments with option-like features.[125]

Stock Appreciation Rights

For purposes of the rules, the term "stock appreciation rights" (SARs) refers to SARs payable in cash or stock, including SARs payable in cash or stock at the election of the registrant or a NEO.[126]

Plan

For purposes of the rules, the term "plan" includes, but is not limited to, any plan, contract, authorization, or arrangement, whether or not set forth in any formal document, pursuant to which cash, securities, similar instruments, or any other property may be received.[127] A plan may be applicable to one person.[128]

Not with standing this expansive definition, registrants may omit information regarding group life, health, hospitalization, or medical reimbursement plans that do not discriminate in scope, terms, or operation in favor of executive officers or directors of the registrant and that are available generally to all salaried employees.[129] In addition, the SEC Staff has indicated that this exclusion applies to broad-based

---

124. *See* Item 402(a)(6)(i) and, in the case of smaller reporting companies, Item 402(m)(5)(i).

125. *See* Item 402(a)(6)(i) and, in the case of smaller reporting companies, Item 402(m)(5)(i).

126. *See* Item 402(a)(6)(i) and, in the case of smaller reporting companies, Item 402(m)(5)(i). This definition is identical to the definition in the former rules. *See* former Item 402(a)(7)(i).

127. *See* Item 402(a)(6)(ii) and, in the case of smaller reporting companies, Item 402(m)(5)(ii). This definition is similar, but not identical, to the definition in the former rules, reflecting the new definitions of the terms "equity," "stock," and "options." *See* former Item 402(a)(7)(ii).

128. *See* Item 402(a)(6)(ii) and, in the case of smaller reporting companies, Item 402(m)(5)(ii).

129. *Id.* This exclusion differs from the former rules, which also expressly excluded "relocation plans" from the definition. This change was prompted by the SEC's concern that these plans, even when generally available to all salaried employees, are susceptible to operation in a discriminatory manner favoring executive officers.

nondiscriminatory disability plans that satisfy these nondiscrimination requirements.[130] While the Staff has not taken a formal position on the matter, it is believed that, subject to this one addition, this exclusion is to be interpreted narrowly. Consequently, a registrant should assume that it is limited to the four identified plan categories and nondiscriminatory disability plans. It is not clear whether a plan in one of these four identified categories (or a disability plan) that excluded foreign employees, where the registrant cannot offer certain benefits to such employees due to the laws of the employees' jurisdiction, would qualify for the exclusion. It may be arguable that, in this situation, however, the exclusion should be available where the omission of these employees is not material to the fulfillment of the underlying rationale for the exclusion.

Incentive Plan

For purposes of the rules, the term "incentive plan" means any plan providing compensation intended to serve as incentive for performance to occur over a specified period, whether such performance is measured by reference to financial performance of the registrant or an affiliate, the registrant's stock price, or any other performance measure.[131]

Equity Incentive Plan

For purposes of the rules, an "equity incentive plan" is an incentive plan or portion of an incentive plan under which awards are granted that fall within the scope of Financial Accounting Standards Board Accounting Standards Codification Topic 718, *Compensation – Stock Compensation* (FASB ASC Topic 718).[132] Consequently, the category of equity incentive plans includes performance-based equity plans, whether the relevant performance criteria involve a performance or a market condition.[133] As defined in FASB ASC Topic 718,[134] a "performance condition" is

---

130. *See* the Current Staff Guidance, *supra* note 13, at Q&A 117.07. *See also* Questions and Answers, Technical Session between the SEC Staff and the Joint Committee on Employee Benefits (May 3, 2011), *available at* http://www.americanbar.org/content/dam/aba/events/employee_benefits/2010_sec_qas.final.110811.authcheckdam.pdf, at Question No. 1.

131. *See* Item 402(a)(6)(iii) and, in the case of smaller reporting companies, Item 402(m)(5)(iii).

132. *See* Item 402(a)(6)(iii) and, in the case of smaller reporting companies, Item 402(m)(5)(iii).

133. *See* the Adopting Release, *supra* note 1, at n.167.

134. See FASB ASC Paragraph 718-10-20 *Glossary.*

a condition affecting the vesting, exercisability, exercise price, or other pertinent factors used in determining the fair value of an award that relates to both (a) an employee's rendering service for a specified (either explicitly or implicitly) period of time and (b) achieving a specified performance target that is defined solely by reference to the employer's own operations (or activities). Attaining a specified growth rate in return on assets, obtaining regulatory approval to market a specified product, selling shares in an initial public offering or other financing event, and a change in control are examples of performance conditions for purposes of this Statement. A performance target also may be defined by reference to the same performance measure of another entity or group of entities. For example, attaining a growth rate in earnings per share that exceeds the average growth rate in earnings per share of other entities in the same industry is a performance condition for purposes of this Statement. A performance target might pertain either to the performance of the enterprise as a whole or to some part of the enterprise, such as a division or an individual employee.

In contrast, a "market condition" is

a condition affecting the exercise price, exercisability, or other pertinent factors used in determining the fair value of an award under a share-based payment arrangement that relates to the achievement of (a) a specified price of the issuer's shares or a specified amount of intrinsic value indexed solely to the issuer's shares or (b) a specified price of the issuer's shares in terms of a similar (or index of similar) equity security (securities).[135]

An award with accelerated vesting upon a change in control of the registrant is not considered an award under an equity incentive plan if the award contains no other performance or market conditions and the award would otherwise vest based on the completion of a specified employee service period.[136]

Nonequity Incentive Plan

For purposes of the rules, a "nonequity incentive plan" is an incentive plan or portion of an incentive plan that is not an equity incentive plan.[137]

---

135. Total shareholder return is an example of a performance measure that is considered to be a "market condition" condition for financial reporting purposes.

136. *Id.*

137. *See* Item 402(a)(6)(iii) and, in the case of smaller reporting companies, Item 402(m) (5)(iii).

Incentive Plan Award

For purposes of the rules, the term "incentive plan award" means an award provided under an incentive plan.[138]

Date of Grant/Grant Date

For purposes of the rules, the terms "date of grant" or "grant date" refer to the grant date determined for financial statement reporting purposes pursuant to FASB ASC Topic 718.[139]

Closing Market Price

For purposes of the rules, "closing market price" is defined as the price at which the registrant's security was last sold in the principal U.S. market for such security as of the date for which the closing market price is determined.[140]

Plain English Requirement

Under the rules, the disclosure must be provided in plain English.[141] Application of the plain English principles[142] is intended to ensure that the CD&A and the narrative discussions that accompany the compensation tables are clear and understandable, and to facilitate more informed investing and voting decisions in the face of complex information about executive and director compensation andother areas.

While some of the SEC Staff's comments during its review of the disclosures from the 2007 proxy season appeared to be at odds with aspects of the plain English principles (for example, requests for additional and more detailed analysis of compensation policies and practices and individual pay decisions), the Staff has indicated that this

---

138. *Id.*

139. *See* Item 402(a)(6)(iv) and, in the case of smaller reporting companies, Item 402(m)(5)(iv).

140. *See* Item 402(a)(6)(v) and, in the case of smaller reporting companies, Item 402(m)(5)(v).

141. *See* Exchange Act Rules 13a-20 and 15d-20 (17 C.F.R. 240.13a-20 and 240.15d-20).

142. *See* Plain English Disclosure, Release Nos. 33-7497, 34-39593, IC-23011 (Jan. 28, 1998), 63 Fed. Reg. 6369 (Feb. 6, 1998), adopting revisions to Securities Act Rule 421 (17 C.F.R. 230.421). The plain English requirements were first adopted in connection with the preparation of prospectuses under the Securities Act.

additional analysis need not result in longer disclosure. In its view, with careful drafting, a registrant can provide succinct and effective disclosure that embraces the plain English principles.[143] Under the SEC's plain English principles, compensation information must be presented in a clear, concise, and understandable manner. Accordingly, the disclosure must be prepared using the following standards:[144]

- Present information in clear, concise sections, paragraphs, and sentences.
- Use short sentences.
- Use definite, concrete, everyday words.
- Use the active voice.
- Avoid multiple negatives.
- Use descriptive headings and subheadings.
- Use a tabular presentation or bullet lists for complex material, wherever possible.
- Avoid legal jargon and highly technical business and other terminology.
- Avoid frequent reliance on glossaries or defined terms as the primary means of explaining information.
- Define terms in a glossary or other section of the document only if the meaning is unclear from the context.
- Use a glossary only if it facilitates understanding of the disclosure.
- In designing the presentation of the information, include pictures, logos, charts, graphs, and other design elements so long as the design is not misleading and the required information is clear, understandable, consistent with applicable disclosure requirements and any other included information, drawn to scale, and not misleading. Use tables, schedules, charts, and graphic illustrations that present relevant data in an understandable manner, so long as such presentations are consistent with applicable disclosure requirements and

---

143. *See* John W. White, Director, Division of Corporation Finance, U.S. Securities & Exchange Comm'n, *Where's the Analysis?*, Remarks Before the Second Annual Proxy Disclosure Conference: Tackling Your 2008 Compensation Disclosures (Oct. 9, 2007), *available at* http://www.sec.gov/news/speech/2007/spch100907jww.htm.

144. *See* Exchange Act Rules 13a-20(a) and 15d-20(a) (17 C.F.R. 240.13a-20(a) and 240.15d-20(a)).

any other included information, drawn to scale, and not misleading.

The Exchange Act rules provide guidance on drafting disclosure that would comply with plain English principles, including guidance as to the following practices that companies should avoid:

- legalistic or overly complex presentations that make the substance of the disclosure difficult to understand;
- vague "boilerplate" explanations that are imprecise and readily subject to different interpretations;
- complex information copied directly from legal documents without any clear and concise explanation of the provision or provisions; and
- disclosure repeated in different sections of the document that increases the size of the document but does not enhance the quality of the information.[145]

Under the rules, if executive compensation disclosure is incorporated by reference into an Exchange Act report from a registrant's proxy or information statement, the disclosure is required to be in plain English in the proxy or information statement.[146]

---

145. *See* the Note to Exchange Act Rule 13a-20 (17 C.F.R. 240.13a-20 Note) and the Note to Exchange Act Rule 15d-20 (17 C.F.R. 240.15d-20 Note).

146. *See,* for example, General Instruction G(3) to Form 10-K (specifying the information that may be incorporated by reference from a proxy or information statement in an annual report on Form 10-K).

3

Compensation Discussion and Analysis

General

When introduced, the Compensation Discussion and Analysis (CD&A) represented a wholly new approach to the presentation of executive compensation information. Now, after six years, it has become the centerpiece of a registrant's message about its approach to executive compensation to investors and the public generally.

A narrative discussion of the specific compensation awarded to, earned by, or paid to the named executive officers (NEOs) of a registrant[1] during the last completed fiscal year, the CD&A is intended to provide investors with an overview of the registrant's executive compensation

---

1. Item 402(b). A smaller reporting company is not required to provide a CD&A as part of its executive compensation disclosure. *See* Executive Compensation and Related Person Disclosure, Release Nos. 33-8732A, 34-54302A, IC-27444A (Aug. 29, 2006), 71 Fed. Reg. 53,158 (Sept. 8, 2006) [hereinafter Adopting Release], *available at* http://www.sec.gov/rules/final/2006/33-8732a.pdf, at Section II.D.1; and Smaller Reporting Company Regulatory Relief and Simplification, Release Nos. 33-8876, 34-56994, 39-2451 (Dec. 19, 2007), 73 Fed. Reg. 934 (Jan. 4, 2008) [hereinafter Small Company Release], *available at* http://www.sec.gov/rules/final/2007/ 33-8876.pdf, at Section III.C.1. Similarly, an emerging growth company that elects to follow the executive compensation disclosure requirements for smaller reporting companies is not required to provide a CD&A as part of its executive compensation disclosure. *See* the Jumpstart Our Business Startups Act, Pub. L. No. 112-106, 126 Stat. 306 (April 5, 2012), at Section 102(c).

policies and decisions and to put into perspective the compensation tables and their accompanying narrative.[2] It should analyze and explain the material factors that underlie these policies and that resulted in the specific pay decisions for the fiscal year, thereby putting into context the information presented in the compensation tables. In sum, it should provide investors with an understanding of a registrant's executive compensation decision-making process for the last completed fiscal year as seen "though the eyes of" the board compensation committee.

The CD&A represents a radical departure from the former Board Compensation Committee Report.[3] That report, which essentially supplemented the Summary Compensation Table, was supposed to describe a registrant's executive compensation policies for the last completed fiscal year[4] and discuss the bases for the chief executive officer's compensation for the last completed fiscal year, including the factors and criteria upon which his or her compensation was based.[5] Over the years, however, the effectiveness of the Compensation Committee Report became diluted, leading to a generalized discussion that, in the Securities and Exchange Commission's (SEC's) view, was of little benefit to investors.[6]

Consequently, it was scrapped in favor of the CD&A, which is to set up, rather than merely supplement, the compensation tables.

At its essence, the CD&A is to present a comprehensive discussion and analysis of the material factors underlying the compensation policies and decisions that are reflected in the compensation tables. Simply put, it is to focus on "how" and "why" a registrant reached its executive compensation decisions for the last completed fiscal year. Necessarily, this analysis will involve an explanation of the factors that

---

2. *See* Instruction 1 to Item 402(b). The CD&A should focus on the material principles underlying a registrant's executive compensation policies and decisions and the most important factors relevant to analysis of those policies and decisions. *See* Instruction 3 to Item 402(b).

3. *See* former Item 402(k).

4. *See* former Item 402(k)(1). This description, which covered all of the registrant's executive officers (not just the NEOs), also was to address the specific relationship of corporate performance to executive compensation. *Id.*

5. *See* former Item 402(k)(2). This discussion also was to address the relationship of the registrant's performance to the chief executive officer's compensation for the last completed fiscal year, describing each measure of the registrant's performance, whether qualitative or quantitative, on which his or her compensation was based. *Id.*

6. *See* Executive Compensation and Related Party Disclosure, Release Nos. 33-8655, 34-53185, IC-27218 (Jan. 27, 2006), 71 Fed. Reg. 6542 (Feb. 8, 2006) [hereinafter Proposing Release], *available at* http://www.sec.gov/rules/proposed/33-8655.pdf, at Section II.A.4.

were considered and how they influenced the amounts that were paid or awarded under each compensation element, as well as an explanation of how these elements (both individually and in the aggregate) affected the decisions about amounts paid or awarded under other compensation elements.[7] Consequently, the CD&A should be analytical rather than merely descriptive. As the SEC indicated in finalizing the executive compensation disclosure rules, the CD&A "should focus on the material principles underlying the registrant's executive compensation policies and decisions and the most important factors relevant to an analysis of those policies and decisions."[8]

As envisioned by the SEC, the CD&A should lead a registrant's executive compensation disclosure, putting into perspective for investors the numbers and narrative discussion that follow.[9]

Guiding Tenets

The CD&A is predicated on two fundamental tenets: It is to be "principles-based,"[10] and it is to be written in plain English. The former concept is intended to ensure that the discussion encompasses each and every material element of a registrant's executive compensation

7. See John W. White, Director, Division of Corporation Finance, U.S. Securities & Exchange Comm'n, *Where's the Analysis?*, Remarks Before the 2nd Annual Proxy Disclosure Conference: Tackling Your 2008 Compensation Disclosures (Oct. 9, 2007) [hereinafter White Analysis Speech], *available at* http://www.sec.gov/news/speech/2007/spch100907jww.htm. As noted by Mr. White in his remarks, the absence of meaningful analysis represented the biggest shortcoming in the CD&As filed during the 2007 proxy season. This concern continues to be a primary focus of the SEC Staff's review of registrants' executive compensation disclosure. See Shelley Parratt, Deputy Director, Division of Corporation Finance, U.S. Securities & Exchange Comm'n, *Executive Compensation Disclosure: Observations on the 2009 Proxy Season and Expectations for 2010*, Remarks Before the 4th Annual Proxy Disclosure Conference: Tackling Your 2010 Compensation Disclosures (Nov. 9, 2009) [hereinafter Parratt 2009 Speech], *available at* http://www.sec.gov/news/speech/2009/spch110909sp.htm.

8. *Id.*

9. *See* the Adopting Release, *supra* note 1, at Section II.B.1. Further, as noted in Division of Corporation Finance, *Staff Observations in the Review of Executive Compensation Disclosure* (Oct. 9, 2007) [hereinafter Staff Report], *available at* http://www.sec.gov/divisions/corpfin/guidance/execcompdisclosure.htm, the CD&A is to precede, rather than follow, the compensation tables.

10. In this regard, the CD&A is similar to the Management's Discussion and Analysis of Financial Condition and Results of Operation in the annual report on Form 10-K. See Item 7 of Part II of Form 10-K and Item 301 of Regulation S-K (17 C.F.R. 229.301). *See also* the White Analysis Speech, *supra* note 7. Generally, the MD&A presents a narrative discussion of the registrant's financial condition and operating results focusing on the events, risks, trends, and opportunities that are material to an investor's understanding of the registrant's financial position and results.

program, even where an item may not fit neatly into one of the described disclosure categories, as well as to provide sufficient flexibility to address future forms of compensation as they develop.[11] The latter concept is intended to ensure that the discussion is accessible to investors and provides information that is both meaningful and useful.[12] In taking this approach, the SEC is looking to produce more robust disclosure that is less susceptible to "boilerplate" presentations.

Principles-Based Disclosure

The rules take a "principles-based" approach to the CD&A. That is, they start by laying out the key reporting objectives and then providing guidance explaining the purpose of the objectives and demonstrating how they apply to some common examples.[13] In this regard, the rules identify several general disclosure concepts and then provide a series of illustrative examples of the type of information that may be disclosed within the framework of these concepts. The disclosure concepts are contained in seven specific items that a registrant must address to explain "how" and "why" its compensation decisions were reached.[14]

The illustrative examples are just that. They neither encompass the universe of possible required disclosures, nor are they mandatory.[15] In some instances, an example may not be material, or even relevant, to a registrant and, therefore, disclosure predicated on that example is not required. The application of a particular example must be tailored to a registrant's circumstances.[16] In other words, the registrant must assess the materiality to investors of the information that is described in the

---

11. *See* the Adopting Release, *supra* note 1, at Section II.B.1.

12. For a discussion of the SEC's "plain English" requirements, see "Plain English Requirement" in Chapter 2.

13. *See* John W. White, Director, Division of Corporation Finance, U.S. Securities & Exchange Comm'n, *Principles Matter*, Remarks Before the Practising Law Institute Conference (Sept. 6, 2006) [hereinafter White Principles Matter Speech], *available at* http://www.sec. gov/news/speech/2006/spch090606jww.htm, citing Robert Herz, Chairman of the Financial Accounting Standards Board, Remarks before the Financial Executives International Current Financial Reporting Issues Conference (Nov. 4, 2000): "Under a principles-based approach, one starts with laying out the key objectives of good reporting in the subject area, and then provides guidance explaining the objective and relating it to some common examples. While rules are sometimes unavoidable, the intent is not to try to provide specific guidance, or rules, for every possible situation. Rather, if in doubt, the reader is directed back to the principles."

14. *See* "Required Discussion Topics," *infra*.

15. *See* the White Analysis Speech, *supra* note 7.

16. *See* the Adopting Release, *supra* note 1, at Section II.B.1.

example in light of its own particular situation.[17] Alternatively, there may be aspects of a registrant's executive compensation program not reflected in the examples that are material to an investor's understanding of the registrant's compensation policies and decisions. In this case, the registrant must address these items in its CD&A, even though they fall outside the scope of the examples.

Plain English Disclosure

As the staff of the SEC's Division of Corporation Finance (SEC Staff) has noted, a plain English discussion involves more than just using small words and short sentences. It also means providing a clear and concise explanation of how and why specific compensation actions were taken and decisions were made.[18] Typically, this will require a discussion of many of the subjects set out in the illustrative examples to the CD&A as applied to the registrant's own particular facts and circumstances. It also will require that the lengthy and oft en complex provisions of compensatory plans and agreements be rewritten in a clear and understandable manner.[19] Finally, it will require that the discussion be responsive to the disclosure item being addressed (essentially, providing the required analysis of the executive compensation program). As the Staff has observed, "[i]t is important to recognize that disclosure can be clear and understandable yet not meaningful or responsive to disclosure requirements."[20]

Scope of Disclosure

The CD&A is to address a registrant's entire executive compensation program. Consequently, it must address postemployment, as well as current, compensation arrangements.[21] It should address the information presented in the compensation tables and otherwise disclosed under the rules.[22] Because it is intended to provide meaningful analysis,

---

17. *Id.*

18. *See* the Staff Report, *supra* note 9, under the heading "Clarity."

19. *Id.*

20. *Id.*

21. As specified in n.86 of the Adopting Release, *supra* note 1, any forward-looking information in the CD&A fits within the "safe harbor" for the disclosure of such information. *See* Section 27A of the Securities Act (15 U.S.C. § 77z-2) and Section 21E of the Exchange Act (15 U.S.C. § 78u-5).

22. *See* Instruction 2 to Item 402(b).

it may specifically refer to the tabular or other disclosures where helpful to make the discussion more robust.[23]

As the SEC Staff discovered in its initial review of proxy statements containing executive compensation disclosure prepared under the then-new rules, the CD&As tended to provide summaries of the terms and conditions of compensatory plans and arrangements, as well as the mechanics of the compensation-setting process, without delving deeply into the underlying reasons for a registrant's pay policies and decisions.[24] While this trend has gradually decreased in subsequent years,[25] it remains a chronic problem and is the basis for many of the Staff's comments when reviewing a registrant's executive compensation disclosure.

As the SEC noted in adopting the CD&A, the discussion "should focus on the material principles underlying the registrant's executive compensation policies and decisions and the most important factors relevant to the analysis of those policies and decisions."[26] Accordingly, the CD&A should avoid repetition of the more detailed information contained in the compensation tables and accompanying narrative disclosures.[27] In fact, registrants would be well served to move many of the merely factual descriptions of the various elements of their executive compensation programs from the CD&A to the narrative disclosure supplementing the compensation tables. This will not only lead to a more analytical discussion, it also may reduce the length of the CD&A.

On the other hand, this dictate is not intended to prohibit or discourage the discussion of specific program-related information that is integral to the analysis being provided.[28] Consequently, a registrant will need to strike a balance between describing its compensation plans and arrangements in language that does not come across as "boilerplate" and weaving this description into the analysis of its pay policies and decisions.

---

23. *See* the Adopting Release, *supra* note 1, at Section II.B.2.

24. *See* the Staff Report, *supra* note 9, under the heading "Compensation Discussion and Analysis—Compensation Philosophies and Decision Mechanics."

25. *See* the Parratt 2009 Speech, *supra* note 7.

26. *See* the Adopting Release, *supra* note 1, at II.B.2.

27. *See* Instruction 3 to Item 402(b).

28. *See* the Adopting Release, *supra* note 1, at n.88 and the accompanying text.

Period Covered

While the CD&A should focus on the compensation of the NEOs during the last completed fiscal year,[29] it is not limited to that time period if additional information is necessary to present a fair understanding of the NEO's compensation for the last fiscal year.[30] Thus, in many cases, the discussion will extend beyond just the most recent fiscal year covered in the Summary Compensation Table. For example, most discussions will cover some executive compensation actions that were taken after the registrant's fiscal year ends (such as decisions about the payment of bonuses or other forms of incentive compensation based on performance during the last completed fiscal year).[31] The discussion also may need to address equity awards that are granted after fiscal year-end, even though these awards may be reported in the subsequent fiscal year's compensation tables, if necessary to present a fair understanding of the NEO's compensation for the last fiscal year.

This requirement to address compensation actions and decisions taken after the end of the last completed fiscal year is not unlimited, however. As the SEC Staff has noted, the requirement to cover actions regarding executive compensation that were taken after the registrant's last fiscal year-end is limited to those actions or steps that could "affect a fair understanding of the named executive officer's compensation for the last fiscal year."[32] Thus, actions or decisions with respect to compensation that is to be paid in the current fiscal year, or in a future fiscal year or years (including, in the case of incentive compensation, performance target levels) do not need to be addressed in the CD&A if they are not relevant to understanding the compensation actions and decisions taken in the last completed fiscal year.

---

29. *See* the Adopting Release, *supra* note 1, at Section II.B.1. *See also* Instruction 2 to Item 402(b).

30. *Id.*

31. *Id.* Other post-fiscal-year-end actions that may need to be addressed include, as examples only, the adoption or implementation of a new compensation plan or arrangement; the material modification of an existing plan or arrangement; the adoption of a new, or material modification of an existing, compensation policy; or any other specific decision that was made or steps that were taken that could affect a fair understanding of the NEO's for the last fiscal year. *Id.*

32. *See* Division of Corporation Finance, Compliance and Disclosure Interpretations – Regulation S-K (July 8, 2011) [hereinafter Current Staff Guidance], *available at* http://www.sec.gov/divisions/corpfin/guidance/regs-kinterp.htm, at Q&A 118.07.

In addition, a discussion of a registrant's existing executive compensation program necessarily will include postemployment compensation arrangements, multiyear incentive compensation plans and awards, and policies that the registrant will apply on a going-forward basis.

Finally, in some situations it may be necessary to discuss prior years' compensation or decisions in order to give context to current amounts or decisions.[33] For example, this need may arise in connection with long-term incentive compensation awards with a multiyear performance period that were granted in a prior fiscal year where the end of the performance period coincides with the end of the last completed fiscal year.

Liability Issues

Unlike the former Board Compensation Committee Report, the CD&A is a registrant, rather than a board compensation committee, report. Although this shift in orientation is easy to state, at times its implementation can be tricky. While the CD&A is to discuss registrant compensation policies and decisions, the SEC has emphatically stated that it need not address the deliberations of the board compensation committee.[34] Nonetheless, the level of expected detail about policy matters and individual compensation decisions has forced registrants to be closely attuned to the committee's deliberations to satisfy their disclosure obligations.[35] As a result, as practice has evolved, the CD&A is typically prepared by the registrant with significant input from the registrant's board of directors and board compensation committee.

To underscore the heightened importance of the CD&A, as well as to ensure that sufficient care and attention is paid to its preparation, the report is treated as "soliciting material" for purposes of the SEC's proxy

---

33. *See* Instruction 2 to Item 402(b).

34. Thus, a registrant's chief executive officer and chief financial officer will not have to certify as to the board compensation committee's deliberations when certifying as to the accuracy and completeness of the CD&A under Exchange Act Rule 13a-14 (17 C.F.R. 240.13a-14). *See* the Adopting Release, *supra* note 1, at Section II.B.3.

35. This tension is further exacerbated by statements in the Staff Report, *supra* note 9, which indicate that the SEC Staff expects registrants to explain in some detail how and why their compensation philosophy resulted in the pay numbers presented in the compensation tables and how their analysis of the relevant pay information resulted in the decisions they made. *See* the Staff Report under the heading "Compensation Philosophies and Decision Mechanics." It appears that responding to these expectations may require a thorough understanding of the board compensation committee's deliberations in order to assess how quantitative and qualitative factors influenced its decisions.

rules and is deemed "filed" with the SEC as part of a registrant's proxy or information statement and any other filing in which it is included. Consequently, it is subject to the proxy rules (including the antifraud provisions of those rules)[36] and to the liabilities of Section 18 of the Exchange Act.[37]

This represents another key difference from the former Board Compensation Committee Report, which was considered "furnished," rather than "filed," with the SEC.[38] While, in theory, "furnished" rather than "filed" status was intended to eliminate liability concerns that were thought to inhibit full and forthcoming discussions,[39] as the SEC noted throughout the rule-making process, nothing in its experience with the former report indicated that this treatment had resulted in more full and transparent disclosure.[40] Consequently, this special treatment was eliminated. In most instances, the SEC's belief that it is appropriate for registrants to take responsibility for disclosure involving board matters as with other disclosure has not presented undue difficulties in preparing the CD&A.

Another significant consequence of the CD&A's "filed" status is that, as part of a registrant's annual report on Form 10-K, it is covered by the chief executive officer and chief financial officer's annual certification of the accuracy and completeness of that report.[41] Thus, these individuals have direct liability for the information contained in the CD&A,

36. *See* Exchange Act Rule 14a-9 (17 C.F.R. 240.14a-9).

37. 15 U.S.C. § 78r.

38. *See* former Item 402(a)(9).

39. In adopting the former Board Compensation Committee Report in 1992, the SEC had taken into account comments that the report should be "furnished" rather than "filed" to stem the potential for litigation, particularly in light of the report's signature requirements. *See* Executive Compensation Disclosure, Release Nos. 33-6962, 34-31327, IC-19032 (Oct. 16, 1992), 57 Fed. Reg. 48,126 (Oct. 21, 1992), as modified, Executive Compensation Disclosure: Correction, Release Nos. 33-6966, 34-31420, IC-19085 (Nov. 9, 1992), 57 Fed. Reg. 53, 985 (Nov. 9, 1992), at Section II.H.

40. *See* the Proposing Release, *supra* note 6, at Section II.A.3.

41. *See* Exchange Act Rules 13a-14 (17 C.F.R. 240.13a-14) and 15d-14 (17 C.F.R. 240.15d-14). *See also* Release No. 34-46427, *Certification of Disclosure in Companies' Quarterly and Annual Reports* (Aug. 29, 2002), 67 Fed. Reg. 57,275 (Sept. 9, 2002), *available at* http://www.sec.gov/rules/final/33-8124.htm, at n.35 (stating that "the certification in the annual report on Form 10-K or 10-KSB would be considered to cover the Part III information in a registrant's proxy or information statement as and when filed"). While the CD&A will be included in a registrant's proxy statement, it will be incorporated by reference into the registrant's annual report on Form 10-K which, typically, will be filed with the SEC before the proxy statement. Consequently, it may be advisable for a registrant to have its CD&A substantially complete before finalizing its annual report on Form 10-K.

placing a premium on, if not their involvement in its preparation, their familiarity and agreement with its content. This fact has motivated most registrants to ensure that they have established and maintain an effective system of disclosure controls and procedures[42] so that critical information is collected, analyzed, and timely reported.

In addition, although most registrants use the common technique of "forward incorporation by reference" to the proxy statement to satisfy the executive compensation disclosure requirement in the annual report on Form 10-K,[43] the presence of this certification requirement has caused these registrants to have their CD&A, as well as the related compensation tables, in fairly final form at the time that the Form 10-K—and the required certifications—is filed with the SEC.

Disclosure Format

While the CD&A is intended to be a narrative discussion,[44] it need not be exclusively so. In fact, over the years, many registrants have used an assortment of charts, tables, and graphs to enhance the discussion of their executive compensation program.[45] This trend has accelerated in recent years with the introduction of the shareholder advisory vote on executive compensation.

Until the executive compensation disclosure rules were amended in December 2009 to change the reporting treatment of stock and option awards in the Summary Compensation Table,[46] many of these disclosures took the form of an "alternative" summary compensation table. Initially, these alternative tables were used by registrants to present the total compensation of their NEOs in a manner that better conformed to how their board compensation committees calculated and used total pay in reaching compensation decisions or to contrast total compensation

---

42. See Exchange Act Rules 13a-15 (17 C.F.R. 240.13a-15) and 15d-15 (17 C.F.R. 240.15d-15).

43. *See* Item 11 of Part III of Form 10-K.

44. *See*, for example, the introductory paragraph of Section II.B. of the Adopting Release, *supra* note 1.

45. The SEC Staff has indicated that approximately two-thirds of the registrants that it reviewed in 2007 included charts, tables, and graphs that were not specifically required by the rules. *See* the Staff Report, *supra* note 9, under the heading "Format." Many of these charts, tables, and graphs were presented as part of the CD&A.

46. *See* the discussion of stock awards and option awards in Chapter 4.

with the amount reported in the required Summary Compensation Table. More recently, these alternative tables have been used to support a registrant's discussion of the alignment of corporate performance and executive compensation and, in particular, to demonstrate how the realizable value of the equity awards previously granted to a registrant's NEOs correlate with the value of investor holdings.

While the SEC Staff condoned the use of these alternative summary compensation tables, where it has found the presentation to be confusing or to include compensation amounts that were calculated differently than under the rules, it has requested that the registrant "de-emphasize" the alternative table and make it no more prominent that the required Summary Compensation Table.[47] With this in mind, the Staff has provided the following guidance in presenting an alternative summary compensation table:[48]

- the title of the table should be sufficiently clear so as to not lead a reader to assume that the table is part of the required compensation tables;
- it may be appropriate to state (presumably in the introduction to the alternative table) that the table is not a substitute for the information required by the rules; and
- the use of an alternative table may necessitate an explanation of the differences between the compensation amounts presented in the table and the compensation amounts presented in the required Summary Compensation Table.

Required Discussion Topics

The CD&A should explain all material elements of the registrant's compensation of its NEOs.[49] To ensure this, the discussion must address seven broad topics that are intended to draw out the following information:

---

47. *See* the Staff Report, *supra* note 9, under the heading "Format." This concern about detracting from the required Summary Compensation Table has not prevented registrants from including an "alternative" summary compensation table in the CD&A, which is required to precede the compensation tables.

48. *See* the Staff Report, *supra* note 9, under the heading "Format."

49. Item 402(b)(1).

- the objectives of the registrant's compensation programs;[50]
- what the compensation program is designed to reward;[51]
- each element of compensation;[52]
- why the registrant chooses to pay each element;[53]
- how the registrant determines the amount of (and, where applicable, the formula for) each element;[54]
- how each compensation element and the registrant's decisions regarding that element fit into the registrant's overall compensation objectives and affect decisions regarding other elements;[55] and
- whether and, if so, how the registrant has considered the results of the most recent shareholder advisory vote on executive compensation required by Section 14A of the Exchange Act[56] in determining compensation policies and decisions and, if so, how that consideration has affected the registrant's executive compensation decisions and policies.[57]

While the discussion in the CD&A need focus only on a registrant's NEOs, in most instances the responses to these topics likely will cover all of its senior executives, the group from which the NEOs will be drawn.

Program Objectives

This discussion should address the objectives of a registrant's executive compensation program. Typically, this disclosure has involved some variation of the conventional statement that the program is intended to attract, maintain, and motivate the registrant's executives to perform in a manner that ensured the long-term success of the organization and enhanced the value of shareholders' investments.

---

50. Item 402(b)(1)(i).

51. Item 402(b)(1)(ii). As proposed, this topic also would have required a discussion of what the program was designed not to reward. Given the potentially open-ended nature of this discussion, this requirement was dropped. *See* the Adopting Release, *supra* note 1, at n.74 and the accompanying text.

52. Item 402(b)(1)(iii).

53. Item 402(b)(1)(iv).

54. Item 402(b)(1)(v).

55. Item 402(b)(1)(vi).

56. 15 U.S.C. 78n-1. *See also* Exchange Act Rule 14a-21(a) (17 C.F.R. 240.14a-21(a)).

57. Item 402(b)(1)(vii).

An effective discussion should explain the objectives of the registrant's executive compensation program in the context of its overall business objectives, both strategic and operational. This discussion should cover both short-term and long-term business objectives, which, in most programs, will be reflected in the registrant's incentive compensation plans and arrangements.

Behaviors Rewarded

This discussion should focus on the specific behaviors and results that the registrant is seeking to obtain from its NEOs. While in the case of some compensation elements (for example, base salary and perquisites and other personal benefits), these behaviors may be general in nature, in the case of other elements (for example, performance-based incentive compensation plans and awards), the discussion may need to address the specific results (both quantitative and qualitative) that the compensation is intended to encourage.

Compensation Elements

This discussion should identify each of the current and long-term compensation elements that comprise a registrant's executive compensation program. Typically, this will include base salary, bonuses and annual incentive compensation, long-term compensation (whether in the form of long-term cash or equity-based incentive compensation and/or equity awards, such as stock and stock options), retirement arrangements, perquisites and other personal benefits, and nonqualified deferred compensation arrangements.

It also will include any postemployment compensation arrangements (including severance payments) and any arrangements for payments and benefits in the event of a change in control of the registrant. Finally, consideration should be given to discussing whether the registrant enters into employment agreements with some or all of its NEOs, the reasons for using such agreements, and how they fit into the registrant's overall compensation objectives.

Reasons for Paying Each Element

This discussion, which is contingent on the compensation elements that comprise a registrants' executive compensation program, should explain why the registrant uses the particular compensation element and how it furthers the overall objectives of the program. This discussion may also entail an explanation of the relationship between different compensation elements, particularly where they are being used together to achieve a specific objective or promote a desired behavior.

Amount of Each Element

This discussion should explain how the registrant arrives at the specific amounts that it pays to its NEOs under each compensation element. This explanation will vary from element to element, and its complexity will depend on the design and structure of each individual compensation element. The discussion of performance-based compensation awards and arrangements likely will be more involved than the discussion of most service-based compensation awards and arrangements. Similarly, in the case of plans and arrangements providing payments and benefits upon a termination of employment or following a change in control of the registrant, it will be necessary to explain how and why the amount (or, where applicable, the formula for determining the amount) was selected.[58]

Relationship to Overall Compensation Objectives

This discussion should tie together the various elements that comprise a registrant's executive compensation program and explain their interrelationship, if any. Essentially, this discussion should address the interrelationship of the various elements of the program and explain how they work together to further the registrant's compensation objectives. For example, it should address how the registrant's executive retirement and other postemployment plans and arrangements (including severance arrangements) fit into its overall compensation objectives.

The discussion also should place in context how and why the decisions that were made with respect to one compensation element may or may not have influenced decisions made with respect to other elements that were considered or actually awarded.[59]

This topic represents a key aspect of the required analysis of compensation policies and decisions. It should unify for an investor the registrant's reasons for deciding the amount of each individual pay

---

58. *See* the Staff Report, *supra* note 9, under the heading "Change-in-Control and Termination Arrangements."

59. *See* the Staff Report, *supra* note 9, under the heading "Compensation Philosophies and Decision Mechanics."

element and present the rationale for how these elements contributed to the total compensation that was targeted and ultimately paid or awarded to the NEOs.

In some cases, this will involve a discussion of the effect, if any, that one pay element had on other elements. It also may involve an explanation of subjective factors that influenced compensation actions or decisions in a way that is not apparent from a general understanding of the underlying plan or arrangement. The scope and detail of the discussion needed to adequately address this topic will vary from registrant to registrant and is likely to involve questions of materiality that will turn on highly nuanced factual situations.[60]

Impact of Most Recent Shareholder Advisory Vote on Executive Compensation

At the same time as it adopted rules[61] implementing the requirement of the Dodd-Frank Wall Street Reform and Consumer Protection Act that a registrant conduct a shareholder advisory vote on its executive compensation program,[62] the SEC also amended the list of broad discussion topics that must be addressed in the CD&A to include a discussion of the impact of the most recent shareholder advisory vote on executive compensation on the registrant's executive compensation policies and decisions.[63]

Specifically, a registrant is required to disclose in its CD&A whether and, if so, how it has considered the results of the most recent shareholder advisory vote on executive compensation in determining its compensation policies and decisions and, if so, how that consideration has affected the registrant's executive compensation decisions and policies.[64] For most registrants, this requirement first became applicable during the 2012 proxy season, the year following their initial shareholder advisory vote on executive compensation in 2011.

---

60. *See* Keith F. Higgins, *Executive Compensation Disclosure: What the Guidance Tells Us* (materials for 35th Annual Securities Regulation Institute (Jan. 23, 2007)) [hereinafter Higgins].

61. See Exchange Act Rule 14a-21(a) (17 C.F.R. 240.14a-21(a)).

62. *See* Section 951 of the Dodd-Frank Wall Street Reform and Consumer Protection Act (Pub. L. No. 111-203, 124 Stat. 1376 (July 21, 2010)) codified at Section 14A(a)(1) of the Exchange Act (16 U.S.C. § 78n-1(a)(1)).

63. Item 402(b)(1)(vii).

64. *Id.*

Typically, a registrant will seek to satisfy this discussion topic by disclosing the results of its most recent shareholder advisory vote on executive compensation (frequently stating the percentage of votes cast in favor of the executive compensation program) and then stating whether the vote had any impact on its subsequent compensation actions and decisions (through the date of filing of the registrant's proxy materials). In situations where the registrant received widespread approval of its executive compensation program, it is common for the registrant to make a statement indicating that the vote had no impact on the actions or decisions involving its executive compensation program.[65]

On the other hand, where a majority of the votes cast on a registrant's advisory vote proposal were against the executive compensation program, or the proposal received significant opposition, it is customary for the registrant to describe the actions taken in response to the vote. Typically, this will involve a summary of any efforts to contact shareholders to understand the reasons for the negative vote and to identify any problematic compensation policies or practices or other concerns, and a description of the actions taken by the registrant to address these policies and practices and resolve the identified concerns.[66] Although "best practices" in this area are still evolving, some registrants have used this discussion topic as a place to also describe their ongoing investor communication activities, particularly as they relate to executive compensation matters.

Other Material Information

In addition to a discussion of the seven required topics, the CD&A also must contain any other information that is material to an investor's understanding of the registrant's executive compensation program. Essentially, a registrant must assess the specific features and elements of its executive compensation program, identify the material items that investors would need to understand the program, and provide this

---

65. *See, e.g.,* the Corning, Incorporated Definitive Proxy Statement (Form 14A) filed Mar. 13, 2012 (file no. 001-03247).

66. *See, e.g.,* the Hewlett-Packard Company Definitive Proxy Statement (Form 14A) filed Feb. 3, 2012 (file no. 001-04423).

information. Consequently, this information will vary from registrant to registrant depending on each one's particular facts and circumstances.[67]

To assist in identifying the kind of topics the SEC considers potentially material to the discussion in the CD&A, the rules contain a nonexclusive list of 15 examples of the types of information that registrants should consider providing. In some cases, an example may not be material to a particular registrant and, therefore, no disclosure about the type of information identified in the example is required.[68] Conversely, since the CD&A is intended to be a comprehensive analysis of the executive compensation program, a registrant must address the specific compensation policies it applies, even if they are not included among the examples.[69]

These examples consist of the following topics:

- the policies for allocating between long-term and current compensation;[70]
- the policies for allocating between cash and noncash compensation, and among different forms of noncash compensation;[71]
- for long-term compensation, the basis for allocating compensation to each different form of award;[72]
- how the determination is made as to when awards are granted, including equity-based awards such as stock options;[73]
- what specific items of corporate performance are taken into account in setting compensation policies and making compensation decisions;[74]
- how specific forms of compensation are structured and implemented to reflect these items of the registrant's performance, including whether discretion can be or has been

---

67. Item 402(b)(2).

68. *See* the Adopting Release, *supra* note 1, at Section II.B.1. *See also* the White Principles Matter Speech, *supra* note 13; the White Analysis Speech, *supra* note 7; and Cleary Gottlieb Steen & Hamilton LLP, *Common Questions: Navigating the SEC's New Compensation Rules* (Jan. 19, 2007) [hereinafter Cleary Memorandum], at Q&A 3.

69. *Id.*

70. Item 402(b)(2)(i).

71. Item 402(b)(2)(ii).

72. Item 402(b)(2)(iii).

73. Item 402(b)(2)(iv). As proposed, this example did not make a specific reference to stock options. *See* Proposed Item 402(b)(2)(iv).

74. Item 402(b)(2)(v).

exercised, identifying any particular exercise of discretion, and stating whether it applied to one or more specified NEOs or to all compensation subject to the relevant performance goal or goals;[75]

- how specific forms of compensation are structured and implemented to reflect the NEO's individual performance and/or individual contribution to these items of the registrant's performance, describing the elements of individual performance and/or contribution that are taken into account;[76]

- registrant policies and decisions regarding the adjustment or recovery of awards or payments if the relevant registrant performance measures upon which they are based are restated or otherwise adjusted in a manner that would reduce the size of an award or payment;[77]

- the factors considered in decisions to increase or decrease compensation materially;[78]

- how compensation or amounts realizable from prior compensation are considered in setting other elements of compensation;[79]

- with respect to any contract, agreement, plan, or arrangement, whether written or unwritten, that provides for payment or payments at, following, or in connection with any termination of employment or change in control of the registrant, the basis for selecting particular events as triggering payment (for example,

---

75. Item 402(b)(2)(vi). As proposed, this example did not refer to either the implementation of specific forms of compensation to reflect items of corporate performance or the actual exercises of discretion and identification of the details of that exercise. *See* Proposed Item 402(b)(2)(vii). This latter subject was intended to be addressed as part of the narrative disclosure to accompany the Summary Compensation Table. *See* Proposed Item 402(f)(1)(iv). These modifications were made (and Proposed Item 402(f)(1)(iv) eliminated) based on commenter suggestions. *See* the Adopting Release, *supra* note 1, at Section II.B.1.

76. Item 402(b)(2)(vii). As proposed, this example did not refer to the implementation of specific forms of compensation to reflect items of individual performance. *See* Proposed Item 402(b)(2)(vi). This modification was made based on commenter suggestions. *See* the Adopting Release, *supra* note 1, at Section II.B.1.

77. Item 402(b)(2)(viii). This example was not included at the proposing stage, but was added to the item in response to commenter suggestions.

78. Item 402(b)(2)(ix).

79. Item 402(b)(2)(x).

the rationale for providing a single trigger for payment in the event of a change in control);[80]

- the impact of the accounting and tax treatments of the particular form of compensation;[81]
- the registrant's equity or other security ownership requirements or guidelines, and any registrant policies regarding hedging the economic risk of such ownership;[82]
- whether the registrant engaged in any benchmarking of total compensation, or any material element of compensation, identifying the benchmark and, if applicable, its components (including component companies);[83] and
- the role of executive officers in determining executive compensation.[84]

To this list, the SEC added an overriding principle that applies across the enumerated examples: a CD&A should be sufficiently precise to identify material differences in compensation policies and decisions for individual NEOs, if and where appropriate.[85] Throughout its focused review project in 2007, the SEC Staff raised this comment in the context of individual compensation elements, severance and change-in-control arrangements, and total compensation, clearly signaling to registrants that they should carefully evaluate their compensation policies and decisions for this potential disclosure.

Where the policies or decisions are materially similar, the discussion of the NEOs may be grouped together.[86] On the other hand, where a compensation policy for a NEO materially differs from the policy for other executive officers, his or her compensation is to be discussed separately.[87] This principle reflects notions of internal pay equity and appears to be getting at the question of whether a registrant treats some of its executives, particularly its chief executive officer, differently from other executives.

---

80. Item 402(b)(2)(xi). This example was not included at the proposing stage, but was added to the item in response to commenter suggestions.

81. Item 402(b)(2)(xii).

82. Item 402(b)(2)(xiii).

83. Item 402(b)(2)(xiv).

84. Item 402(b)(2)(xv).

85. *See* the Adopting Release, *supra* note 1, at Section II.B.1.

86. *Id.*

87. *Id.*

The significance of this principle to a fair understanding of a registrant's executive compensation program was underscored by the attention devoted to it in the Staff Report.[88] Accordingly, registrants should be aware that where their disclosure, including that in the Summary Compensation Table, suggests that different compensation policies and decisions led to the amounts being reported for the NEOs, these differences are to be discussed if they are material.[89]

Allocations between Current and Long-Term Compensation

This example addresses the allocation of compensation between current and long-term pay. This disclosure may be material to explaining the different compensation elements employed by the registrant in its executive compensation program and how those elements enable the registrant to implement its pay policies and achieve its compensation objectives and policies. Generally, registrants have tended to discuss this subject, if at all, in the course of explaining the relative weighting of the primary compensation elements provided to their NEOs.

Allocations between Cash and Noncash Compensation

This example addresses the allocation of compensation between cash and other forms of compensation, such as equity and other equity-based awards and arrangements. Further, the example addresses the allocation between different forms of noncash compensation. This disclosure may be material to explaining the different compensation elements employed by the registrant in its executive compensation program and how those elements enable the registrant to implement its pay policies and achieve its compensation objectives. Generally, registrants have tended to discuss this subject, if at all, in the course of explaining the relative weighting of the primary compensation elements provided to their NEOs.

Long-Term Compensation Allocations

This example addresses the bases, in the case of long-term compensation, for allocating compensation to each different form of award used by the

88. *See* the Staff Report, *supra* note 9, under the heading "Differences in Compensation Policies and Decisions."

89. The fact that a NEO was paid more than his or her counterparts does not, in and of itself, require disclosure, unless the disparity is the result of different policies or methodologies. *See* Higgins, *supra* note 60.

registrant. This disclosure should address such factors as the relationship of the award to the achievement of the registrant's long-term objectives, management's exposure to downside equity performance risk, and the correlation between the cost and expected benefits to the registrant. Generally, this subject arises only where a registrant awards multiple forms of long-term incentive or equity compensation to its NEOs.

Award Determinations

This example addresses how and why a registrant decides when awards are made to its NEOs. This disclosure covers all awards, including equity awards such as stock options, restricted stock, and other nonoption equity awards, and involves an explanation of the reasons that the registrant selects particular grant dates for its equity awards.[90] As a practical matter, a registrant's policies, programs, and practices regarding the granting of stock options and other equity-based awards may require disclosure in the CD&A if it is material to understanding the registrant's executive compensation objectives and policies.[91]

It is important to note that the CD&A may need to cover equity awards that are granted after fiscal year-end if material to an investor's understanding of a registrant's compensation policies and decisions for the last completed fiscal year. Given the required reporting of equity awards, it is likely that these awards may not be reflected in the Summary Compensation Table or the Grants of Plan-Based Awards Table for the last completed fiscal year. Thus, it has become common for a registrant's discussion of its long-term incentive compensation plans and arrangements or the target (and actual) total direct compensation of its NEOs in the CD&A to vary from the amounts reported in these tables.

Corporate Performance Items in Compensation Policies and Decisions

This example addresses the use of corporate performance metrics by a registrant in its executive compensation program. Typically, this consideration will arise when discussing a registrant's annual and long-term performance-based incentive compensation plans and

---

90. *See* the Current Staff Guidance, *supra* note 32, at Q&A 118.01.

91. *See* the Adopting Release, *supra* note 1, at Section II.B.1. For an additional discussion of this example, see "Equity Award Disclosure," *infra*.

performance-based equity awards. This disclosure involves identifying and discussing the material items of corporate performance that a registrant takes into account in setting its compensation policies and making individual compensation decisions. In other words, for each performance-based compensation plan and arrangement, a registrant should describe the material corporate performance metrics that were used to determine or influenced the specific amounts or awards that are reported in the compensation table or decided by the board compensation committee.

This discussion of material corporate performance metrics used by a registrant will typically involve identifying the specific performance measures selected (and explain why they were selected) and may require disclosure of the target levels established for each measure. While a determination of what must be disclosed will vary from registrant to registrant, and from arrangement to arrangement, several themes have emerged that provide a general framework with which to work.

For example, typical performance measures tend to be financial, strategic, or operational in nature. Where a registrant uses a financial measure (for example, net income or return on equity) that corresponds or is similar to the measures upon which it provides guidance to the market about its results and prospects or which are reported in its financial statements, generally it will need to disclose this item in its discussion. Where the measure is strategic (for example, achieve a 10 percent market share) or operational (for example, achieve sales of 100,000 units for the fiscal year), disclosure will turn on whether the registrant has a basis for claiming that revealing this specific information will result in competitive harm.

While the disclosure of performance measures has been relatively uncontroversial, a more difficult question is presented when it comes to disclosing the specific target levels that have been established for these measures. Initially, many registrants raised concerns about the disclosure of this information, which they viewed as either proprietary (and, thus, confidential) or sufficiently sensitive as to result in competitive harm if revealed.

In deciding the extent to which target levels must be disclosed, a registrant will need to assess whether a discussion of this information is material to an investor's understanding of the compensation element being discussed (or the matters being presented at the meeting for which the information is being provided), for what years the information is relevant, and whether its disclosure will result in competitive harm.

Materiality of Target Levels

While disclosure of the specific performance measures for a given compensation element will typically be straightforward (except, perhaps, in the case of strategic or operational measures), disclosure of the related target levels may present more challenging business, if not legal, issues. At the outset, disclosure will turn on the materiality of this information to an investor's understanding of the compensation element or decision being discussed. In resolving this question, a registrant must be mindful of the requirement that the CD&A describe how it determines the amount that it will pay for each compensation element.[92]

So, for example, in the case of an annual incentive plan where a NEO will receive a cash payment only if the registrant achieves a stipulated net income target for the fiscal year, the target level is clearly material. Further, the materiality of the information should be considered with respect to a shareholder who is being asked to vote on a matter to be presented at the meeting for which the information is being provided (for example, the election of directors). On the other hand, the question becomes problematic as the relative sophistication of the compensation plan or arrangement increases.[93] Ultimately, a determination of whether the target levels are material, and, accordingly, must be disclosed, will depend on the particular design and operation of each plan or arrangement.

While the fact that a performance target was not met or was otherwise disregarded may be a factor to consider in the materiality determination, it is not dispositive. Even where it does not result in an actual payout, a performance measure target level may be material if, based on a registrant's specific facts and circumstances, it plays an important role in the way the registrant incentivizes its NEOs.[94] Moreover, where a registrant pays its NEOs incentive compensation even though the relevant target levels were not met, it may suggest that the target levels, and compensation, were not sensitive to risk since the compensation was paid without regard to the risk outcome.[95] Accordingly, in most

---

92. See Item 402(b)(1)(v).

93. For a helpful discussion of the materiality of performance targets, see Cleary Gottlieb Steen & Hamilton LLP, *The Materiality of Performance Targets in Proxy Disclosure* (Sept. 14, 2007). See also Higgins, *supra* note 60.

94. See the Parratt 2009 Speech, *supra* note 7.

95. *Id.* In this situation, the SEC Staff has noted that, in the absence of disclosure about these target levels, it questions whether shareholders are presented with the complete picture with which they can judge whether the board of directors is acting in their best interests.

cases, it appears that the SEC Staff expects to see registrants disclose and discuss such target levels in their CD&A.

Relevant Time Period

The rules require a registrant to address in its CD&A compensation actions taken after the end of the fiscal year if relevant to an understanding of the amounts paid or decisions made during the last completed fiscal year.[96] In the case of the target levels for a specific performance measure, in many cases it is unlikely that an explanation of the target levels for the current fiscal year will be needed to assist investors in understanding the amounts paid or decisions made for the prior fiscal year. Nonetheless, the SEC Staff has indicated that this is a matter that registrants should consider in preparing the disclosure about their performance-based compensation arrangements.[97]

There are at least two situations, however, where current-year target levels may be necessary to place the required disclosure in context or to provide a fair understanding of a NEO's compensation. These include a situation where a registrant has a multiple-year compensation plan and a situation where the target levels materially change between fiscal years.[98] In addition, in the context of an initial public offering of securities, the SEC Staff has requested that registrants disclose the target levels for the current fiscal year as part of their discussion of their incentive compensation plans.

---

96. *See* Instruction 2 to Item 402(b).

97. *See* the Staff Report, *supra* note 9, under the heading "Performance Targets." The SEC Staff has stated that disclosure will always depend on each registrant's particular facts and circumstances. *Id.*

98. *Id.* It is not readily apparent under what circumstances these situations would compel disclosure of current fiscal year target levels. Disclosure may not be necessary where a multiyear compensation plan or arrangement involves a performance metric or metrics that are evaluated only at the end of the performance period. Similarly, where a multiyear plan or arrangement had discrete annual target levels, it is not clear that knowledge of the current year's target level would be needed to understand the prior year's compensation. Further, in the case of a change in performance metrics from one year to the next, it is more likely that a change in measures would be more significant to investors than a change in target levels. *See* Higgins, *supra* note 60.

Competitive Harm Exclusion

Where a registrant determines that the target levels for its performance measures are material, then it must specifically—and if applicable, quantitatively—disclose these target levels, unless this disclosure would cause it substantial competitive harm. Specifically, the rules provide that a registrant need not disclose the target levels with respect to specific quantitative or qualitative factors considered by the board compensation committee or the board of directors, or any other factors or criteria involving confidential trade secrets or confidential commercial or financial information, if disclosure of this information would result in competitive harm for the registrant.[99]

The standard to be used to determine whether disclosure would cause competitive harm for the registrant is the same standard that applies when a registrant requests confidential treatment of confidential trade secrets or confidential commercial or financial information.[100] Thus, to the extent that a performance target has otherwise been disclosed publicly (for example, where a registrant provides guidance using the same metrics that inform its incentive plan), a registrant will not be able to withhold this information if it is material to an investor's understanding of the compensation award or arrangement.[101]

A registrant is not required to actually seek confidential treatment if it determines that the disclosure would cause competitive harm.[102] Instead, the registrant simply must make its own determination based on the established standards for what constitutes confidential commercial or financial information, the disclosure of which would cause competitive harm.

Whether disclosure will cause competitive harm is a question that must be analyzed based on the registrant's specific facts and circumstances. As a practical matter, it has been difficult for registrants

---

99. *See* Instruction 4 to Item 402(b).

100. *Id. See* Securities Act Rule 406 (17 C.F.R. 230.406) and Exchange Act Rule 24b-2 (17 C.F.R. 240.24b-2). These rules each incorporate the criteria for nondisclosure when relying on Exemption 4 of the Freedom of Information Act (5 U.S.C. § 552(b)(4)) and Exchange Act Rule 80(b)(4) (17 C.F.R. 200.80(b)(4)). These standards have been articulated in case law, including *National Parks and Conservation Association v. Morton*, 498 F.2d 765 (D.C. Cir. 1974); *National Parks and Conservation Association v. Kleppe*, 547 F.2d 673 (D.C. Cir. 1976); and *Critical Mass Energy Project v. NRC*, 931 F.2d 939 (D.C. Cir. 1991), *vacated & reh'g en banc granted*, 942 F.2d 799 (D.C. Cir. 1991), *grant of summary judgment to agency aff'd en banc*, 975 F.2d 871 (D.C. Cir. 1992).

101. *See* the Current Staff Guidance, *supra* note 32, at Q&A 118.04.

102. *Id.*

to persuade the SEC Staff that they were justified in withholding the target levels related to general corporate financial measures, although somewhat easier when using specific strategic or operational measures. In the former case, this type of information is generally understood by the market to be a common indicator of a registrant's progress against its operating plan or budget, and, in most instances, lacks the characteristics that would make this information unique or proprietary.[103] In the latter case, this type of information may involve an internal metric which, if disclosed, would provide competitors with insight into the registrant's short-term or long-term business plan and objectives.

In the case of some compensation arrangements, the competitive harm exclusion may not be necessary since the required disclosure is being made on an after-the-fact basis (for example, in the case of an annual incentive plan), after the performance period has been completed and the related performance has been measured. This will not always be the case, however, particularly where the same performance metrics are used in successive fiscal years or the measures and/or target levels are based on proprietary, competitively sensitive business information that may be useful to competitors.

Moreover, in the case of long-term incentive plans and awards, registrants are much more likely to have competitive harm concerns because potential disclosure will involve performance metrics that are still in use. While some observers predicted that a narrow application of the competitive harm exclusion would lead to the use of more generic target levels in performance-based incentive plans and arrangements, this has not occurred.

Difficulty in Achieving Undisclosed Targets

If the registrant uses target levels for specific quantitative or qualitative performance-related factors, or other factors or criteria that it does not

---

103. As the SEC Staff has observed, it is more difficult for a registrant to make a persuasive argument that the disclosure of performance target levels will result in competitive harm *after* it has disclosed the information. This is especially true for target levels that are tied to organization-wide financial results that are publicly reported—such as target levels tied to a registrant's earnings-per-share. *See* the Parratt 2009 Speech, *supra* note 7. In this regard, the Staff has indicated that it has yet to see any persuasive analyses explaining how competitors could pull together sufficiently specific information about a registrant's future operations and strategy from the disclosure of these types of target levels to cause the registrant competitive harm. Accordingly, absent highly unusual circumstances, registrants should plan to disclose these kinds of performance target levels if material to their compensation policies and decisions. *Id.*

disclose in reliance on the competitive harm exception, it must explain how difficult it will be for the executive or how likely it will be for the registrant to achieve the undisclosed target levels or other factors.[104] In this regard, a general statement about difficulty is not sufficient. A more focused discussion, perhaps describing whether the registrant achieved or failed to achieve similar targets in prior fiscal years, may be an appropriate way to put the undisclosed targets into a meaningful context.[105] For example, where a registrant's performance metrics and its approach to setting target levels have been historically consistent, it may be appropriate to describe the approach and discuss the historic levels of achievement compared to the past targets.[106]

In any event, if a registrant withholds its performance targets it may be required to demonstrate to the SEC or the SEC Staff that the particular factors or criteria involve confidential trade secrets or confidential commercial or financial information and explain why disclosure would result in competitive harm.[107] If it is ultimately determined that a registrant has not met this standard, and if the information is material, then the registrant will be required to disclose publicly the factors or criteria used.[108]

Non-GAAP Financial Measures

Under the rules, the disclosure of target levels that involve non-GAAP (generally accepted accounting principles) financial measures is not subject to the general rules regarding the disclosure of non-GAAP measures.[109] Nonetheless, a registrant must explain how the number is calculated from its audited financial statements.[110] So, for example, if a registrant uses total shareholder return as a performance metric, it must describe how it calculates total shareholder return and how this measure influences its compensation decisions.[111]

---

104. *See* Instruction 4 to Item 402(b).

105. *See* the Staff Report, *supra* note 9, under the heading "Performance Targets."

106. *See* the Cleary Memorandum, *supra* note 60, at Q&A 5.

107. *See* the Adopting Release, *supra* note 1, at n.94. *See also* the Current Staff Guidance, *supra* note 32, at Q&A 118.04.

108. *See* the Adopting Release, *supra* note 1, at Section II.B.2.

109. *See* Instruction 5 to Item 402(b). These requirements are contained in Regulation G (17 C.F.R. 244.100–102) and Item 10(e) of Regulation S-K (17 C.F.R. 229.10(e)).

110. *Id.*

111. *See* the Staff Report, *supra* note 9, under the heading "Performance Targets."

This exception to the GAAP reconciliation requirements is to be construed narrowly, however. As the SEC Staff has stated, the exception is limited to the disclosure in the CD&A of target levels that involve non-GAAP financial measures.[112] In other words, the exception does not extend to non-GAAP financial information that does not relate to the disclosure of target levels but is nevertheless included in the CD&A (or, for that matter, other parts of the registrant's proxy statement). Thus, it would not apply to the use of non-GAAP financial information in the Executive Summary of a CD&A to explain the correlation between executive compensation and a registrant's financial performance. The Staff has indicated that, if non-GAAP financial measures are presented in the CD&A (or any other part of the proxy statement) for any other purpose (such as to explain the relationship between pay and performance or to justify certain levels or amounts of pay), these non-GAAP financial measures are subject to the requirements of Regulation G[113] and Item 10(e) of Regulation S-K.

The SEC Staff has indicated, however, that, in these compensation-related circumstances only, it will not object if a registrant included the required GAAP reconciliation and other information in an annex to the proxy statement, provided the registrant includes a prominent cross reference to the annex.[114] Similarly, if the non-GAAP financial measures are the same as those included in the annual report on Form 10-K that is incorporating by reference the proxy statement's Item 402 disclosure as part of its Part III information, the Staff will not object if the registrant complies with Regulation G and Item 10(e) by providing a prominent cross-reference to the pages in the Form 10-K containing the required GAAP reconciliation and other information.[115]

Performance-Based Compensation—Corporate Performance

This example addresses how a registrant structures and implements specific forms of compensation to reflect the specific items of corporate performance that it takes into account in setting its compensation policies and making individual compensation decisions.

---

112. *See* the Current Staff Guidance, *supra* note 32, at Q&A 118.08.

113. 17 C.F.R. 244.100–102.

114. *See* the Current Staff Guidance, *supra* note 32, at Q&A 118.08. For an example of this approach, *see* PVH, Inc. Definitive Proxy Statement (Form 14A) filed May 11, 2011 (file no. 001-07572).

115. *See* the Current Staff Guidance, *supra* note 32, at Q&A 118.08.

Where a registrant can exercise discretion or has exercised discretion, either to award compensation even though the relevant performance goal or goals have not been achieved or to reduce or increase the size of any award or payout, the disclosure should identify this particular exercise of discretion, and state whether it applied to one or more specified NEOs or to all compensation subject to the relevant performance goal or goals.

In addition, the same considerations with respect to the disclosure of target levels based on corporate performance items apply to this disclosure.[116]

Performance-Based Compensation—Individual Performance

This example addresses the use of individual performance metrics by a registrant in its executive compensation program, which most often will involve its annual and long-term performance-based incentive compensation plans and arrangements. This disclosure is to explain how a registrant structures and implements specific forms of compensation to reflect the specific items of individual performance or individual contribution to these items of corporate performance, describing these elements of individual performance or individual contributions. Consequently, it may involve a discussion of the specific quantitative and qualitative performance measures used by the registrant, including the performance target levels established for each measure, to the extent that they are material to an investor's understanding of the plan or arrangement being discussed.

This disclosure will be more challenging where the specific items of individual performance or individual contributions are largely or exclusively qualitative in nature. In some instances, these factors may be difficult to describe or quantify, and may involve sensitive business or personnel issues. Because the SEC Staff is sensitive to these considerations, a registrant does not need to provide an objective or quantitative explanation of the decisions that involve subjective assessments of individual performance.[117] Registrants are expected

---

116. See "Other Material Information—Corporate Performance Items in Compensation Policies and Decisions," *supra*.

117. *See* the White Analysis Speech, *supra* note 7.

to explain, however, the way these qualitative factors are ultimately translated into objective pay determinations.[118]

While it is not entirely clear what needs to go into this explanation, some practical themes have developed. While the discussions presented by most registrants have described the items of individual performance that were being evaluated, these registrants have not disclosed the board compensation committee's assessment of a NEO's actual performance against these items. It appears that it is sufficient to provide a general description of the individual performance metrics that were used, along with an explanation of how the NEO's performance (as measured by these metrics) affected the type of amount of compensation paid or awarded.[119]

In addition, the same considerations with respect to the disclosure of target levels based on corporate performance items apply to this disclosure.[120]

Compensation Recovery Policies and Decisions

This example addresses any policy, provision, or arrangement that a registrant may have for adjusting or recouping previously earned or paid performance-based compensation that is subsequently determined to have been erroneously credited or paid to one or more of the registrant's executives. This type of policy became more prevalent following the enactment of the Sarbanes-Oxley Act of 2002, which contained a provision[121] requiring a registrant to recover certain compensation and realized profits from its chief executive officer and chief financial officer if it is required to prepare an accounting restatement due to the registrant's material noncompliance, as a result of misconduct, with any financial reporting requirement under the federal securities laws. Pursuant to this provision, the registrant's chief executive officer and chief financial officer must reimburse the registrant for any bonus or other incentive-based or equity-based compensation that they received from the registrant during the 12-month period following the first public issuance or filing with the SEC (whichever first occurs) of the financial document embodying such financial reporting requirement. These executives also must reimburse

---

118. *Id.*

119. *See* Higgins, *supra* note 57.

120. See "Other Material Information—Corporate Performance Items in Compensation Policies and Decisions," *supra.*

121. See the Sarbanes-Oxley Act of 2002, Section 304 (codified at 15 U.S.C. § 7243).

the registrant for any profits they realized from the sale of its securities during that 12-month period.

Subsequently, the Dodd-Frank Act contains a provision requiring the SEC, by rule, to direct the national securities exchanges and national securities associations to prohibit the listing of any security of a registrant that does not have a policy that provides for compensation recovery from any current or former executive officer who received incentive-based compensation (including stock options) during the three-year period preceding the date when the registrant is required to restate its financial statements due to material noncompliance with any financial reporting requirement.[122] While this provision has yet to take effect, it has further underscored the need for registrants to incorporate such policies into their executive compensation programs.

A number of registrants have adopted policies or included provisions in plans and arrangements that provide for a similar adjustment or recovery under a variety of scenarios. Some of these provisions apply to other executives as well as to the registrant's chief executive officer and chief financial officer. Others cover situations involving any overpayment, not just transactions involving fraud or other misconduct. Still others do not require a financial restatement to become operative. In keeping with the variety of policies and provisions that have been implemented, the example in the rules is not intended to be limited to policies and provisions that mirror the situation addressed in the Sarbanes-Oxley Act[123] or, for that matter, the Dodd-Frank Act.

While this is just an example of the type of information registrants should consider disclosing, in view of the numerous instances of corporate fraud in recent years and the pending requirement of the Dodd-Frank Act, a registrant's plans with respect to adopting a compensation recovery policy are likely to be material to investors. Consequently, as with equity award grant practices, this is a topic that registrants should consider addressing in their CD&A each year, even in advance of taking action to implement a formal compensation recovery policy.

In addition to policies, the example also covers actual decisions by a registrant to adjust or recover awards or payments if the relevant performance measures upon which they are based are restated or are

---

122. *See* Section 954 of the Dodd-Frank Act. *See also* Section 10D(b) of the Exchange Act (15 U.S.C. § 78j-4(h)).

123. *See* the Adopting Release, *supra* note 1, at n.83.

otherwise adjusted in a way that reduces the size of the award or the amount of the payment. Consequently, even where a registrant does not have a formal policy or arrangement for compensation adjustment or recovery, to the extent that it actually adjusts or recovers a previously earned or paid award or amount, disclosure should be considered.

Material Compensation Adjustments

This example addresses any decision a registrant made to materially increase or decrease compensation paid or payable to a NEO and the factors that influenced or compelled that decision. This would cover decisions that are permitted under a registrant plan or arrangement, as well as any decisions that are made through the exercise of discretion by the board compensation committee (although in the case of performance-based compensation, any such adjustments are the subject of a separate example).

Where a board compensation committee has the discretion to adjust or change the amount that would otherwise be payable to its NEOs, this fact should be disclosed. Of course, where the committee actually exercises this discretion, this should be noted in the discussion of the relevant compensation element, and the specific factors, both quantitative and qualitative, that influenced the committee's action disclosed.

While adjustments can arise in a variety of situations, one potential area where this disclosure may be relevant involves the amounts payable under an annual incentive plan that is designed to comply with Section 162(m) of the Internal Revenue Code.[124] Where the board compensation committee has reserved the ability to reduce the size of awards that would otherwise be payable (so-called "negative discretion"), a discussion of the exercise of this discretion may be warranted.

Influence of Prior Compensation in Current Decision-Making

This example addresses the impact, if any, that amounts previously earned or amounts potentially realizable from prior compensation awards are taken into consideration in determining whether to provide other compensation elements or influence the amount of any such compensation elements. For example, the rules cite a situation where

---

124. 26 U.S.C. § 162m.

gains (either realized or realizable) from previously granted stock option or other stock awards may be considered when determining an executive's retirement benefits. While not strictly a wealth accumulation analysis, this disclosure is aimed at helping investors understand the extent, if any, that a registrant factors an executive's prior compensation history and the amounts that he or she has earned or stands to receive from outstanding awards into current compensation decisions.

To the extent that a board compensation committee uses a "tally sheet" or similar compensation aggregation tool in its decision-making process, this information, as it relates to historical compensation, may be material to investors' understanding of some or all of the amounts reported in the compensation tables. Consequently, where a tally sheet is used, it may be necessary to explain what this information was and how it affected compensation decisions.[125]

Postemployment and Change-in-Control Arrangements

This example addresses the reason for and operation of any severance or other postemployment plans and arrangements that a registrant maintains for its NEOs, as well as any plans or arrangements that provide for payments and/or benefits upon a change in control of the registrant. The example covers provisions in executive employment agreements and stand-alone plans and arrangements. It also covers informal, as well as formal, policies and practices.

Initially, many of the disclosures in response to this example consisted of lengthy factual descriptions of a registrant's severance and change-in-control provisions, rather than an analysis of how these provisions fit into the registrant's executive compensation program. In response, the SEC Staff reminded registrants that this disclosure should be more analytical than descriptive. As a practical matter, the disclosure should complement the descriptive information required by the rules about potential payments upon a termination of employment or change in control of the registrant.[126]

As noted by the SEC Staff, the disclosure should address the reason or reasons for the specific design and structure of these plans and arrangements. For example, this may require an analysis of how actual

---

125. *See* the Staff Report, *supra* note 9, under the heading "Compensation Philosophies and Decision Mechanics."

126. See Chapter 12.

postemployment payments and benefits are determined and why specific amounts, or formulas for calculating these amounts, were selected.[127]

In addition, the relationship, if any, between the potential payments and benefits under these plans and arrangements to decisions that were made about other compensation elements, as well as how these plans and arrangements fit into the registrant's overall compensation objectives, may need to be addressed.[128] Further, if there are significance differences in the terms and conditions of, or the amounts payable under, these plans and arrangements between NEOs, the reasons for these differences may need to be discussed as well.

Tax and Accounting Considerations

This example addresses the actual or potential tax and accounting considerations that affected a registrant's executive compensation policies or individual pay decisions. Thus, to the extent that a registrant's policies or decisions were materially influenced by any relevant federal tax provision (such as Section 409A of the Internal Revenue Code)[129] or applicable accounting standard (such as Financial Accounting Standards Board Accounting Standards Codification Topic 718, *Compensation – Stock Compensation* (FASB ASC Topic 718), disclosure should be considered. In the case of tax considerations, this example applies both to the registrant and to the NEOs.[130]

While this example does not make specific reference to a discussion of a registrant's policy regarding Section 162(m) of the Internal Revenue Code,[131] the provision that limits the deductibility of remuneration paid to a registrant's NEOs to $1 million annually, the SEC indicated in the Adopting Release that the adoption of this example should not be construed to eliminate this discussion.[132] Thus, if material to an investor's

---

127. This could involve explaining why a specific pay multiple of base salary and bonus is used to calculate a severance payment and why the vesting of equity awards is to be accelerated upon the occurrence of a designated triggering event.

128. *See* the Staff Report, *supra* note 9, under the heading "Change-in-Control and Termination Arrangements."

129. 26 U.S.C. § 409A.

130. *See* the Adopting Release, *supra* note 1, at Section II.B.1.

131. 26 U.S.C. § 162(m).

132. *See* the Adopting Release, *supra* note 1, at n.82 and the accompanying text. Disclosure of this policy in the Board Compensation Committee Report was required under the former rules. *See* Executive Compensation Disclosure; Securityholder Lists and Mailing Requests, Release Nos. 33-7032, 34-33229 (Nov. 22, 1993), 58 Fed. Reg. 63,010 (Nov. 29, 1993), at Section III.

understanding of a registrant's executive compensation program or specific compensation decisions, a discussion of the registrant's Section 162(m) policy may be warranted.

Other federal tax provisions that may merit discussion include Sections 280G and 4999 of the Internal Revenue Code,[133] which limit the deductibility of, and impose an excise tax on, amounts that constitute "excess parachute payments," and Section 274(e) of the Internal Revenue Code,[134] which limits the deductibility of the expenses associated with the personal use of corporate aircraft by a registrant's executives for entertainment purposes.[135]

Equity Ownership Requirements or Guidelines

This example addresses any registrant requirement or guideline concerning equity or other security ownership for its NEOs. If such a requirement or guideline is disclosed, the discussion should specify the applicable amounts that must or should be owned by each executive or category of executive, as well as the forms of ownership that will satisfy the requirement or guidelines.

In addition, if a registrant has a policy prohibiting or limiting the ability of its executives to hedge the economic risk of their equity or other security ownership, disclosure of this policy may be warranted. The Dodd-Frank Act contains a provision requiring the SEC to adopt rules mandating disclosure in the proxy materials for any annual meeting of shareholders regarding whether any employee or member of the board of directors of a registrant, or designee of such persons, is permitted to purchase financial instruments, including prepaid variable forwards, equity swaps, collars, and exchange funds, that are designed to hedge or offset any decrease in the market value of equity securities granted as compensation or held, directly or indirectly, by the employee or director.[136] While this provision has yet to take effect, it has further underscored the importance of this subject when addressing the policies and practices that make up a registrant's executive compensation program.

---

133. 26 U.S.C. §§ 280G and 4999.

134. 26 U.S.C. § 274(e).

135. *See, e.g.*, Ameriprise Financial Inc. Definitive Proxy Statement (Form 14A) filed Mar. 19, 2010 (file no. 001-32525) (discussion of Section 274(e) in CD&A).

136. *See* 955 of the Dodd-Frank Act. *See also* Section 14(j) of the Exchange Act (15 U.S.C. § 78n(j)).

Benchmarking and Peer Group Comparisons

This example addresses the use of benchmarking and other peer group comparisons as part of the compensation-setting process. For these purposes, the SEC Staff considers "benchmarking" to generally entail "using compensation data about other companies as a reference point on which—either wholly or in part—to base, justify or provide a framework for a compensation decision."[137] According to the Staff, benchmarking does not include a situation in which a registrant reviews or considers a broad-based third-party survey for a more general purpose, such as to obtain a general understanding of current compensation practices.[138]

If benchmarking is a material factor in how a registrant makes decisions regarding the total compensation of its executives, or any material individual compensation element, then it should identify and describe the benchmark.[139] In addition, if applicable, the registrant should identify the benchmark components (including individual component companies) and explain how and why these companies were selected.[140]

This disclosure should define and explain how comparative information was actually used in connection with the decisions reflected in the compensation tables and the extent, if any, to which this information influenced specific compensation decisions.[141] This may require discussing how the information is used for each individual compensation element, as well as whether it is used for assessing the NEOs' total compensation. The disclosure also should address the nature and extent to which the board compensation committee retains the discretion to deviate from the outcomes suggested or required by the benchmarking process and whether and how that discretion has been exercised in making specific pay decisions.[142] Further, where a registrant targets total compensation, or individual compensation elements, as a percentile of the benchmarked companies or within a quartile range, the SEC Staff expects that the registrant will disclose

---

137. *See* the Current Staff Guidance, *supra* note 32, at Q&A 118.05.

138. *Id.*

139. *See* the Cleary Memorandum, *supra* note 68, at Q&A 6.

140. *See, e.g.,* Seagate Technology plc Definitive Proxy Statement (Form 14A) filed Sept. 26, 2011 (file no. 001-31560) (listing identities, industry classification, and financial results of peer companies).

141. *See* the Staff Report, *supra* note 9, under the heading "Benchmarks."

142. *Id.*

where actual total compensation, or such individual pay element, came out against the target percentile or fell within the targeted range.

Where a registrant uses a peer group of companies to benchmark compensation, it should identify the companies that composed the peer group as well as the compensation components used in that comparison.[143] It also should explain the selection process and why these companies are an appropriate group for making pay comparisons. This may involve a discussion of the selection criteria, such as industry, size (whether measured on the basis of revenue, market capitalization, number of employees, or some other metric), complexity, business model, product or service sales cycle, or performance, that resulted in the formulation of the peer group. Further, where a registrant uses a compensation survey or surveys for comparative purposes, it should identify the survey, and explain how the survey was developed.[144] It also should describe how the survey was used and explain why the survey is an appropriate tool for compensation-setting purposes.

Role of Executive Officers in Compensation Decisions

This example addresses the role of the registrant's executives, principally its chief executive officer, in the executive compensation-setting process. It is common for a registrant's chief executive officer to be involved in formulating the compensation for the other members of his or her management team. Where this individual (or any other executive) plays a significant role in either recommending or deciding the amounts that will be paid or awarded to the NEOs, or in assessing the performance of the NEOs in the case of performance-based compensation, this information may be material to an investor's understanding of the compensation amounts or decisions that were made for the last completed fiscal year.

While the level of detail needed to complete this disclosure will vary among registrants, the registrant should probably identify each executive who plays a role in the assessment, design, or recommenda-

---

143. *Id.*

144. While the SEC Staff has indicated that a registrant should identify all of the constituent companies in a survey, in situations where the survey involves a large number of companies, it may be sufficient to simply identify the industry sector and/or other criteria used to select the companies.

tion of compensation plans, arrangements, or awards for the NEOs; describe the nature of his or her involvement; and explain how the board compensation committee made use of the recommendations or information provided in formulating its final compensation decisions. This also may involve identifying which executives, if any, attend meetings of the board compensation committee and describing any delegation of authority from the committee to an executive or executives.

Role of Compensation Advisors in Compensation Decisions

While not included as a specific example of the type of material items that investors may need to understand a registrant's executive compensation program, most registrants address the role of the advisors to the compensation committee in the executive compensation-setting process in their CD&As. As a practical matter, this disclosure is relevant, given the prominent role that compensation consultants, legal counsel, and other advisors frequently play in assisting the compensation committee in analyzing executive compensation market practices and trends, designing compensation plans and arrangements, and formulating the compensation of a registrant's executive officers.

Some of this information may overlap the general disclosure that is required by the SEC's rules about corporate governance in a registrant's proxy materials.[145] Specifically, this involves the required disclosure about a registrant's processes and procedures for the consideration and determination of executive and director compensation by the registrant's standing compensation committee (or committee performing similar functions).[146]

The SEC Staff has indicated that, with respect to the disclosure in the CD&A, a registrant need discuss the role of a compensation consultant only to the extent that the consultant has played a material role in the registrant's compensation-setting practices and decisions.[147] While the

---

145. See Item 7(d) of Schedule 14A (17 C.F.R. 240.14a-101) and Item 1 of Schedule 14C (17 C.F.R. 240.14c-101). See also Item 407(e)(3) of Regulation S-K (17 C.F.R. 229.407(e)(3)).

146. Item 407(e)(3)(iii).

147. See the Current Staff Guidance, supra note 32, at Q&A 118.06. (See also the Current Staff Guidance, supra note 32, at Q&A 133.08). In the SEC Staff's view, the information regarding "any role of compensation consultants in determining or recommending the amount or form of executive and director compensation" required by Item 407(e)(3)(iii) is to be provided as part of a registrant's Item 407(e)(3) compensation committee disclosure. See the Adopting Release, supra note 1, at Section V.D.

Staff guidance is clearly addressing the role of a compensation consultant in the compensation actions and decisions for the last completed fiscal year, it appears that it may also extend to actions taken after the end of the fiscal year if relevant to a fair understanding of the compensation actions and decisions taken in the last completed fiscal year.

Equity Award Disclosure

The rules are intended to ensure the proper disclosure of executives' stock option grants and other equity awards.[148] In the case of the CD&A, this means that a registrant should consider discussing its policies and practices for timing and pricing its stock option grants and other equity awards.[149] This is in addition to the broader example that addresses how a registrant determines when its awards to executives are to be granted.[150]

Timing Practices

Where a registrant has a program, plan, or practice to select equity award grant dates for its executives in coordination with the release of material nonpublic information, it should disclose this arrangement

---

148. Much of this information is provided in tabular form. For example, stock options and other equity awards must be disclosed in the Grants of Plan-Based Awards Table at their grant date fair value (as determined under FASB ASC Topic 718) (see Item 402(d)(2)(viii)). This table also requires disclosure of the equity award's grant date, and, if the exercise price is less than the closing market price of the underlying security on the date of the grant, the registrant must disclose both that market price on the grant date and the methodology that was used to set the exercise price (see Item 402(d)(2)(vii) and Instruction 3 to Item 402(d)).

149. While the discussion in the Adopting Release, *supra* note 1, speaks in terms of stock options, the SEC Staff has indicated that this discussion also covers other forms of equity compensation, such as restricted stock and other nonoption equity awards. *See* the Current Staff Guidance, *supra* note 32, at Q&A 118.01.

150. *See* Item 402(b)(iv). The SEC Staff has taken the position that this broader disclosure should cover programs, plans, or practices that occurred beyond the scope of the information presented in the compensation tables. *See* the Current Staff Guidance, *supra* note 32, at Q&A 118.02. Thus, depending on a registrant's particular circumstances, this disclosure may need to address programs, plans, or practices affecting nonexecutive employees, as well as periods before and after the information presented in the compensation tables. *See also* the Current Staff Guidance, *supra* note 32, at Q&A 118.03 (registrants are required to include disclosure about programs, plans, or practices relating to option grants in their CD&As for fiscal years ending on or after Dec. 15, 2006, as well as any other periods where necessary as contemplated by Instruction 2 to Item 402(b)).

in its CD&A.[151] For example, a registrant may grant equity awards (particularly stock options) when it knows of material nonpublic information that is likely to result in an increase in its stock price, such as immediately prior to a significant positive earnings or product development announcement.[152] Alternatively, a registrant may coordinate its grant of equity awards (particularly stock options) with the release of negative material nonpublic information.[153]

Regardless of the reasons for these actions, the SEC has stated that the existence of a program, plan, or practice to time the grant of equity awards to executives in coordination with material nonpublic information is material to investors and, thus, should be fully disclosed in the CD&A. If the registrant has such a program, plan, or practice, it should disclose that the board of directors or board compensation committee may grant equity awards at times when the board or committee is in possession of material nonpublic information.

A registrant may also need to consider disclosure about how the board of directors or board compensation committee takes such information into account when determining whether and in what amount to make those awards. In the Adopting Release, the SEC provided a nonexhaustive list of some elements and questions about equity award timing to which a registrant should pay particular attention when drafting its disclosure:

- Does the registrant have a program, plan, or practice to time equity awards to its executives in coordination with the release of material nonpublic information?
- How does any program, plan, or practice to time the grant of equity awards to executives fit in the context of the registrant's program, plan, or practice, if any, with regard to grants of equity

---

151. *See* the Adopting Release, *supra* note 1, at Section II.A.2.b.i.

152. Such timing could occur in at least two ways: The registrant grants stock options just prior to the release of material nonpublic information that is likely to result in an increase in its stock price (whether the date of that release of material nonpublic information is a regular date or otherwise preannounced, or not), or the registrant chooses to delay the release of material nonpublic information that is likely to result in an increase in its stock price until after a stock option grant date (so-called "spring-loading").

153. Such timing could occur in at least two ways: The registrant delays granting stock options until after the release of material nonpublic information that is likely to result in a decrease in its stock price, or the registrant chooses to release material nonpublic information that is likely to result in a decrease in its stock price prior to an upcoming stock option grant (so-called "bullet-dodging").

awards to employees generally?

- What was the role of the board compensation committee in approving and administering such a program, plan, or practice?
- How did the board of directors or board compensation committee take such information into account when determining if and in what amount to make grants?
- Did the board compensation committee delegate any aspect of the actual administration of a program, plan, or practice to any other person (such as an executive officer)?
- What was the role of executive officers in the registrant's program, plan, or practice of equity award timing?
- Does the registrant set the grant date of its stock options or other equity awards to new executives in coordination with the release of material nonpublic information?
- Does a registrant plan to time, or has it timed, its release of material nonpublic information for the purpose of affecting the value of executive compensation?[154]

While these questions are largely couched in terms of potentially manipulative practices, a registrant should consider disclosing its equity award grant practices in its CD&A each year even if it does not engage in activities that raise some of the concerns that prompted the SEC to address this subject in the Adopting Release. In view of the number of stock option backdating problems that have been exposed over the past few years, these practices may be material to investors without regard to whether a registrant considers them to be an integral part of its executive compensation program.

Exercise Price Selection

If a registrant has a program, plan, or practice of granting stock options and setting the exercise price based on the market price of the underlying stock on a date other than the actual grant date, this also should be disclosed and explained in the CD&A.[155] As with equity award timing practices, registrants should consider their own facts and circumstances and include all relevant material information in this disclosure.

---

154. *See* the Adopting Release, *supra* note 1, at Section II.A.2.b.i.
155. *See* the Adopting Release, *supra* note 1, at Section II.A.2.b.ii.

Some registrants have provisions in their stock option plans or have followed practices for determining the option exercise price by using formulas based on average prices (or lowest prices) of the underlying stock in a period preceding, surrounding, or following the grant date. In some cases, these provisions may increase the likelihood that recipients will be granted "in-the-money"[156] options. The SEC considers these provisions or practices to relate to a material term of a stock option grant that should be discussed in the CD&A.[157]

Compensation Committee Report

General

The SEC's decision to make the CD&A a registrant, rather than a board compensation committee, raised investor concerns that the committee could be marginalized or excluded from the process of preparing this disclosure. To allay these concerns by ensuring that the committee will remain involved in compensation disclosure matters, the SEC adopted a requirement that a Compensation Committee Report accompany the CD&A.[158] This report also is intended to serve as a basis for the chief executive officer and chief financial officer's certification of the CD&A, particularly to the extent that the CD&A addresses information and/or decisions to which these executive may not have had direct access.

The Compensation Committee Report is considered to be furnished to, rather than filed with, the SEC.[159] Further, it is required only in a registrant's annual report on Form 10-K and a proxy or information statement.[160] In this latter situation, this ensures that it will be presented

---

156. An "in-the-money" stock option is one where the market value of the underlying stock on the grant date exceeds the exercise or base price of the option.

157. *See* the Adopting Release, *supra* note 1, at Section II.A.2.b.ii.

158. *See* the Adopting Release, *supra* note 1, at Section II.B.3. This requirement does not apply to small business issuers since they are not required to include a CD&A as part of their executive compensation disclosure. *See* the Small Company Release, *supra* note 1.

159. *See* Instruction 1 to Item 407(e)(5). Thus, it will not be deemed to be "soliciting material" or to be "filed" with the SEC or subject to Regulation 14A or 14C (17 C.F.R. 240.14a-1 through 240.14b-2 or 240.14c-1 through 240.14c-101), other than as provided in the item, or to the liabilities of Section 18 of the Exchange Act (15 U.S.C. § 78r), except to the extent that the registrant specifically requests that it be treated as soliciting material or specifically incorporates it by reference into a document filed under the Securities Act or the Exchange Act. *Id.*

160. *See* Instruction 2 to Item 407(e)(5) of Regulation S-K (17 C.F.R. 229.407(e)(5)). The report will not be deemed to be incorporated by reference into any filing under the Securities

along with the CD&A when that disclosure is provided in the Form 10-K or incorporated by reference from a proxy or information statement.[161]

Disclosure Requirements

The Compensation Committee Report is to accompany the CD&A and must state whether the board compensation committee[162] has reviewed and discussed the CD&A with management and, based on that review and discussion, has recommended to the registrant's board of directors that the CD&A be included in the registrant's annual report on Form 10-K and, as applicable, its proxy or information statement.[163] The report is to be captioned "Compensation Committee Report,"[164] and the name of each committee member (or the name of each member of the other board committee performing equivalent functions or, in the absence of any such committee, the entire board of directors)[165] must appear below

---

Act or the Exchange Act, except to the extent that the registrant specifically incorporates it by reference. *Id.* If a registrant elects to incorporate the report by reference from the proxy or information statement into its annual report on Form 10-K pursuant to General Instruction G(3) to Form 10-K, the report will be deemed "furnished" in the annual report on Form 10-K and will not be deemed incorporated by reference into any filing under the Securities Act or the Exchange Act as a result of furnishing the report in this manner. *Id.*

161. *See* the Adopting Release, *supra* note 1, at Section II.B.3.

162. Or other board committee performing equivalent functions or, in the absence of any such committee, the entire board of directors. *See* Item 407(e)(5)(i) of Regulation S-K (17 C.F.R. 229.407(e)(5)(i)).

163. *See* Item 407(e)(5)(i)(A) and (B) of Regulation S-K (17 C.F.R. 229.407(e)(5)(i)(A) and (B)). The SEC Staff has permitted little variation in the wording of this statement.

164. *See* Item 407(e)(5) of Regulation S-K (17 C.F.R. 229.407(e)(5)).

165. Under the former rules, the Board Compensation Committee Report was to be published over the names of the members of the board compensation committee (or the full board of directors) who participated in the deliberations concerning the compensation reported for the last fiscal year. Accordingly, new members who did not participate in the deliberations and departed committee members who were no longer directors need not be included. *See* the Manual of Publicly Available Telephone Interpretations compiled by the Officer of the Chief Counsel, Division of Corporation Finance, Item 402, No. 29. In addition, members who resigned from the compensation committee during the course of the fiscal year, but who remained directors of the registrant, may need to be made responsible for the report. This interpretation was not included in the Staff Guidance. Nonetheless, the interpretation would appear to be relevant under the rules. Thus, the required signatories would include a director who served on the board compensation committee for a portion of the last completed fiscal year and who subsequently resigns from the committee while remaining a director. On the other hand, a director who joined the board compensation committee after the end of the last completed fiscal year and who did not participate in any deliberations involving the NEOs' compensation for that fiscal year would not need to sign the report.

the report.[166] This disclosure need be provided only one time during any fiscal year.[167]

The SEC Staff has indicated that the members of the compensation committee (or the entire board of directors) who participated in the review, discussions, and recommendation with respect to the CD&A must be identified.[168] New members of the compensation committee (or the entire board of directors) who did not participate in such activities and departed members who are no longer directors need not be identified.[169] Members who resigned from the compensation committee during the course of the year, but remain directors of the registrant, may need to be named under the disclosure in the Compensation Committee Report.[170]

While the rules do not preclude a board compensation committee from including additional information in the Compensation Committee Report, only a few committees have taken advantage of this flexibility to supplement the required disclosure since the rules were adopted.[171]

Other Considerations

Although a registrant's audit committee does not have a formal role in preparing the Compensation Committee Report, it will need to coordinate with the registrant's auditors for their review of the CD&A and the compensation tables. In addition, the auditors will need to evaluate the registrant's internal controls over financial reporting to ensure that the registrant has an effective system for collecting, analyzing, and reporting the data and other information that is reported in the CD&A and compensation tables. Consistent with existing practice, any such supplemental disclosure must not distort or distract from the required disclosure.

---

166. *See* Item 407(e)(5)(ii) of Regulation S-K (17 C.F.R. 229.407(e)(5)(ii)). While this "signing" requirement is comparable to the requirement for the former Board Compensation Committee Report (*see* former Item 402(k)(3)), that is the only similarity between the two reports.

167. *See* Instruction 3 to Item 407(e)(5) of Regulation S-K (17 C.F.R. 229.407(e)(5), Instruction 3).

168. *See* the Current Staff Guidance, *supra* note 32, at Q&A 133.07.

169. *Id.*

170. *Id.*

171. For an example of a registrant with an expanded Compensation Committee Report, *see* AT&T Inc. Definitive Proxy Statement (Form 14A) filed Mar. 22, 2007 (file no. 001-08610). Consistent with existing practice, any such supplemental disclosure must not distort or distract from the required disclosure.

4

Summary Compensation Table

General

Under the executive compensation disclosure rules, the Summary Compensation Table is the centerpiece of the required executive compensation disclosure.[1] This table is intended to disclose all of the compensation awarded, earned, and received by a registrant's named executive officers (NEOs). Thus, it presents their full compensation, broken out by category, for the last completed fiscal year, whether or not actually paid out, and, for comparative purposes, their compensation for the two preceding fiscal years.

Each compensation element is disclosed only once in a covered fiscal year, although an element may also be disclosed in one or more of the other compensation tables.[2] Compensation elements are to be reported in seven separate categories, including a column disclosing a figure

---

1. The requirements for the Summary Compensation Table are set forth in Item 402(c). For the requirements applicable to smaller reporting companies, see Item 402(n).

2. This timing approach is the same as that used in the Summary Compensation Table under the former rules. *See* Executive Compensation Disclosure, Release Nos. 33-6962, 34-31327, IC-19032 (Oct. 16, 1992), 57 Fed. Reg. 48,126 (Oct. 21, 1992), *as modified,* Executive Compensation Disclosure: Correction, Release Nos. 33-6966, 34-31420, IC-19085 (Nov. 9, 1992), 57 Fed. Reg. 53,985 (Nov. 9, 1992) [hereinafter 1992 Release]. *See also* Executive Compensation Disclosure Release Nos. 33-6940, 34-30851 (June 23, 1992), 57 Fed. Reg. 29,582

representing the total compensation of each NEO for each covered fiscal year.[3] This column aggregates the total dollar value of each different compensation element quantified in the other columns of the table.[4]

This information has not yet proven to be the panacea that investors expected. Because the amounts reported in the table reflect dissimilar pay elements that are intended to compensate executives at different times and that are valued using different methodologies, it is not always clear what this total compensation figure means. This concern was further exacerbated in December 2006 when the Securities and Exchange Commission (SEC) abruptly revised how equity awards are to be reported in the table,[5] a change that was subsequently reversed in December 2009.[6]

While there are numerous ways to characterize the different pay elements presented in the table, generally they fall into two broad categories:

- compensation that has been earned (and often paid) during the covered fiscal year ("earned compensation"); and
- compensation awarded during the covered fiscal year that may be earned (and paid) in a future fiscal year ("contingent compensation").[7]

(July 2, 1992), *as modified,* Executive Compensation Disclosure, Release Nos. 33-6941, 34-80852 (July 10, 1992), 57 Fed. Reg. 31, 156 (July 14, 1992).

3. To facilitate this information, all compensation must be reported in dollars in the table. See "Tabular Format," *infra.* The Summary Compensation Table is accompanied by a supplemental table providing additional detail about several of the compensation elements reported therein (see Chapter 6), as well as by supplemental narrative disclosure of material information necessary to an understanding of the information presented in the table (see Chapter 7).

4. As the SEC noted, this change was widely acclaimed by investors. Among other commenters, the SEC received over 20,000 form letters from individuals specifically supporting the addition of a Total Compensation column to the table. *See* Executive Compensation and Related Person Disclosure, Release Nos. 33-8732A, 34-54302A, IC-27444A (Aug. 29, 2006), 71 Fed. Reg. 53,158 (Sept. 8, 2006) [hereinafter Adopting Release], *available at* http://www.sec. gov/rules/final/2006/33-8732a.pdf, at n.127.

5. *See* Executive Compensation Disclosure, Release Nos. 33-8765, 34-55009 (Dec. 22, 2006), 71 Fed. Reg. 78,338 (Dec. 29, 2006) [hereinafter December 2006 Release], *available at* http://www.sec.gov/rules/final/2006/33-8765.pdf. See also the discussion at "Stock Awards—Amount to be Reported," *infra.*

6. *See* Proxy Disclosure Enhancements, Release Nos. 33-9089, 34-61175, IC-29092 (December 16, 2009), 74 Fed. Reg. 68,334 (December 23, 2009) [hereinafter 2009 Adopting Release], *available at* http://www.sec.gov/rules/final/33-9089.htm.

7. For example, nonequity incentive plan compensation (see "Nonequity Incentive Plan Compensation," *infra*) is reported in the table when earned, while the reporting of equity

Several of the other compensation tables are intended to track and report on contingent compensation items.[8] As a result of this dichotomy, as well as concerns on the part of some registrants that this total compensation figure is not representative of total pay as more commonly understood by investors or the registrant's board of directors or board compensation committee, some registrants include "alternative" tables disclosing a reformulated total compensation figure and its constituent elements as part of their executive compensation disclosure.[9]

In the SEC's defense, it should be noted that there is probably not a single disclosure approach that would effectively eliminate the issue described above. Differences in how various executive compensation arrangements are designed and operate make it difficult, if not impossible, to harmonize the reporting of all pay elements and to adopt a single consistent approach across all forms of compensation.

Another major structural feature of the Summary Compensation Table is the absence of any differentiation between annual and long-term compensation. Under the former rules, the different reporting categories were placed under one caption or the other. However, this distinction did not prove to be useful to investors and was often confusing for registrants.[10] Instead, the different reporting categories are now presented uniformly in the table and differences in the nature of the compensation being reported are to be addressed in the Compensation Discussion and Analysis (CD&A).

Finally, the table includes a separate column to report the annual change in value of retirement plan benefits and above-market or preferential earnings on nonqualified deferred compensation.[11] The segregation of these compensation elements in their own column is intended to highlight these items—which, for the most part, relate principally to tenure—for investors and to reinforce the fact that they

---

compensation is triggered by the grant of the award, whether or not it has been actually earned or paid (see "Stock Awards" and "Option Awards," *infra*).

8. See, for example, the Outstanding Equity Awards at Fiscal Year-End Table (Chapter 8) and the Option Exercises and Stock Vested Table (Chapter 9).

9. *See* Division of Corporation Finance, *Staff Observations in the Review of Executive Compensation Disclosure* (Oct. 9, 2007), *available at* http://www.sec.gov/divisions/corpfin/guidance/execcompdisclosure.htm, under the heading "Format." An example of a registrant providing such "alternative" tables is the Bank of America Corporation (see its Definitive Proxy Statement (Form 14A) filed Mar. 30, 2011 (file no. 001-06523)).

10. *See* the Adopting Release, *supra* note 4, at Section II.C.1.a.

11. See "Pension Value Changes and Above-Market and Preferential Earnings," *infra*.

are not to be included in determining which of a registrant's executives are included in the disclosure.

Tabular Format

The Summary Compensation Table is to be presented in the following tabular format:

SUMMARY COMPENSATION TABLE

Name and Principal Position	Year	Salary ($)	Bonus ($)	Stock Awards ($)	Option Awards ($)	Non-equity Incentive Plan Compensation ($)	Change in Pension Value and Non-qualified Deferred Compensation Earnings ($)	All Other Compensation ($)	Total ($)
(a)	(b)	(c)	(d)	(e)	(f)	(g)	(h)	(i)	(j)
Principal Executive Officer (PEO)									
Principal Financial Officer (PFO)									
A									
B									
C									

The table includes the following information for the last completed fiscal year and the two preceding fiscal years:

- the name and principal position of the NEO (column (a));[12]
- the fiscal year covered (column (b));[13]
- the dollar value of base salary (cash and noncash) earned by the NEO during the fiscal year covered (column (c));[14]
- the dollar value of bonus (cash and noncash) earned by the NEO during the fiscal year covered (column (d));[15]

---

12. Item 402(c)(2)(i).
13. Item 402(c)(2)(ii).
14. Item 402(c)(2)(iii).
15. Item 402(c)(2)(iv).

- the aggregate grant date fair value computed in accordance with Financial Accounting Standards Board (FASB) Accounting Standards Codification Topic 718, *Compensation – Stock Compensation* (FASB ASC Topic 718) for all stock awards (column (e));[16]
- the aggregate grant date fair value computed in accordance with FASB ASC Topic 718 for all stock option awards (column (f));[17]
- the dollar value of all earnings for services performed during the fiscal year pursuant to nonequity incentive plans, and all earnings on any outstanding awards (column (g));[18]
- the sum of

  - the aggregate change in the actuarial present value of the NEO's accumulated benefit under all defined benefit and actuarial pension plans (including supplemental plans);[19] and
  - above-market or preferential earnings on nonqualified deferred compensation, including any such earnings on nonqualified defined contribution plans (column (h));[20]

- all other compensation for the covered fiscal year that the registrant could not properly report in any other column of the table (column (i));[21] and
- the dollar value of total compensation for the covered fiscal year (column (j)).[22]

As with most of the disclosure tables, the last completed fiscal year is to be added to the title of the table.[23] Any column in the table for which there is no information to be reported may be omitted.[24]

The compensation values to be reported in the Summary Compensation Table must be reported in dollars and rounded to the

---

16. Item 402(c)(2)(v).
17. Item 402(c)(2)(vi).
18. Item 402(c)(2)(vii).
19. Item 402(c)(2)(viii)(A).
20. Item 402(c)(2)(viii)(B).
21. Item 402(c)(2)(ix).
22. Item 402(c)(2)(x).
23. *See* the Instruction to Item 402.
24. *See* Item 402(a)(5).

nearest dollar.[25] In addition, reported compensation values must be reported numerically, providing a single numerical value for each grid in the table.[26] Under the former rules, some stock-based compensation was disclosed on the basis of number of shares rather than in dollar amounts.

Where compensation was paid to or received by a NEO in a currency other than dollars, a footnote to the table must be provided to identify that currency and describe the rate and methodology used to convert the payment amounts to dollars.[27]

Where an instruction to the Summary Compensation Table does not specifically limit footnote disclosure to compensation for the registrant's last fiscal year, footnote disclosure for the other years reported in the table is required only if it is material to an investor's understanding of the compensation reported in the Summary Compensation Table for the company's last fiscal year.[28]

Any amounts that are deferred, whether pursuant to a Section 401(k) plan or otherwise, are to be included in the appropriate column of the table for the covered fiscal year.[29] This treatment applies to all compensation elements (not just base salary and bonus as under the former rules), and without regard to the reason for the deferral. Thus, it applies to both elective and mandatory deferrals.[30]

While the SEC had initially proposed that deferred amounts be disclosed in a footnote to the applicable column,[31] in view of the requirement to report deferred amounts in the Nonqualified Deferred Compensation Table and in response to concerns about potential

---

25. *See* Instruction 2 to Item 402(c). Under the former rules, information about stock options and stock appreciation rights was reported in number of shares, rather than in dollars. *See* former Item 402(b)(2)(iv)(B).

26. *Id.*

27. *Id.* The rules do not mandate that registrants use a particular currency conversion rate or methodology to perform this calculation. Reasonable methods may include using the currency conversion rate on the last day of the fiscal year (provided that this rate did not fluctuate dramatically during the year), using the average conversion rate over the entire fiscal year, and using the methodology used for financial reporting purposes. *See* Cleary Gottlieb Steen & Hamilton LLP, *Common Questions: Navigating the SEC's New Compensation Rules* (Jan. 19, 2007), at Q&A 32.

28. See Division of Corporation Finance, Compliance and Disclosure Interpretations – Regulation S-K (July 8, 2011) [hereinafter Current Staff Guidance], *available at* http://www.sec.gov/divisions/corpfin/guidance/regs-kinterp.htm, at Q&A 119.14.

29. *See* Instruction 4 to Item 402(c).

30. *See* the Adopting Release, *supra* note 4, at n.142.

31. *See* Instruction 4 to Proposed Item 402(c).

"double counting," the proposal was not adopted.[32] Still, in some situations a registrant may find it advisable to include a footnote to the applicable column indicating the amount that has been deferred.

Compensation Subject to Reporting

General

All compensation that has been earned, paid, or awarded for services performed as a NEO must be reported in the table. As noted in the next section, however, this general principle is not all-encompassing.[33]

Where a NEO also is a director of the registrant and is compensated for serving as a director, his or her director compensation is to be fully reported in this table rather than in the Director Compensation Table.[34] In this situation, a registrant should provide a footnote to the table identifying this pay as director compensation and itemizing the amounts.[35]

Special Situations

Determining what compensation needs to be reported where there has been a significant corporate transaction during the last completed fiscal year can be challenging. The staff of the SEC's Division of Corporation Finance (SEC Staff) has addressed a number of common scenarios that are instructive in deciding the amounts that must be reported in the Summary Compensation Table and the related tables.[36]

Whether a spin-off is to be treated like the initial public offering of the new "spun-off" registrant for purposes of the rules depends on the particular facts and circumstances.[37] To determine whether

---

32. *See* the Adopting Release, *supra* note 4, at Section II.C.1.b.

33. There are three additional qualifications to this principle. Perquisites and other personal benefits received by a NEO do not need to be disclosed to the extent that their total value is less than $10,000. Further, the disclosure of earnings on nonqualified deferred compensation is limited to the above-market or preferential portion of such earnings. Finally, registrant payments regarding broad-based, nondiscriminatory group life, health, hospitalization, and medical reimbursement plans do not need to be disclosed.

34. *See* Instruction 3 to Item 402(c).

35. *Id.* A registrant is to use the categories in the Director Compensation Table to itemize the reported amounts. *See* Item 402(k)(2).

36. Most of these positions were carried over to the rules from prior SEC Staff positions under the former rules as reflected in the Telephone Interpretations Manual.

37. *See* the Current Staff Guidance, *supra* note 28, at Interpretation 1.01.

compensation earned, paid, or awarded before the spin-off must be disclosed, the SEC Staff has taken the position that the "spun-off" registrant should consider whether it was a reporting company or a separate division before the spin-off, as well as its continuity of management. For example, if a parent company spun off a subsidiary that conducted one line of the parent company's business, and before and after the spin-off the executive officers of the subsidiary (a) were the same, (b) provided the same type of services to the subsidiary, and (c) provided no services to the parent, historical compensation disclosure likely would be required.[38] In contrast, if a parent company spun off a newly formed subsidiary consisting of portions of several different parts of the parent's business and having new management, it is more likely that the spin-off could be treated as the initial public offering of a new "spun-off" registrant.[39]

Further, the rules do not recognize a concept of "successor" compensation following a merger among operating companies. Therefore, the SEC Staff has indicated that the surviving registrant in the merger need not report on compensation paid by predecessor corporations that disappeared in the merger.[40] Similarly, a parent corporation would not pick up compensation paid to an employee of its subsidiary prior to the time the subsidiary became a subsidiary (that is, when it was a target).[41] Moreover, income paid by such predecessor companies need not be counted in computing whether an individual is a NEO of the surviving registrant.[42] The Staff has indicated that a different result may apply, however, in situations involving an amalgamation or combination of companies.[43]

---

38. *Id.*

39. *Id.*

40. *See* the Current Staff Guidance, *supra* note 28, at Interpretation 217.02.

41. *Id.*

42. *Id.*

43. *Id.* A different result also applies where an operating company combines with a shell company (as defined in Securities Act Rule 405 (17 C.F.R. 230.405)). Where the shareholders of a shell company will vote on combining the shell company with an operating company, the effect of which will make the operating company subject to the reporting requirements of Section 13(a) or 15(d) of the Exchange Act (15 U.S.C. § 78m(a) or § 78o(d)), the disclosure document soliciting shareholder approval of the combination (whether a proxy statement, Form S-4, or Form F-4) needs to disclose (a) Item 402 disclosure for the shell company before the combination; (b) Item 402 disclosure regarding the operating company that the operating company would be required to make if filing an Exchange Act registration statement, including a CD&A; and (c) Item 402 disclosure regarding each person who will serve as a director or an executive officer of the surviving company required by Item 18(a)(7)(ii) or 19(a)(7)(ii) of Form

Finally, where a subsidiary of a public company is going public and the officers of the subsidiary previously were officers of the parent, and, in some cases, all of the work that they did for the parent related to the subsidiary, the SEC Staff has taken the position that the registration statement of the subsidiary does not need to include compensation previously awarded by the parent corporation.[44] Instead, the subsidiary would start reporting as of the initial public offering date.[45]

Identification of Named Executive Officers and Principal Position

Column (a) of the table is to list each of the registrant's NEOs for the last completed fiscal year and to indicate their principal position with the registrant.

Fiscal Years Covered

General

Column (b) of the table is to list each fiscal year for which compensation information is being presented. The table requires three years of information.[46] As under the former rules, a registrant need not provide information for a fiscal year prior to the last completed fiscal year if it was not a reporting company pursuant to Exchange Act Section 13(a) or 15(d)[47] *at any time* during that year, unless the registrant previously was required to provide information for any such year in response to a SEC filing requirement.[48]

S-4, including a CD&A that may emphasize new plans or policies (as provided in the Adopting Release, *supra* note 4, at n.97). *See* the Current Staff Guidance, *supra* note 28, at Interpretation 217.12. The annual report on Form 10-K of the combined entity for the fiscal year in which the combination occurs must provide Item 402 disclosure for the NEOs and directors of the combined entity, complying with Item 402(a)(4) of Regulation S-K and Instruction 1 to Item 402(c) of Regulation S-K. *Id.*

44. *See* the Current Staff Guidance, *supra* note 28, at Interpretation 217.03.

45. *Id.*

46. *See* Item 402(c)(1). In the case of a smaller reporting company, the table need only provide disclosure for two years. *See* Item 402(n)(1).

47. 15 U.S.C. § 78m(a) or § 780(d).

48. *See* Instruction 1 to Item 402(c).

Transition

To ease transition to the rules, the SEC elected to phase in compliance with the revised Summary Compensation Table. Thus, registrants were not required to "restate" compensation disclosure for fiscal years in which they previously applied the former rules. Consequently, in 2007, the initial year that the rules were effective, registrants were required to reflect only the last completed fiscal year in the table and did not have to provide information for the two fiscal years preceding the last completed fiscal year. For the subsequent year, registrants were required to present only the most recent two fiscal years in the table, and for the next and all subsequent years were required to present the last completed fiscal year and the two preceding fiscal years in the table.[49] Thus, in the case of a registrant with a calendar year fiscal year-end, the first year in which it presented a full three-year Summary Compensation Table was 2009, presenting compensation information for fiscal years 2006, 2007, and 2008.

Stub Periods

If a registrant changes its fiscal year, the SEC Staff takes the position that the registrant should report compensation for the "stub period."[50] It should not annualize or restate compensation. In addition, the registrant should report compensation for the last three full fiscal years, in accordance with the rules (assuming that transition to the full three-year Summary Compensation Table has been completed).

For example, in late 2012 a registrant changes its fiscal year-end from June 30 to December 31. In the Summary Compensation Table, the registrant would provide disclosure for each of the following four periods: July 1, 2012, to December 31, 2012; July 1, 2011, to June 30, 2012; July 1, 2010, to June 30, 2011; and July 1, 2009, to June 30, 2010.[51] The registrant would continue providing such disclosure for four periods (three full fiscal years and the stub period) until there is disclosure for three full fiscal years after the stub period (until December 31, 2015, in the example). If the registrant was not a reporting company and was to do an initial public offering in February 2012, it would furnish disclosure

---

49. *See* the Adopting Release, *supra* note 4, at n.547 and the accompanying text.
50. *See* the Current Staff Guidance, *supra* note 28, at Interpretation 217.05.
51. *Id.*

for both of the following periods in the Summary Compensation Table: July 1, 2011, to December 31, 2011; and July 1, 2010, to June 30, 2011.[52]

Impact of Reporting Multiple Years

There are various practical considerations that come into play when reporting compensation in the table for multiple fiscal years. For example, in the event of a stock split or similar event, it is advisable to consider adjusting the number of shares and per share information for previously disclosed fiscal years in the current fiscal year's table to reflect the event and make the presentation more understandable for investors.[53] Similarly, if a registrant changes the valuation methodology that it uses for its perquisites disclosure from one fiscal year to the next, it is advisable to consider restating the computations from the prior fiscal year or years (even though this will likely result in different amounts than were reported in the prior Summary Compensation Table or tables) to promote comparability.[54] In this situation, it is also advisable to explain the reason for the difference in the reported amounts in a footnote to the All Other Compensation column of the table.

Base Salary

General

Column (c) of the table is to report the base salary of each NEO for each covered fiscal year. Base salary that is earned is to be reported in the column even though a NEO may have elected to defer receipt of this compensation until a subsequent year.[55] While the question has not been

---

52. *Id.*

53. *See* W. Alan Kailer, *The Securities and Exchange Commission's Executive Compensation Rules—Preparing the Executive Compensation Tables* (Jan. 2012) [hereafter Kailer], at A-35.

54. *See id.* at A-37.

55. *See* Instruction 4 to Item 402(c). Any amount deferred, whether pursuant to a Section 401(k) plan or otherwise, is to be included in the appropriate column for the fiscal year in which earned. Further, the SEC Staff has informally indicated that, where an executive officer is permitted to defer his base salary into the stock fund of a Section 401(k) plan, this deferral right is considered a separate arrangement which does not bring the executive officer's base salary within the scope of FASB ASC Topic 718 for purposes of Q&A 119.03 of the Current Staff Guidance. *See* Questions and Answers, Technical Session Between the SEC Staff and the Joint Committee on Employee Benefits (May 4, 2010) [hereinafter 2010 JCEB Questions], *available at* http://www.americanbar.org/content/dam/aba/events/employee_benefits/2010_sec_qa.authcheckdam.pdf, at Question No. 10.

formally addressed under the rules, it appears that sales commissions paid to a NEO should generally be reported in this column, as was the case under the former rules.[56] Similarly, the SEC Staff has informally suggested that a cash payment in lieu of accrued vacation is to be reported in this column.[57]

Forgone Salary

A registrant is to include in this column any amount of base salary that is forgone at the election of a NEO under which stock, equity-based, or another form of noncash compensation instead has been received by the executive.[58] The receipt of any such noncash compensation instead of salary must be disclosed in a footnote added to the column.[59] In addition, where applicable, this footnote should refer to the Grants of Plan-Based Awards Table where the stock, option, or nonequity incentive plan award elected by the NEO is reported.[60]

If the amount of base salary forgone at the election of the NEO was less than the value of the equity-based compensation received, or if the agreement pursuant to which the executive had the option to elect settlement in stock or equity-based compensation was within the scope of FASB ASC Topic 718, then different reporting treatment results. In the former situation, the incremental value of an equity award is to be reported in the Stock Awards or Option Awards column of the table, as the case may be,[61] and, in the latter situation, the award is to be reported in total in the Stock Awards or Option Awards column, as the case may be, instead of in this column.[62]

In both of these special cases, footnote disclosure would be provided reporting the circumstances of the award or awards.[63] Further, appropriate disclosure about the equity-based compensation received

---

56. *See* Questions and Answers, Technical Session Between the SEC Staff and the Joint Committee on Employee Benefits (May 1997), at Question No. 15.

57. This position is based on a review of SEC Staff comment letters from the mid-1990s.

58. *See* Instruction 2 to Item 402(c)(2)(iii) and (iv).

59. *Id.*

60. *Id.*

61. By implication, if the value of the equity award (or other form of noncash compensation) is that same as the value of the forgone base salary, the amount is reported only in this column and not in any other column of the Summary Compensation Table. *See* the Current Staff Guidance, *supra* note 28, at Q&A 119.03.

62. *Id.*

63. *Id.*

instead of base salary also must be provided in the Grants of Plan-Based Awards Table, the Outstanding Equity Awards at Fiscal Year-End Table, and the Option Exercises and Stock Vested Table, as applicable.[64]

Determining whether an arrangement is within the scope of FASB ASC Topic 718 will not always be easy. To clarify the intent of the rules, the SEC Staff has indicated that an arrangement is likely to be considered within the scope of FASB ASC Topic 718 if the right to stock settlement is "embedded"[65] in the terms of the award.[66] Although the accounting rules do not use the "embedded" terminology, the Staff has indicated that it is simply a shorthand way of referring to Paragraph 4 of SFAS 123R (now codified as FASB ASC Topic 718); that is, a way to determine whether the right to payment in the form of stock or equity-based compensation is inherent in the award itself.[67]

Based on this interpretation, it is probably the case that if a NEO has the ability to receive his or her base salary either in cash or equity, this choice is established at the outset of the compensation arrangement, and if he or she elects to receive equity, the compensation is to be reported in the Stock Awards or Option Awards column, as applicable. On the other hand, if at the end of the fiscal year, or after the compensation has been earned, a registrant extends to its NEOs the option of taking all or a portion of their base salary in the form of equity, this amount is to be reported in this column. Because of the complexities associated with applying the principles of FASB ASC Topic 718, registrants should consult with their accounting advisors before deciding how to report these arrangements in the table.

Indeterminate Salary

Where a NEO's base salary for the last competed fiscal year cannot be calculated as of the most recent practicable date, the amount will not

---

64. See Chapters 6, 8, and 9, respectively.

65. The "embedded" concept contemplates a situation where, at the time an award is granted, the NEO has the right to elect to receive payment in the form of stock or equity-based compensation. Such an arrangement is within the scope of FASB ASC Topic 718. On the other hand, where the NEO has no right to receive stock or equity-based compensation at the time an award is granted, but he or she later obtains the right to make such an election, the award is not within the scope of FASB ASC Topic 718.

66. See the Current Staff Guidance, *supra* note 28, at Q&A 119.03. *See also* Questions and Answers, Technical Session Between the SEC Staff and the Joint Committee on Employee Benefits (May 8, 2007) [hereinafter 2007 JCEB Questions], *available at* http://www.abanet.org/jceb/2007/SEC07Final.pdf, at Question No. 1.

67. See the 2010 JCEB Questions, *supra* note 55, at Question No. 10.

be reportable in the table. Instead, a registrant must include a footnote to the column indicating that the amount is not calculable through the latest practicable date and giving the date that the NEO's salary is expected to be determined.[68]

When the base salary amount is calculated, either in whole or in part (either through an actual payment or a decision or other occurrence that fixes the amount), the registrant must file a current report on Form 8-K disclosing the salary amount and providing a new recomputed total compensation figure for the NEO that includes this amount.[69]

Bonus

General

Column (d) of the table is to report the bonus received by each NEO for each covered fiscal year. A bonus that is earned for a covered fiscal year is to be reported in the column even if it is paid in the subsequent fiscal year[70] or even though a NEO may have elected to defer receipt of this compensation until a subsequent year.[71]

---

68. *See* Instruction 1 to Item 402(c)(2)(iii) and (iv). The SEC Staff has applied this position to a situation where a document including executive compensation information was filed on January 2 with respect to a fiscal year ended on December 31 and where compensation information could not be incorporated by reference into the filing. *See* the Current Staff Guidance, *supra* note 28, at Interpretation 217.11. In this instance, the SEC Staff indicated that the compensation information for the last completed fiscal year should be included in the filing, subject to the application of this Instruction in the case of indeterminate bonus amounts. The Staff went on to note, however, that, to the extent that the compensation disclosure was dependent on assumptions used in the registrant's financial statements and those financial statements have not yet been audited, it was permissible for the registrant to note this fact in its disclosure. *Id.*

69. *Id. See also* Item 5.02(f) of Form 8-K (17 C.F.R. 249.308). Under the former rules, if a NEO's base salary was not determinable at the time the disclosure was being prepared, generally a registrant would report the amount in its next annual report on Form 10-K or proxy statement for the subsequent fiscal year. *See* Instruction 1 to former Item 402(b)(2)(iii)(A) and (B). *See also* the 2007 JCEB Questions, *supra* note 66, at Question No. 2.

70. *See* Instruction 1 to Item 402(c)(2)(iii) and (iv). Note that this principle does not necessarily apply when reporting equity awards. See "Covered Compensation—Timing of Reporting" in Chapter 2.

71. *See* Instruction 4 to Item 402(c). Any amount deferred, whether pursuant to a Section 401(k) plan or otherwise, is to be included in the appropriate column for the fiscal year in which earned. *See also* the Adopting Release, *supra* note 4, at n.141 and the accompanying text. Further, the SEC Staff has informally indicated that, where an executive officer is permitted to defer his bonus into the stock fund of a Section 401(k) plan, this deferral right is considered a separate arrangement which does not bring the executive officer's

Relationship to Nonequity Incentive Plan Compensation

The characterization of an amount as a bonus is based largely on the type of plan or arrangement pursuant to which the amount is being determined and paid. Amounts that are awarded or payable under many performance-based cash plans, without regard to the length or duration of the performance period, are considered to be "nonequity incentive plan compensation" for purposes of the rules[72] and, accordingly, are to be reported in the Nonequity Incentive Plan Compensation column of the table as earned.[73]

Because nonequity incentive plan compensation encompasses both annual and long-term awards, most conventional bonus arrangements (which are typically based on preestablished performance criteria) are no longer reported in this column. As a practical matter, the amounts reported in this column include guaranteed payments (for example, a "signing" or "retention" bonus)[74] and purely discretionary payments (for example, non-performance-based bonuses and bonuses that are not based on the satisfaction of preestablished performance criteria).[75] Consequently, a registrant may find that, in a covered fiscal year, it has nothing to report in this column for one or more of its NEOs.[76]

---

bonus within the scope of FASB ASC Topic 718 for purposes of Q&A 119.03 of the Current Staff Guidance. *See* the 2010 JCEB Questions, *supra* note 55, at Question No. 10.

72. Under an interrelated set of definitions, a "nonequity incentive plan" is defined as "an incentive plan or portion of an incentive plan that is not an equity incentive plan." For these purposes, an "incentive plan" is defined as "any plan providing compensation intended to serve as incentive for performance to occur over a specified period, whether such performance is measured by reference to financial performance of the registrant or an affiliate, the registrant's stock price, or any other performance measure," while an "equity incentive plan" is defined as "an incentive plan or portion of an incentive plan under which awards are granted that fall within the scope of FASB ASC Topic 718." *See* Item 402(a)(6)(iii). Taken together, a nonequity incentive plan is a performance-based plan that does not involve equity or other amounts that are within the scope of FASB ASC Topic 718.

73. Item 402(c)(2)(vii). See "Nonequity Incentive Plan Compensation," *infra*.

74. In the case of a one-time retention bonus, where payment is tied to multiple years of service, the bonus is reportable in the fiscal year in which the performance condition is satisfied. See the Current Staff Guidance, *supra* note 28 at Q&A 119.17.

75. *See* the Current Staff Guidance, *supra* note 28, at Q&A 119.02. See also "Nonequity Incentive Plan Compensation," *infra*.

76. If there is no compensation awarded to, earned, or received by any of the NEOs in any fiscal year covered by that column, the column may be omitted. *See* Item 402(a)(5).

Forgone Bonus Amounts

A registrant is to include in this column any bonus amount that is forgone at the election of a NEO under which stock, equity-based, or another form of noncash compensation instead has been received by the executive.[77] The receipt of any such noncash compensation instead of bonus must be disclosed in a footnote added to the column.[78] In addition, where applicable, this footnote also should refer to the Grants of Plan-Based Awards Table where the stock, option, or nonequity incentive plan award[79] elected by the NEO is reported.[80]

If the bonus amount forgone at the election of the NEO was less than the value of the equity-based compensation received, or if the agreement pursuant to which the executive had the option to elect settlement in stock or equity-based compensation was within the scope of FASB ASC Topic 718, then, as previously described in the case of forgone base salary, different reporting treatment results.[81]

Indeterminate Bonus Amounts

Where a NEO's bonus for the last competed fiscal year cannot be calculated as of the most recent practicable date, the amount will not be reportable in the table. Instead, a registrant must include a footnote to the column indicating that the amount is not calculable through the latest practicable date and giving the date that the NEO's bonus is expected to be determined.[82]

When the bonus amount is calculated, either in whole or in part (either through an actual payment or a decision or other occurrence that fixes the amount), the registrant must file a current report on Form

---

77. *See* Instruction 2 to Item 402(c)(2)(iii) and (iv).

78. *Id.*

79. Note that the language in the Instruction is not symmetrical. While the first sentence of Instruction 2 refers to "stock, equity-based, or another form of noncash compensation" that is received in lieu of the forgone bonus, the second sentence refers to the "stock, option, or nonequity incentive plan award" elected by the NEO that is to be reported in the Grants of Plan-Based Awards Table. Presumably, this distinction simply acknowledges that not all forms of noncash compensation are subject to reporting in the Grants of Plan-Based Awards Table.

80. *Id.*

81. See the discussion in "Base Salary," *supra.*

82. *See* Instruction 1 to Item 402(c)(2)(iii) and (iv).

8-K disclosing the bonus amount and providing a new recomputed total compensation figure for the NEO that includes this amount.[83]

Retention Bonus

A registrant is to include in this column a bonus received by a NEO that is predicated on continued service and is not considered a "non-equity incentive plan award." The SEC Staff has indicated that, where a registrant enters into a retention agreement in which it agrees to pay a NEO a cash retention bonus, conditioned on the NEO remaining employed by the registrant through the end of a subsequent fiscal year, the cash retention bonus is reportable in column (d) for the fiscal year in which the employment condition[84] has been satisfied.[85]

The SEC Staff has further indicated that same analysis applies to any interest the registrant is obligated to pay on the cash retention bonus, assuming the interest is not payable unless and until the employment condition has been satisfied. Before the employment condition has been satisfied, the bonus would not be required to be reported in column (d) as a bonus that has been earned but deferred, nor would it be reportable in the Nonqualified Deferred Compensation Table.[86]

Impact of Bonus "Clawback"

The introduction of compensation recovery ("clawback") policies has raised the possibility that, in a given fiscal year, a registrant may recoup all or a portion of a bonus previously paid to a NEO. The SEC Staff has indicated that, in a situation where, in Year Two, a registrant recovers (or "claws back") a portion of a bonus paid to an executive officer in Year One, the portion of the Year One bonus recovered in Year Two should not be deducted from the amounts otherwise reported in column (d)

---

83. *Id. See also* Item 5.02(f) of Form 8-K (17 C.F.R. 249.308). Under the former rules, if a NEO's bonus was not determinable at the time the disclosure was being prepared, generally a registrant would report the amount in its next annual report on Form 10-K or proxy statement for the subsequent fiscal year. *See* Instruction 1 to former Item 402(b)(2)(iii)(A) and (B).

84. While the SEC Staff guidance refers to the continued service of the NEO as a "performance" condition, subsequently the Staff confirmed that this reference was meant to refer to the employment condition described in the related question and was not intended to mean a performance condition within the scope of FASB ASC Topic 718. *See* the 2010 JCEB Questions, *supra* note 55, at Question No. 11.

85. *See* the Current Staff Guidance, *supra* note 28, at Q&A 119.17.

86. *Id.* The registrant should discuss the cash retention bonus in its CD&A, however, for the fiscal year in which the retention agreement was entered into, as well as the subsequent fiscal years through completion of the performance necessary to earn the bonus. *Id.*

(or in total compensation for purposes of determining whether the executive officer is a NEO for Year Two).[87]

If the executive officer is a NEO for the last completed fiscal year (Year Two), the registrant should report in the Summary Compensation Table for the fiscal year preceding the last completed fiscal year (Year One), in column (d) and in column (j), amounts that are adjusted to reflect the compensation recovery (or clawback), with footnote disclosure of the amount recovered.[88]

Declined Bonus

The SEC Staff has indicated that, where a registrant has a practice of granting discretionary bonuses to its executive officers and, before the board of directors takes action to grant such bonuses for a fiscal year, an executive officer advises the board of directors that he or she will not accept a bonus for that year, the registrant does not need to report this anticipated award in the Summary Compensation Table.[89] In the Staff's view, since the executive officer declined the bonus before it was granted, no reportable compensation was received (since no bonus was actually granted).[90]

Stock Awards

General

Column (e) of the table is to report the aggregate grant date fair value, computed in accordance with FASB ASC Topic 718, for all stock awards granted to each NEO with respect to each covered fiscal year, including stock awards granted pursuant to an equity incentive plan.[91] For purposes of the rules, the scope of this column is quite broad and encompasses any stock-related award that derives its value from the registrant's equity

---

87. *See* the Current Staff Guidance, *supra* note 28, at Q&A 117.03.

88. *Id.* As the instruction to Item 402(b) provides, if "necessary to an understanding of the registrant's compensation policies and decisions regarding the named executive officers," the CD&A should discuss the reasons for the clawback" and how the amount recovered was determined. *Id.*

89. *See* the Current Staff Guidance, *supra* note 28, at Q&A 119.26. Similarly, no amount need be included in total compensation for purposes of determining if the executive officer is a NEO. *Id.*

90. *Id.*

91. *See* the Adopting Release, *supra* note 4, at n.147 and the accompanying text.

securities or that permits settlement by issuing the registrant's equity securities and, consequently, is within the scope of FASB ASC Topic 718 for financial reporting purposes.[92] This includes both service-based and performance-based stock awards,[93] as well as awards that have been transferred.[94] Since, as explained below, the amount reported is based on the grant date fair value computed by the registrant for financial statement reporting purposes, generally stock awards will be reported in the fiscal year granted, rather than the fiscal year to which the award relates.[95]

Amount to Be Reported

As originally adopted, a registrant would have been required to report the aggregate grant date fair value of all stock awards granted to a NEO with respect to each covered fiscal year in this column. This requirement has been changed twice since the rules were adopted in 2006.

Initially, this requirement was changed in December 2006.[96] At that time, the SEC was persuaded that disclosure of just a proportionate amount of a stock award's total grant date fair value that was recognized

---

92. Under the rules, the term "stock" means instruments such as common stock, restricted stock, restricted stock units, phantom stock, phantom stock units, common stock equivalent units, or any similar instruments that do not have option-like features. *See* Item 402(a)(6)(i). Generally speaking, a restricted stock award is an award of stock subject to performance-based or service-based vesting conditions. Typically, phantom stock, phantom stock units, common stock equivalent units, and other similar awards are awards where an executive obtains a right to receive payment in the future of an amount based on the value of a hypothetical, or notional, amount of shares of common equity (or in some cases stock based on that value). *See* the Adopting Release, *supra* note 4, at n.146. If the terms of phantom stock, phantom stock units, common stock equivalents, or other similar awards contain option-like features, the awards must be included in the Option Awards column rather than this column. *Id.*

93. *See* the Adopting Release, *supra* note 4, at n.147 and the accompanying text. Under the former rules, alternatively performance-based stock awards could be reported as Long-Term Incentive Plan awards. *See* Instruction 1 to former Item 402(b)(2)(iv). This alternative was eliminated under the current rules.

94. *See* Kailer, *supra* note 53, at B-4.

95. See "Covered Compensation—Timing of Reporting" in Chapter 2.

96. *See* the December 2006 Release, *supra* note 5. Essentially, the SEC, upon reconsideration of the original rules, concluded that a combination of disclosure of the compensation cost associated with equity awards as that cost was recognized for financial statement reporting purposes in the Summary Compensation Table, combined with disclosure of the grant date fair value of those awards on an award-by-award basis in the Grants of Plan-Based Awards Table, would provide investors with a more complete and more useful picture of executive compensation than the original rules. *See id.* at Section II. These changes were adopted as interim final rules. In addition, at that time, the information about an award's full grant date fair value was not eliminated. Instead, it was moved to the Grants of Plan-Based Awards Table.

in a registrant's financial statements for each covered fiscal year was the most accurate way to present the compensation attributable to the services rendered by a NEO for that year. As some commenters had argued at the time the rules were originally adopted, the reporting of the full grant date fair value of a stock award would overstate compensation earned related to service rendered for the year, and might confuse the discussion and analysis of a registrant's compensation policies and practices. This result was considered to be particularly problematic in the case of a performance-based stock award. Acknowledging that no one approach to the disclosure of stock and stock option awards addressed all of the issues regarding disclosure of these forms of compensation, the SEC decided to reverse its original decision and implement an approach providing for the disclosure of compensation cost of these awards over their requisite service period, as described in FASB ASC Topic 718.[97]

While an award's reportable value was still to be determined in accordance with FASB ASC Topic 718,[98] the amount reported in column (e) of the table was to be based solely on the dollar amount recognized for financial statement reporting purposes during the covered fiscal year.[99] Since the grant date fair value of most stock awards was recognized over the award's requisite service period for financial statement reporting purposes,[100] to the extent that an award had a service period longer than one year (for example, a multiple-year vesting schedule), the amount reported in column (e) in any given year was likely to encompass multiple awards, including awards that were granted in prior fiscal years.

Notwithstanding its stated objective of enhanced clarity, for several reasons the December 2006 change resulted in significantly more complexity in computing the amounts to be reported. Most importantly, the change placed a premium on understanding the proper accounting treatment of individual stock awards to ensure accurate reporting in column (e). For example, under FASB ASC Topic 718, the classification of an award as an equity or liability instrument affects the measurement

---

97. *Id.*

98. Under the former rules, restricted stock awards were valued for purposes of the Summary Compensation Table by multiplying the closing market price of the registrant's unrestricted stock on the date of grant by the number of shares awarded. *See* former Item 402(b)(2)(iv)(A).

99. The amount to be reported was to include both the amounts recorded as compensation expense in the income statement for the covered fiscal year as well as any amounts earned by a NEO that had been capitalized on the balance sheet for that year.

100. FASB ASC Topic 718 defines the requisite service period as the period or periods during which an employee is required to provide service in exchange for an award under a share-based payment arrangement. *See* Appendix E of SFAS 123(R).

of its related compensation expense over the award's service period. Awards that are settled in cash or that contain repurchase or other features that do not result in the holder bearing the risks and rewards normally associated with share ownership for a specified period of time are classified as liability awards under FASB ASC Topic 718.

While the compensation expense recognized for an award classified as an equity instrument is fixed as of the grant date and, absent modification, is not revised with subsequent changes in the market price of the registrant's securities or the other assumptions used to initially value the award, awards classified as liability instruments receive starkly different treatment. While the fair value of a liability award is initially measured on the grant date, for financial statement reporting purposes the instrument is then remeasured at each subsequent reporting date until it is ultimately settled. Thus, unlike an award classified as an equity instrument, which had a fixed and consistent amount recognized (and correspondingly reported) each year over its service period, the amount recognized (and correspondingly reported) for an award classified as a liability instrument fluctuated from fiscal year to fiscal year and, in some situations, increased over time.[101]

Further, in the case of a stock award containing a performance-based vesting condition, compensation expense was reported in this column only if it was probable that the performance condition would be achieved. If the achievement of the performance condition was not probable at the grant date but later became probable, the proportionate amount of compensation expense based on the service previously rendered by the NEO was reported in the column during the period in which achievement of the performance condition became probable.[102]

Another troublesome variation in the reporting treatment of a NEO's stock rewards involved a retirement-eligible executive. Under FASB ASC Topic 718, an award granted to a retirement-eligible employee who is entitled to retain the award at retirement generally is not considered to have a substantive service requirement, since the recipient can keep the benefit of the award without performing services, regardless of its stated vesting terms. Thus, for financial statement reporting purposes, the full grant date fair value of the award was recognized in the registrant's

---

101. *Id.* at n.32 and the accompanying text.

102. Conversely, as discussed below, if the achievement of a performance condition was previously considered probable but subsequently, in a later period, was no longer considered probable, the amount of compensation expense previously reported was to be reversed during the period in which it was determined that achievement of the performance condition is no longer probable.

financial statements in the year of grant, notwithstanding the presence of a vesting schedule for the award.[103]

For many registrants—and investors—these complexities made it more difficult to understand what the amounts reported in column (e) actually represented. In response to this challenge, registrants were frequently required to provide lengthy and, at times, dense explanations of how these amounts were calculated. In addition, it was often necessary to devote attention in the CD&A to the difference between an award's full value (which was what the compensation committee was using to make compensation decisions) and the amounts reported in the table.

Ultimately, the SEC decided to reverse its position once again and, in December 2009, changed the reporting treatment of stock and option awards back to its original formulation.[104] As changed, the amount reported in column (e) is the aggregate grant date fair value of all stock awards granted during[105] a covered fiscal year, computed in accordance with FASB ASC Topic 718.[106]

---

103. Thus, the interim final rules did not substantively change the requirements for computing the amount to report in the Stock Awards and Option Awards columns for retirement-eligible executives.

104. *See* the 2009 Adopting Release, *supra* note 6, at Section II.A.2. To implement the 2009 change, the SEC required registrants providing Item 402 disclosure for a fiscal year ending on or after December 20, 2009 to present recomputed disclosure for each preceding fiscal year required to be included in the table, so that the stock awards and option awards columns presented the applicable full grant date fair values, and the total compensation column was correspondingly recomputed. *Id.*, at Section II.A.2.d. Column (e) amounts were to be computed based on the individual award grant date fair values reported in the applicable fiscal year's Grants of Plan-Based Awards Table, except that awards with performance conditions were to be recomputed to report grant date fair value based on the probable outcome as of the grant date, consistent with FASB ASC Topic 718. *Id.* In addition, if a person who would be a NEO for the most recent fiscal year (2009) also was disclosed as a NEO for 2007, but not for 2008, the NEO's compensation for each of those three fiscal years was to be reported pursuant to the 2009 change. Registrants were not required, however, to include different NEOs for any preceding fiscal year based on recomputing total compensation for those years pursuant to the 2009 change. *Id.*

105. While some commenters pressed for a rule that would require disclosure of the aggregate grant date fair value of equity awards granted *for* services performed in the covered fiscal year, even if granted *after* fiscal year-end, rather than awards granted *during* the covered fiscal year, the SEC declined to adopt this approach because of concerns that, since multiple subjective factors, which could vary significantly from registrant to registrant, influence equity awards granted after fiscal year-end, this approach to reporting could result in inconsistencies that would erode comparability. *See* the 2009 Adopting Release, *supra* note 6, at Section II.A.2.c.

106. Item 402(c)(2)(v). In the case of smaller reporting companies, *see* Item 402(n)(2)(v). As the SEC noted in the 2009 Adopting Release, the presentation of this information will allow investors to consider the decision of the compensation committee to grant a stock award or

To address the special challenge in reporting performance-based stock awards (which was, in part, the impetus for the December 2006 rule change[107]), the rules provide that the value of performance-based awards reported in the Summary Compensation Table, Grants of Plan-Based Awards Table are to be reported in column (e) based upon the probable outcome of the performance condition or conditions as of the grant date.[108] This amount is to be consistent with the grant date estimate of compensation cost to be recognized over the service period, excluding the effect of forfeitures.[109] In the SEC's view, this value better reflects how compensation committees take performance-contingent vesting conditions into account in granting such awards.

To provide investors additional information about an award's potential maximum value subject to changes in performance outcome, the rules also require footnote disclosure to column (e) of the maximum value of a stock award, assuming the highest level of performance conditions is probable.[110] For purposes of this calculation, if the award's performance condition is a "market condition" (for example, relative total shareholder return), it will be factored into the calculation of the award's grant date fair value and, thus, will not require footnote disclosure of the award's potential maximum value.[111] In other words, the impact of the market condition is embedded in the fair value calculation. Consequently, unlike the performance condition referenced in the rules, it does not require footnote disclosure of the award's potential maximum value.[112]

---

awards in a given fiscal year to a NEO as part of his or her overall compensation when making voting and investment decisions.

107. In 2006, commenters had criticized the reporting of the grant date fair value for performance-based awards at the maximum performance level. Noting that, typically, such awards are designed to incentivize attainment of target performance and generally set a higher maximum performance level as a "cap" on attainable compensation, these commenters asserted that requiring disclosure of an award's value to always be based on maximum performance would overstate the intended level of compensation and result in investor misinterpretation of compensation decisions. They also expressed concern that such a reporting requirement could discourage the grant of awards with difficult—or any—performance conditions, and lead to inflated benchmarking values used to set equity award or total compensation levels at other registrants.

108. *See* Instruction 3 to Item 402(c)(2)(v). In the case of smaller reporting companies, *see* Instruction 3 to Item 402(n)(2)(v).

109. *Id.*

110. *Id.*

111. *See* the 2010 JCEB Questions, *supra* note 55, at Question No. 6.

112. *Id.*

Many registrants grant performance-based stock awards (such as performance share awards) which provide for threshold, target, and maximum payout amounts depending on the level of achievement of the award's performance condition (or conditions) as determined at the conclusion of the performance period. Where, following the completion of the performance period, the board of directors (or compensation committee) determines that the executive officer has earned a number of shares that exceeds the target payout amount, the SEC Staff has informally indicated that, as long as the value of the award at the grant date assuming that the highest level of the performance conditions will be achieved (if an amount less than the maximum value was reported in column (e)) has been reported in a footnote to the column, the value of the additional shares earned in excess of the target payout amount need not be reported in the Summary Compensation Table following the completion of the performance period.[113] The additional shares that are received at the completion of the performance period are to be reported in the Option Exercises and Stock Vested Table for the fiscal year in which the performance period ended.[114] Also, the payout should be discussed in the CD&A.

Where a performance-based stock award has a single-year performance period, the amount to be reported in column (e) is to be based on the probable outcome of the performance condition or conditions as of the award's grant date, even if the actual outcome of the performance condition or conditions, and, therefore, the number of shares actually awarded for the performance period is known at the time the Summary Compensation Table is being prepared.[115]

The SEC Staff has indicated that if a registrant grants a stock award to an executive officer in a fiscal year and the same award is forfeited

---

113. *Id.*

114. *Id.*

115. *See* the Current Staff Guidance, *supra* note 28, at Q&A 119.28. The question presented to the SEC Staff was as follows: At the beginning of Year One, the compensation committee sets the threshold, target, and maximum levels for the number of shares that may be earned for Year One under the registrant's performance-based equity incentive plan. Incentive awards are paid in the form of restricted shares, which are issued early in Year Two after the compensation committee has certified the registrant's Year One performance results. As described in the text, in response to an inquiry as to how to calculate the amount to be reported in column (e), the Staff took the position that the grant date fair value for stock awards (as well as option awards) subject to performance conditions must be reported based on the probable outcome of the performance conditions as of the grant date, even though the actual outcome of the performance conditions and, therefore, in this case, the number of restricted shares actually awarded for Year One was known by the time of the filing of the proxy statement.

later during the same fiscal year because the executive officer leaves the registrant, the grant date fair value of this award is to be included for purposes of determining the executive officer's total compensation for that fiscal year (as well as for purposes of identifying the NEO group for that fiscal year).[116]

Timing of Reporting

Under the current rules, a stock award is to be reported in column (e) in the fiscal year in which the registrant calculates and begins to recognize compensation expense for the award for financial reporting purposes (essentially, the year in which the award is granted). Consequently, a registrant that makes compensation decisions about equity awards after fiscal year-end will typically report these awards in the fiscal year in which they are granted even though their size (or even the decision to make the award) may be closely tied to the prior fiscal year's service or performance.

Recently, the parameters of this general reporting principle were called into question when the SEC Staff was asked to provide guidance in the following situation. In 2010, a registrant granted an executive officer an equity incentive plan award with a three-year performance period commencing at the beginning of 2010. The plan under which the equity incentive plan award was granted allows the board of directors (or compensation committee) to exercise its discretion to reduce the amount earned pursuant to the award, consistent with Section 162(m) of the Internal Revenue Code. Under FASB ASC Topic 718, the fact that the board of directors (or compensation committee) had the right to exercise so-called "negative" discretion (to reduce the amount of the award actually earned) may cause, in certain circumstances, the grant date of the award to be deferred until the end of the three-year performance period, after the board of directors (or compensation committee) had determined whether to exercise its discretion to reduce the amount of the award.

In analyzing this situation, the SEC Staff initially noted that the use of grant date fair value reporting for purposes of the executive compensation disclosure rules generally assumes that, as stated in FASB ASC Topic 718, "[t]he service inception date usually is the grant date." The Staff then went on to note that the service inception

---

116. *See* the Current Staff Guidance, *supra* note 28, at Q&A 117.04.

date may precede an award's grant date, however, if the equity incentive plan award is authorized but service begins before a mutual understanding of the key terms and conditions of the award has been reached. Accordingly, in a situation in which the board of directors' (or compensation committee's) right to exercise "negative" discretion may preclude, in certain circumstances, a grant date for the award during the fiscal year in which the board of directors (or compensation committee) communicated the terms of the award and the performance target levels to the executive officer and in which the service inception date begins, the Staff indicated that the award should be reported in column (e) as compensation for the year in which the service inception date began.[117]

Essentially, the SEC Staff determined that, notwithstanding the award's accounting treatment, the reporting of the award in this manner would better reflect the board of directors' (or compensation committee's) decisions with respect to the award. The Staff went on to state that the amount to be reported should be the fair value of the award at the service inception date, based on the then-probable outcome of the performance conditions.[118]

At the present time, it is unclear whether this SEC Staff guidance has implications beyond the scope of the specific situation presented for analysis. The Staff has informally indicated that the application of the principles reflected in its guidance will depend on the specific facts and circumstances of each situation.[119] Further, where, in practice, a registrant faces a situation where the service inception date precedes the grant date of an equity-based award for purposes of FASB ASC Topic 718 and the selection of the grant date as of the time for reporting the award would result in reporting in a fiscal year other than the fiscal year of board of directors' (or compensation committee) action, registrants are encouraged to contact the Staff for assistance.[120]

---

117. *See* the Current Staff Guidance, *supra* note 28, at Q&A 119.24. This reporting treatment would also apply to the Grants of Plan-Based Awards Table. *Id.*

118. *Id.* Similarly, this amount should be included in total compensation for purposes of determining whether the executive officer is a NEO for the year in which the service inception date occurs. *Id.*

119. *See* the 2010 JCEB Questions, *supra* note 55, at Question No. 13.

120. *Id.* So, for example, if the grant of an equity-based award is subject to shareholder approval and, therefore, is not subject to the recognition of compensation expense for purposes of FASB ASC Topic 718 (and, correspondingly, not reported under Section 16(a) of the Exchange Act of 1934) until the date shareholder approval is obtained, a registrant is advised to consult the SEC Staff as to whether the award should be reported as of the date of board of

Nor is it clear whether the SEC Staff guidance is applicable to a cash-based award that is subject to the exercise of "negative discretion" by a board of directors (or compensation committee) for purposes of Section 162(m) of the Internal Revenue Code. The Staff has indicated that the guidance was intended to achieve a reasonable reporting result in a situation where the treatment of the award under FASB ASC Topic 718 would have led to a reporting result that would not have been in the best interests of shareholders.[121] Consequently, in the case of a cash-based award where the number of shares to be received by an executive officer is not determinable until the end of the performance period, once again the reporting of the award will depend on its treatment under the applicable accounting standards. Where the award is considered a "liability" within the scope of FASB ASC Topic 718, then the same principles as those reflected in the guidance apply. Where the award is not within the scope of FASB ASC Topic 718, however, then the concept of a "service inception date" is not relevant to its reporting treatment.[122]

Award Modifications

If a stock award is modified during the covered fiscal year, the incremental fair value resulting from the modification determined as of the modification date in accordance with FASB ASC Topic 718 is to be reported in this column to the extent that this amount is recorded in the registrant's financial statements.[123]

The proper reporting treatment can be problematic where the modification occurs in the fiscal year in which the stock award is granted. In 2010, the SEC Staff was presented with just such a situation. In April 2010, a registrant had granted an equity award to an executive officer with a grant date fair value of $1,000. The terms of the award did not provide for acceleration of vesting if the executive officer terminated his employment with the registrant. In November 2010, the executive officer terminated his employment with the registrant and, at that time, the registrant modified this equity award to provide for acceleration of vesting upon his departure. As modified, the fair value of the award,

---

directors' (or compensation committee) action (assuming that this date is the service inception date) or as of the date of shareholder approval of the award.

121. *Id.*

122. *Id.*

123. *See* Instruction 2 to Item 402(c)(2)(v) and (vi). In the case of smaller reporting companies, *see* Instruction 2 to Item 402(n)(2)(v) and (n)(2)(vi).

computed in accordance with FASB ASC Topic 718, was $800, reflecting a decline in the market price of the registrant's stock.

The SEC Staff took the position that both the incremental fair value of the modified award, computed as of the modification date in accordance with FASB ASC Topic 718,[124] *as well as* the grant date fair value of the original award must be reported in column (e)[125] of the Summary Compensation Table.[126] In the Staff's view, the sum of these two events— the original grant ($1,000) and the subsequent modification ($800) is to be reported since this reflects the two compensatory decisions the registrant made for this award during 2010.[127]

If both the award modification and the executive officer's termination of employment occur in the fiscal year following the fiscal year in which the equity award is granted, the registrant is to report $1,000 (the grant date fair value of the original award) in column (e) of the table for the fiscal year in which the award was granted and $800 (the incremental fair value of the modified award) in column (e) of the table for the fiscal year in which the award is modified.[128]

Impact of Estimated Forfeitures

If the stock award being reported is subject to performance conditions, the effect of estimated forfeitures is to be disregarded.[129] The SEC Staff has indicated that the grant date fair value reported for stock awards

---

124. This aspect of the reporting treatment is mandated by Instruction 2 to Item 402(c)(2)(v) and (vi).

125. If the equity award was a stock option, presumably both the incremental fair value of the modified award and the grant date fair value of the original award would be reported in column (f) of the table.

126. *See* the Current Staff Guidance, *supra* note 28, at Q&A 119.21. Applying the guidance in paragraph 55-116 of FASB ASC Section 718-20-55, the "incremental fair value" of the modified award is computed as follows: the incremental fair value of the modified award is equal to the fair value of the modified award at the date of modification less the fair value of the original award at the date of modification. As the SEC Staff went on to note, in the fact pattern presented, the fair value of the original award at the date of modification is zero, since the executive officer left the registrant in November and the original award would not have vested. Therefore, the incremental fair value of the modified award is the full $800 calculated as of the modification. When added to the grant date fair value of the original award ($1,000), the total amount reported in column (e) is $1,800.

127. This amount is also to be included in the executive officer's total compensation for the fiscal year for purposes of identifying the registrant's NEOs for the fiscal year pursuant to Item 402(a)(3)(iii) and (iv) of Regulation S-K. *Id.*

128. *Id.*

129. *See* Instruction 3 to Item 402(c)(2)(v) and (vi).

subject to time-based vesting should also exclude the effect of estimated forfeitures.[130]

Consequently, a registrant must take care to ensure that it is reporting the correct amount. If the amount recognized for financial statement reporting purposes has been adjusted to taken into account a *pro rata* portion of the registrant's forfeiture estimate for a group of awards, that amount must be added back for disclosure purposes.

Assumptions Used in Valuation

A registrant must disclose in a footnote (attached to column (e)) all assumptions made in the valuation of the stock awards reported in the column.[131] While the rules indicate that this disclosure should be made by reference to a discussion of those assumptions in the registrant's financial statements, footnotes to the financial statements, or discussion in the Management's Discussion and Analysis,[132] the SEC Staff has informally indicated that it is also permissible to set out the assumptions in the footnote itself. The Staff also has indicated that a registrant may provide the assumption information for stock awards granted in the registrant's most recent fiscal year by reference to the Grants of Plan-Based Awards Table if the registrant chooses to report that assumption information in that table.[133]

Depending on the nature of the stock awards being reported, the assumption disclosure may be minimal. Under FASB ASC Topic 718, the grant date fair value of many stock-based awards is based on the market price of the registrant's securities on the date of grant. In this instance, there may not be any assumptions to disclose.

Treatment of Dividends

Under FASB ASC Topic 718, the value of the right to receive dividends is factored into the grant date fair value of most stock awards as reported

---

130. *See* the Current Staff Guidance, *supra* note 28, at Q&A 119.20. The amount to be reported is the grant date fair value. FASB ASC Paragraph 718-10-30-27 provides, in relevant part, that "service conditions that affect vesting are not reflected in estimating the fair value of an award at the grant date because those conditions are restrictions that stem from the forfeitability of instruments to which employees have not yet earned the right." *Id.*

131. See Instruction 1 to Item 402(c)(2)(v) and (vi). In the case of smaller reporting companies, *see* Instruction 1 to Item 402(n)(2)(v) and (n)(2)(vi).

132. *Id.* The sections so referenced are deemed part of the disclosure provided pursuant to Item 402.

133. *See* the Current Staff Guidance, *supra* note 28, at Q&A 119.16.

in the Grants of Plan-Based Awards Table. Consequently, dividends and other earnings paid on stock awards generally are not required to be separately reported in this column.[134] If the value of the right to receive dividends is not factored into a stock award's grant date fair value, then the dollar value of any dividends or other earnings paid on the award is to be reported in the All Other Compensation column of the table.[135]

Option Awards

General

Column (f) of the table is to report the aggregate grant date fair value, computed in accordance with FASB ASC Topic 718, for all stock options[136] granted to each NEO with respect to each covered fiscal year, including options granted pursuant to an equity incentive plan. For purposes of the rules, the column encompasses any award with option-like features that is within the scope of FASB ASC Topic 718 for financial reporting purposes.[137] This includes both service-based and performance-based options.

Options are reportable in this column whether or not they are accompanied by tandem stock appreciation rights (SARs).[138] Options or other rights to purchase securities of the parent or a subsidiary of a registrant should be reported in the same manner as compensatory options to purchase registrant securities.[139] Since, as explained below, the amount reported is based on the grant date fair value computed by

---

134. See the Adopting Release, *supra* note 4, at nn.163 & 164 and the accompanying text. Further, changes in the assumed dividend rights on a stock award will not require a revaluation of the award. See FASB ASC Topic 718 at para. A12 and Kailer, *supra* note 53, at B-4.

135. See Item 402(c)(2)(ix)(G). See also "All Other Compensation—Dividends and Earnings on Equity Awards," *infra*. As proposed, dividends and earnings on stock awards would have been included in the Stock Awards column. See Proposed Item 402(c)(2)(vi). This proposal was not adopted. See the Adopting Release, *supra* note 4, at nn.163 & 164 and the accompanying text.

136. For these purposes, the term "option" means instruments such as stock options, stock appreciation rights, and similar instruments with option-like features. See Item 402(a)(6)(i).

137. As described in the Adopting Release, a stock appreciation right usually gives an executive the right to receive the value of the increase in the value of a specified number of shares over a specified period of time, and may be settled in cash or in shares. See the Adopting Release, *supra* note 4, at n.148. For a definition of the term "stock appreciation right," see Item 402(a)(6)(i).

138. See Item 402(k)(2)(iv).

139. See the Current Staff Guidance, *supra* note 28, at Interpretation 217.13.

the registrant for financial statement reporting purposes, generally stock options will be reported in the fiscal year granted, rather than the fiscal year to which the award relates.[140]

Amount to Be Reported

As originally adopted, a registrant would have been required to report the aggregate grant date fair value of all stock options granted to a NEO with respect to each covered fiscal year in this column. As with stock awards, this requirement was changed in December 2006[141] and again in December 2009.[142] Following these two changes, the reported amount is to be determined in accordance with FASB ASC Topic 718,[143] and represents the aggregate grant date fair value of each stock option granted during the covered fiscal year.

As discussed in the "Stock Awards" section above, the December 2006 change put a premium on understanding the proper accounting treatment of individual stock options to ensure accurate reporting in this column. And, as previously discussed, the difficulty associated with analyzing and explaining these complexities contributed to the SEC's decision to reverse the 2006 change and, in December 2009, change the reporting treatment of stock and option awards back to its original formulation.[144]

The SEC Staff has indicated that if a registrant grants a stock option award to an executive officer in a fiscal year and the same award is forfeited later during the same fiscal year because the executive officer leaves the registrant, the grant date fair value of this award is to be included for purposes of determining the executive officer's total compensation for that fiscal year (as well as for purposes of identifying the NEO group for that fiscal year).[145]

---

140. See "Covered Compensation—Timing of Reporting" in Chapter 2.

141. *See* the December 2006 Release, *supra* note 5.

142. *See* the 2009 Adopting Release, *supra* note 6.

143. Under the former rules, only the number of securities underlying stock options granted during the covered fiscal year had to be reported in the Summary Compensation Table. *See* former Item 402(b)(2)(iv)(B). Under the current rules, this information is now disclosed in the Grants of Plan-Based Awards Table.

144. *See* the 2009 Adopting Release, *supra* note 6, at Section II.A.2.

145. *See* the Current Staff Guidance, *supra* note 28, at Q&A 117.04.

Award Modifications

If an option award is modified during the covered fiscal year, the incremental fair value resulting from the modification determined as of the modification date in accordance with FASB ASC Topic 718 is to be reported in this column to the extent that this amount is recorded in the registrant's financial statements.[146]

For the proper reporting treatment when an option award is granted and modified in the same fiscal year, see Stock Awards above.[147]

Impact of Estimated Forfeitures

If the stock option being reported is subject to performance conditions, the effect of estimated forfeitures is to be disregarded.[148] The SEC Staff has indicated that the grant date fair value reported for stock option awards subject to time-based vesting should also exclude the effect of estimated forfeitures.[149]

Consequently, a registrant must take care to ensure that it is reporting the correct amount. If the amount recognized for financial statement reporting purposes has been adjusted to taken into account a pro rata portion of the registrant's forfeiture estimate for a group of awards, that amount must be added back for disclosure purposes.

Assumptions Used in Valuation

A registrant must disclose in a footnote (attached to column (f)) all assumptions made in the valuation of the stock options reported in the column.[150] While the rules indicate that this disclosure should be made by reference to a discussion of those assumptions in the registrant's

---

146. *See* SFAS 123(R) at para. 51.

147. *See* note 123 *supra* and the accompanying text.

148. *See* Instruction 3 to Item 402(c)(2)(v) and (vi).

149. *See* the Current Staff Guidance, *supra* note 28, at Q&A 119.20. The amount to be reported is the grant date fair value. FASB ASC Paragraph 718-10-30-27 provides, in relevant part, that "service conditions that affect vesting are not reflected in estimating the fair value of an award at the grant date because those conditions are restrictions that stem from the forfeitability of instruments to which employees have not yet earned the right." *Id.*

150. *Id.* While the rules contemplate that the grant date fair value of an equity award for reporting purposes will be generated using the same assumptions that are used for financial statement reporting purposes and, thus, are not intended to change the method that a registrant uses to value employee stock options or to affect the registrant's judgments as to reasonable groupings for purposes of determining the expected term assumption required by FASB ASC Topic 718, the SEC does indicate that, where a registrant uses more than one group for assessing exercise or postvesting employment termination behaviors, the grant date fair

financial statements, footnotes to the financial statements, or discussion in the Management's Discussion and Analysis,[151] the SEC Staff has informally indicated that it is also permissible to set out the assumptions in the footnote itself. The Staff also has indicated that a registrant may provide the assumption information for stock awards granted in the registrant's most recent fiscal year by reference to the Grants of Plan-Based Awards Table if the registrant chooses to report that assumption information in that table.[152]

Depending on the number of stock options being reported, a registrant may find it advisable to set out the assumptions relating to its reported options in this required footnote.

Reload Stock Options

The SEC Staff has taken the position that where a NEO exercises a "reload" stock option and received additional options as a result of the exercise, a registrant must report the additional options as a plan-based award in the Grants of Plan-Based Awards Table. In this column, the registrant would report the grant date fair value of the additional options for financial statement reporting purposes in accordance with FASB ASC Topic 718 in the aggregate amount reported.[153]

Option Repricings

Though the SEC had initially required disclosure of the incremental fair value (as determined in accordance with FASB ASC Topic 718) resulting from the repricing of an option (or an SAR or other similar option-like instrument) during the last completed fiscal year,[154] that disclosure was rescinded as part of the December 2006 changes.[155] It was subsequently restored to the rule in December 2009. Under the rule, if at any time during the last completed fiscal year, the registrant has adjusted or amended the exercise price of options or SARs previously awarded

value for reporting purposes should be derived using the expected term assumption for the group that includes the NEOs. *See* the Adopting Release, *supra* note 4, at n.154.

151. *Id.* The sections so referenced are deemed part of the disclosure provided pursuant to Item 402.

152. *See* the Current Staff Guidance, *supra* note 28, at Q&A 119.16.

153. *See* the Current Staff Guidance, *supra* note 28, at Interpretation 220.01. *See also* the Adopting Release, *supra* note 4, at n.162 and the accompanying text.

154. *See* Instruction 2 to former Item 402(c)(2)(v) and (vi) of Regulation S-K and Instruction 2 to former Item 402(b)(2)(v) and (vi) of Regulation S-B.

155. *See* the December 2006 Release, *supra* note 5, at n.30 and the accompanying text.

to a NEO, whether through amendment, cancellation or replacement grants, or any other means ("repriced"), the registrant is to include, as awards required to be reported in column (f), the incremental fair value, computed as of the repricing date in accordance with FASB ASC Topic 718, with respect to that repriced or modified award.[156]

Options Assumed in Merger Transaction

The SEC Staff has indicated that, where in connection with a merger or other acquisition transaction and as part of the merger consideration, the acquiring entity agrees to assume all of the outstanding stock options of the acquired entity and the options have not been modified other than to adjust their exercise price to reflect the merger exchange ratio, the acquiring entity needs to report the assumed options in column (f) of its Summary Compensation Table in the case of executives of the acquired entity who become NEOs of the acquiring entity.[157] This position is based on the fact that the awards do not reflect compensation decisions that were made by the compensation committee of the acquiring entity.[158]

Treatment of Dividends

Under FASB ASC Topic 718, the value of the right to receive dividends is factored into the grant date fair value of most stock options as reported in the Grants of Plan-Based Awards Table. Consequently, dividends and other earnings paid on stock options generally are not required to be separately reported in this column.[159] If the value of the right to receive dividends is not factored into a stock option's grant date fair value, then

---

156. Instruction 2 to Item 402(c)(2)(v) and (vi). In the case of smaller reporting companies, *see* Instruction 2 to Item 402(n)(2)(v) and (n)(2)(vi).

157. *See* the Current Staff Guidance, *supra* note 28, at Q&A 119.27. Nor should the value of the stock options be included in "total compensation" for purposes of determining whether an executive of the acquired entity is a NEO of the acquiring entity. *Id.*

158. *Id.* Since the assumed stock options are now options of the acquiring entity, however, they should be included in the acquiring entity's Outstanding Equity Awards at Fiscal Year-End Table and Options Exercised and Stock Vested Table, as applicable, for the fiscal year in which they were assumed and subsequent fiscal years, with footnote disclosure describing their assumption.

159. *See* the Adopting Release, *supra* note 4, at nn.163 & 164 and the accompanying text. Further, changes in the assumed dividend rights on a stock option will not require a revaluation of the award. *See* SFAS 123(R) at para. A12 and Kailer, *supra* note 53, at B-4.

the dollar value of any dividends or other earnings paid on the option is to be reported in the All Other Compensation column of the table.[160]

Nonequity Incentive Plan Compensation

General

Column (g) of the table is to report the dollar value of all amounts earned by a NEO during the fiscal year pursuant to nonequity incentive plan[161] awards for services performed. The amount to be reported is the amount earned during the last completed fiscal year regardless of when the related services were performed.[162] Thus, unlike the Stock Awards and Option Awards columns, a registrant does not report the grant of nonequity incentive plan awards in this table.[163]

This column complements the Stock Awards and Option Awards columns by requiring disclosure of all of a registrant's incentive plan awards that are not equity-based.[164] Finally, the dollar value of all

---

160. *See* Item 402(c)(2)(ix)(G). *See also* "All Other Compensation—Dividends and Earnings on Equity Awards," *infra*. As proposed, dividends and earnings on stock options would have been included in the Option Awards column. *See* Proposed Item 402(c)(2)(vi). This proposal was not adopted. *See* the Adopting Release, *supra* note 4, at nn.163 & 164 and the accompanying text.

161. A "nonequity incentive plan" is a plan providing compensation intended to serve as incentive for performance to occur over a specified period, whether such performance is measured by reference to financial performance of the registrant or an affiliate, the registrant's stock price, or any other performance measure (an "incentive plan"), or portion of an incentive plan, under which awards are granted that fall outside the scope of FASB ASC Topic 718. *See* Item 402(a)(6)(iii). In other words, they are performance-based cash incentive plans.

162. While, at the proposing stage, the SEC was urged to take a grant date fair value approach for reporting nonequity incentive plan awards in the Summary Compensation Table, because of the absence of a clearly required or accepted standard for measuring the grant date value of these awards that took into consideration the applicable performance contingencies, the SEC chose to require amounts to be reported when earned. *See* the Adopting Release, *supra* note 4, at n.173 and the accompanying text. This approach is also consistent with the treatment of long-term incentive plan awards under the former rules. *See* former Items 402(b)(2)(iv)(C) and 402(e).

163. *See* the Adopting Release, *supra* note 4, at nn.135, 170, 171, 172 and 173 and the accompanying text. Instead, the grant of a nonequity incentive plan compensation award is reported in the Grants of Plan-Based Awards Table.

164. As noted in the Adopting Release, the awards to be reported in the column are awards that do not involve share-based payment arrangements and, consequently, are not covered by FASB ASC Topic 718 for financial statement reporting purposes. *See* the Adopting Release, *supra* note 4, at n.170.

earnings on any outstanding nonequity incentive plan awards is also to be reported in this column.[165]

Compensation Reported When Earned

Compensation awarded under a nonequity incentive plan is to be disclosed in this column in the covered fiscal year when the relevant performance measure under the plan is satisfied and the compensation earned, whether or not payment is actually made to the NEO in that year.[166] In the case of a plan with separate performance criteria for periods within the framework of a multiyear performance measure, each award installment is to be reported as earned when the applicable performance criteria have been satisfied.

Once this disclosure has been made, no further reporting is specifically required when payment is actually made to the NEO.[167] Consequently, in the case of an earned award that is subject to further contingencies (such as, for example, a service-based vesting condition or a requirement providing for forfeiture based on the future performance of the registrant), this amount will be considered part of the NEO's total compensation for the covered fiscal year even if, ultimately, he or she does not receive this previously reported amount.

While the SEC encourages registrants to use the related narrative discussion accompanying the Summary Compensation Table to disclose subsequent forfeitures of amounts that were reported in this column (and in the Summary Compensation Table generally) with respect to previous fiscal years,[168] the rules do not require such disclosure. If compensation is deferred in the form of and reported in the year earned in the Grants of Plan-Based Awards Table as nonequity incentive plan compensation, then the payout of the compensation is to be reported in this column.[169]

---

165. This includes all earnings, not just the above-market or preferential amounts. These earnings are to be identified and quantified in a footnote to this column. *See* Instruction 2 to Item 402(c)(2)(vii). This reporting is required whether these earnings were paid during the covered fiscal year, payable during the period but deferred at the election of the NEO, or payable by the terms of the award at a later date. *Id.*

166. *See* Instruction 1 to Item 402(c)(2)(vii). *See also* the Adopting Release, *supra* note 4, at n.174 and the accompanying text.

167. *Id.* This assumes that the award has been properly reported in the Grants of Plan-Based Awards Table.

168. *See* the Adopting Release, *supra* note 4, at n.175 and the accompanying text.

169. *See* Kailer, *supra* note 53, at B-6.

Nonequity Incentive Plans

The defining characteristic of a nonequity incentive plan is whether the compensation is intended to serve as an incentive for performance, rather than the length of the period over which this performance is to occur (as was the focus under the former rules). As a result, amounts earned under both annual and long-term incentive plans are to be reported in this column.[170] To the extent that a NEO earns amounts under more than one nonequity incentive plan during a covered fiscal year, a registrant may find it advisable to include a footnote to the column itemizing the amount that was earned under each plan.

This disregard for the term of an award granted under an incentive plan has other unusual effects. Under the rules, the grant of a nonequity incentive plan award is to be disclosed in the Grants of Plan-Based Awards Table in the year of grant.[171] In the case of a long-term incentive award, this may be one or more years prior to the year in which compensation earned under the award is reported in the Summary Compensation Table, setting up a situation where an award is reported in a supplemental compensation table before it is reported in the Summary Compensation Table itself.

Further, in the case of an annual incentive award, typically the outcome of an award will be known at the time the registrant is preparing its executive compensation disclosure. Nonetheless, the SEC Staff has indicated that a registrant must include grant-related information in the Grants of Plan-Based Awards Table.

Relationship to Bonuses

The characterization of an amount as nonequity incentive plan compensation rather than a bonus depends both on whether the amount is awarded or payable under a performance-based cash plan[172] and on the nature of the relevant performance target. To be considered nonequity incentive plan compensation, an award must be "intended to serve as an incentive for performance to occur over a specified period." An award will be considered to satisfy this condition if the outcome with respect to the relevant performance target is substantially uncertain at the time

---

170. *See* the Current Staff Guidance, *supra* note 28, at Q&A 119.02.

171. See Chapter 6.

172. If the amount is awarded or paid under a service-based cash plan, it is reportable in the Summary Compensation Table as a bonus.

the performance target is established and the target is communicated to the executive.[173]

In addition, a plan that otherwise satisfies the definition of a nonequity incentive plan, but that permits the exercise of so-called "negative discretion" in determining the amount that will be paid to executives, is still to be reported in this column.[174] If, in the exercise of discretion, an amount is paid over and above the amounts earned by meeting the relevant performance measure, that excess amount should be reported in the Bonus column of the Summary Compensation Table.[175]

Although not expressly addressed in the rules, presumably amounts that would otherwise be reported as nonequity incentive plan compensation (rather than a bonus) for the last completed fiscal year that cannot be calculated as of the most recent practicable date are covered by the instruction for reporting indeterminate bonus amounts.[176] Under this instruction, a registrant must include a footnote to the column indicating that the amount is not calculable through the latest practicable date and giving the date that the amount of the NEO's nonequity incentive plan award is expected to be determined.[177]

When the amount is calculated, either in whole or in part (either through an actual payment or a decision or other occurrence that fixes the amount), the registrant must file a current report on Form 8-K disclosing the amount and providing a new recomputed total compensation figure for the NEO that includes the nonequity incentive plan compensation.[178]

---

173. *See* the Adopting Release, *supra* note 4, at Section II.C.1.f. On the other hand, if the performance target for a cash incentive award is not preestablished and communicated, or if the outcome is not substantially uncertain at the beginning of the performance period, the award is reportable in the Summary Compensation Table as a bonus. *See also* the Current Staff Guidance, *supra* note 28, at Q&A 119.02.

174. *Id.* As noted by the SEC Staff, the use of various performance targets and negative discretion to determine the amounts earned by and payable to a NEO may be material information that should be discussed in the CD&A. *Id.*

175. *Id.*

176. *See* Instruction 1 to Item 402(c)(2)(iii) and (iv).

177. *Id.*

178. *Id.*

Forgone Nonequity Incentive Plan Compensation

Although not expressly addressed in the rules, the SEC Staff has indicated that a registrant is to include in this column any amount of nonequity incentive plan compensation that is forgone at the election of a NEO under which stock instead has been received by the executive, to reflect the compensation that the registrant awarded.[179] In addition, the future settlement of the award in stock instead of nonequity incentive plan compensation must be disclosed in a footnote added to the column.[180]

Similarly, where applicable, this footnote also should refer to the Grants of Plan-Based Awards Table where the registrant should report the award in the Estimated Future Payouts under Non-Equity Incentive Plan Awards columns (columns (c)-(e)) of the table.[181] (Although not expressly addressed by the SEC Staff, presumably the same reporting treatment would result where the NEO elects to receive any form of equity-based compensation or another form of noncash compensation in lieu of a nonequity incentive plan award.) The shares of stock received upon settlement of the award should not subsequently be reported in the Grants of Plan-Based Awards Table since to do so would "double count" the award.[182]

As the SEC Staff has noted informally, the reporting of an award, such as a nonequity incentive plan award, should be consistent with its character.[183] Thus, the character of a cash award doesn't change simply because a NEO has elected to receive payment of the award in the form of stock or equity-based compensation. In this situation, a registrant should report what the Compensation Committee awarded, including, in the case of a nonequity incentive plan award, the intended threshold, target, and maximum payout levels. In the Staff's view, it would be

---

179. See the Current Staff Guidance, *supra* note 28, at Q&A 119.22. This guidance was provided in response to a situation where a registrant had granted an annual incentive plan award to one of its NEOs. Since no right to stock settlement was embedded in the terms of the award, the award was not within the scope of FASB ASC Topic 718. Therefore, the registrant had concluded that it was a nonequity incentive plan award as defined in Item 402(a)(6)(iii). The NEO elected to receive the award in shares of the registrant's stock. Technically, Instruction 2 to Item 402(c)(2)(iii) and (iv) does not apply because the award was an "incentive plan award" rather than a "bonus."

180. *Id.* This footnote disclosure should also state that the decision to settle the nonequity incentive plan compensation in shares of stock was made at the election of the NEO.

181. *Id.*

182. *Id.*

183. See 2010 JCEB Questions, *supra* note 55, at Question No. 5.

insufficient to provide information about the compensation committee's decision if a registrant simply reports the amount of the actual award payout without reporting the related information in the Grants of Plan-Based Awards Table.[184]

Note that this reporting treatment differs in one significant respect from the reporting treatment when a NEO elects to forego the receipt of a bonus in exchange for stock, equity-based, or another form of noncash compensation.[185] As described in the preceding paragraph, in the case of a forgone nonequity incentive plan award, the registrant must also report the award in the Estimated Future Payouts under Non-Equity Incentive Plan Awards columns (columns (c)-(e)) of the Grants of Plan-Based Awards Table.[186] In the case of a forgone bonus, however, there is no corresponding requirement to report the forgone bonus in the Grants of Plan-Based Awards Table, as there is no column in that table in which to provide supplemental information about a bonus payment. Instead, the stock, option, or nonequity incentive plan award elected by the NEO in lieu of a forgone bonus is to be reported as such in the Grants of Plan-Based Awards Table.[187]

Election to Receive Annual Incentive Award in Stock

If a registrant grants an annual incentive award to its executive officers, giving them at the time of the award the ability to elect whether to receive payment of the award in either cash or shares of stock, the SEC Staff has indicated that the reporting of the award will depend on the executive officer's choice of the form of payment. Specifically, the Staff was asked to provide guidance in the following situation: During 2010, a registrant grants annual incentive plan awards to its NEOs. The awards permit each NEO to elect payment of the award for 2010 performance in shares of the registrant's stock rather than cash, with the election to be made during the first 90 days of 2010. If payment in stock is elected, the shares will have a grant date fair value equal to 110 percent of the value of the award that would be paid in cash.

---

184. *Id.*

185. *See* Instruction 2 to Item 402(c)(2) (iii) and (iv). In the SEC Staff's view, there is no reason that the disclosure with respect to nonequity incentive plan awards must be symmetrical with the disclosure of bonuses. *See* the 2010 JCEB Questions, *supra* note 55, at Question No. 5.

186. Since the situation presented to the SEC Staff involved, upon its facts, an award that was defined as a nonequity incentive plan award, the award would continue to be reported as a nonequity incentive plan award in the Grants of Plan-Based Awards Table.

187. *Id.*

In the case of a NEO who elects to receive payment of the award in shares of stock, the SEC Staff indicated that the award is to be reported in the Summary Compensation Table and the Grants of Plan-Based Awards Table as an equity incentive award.[188] In the case of a NEO who elects to receive payment of the award in cash, the Staff indicated that the award is to be reported in these tables as a nonequity incentive plan award.[189]

It is important to note that the SEC Staff differentiates this situation from one in which the award, by its terms, allows an executive officer to select whether to receive an earned award in the form of cash or shares of stock at the end of the performance period (in this case, an annual performance period). In this latter case, the Staff takes the position that since the right to receive payment in either cash or shares of stock is an integral feature of the award itself (in other words, is "embedded" in the award), it brings the award within the scope of FASB ASC Topic 718, resulting in its treatment as an equity incentive award without regard to the form of payment that the executive officer ultimately chooses.[190]

In the former situation, the compensation committee has essentially given the executive officer a choice between two awards—a cash award or a stock award. Thus, the SEC Staff's analysis focused on the actions of the compensation committee in offering the executive officer a clear choice between the receipt of cash or equity at the time the award is granted. The Staff analyzed the fact pattern on the basis of the form of award selected by the executive officer (as opposed to an award where the choice to receive cash or equity was embedded in the award itself).

Decision to Forgo Receipt of Annual Incentive Award

The SEC Staff has been asked to provide the proper reporting treatment in a situation where a registrant has granted annual nonequity incentive plan awards to its executive officers and, subsequently, one of the recipients decides not to receive any payment of the amounts earned pursuant to the award. The facts of the situation were as follows: A registrant granted annual nonequity incentive plan awards to its executive officers

---

188. *See* the Current Staff Guidance, *supra* note 28, at Q&A 119.23. The SEC Staff indicated that the award should be treated as an equity incentive award even if the amount of the award is not determined until early in the year following the year of grant since all registrant decisions necessary to determine the value of the award are made in the year of grant. *Id.*

189. *Id.*

190. *See* the 2010 JCEB Questions, *supra* note 55, at Question No. 12.

in January 2010. The awards' performance criteria were communicated to the executive officers at that time and were based on the registrant's financial performance for the year. The executive officers did not know the total amount earned pursuant to the awards until the end of the year, when the compensation committee would determine whether, and to what extent, the performance criteria had been satisfied. In other words, after the end of the year, the amounts earned pursuant to the awards would be determined and communicated to the executive officers.

As noted, one of the executive officers decided not to receive any payment of earnings pursuant to the award. The SEC Staff indicated that the executive officer's decision not to accept payment of the award does not change the fact that the award was granted in, and earned for, services performed during 2010. Accordingly, the earnings pursuant to the award, even though declined, should be included in total compensation for purposes of determining if the executive officer is a NEO for 2010 and reported in the Summary Compensation Table.[191]

The registrant would disclose the executive officer's decision not to accept payment of the award, which it can do either by adding a column next to column (g) reporting the amount of nonequity incentive plan compensation declined, or by providing an appropriate footnote to the column.[192] Finally, the registrant should discuss the effect, if any, of the executive officer's decision on how it structures and implements compensation to reflect performance in its CD&A.[193]

Modification or Waiver

If a registrant materially modifies or waives any term or condition under a nonequity incentive plan award during the covered fiscal year (for example, an extension of the exercise period, a change in the vesting or forfeiture schedule, a change of the performance criteria, or a waiver of the performance targets or conditions to payment), then it must disclose the modification or waiver in the narrative to accompany the Summary Compensation Table.[194]

---

191.   *See* the Current Staff Guidance, *supra* note 28, at Q&A 119.25. In addition, the grant of the award should also be included in the Grants of Plan-Based Awards Table, which will reflect the compensation committee's decision to grant the award in 2010. *Id.*

192.   *Id.*

193.   *Id.*

194.   *See* Item 402(e). See also Chapter 7.

Pension Value Changes and Above-Market and Preferential Earnings

General

Column (h) of the table is to report the sum of two distinct compensation items: the aggregate change in the actuarial present value of each NEO's accumulated benefit under the registrant's defined benefit and actuarial pension plans in which he or she is a participant, and any above-market or preferential earnings on nonqualified deferred compensation, including earnings on nonqualified defined contribution plans. Given the increased prominence of retirement benefits in executive compensation packages, the SEC decided to include the annual increase in the actuarial value of these accumulated benefits as part of each NEO's total compensation.[195] Similarly, to the extent that a registrant contributes to the growth of its NEOs' nonqualified deferred compensation accounts (through the payment of above-market or preferential earnings), those amounts are to be included in total compensation as well.

If a registrant has both types of compensation to report for a covered fiscal year, each separate amount must be identified and quantified in a footnote to this column.[196] If the amount of the pension value change for a covered fiscal year is a negative number, it should be disclosed in a footnote to this column, but should not be reflected in the sum reported in the column itself.[197]

As proposed, all earnings on nonqualified deferred compensation, not just above-market or preferential amounts, would have been included in the All Other Compensation column of the table, as would have been the pension plan information.[198] In response to concerns that this information should not be considered when determining a registrant's most highly compensated executive officers, however, the SEC decided to present the information in a separate column.[199] Thus, while this compensation is not used when determining the NEO

---

195. As the SEC noted, this disclosure also provides investors with a better understanding of a registrant's compensation obligations to its NEOs. *See* the Adopting Release, *supra* note 4, at Section II. C.1.d.ii.

196. *See* Instruction 3 to Item 402(c)(2)(viii).

197. *Id.*

198. *See* Proposed Items 402(c)(ix)(B) and (G).

199. See the discussion in "Persons Covered—Named Executive Officers—Most Highly Compensated Executive Officers" in Chapter 2.

group, it is reported in the Summary Compensation Table and included in each NEO's total compensation figure.

Pension Plan Value Changes

A registrant must report the aggregate change in the actuarial present value of each NEO's accumulated benefits under its defined benefit and actuarial plans.[200] The required disclosure applies to each plan that provides for the payment of retirement benefits, or benefits that will be paid primarily following retirement, including, but not limited to, tax-qualified defined benefit plans and supplemental executive retirement plans (SERPs).[201] It does not apply to tax-qualified defined contribution plans and nonqualified defined contribution plans.[202] It does apply to cash balance plans in which a NEO's benefit may be determined by the amount represented in an account rather than based on a formula that is tied to the executive's base salary while still employed.

The change in value for a defined benefit or actuarial plan will reflect any increase in value due to an additional year of service, compensation increases, and changes to the underlying defined benefit plan itself (if any), as well as any increase (or decrease) in value attributable to interest.[203] In situations where the changes attributable to adjustments to the applicable interest rate exceed the increase resulting from additional service and other factors, the change in value for the covered fiscal year may be a negative number (for example, where a NEO has reached his or her maximum benefit accrual and there has been an increase in the discount rates during the fiscal year).

In contrast to the disclosure of equity awards, a negative number is not to be reported in the sum disclosed in the column itself.[204] Instead,

---

200. As proposed, registrants would have been required to disclose the aggregate annual increase in the actuarial value of all defined benefit and actuarial pension plans in the All Other Compensation column of the table. *See* Proposed Item 402(c)(2)(ix)(G). As described in the Adopting Release, *supra* note 4, that proposal was modified to create the current disclosure requirement.

201. *See* Instruction 1 to Item 402(c)(2)(viii). A typical defined benefit plan is a retirement plan in which the registrant pays the executive specified amounts at retirement which are not tied to the investment performance of the contributions that fund the plan. *See* the Adopting Release, *supra* note 4, at n.188.

202. *See* Instruction 1 to Item 402(c)(2)(viii). A typical defined contribution plan is a retirement plan in which the registrant and/or the executive makes contributions of a specified amount, and the amount that is paid out to the executive depends on the return on investments from the contributed amounts. *See* the Adopting Release, *supra* note 4, at n.188.

203. *See* the Adopting Release, *supra* note 4, at Section II.C.1.b.ii.

204. *See* Instruction 3 to Item 402(c)(2)(viii).

it is simply reported in a footnote to the column. Where a registrant aggregates all of the decreases and increases in the value of a NEO's individual pension plans, the registrant may offset negative values against positive values, and apply the "no negative number" position of the rules for the final number after aggregating the values of all plans.[205]

The amount to be reported in the column will be the difference between the amount that is required to be reported for a NEO for the covered fiscal year in the Pension Benefits Table[206] and the amount that was required to be reported for the NEO in that table for the prior completed fiscal year.[207] Accordingly, this actuarial present value of the accumulated benefits is to be calculated from the pension plan measurement date used for financial statement reporting purposes with respect to the registrant's audited financial statements for the completed fiscal year prior to the pension plan measurement date used for financial statement reporting purposes with respect to the registrant's audited financial statements for the covered fiscal year.[208] In computing the amount to be disclosed, the company must use the same assumptions it uses for financial statement reporting purposes under generally accepted accounting principles.[209]

For purposes of column (h), the aggregate change in the actuarial present value of each NEO's accumulated benefits are to be computed as of the same pension plan measurement date used for financial statement reporting purposes with respect to a registrant's audited financial statements for the last completed fiscal year. This reference to the same pension plan measurement date as is used for financial statement reporting purposes is intended to simplify compliance by making clear that the registrant would not have to use different assumptions when computing the present value for disclosure purposes and financial reporting purposes.

---

205. *See* the Current Staff Guidance, *supra* note 28, at Q&A 119.06. Under this approach, if one plan had a $500 increase and another plan had a $200 decrease, the net change in the actuarial present value of the accumulated pension benefits would be $300.

206. This is the amount required to be disclosed pursuant to Item 402(h)(2)(iv).

207. *See* Instruction 1 to Item 402(c)(2)(viii).

208. Item 402(c)(2)(viii)(A).

209. *See* Instruction 1 Item 402(c)(2)(viii) and Instruction 2 to Item 402(h)(2). As discussed in Chapter 10, a registrant must use the same assumptions as it applies pursuant to FASB ASC Topic 715, *Compensation – Retirement Plans* both for this column and the Pension Benefits Table. *See* the Adopting Release, *supra* note 4, at n.194.

At the time the rules were adopted in 2006, the pension plan measurement date for most pension plans was September 30, which, in the case of registrants with a calendar-year fiscal year, did not correspond with the registrant's fiscal year. This meant that, for these registrants, the pension benefit information was presented for a period that differed from the fiscal-year period covered by their executive compensation disclosure. Subsequently, as a result of changes in pension accounting standards, the pension measurement date was changed to be the same as the end of the registrant's fiscal year.

The SEC Staff has indicated that, in the year in which a registrant changes its pension measurement date, the registrant may use an annualized approach for the disclosure of the change in the value of the accumulated pension benefits in the Summary Compensation Table (thereby adjusting the 15-month period to a 12-month period) when the transition in pension plan measurement date occurs, so long as the registrant includes a disclosure explaining it has followed this approach.[210]

The SEC Staff has taken the position that where a change in the actuarial present value of a NEO's accumulated pension benefit is offset by a distribution during the fiscal year, the change should be reported in the column without regard to the distribution.[211] For example, where the actuarial present value of a NEO's accumulated pension benefit on the pension measurement date of the prior fiscal year was $1 million, and the present value of the accumulated pension benefit on the pension measurement date of the most recently completed fiscal year is also $1 million, but during the most recently completed fiscal year the NEO earned and received an in-service distribution of $200,000, then $200,000 should be reported as the change in pension value in this column.[212]

Above-Market and Preferential Earnings

A registrant must report all above-market and preferential earnings on nonqualified deferred compensation and from nonqualified defined contribution plans paid to or accrued by a NEO during the

---

210. *See* the Current Staff Guidance, *supra* note 28, at Interpretation 219.03. The actuarial present value computed on the new measurement date should be reported in the Pension Benefits Table. *Id.*

211. *See* the Current Staff Guidance, *supra* note 28, at Interpretation 219.04.

212. *Id.*

covered fiscal year.[213] This includes investment earnings paid at "above-market" or "preferential" rates on both elective deferrals and registrant contributions. As under the former rules, interest on nonqualified deferred compensation is above-market only if the rate of interest exceeds 120 percent of the applicable federal long-term rate, with compounding[214] at the rate that corresponds most closely to the rate under the registrant's plan at the time the interest rate or formula is set.[215] Only the above-market portion of the interest must be reported in the column.[216]

Disclosure is required even if the nonqualified deferred compensation arrangement is unfunded and, thus, subject to the risk of loss of the principal.[217] If the applicable interest rates vary depending on conditions such as a minimum period of continued service, the reported amount should be calculated assuming satisfaction of all conditions to receiving interest at the highest rate.[218] A registrant may, but is not required to, provide footnote or narrative explaining its criteria for determining any portion of the earnings considered to be above-market.[219]

Similarly, as under the former rules, dividends (and dividend equivalents) on deferred compensation denominated in shares of the registrant's stock are "preferential" only if earned at a rate higher than dividends on the registrant's common stock.[220] Again, only the

---

213. As proposed, registrants would have been required to disclose *all* earnings on nonqualified deferred compensation and from nonqualified defined contribution plans in the All Other Compensation column of the table. *See* Proposed Item 402(c)(2)(ix)(B). That proposal was not adopted. Thus, the required disclosure conforms to the requirements of the former rules. *See* former Item 402(b)(2)(C)(2) and Instruction 3 to former Item 402(b)(2)(iii) (C). Earnings under tax-qualified Section 401(k) plans are not disclosed in this table as the disclosure requirement extends only to above-market or preferential earnings on nonqualified deferred compensation. *See* the Current Staff Guidance, *supra* note 28, at Q&A 119.10.

214. As prescribed under Section 1274(d) of the Internal Revenue Code (26 U.S.C. § 1274(d)).

215. *See* Instruction 2 to Item 402(c)(2)(viii). In the event of a discretionary reset of the interest rate, the requisite calculation must be made on the basis of the interest rate at the time of such reset, rather than when originally established. *Id.*

216. *Id.*

217. *See* the Current Staff Guidance, *supra* note 28, at Interpretation 229.01.

218. *Id.*

219. *Id.*

220. *Id.*

preferential portion of the dividends or equivalents need be reported in the column.[221]

Notwithstanding that only above-market and preferential earnings on nonqualified deferred compensation are to be reported in the Summary Compensation Table, all earnings (including the above-market and preferential portions reported in this column) are to be disclosed in the Nonqualified Deferred Compensation Table.[222]

The primary challenge in complying with this disclosure requirement is identifying when earnings are to be considered above-market or preferential. While this analysis is fairly straightforward when dealing with investments that pay interest or dividends only, it becomes increasingly more complex when other types of investments are involved. Historically, the SEC Staff has taken the position that a registrant need not report earnings on nonqualified deferred compensation as above-market or preferential earnings where the return on such earnings is calculated in the same manner and at the same rate as earnings on externally managed investments to employees participating in a tax-qualified plan providing for broad-based employee participation.[223] As the Staff notes, many issuers provide for deferral of salary or bonus amounts not covered by tax-qualified plans where the return is the same as the return paid on amounts invested in an externally managed investment fund, such as an equity mutual fund, available to all employees participating in a nondiscriminatory, tax-qualified plan (for example, a Section 401(k) plan).

The SEC Staff goes on, however, to indicate that, although this position generally will be available for so-called "excess benefit plans" (as defined for Exchange Act Rule 16b-3(b)(2)[224] purposes), it may not

---

221. *Id.*

222. See Chapter 11. Further, where plan earnings are calculated by reference to the actual earnings of mutual funds or other securities, such as registrant stock, the SEC has indicated that it is sufficient to identify the reference security and quantify its return in the narrative accompanying the Nonqualified Deferred Compensation Table. *See* the Adopting Release, *supra* note 4, at n.311 and the accompanying text. This disclosure may be aggregated to the extent that the same measure applies to more than one NEO. *Id.*

223. *See* the Current Staff Guidance, *supra* note 28, at Interpretation 219.01, citing the 1992 Release, *supra* note 2, at n.43, and the SEC Staff's letter to the American Society of Corporate Secretaries (Jan. 6, 1993). *See also* the 2007 JCEB Questions, *supra* note 66, at the Topic for Discussion.

224. 17 C.F.R. 240.16b-3(b)(2).

be appropriately applied in the case of a pure "top-hat" plan or SERP that bears no relationship to a tax-qualified plan of the issuer.[225]

Some registrants have a benign attitude about reporting these types of investments, rationalizing their position on the bases that the amounts reported in this column are not included in total compensation for purposes of identifying their most highly compensated executive officers and all earnings must be disclosed in the Nonqualified Deferred Compensation Table. Nonetheless, some investors have expressed a desire for greater transparency in this area to highlight arrangements where fixed or above-markets returns are being provided.

All Other Compensation

General

Column (i) of the table is to report each compensation item that is not otherwise properly reportable in columns (c) through (h) as previously described.[226] This requirement applies to all compensatory items, regardless of their amount.[227] In other words, there is generally no *de minimis* threshold below which disclosure is not required. All items of compensation are required to be included in the Summary Compensation Table without regard to whether such items are required to be identified other than as specifically required by the rules.[228] Any compensation item reported in this column for a NEO that is not a perquisite or personal benefit and whose value exceeds $10,000 must be

---

225. If in doubt about the proper characterization of nonqualified deferred compensation earnings, registrants are encouraged to contact the SEC Staff for guidance.

226. To simplify the Summary Compensation Table and consistent with the SEC's decision to eliminate distinctions based on annual and long-term compensation, this column combines the separate "Other Annual Compensation" column (*see* former Item 402(b)(2)(iii)(c)) and the "All Other Compensation" column (*see* former Item 402(b)(2)(v)) under the former rules.

227. *See* Item 402(c)(2)(ix). Note the separate standard for disclosure and identification of perquisites and other personal benefits. See "All Other Compensation—Perquisites," *infra*. Further, the disclosure of nonqualified deferred compensation earnings is limited to the above-market or preferential portion of such earnings. Finally, a registrant is not required to disclose information regarding group life, health, hospitalization, and medical reimbursement plans that do not discriminate in scope, terms, or operation in favor of executive officers or directors of the registrant and that are available generally to all salaried employees. *See* Item 402(a)(6)(ii). *See also* the Adopting Release, *supra* note 4, at n.198.

228. *See* Instruction 3 to Item 402(c)(2)(ix).

identified and quantified in a footnote to this column.[229] In other words, compensation items with a value less than $10,000 are to be included in the total reported in this column, but need not be identified by type and amount. Several registrants use a supplemental table to present and itemize the compensation reported in this column.[230]

Required Disclosure Items

The rules provide a nonexclusive list of the type of compensation items that must be disclosed in this column for each NEO:

- perquisites and other personal benefits, or property, unless the aggregate amount of such items is less than $10,000;[231]
- "gross-ups" or other amounts reimbursed during the covered fiscal year for the payment of taxes;[232]
- registrant securities (or the securities of its subsidiaries) purchased at a discount from their market price;[233]
- amounts paid or accrued pursuant to a plan or arrangement in connection with his or her resignation, retirement, or any other termination of service, or a change in control of the registrant;[234]
- registrant contributions or other allocations to vested and unvested defined contribution plans;[235]
- the dollar value of any insurance premiums paid by, or on behalf of, the registrant during the covered fiscal year with respect to life insurance for his or her benefit;[236] and

---

229. *Id.* The requirement is somewhat different for smaller reporting companies. Item 402(o)(7) requires a smaller reporting company to identify to the extent material any item included in the All Other Compensation column of the Summary Compensation Table. Identification of an item will not be considered material, however, if the item does not exceed the greater of $25,000 or 10 percent of all items included in the specified category. Nonetheless, all compensation items are required to be included in the table without regard to whether these items are required to be identified. *Id.*

230. *See, e.g.*, the Midland Company Definitive Proxy Statement (Form 14A) filed Mar. 23, 2007 (file no. 001-06026).

231. Item 402(c)(2)(ix)(A).

232. Item 402(c)(2)(ix)(B).

233. Item 402(c)(2)(ix)(C).

234. Item 402(c)(2)(ix)(D).

235. Item 402(c)(2)(ix)(E).

236. Item 402(c)(2)(ix)(F).

- the dollar value of any dividends or other earnings paid on stock or option awards, when those amounts were not factored into the grant date fair value required to be reported for the stock or option award.[237]

Perquisites

Perquisites and other personal benefits a NEO receives are to be reported in this column if the total value of all perquisites and personal benefits for the executive during the covered fiscal year is $10,000 or more.[238] Where this disclosure threshold is met, then each perquisite or personal benefit, regardless of its amount, must be specifically identified by type.[239] In identifying perquisites, each item must be described in a manner that identifies the particular nature of the benefit received.[240]

The SEC Staff has indicated that in the case of any item for which the NEO has actually fully reimbursed the registrant, such item does not need to be considered a perquisite or other personal benefit and, therefore, does not need to be separately identified by type.[241] Reliance on the Staff's position depends on compliance with two conditions. First, there must be "actual" reimbursement. While the Staff has not interpreted the meaning of this term, it is possible that it is intended to require an actual economic payment from the NEO to the registrant. Under this view, a credit or offset, or a notional entry representing the NEO's payment of the cost, may not be sufficient.

Second, there must be "full" reimbursement. An earlier version of the SEC Staff's guidance stated that the reimbursement must be of the item's "total cost," suggesting that this amount differed from its "incremental

---

237. Item 402(c)(2)(ix)(G).

238. For more information about perquisites, see Chapter 5. Under the former rules, the disclosure threshold for perquisites was the lesser of $50,000 or 10 percent of the NEO's annual salary and bonus as reported in the Summary Compensation Table. *See* former Item 402(b)(2)(iii)(C)(1). This change increased the instances in which perquisites must be disclosed.

239. *See* Instruction 4 to Item 402(c)(2)(ix). If the $10,000 disclosure threshold is otherwise exceeded, a perquisite or other personal benefit must be separately identified by type even if the provision of the perquisite or personal benefits involved no aggregate incremental cost to the registrant. *See* the Current Staff Guidance, *supra* note 28, at Q&A 119.03.

240. For example, it is insufficient to characterize generally as "travel and entertainment" different registrant-financed benefits, such as clothing, jewelry, artwork, theater tickets, and housekeeping services. *See* the Adopting Release, *supra* note 4, at n.204 and the accompanying text.

241. *See* the Current Staff Guidance, *supra* note 28, at Q&A 119.07.

cost."[242] While it is unclear whether the subsequent deletion of this reference was intended to signal that the Staff is willing to accede to the position that reimbursement of an item's incremental cost is sufficient to change its characterization as a perquisite, it's certainly a reasonable conclusion.

Beyond this revision to the guidance, the SEC Staff has declined to provide a specific definition of how "full reimbursement" is to be determined. The Staff has indicated, however, by way of example, that if a registrant pays for country club annual dues as well as for meals and incidentals and an executive officer reimburses the cost of the meals and incidentals, then the registrant need not report the meals and incidentals as perquisites, although it would continue to report the country club annual dues. If there was no such reimbursement, then the registrant would need to also report the meals and incidentals as perquisites.[243]

Where perquisites and personal benefits are required to be reported for a NEO, then each perquisite or personal benefit that exceeds the greater of $25,000 or 10 percent of the total amount of perquisites and personal benefits for that executive must be quantified and specifically identified in a footnote to this column.[244]

Perquisites and other personal benefits are to be valued on the basis of the aggregate incremental cost to the registrant.[245] In the case of a perquisite or other personal benefit for which footnote quantification is required, a registrant also must describe in the footnote its methodology for computing the aggregate incremental cost of the item.[246]

While reimbursements of taxes owed with respect to perquisites or other personal benefits are to be reported in this column,[247] they are subject to separate quantification and identification as tax reimbursements[248] even if the associated perquisites or other personal benefits are not required to be reported because the total amount of all perquisites or personal benefits for the NEO is less than $10,000

---

242. See the 2007 JCEB Questions, supra note 66, at Question No. 6 for a discussion of the differences between total cost and aggregate incremental cost.

243. Id.

244. Id. Under the former rules, a perquisite had to be separately identified and quantified only if its value exceeded 25 percent of the total amount of disclosable perquisites. See Instruction 1 to former Item 402(b)(2)(iii)(C).

245. Id.

246. Id.

247. See Item 402(c)(2)(ix)(B).

248. Id.

or are required to be identified but are not required to be separately quantified.[249]

Tax Payments

Any tax payment made to or for a NEO during a covered fiscal year, whether in the nature of a "gross-up" payment or other tax reimbursement, is to be reported in this column. This will include any "gross-up" payments or reimbursements of taxes owed with respect to perquisites or other personal benefits and, subject to the $10,000 disclosure threshold, separately identified and quantified.[250] It also covers "gross-up" payments and reimbursements that are linked to other types of compensation as well.[251]

The SEC Staff has indicated that, where a NEO for a covered fiscal year is entitled to receive a "gross-up" payment in respect of taxes on perquisites or other compensation provided during that fiscal year, but the "gross-up" payment is not payable by the registrant until the following fiscal year, the "gross-up" payment should be reported in the Summary Compensation Table for the same fiscal year as the related perquisite or other compensation.[252] In the Staff's view, disclosing these items in the same fiscal year will provide investors with a clearer view of all costs to the registrant associated with providing the perquisites or other compensation for which the tax "gross-up" payment was made.

Discount Securities Purchases

If a NEO purchases any security of the registrant or any of its subsidiaries from the registrant or a subsidiary, as the case may be, whether directly or indirectly through the deferral of base salary or bonus or otherwise, at a discount from the securities' market price at the date of purchase, the compensation cost of the security, computed in accordance with FASB ASC Topic 718, is to be reported in this column unless that discount is available generally either to all security holders or to all salaried employees of the registrant.

In the case of a Section 423 employee stock purchase plan, the SEC Staff has taken the position that, since Section 423 plans must be

---

249. *See* Instruction 4 to Item 402(c)(2)(ix).

250. *See* Instructions 3 and 4 to Item 402(c)(2)(ix).

251. *See* the Adopting Release, *supra* note 4, at n.204 and the following text. *See also* Kailer, *supra* note 53, at B-8.

252. *See* the Current Staff Guidance, *supra* note 28, at Q&A 119.19.

broad-based and nondiscriminatory to qualify for favorable income tax treatment, they would be within the scope of the exception to this disclosure requirement.[253]

Severance and Change-in-Control Payments

To the extent that a NEO is paid an amount or has an amount accrued for his or her benefit pursuant to a plan or arrangement in connection with his or her resignation, retirement, or any other termination of service with the registrant, or in connection with a change in control of the registrant, the amount is to be reported in this column. This will include any severance payment, and any other payment or benefit that is paid to or accrued for the NEO. It may also include the intrinsic value of any acceleration of vesting of stock and option awards that is triggered by the termination or change in control. While "gross-up" payments and other tax reimbursements related to a severance or other payment are reportable in this column, these amounts are to be separately identified and quantified.[254]

For purposes of this provision, an "accrued" amount is an amount for which payment has become due.[255] The SEC Staff has indicated that, for purposes of determining whether an amount is reportable because it is accrued, if a NEO's performance necessary to earn an amount is complete, it is an amount that should be reported.[256] In contrast, if an amount will be payable two years after a termination event if the NEO cooperates with (or complies with a covenant not to compete with) the registrant during that period, the amount is not reportable because the executive's performance is still necessary for the payment to become due.[257]

---

253. *See* the Current Staff Guidance, *supra* note 28, at Q&A 119.08. The SEC Staff takes this position even if the plan requires some minimum number of work hours in order to be eligible to participate or if the purchase price discount is greater than 5 percent. Footnote 221 of the Adopting Release, *supra* note 4, is not to be read to mean that the recognition of compensation expense for financial statement reporting purposes in connection with the plan disqualifies it from the exception. *Id.*

254. *See* Item 402(c)(2)(ix)(B).

255. *See* Instruction 5 to Item 402(c)(2)(ix).

256. *See* the Current Staff Guidance, *supra* note 28, at Q&A 119.13. For example, if a NEO has completed all performance to earn an amount, but payment is subject to a six-month deferral in order to comply with Section 409A of the Internal Revenue Code (26 U.S.C. § 409A), the amount would be an accrued amount subject to disclosure.

257. *Id.* As noted in the Adopting Release, amounts that are payable in the future, as well as amounts reportable under this provision, are to be reported under Item 402(j). *See*

In addition to this required disclosure, if payments or benefits are reported in this column, these amounts must be addressed in the narrative discussion that is to accompany the Summary Compensation Table.[258] Otherwise, the termination and change-in-control provisions are to be discussed as part of the required Potential Payments Upon Termination or Change-in-Control disclosure.[259]

Benefits that are payable pursuant to a defined benefit or actuarial plan are not reportable in this column unless they are accelerated as a result of the change in control of the registrant.[260] Similarly, a lump-sum distribution from a Section 401(k) plan is not reportable in the Summary Compensation Table, as the compensation that is deferred into such a plan has already been disclosed in the table, as have any registrant matching contributions.[261]

Any tax reimbursement or "gross-up" payment that is associated with any severance payment must be included in this column and, subject to the $10,000 disclosure threshold, separately identified and quantified as a tax payment in a footnote to the column.[262]

The SEC has indicated that compensation paid to a NEO as a result of a business combination that does not involve a termination of employment or a change in control of the registrant, such as a retention bonus, the acceleration of stock or option vesting arrangements, or performance-based compensation, that is intended to serve as an inducement for entering into the transaction is to be reported in the appropriate column of the Summary Compensation Table and also in any other compensation table or accompanying narrative where the particular compensation element is required to be disclosed.[263]

The SEC Staff has informally indicated that, where a registrant maintains a "death benefit only" plan (that is, a plan that provides for the

---

the Adopting Release, *supra* note 4, at n.217. Where a payment is to be made over a period of several years, the total amount payable should be reported. See the 2007 JCEB Questions, *supra* note 66, at Question No. 14.

258. See the Adopting Release, *supra* note 4, at n.255 and the accompanying text referencing Item 402(e).

259. *Id.* See Item 402(j) and Chapter 12.

260. See Instruction 2 to Item 402(c)(2)(ix). Instead, information about these plans is reportable in the Pension Value Changes and Above-Market or Preferential Earnings column of the table.

261. See the Current Staff Guidance, *supra* note 28, at Q&A 119.10.

262. See Item 402(c)(2)(ix)(B).

263. See the Adopting Release, *supra* note 4, at n.217.

payment of a death benefit to designated beneficiaries equal to a multiple of an executive officer's final base salary in the event of a termination of employment due to death),[264] where there is no life insurance involved, in the event of an actual termination of employment due to death, any payment or accrual under the plan is to be reported in this column for the fiscal year in which the NEO dies.[265] It also should be noted that, given investor concerns about the use of so-called "golden coffin" arrangements, an analysis of a registrant-sponsored death benefits only plan, including the reasons for the arrangement, should be included in the CD&A.[266]

Defined Contribution Plan Amounts

All registrant contributions or other allocations to tax-qualified and nonqualified defined contribution plans, whether vested or unvested, must be reported in this column. This includes matching contributions.

Life Insurance Premiums

The dollar value of any insurance premiums paid by, or on behalf of, the registrant during the covered fiscal year with respect to life insurance for the benefit of a NEO is to be reported in this column.[267]

Dividends and Earnings on Equity Awards

The dollar value of any dividends or other earnings paid on stock or option awards, when those amounts were not factored into the grant

---

264. Unlike a nonequity split-dollar life insurance arrangement, in which the designated beneficiaries directly receive life insurance proceeds, the benefits under a death benefits only plan are paid directly by the registrant from its general assets. The registrant may, but is not required to, purchase a life insurance policy to hedge against this future liability.

265. See 2010 JCEB Questions, supra note 55, at Question No. 1. In the event that a registrant has purchased a life insurance policy on a NEO to help fund the future liability, whether disclosure of the ongoing arrangement is required in the Summary Compensation Table will depend on the particular facts and circumstances. For example, if there is a direct relationship between the life insurance policy and the required death benefit payment, such that the registrant is simply serving as a conduit for the payment of the life insurance policy proceeds, then the arrangement should be reported as a current benefit to the NEO (presumably on the basis of the dollar value of the associated premium payments). In any event, the substance rather than the form of the arrangement should control the reporting treatment in this situation. Id.

266. Id.

267. On the other hand, the proceeds of a life insurance policy funded by the registrant and paid to the deceased executive officer's estate need not be reported in this column or elsewhere in the Summary Compensation Table. See the Current Staff Guidance, supra note 28, at Interpretation 217.14.

date fair value required to be reported for the stock or option award in column (e) or (f) is to be reported in this column.[268] In contrast, earnings on nonequity incentive plan awards are required to be reported in the Nonequity Incentive Plan Compensation column of the table and are not to be reported in this column.[269]

The SEC Staff takes the position that if a registrant credits stock dividends on unvested restricted stock units, but does not actually pay them out until the restricted stock units vest, those dividends should be reported in the fiscal year credited, rather than the fiscal year vested (and actually paid).[270]

In the case of equity awards that were granted prior to the effective date of the rules (and, thus, that have not previously been reported in the Grants of Plan-Based Awards Table), the SEC Staff took the position that the reporting of dividends, dividend equivalents, or other earnings on such awards depended on an analysis of whether these amounts would have been factored into the grant date fair value of the related award in accordance with Statement of Financial Accounting Standards 123(R) (SFAS 123(R)), the predecessor to FASB ASC Topic 718.[271] In this regard, the disclosure depended on how the dividend rights were structured and whether or not that brought them within the scope of SFAS 123(R) for purposes of the grant date fair value calculation.[272]

Other Items

Charitable Matching Programs

The SEC Staff has indicated that even where a charitable matching program is available to all employees of the registrant, the program must be reported in this column.[273] The reportable item applies to "the annual costs of payments and promises of payments pursuant to director legacy

---

268. As proposed, all earnings on equity awards, including dividends, were to be reported in the Stock Awards or Option Awards column, as the case may be, when paid. *See* Proposed Items 402(c)(2)(vi) and (vii). Acknowledging that, under FASB ASC Topic 718, the right to receive dividends is factored into an award's grant date fair value, however, the SEC revised the proposal to require this disclosure. This provision was revised in December 2006 (*see* the December 2006 Release, *supra* note 5, at Section II.B) and then again in December 2009 (*see* the 2009 Adopting Release, *supra* note 6, at Section VII).

269. *See* Instruction 1 to Item 402(c)(2)(ix).

270. *See* the Current Staff Guidance, *supra* note 28, at Interpretation 219.02.

271. *See* the Current Staff Guidance, *supra* note 28, at Q&A 119.09.

272. *Id.*

273. *See* the Current Staff Guidance, *supra* note 28, at Q&A 127.05.

programs and similar charitable award programs." In the Staff's view, any registrant-sponsored charitable award program in which a director or a NEO can participate would be a "similar charitable award program."[274]

Retirement Plans and Arrangements

Amounts paid or distributed under a defined benefit or actuarial plan during a covered fiscal year are not reportable in this column unless their receipt has been accelerated pursuant to a change in control of the registrant.[275] Similarly, the SEC Staff has taken the position that distributions or payouts from nonqualified defined contribution plans and nonqualified deferred compensation plans or arrangements are not to be reported in the Summary Compensation Table.[276] Instead, these distributions and payouts are to be reported in the Aggregate Withdrawals/Distributions column (column (e)) of the Nonqualified Deferred Compensation Table.[277]

Further, a lump sum distribution from a Section 401(k) plan is not to be reported in the table, since the compensation that was contributed to the plan has already been reported in the table, as would be any registrant matching contributions.[278] Finally, the earnings generated from a Section 401(k) plan account do not have to be reported in the table except to the extent that they are above-market or preferential earnings, and then only to the extent that they are above-market or preferential.[279]

Life Insurance Proceeds

If an executive officer dies during the last completed fiscal year, the proceeds of a life insurance policy funded by the registrant and paid to the deceased executive officer's estate need not be taken into consideration in determining the compensation to be reported in the Summary Compensation Table.[280]

---

274. *Id.* In the SEC Staff's view, the exclusion for "information regarding group life, health, hospitalization, or medical reimbursement plans that do not discriminate in scope, terms, or operation, in favor of executive officers or directors of the registrant and that are available generally to all salaried employees" in Item 402(a)(6)(ii) is not available here. *Id.*

275. *See* Instruction 2 to Item 402(c)(2)(ix). Instead, information about these plans is reportable pursuant to Item 402(c)(2)(viii) and Item 402(h).

276. *See* the Current Staff Guidance, *supra* note 28, at Q&A 119.10.

277. See Chapter 11.

278. *See* the Current Staff Guidance, *supra* note 28, at Q&A 119.10.

279. *Id.*

280. *See* the Current Staff Guidance, *supra* note 28, at Interpretation 217.14.

Total Compensation

Column (j) of the table is to report the dollar value of the total compensation of each NEO for each covered fiscal year. With respect to each NEO, this total will be the sum of all of the amounts reported in columns (c) through (i) of the table.[281]

As proposed, this column would have been the first column providing compensation information in the table.[282] In response to comments that this information more logically should follow, rather than precede, the relevant compensation numbers, the SEC shifted the column to the end of the table.

Common Reporting Issues

Bonus Payable in Shares of the Registrant's Stock

From time to time, a registrant will extend a bonus opportunity to its executive officers that is initially denominated in cash (such as a percentage of base salary) but, subsequently, the bonus will be paid in the form of equity, typically in shares of the registrant's common stock. Since the adoption of the rules, several permutations of this common fact pattern have arisen, with each variation potentially altering the proper reporting treatment of these awards. The following summarizes the disclosure principles that apply in these situations.

Decision to Pay Award in Fully Vested Shares of Stock Made at Time of Award Payout

A registrant establishes an annual bonus opportunity under a nonequity incentive plan as a dollar amount. After the end of the year (the performance period), the board of directors (or the compensation committee) decides to pay a portion of the bonus actually earned in fully vested shares of the registrant's common stock.

---

281. "Total" compensation is not, in fact, total, since, given the minimum $10,000 disclosure threshold for perquisites and other personal benefits, the amount reported in this column may be slightly less than a complete accounting of a NEO's total compensation for the covered fiscal year.

282. *See* Proposed Item 402(c)(2)(iii).

When presented with this fact pattern, the SEC Staff has indicated that the reporting treatment of the award is problematic.[283] A tension arises between the general principle that the reporting treatment of an equity award should follow the accounting of the award and the general objective of "principles-based" disclosure to reflect the intent of the board of directors (or the compensation committee) in making its compensation decisions. Strict adherence to the former principle may result in the stock award being reported for the fiscal year in which the award was granted, rather than the fiscal year to which the award relates (that is, the year in which the underlying performance occurred). This may create an anomaly in reporting the compensation of the registrant's NEOs, with all (or a portion) of their annual incentive compensation being reported in the Summary Compensation Table and Grants of Plan-Based Awards Table for the fiscal year following the fiscal year to which the performance relates (in other words, a year in arrears). In this situation, the registrant will need to address the terms and conditions of the award and its amount and form of payment in the CD&A.

As a practical matter, it is often the case that, at the time the bonus opportunity is granted, the registrant fully intends that the award payout will be made in cash, but subsequently determines that it does not have sufficient cash to pay the awards and, thus, decides to make payment in the form of shares of the registrant's common stock. In this situation, particularly given the potentially problematic nature of the accounting treatment of such a situation, it may be clearer to simply report the payment as a nonequity incentive plan award, with footnote disclosure that all (or a portion) of the award was paid in shares of the registrant's common stock. It should be noted that this reporting treatment is similar to that reflected in the SEC Staff's guidance for reporting a bonus where an executive officer elects to forgo a cash bonus in exchange for stock, equity-based, or another form of noncash compensation.[284]

---

283. *See* the Questions and Answers, Technical Session Between the SEC Staff and the Joint Committee on Employee Benefits (May 6, 2008) [hereinafter 2008 JCEB Questions], *available at* http://www.americanbar.org/content/dam/aba/migrated/2011_build/employee_benefits/sec_2008.authcheckdam.pdf, at Question No. 3.

284. *See* the Current Staff Guidance, *supra* note 28, at Q&A 119.03.

Decision to Pay Award in Restricted Stock or Restricted Stock Units Made at Time of Award Payout

A registrant establishes an annual bonus opportunity under a nonequity incentive plan as a dollar amount. After the end of the year (the performance period), the board of directors (or the compensation committee) decides to pay the bonus actually earned in restricted stock or restricted stock units which will be paid in shares of the registrant's common stock subject to an additional service-based vesting requirement.

When presented with this fact pattern, the SEC Staff has indicated that the reporting treatment of the award is problematic.[285] The analysis of this situation is similar to the analysis above for a bonus payout in fully vested shares of the registrant's common stock.

Decision to Pay Award in Fully Vested Shares of Stock Made at Time of Grant

At the time of establishing the bonus opportunity, the board of directors (or the compensation committee) decides that the dollar amount of any bonus actually earned will be converted into fully vested shares of the registrant's common stock based on the market price of the registrant's common stock on a specified date when the amount of the bonus is determined (such as, for example, the date of payment or the last day of the fiscal year for which the bonus was earned).

In this situation, where, at the time of establishing the bonus opportunity the registrant decides that the amount of the bonus earned will be determined as a dollar amount but paid in the form of equity, the compensation opportunity is considered an equity incentive plan award since it is within the scope of FASB ASC Topic 718. Accordingly, the compensation opportunity should be reported as a stock award in column (e) of the Summary Compensation Table.[286] In addition, the compensation should be reported as an equity incentive plan award in the Grants of Plan-Based Awards Table.[287]

---

285. *See* the 2008 JCEB Questions, *supra* note 289, at Question 3.

286. *Id.*

287. *Id.* Although columns (f), (g), and (h) of the Grants of Plan-Based Awards Table provides for the reporting of a number of shares that could be earned at each level of performance, in this case, where the potential bonus is stated in dollars, it will be permissible to change the column heading and report the potential payouts in dollars.

Decision to Pay Award in Restricted Stock or Restricted Stock Units Made at Time of Grant

At the time of establishing the bonus opportunity, the board of directors (or the compensation committee) decides that the dollar amount of any bonus actually earned will be converted into restricted stock or restricted stock units which will be paid in shares of the registrant's common stock subject to an additional service-based vesting requirement. The number of shares of the registrant's common stock subject to the award will be based on the market price of the registrant's common stock on a specified date when the amount of the bonus is determined (such as, for example, the date of payment or the last day of the fiscal year for which the bonus was earned), neither of which is known at the time the bonus opportunity is established.

In this situation, where, at the time of establishing the bonus opportunity the registrant decides that the amount of the bonus earned will be determined as a dollar amount but paid in the form of equity, the compensation opportunity is considered an equity incentive plan award since it is within the scope of FASB ASC Topic 718. Accordingly, the compensation opportunity should be reported as a stock award in column (e) of the Summary Compensation Table.[288] In addition, the compensation should be reported as an equity incentive plan award in the Grants of Plan-Based Awards Table.[289]

Decision to Pay Award in Shares of Phantom Stock Made at Time of Grant

At the time of establishing the bonus opportunity, the board of directors (or the compensation committee) decides that the dollar amount of any bonus actually earned will be converted into shares of phantom stock which will be paid in cash subject to an additional service-based vesting requirement. The number of shares will be based on the market price of the registrant's common stock on a specified date when the amount of the bonus is determined (such as, for example, the date of payment or the last day of the fiscal year for which the bonus was earned), neither of which is known at the time the bonus opportunity is established.

---

288. *See* the 2008 JCEB Questions, *supra* note 283, at Question No. 3.

289. *Id.* Although columns (f), (g), and (h) of the Grants of Plan-Based Awards Table provide for the reporting of a number of shares that could be earned at each level of performance, in this case, where the potential bonus is stated in dollars, it will be permissible to change the column heading and report the potential payouts in dollars.

In this situation, where, at the time of establishing the bonus opportunity the registrant decides that the amount of the bonus earned will be determined as a dollar amount but converted to an equity-based vehicle payable in cash, the compensation opportunity is considered an equity incentive plan award since it is within the scope of FASB ASC Topic 718. Accordingly, the compensation opportunity should be reported as a stock award in column (e) of the Summary Compensation Table.[290] In addition, the compensation should be reported as an equity incentive plan award in the Grants of Plan-Based Awards Table.[291]

Discretionary Bonus Payable in Stock

Where the "bonus" is purely discretionary—that is, the compensation opportunity does not qualify as "nonequity incentive plan compensation,"[292] and, thus, is generally reportable in column (d) rather than in column (g), a decision by the board of directors (or the compensation committee) to pay the bonus in shares of the registrant's common stock should be reported in column (e) of the Summary Compensation Table.[293]

---

290. *See* the 2008 JCEB Questions, *supra* note 283, at Question No. 3.

291. *Id.* Although columns (f), (g), and (h) of the Grants of Plan-Based Awards Table provides for the reporting of a number of shares that could be earned at each level of performance, in this case, where the potential bonus is stated in dollars, it will be permissible to change the column heading and report the potential payouts in dollars.

292. Item 402(a)(60(iii).

293. *See* the 2008 JCEB Questions, *supra* note 283, at Question No. 3. In addition, the award would be reported as a stock award in the Grants of Plan-Based Awards Table.

5

Perquisites

General

Over the years, perhaps no compensation disclosure area has been more vexing to registrants than the reporting of perquisites and other personal benefits. While executive perquisites typically make up only a small portion of an individual executive's overall compensation package and collectively represent just a fraction of the total amount that a registrant is spending on executive pay, more time and effort probably is devoted to determining whether an item is a disclosable perquisite and, if so, to ascertaining its value than to any other compensation item.

Belying their standing in the compensation hierarchy, investors have a keen interest in a registrant's perquisite policies and practices.[1]

---

1. A registrant should address its perquisite policies in its Compensation Discussion and Analysis (CD&A). *See* John W. White, Director, Division of Corporation Finance, U.S. Securities & Exchange Comm'n, *Principles Matter*, Remarks Before the Practising Law Institute Conference (Sept. 6, 2006) [hereinafter White Principles Matter Speech], *available at* http://www.sec.gov/news/speech/2006/spch090606jww.htm. It is advisable for a registrant to address its perquisite policies and practices even if it is not required to actually disclose perquisites in the Summary Compensation Table (because the amount received by each named executive officer during the last completed fiscal year is less than $10,000). This is because the CD&A is to be used to explain each element of a registrant's executive compensation program, why it chooses to pay each element, and how each element fits into its overall compensation objectives. Consequently, even if the level of benefits received in a given fiscal year is below

173

Some investors view executive perquisites as an effective way to assess a registrant's general approach to executive pay, as well as a tool for understanding the attitude of its board of directors or board compensation committee towards the allocation and use of corporate assets. In addition, the media, analysts, and other market observers use a registrant's perquisite practices as a way to gauge the strength of its corporate governance structure, its commitment to transparency, and, in many cases, the health of its business and financial condition. In spite (or perhaps because) of this scrutiny, registrants have often struggled to identify which of the benefits and other items offered to their executives and directors are perquisites. With the reduction of the minimum threshold for perquisite disclosure from $50,000 to $10,000, this challenge is only likely to increase.

Traditionally, the Securities and Exchange Commission (SEC) has taken a largely "hands off " approach to perquisites,[2] other than to set the basic disclosure framework[3] and, from time to time, bring the occasional enforcement action where a registrant's compliance efforts failed to meet the spirit of the disclosures requirements.[4] In adopting the executive compensation disclosure rules, however, the SEC, for the first time in 25 years, provided guidance on the factors to be considered in

---

the disclosure threshold, if the registrant offers perquisites to its executives, a discussion of the related policies and practices may be material to an investor's understand of the registrant's executive compensation program.

2. In the 1970s and early 1980s, the SEC issued several interpretive releases addressing executive compensation disclosure, including the disclosure of perquisites and other personal benefits. See Disclosure of Management Remuneration, Release No. 33-5856 (Aug. 18, 1977), 42 Fed. Reg. 43,058; Disclosure of Management Remuneration, Release No. 33-5904 (Feb. 6, 1978), 43 Fed. Reg. 6060; Disclosure of Management Remuneration, Release No. 33-6027 (Feb. 22, 1979), 44 Fed. Reg. 16,368; Disclosure of Management Remuneration, Release No. 33-6166 (Dec. 12, 1979), 44 Fed. Reg. 74,803; and Interpretation of Rules Relating to Disclosure of Management Remuneration, Release No. 33-6364 (Dec. 3, 1981), 46 Fed. Reg. 60,421. In Disclosure of Executive Compensation, Release Nos. 33-6486, 34-20220, 35-23069, IC-13529 (Sept. 23, 1983), 48 Fed. Reg. 44,467 (Sept. 29, 1983), as part of a major revision to Item 402, the SEC rescinded these interpretive releases. Subsequently, neither the SEC nor the SEC Staff had published interpretations addressing what must be disclosed as a perquisite. See Executive Compensation and Related Party Disclosure, Release Nos. 33-8655, 34-53185, IC-27218 (Jan. 27, 2006), 71 Fed. Reg. 6542 (Feb. 8, 2006) [hereinafter Proposing Release], available at http://www.sec.gov/rules/proposed/33-8655.pdf, at n.111.

3. For a discussion of the disclosure requirements for perquisites and other personal benefits, see "All Other Compensation—Perquisites" in Chapter 4.

4. See, e.g., In the Matter of Tyson Foods, Inc. and Donald Tyson, Litigation Release No. 19208 (Apr. 28, 2005).

determining whether an item is a perquisite or other personal benefit.[5] While this guidance does not define the term "perquisite" or establish a bright-line test for perquisite identification,[6] it does establish a two-step analytical framework that registrants should find helpful in identifying perquisites. This framework first examines an item's connection to the performance of an executive's duties, and then the degree to which the benefit derived from the item is personal in nature. Nonetheless, the ultimate determination of whether a particular benefit is a perquisite will depend on the specific facts and circumstances of the item being analyzed.[7]

Once all of the perquisites have been identified for an executive, they must be valued to as part of the calculation of the executive's total compensation for purposes of determining whether he or she is a named executive officer (NEO) and, if so, disclosed in the All Other Compensation column of the Summary Compensation Table. For a discussion of the disclosure requirements for perquisites, see Chapter 4.[8]

Identifying Perquisites

To assist registrants in identifying perquisites, the SEC has articulated a two-step analysis for examining an item. First, an item *is not* a perquisite if it is "integrally and directly related" to the performance of the executive's duties. Second, if the item is not essential to the performance of an executive's duties, it *is* a perquisite if it confers a "direct or indirect benefit that has a personal aspect" on the executive that is

---

5. *See* the Proposing Release, *supra* note 2, at Section II.B.1.d.iii, and Executive Compensation and Related Person Disclosure, Release Nos. 33-8732A, 34-54302A, IC-27444A (Aug. 29, 2006), 71 Fed. Reg. 53,158 (Sept. 8, 2006) [hereinafter Adopting Release], *available at* http://www.sec.gov/rules/final/2006/33-8732a.pdf, at Section II.C.1.e.i.

6. This policy is based on the belief that a bright-line definition would provide an incentive to characterize perquisites or personal benefits in ways that would attempt to circumvent the definition and in recognition that, in a dynamic and evolving compensation environment, any definition would quickly become outdated. *See* the Adopting Release, *supra* note 5, at Section II.C.1.e.i.

7. While this chapter speaks in terms of executive perquisites, the same two-step framework applies to identifying director perquisites as well. It also applies to perquisites and other personal benefits to be provided to a named executive officer following termination of employment or in connection with a change in control of the registrant. *See* Chapter 12.

8. See "All Other Compensation—Perquisites" in Chapter 4 for a discussion of the disclosure requirements for perquisites and other personal benefits.

not generally available to other employees. It should be noted that, as framed by the SEC, these two standards are just "among the factors" to be considered in determining whether an item is a perquisite. While this strongly suggests that there may be other considerations that are relevant to the analysis in a specific situation, as a practical matter most registrants and their advisors have quickly moved to this two-step analysis as the sole basis for evaluating an item's treatment as a perquisite.

Integrally and Directly Related

The first step of the analysis requires a determination of whether the item in question is integrally and directly related to the performance of the executive's duties; in other words, does the executive need the item to do his or her job? If it is an essential item without which the executive would not be able to carry out his or her responsibilities, then the analysis is concluded—the item is not a perquisite and no compensation disclosure is required.[9] As the SEC had noted, the analysis makes a critical distinction between an item that a registrant provides because the executive needs it to do his or her job and an item provided for some other reason, even where that other reason includes a business, as well as a personal, benefit.

As the SEC noted in both the Proposing and Adopting Releases, the "internally and directly related" standard is a narrow one. Applying this standard, typically the following items *will not* be considered perquisites:

- office space at a registrant business location;[10]
- a reserved parking space that is closer to business facilities but not otherwise preferential;
- travel to and from business meetings and other business travel;
- business entertainment;
- security during business travel;
- itemized expense accounts limited to business use;
- additional clerical or secretarial services devoted to registrant matters;[11] and

---

9. Since there is an integral and direct connection to job performance, the second step of the analysis (whether there is also a personal benefit that is not generally available to other employees) need not be considered.

10. Office space at a registrant business location, even if larger than that of other employees, is integrally and directly related to performance of an executive's duties.

11. Secretarial services used for business purposes, even if at a higher level than other employees, are integrally and directly related to performance of an executive's duties. On the

- a BlackBerry device or a laptop computer where the registrant believes that it is an integral part of the executive's duties to be accessible by e-mail to colleagues and clients when out of the office.[12]

If an item is integrally and directly related to the performance of an executive's duties, the registrant is not required to disclose any incremental cost over a less expensive alternative.[13]

Personal Benefit

An item that is not excluded from perquisite status by virtue of the first step of the framework then must be analyzed under the second step. At this stage, however, the analysis is reversed. Instead of considering whether the item should be excluded from perquisite treatment, it is examined to determine whether it confers a benefit on the executive that has some personal aspect to it. If so, is the benefit generally available on a nondiscriminatory basis to all employees? If the answer to the first inquiry is "yes," the answer to the second question also must be in the affirmative to avoid perquisite status.

In contrast to the "integrally and directly related" standard, this standard is to be construed broadly. As a result, the presence of a personal benefit may mean that the item in question is a perquisite even though it is provided for a business reason or the registrant's convenience,[14] unless it is generally available on a nondiscriminatory basis to all employees.

Nor is the tax treatment of an item dispositive for disclosure purposes. As the SEC noted in the Proposing Release, although a registrant may have determined that an expense is an "ordinary" or "necessary" business expense for federal income tax or other purposes, that determination is not responsive to the inquiry as to whether the

---

other hand, provision of additional secretarial services, such as a second secretary, that are not directly related to performance of an executive's duties is a perquisite.

12. *See* the Adopting Release, *supra* note 5, at Section II.C.1.e.i.

13. While the example given in the Adopting Release to illustrate this principle involves, in the case of business travel, the cost differential between renting a midsize car over a compact car, its most obvious applications are the cost differential between business-related first-class and economy air travel and the cost differential between a suite and a standard hotel room when on a business trip.

14. The SEC uses an example of a registrant's provision of a helicopter service for an executive to commute to and from work as an example of an item that is not integrally and directly related to job performance, even though reducing the executive's commute benefits the registrant.

item provides a perquisite or other personal benefit for disclosure purposes. Whether the registrant should pay for an expense or it is deductible for tax purposes relates principally to questions of state law regarding use of corporate assets and to questions of tax law; the disclosure requirements are triggered by different and broader concepts.

An item is considered to be generally available to all employees on a nondiscriminatory basis if it is available to those employees to whom it lawfully may be provided. For these purposes, a registrant is permitted to recognize jurisdictionally based legal restrictions (such as in the case of foreign employees) or the employee's "accredited investor" status.[15] In contrast, merely providing a benefit consistent with its availability to employees in the same job category or at the same pay scale does not establish that it is generally available on a nondiscriminatory basis to all employees.

Applying this standard, typically the following items *will be* considered perquisites:

- personal travel on registrant-provided (owned or leased) aircraft or watercraft;[16]
- personal travel using registrant-owned or -leased vehicles;
- any other personal travel otherwise financed by the registrant;
- personal use of other property owned or leased by the registrant;
- commuting expenses or commuter transportation services;
- additional clerical or secretarial services devoted to personal matters;
- personal financial, tax, or investment management services;
- club memberships not exclusively used for business entertainment purposes;
- housing and other living expenses (including, but not limited to, relocation assistance and payments to an executive to stay at his or her personal residence);[17]

---

15. The term "accredited investor" is defined in Securities Act Rule 501(a) (17 C.F.R. 230.501(a)) for purposes of Regulation D (17 C.F.R. 230.500–508).

16. While the SEC Staff has not addressed the question, it is advisable to treat the use of registrant-provided aircraft to attend meetings of the board of directors or board committees of which a named executive officer is a member as personal travel unless a different conclusion is warranted after applying the SEC's two-step analysis.

17. *See* "Other Issues—Relocation Expenses," *infra*.

- security provided at a personal residence or during personal travel; and
- discounts on registrant products and services not generally available on a nondiscriminatory basis to all employees.

Valuing Perquisites

The rules retain the former approach[18] that perquisites are to be valued for disclosure purposes on the basis of their aggregate incremental cost to the registrant.[19] After soliciting comment on whether to provide guidance on how to determine this amount,[20] the SEC decided to take no action in this area. Consequently, registrants must make their own assessments of the aggregate incremental cost of these items.[21] In many instances, an item's incremental cost to the registrant will be obvious, particularly where the registrant has to procure the item in a retail context.[22] Where the item involves the use of corporate property or services, however, the valuation will be more difficult and may involve the exercise of significant judgment by the registrant. In the case of a perquisite or other personal benefit for which footnote quantification is required, a registrant also must describe in the footnote its methodology for computing the aggregate incremental cost of the item.[23]

As the SEC noted in the Proposing Release, the amount attributed to a perquisite for federal income tax purposes is not the incremental cost for purposes of the disclosure rules unless, independent of the tax

---

18. *See* Instruction 2 to former Item 402(b)(2)(iii)(C).

19. *See* Instruction 4 to Item 402(c)(2)(ix).

20. *See* the Proposing Release, *supra* note 2, at Section II.B.1.d.iii.

21. While the SEC declined to take a position on *how* to determine aggregate incremental cost, it did offer guidance on *how not* to determine it. In this regard, the SEC has indicated that the amount attributable to an executive for federal income tax purposes is generally not the incremental cost to the registrant, particularly in the case of the personal use of registrant-provided aircraft. *See* the Proposing Release, *supra* note 2, at Section II.B.1.d.iii.

22. In these situations, the retail price of the item, or the retail price of a commercially available equivalent, will probably suffice to value the item. Note, however, that, in the SEC's view, this approach will not work for every benefit category. For example, in the case of personal use of registrant-provided aircraft, the retail price of a commercially available equivalent will be the retail price to charter the same model aircraft, not first-class airfare for the equivalent journey.

23. *See* Instruction 4 to Item 402(c)(2)(ix). This disclosure is aimed at improving investors' ability to compare the cost of perquisites from registrant to registrant.

characterization, it constitutes the incremental cost. For example, the cost of personal travel on registrant-provided aircraft attributed to an executive for federal income tax purposes is not generally the incremental cost of this benefit for disclosure purposes.[24]

Where a registrant changes its valuation methodology from one fiscal year to the next, it is advisable to consider restating the computations from the prior fiscal year or years (even though this will likely result in different amounts than were reported in the prior Summary Compensation Table or tables) to promote comparability.[25] In this situation, it is also advisable to explain the reason for the difference in the reported amounts in a footnote to the All Other Compensation column.

Perquisite Reimbursement and "No Cost" Perks

In some instances, an executive may desire to avoid the perquisites disclosure requirement of the rules. This has led to questions with respect to the disclosure of perquisites or other personal benefits with no aggregate incremental cost of the registrant. Similarly, an executive may desire to reimburse the registrant for the cost of a perquisite or other personal benefit to avoid disclosure.

The staff of the SEC's Division of Corporation Finance (SEC Staff) has taken the position that, if the $10,000 disclosure threshold is otherwise exceeded,

- even if a perquisite or other personal benefit has no aggregate incremental cost to the registrant, it still must be separately identified by type as part of the perquisite disclosure for the affected NEO and

---

24. *See* IRS Regulation § 1.61-21(g) (26 C.F.R. 1.61-21(g)) regarding Internal Revenue Service guidelines for imputing taxable personal income to an employee who travels for personal reasons on corporate aircraft.

25. *See* W. Alan Kailer, Hunton & Williams, *The Securities and Exchange Commission's Executive Compensation Rules—Preparing the Executive Compensation Tables* (Jan. 2012), at A-37.

- no disclosure is required in the case of a perquisite or other personal benefit as to which the NEO has fully reimbursed the registrant for the cost of the item.[26]

Thus, in this latter case, the item for which the NEO has actually fully reimbursed the registrant would not be considered a perquisite or other personal benefit and, therefore, need not be included or separately identified by type as part of the perquisite disclosure for the affected NEO.[27]

As with the concept of "incremental cost," the SEC Staff has not taken a position as to what constitutes "full reimbursement" of the cost of a perquisite or other personal benefit that is, whether full reimbursement of the registrant's aggregate incremental cost for the item is sufficient or whether full reimbursement requires payment of the item's retail cost or value. Consequently, a registrant must make its own assessment of the amount that a NEO must pay to avoid disclosure of the item as a perquisite. In many cases, the registrant's aggregate incremental cost to provide a specific personal benefit and its economic value to the recipient (for example, the costs associated with a physical examination) may be the same. Thus, the amount that must be paid to constitute full reimbursement will not be problematic. In other cases, however, the item's aggregate incremental cost to the registrant and its economic value to the recipient may be significantly different (for example, the costs associated with the personal use of corporate aircraft). In this instance, it may be difficult for a registrant to get comfortable with the notion that a NEO has satisfied the full reimbursement requirement.

---

26. *See* Division of Corporation Finance, Compliance and Disclosure Interpretations – Regulation S-K (July 8, 2011) [hereinafter Current Staff Guidance], *available at* http://www.sec.gov/divisions/corpfin/guidance/regs-kinterp.htm, at Q&A 119.07.

27. *Id.* In this regard, for example, if a registrant pays for country club annual dues as well as for meals and incidentals and a named executive officer reimburses the cost of meals and incidentals, then the registrant need not report meals and incidentals as perquisites, although it would continue to report the country club annual dues. If there was no such reimbursement, then the registrant would need to also report the meals and incidentals as perquisites.

Other Issues

Security-Related Items

The treatment of security-related costs should be analyzed under the SEC's two-step framework. As the SEC has stated, unless the costs are integrally and directly related to the executive's job performance, the fact that there is a business purpose for providing the security does not affect its characterization as a perquisite. Thus, registrant policy that, for security purposes, its chief executive officer or some other executive (or the executive and his or her family) must use registrant-provided aircraft or other means of travel for both business and personal travel, or must use registrant or registrant-provided property for vacations, does not preclude the item from being considered a perquisite.[28] The result is the same whether or not the use of registrant-provided transportation is required under a formal security policy.

Personal Aircraft Use

Since the SEC has not provided guidance on how to calculate a perquisite's aggregate incremental cost to the registrant, valuation methodologies vary significantly from registrant to registrant, particularly when it comes to valuing the personal use of corporate aircraft.[29] As a result of the requirement that registrants disclose the valuation methodology for perquisites with a value in excess of $25,000 and given the significant expense often associated with personal aircraft use, information about this item began to appear for the first time during the 2007 proxy season. It appears that for most registrants, the decision as to whether to include an amount as part of the aggregate incremental cost depends on whether the amount represents a fixed or variable cost.

---

28. *See* Questions and Answers, Technical Session Between the SEC Staff and the Joint Committee on Employee Benefits (May 8, 2007) [hereinafter 2007 JCEB Questions], *available at* http://www.abanet.org/jceb/2007/SEC07Final.pdf, at Question No. 19(b). *See also* the Adopting Release, *supra* note 5, at the text following n.209.

29. Generally, the Standard Industry Fare Level (SIFL) rate guidelines imposed by the Internal Revenue Service for purposes of imputing taxable personal income to an employee who travels for personal reasons on corporate aircraft are not an appropriate valuation methodology for determining the aggregate incremental cost of personal aircraft use for disclosure purposes. *See* the Adopting Release, *supra* note 5, at n.213. *See also* the 2007 JCEB Questions, *supra* note 28, at Question No. 19(a).

Personal Travel on Registrant-Owned Aircraft

Generally, when an executive makes personal use of a registrant-owned aircraft primarily used for business travel, many companies exclude the direct and indirect fixed costs associated with owning and maintaining the aircraft from the aggregate incremental cost. Examples of the types of fixed expenses (that is, expenses that do not vary based on use) that generally *are not* reported include:

- pilots' and other employees' salaries;
- purchase costs of the aircraft;
- aircraft-related insurance; and
- non-trip-related hangar expenses.

The treatment of maintenance costs (parts and labor, including inspections and repairs) presents a more difficult question. While those may be considered fixed costs, there is no question that at least a portion of their amount is directly related to use. Thus, it may be advisable to attribute a portion of the annual maintenance costs for operating the aircraft to the personal use using a reasonable valuation methodology. Similarly, the depreciation of the aircraft raises some issues. While the depreciation associated with an individual flight may be minimal, presumably where an executive makes use of a registrant-owned aircraft for significant personal use, it may be appropriate to include a portion of the aircraft's annual depreciation as part of the cost that is attributable to the executive.

In addition, many companies include all of the direct and indirect variable costs associated with the personal use of the aircraft in the aggregate incremental cost.[30] Generally, these include all flight-related expenses, such as

- hangar and tie-down costs away from the aircraft's home base;
- landing fees, airport taxes, and similar assessments;
- flight planning and weather contract services;
- crew travel expenses (food, lodging, and ground transportation);
- in-flight supplies and catering (food and beverages); Insurance obtained for the specific flight (such as engine insurance);

---

30. *See, e.g.,* the Bank of America Definitive Proxy Statement (Form 14A) filed Mar. 30, 2011 (file no. 001-06523).

- aircraft fuel (fuel, oil, lubricants, and other additives);[31]
- aircraft accrual expenses per hour of flight;
- customs expenses, foreign permits, and similar fees directly related to the flight; and
- passenger ground transportation and trip-related maintenance.

Also, the costs associated with any "deadhead" flights[32] related to the personal use of registrant-owned aircraft should be included in the aggregate incremental cost of the executive's use.[33] Further, some registrants include the amount of any income tax deduction forgone by the registrant as a result of the cost of the personal use exceeding the amount reported by the executive as income for federal income tax purposes as an additional incremental cost of the use.[34]

Travel by Family or Guest

When family members or guests accompany an executive on a flight (whether business-related or personal), there are at least two ways to value the aggregate incremental cost of this benefit. Under a pure "incremental cost" approach, only those costs directly attributable to the additional passengers (in-flight food and beverages, any additional weight-related charges) would be taken into account. Under a "value received" approach, the benefit of not having to pay for the travel costs of these individuals (that is, the commercial airfare) would be taken into account. While the latter approach usually results in a higher reportable amount, this methodology may overstate the intended amount since only the registrant's actual incremental cost needs to be taken into account. If an executive's family members or guests are the sole passengers on the flight, however, then the full aggregate incremental cost approach that would be applicable to the executive him or herself should be used.

Relocation Expenses

The expenses associated with the relocation of a NEO, whether payable pursuant to a formal relocation plan or on an *ad hoc* basis, may constitute

---

31. These amounts are often calculated on a per-flight-hour basis.
32. A "deadhead" flight is an outgoing or return flight that does not have any passengers where the complementary leg of the flight is for the purpose of transporting an executive.
33. *See* the White Principles Matter Speech, *supra* note 1.
34. *See* Internal Revenue Code § 274(e) (26 U.S.C. § 274(e)).

a reportable perquisite. Under the former rules, such expenses, to the extent that they were payable pursuant to a broad-based plan that did not discriminate in scope, terms, or operation, were not subject to disclosure.[35] The current rules intentionally omitted relocation programs from the type of plans for which disclosure is not required.[36] Further, the Commission expressly included relocation assistance as an example of the type of item requiring disclosure as a perquisite or personal benefit under the rules.[37]

While the SEC Staff has indicated that this explicit reference to relocation assistance is intended to mean that relocation expenses, by their nature, are always a perquisite,[38] some registrants believe that, applying the SEC's two-step analysis as described above, there may be situations where a relocation arrangement would not be considered a perquisite or personal benefit (for example, where a registrant requires an executive to relocate overseas to manage a particular segment of the registrant's business). Still, reaching such a conclusion may be an insurmountable obstacle in view of the current Staff position.[39]

Reimbursement of Legal Expenses

The SEC Staff has taken the position that a registrant's reimbursement to an executive officer of legal expenses with respect to a lawsuit in which the executive was named as a defendant, in his or her capacity as an officer, is not disclosable under the current rules.[40] On the other hand, the payment or reimbursement of legal expenses for matters that are personal to an executive, such as the negotiation of an employment agreement, are likely to be considered perquisites under the two-step

---

35. *See* former Item 402(a)(7)(ii).

36. *See* Item 402(a)(6)(ii). This change was made as a result of the SEC's belief that even broad-based, nondiscriminatory plans were susceptible to operation in a discriminatory manner favoring executive officers, and, therefore, an exclusion could potentially deprive investors of information about significant compensatory benefits. *See* the Adopting Release, *supra* note 5, at n.340 and the accompanying text.

37. *See* the Adopting Release, *supra* note 5, at the text following n.210.

38. *See* the 2007 JCEB Questions, *supra* note 28, at Question No. 7.

39. *Id.* It appears that the SEC Staff based its informal response to this question on an application of the two-step analysis, stating its belief that since relocation expenses involve the provision of housing, this is a personal rather than a business expense, even where it relates to an overseas assignment. *See also* the Adopting Release, *supra* note 5, at n.340 and the accompanying text.

40. *See* the Current Staff Guidance, *supra* note 26, at Interpretation 217.10.

analysis and, thus, would be reportable.[41] Another area where this issue arises involves the assistance that a registrant provides to its executive officers in complying with their reporting obligations under Section 16(a) of the Exchange Act. Here, applying the two-step analysis would suggest that the cost of such assistance is not a reportable perquisite since the reporting obligation arises solely as a result of the individual's status as an executive officer of the registrant.[42]

Perquisite Allowances

Where a registrant provides its executive officers with a pool of money (either fixed or discretionary in amount) that may be used to purchase (either from the registrant or one or more third parties) personal benefits, this "perquisite allowance" should be reported in the All Other Compensation column of the Summary Compensation Table. This would be true whether expenditures are to be selected from a list of designated items or may involve any item of the executive's choosing.

The amount actually expended during the covered fiscal year should be reported in the column subject to all of the rules.[43] Thus, the benefits actually obtained as a result of using an allowance that is provided to purchase from a list of designated items should be itemized and quantified.[44] A registrant should also address the reasons for the providing the perquisite allowance and how it furthers its overall compensation objectives in the CD&A.

Medical Benefits

Under the rules, benefits provided under a life, health, hospitalization, or medical reimbursement plan are not reportable (as a perquisite or otherwise) if the plan does not discriminate in scope, terms, or operation in favor of executive officers or directors and the plan is generally available to all salaried employees of the registrant.[45] Where a medical plan does not meet these criteria, then the benefits received by a NEO must be reported, either as a perquisite or, in the case of life insurance

---

41. *See* Kailer, *supra* note 25, at B-8.

42. *Id.*

43. *See* Instruction 4 to Item 402(c)(2)(ix).

44. *See* the Adopting Release, *supra* note 5, at Section II.C.1.e.i.

45. *See* Item 402(a)(6)(ii).

premiums, as a separate item in the All Other Compensation column of the Summary Compensation Table.[46]

Relationship to Tax "Gross-Ups" or Reimbursements

Frequently, a registrant may agree to cover the income and other taxes, if any, associated with the receipt of a perquisite or other personal benefit. It is important to note that, while a reimbursement of taxes owed with respect to a perquisite or other personal benefit is to be reported (along with the perquisite) in the All Other Compensation column of the Summary Compensation Table,[47] it is subject to separate quantification and identification as a tax reimbursement.[48] In other words, the perquisite and associated tax reimbursement are not aggregated for purposes of determining whether the perquisite exceeds the $10,000 disclosure threshold. Even if the associated perquisite or other personal benefit is not required to be reported because the total amount of all perquisites and other personal benefits for a NEO is less than $10,000, the associated tax reimbursement must still be disclosed.[49]

In a situation where an executive officer who is determined to be a NEO for 2011 (Year One) is entitled to receive a "gross-up" payment with respect to taxes associated with a perquisite or other personal benefit provided during the year, but the tax "gross-up" payment is not payable by the registrant until 2012 (Year Two), the SEC Staff has taken the position that, to provide investors with a clearer view of all costs to the registrant associated with providing the perquisites or other personal benefit for which tax "gross-up" payments are being made, the tax "gross-up" payment should be reported in the Summary Compensation Table for the same fiscal year as the related perquisites or other personal benefit.[50]

---

46. *See* Item 402(c)(2)(ix)(F).
47. *See* Item 402(c)(2)(ix)(B).
48. *Id.*
49. *See* Instruction 4 to Item 402(c)(2)(ix).
50. *See* the Current Staff Guidance, *supra* note 26, at Q&A 119.19.

6

Grants of Plan-Based Awards Table

General

The Summary Compensation Table is to be accompanied by the Grants of Plan-Based Awards Table,[1] the first of three tables intended to provide investors with supplemental information about the incentive and equity awards provided to and held by the named executive officers (NEOs). This table presents, on a grant-by-grant basis for each NEO, additional information about the incentive and equity awards made during the last completed fiscal year under any plan.[2]

---

1. Item 402(d). A smaller reporting company is not required to provide a Grants of Plan-Based Awards Table as part of its executive compensation disclosure. *See* Executive Compensation and Related Person Disclosure, Release Nos. 33-8732A, 34-54302A, IC-27444A (Aug. 29, 2006), 71 Fed. Reg. 53,158 (Sept. 8, 2006) [hereinafter Adopting Release], *available at* http://www.sec.gov/rules/final/2006/33-8732a.pdf, at Section II.D.1 and Smaller Reporting Company Regulatory Relief and Simplification, Release Nos. 33-8876, 34-56994, 39-2451 (Dec. 19, 2007), 73 Fed. Reg. 934 (Jan. 4, 2008), *available at* http://www.sec.gov/rules/final/33-8876.pdf, at Section III.C.1.

2. As originally proposed, the Summary Compensation Table would have been supplemented with two additional tables intended to explain the information in the Summary Compensation Table. The first supplemental table would have included information about nonstock grants of incentive plan awards, stock-based incentive plan awards, and awards of performance-based options, restricted stock, and similar instruments (*see* Proposed Item 402(d)), while the second suppelmental table would have included equity-based compensation

189

While the table is intended to help explain the information in the Summary Compensation Table, it actually serves four distinct purposes:

- It provides detailed information about the potential annual and long-term incentive award opportunities for awards granted to the NEOs during the last completed fiscal year under both equity incentive and nonequity incentive plans. Thus, it enables investors to evaluate the performance targets established by the registrant for its incentive awards and to compare these amounts with the actual award payouts.

- It provides the number of shares or other securities covered by stock and option awards made to the NEOs during the last completed fiscal year.[3]

- It highlights the registrant's equity award grant practices as they relate to equity awards made to the NEOs during the last completed fiscal year, by differentiating between an award's authorization date and its actual grant date, and, in the case of options, between the exercise or base price and the market price of the underlying securities on the grant date. Thus, it enables investors to monitor a registrant's practices for possible manipulation of option grant dates to achieve below-market exercise prices.

- It provides the full grant date fair value of all stock and option awards made to the NEOs during the last completed fiscal year.

As a result, preparation of the table can be quite complex. To simplify the presentation of information, a registrant may omit any column or

---

awards that were not performance-based, such as stock, options, or similar instruments where the payout or future value was tied to the company's stock price, and not to other performance criteria (*see* Proposed Item 402(e)). (In the case of this latter table, much of this information had previously been required in the Option/SAR Grants in Last Fiscal Year Table (*see* former Item 402(c))). Since much of the information contained in the proposed tables was consistent, the SEC decided to combine the proposed disclosure into a single table and simplify the disclosure requirements. *See* the Adopting Release, *supra* note 1, at n.232 and the accompanying text.

3. The SEC Staff has observed informally that the table, as a complement to the Summary Compensation Table, focuses on what the registrant's compensation committee decided, rather than on what the NEO received. *See* Questions and Answers, Technical Session Between the SEC Staff and the Joint Committee on Employee Benefits (May 4, 2010), *available at* http://www.americanbar.org/content/dam/aba/events/employee_benefits/2010_sec_qa.authcheckdam.pdf, at Question No. 5.

columns for which there has been no compensation awarded to any of the NEOs during the last completed fiscal year.[4]

Tabular Format

The Grants of Plan-Based Awards Table is to be presented in the following tabular format:

GRANTS OF PLAN-BASED AWARDS

Name	Grant Date	Estimated Future Payouts Under Nonequity Incentive Plan Awards			Estimated Future Payouts Under Equity Incentive Plan Awards			All Other Stock Awards: Number of Shares of Stock or Units (#)	All Other Option Awards: Number of Securities Underlying Options (#)	Exercise or Base Price of Option Awards ($/Sh)	Grant Date Fair Value of Stock and Option Awards
		Thresh-old ($)	Target ($)	Maximum ($)	Thresh-old (#)	Target (#)	Maximum (#)				
(a)	(b)	(c)	(d)	(e)	(f)	(g)	(h)	(i)	(j)	(k)	(l)
Principal Executive Officer (PEO)											
Principal Financial Officer (PFO)											
A											
B											
C											

The table includes the following information for the last completed fiscal year:

- the name of the NEO (column (a));[5]
- the grant date for any equity awards reported in the table (column (b)).[6] Where the grant date differs from the date on which the board compensation committee (or a committee of the board of directors performing a similar function or the full board of directors) takes action (or is deemed to take action) to grant such awards, a separate, adjoining column is to be added between columns (b) and (c) showing the date of the committee (or board) action;[7]

---

4. *See* Instruction 5 to Item 402(a)(3).
5. Item 402(d)(2)(i).
6. Item 402(d)(2)(ii).
7. *Id.*

- the dollar value of the estimated future payout upon satisfaction of the conditions in question under nonequity incentive plan[8] awards granted in the fiscal year, or the applicable range of estimated payouts denominated in dollars (threshold, target, and maximum amount) (columns (c) through (e));[9]

- the number of shares of stock[10] or the number of shares underlying options[11] to be paid out or vested upon satisfaction of the conditions in question under equity incentive plan awards granted in the fiscal year, or the applicable range of estimated payouts denominated in the number of shares of stock, or the number of shares underlying options under the award (threshold, target, and maximum amount) (columns (f) through (h));[12]

- the number of shares of stock granted in the fiscal year that are not required to be disclosed in columns (f) through (h) (column (i));[13]

- the number of securities underlying options granted in the fiscal year that are not required to be disclosed in columns (f) through (h) (column (j));[14]

- the per-share exercise or base price of the options granted in the fiscal year (column (k));[15] If such exercise or base price is less than the closing market price of the underlying security on the date of grant, a separate, adjoining column showing the

---

8. A "nonequity incentive plan" is a plan providing compensation intended to serve as incentive for performance to occur over a specified period, whether such performance is measured by reference to financial performance of the registrant or an affiliate, the registrant's stock price, or any other performance measure (an "incentive plan"), or portion of an incentive plan, under which awards are granted that fall outside the scope of FASB ASC Topic 718. *See* Item 402(a)(6)(iii). Consequently, such a plan is most commonly a cash-based incentive plan.

9. Item 402(d)(2)(iii).

10. For these purposes, the term "stock" means instruments such as common stock, restricted stock, restricted stock units, phantom stock, phantom stock units, common stock equivalent units, or any similar instruments that do not have option-like features. *See* Item 402(a)(6)(i).

11. For these purposes, the term "option" means instruments such as stock options, stock appreciation rights, and similar instruments with option-like features. *See* Item 402(a)(6)(i).

12. Item 402(d)(2)(iv).

13. Item 402(d)(2)(v).

14. Item 402(d)(2)(vi).

15. Item 402(d)(2)(vii).

closing market price on the date of grant is to be added between columns (k) and (l);[16] and

- the grant date fair value of each equity award reported in the table, computed in accordance with Financial Accounting Standards Board (FASB) Accounting Standards Codification Topic 718, *Compensation – Stock Compensation* (FASB ASC Topic 718) (column (l)).[17]

Each award, regardless of type, made to a NEO during the last completed fiscal year is to be reported on a separate line in the table.[18] This includes awards that subsequently have been transferred as well as awards that are still held.[19]

If awards were made to a NEO during the last completed fiscal year under more than one plan, the registrant must identify the particular plan under which each different award was made.[20] This may be done in the table itself (through the insertion of an additional column) or with one or more footnotes. Finally, if a NEO has paid any consideration for an award reported in the table, the dollar amount of such consideration is to be reported in a footnote to the appropriate column.[21]

As with most of the disclosure tables, the applicable fiscal year is to be added to the title of the table.[22]

Identification of Named Executive Officers

Column (a) of the table is to list each of the registrant's NEOs for the last completed fiscal year. Unlike the Summary Compensation Table,

---

16. *Id.*

17. Item 402(d)(2)(viii).

18. *See* Instruction 1 to Item 402(d). As proposed, the table would have permitted the aggregation of option grants with the same exercise or base price. However, because of disclosure concerns regarding stock option grant practices, this approach was not adopted. *See* the Adopting Release, *supra* note 1, at Section II.C.1.c.i.

19. *See* Item 402(d)(1).

20. *Id.*

21. *See* Instruction 5 to Item 402(d). As proposed, this information would have been reported in a column of the table itself. *See* Proposed Item 402(d)(2)(v). This requirement was changed in the rules in recognition of the fact that consideration is only rarely paid for an award.

22. *See* the Instruction to Item 402.

it is not necessary to include the executive's principal position when he or she is being identified.

Equity Award Grant Dates

Column (b) of the table is to report the grant date for any equity award (whether a stock award or option award) reported in the table. For this purpose, an award's grant date will be the date determined for financial statement reporting purposes pursuant to FASB ASC Topic 718.[23]

Where an equity award's grant date differs from the date on which the board compensation committee (or a committee of the board of directors performing a similar function or the full board of directors) took action (or was deemed to have taken action) to grant the award, a registrant must insert a separate, adjoining column between columns (b) and (c) of the table and report this additional date. This disclosure requirement reflects the significance of grant date issues in grants of stock options and other equity awards, and was added to the executive compensation disclosure rules in response to concerns that if the date on which the board compensation committee takes action to grant an equity-based award differs from its date of grant for financial statement reporting purposes, this is information that would be relevant to investors.

---

23. *See* Instruction 6 to Item 402(a)(3). Under FASB ASC Topic 718, the term "grant date" means the date at which an employer and an employee reach a mutual understanding of the key terms and conditions of a share-based payment award. *See* FASB ASC 718-10-20. Practice has developed such that the grant date of an award is generally the date the award is approved in accordance with an entity's corporate governance provisions, so long as the approved grant is communicated to employees within a relatively short time period after the date of approval. *See* FASB ASC 718-10-55-81 through 55-83. FASB ASC 718-10-55-81 provides guidance on the application of the term "mutual understanding" in fixing the grant date of an award of employee stock-based compensation and states that a mutual understanding of the key terms and conditions of an award to an individual employee shall be presumed to exist at the date the award is approved in accordance with the relevant corporate governance requirements (that is, by the board or management with the relevant authority) if both of the following conditions are met: (1) the award is a unilateral grant and, therefore, the recipient does not have the ability to negotiate the key terms and conditions of the award with the employer, and (2) the key terms and conditions of the award are expected to be communicated to an individual recipient within a relatively short time period from the date of approval. *Id.* A "relatively short time period" is that period in which an entity could reasonably complete all actions necessary to communicate the awards to the recipients in accordance with the entity's customary human resource practices. *Id.*

Nonequity Incentive Plan Award Disclosure

Columns (c), (d), and (e) of the table are to report specified information about any nonequity incentive plan awards made to the NEOs during the last completed fiscal year. The information to be reported is the value of the estimated future payout upon satisfaction of the awards' performance conditions, or the applicable range of estimated payouts.[24] These columns encompass both annual and long-term nonequity incentive plan awards. They are to reflect any nonstock grants of incentive plan awards made during the last completed fiscal year that are performance-based[25] and, thus, provide the opportunity for future compensation if the specified performance conditions are satisfied.[26]

Given the Summary Compensation Table's reporting requirements for nonequity incentive plan compensation—awards are disclosed only as they are earned—the executive compensation disclosure rules operate somewhat differently in the case of annual, as opposed to long-term, awards.

In the case of an annual nonequity incentive plan award, typically the award's performance period will have been completed by the time the table is prepared. Thus, the actual amount earned under the award opportunity will be known. Nonetheless, the staff of the Securities and Exchange Commission's (SEC's) Division of Corporation Finance (SEC Staff) has indicated that the rules require a registrant to report in the table the available information about the potential award opportunity as it was established at the beginning of the performance period.

Given that the award payout will probably be concurrently reported in the Summary Compensation Table, the heading for this set of columns, "Estimated Future Payouts Under Nonequity Incentive Plan Awards," could potentially be misleading. As a result, the SEC Staff has indicated that, where all of the nonequity incentive plan awards made during the last completed fiscal year were made for annual plans and, thus, the awards payable have already been earned, it is permissible to

---

24. See W. Alan Kailer, *The Securities and Exchange Commission's Executive Compensation Rules—Preparing the Executive Compensation Tables* (Jan. 2012), at B-12.

25. This would include awards with performance, market, and other conditions affecting the terms of the award (exercise price, for example) rather than service-based vesting conditions.

26. This is similar to the approach taken in the former Long-Term Incentive Plan Awards Table. *See* former Item 402(e).

change the heading over columns (c), (d), and (e) to read "Estimated Possible Payouts Under Nonequity Incentive Plan Awards."[27]

In the case of a long-term nonequity incentive plan award, typically the award's performance period will extend for two or more years. Thus, the actual amount earned under the award opportunity, if any, will not be known for some period of time. As a result, the information about these awards reported in the table will not be reflected concurrently in the Summary Compensation Table, belying the SEC's notion that the table fully complements the information reported in that table.

The information called for by columns (c), (d), and (e) needs to be reported only to the extent that it is reflected in the applicable plan or arrangement.[28] If a plan or arrangement does not include thresholds or maximums (or equivalent items), the registrant need not include arbitrary sample threshold and maximum amounts.[29]

For purposes of columns (c), (d), and (e), the term "threshold" in column (c) refers to the minimum amount payable for a certain level of performance under the plan or arrangement, the term "target" in column (d) refers to the amount payable if the specified performance target or targets are achieved, and the term "maximum" in column (e) refers to the maximum payout possible under the plan or arrangement.[30] If an award provides only for a single estimated payout, that amount must be reported in column (d) as the target amount.[31] In the case of some long-term nonequity incentive awards, the target amount may not be determinable at the time the table is prepared. In these instances, the registrant must provide a representative amount based on the previous

---

27. *See* Division of Corporation Finance, Compliance and Disclosure Interpretations – Regulation S-K (July 8, 2011) [hereinafter Current Staff Guidance], *available at* http://www.sec. gov/divisions/corpfin/guidance/regs-kinterp.htm, at Q&A 120.02. This change is permissible as long as the awards were made in the same year that they were earned and, therefore, the earned amounts are disclosed in the Summary Compensation Table.

28. *See* Instruction 2 to Item 402(d).

29. *See* the Current Staff Guidance, *supra* note 27, at Interpretation 220.02. For example, in the case of a nonequity incentive plan that does not specify threshold or maximum payout amounts (for example, a plan in which each unit entitles a NEO to $1.00 of payment for each $.01 increase in earnings per share during the performance period), threshold and maximum levels need not be shown as "0" and "N/A" because the payouts theoretically may range from nothing to infinity. Rather, an appropriate footnote should state that there are no thresholds or maximums (or equivalent items).

30. *Id.*

31. *Id.*

fiscal year's performance in column (d).[32] For this purpose, the SEC Staff has informally indicated that the "previous fiscal year" means the last completed fiscal year, not the fiscal year preceding that year.[33]

If a nonequity incentive plan award is denominated in units or other rights, a separate, adjoining column is to be added between columns (b) and (c) quantifying the units or other rights awarded.[34] The material modification of a nonequity incentive plan award does not have to be reported in this column (or in the table).[35]

The SEC Staff has taken the position that, where a NEO elects to receive settlement of a nonequity incentive compensation plan award in shares of the registrant's stock, the award should be reported in columns (c) through (e) of the table, rather than in the columns reserved for stock or option awards.[36] The shares of stock subsequently received upon settlement of the award should not also be reported in the table, however, because that would result in "double counting" the award.[37]

The SEC Staff has also taken the position that, where a NEO is granted an annual incentive award that permits him or her to elect, at the time of the award, whether to receive payment of the award in either cash or shares of stock, the reporting of the award will depend on the executive officer's choice of the form of payment. In the case of a NEO who elects to receive payment of the award in cash, the Staff has indicated that the award is to be reported in columns (c), (d), and (e) of the table as a nonequity incentive plan award.[38] In the case of a NEO who elects to receive payment of the award in shares of stock, the Staff has indicated that the award is to be reported in columns (f), (g), and (h) of the table as an equity incentive award.[39]

---

32. *Id.* For example, the amount of a registrant's increase in earnings-per-share experienced in the prior fiscal year. *See* Kailer, *supra* note 24, at B-12.

33. *See* Questions and Answers, Technical Session Between the SEC Staff and the Joint Committee on Employee Benefits (May 8, 2007) [hereinafter 2007 JCEB Questions], *available at* http://www.abanet.org/jceb/2007/SEC07Final.pdf, at Question No. 9.

34. *See* Instruction 6 to Item 402(d).

35. *See* the Adopting Release, *supra* note 1, at n.241 and the accompanying text.

36. *See* the Current Staff Guidance, *supra* note 27, at Q&A 119.22.

37. *Id.*

38. *See* the Current Staff Guidance, *supra* note 27, at Q&A 119.23. The award would also be treated as a nonequity incentive plan award for purposes of the Summary Compensation Table. *Id.*

39. *Id.* The SEC Staff further indicated that the award should be treated as an equity incentive award even if the amount of the award is not determined until early in the year

Equity Incentive Plan Award Disclosure

Columns (f), (g), and (h) of the table are to report specified information about any awards made under equity incentive plans to the NEOs during the last completed fiscal year. Thus, these columns encompass both stock and option awards with performance-based vesting conditions. The number of shares of stock (or shares underlying options) or dollar amount of estimated future payouts, or the range of estimated payouts, expressed as threshold, target, and maximum payout amounts, must be reported for all types of equity incentive plan awards.

As in the case of nonequity incentive plan awards, the information called for by columns (f), (g), and (h) needs to be reported only to the extent that it is reflected in the applicable plan or arrangement.[40] Again, the term "threshold" in column (f) refers to the minimum amount payable for a certain level of performance under the plan or arrangement, the term "target" in column (g) refers to the amount payable if the specified performance target or targets are achieved, and the term "maximum" in column (h) refers to the maximum payout possible under the plan or arrangement.[41] If an award provides only for a single estimated payout, that amount must be reported in column (g) as the target amount.[42] In the case of some long-term equity incentive awards, the target amount may not be determinable at the time the table is prepared. In these instances, the registrant must provide a representative amount based on the previous fiscal year's performance in column (g).[43] For this purpose, the SEC Staff has informally indicated that the "previous fiscal year" means the last completed fiscal year, not the fiscal year preceding that year.[44]

An equity incentive plan award may be denominated in dollars but payable in stock. This presents a potential disclosure issue since the headings for columns (f), (g), and (h) refer only to numbers and not dollars. The SEC Staff has indicated that such an award should be reported in the table by including its dollar value and using a footnote

---

following the year of grant since all registrant decisions necessary to determine the value of the award are made in the year of grant. *Id.*

40. *See* Instruction 2 to Item 402(d).

41. *Id.*

42. *Id.*

43. *Id.*

44. *See* the 2007 JCEB Questions, *supra* note 33, at Question No. 9.

to the appropriate column or columns to explain that the award will be paid out in stock in the form of whatever number of shares that amount translates into at the time of the payout. In addition, in this limited circumstance, and where all of the awards to be reported in these columns are structured in this manner, it is permissible to change the captions for columns (f), (g), and (h) to show "($)" instead of "(#)."[45]

The material modification of an equity incentive plan stock award does not have to be reported in this column (or in the table).[46] The repricing or material modification of an equity incentive plan option award must be reported, however.[47]

Stock Awards Disclosure

Column (i) of the table is to disclose the number of shares of stock that were granted to each of the NEOs during the last completed fiscal year that were not equity incentive plan awards. Accordingly, this column is used to separately report each service-based stock award made during the last completed fiscal year. The number to be reported is the actual number of shares of stock subject to the award.

Where an award consists of a tandem grant of two instruments, only one of which is granted under an incentive plan, such as a restricted stock award granted in tandem with a performance share, the award is to be reported in the table only once, and only the instrument that is not granted under an incentive plan is disclosed (in column (i)), with the tandem feature noted.[48] For example, a restricted stock award granted in tandem with a performance share is to be reported only as a stock award in column (i), with the tandem feature noted either by a footnote to the column or in the textual narrative accompanying the table.

Where a NEO exercises a "reload" stock option and receives additional stock options upon such exercise, a registrant is required to report the additional options as an option grant in the table.[49]

---

45. *See* the Current Staff Guidance, *supra* note 27, at Q&A 120.01.

46. *See* the Adopting Release, *supra* note 1, at n.241 and the accompanying text.

47. *See* Instruction 7 to Item 402(d).

48. *See* Instruction 4 to Item 402(d).

49. *See* the Current Staff Guidance, *supra* note 27, at Interpretation 220.01. The registrant would also include the grant date fair value of the additional options in the aggregate amount reported in the Summary Compensation Table. *Id.*

The material modification of a stock award does not have to be reported in this column (or in the table).[50]

Option Awards Disclosure

Column (j) of the table is to disclose the number of securities underlying stock options, stock appreciation rights (SARs), and similar instruments that were granted to each of the NEOs during the last completed fiscal year that were not equity incentive plan awards. Accordingly, this column is used to separately report each service-based option grant made during the last completed fiscal year. The number to be reported is the gross number of securities underlying the option, SAR, or other similar instrument.

Where an award consists of a tandem grant of two instruments, only one of which is granted under an incentive plan, such as a stock option granted in tandem with a performance share, the award is to be reported in the table only once, and only the instrument that is not granted under an incentive plan is disclosed (in column (j)), with the tandem feature noted.[51] For example, an option granted in tandem with a performance share is to be reported only as an option award in column (j), with the tandem feature noted either by a footnote to the column or in the textual narrative accompanying the table.

Where a NEO exercises a "reload" stock option and receives an additional option upon the exercise, a registrant is required to report the additional option as a stock option grant in this column.[52] Each reload exercise triggers a separate option grant that should be reported on a separate line of the table.[53]

The repricing or material modification of a stock option award must be reported.[54]

---

50. *See* the Adopting Release, *supra* note 1, at n.241 and the accompanying text.

51. *See* Instruction 4 to Item 402(d).

52. *See* the Current Staff Guidance, *supra* note 27, at Interpretation 220.01. The dollar amount recognized for the additional stock options for financial statement reporting purposes with respect to the fiscal year in accordance with FASB ASC Topic 718 is to be reported in the Summary Compensation Table. *Id.*

53. *See* Kailer, *supra* note 24, at B-11.

54. *See* Instruction 7 to Item 402(d).

Exercise or Base Price Information

Column (k) of the table is to disclose the exercise or base price of any stock option granted to a NEO during the last completed fiscal year that has been reported in the table.

An additional purpose for this column is to highlight irregular or potentially abusive option grant practices.[55] To bring to investors' attention situations where an option's exercise or base price differs from the market price of the underlying security on the option's grant date, the registrant must highlight any such discrepancy in the table. If the per-share exercise or base price of an option is less than the closing market price[56] of the underlying security on the grant date, a separate column must be added after column (k) and before column (l) reporting the closing market price of the registrant's securities on the grant date. In addition, if the exercise or base price is not the grant date closing market price per share, the registrant must describe the methodology used to determine the exercise or base price either in a footnote to the table or in the textual narrative accompanying the table.[57]

The decision to use the closing market price to trigger this additional disclosure was controversial. Previously, the SEC's rules permitted the use of a range of different formulas to determine a security's "fair market value," even for securities traded on an established market. Ultimately, the SEC determined that the significance of the issues involving equity award grant practices warranted the move to a single standard.

Thus, as a practical matter, a registrant that uses a different methodology to determine the fair market value of its securities when granting stock options (for example, the average market price on the grant date, the average market price for a specified range of days either before or after the grant date, or the closing market price of the underlying security on the date preceding the grant date) will find that it almost always needs to include both columns in the table. Even where a registrant does not use the closing market price on the grant date to

---

55. *See* the Adopting Release, *supra* note 1, at Section II.A.

56. For these purposes, "closing market price" means the price at which the registrant's security was last sold in the principal U.S. market for such security as of the date for which the closing market price is determined. *See* Instruction 6 to Item 402(a)(3). A foreign company complying with this requirement may look to the principal foreign market in which the underlying securities trade for the appropriate closing market price. *See* the Adopting Release, *supra* note 1, at n.247.

57. *See* Instruction 3 to Item 402(d).

determine fair market value, however, the additional column will not always be necessary. Where the closing market price on the grant date *is less than* the per-share exercise or base price of an option, the additional column is not required.

In determining if the exercise or base price of an option is less than the closing market price of the underlying security on the date of the grant, the registrant may use either the closing market price in the principal U.S. market for such security as of the date for which the closing market price is determined,[58] or if no market exists for the security, any other formula prescribed for the security.[59]

Grant Date Fair Value Information

Column (l) of the table is to disclose the grant date fair value of each equity award reported in the table. This fair value amount is to be computed in accordance with FASB ASC Topic 718. In reporting this amount, a registrant is to disregard any estimate of forfeitures related to service-based vesting conditions.[60] Where the number of shares or stock options that will vest is tied to the achievement of performance conditions, the amount to be reported in this column should be the grant date fair value for the number of shares or options that reflect the probable outcome of the conditions that could be earned.[61]

As the rules were originally adopted, the aggregated fair value of stock and option awards was to be reported in the Summary Compensation Table.[62] In December 2006, as part of a series of changes to that table,[63] this disclosure was moved to the Grants of Plan-Based Awards Table.[64] Consistent with the presentation of other information in this table, these fair value amounts are to be provided on a grant-by-grant basis.[65] Thus,

---

58. *See* Instruction 6 to Item 402(a)(3).

59. *See* Instruction 3 to Item 402(d).

60. Technically, since the adjustment for forfeitures related to service-based vesting conditions permitted under FASB ASC Topic 718 is a recognition, rather than a valuation, principle, it should not come into play in reporting fair value amounts in column (l).

61. *See* Instruction 8 to Item 402(d). *See also* the Current Staff Guidance *supra* note 27, at Q&A 119.20.

62. *See* the Adopting Release, *supra* note 1, at Section II.C.1.c.i.

63. *See* Executive Compensation Disclosure, Release Nos. 33-8765, 34-55009 (Dec. 22, 2006), 71 Fed. Reg. 78,338 (Dec. 29, 2006) [hereinafter December 2006 Release], *available at* http://www.sec.gov/rules/final/2006/33-8765.pdf.

64. *See* Item 402(d)(2)(vii).

65. *See* the December 2006 Release, *supra* note 57, at Section II.B.

this information supplements the number of shares underlying an award and the other details about the award included in the table. When the SEC reversed the reporting treatment of stock and option awards in the Summary Compensation Table in December 2009,[66] it retained column (l), largely because of its grant-by-grant presentation.[67]

Where, at any time during the last completed fiscal year, a registrant has repriced[68] the exercise or base price of an option previously awarded to a NEO, or otherwise materially modified such an award, the incremental fair value of the repriced option or modified award, computed in accordance with FASB ASC Topic 718 as of the repricing or modification date, is also to be reported in column (l).[69] Consistent with the presentation of other information in the table, this disclosure is also to be made on a grant-by-grant basis.[70]

The SEC Staff has taken the position that, in the case of a long-term incentive plan where a NEO receives an award for a target number of shares at the start of a three-year period, with one-third of this amount allocated to each of the three single-year performance periods, for purposes of the disclosure required by column (l) of the table the grant

---

66. *See* Proxy Disclosure Enhancements, Release Nos. 33-9089, 34-61175, IC-29092 (Dec. 16, 2009), 74 Fed. Reg. 68,334 (Dec. 23, 2009) [hereinafter 2009 Adopting Release], *available at* http://www.sec.gov/rules/final/2009/33-9089.pdf.

67. As proposed, the SEC contemplated rescinding the requirement to report the full grant date fair value of each individual equity award in the Grants of Plan-Based Awards Table because this disclosure could have been considered duplicative of the aggregate grant date fair value to be provided in the amended Summary Compensation Table. *See* Proxy Disclosure and Solicitation Enhancements, Release Nos. 33-9052, 34-60280, IC-28817 (July 10, 2009), 74 Fed. Reg. 35,076 (July 17, 2009), *available at* http:www.sec.gov/rules/proposed/2009/33-9052.pdf, at Section II.A.2. Based on the comments received, however, the SEC decided to retain this requirement because this disclosure reveals the value associated with each type of equity award granted and the mix of values among various awards with different incentive effects, thereby helping investors better evaluate the decisions of the compensation committee. *See* the 2009 Adopting Release, *supra* note 66, at Section II.A.2.c.

68. For these purposes, the term "reprice" means to adjust or amend the exercise price of an option, whether through amendment, cancellation, or replacement grants, or any other means. *See* Item 402(d)(2)(vii).

69. *Id. See also* Instruction 7 to Item 402(d). *See also* the Current Staff Guidance, *supra* note 27, at Q&A 120.07. This disclosure does not apply to any repricing that occurs through a preexisting formula or mechanism in the plan or award that results in the periodic adjustment of the option's exercise or base price, an antidilution provision in a plan or award, or a recapitalization or similar transaction equally affecting all holders of the class of securities underlying the options. *Id.* Nor does it apply, consistent with FASB ASC Topic 718, to any modification that equalizes the fair value of an award before and after the modification. *See* the December 2006 Release, *supra* note 63, at Section II.B.

70. *See* the December 2006 Release, *supra* note 63, at Section II.B.

date fair value of the award is to be determined as provided in FASB ASC Topic 718 as follows:

- If all of the annual performance targets are set at the start of the three-year period, the amount to be reported is the grant date fair value for the entire award.[71] In other words, the grant date fair value for all three tranches of the award would be measured at that time and reported in column (l).[72]
- If each annual performance target is to be set at the start of each respective single-year performance period, each of these dates is considered to be a separate grant date for purposes of measuring the grant date fair value of the respective tranche.[73] In this instance, only the grant date fair value for the first year's performance period would be measured as reported in column (l).[74]

Transferred Awards

For several years, registrants have offered their employees, particularly their executives, the ability to transfer their equity awards. While traditionally this feature has been offered to facilitate tax and estate planning, recently a few registrants have begun to permit employees to transfer their awards, particularly options, for value to one or more designated third parties, typically a financial institution. If a NEO receives an award during the last completed fiscal year that is subsequently transferred, whether or not for value, that award must still be reported in the table.[75]

---

71. *See* FASB ASC Topic 718-55-Example 3-Case A.
72. *See* the Current Staff Guidance, *supra* note 27, at Q&A 120.06.
73. See FASB ASC Topic 718-55-Example 3-Case B.
74. *See* the Current Staff Guidance, *supra* note 27, at Q&A 120.06.
75. Item 402(d)(1).

7

Supplemental Narrative Disclosure

General

A key aspect of the executive compensation disclosure rules is the Securities and Exchange Commission's (SEC's) decision to separate the analysis of a registrant's executive compensation program (which is to be addressed in the Compensation Discussion and Analysis (CD&A)) from the summary descriptions of individual program elements. One of the major disappointments of the former Board Compensation Committee Report was its gradual devolution into a "boilerplate" recitation of the principal terms and conditions of the plans and arrangements comprising a registrant's executive compensation program. To avoid a repeat of this result with the CD&A, and to ensure that it will focus instead on a discussion of the policies and reasons for a program's components and individual pay decisions, the rules require that much of this descriptive information accompany the compensation tables where it can give context to the tabular disclosure.[1]

---

1. *See* Executive Compensation and Related Person Disclosure, Release Nos. 33-8732A, 34-54302A, IC-27444A (Aug. 29, 2006), 71 Fed. Reg. 53,158 (Sept. 8, 2006) [hereinafter Adopting Release], available at http://www.sec.gov/rules/final/2006/33-8732a.pdf, at Section II.C.3.

Thus, under the rules, a registrant is required to supplement the Summary Compensation Table and the Grants of Plan-Based Awards Table with a narrative description of the material[2] factors necessary to an understanding of the information disclosed in the tables.[3] Unlike the CD&A, which is to focus on broader topics concerning the objectives and implementation of a registrant's executive compensation policies, this narrative disclosure is to focus on the specific context to the quantitative information in the compensation tables, addressing any material factors necessary to an investor's understanding of this information. For example, as noted in the Adopting Release, the narrative disclosure following a compensation table might explain the material aspects of a plan that are not evident from the quantitative tabular disclosure and are not addressed in the CD&A.[4] Requiring this disclosure in proximity to the Summary Compensation Table and the Grants of Plan-Based Awards Table is intended to make the tabular disclosure more meaningful, as is presenting the information in a prominent narrative discussion rather than a footnote to the relevant table. While the rules expressly cover the Summary Compensation Table and Grants of Plan-Based Awards Table, this directive to supplement tabular disclosure with additional narrative disclosure if necessary to make the information presented meaningful can be found throughout the required compensation table disclosures.[5]

Necessarily, these material factors will vary among registrants depending on the particular facts and circumstances. To assist registrants in assessing the type of information to be included in the required

---

2. The standard of materiality that applies in Item 402(e) is that of *Basic v. Levinson*, 485 U.S. 224 (1988), and *TSC Industries v. Northway*, 426 U.S. 438 (1976). Under this standard, information is considered "material" if there is "a substantial likelihood that the disclosure of the [information] would have been viewed by the reasonable investor as having significantly altered the 'total mix' of information made available." *Basic*, 485 U.S. at 240.

3. Item 402(e)(1) of Regulation S-K. *See also* Item 402(o), which, in the case of smaller reporting companies, references the Summary Compensation Table only because a smaller reporting company is not required to provide a Grants of Plan-Based Awards Table.

4. *See* the Adopting Release, *supra* note 1, at Section II.C.3.

5. For example, if the exercise price of an employee stock option is based on something other than the closing market price on the date of grant, this must be disclosed and explained. *See* Instruction 3 to Item 402(d). Similarly, a registrant must provide a succinct narrative description of any material factors necessary to an understanding of any defined benefit pension and actuarial plans and any nonqualified defined contribution and other nonqualified deferred compensation plans in which the NEOs participate. *See* Item 402(h)(3) and Item 402(i)(3).

narrative description, the rules contain a nonexhaustive list of examples of the type of factors that may warrant discussion:[6]

- the material terms of each named executive officer's (NEO's) employment agreement or arrangement, whether written or unwritten;[7]

- if at any time during the last fiscal year, any outstanding stock option or other equity-based award was repriced or otherwise materially modified, a description of each such repricing or other material modification;[8]

- the material terms of any award reported in the Grants of Plan-Based Awards Table,[9] including a general description of the formula or criteria to be applied in determining the amounts payable, and the vesting schedule. For example, a registrant should state where applicable that dividends will be paid on stock, and if so, the applicable dividend rate and whether that rate is preferential. The registrant should also describe any performance-based conditions, and any other material conditions, that are applicable to the award. For purposes of the Grants of Plan-Based Awards Table and this supplemental narrative disclosure, performance-based conditions include both performance conditions and market conditions, as those terms are defined in Financial Accounting Standards Board Accounting Standards Codification Topic 718, *Compensation – Stock Compensation* (FASB ASC Topic 718);[10] and

- an explanation of the amount of salary and bonus in proportion to total compensation.[11]

---

6. A proposed example concerning the waiver or modification of any specified performance target, goal, or condition to payout with respect to any amount included in nonequity incentive plan compensation reported in the Summary Compensation Table, stating whether the waiver or modification applied to one or more specified NEOs or to all compensation subject to the target, goal, or condition (see Proposed Item 402(f)(1)(iv)), was moved to the list of examples of possibly material information to be discussed in the CD&A when the rules were adopted. *See* the Adopting Release, *supra* note 1, at Section II.B.1, and Item 402(b)(2)(vi). This change also expanded the scope of the example so that it is no longer limited to nonequity incentive plan compensation. *Id.*

7. Item 402(e)(1)(i).

8. Item 402(e)(1)(ii).

9. *See* Chapter 6.

10. Item 402(e)(1)(iii). *See* "Definitions—Equity Incentive Plan" in Chapter 2.

11. Item 402(e)(1)(iv).

Initially, many registrants included information that was more properly part of this required narrative disclosure in their CD&A. As the staff of the SEC's Division of Corporation Finance (SEC Staff) made clear following the 2007 proxy season, these discussions should be moved to the narrative following the appropriate compensation tables or the footnotes to those tables.[12] While there has been a noticeable improvement in the presentation of this information in subsequent years, particularly among large registrants, some companies continue to include much of this information in one or more footnotes to the Summary Compensation Table and the Grants of Plan-Based Awards Table rather than in narrative form.

Employment Agreements

Where a registrant has an employment agreement with a NEO, it may be appropriate to describe the material terms of that agreement to provide investors with information necessary to understand of the related tabular disclosure (for example, the base salary set for or size of equity awards granted to the executive).[13] While this discussion will be fairly straightforward in the case of a written employment agreement or arrangement, it may potentially be more difficult with unwritten arrangements (such as, for example, where the registrant has an "understanding" with a NEO).[14] Essentially, a registrant must exercise its judgment to determine and describe the information that an investor would consider important about these agreements and arrangements (whether written or unwritten), including information that may not be evident from the compensation tables.

---

12. See Division of Corporation Finance, *Staff Observations in the Review of Executive Compensation Disclosure* (Oct. 9, 2007), *available at* http://www.sec.gov/divisions/corpfin/guidance/execcompdisclosure.htm, under the heading "Clarity."

13. Disclosure of the terms and conditions of an employment agreement between a registrant and a NEO was previously required by former Item 402(h)(1). While the SEC solicited comment on whether it should require an additional column in the Summary Compensation Table where registrants would indicate by checkmark whether a particular NEO had an employment agreement, so that investors would know to look for disclosure about the agreement in the narrative discussion accompanying the table or to look for the agreement as an exhibit to a SEC filing, it did not adopt such a requirement.

14. As noted in the Adopting Release, depending on the circumstances, the mere filing of an employment agreement (or a summary of an oral agreement) with the SEC may not be adequate to make its material provisions accessible to investors. *See* the Adopting Release, *supra* note 1, at Section II.C.3.a.

A typical provision in many employment agreements will address the postemployment compensation arrangements between the registrant and the NEO. Provisions regarding post employment compensation need be addressed as part of this supplemental narrative disclosure only to the extent that the reporting of this compensation is required in the Summary Compensation Table.[15] In all other situations, these provisions should be addressed as part of the required postemployment compensation disclosure.[16]

Option and Other Equity-Based Award Repricings

In the event that a registrant has repriced stock option or stock appreciation right (SAR) held by a NEO during the last completed fiscal year, it may be necessary to describe the repricing to provide investors with material information necessary to understand of the related tabular disclosure concerning the repriced instrument or instruments.[17] Similarly, if a registrant has modified a material term or condition of an outstanding equity-based award (such as by extension of its exercise periods, the change of vesting or forfeiture conditions, the change or elimination of applicable performance criteria, or the change of the bases upon which returns are determined) held by a NEO during the last completed fiscal year, it may be necessary to describe the modification to provide investors with material information necessary to understand the related tabular disclosure concerning the modified award. The incremental fair value for financial statement reporting purposes of any repricing or modification of an equity award is to be reported in the Summary Compensation Table.[18]

---

15. *See* Item 402(c)(2)(ix)(D). In the case of a NEO who is a former executive officer who terminated employment during the last completed fiscal year, it is probably not necessary to describe the terms and conditions of the employment agreement beyond the severance arrangements, notwithstanding that the individual is technically a NEO.

16. *See* Item 402(j). While the SEC proposed an instruction to this effect (*see* Instruction 1 to Proposed Item 402(f)(1)), this instruction was not adopted.

17. This "principles-based" disclosure is intended to provide investors with more current and relevant information about stock option and SAR repricings and replaces the arguably dated information contained in the former Ten Year Option/SAR Repricings Table. This is why former Item 402(i) was eliminated.

18. *See* Chapter 4.

Note, however, that the contemplated disclosure does not apply to any repricing that occurs through a preexisting formula or mechanism in the applicable plan or award that results in the periodic adjustment of the stock option or SAR exercise or base price, an antidilution provision in a plan or award, or a recapitalization or similar transaction equally affecting all holders of the class of securities underlying the options or SARs.[19]

Performance-Based Compensation

The narrative discussion may need to describe, to the extent material and necessary to understand the related tabular disclosure, the material terms and conditions of the awards reported in the Grants of Plan-Based Awards Table. This could include, for example, a general description of the formula or criteria to be applied in determining the amounts payable, the vesting schedule, a description of the performance-based conditions[20] and any other material conditions applicable to the award, whether dividends or other amounts would be paid, and, if so, the applicable rate and whether that rate is preferential.[21] A reload feature of a stock option may also need to be described in this narrative discussion.[22]

Consistent with the requirements applicable to the CD&A, however, registrants are not required to disclose any target levels with respect to specific quantitative or qualitative performance based-factors considered by the board compensation committee or the board of directors, or any other factors or criteria involving confidential trade secrets or confidential commercial or financial information, the disclosure of which would result in competitive harm for the registrant. For purposes of this analysis, a registrant is to apply the same standards applicable to

---

19. *See* Instruction 1 to Item 402(e)(1).

20. For purposes of this narrative disclosure, the term "performance-based conditions" include both performance conditions and market conditions, as those terms are defined in FASB ASC Topic 718. *See* "Definitions—Equity Incentive Plan" in Chapter 2.

21. Item 402(e)(1)(iii). This provision combines some of the information that had been required by Instruction 2 to former Item 402(b)(2)(iv) with information that had been required by Instruction 1 to former Item 402(e).

22. See W. Alan Kailer, Hunton & Williams, *The Securities and Exchange Commission's Executive Compensation Rules—Preparing the Executive Compensation Tables* (Jan. 2012), at A-12 and B-11.

determining whether similar disclosure in the CD&A would result in competitive harm.[23]

Compensation Mix

To aid investors' understanding of NEOs' total compensation and the use of total pay to determine a registrant's most highly compensated executive officers, the narrative discussion may need to explain the level of a NEO's base salary and bonus in proportion to his or her total compensation.[24]

Smaller Reporting Companies

In the case of a smaller reporting company, the nonexhaustive list of examples of the type of material factors that may warrant discussion differs from that of other registrants, reflecting the scaled disclosure that is required of such issuers. In addition to the employment agreement and equity award repricing and modification examples for regular registrants,[25] the list includes:

- the waiver or modification of any specified performance target, goal, or condition to payout with respect to any amount included in nonequity incentive plan compensation or payouts reported in the Summary Compensation Table,[26] stating whether the waiver or modification applied to one or more specified NEOs or to all compensation subject to the target, goal, or condition;[27]
- the material terms of each grant, including, but not limited to, the date of exercisability, any conditions to exercisability, any tandem feature, any reload feature, any tax-reimbursement

---

23. *See* Instruction 2 to Item 402(e)(1), which expressly refers to Instructions 4 and 5 to Item 402(b). See "Other Material Information Corporate Performance Items in Compensation Policies and Decisions—Competitive Harm Exclusion" in Chapter 3.

24. *See* Item 402(e)(1)(iv).

25. *See* Item 402(o)(1) and (2).

26. *See* Item 402(n)(2)(vii).

27. *See* Item 402(o)(3). A similar item was proposed for regular registrants. *See* Proposed Item 402(f)(1)(iv). The SEC dropped the proposal, however, deeming this information to be better addressed in the CD&A. *See* Item 402(b)(2)(vi) and the Adopting Release, *supra* note 1, at Section II.B.1. This latter disclosure covers both equity and nonequity incentive plans.

feature, and any provision that could cause the exercise price to be lowered;[28]

- the material terms of any nonequity incentive plan award made to a NEO during the last completed fiscal year, including a general description of the formula or criteria to be applied in determining the amounts payable and vesting schedules;[29]

- the method of calculating earnings on nonqualified deferred compensation plans, including nonqualified defined contribution plans;[30] and

- the identification, to the extent material, of any item included in the All Other Compensation column of the Summary Compensation Table.[31]

Two additional narrative disclosure requirements address areas that are covered by specific compensation tables for regular registrants. To the extent material, a smaller reporting company must provide a narrative description of:

- the material terms of each plan that provides for the payment of retirement benefits, or benefits that will be paid primarily following retirement, including, but not limited to, tax-qualified defined benefit plans, supplemental executive retirement plans, tax-qualified defined contribution plans, and nonqualified defined contribution plans;[32] and

- the material terms of each contract, agreement, plan, or arrangement, whether written or unwritten, that provides for a payment or payments to a NEO at, following, or in connection with the resignation, retirement, or other termination of

---

28. *See* Item 402(o)(4).

29. *See* Item 402(o)(5).

30. *See* Item 402(o)(6). A similar proposal, which also would have covered defined benefit plans (including the material assumptions underlying the determination of the amount of increase in actuarial value of such plans), was proposed for regular registrants. *See* Proposed Item 402(f)(1)(v). The SEC decided, however, that this information should be addressed in the narrative disclosure accompanying the Pension Benefits Table and the Nonqualified Deferred Compensation Table. *See* the Adopting Release, *supra* note 1, at Section II.C.3.a.

31. *See* Item 402(o)(7). Identification of an item is not considered material if the item does not exceed the greater of $25,000 or ten percent of all items included in the specified category in question in the All Other Compensation column. *Id.* All items of compensation are required to be included in the Summary Compensation Table without regard to whether such items are required to be identified. *Id.*

32. *See* Item 402(q)(1).

a NEO, or a change in control of the smaller reporting company or a change in the NEO's responsibilities following a change in control, with respect to each NEO.[33]

Nonexecutive Employee Disclosure

As part of its initial proposal, the SEC included a novel reporting item that would have required disclosure for up to three employees who were not executive officers of the registrant during the last competed fiscal year and whose total compensation for the last completed fiscal year was greater than that of any of the NEOs.[34] Ostensibly, the purpose of this disclosure was assets to provide shareholders with information about the use of a registrant's assets to compensate extremely highly paid employees.[35]

This item would have required a registrant to report the amount of each of such employee's total compensation for the last completed fiscal year and to provide a description of his or her job position. These individuals would not have needed to be identified by name. In view of the fact that these employees did not have a policy-making function with the registrant, the SEC decided that more detailed information about these individuals and their compensation was not necessary or appropriate.[36] As proposed, this item would have read as follows:

> For up to three employees who were not executive officers during the last completed fiscal year and whose total compensation for the last completed fiscal year was greater than that of any of the named executive officers, disclose each of such employee's total compensation for that year and describe their job positions.[37]

---

33. *See* Item 402(q)(2).

34. *See* Proposed Item 402(f)(2). A nonexecutive employee's total compensation would have been determined in the same manner as the NEOs. *See* Instruction 1 to Item 402(a)(3).

35. *See* Executive Compensation and Related Party Disclosure, Release Nos. 33-8655, 34-53185, IC-27218 (Jan. 27, 2006), 71 Fed. Reg. 6542 (Feb. 8, 2006) [hereinafter Proposing Release], *available at* http://www.sec.gov/rules/proposed/33-8655.pdf, at Section II.B.3. While not expressly articulated in the Proposing Release, the SEC was also motivated, in part, by a concern about the lack of transparency about the compensation of employees, particularly within large conglomerates, who, whether or not they were executive officers, earned more during the last completed fiscal year than one or more of the NEOs. *See* the Adopting Release, *supra* note 1, at Section II.C.3.b.

36. *Id.*

37. *See* Proposed Item 402(f)(2).

The proposed item was roundly criticized by registrants and investors alike as being burdensome and unnecessary.[38] Most registrants also raised concerns that requiring such disclosure would trigger privacy issues or create competitiveness problems around employee recruitment and retention. Consequently, the proposal was not adopted as part of the final rules.

At the same time, the SEC expressed a continuing belief that some level of disclosure was appropriate so that investors would have information about these highly compensated employees and be able to put into context the type of employees that were compensated at a level higher than the registrant's NEOs and better understand the compensation structure of the NEOs and directors. Thus, the SEC indicated that it intended to give the proposal further consideration and, concurrent with adopting the final executive compensation disclosure rules, requested further comment on a number of potential modifications to the item in an effort to address these concerns.[39] These potential modifications covered two specific areas.

First, given its focus on larger organizations where a key employee might have managerial responsibilities for major portions of the organization's overall business (such as leadership of a subsidiary or business unit generating a disproportionate share of the registrant's total solicited revenue or income), the SEC sought comment on whether it should limit the application of the item to large accelerated filers.[40] This approach would have effectively negated the proposal's impact on smaller registrants, thereby focusing the disclosure on registrants that were more likely to have these additional highly compensated employees (and that were, presumably, better able to track the covered employees)

---

38. While some commenters supported the proposal or suggested that it go further, most expressed concern that it would be of negligible value to investors, yet would involve considerable time and expense to ensure compliance. *See* the Adopting Release, *supra* note 1, at Section II.C.3.b.

39. *See* Executive Compensation Disclosure, Release Nos. 33-8735, 34-54380, IC-27470 (Aug. 29, 2006), 71 Fed. Reg. 53,267 (Sept. 8, 2006) [hereinafter Nonexecutive Employee Disclosure Release], *available at* http://www.sec.gov/rules/proposed/2006/33-8735.pdf.

40. The term "large accelerated filer" is defined in Exchange Act Rule 12b-2 [17 C.F.R. 240.12b-2]. At the time, the SEC estimated that there were approximately 1,700 registrants that were large accelerated filers. *See* the Nonexecutive Employee Disclosure Release, *supra* note 39, at n.13.

and responding to concerns about the potentially disproportionate compliance burden on small businesses.[41]

Second, in response to questions about the materiality to investors of the compensation of nonexecutive employees, the SEC solicited comment on whether it should narrow the scope of the item to only employees who exerted significant policy influence at the registrant or at a significant part of the registrant (such as a subsidiary or a principal business unit, division, or function). This approach was intended to mitigate concerns regarding privacy and competition for employees. Thus, modified to incorporate these changes, the proposal would have read as follows:

> For each of the company's three most highly compensated employees, whether or not they were executive officers during the last completed fiscal year, whose total compensation for the last completed fiscal year was greater than that of any of the named executive officers, disclose each such employee's total compensation for that year and describe the employee's job position, without naming the employee; *provided, however,* that employees with no responsibility for significant policy decisions within the company, a significant subsidiary of the company, or a principal business unit, division, or function of the company are not included when determining who are each of the three most highly compensated employees for the purposes of this requirement, and therefore no disclosure is required under this requirement for any employee with no responsibility for significant policy decisions within the company, a significant subsidiary of the company, or a principal business unit, division, or function of the company.[42]

Notwithstanding these possible modifications, registrants continued to be skeptical about the benefits of this disclosure item. For example, at many registrants the board compensation committee is not responsible for setting the compensation of nonexecutive employees. Consequently, it was unclear how the disclosure of this information would provide investors with insight into the committee's oversight of the registrant's executive compensation program. Nor was it clear whether (and how) this information would be relevant to their investment decisions.

---

41. The SEC estimated that the average compliance cost during the first three years of compliance would be $18,800 per registrant. *See* the Nonexecutive Employee Disclosure Release, *supra* note 39, at n.13 and the accompanying text.

42. *See* the Nonexecutive Employee Disclosure Release, *supra* note 39, at Section III.

In addition, determining whether a nonexecutive employee had responsibility for significant policy decisions was likely to be a difficult subjective judgment for most registrants, particularly given the fine distinctions that the SEC appeared to be making for identifying and delimiting the number of employees whose compensation would be subject to this item.[43] Further, even though nonexecutive employees would not need to be identified under the reconstituted proposal, many critics believed that, given the limited number of employees affected, and the requirement that their job position be described, their identities would be easily ascertained.

Finally, it was not clear that the proposed disclosure was material to investors. During the comment process, many investors expressed ambivalence about the information. Others indicated a preference that registrants devote their attention to the required disclosure about their NEOs, rather than expend effort on largely unrelated information. Even with the proposed limitation of the disclosure to significant policy makers, these questions remained.

Subsequently, the SEC took no action on the proposed item and, over the past three years, has given no indication of an intention to consider the matter further.

---

43. As described in the Nonexecutive Employee Disclosure Release, responsibility for significant policy decisions could consist of, for example, the exercise of strategic, technical, editorial, creative, managerial, or similar responsibilities. *See* the Nonexecutive Employee Disclosure Release, *supra* note 39, at Section II.C.3.b. *See also* the Adopting Release, *supra* note 1, at Section II.C.3.6. Using this approach, examples of employees who might not be executive officers but who might have responsibility for significant policy decisions could include the director of the news division of a major network, the principal creative leader of the entertainment function of a media conglomerate, or the head of a principal business unit developing a significant technological innovation. In contrast, the modified proposal would not be intended to cover a salesperson, entertainment personality, actor, singer, or professional athlete who is highly compensated but who does not have responsibility for significant policy decisions. Nor, as a general matter, would investment professionals (such as a trader, or a portfolio manager for an investment adviser who is responsible for one or more mutual funds or other clients) be deemed to have responsibility for significant policy decisions at the registrant simply as a result of performing the duties associated with those positions. On the other hand, an investment professional, such as a trader or portfolio manager, who does have broader duties within a firm (such as, for example, oversight of all equity funds for an investment adviser) may be considered to have responsibility for significant policy decisions. *Id.*

8

Outstanding Equity Awards at Fiscal Year-End Table

General

Following the grant of an equity award to a named executive officer (NEO), that award becomes part of his or her equity holdings and is reportable on an annual basis as long as he or she continues to be a NEO and the award is outstanding. The Outstanding Equity Awards at Fiscal Year-End Table presents in summary form the number of options and shares of stock that have previously been awarded to each NEO and that are outstanding and unexercised or unvested as of the end of the registrant's last completed fiscal year.[1]

The Outstanding Equity Awards at Fiscal Year-End Table essentially combines into a single format two disclosure items that were separately required under the former rules and expands the scope of what must be reported. Under the former rules, a registrant was required to disclose the total number of unexercised stock options (and stock appreciation rights (SARs)) held at the end of the last completed fiscal year, as well as

---

1. The requirements for the Outstanding Equity Awards at Fiscal Year-End Table are set forth in Item 402(f). The requirements applicable to smaller reporting companies, which are set forth in Item 402(p), are similar to those as described in this chapter.

the aggregate dollar value of the "in-the-money,"[2] unexercised options and SARs, separately identifying the exercisable and unexercisable options and SARs.[3] A registrant was also required to disclose in a footnote to the Summary Compensation Table the number and value of the aggregate restricted stock holdings at the end of the last completed fiscal year.[4] The Outstanding Equity Awards at Fiscal Year-End Table maintains the prominence of the stock option information and expands the coverage of equity awards to include stock awards other than just restricted stock.

The purpose of the table is to provide investors with material information about outstanding equity awards that have been previously granted to the NEOs but that have not yet resulted in the receipt of compensation. In effect, the table discloses amounts that represent potential compensation that may or may not be realized in future years, depending on the outcome of the conditions subject to which the awards have been granted.[5]

As proposed, the table would have included the total number of securities underlying unexercised stock options, SARs, and similar instruments with option-like features held at the end of the last completed fiscal year, as well as the aggregate in-the-money value of such options, SARs, and similar instruments.[6] As a result of comments in response to the proposed rule[7] and consistent with its response to the then-unfolding stock option backdating controversy,[8] however, the Securities and Exchange Commission (SEC) decided to (1) require disclosure of the number and key terms of all options, SARs, and similar instruments (including out-of-the-money instruments), (2) delete the requirement to disclose the value of in-the-money options, SARs, and similar instruments, and (3) require that options, SARs, and similar

---

2. "In-the-money" awards are ones where the fair market value of the underlying security exceeds the exercise or base price of the award.

3. *See* the Aggregated Option/SAR Exercises in Last Fiscal Year and Fiscal Year-End Option/SAR Values Table required by former Items 402(d)(2)(iv) and (v).

4. *See* Instruction 2(a) to former Item 402(b)(2)(iv).

5. These would include either or both service-based and performance-based vesting conditions.

6. *See* Proposed Items 402(g)(2)(ii) and (iii).

7. *See* Executive Compensation and Related Person Disclosure, Release Nos. 33-8732A, 34-54302A, IC-27444A (Aug. 29, 2006), 71 Fed. Reg. 53,158 (Sept. 8, 2006), *available at* http://www.sec.gov/rules/final/2006/33-8732a.pdf, at n.277 and the accompanying text.

8. *See* Chapter 3.

instruments be reported on a grant-by-grant, rather than an aggregated, basis. In the SEC's view, this approach would enable investors, when combined with information about exercise or base price and expiration date, to understand the potential compensation opportunity of each individual award and, in the case of out-of-the-money awards, to see how much a registrant's stock price must rise before an award would have value to the recipient and the amount of time remaining for this to happen.

The decision to require individual, rather than aggregated, reporting of options, SARs, and similar instruments with option-like features has made the Outstanding Equity Awards at Fiscal Year-End Table one of the longer compensation tables. In fact, the propensity of some companies to grant stock options to their executives each year, coupled with the tendency of many executives to hold their options until the end of their contractual term, has resulted in extensive disclosure for many NEOs; often involving ten or more separate option grants.

More problematic is the SEC's decision to omit the disclosure of the unrealized appreciation of in-the-money awards from the table. For many investors, the aggregate intrinsic value of outstanding options, SARs, and similar instruments is the most important piece of information to be derived from this disclosure. Although the tables provide adequate information for investors to make this computation themselves, it is unclear why the SEC chose to drop the requirement from the table.[9] A registrant may add a column to the table to show the unrealized appreciation in outstanding options, SARs, and similar instruments as of the end of the last completed fiscal year,[10] although, to date, few have elected to do so.[11]

---

9. Informally, the SEC Staff has questioned the need for the table to include intrinsic value information as of the end of the last completed fiscal year (which makes the information several months old when it is eventually disclosed), pointing out that investors can make a current—and more meaningful—calculation at any time.

10. It is permissible to add a column to the table to show the unrealized appreciation in outstanding stock options as of the end of the registrant's last completed fiscal year as long as the column does not make the disclosure misleading or unclear. *See* Questions and Answers, Technical Session Between the SEC Staff and the Joint Committee on Employee Benefits (May 8, 2007) [hereinafter 2007 JCEB Questions], *available at* http://www.abanet.org/jceb/2007/SEC07Final.pdf, at Question No. 8.

11. *See, e.g.,* the Staples, Inc. Definitive Proxy Statement (Form 14A) filed May 3, 2007 (file no. 000-17586).

Tabular Format

The Outstanding Equity Awards at Fiscal Year-End Table is to be presented in the following tabular format:[12]

OUTSTANDING EQUITY AWARDS AT FISCAL YEAR-END

Name	Option Awards					Stock Awards			
	Number of Securities Underlying Unexercised Options (#) Exercisable	Number of Securities Underlying Unexercised Options (#) Unexercisable	Equity Incentive Plan Awards: Number of Securities Underlying Unexercised Unearned Options (#)	Option Exercise Price ($)	Option Expiration Date	Number of Shares or Units of Stock That Have Not Vested (#)	Market Value of Shares or Units of Stock That Have Not Vested ($)	Equity Incentive Plan Awards: Number of Unearned Shares, Units, or Other Rights That Have Not Vested (#)	Equity Incentive Plan Awards: Market or Payout Value of Unearned Shares, Units, or Other Rights That Have Not Vested ($)
(a)	(b)	(c)	(d)	(e)	(f)	(g)	(h)	(i)	(j)
Principal Executive Officer (PEO)									
Principal Financial Officer (PFO)									
A									
B									
C									

The table includes the following information concerning unexercised stock options, stock that has not vested, and equity incentive plan awards outstanding as of the end of the registrant's last completed fiscal year:

- the name of the NEO (column (a));[13]
- the number of securities underlying unexercised options,[14] including awards that have been transferred other than for value, that are exercisable and that are not reported in column (d) (column (b));[15]

---

12. Item 402(f)(1).

13. Item 402(f)(2)(i).

14. For these purposes, the term "option" means instruments such as stock options, stock appreciation rights, and similar instruments with option-like features. *See* Item 402(a)(6)(i). The term "Stock Appreciation Rights" (SARs) means SARs payable in cash or stock, including SARs payable in cash or stock at the election of the registrant or a NEO. *Id.*

15. Item 402(f)(2)(ii).

- the number of securities underlying unexercised options, including awards that have been transferred other than for value, that are unexercisable and that are not reported in column (d) (column (c));[16]
- the total number of shares underlying unexercised options awarded under any equity incentive plan that have not been earned (column (d));[17]
- for each option reported in columns (b), (c), and (d), as applicable, its exercise or base price (column (e));[18]
- for each option reported in columns (b), (c), and (d), as applicable, its expiration date (column (f));[19]
- the total number of shares of stock[20] that have not vested and that are not reported in column (i) (column (g));[21]
- the aggregate market value of shares of stock that have not vested and that are not reported in column (i) (column (h));[22]
- the total number of shares of stock, units, or other rights awarded under any equity incentive plan that have not vested and that have not been earned, and, if applicable, the number of shares underlying any such unit or right (column (i));[23] and
- the aggregate market or payout value of shares of stock, units, or other rights awarded under any equity incentive plan that have not vested and that have not been earned (column (j)).[24]

As with most of the disclosure tables, the applicable fiscal year is to be added to the title of the table.[25]

---

16. Item 402(f)(2)(iii).
17. Item 402(f)(2)(iv).
18. Item 402(f)(2)(v).
19. Item 402(f)(2)(vi).
20. For these purposes, the term "stock" means instruments such as common stock, restricted stock, restricted stock units, phantom stock, phantom stock units, common stock equivalent units, or any similar instruments that do not have option-like features. *See* Item 402(a)(6)(i).
21. Item 402(f)(2)(vii).
22. Item 402(f)(2)(viii).
23. Item 402(f)(2)(ix).
24. Item 402(f)(2)(x).
25. *See* the Instruction to Item 402.

Identification of Named Executive Officers

Column (a) of the table is to list each of the registrant's NEOs for the last completed fiscal year. Unlike the Summary Compensation Table, it is not necessary to include the executive's principal position when he or she is being identified.

Option Awards Disclosure

As previously described, each stock option award outstanding as of the end of the registrant's last completed fiscal year is to be reported separately.[26] Multiple option awards may be aggregated where the exercise or base price and the expiration date of the instruments is identical.[27] In the case of a single award consisting of a combination of options, SARs, and/or similar option-like instruments, the award must be reported as separate awards with respect to each tranche with a different exercise or base price or expiration date.[28]

Column (b) of the table is to disclose the number of securities underlying unexercised options that were exercisable as of the end of the last completed fiscal year and that are not equity incentive plan awards. Since an equity incentive plan award is an award that provides compensation intended to serve as incentive for performance to occur over a specified period (whether such performance is measured with reference to the financial performance of the registrant, the registrant's stock price, or any other performance measure), this column is limited to exercisable service-based options.

Column (c) of the table is to disclose the number of securities underlying unexercised options that were not exercisable as of the end of the last completed fiscal year and that are not equity incentive plan awards. Thus, this column is limited to unexercisable service-based options.

---

26. Item 402(f)(2)(ii), (iii), and (iv). This disclosure may need to include stock option awards received as forgone salary or bonus. *See* Division of Corporation Finance, Compliance and Disclosure Interpretations – Regulation S-K (July 8, 2011) [hereinafter Current Staff Guidance], *available at* http://www.sec.gov/divisions/corpfin/guidance/regs-kinterp.htm., at Q&A 119.03.

27. *See* Instruction 4 to Item 402(f)(2).

28. *Id.*

Both column (b) and (c) are to include any options that were previously transferred other than for value (for example, as a gift to a family member, or to a trust for estate planning purposes), since the transfer of such options does not negate their status as compensation awarded to the NEO. In the event that either column includes one or more options that were transferred other than for value, the instrument is to be identified by footnote to the appropriate column, disclosing the nature of the transfer.[29]

Column (d) of the table is to disclose the number of securities underlying options that constitute equity incentive plan awards for reporting purposes and that were unexercised and unearned as of the end of the last completed fiscal year. The inclusion of this column in the table corresponds to the approach taken in the Grants of Plan-Based Awards Table,[30] which differentiates between service-based and performance-based awards.

The final two option award columns provide information that may be material to investors in assessing the potential value of the reported awards, including out-of-the-money awards. Thus, column (e) of the table is to disclose the exercise or base price of the option, while column (f) is to disclose the option's expiration date. Using this information, investors can better understand the potential compensation opportunity of each award.

This may be especially true in the case of out-of-the-money options, where the registrant's stock price must increase in order for the award to have value to the NEO. Depending on the relationship of an option's exercise or base price to the current fair market value of the registrant's stock, as well as the time remaining for exercise, investors can gauge whether an instrument is likely to be considered valuable to the executive and its remaining motivational effect.

---

29. *See* Instruction 1 to Item 402(f)(2). Since stock option that has been transferred for value is not an award for which the outcome remains to be realized, these transactions must be disclosed in the Option Exercises and Stock Vested Table rather than in this table.

30. *See* Chapter 6.

Stock Awards Disclosure

Column (g) of the table is to disclose the number of shares or units that had not vested as of the end of the last completed fiscal year and that are not equity incentive plan awards. Thus, this column is limited to unvested service-based equity awards. Unlike options, outstanding unvested stock awards may be reported on an aggregated basis.[31]

Column (h) of the table is to disclose the market value of the unvested shares or units reported in column (g). The market value of the securities reported in column (h) is to be computed by multiplying the closing market price of the registrant's stock at the end of the last completed fiscal year by the number of unvested shares or units outstanding at fiscal year-end.[32]

Column (i) of the table is to disclose the number of shares, units, or other rights that had not been earned under equity incentive plan awards as of the end of the last completed fiscal year. Thus, this column is for unearned performance-based equity awards. If the number of shares of stock underlying any award denominated in units or other rights is not determined on a one-for-one basis, then the number of shares potentially receivable must also be disclosed in this column. As with the awards reported in column (g), outstanding unearned equity incentive plan awards may be reported on an aggregated basis.

Column (j) of the table is to disclose the market or payout value of the shares, units, or rights reported in column (i) that have not vested and that have not been earned. As with service-based stock awards, the market value of the securities reported in column (j) is to be computed by multiplying the closing market price of the registrant's stock at the end of the last completed fiscal year by the amount of equity incentive plan awards outstanding at fiscal year-end.[33]

---

31. Item 402(f)(2)(vii) and (ix). This disclosure may need to include stock awards received as forgone salary or bonus. *See* the Current Staff Guidance, *supra* note 26, at Q&A 119.03.

32. *See* Instruction 3 to Item 402(f)(2).

33. *Id.*

Estimating the Value of Unearned Performance-Based Awards

Since the outcome of most performance-based equity awards will not be known until the end of the performance period, a registrant will need to estimate the value of these awards on an interim basis. The executive compensation disclosure rules provide that the number of shares or units to be reported in column (i) for equity incentive plan awards and the market or payout value to be reported in column (i) are to be based on achieving threshold performance goals.[34] If the previous fiscal year's performance has exceeded the threshold level, however, the disclosure is to be based on the next higher performance measure (target or maximum) that exceeds the previous fiscal year's performance.[35] For these purposes, "previous fiscal year" means the last completed fiscal year.[36] So, for disclosure being prepared in March 2012 for a registrant with a calendar year fiscal year, the relevant performance would be the performance during fiscal 2011.

In the case of an equity incentive plan award with a multiyear performance period where more than one year has elapsed since the award was granted, the staff of the SEC's Division of Corporation Finance (SEC Staff) has indicated that it is permissible to determine the amount to be disclosed in the table based on the actual multiyear performance through the end of the last completed fiscal year, rather than looking solely at the previous fiscal year.[37] This approach may be used, however, only where the award has been structured to use multiyear performance to determine the market or payout amount for

34. *See* Instruction 3 to Item 402(f)(2).

35. *Id.*

36. *See* the Current Staff Guidance, *supra* note 26, at Q&A 122.05. *See also* the 2007 JCEB Questions, *supra* note 10, at Question No. 9(a).

37. *See* the Current Staff Guidance, *supra* note 26, at Q&A 122.01. So, for example, assume that a registrant has an equity incentive plan pursuant to which it grants awards that will vest, if at all, based on total shareholder return over a three-year period. Awards were granted in fiscal 2005 that will vest based on the registrant's total shareholder return from January 1, 2005, through December 31, 2007. Fiscal 2006 was the second year of the three-year performance period. Performance during fiscal 2005 was well above the maximum level. Performance during fiscal 2006 was below the threshold level. The combined performance for fiscal 2005 and fiscal 2006 would result in a payout at target, however, if the performance period had ended on December 31, 2006. In this situation, the SEC Staff has indicated that it is permissible for the registrant to base its disclosure of the number of shares or units in columns (d) or (i) of the table, and the payout value reported in column (j) of the table, on the actual multiyear performance to date (through the end of the last completed fiscal year). *Id.*

the award. If an award provides only for a single estimated payout, that is the amount that should be reported in column (j). Where the target amount is not determinable, a registrant must provide a representative amount based on the previous fiscal year's performance.

Performance-Based Awards with Service Vesting Conditions

Some equity incentive plan awards require that an executive satisfy a service-based vesting requirement once the performance period has been completed and the market or payout value of the award determined. The rules provide that such an award is to be reported as an equity incentive plan award (whether a stock option or stock award) until the relevant performance condition has been satisfied. At that point, if the option remains unexercised or shares of stock are still unvested, the option or stock should continue to be reported in the appropriate column or columns for service-based awards (columns (b) or (c), in the case of options, or (g) and (h), in the case of stock awards).[38]

For example, the SEC Staff has been asked as to the appropriate reporting treatment in the case of a registrant with a performance-based restricted stock unit (RSU) plan that measured performance over a three-year period (2007 – 2009). After the end of the three-year performance period, the registrant's compensation committee was to evaluate performance to determine the number of shares subject to the RSU award earned by the NEOs. The NEOs must remain by the registrant for a subsequent two-year service-based vesting period (2010 – 2011). Upon the completion of the service-based vesting period, the registrant will distribute to the NEOs the shares subject to the RSU awards. The Staff has taken the position that, in this situation, the number of shares to be reporte in the Outstanding Equity Awards at Fiscal Year-End Table should be based on the actual number of shares underlying the RSU awards that were earned as determined at the end of the three-year

---

38. *See* Instruction 5 to Item 402(f)(2).

performance period.[39] This is the case even if the number of shares will not be determined until after the 2009 fiscal year-end.[40]

Performance-Based Awards With Successive Single-Year Performance Periods

Some registrants use equity incentive plan awards (such as a performance share award) that establish performance objectives and measures performance on an annual basis but that do not pay out until the after the end of s three-year period. Under these plans, the NEOs receive an award for a target number of shares at the commencement of the three-year period, with one-third of this amount allocated to each of the three years. In addition, an annual performance objective is established at the beginning of each fiscal year with performance assessed at the end of each year to determine the number of shares (if any) that have been earned for that period. Any shares earned are held by the registrant for payout at the end of the three-year period. All shares that are earned vest and are paid out at the end of the three-year period, contingent upon the NEO's continued service until that time.[41] Under Financial Accounting Standards Board Accounting Standards Codification Topic 718, *Compensation – Stock Compensation* (FASB ASC Topic 718), the award tranches for fiscal years two and three do not result in any compensation expense for financial statement reporting purposes until fiscal years two and three, respectively.

For purposes of the Outstanding Equity Awards at Fiscal Year-End Table, with respect to the year that the performance award is granted, the total target number of unearned shares subject to the award should be reported in column (i) of the table and the aggregate market or payout value of the shares should be reported in column (j) of the table, respectively. In subsequent years, the number of shares that have been

---

39. *See* the Current Staff Guidance, *supra* note 26, at Q&A 122.03. The shares should not be reported in columns (i) and (j) of the table (the two equity incentive plan awards columns) because they are no longer subject to performance-base conditions. *Id.* Instead, the shares should be reported in columns (g) and (h) of the table (the two general stock awards columns) because they are subject to service-based vesting conditions.

40. *Id.*

41. In other words, the shares (if any) earned for Year One vest two years after the end of Year One. The shares (if any) earned for Year Two vest one year after the end of Year Two. The shares (if any) earned for Year Three vest immediately.

earned under the equity incentive plan awards should be reported in column (g) of the table (along with the aggregate market or payout value of the shares being reported in column (h) of the table) and the total target number of unearned shares remaining subject to the award should be reported in column (i) of the table and the aggregate market or payout value of these shares should be reported in column (j) of the table, respectively.[42]

Disclosure of Award Vesting Schedules

To enable investors to ascertain when an unexercisable stock option or unvested stock award will be earned (in the case of a service-based award) or when the performance period will be completed (in the case of an equity incentive plan award), the registrant must provide a footnote to the applicable column of the table where each outstanding award is reported disclosing the relevant vesting dates of the options, shares of stock, and equity incentive plan awards.[43] To simplify the presentation of the required vesting information, some registrants add a column to the table (after column (a), the identity of the NEOs, and before column (b), the number of securities underlying exercisable but unexercised options) to report the grant date of each award and reference these dates in the footnote description of the vesting schedule.[44] The SEC Staff has taken the position that a registrant may comply with this disclosure requirement by including a column in its Outstanding Equity Awards at Fiscal Year-End Table showing the grant date of each award reported and including a statement of the standard vesting schedule that applies to the reported awards, provided, however, that if there is any different vesting schedule applicable to any of the awards, then table also includes the appropriate disclosure about any such vesting schedule.[45]

---

42. *See* Questions and Answers, Technical Session between the SEC Staff and the Joint Committee on Employee Benefits (May 5, 2009), *available at* http://www.americanbar.org/content/dam/aba/migrated/2011_build/employee_benefits/sec_2009.authcheckdam.pdf, at Question No. 3(c).

43. *See* Instruction 2 to Item 402(f)(2).

44. *See, e.g.,* the Sara Lee Corporation Definitive Proxy Statement (Form 14A) filed Sept. 15, 2011 (file no. 001-03344).

45. *See* the Current Staff Guidance, *supra* note 26, at Q&A 122.02.

Option Awards with an "Early Exercise" Feature

Some stock options are structured to allow for immediate exercise in full as of the date of grant subject to a "reverse" vesting schedule; that is, if the optionee terminates his or her employment with the registrant prior to the vesting date, the registrant may repurchase any exercised but unvested shares at their original cost (that is, option exercise or base price). Typically, this right of repurchase lapses on a periodic basis over a specified schedule (generally, three or four years). As a result, if a NEO exercises the option before the repurchase restrictions have lapsed, he or she effectively receives shares of restricted stock that are subject to forfeiture (through repurchase) until the shares vest. Because this type of instrument possesses the characteristics of both an option and a restricted stock award, its disclosure in the Outstanding Equity Awards at Fiscal Year-End Table is not obvious.

The SEC Staff has indicated that options with an "early exercise" feature should be reported in the Outstanding Equity Awards at Fiscal Year-End Table as options until exercised, at which time the shares received as stock awards that have not vested (in columns (g) (number of shares or units that have not vested as of the end of the last completed fiscal year) and (h) (until the repurchase restriction lapses.[46] This information would be supplemented with a footnote disclosing that the acquired shares are subject to vesting conditions and, thus, may be forfeited by the NEO.[47]

In-Kind Earnings

In recent years, it has become common for a registrant to pay dividends or dividend equivalents on some stock awards, such as restricted stock awards, during the vesting period. While occasionally these amounts will

---

46. *See* the Current Staff Guidance, *supra* note 26, at Interpretation 222.01. *See also* the 2007 JCEB Questions, *supra* note 10, at Question No. 10.

47. In subsequent years, the shares acquired on exercise, which have the characteristics of restricted stock, would be reported in columns (d) (the number of shares) and (e) (the value realized upon vesting), respectively, of the Option Exercises and Stock Vested Table as the shares vest, once again supplemented with a footnote disclosing that the shares are from a previously exercised (and reported) option and providing the dollar amount that was originally realized upon exercise.

be distributed on an ongoing basis, in most cases, they are accumulated and held by the registrant pending the outcome of the award. The SEC Staff has taken the position that outstanding in-kind earnings, such as share dividends and share dividend equivalents, that have not vested (or otherwise been earned) as of the end of the last completed fiscal year should be included in the table.[48]

---

48. *See* the Current Staff Guidance, *supra* note 26, at Q&A 122.04. In-kind earnings that vested during the fiscal year, or in-kind earnings that are already vested when the dividends are declared, however, should be reported in the Option Exercises and Stock Vested Table.

9

Option Exercises and Stock Vested Table

General

The final member of the trio of supplemental equity award disclosure tables is the Option Exercises and Stock Vested Table.[1] This table presents, on an aggregated basis for each named executive officer (NEO), a summary of the amounts realized from the exercise of stock options and the vesting of stock awards during the last completed fiscal year.[2] This includes awards that were granted by the registrant to the NEOs, as

---

1. Item 402(g). A smaller reporting company is not required to provide an Option Exercises and Stock Vested Table as part of its executive compensation disclosure. *See* Executive Compensation and Related Person Disclosure, Release Nos. 33-8732A, 34-54302A, IC-27444A (Aug. 29, 2006), 71 Fed. Reg. 53,158 (Sept. 8, 2006) [hereinafter Adopting Release], *available at* http://www.sec.gov/rules/final/2006/33-8732a.pdf, at Section II.D.1, and Smaller Reporting Company Regulatory Relief and Simplification, Release Nos. 33-8876, 34-56994, 39-2451 (Dec. 19, 2007), 73 Fed. Reg. 934 (Jan. 4, 2008), *available at* http://www.sec.gov/rules/final/2007/33-8876.pdf, at Section III.C.1.

2. The reporting of stock option or stock award forfeitures is not required in this table. *See* W. Alan Kailer, Hunton & Williams, *The Securities and Exchange Commission's Executive Compensation Rules—Preparing the Executive Compensation Tables* (Jan. 2012), at B-16.

well as equity awards received at the election of a NEO in lieu of salary or bonus that he or she has earned for the fiscal year.[3]

The Option Exercises and Stock Vested Table combines two disclosure items from the former rules, enhances one of them to provide new information long requested by investors, and reformats the columns to make the presentation of stock option and stock awards consistent. Under the former rules, a registrant was required to disclose the number of shares received upon the exercise of stock options (or tandem stock appreciation rights (SARs)) and freestanding SARs during the last completed fiscal year (or, if no shares were received, the number of securities with respect to which the options or SARs were exercised) and the aggregate dollar value realized upon exercise.[4] In addition, in preparing the Summary Compensation Table a registrant was required to disclose in a footnote to the table the number and value of the aggregate restricted stock holdings of each NEO at the end of the last completed fiscal year.[5] While investors found this disclosure useful, they pointed out that the disclosure omitted the most important piece of information concerning a restricted stock award—the market value of the shares on their vesting date. As adopted, the Option Exercises and Stock Vested Table shows the amounts received by the NEOs upon the exercise of stock options, SARs, or similar instruments and from the vesting of shares of stock, including restricted stock, restricted stock units, and similar instruments, during the late completed fiscal year. Thus, investors are able to see in a single location the amounts that a NEO realized from equity awards during the covered fiscal year. Unlike the accounting-based values reported in the Summary Compensation Table, these amounts represent the actual economic benefit received from these awards.[6]

---

3. See Division of Corporation Finance, Compliance and Disclosure Interpretations – Regulation S-K (July 8,2011) [hereinafter Current Staff Guidance], *available at* http://www.sec.gov/divisions/corpfin/guidance/regs-kinterp.htm, at Q&A 119.03.

4. See former Items 402(d)(2)(ii) and (iii). This table did not include the vesting of shares of stock.

5. See Instruction 2(a) to former Item 402(b)(2)(iv).

6. As proposed, the Option Exercises and Stock Vested Table would have had an additional column showing the grant date fair value previously reported in the Summary Compensation Table for the stock options, SARs, and similar instruments that were exercised and the shares of stock that vested during the covered fiscal year. See Proposed Item 402(h)(2)(iv). The purpose of this column was to eliminate the impact of "double disclosure" by providing for a comparison of the amount reported in the year of grant with the amount realized in the year of exercise or vesting. See Executive Compensation and Related Party Disclosure, Release Nos.

Tabular Format

The Option Exercises and Stock Vested Table is to be presented in the following tabular format:

OPTION EXERCISES AND STOCK VESTED

Name	Option Awards		Stock Awards	
	Number of shares acquired on exercise (#)	Value realized on exercise ($)	Number of shares acquired on vesting (#)	Value realized on vesting ($)
(a)	(b)	(c)	(d)	(e)
Principal Executive Officer (PEO)				
Principal Financial Officer (PFO)				
A				
B				
C				

The table includes the following information for the last completed fiscal year:

- the name of the NEO (column (a));[7]
- the number of securities for which options[8] were exercised (column (b));[9]

33-8655, 34-53185, IC-27218 (Jan. 27, 2006), 71 Fed. Reg. 6542 (Feb. 8, 2006), *available at* http://www.sec.gov/rules/proposed/33-8655.pdf, at Section II.B.4.b. In response to concerns that such a column would actually confuse investors and increase the potential for double counting, however, it was omitted from the final rule. *See* the Adopting Release, *supra* note 1, at Section II.C.4.b.

7. Item 402(g)(2)(i).

8. For these purposes, the term "option" means instruments such as stock options, stock appreciation rights, and similar instruments with option-like features. *See* Item 402(a)(6)(i). The term "stock appreciation rights" (SARs) means SARs payable in cash or stock, including SARs payable in cash or stock at the election of the registrant or a NEO. *Id.*

9. Item 402(g)(2)(ii).

- the aggregate dollar value realized upon exercise of options, or upon the transfer of an award for value (column (c));[10]
- the number of shares of stock[11] that vested (column (d));[12] and
- the aggregate dollar value realized upon the vesting of stock, or upon the transfer of an award for value (column (e)).[13]

As with most of the disclosure tables, the applicable fiscal year is to be added to the title of the table.[14]

Identification of Named Executive Officers

Column (a) of the table is to list each of the registrant's NEOs for the last completed fiscal year. Unlike the Summary Compensation Table, it is not necessary to include the executive's principal position when he or she is being identified.

Option Awards Disclosure

Column (b) of the table is to disclose the number of shares acquired upon the exercise of each stock option, settlement of each SAR, or exercise or settlement of each similar instrument during the last completed fiscal year. This disclosure covers both service-based options and options granted under equity incentive plans. The number to be reported is the gross number of shares underlying the exercised option or settled SAR, rather than the net number of shares received upon exercise or settlement.[15] For example, in the case of a cashless exercise of a stock option for 100 shares of stock with an exercise price of $5.00 per share at a time when the market price of the registrant's stock is $10.00 per share,

---

10. Item 402(g)(2)(iii).

11. For these purposes, the term "stock" means instruments such as common stock, restricted stock, restricted stock units, phantom stock, phantom stock units, common stock equivalent units, or any similar instruments that do not have option-like features. *See* Item 402(a)(6)(i).

12. Item 402(g)(2)(iv).

13. Item 402(g)(2)(v).

14. *See* the Instruction to Item 402.

15. *See* the Current Staff Guidance, *supra* note 3, at Q&A 123.01. A footnote or a narrative statement accompanying the table may be used to explain and quantify the net number of shares received. *Id.*

the number to be reported in column (b) would be the full 100 shares exercised, rather than the 50 shares actually received after the remaining shares were used to cover the option exercise price.[16]

Column (c) of the table is to disclose the aggregate dollar amount realized by a NEO upon the exercise of a stock option, settlement of an SAR, or exercise or settlement of any similar instrument during the last completed fiscal year. The dollar amount realized upon exercise is to be computed by determining the difference between the market price of the underlying securities at the time of exercise and the exercise or base price of the option or SAR.[17] While the executive compensation disclosure rules do not define how the market price is to be determined, many registrants, in reliance on Item 402(d)(2)(vii),[18] use the closing market price of the underlying security on the date of exercise for this purpose.[19] The value of any related payment or other consideration provided (or to be provided) by the registrant to or on behalf of a NEO, whether in payment of the exercise price or related taxes, is not to be included as part of the disclosed amount.[20] Thus, a tax reimbursement payment provided to a NEO in connection with the exercise of an option would not be disclosed in this table.

The dollar amount realized on exercise or settlement is reported on a pretax basis (that is, the amount reported is the gross amount realized from the transaction, not the net amount received by the NEO

---

16. The same result would apply in the case of the settlement of a cash- or stock-settled SAR.

17. *See* the Instruction to Item 402(g)(2).

18. Instruction 1 to former Item 402(d)(2) used the term "fair market value," instead of "market price," in describing how to calculate the value realized upon exercise, which suggests that under the rules, the SEC is looking for an objective standard for determining the economic value of the acquired securities. Given the stated preference for "closing market price" in Item 402(d)(2)(vii) when highlighting the implied reasonableness of a stock option exercise price, many companies have opted to use this methodology to satisfy the "market price" requirement.

19. Under their stock option administration policies and procedures, some registrants use different methodologies for determining the market price of their securities depending on the nature of the exercise transaction (for example, a cash exercise, stock swap exercise, or a broker-assisted cashless exercise). In this situation, the valuation methodology used for disclosure purposes may vary based on the nature of the underlying transaction. If this is the case, it may be advisable for a registrant to describe the specific methodology or methodologies being used (if they differ from the closing market price) so that investors can understand any discrepancies between the registrant's and their own calculations.

20. *See* the Instruction to Item 402(g)(2). Instead, any such payment or other consideration provided by the registrant is to be disclosed in the All Other Compensation column of the Summary Compensation Table in accordance with the requirements of Item 402(c)(2)(ix). *Id.*

following satisfaction of any tax withholding obligations arising from the transaction).

Stock Awards Disclosure

Column (d) of the table is to disclose the number of shares of stock acquired upon the vesting of each stock award during the last completed fiscal year. As with option awards, the number to be reported is the gross number of shares that vested, rather than the net number of shares received (for example, after taking into consideration shares withheld to satisfy any tax withholding obligation arising in connection with the vesting of the shares).[21] The type of award subject to disclosure is broader than just restricted stock awards and restricted stock units. Any stock award, including both service-based awards and performance-based awards—such as performance shares and performance units—that vested during the last completed fiscal year would need to be disclosed.[22]

If a registrant pays dividends or dividend equivalents on restricted stock awards and those earnings are reinvested in additional restricted shares, then these additional shares should be reported in the table when they vest.[23] If these additional shares are vested at the time the dividend was declared, they are reportable in the table when the dividend is declared.[24]

Column (e) of the table is to disclose the aggregate dollar amount realized by a NEO upon the vesting of the shares of stock (or the transfer of the award for value) during the last completed fiscal year. The dollar amount realized upon vesting is to be computed by multiplying the number of shares of stock or units vesting by the market value of the underlying shares on the vesting date.[25] Presumably, this reportable amount would be reduced by the purchase price, if any, that a NEO must pay to acquire the shares. Finally, since the rules do not define how the market value of the underlying shares is to be determined, many

---

21. *See* the Current Staff Guidance, *supra* note 3, at Q&A 123.01.

22. Essentially, any stock award reportable in the Stock Awards column of the Summary Compensation Table must be disclosed in these columns. Presumably, this would also include a stock award that is vested in whole or in part at the time of grant.

23. *See* the Current Staff Guidance, *supra* note 3, at Q&A 122.01.

24. *Id.*

25. *See* the Instruction to Item 402(g)(2).

registrants, in reliance on Item 402(d)(2)(vii), use the closing market price of the underlying security on the vesting date for this purpose.

Transferred Awards

For several years, registrants have offered their employees, particularly their executives, the ability to transfer their equity awards. While traditionally this feature has been offered to facilitate tax and estate planning, some registrants permit employees to transfer their awards, particularly stock options, for value to one or more designated third parties, typically a financial institution. Such transfers present their own reporting issues.

Under the rules, the transfer of a stock option or stock award for value is also treated as a realization event for purposes of the table.[26] Thus, any amount received by a NEO upon or in connection with a transfer for value of a stock option must be reported in column (c) of the table, while the transfer of a stock award for value must be reported in column (e).[27] Further, although the rules are silent on this point, the number of shares underlying a stock option or covered by a stock award that is transferred for value may need to be reported in column (b) or column (d), respectively, of the table.[28]

Further, while the rules are silent on this point, presumably the exercise of a stock option or the vesting of a stock award that was previously transferred without value would not be reportable in column (b) or (d) of the table, as the case may be. While the rules contemplate that the transfer of a stock award for value will be treated as a realization event for purposes of the table in the case of a transfer without value, since the NEO doesn't receive any compensation from the exercise or vesting event, it would not appear that this information would be important to investors.

---

26. Item 402(g)(2)(iii). Some registrants permit such transfers as an alternative means for an optionee to realize an economic benefit from a stock option.

27. Item 402(g)(2)(v).

28. Alternatively, a registrant may want to provide a narrative statement to accompany the table to explain the discrepancy between the information in columns (b) and (c) or (d) and (e), as the case may be.

Option Awards with an "Early Exercise" Feature

Some stock options are structured to allow for immediate exercise in full as of the date of grant subject to a "reverse" vesting schedule; that is, if the optionee terminates his or her employment with the registrant prior to the vesting date, the registrant may repurchase any exercised but unvested shares at their original cost (that is, option exercise or base price). Typically, this right of repurchase lapses on a periodic basis over a specified schedule (generally, three or four years). As a result, if a NEO exercises the option before the repurchase restrictions have lapsed, he or she effectively receives shares of restricted stock that are subject to forfeiture (through repurchase) until the shares vest. Because this type of instrument possesses the characteristics of both an option and a restricted stock award, its disclosure in the Option Exercises and Stock Vested Table is not obvious.

The staff of the Securities and Exchange Commission's Division of Corporation Finance (SEC Staff) has indicated that options with an "early exercise" feature should always be reported in the Option Exercises and Stock Vested Table since the exercise is a volitional transaction. If the option is exercised before the repurchase restrictions have lapsed, it is to be reported in the following manner.[29] It is to be reported in the table for the fiscal year in which the exercise occurs, showing the number of shares acquired in column (b) and the value realized upon exercise (if any) in column (c). This information would be supplemented with a footnote disclosing that the acquired shares are subject to vesting conditions and, thus, may be forfeited by the NEO.[30] As the shares vest, the number of shares and the value realized upon vesting would be reported in columns (d) and (e), respectively, of the table, once again supplemented with a footnote disclosing that the shares are from a previously exercised (and reported) option and providing the dollar amount that was originally realized upon exercise. While this may lead to some or all of the award

---

29. *See* the Current Staff Guidance, *supra* note 3, at Interpretation 222.01. *See also* Questions and Answers, Technical Session Between the SEC Staff and the Joint Committee in Employee Benefits (May 8, 2007), *available at* http://www.abanet.org/jceb/2007/SEC07Final.pdf, at Question No. 10.

30. In subsequent years, the shares acquired on exercise, which have the characteristics of restricted stock, would be reported in columns (g) and (h) of the Outstanding Equity Awards at Fiscal Year-End Table until the repurchase restrictions have lapsed. Footnotes would be used to explain what is being reported.

being reported in the table twice, any potential "double counting" issues could be addressed in a footnote to the relevant entry.

If the stock option is exercised after the repurchase restrictions have lapsed, it is to be reported solely as an option exercise in the following manner. It is to be reported in the table for the fiscal year in which the exercise occurs, showing the number of shares acquired in column (b) and the value realized upon exercise (if any) in column (c). While this information may be supplemented with a footnote disclosing that the option was originally granted with an "early exercise" feature, this information would not be required since that feature was not relevant to the acquisition of the underlying option shares.

Deferral of Receipt of Gain

If a NEO elected to defer the receipt of any amount realized upon the exercise of an option or the vesting of a stock award, the registrant must provide a footnote to the table quantifying the amount deferred and disclosing the terms of the deferral.[31] Presumably, this amount would also be reportable in the Nonqualified Deferred Compensation Table in the year of the deferral and thereafter.[32]

---

31. *See* the Instruction to Item 402(g)(2).
32. *See* Chapter 11.

10

Pension Benefits Table

General

The Pension Benefits Table is the first of two required postemployment disclosure tables.[1] It is intended to provide investors with a comprehensive summary of the potential future compensation, in the form of retirement payments, that a registrant's named executive officers (NEOs) may receive under the various defined benefit pension plans that the registrant maintains for its executives. This table presents, on a plan-by-plan basis for each NEO, the actuarial present value of his or her accumulated pension benefits under each tax-qualified and nonqualified defined benefit pension and actuarial plan that was maintained by the registrant as of the end of the last completed fiscal year, assuming that benefits are paid at normal retirement age and based on current compensation levels. The computation of this amount has essentially

---

1. Item 402(h). A smaller reporting company is not required to provide a Pension Benefits Table as part of its executive compensation disclosure. *See* Executive Compensation and Related Person Disclosure, Release Nos. 33-8732A, 34-54302A, IC-27444A (Aug. 29, 2006), 71 Fed. Reg. 53,158 (Sept. 8, 2006) [hereinafter Adopting Release], *available at* http://www.sec.gov/rules/final/2006/33-8732a.pdf, at Section II.D.1, and Smaller Reporting Company Regulatory Relief and Simplification, Release Nos. 33-8876, 34-56994, 39-2451 (Dec. 19, 2007), 73 Fed. Reg. 934 (Jan. 4, 2008), *available at* http://www.sec.gov/rules/final/2007/33-8876.pdf, at Section III.C.1. But *see* "Smaller Reporting Companies," *infra*.

been standardized, as it is determined without regard to the particular form or forms of benefit payment (for example, lump sum or annual annuity) available under the plan or selected by a NEO.

This approach represents a pronounced departure from that of the former rules, which required only generalized disclosure about the amounts payable under executive retirement plans. While the former rules required disclosure about executive retirement benefits, investors did not find the general and largely imprecise nature of the former pension plan table and alternative plan disclosure[2] to be very useful. In fact, of the various items reported under the former rules, the pension benefits disclosure was often the most frequently criticized for its virtual labyrinth of confusing numbers that were not directly tied to the potential benefits for individual NEOs. In addition, in recent years, as executive retirement packages have begun to represent a larger portion of an executive's overall compensation, investors began to request more and better information about the nature and scope of these arrangements.

In response, the Securities and Exchange Commission (SEC) decided to replace the existing disclosure requirements with a table reflecting the specific potential pension benefits for each NEO as of fiscal year-end and enhanced narrative disclosure to help investors better understand this information. Initially, the SEC proposed a new table that would have required disclosure of the estimated retirement benefits payable to each NEO at normal retirement age and, if available, early retirement, under the registrant's defined benefit plans.[3] In response to comments that the proposed approach would result in disclosure that would not be readily

---

2. *See* former Item 402(f)(1). This item required registrants to present a table showing estimated annual benefits under each defined benefit or actuarial plan payable upon retirement (including amounts attributable to supplementary or excess pension award plans) for specified compensation levels and years of service. The table did not require disclosure of this information for any specific NEO. This requirement applied to plans under which benefits were determined primarily by final compensation (or average final compensation) and years of service, and included a limited amount of additional narrative disclosure. If NEOs participated in other plans under which benefits were not determined primarily by final compensation (or average final compensation), a registrant was required to provide narrative disclosure of the benefit formula and estimated annual benefits payable to the executives upon retirement at normal retirement age. *See* former Item 402(f)(2).

3. *See* Proposed Item 402(i). Under the proposal, each NEO's benefits would have been quantified based on the form of benefit currently elected by the executive (such as joint and survivor annuity or single life annuity). In addition, where a NEO was not yet eligible to retire, the dollar amount of annual benefits to which he or she would have been entitled upon becoming eligible would have been computed assuming that the NEO continued to earn the same amount of compensation as reported for the registrant's last fiscal year.

comparable and could necessitate complicated explanations that would hinder transparency,[4] however, the SEC opted to simplify the required disclosure and to promote comparability and transparency by requiring presentation of the economic value of the benefit that each NEO has accumulated through plan participation.

Specifically, a registrant must disclose the present value of the current accrued benefit under each plan for each NEO computed as of the end of the registrant's last completed fiscal year. Ultimately, the SEC chose to ensure a minimum level of comparability by requiring registrants to report the amount each NEO has accumulated through the plan.[5] This disclosure requirement applies without regard to the particular form or forms of benefit payment actually available under a plan.[6] This is intended to provide investors with a sense of the potential cost of the future benefits that have been promised to the NEO on a present value basis. Further, as explained in the Adopting Release, basing pension plan disclosure on the accumulated benefit is consistent with nonqualified deferred compensation plan disclosure, which is reported on the basis of an aggregate account balance.[7]

The actuarial present value of the accumulated pension benefit reported in the Pension Benefits Table correlates to the change in pension value information required to be disclosed in the Summary Compensation Table.[8] In fact, the aggregated amount reported in the Change in Pension Value and Nonqualified Deferred Compensation

---

4. As proposed, a benefit calculation would have depended heavily on factors specific to each individual executive, such as the form of benefit payment, martial status, and the actuarial assumptions used in the calculation. Given variations between registrants and between plans, this would have impeded comparability and hindered transparency.

5. The SEC also considered, but ultimately discarded, an approach advocated by some commenters that would have required "normalized" disclosure based on a series of hypothetical annual benefit assumptions prescribed by the SEC. This approach, which would have produced a hypothetical benefit value, was thought to be too similar to the former disclosure requirements in that the assumptions selected might bear no relationship to the assumptions that the registrant actually applied with respect to the actual plan.

6. *See* the Adopting Release, *supra* note 1, at n.295 and the accompanying text. The burden associated with preparing the disclosure was also lessened by requiring that the actuarial present value of the accumulated pension benefits be computed using, with the exception of the retirement age, the same assumptions that the registrant uses for financial statement reporting purposes and computed as of the same pension plan measurement date for financial statement reporting purposes with respect to the audited financial statements for the last completed fiscal year.

7. *See* the Adopting Release, *supra* note 1, at n.296.

8. *See* Item 402(c)(2)(viii)(A) and the discussion in "Pension Value Changes and Above-Market and Preferential Earnings" in Chapter 4.

Earnings column of the Summary Compensation Table will be the difference between the sum of the actuarial present value amount reported in the Pension Benefits Table for each plan presented for a NEO from one fiscal year to the next...

As previously noted, the new table is to be followed by a narrative description of the material factors necessary to an understanding of each plan disclosed in the table.

Tabular Format

The Pension Benefits Table is to be presented in the following tabular format:

PENSION BENEFITS

Name	Plan Name	Number of Years Credited Service (#)	Present Value of Accu-mulated Benefit ($)	Payments During Last Fiscal Year ($)
(a)	(b)	(c)	(d)	(e)
Principal Executive Officer (PEO)				
Principal Financial Officer (PFO)				
A				
B				
C				

The table includes the following information for the last completed fiscal year:

- the name of the NEO (column (a));[9]
- the name of the plan (column (b));[10]

---

9. Item 402(h)(2)(i).
10. Item 402(h)(2)(ii).

- the number of years of service credited to the NEO under the plan (column (c));[11]
- the actuarial present value of the NEO's accumulated benefit under the plan (column (d));[12] and
- the dollar amount of any payments and benefits paid to the NEO during the registrant's last completed fiscal year (column (e)).[13]

As with most of the disclosure tables, the applicable fiscal year is to be added to the title of the table.[14]

Identification of Named Executive Officers

Column (a) of the table is to list each of the registrant's NEOs for the last completed fiscal year. Unlike the Summary Compensation Table, it is not necessary to include the executive's principal position when he or she is being identified.

Name of Plan

Column (b) of the table is to identify each plan that provides for one or more of the NEOs to receive payments or other benefits at, following, or in connection with retirement. Disclosure is required for each plan[15] that provides for specified retirement payments and benefits, or payments and benefits that will be provided primarily following retirement, including, but not limited to, tax-qualified defined benefit plans (including cash balance plans) and supplemental executive retirement plans (SERPs).[16]

---

11. Item 402(h)(2)(iii).

12. Item 402(h)(2)(iv).

13. Item 402(h)(2)(v).

14. *See* the Instruction to Item 402.

15. For these purposes, the term "plan" includes, but is not limited to, any plan, contract, authorization, or arrangement, whether or not set forth in any formal document, pursuant to which cash, securities, similar instruments, or any other property may be received. *See* Item 402(a)(6)(ii). A plan may be applicable to one person. *Id.*

16. *See* Instruction 1 to Item 402(h)(2). Thus, the disclosure covers both tax-qualified and non-tax-qualified, or "discriminatory" plans, including excess, or "restoration," benefit plans and SERPs that are designed to restore the benefits that are ineligible for tax-qualified plan coverage by virtue of Internal Revenue Code Sections 401 and 415 (26 U.S.C. §§ 401 and

This disclosure does not include payments receivable pursuant to a tax-qualified or nonqualified defined contribution plan.[17]

If a NEO participates in more than one retirement plan, a registrant must provide a separate row for each such plan.[18] Since many registrants maintain multiple defined benefit pension plans for their executives—a tax-qualified defined benefit plan, an "excess" retirement plan, and, possibly, a supplemental executive retirement plan, it will be common to have multiple entries for each NEO.[19] For purposes of allocating the current accrued benefit between tax-qualified defined benefit plans and related supplemental plans, a registrant is to apply the limitations applicable to tax-qualified defined benefit plans established by the Internal Revenue Code and the associated income tax regulations that applied as of the relevant pension plan measurement date.[20]

Number of Years of Credited Service

Column (c) of the table is to report the number of years of service credited to a NEO under each disclosed plan. The years of credited service are to be computed as of the same pension plan measurement date used for financial statement reporting purposes with respect to the registrant's audited financial statements for the last completed fiscal year.[21] This number will include both years of service actually worked by the NEO and any additional years of service credited to the executive under the plan or any other arrangement.[22]

If a NEO's number of years of credited service under any plan differs from his or her number of actual years of service with the registrant, this

---

415) (which, generally, impose prescribed dollar limitations on the compensable benefits and estimated annual benefits that can be paid to employee-participants).

17. *Id.* The disclosure requirements for defined contribution plans are located in Items 402(c)(2)(ix)(E) and 402(i).

18. *See* Instruction 1 to Item 402(h)(2).

19. Since some defined benefit pension plans have been bifurcated to "grandfather" pre-January 1, 2005, benefits for purposes of Internal Revenue Code Section 409A (26 U.S.C. § 409A), it is possible that these plan variants may need to be reported as separate plans for disclosure purposes. Alternatively, it may be possible to simply highlight these variations in the narrative disclosure accompanying the table.

20. *See* Instruction 3 to Item 402(h)(2).

21. Item 402(h)(2)(iii).

22. *See* Instruction 4 to Item 402(h)(2).

fact must be noted and any resulting benefit augmentation (increase) quantified in a footnote to the table.[23]

Actuarial Present Value of Accumulated Benefit

Column (d) of the table is to report the actuarial present value of the NEO's accumulated benefit under each disclosed plan. Essentially, this figure is an estimate of the expected future value of the NEO's retirement benefit under a plan discounted to reflect the time value of money. The accumulated benefit amount is to be computed as of the same pension plan measurement date used for financial statement reporting purposes with respect to the registrant's audited financial statements for the last completed fiscal year.[24]

Until recently, the pension plan measurement date for most pension plans was September 30, which, in the case of many registrants (including all calendar-year registrants), did not correspond with the registrant's fiscal year. As a result, the pension benefit information was presented for a period that differed from the fiscal year period covered by the disclosure.[25] In the past few years, however, under recent changes in pension accounting standards, the pension plan measurement date for most companies has changed to be the same as the end of a registrant's fiscal year. The staff of the SEC's Division of Corporation Finance (SEC Staff) has taken the position that, in the year in which a registrant changes its pension plan measurement date, it may use an annualized approach for the disclosure of the change in the actuarial present value of the accumulated pension benefits in the Summary Compensation Table (thereby adjusting the 15-month period to a 12-month period) when the transition in pension plan measurement date occurs, so long as the registrant includes disclosure (presumably in a footnote to column (h)

---

23. *Id.*

24. *See* Item 402(h)(2)(iv). The pension plan measurement date as used for financial statement reporting purposes was selected for this calculation so that registrants would not have to use different assumptions when computing the present value for executive compensation disclosure and financial reporting purposes. *See* Division of Corporation Finance, Compliance and Disclosure Interpretations – Regulation S-K (July 8, 2011) [hereinafter Current Staff Guidance], *available at* http://www.sec.gov/divisions/corpfin/guidance/regs-kinterp.htm, at Interpretation 219.03.

25. *See* the Current Staff Guidance, *supra* note 24, at Interpretation 219.03.

of the Summary Compensation Table) explaining that it has followed this approach.[26] The actuarial present value of the accumulated pension benefits computed on the new measurement date should be reported in this table.[27]

For purposes of computing the actuarial present value of an accumulated benefit, a registrant must use the same assumptions (for example, interest rate assumptions) that are used to compute the amounts disclosed in its audited financial statements under generally accepted accounting principles, except that retirement age is to be assumed to be the normal retirement age as defined in the plan, or, if not so defined, the earliest time at which a participant may retire under the plan without any benefit reduction due to age.[28] The SEC Staff has indicated that where a plan has a stated "normal" retirement age and also a younger age at which retirement benefits may be received without any reduction in benefits, the younger age should be used for determining pension benefits.[29] Further, the computation is to be based on current compensation levels, and, accordingly, future compensation levels need not be estimated for purposes of the calculation.[30]

Whether or not the plan allows for a lump-sum payment, presentation of the present value of the accrued plan benefit provides investors an understanding of the cost of promised future benefits in present value terms. Other than the single concession concerning retirement age, the SEC Staff has been steadfast in insisting that registrants base the required actuarial computations on the assumptions that they use for financial statement reporting purposes,[31] even though

---

26. *Id.*

27. *Id.*

28. *See* Instruction 2 to Item 402(h)(2). Specifically, a registrant must use the same assumptions regarding such key items as discount rate, interest rate, form of benefit, number of years of service, level of compensation used to determine the benefit, payment distribution, and postretirement mortality as it applies pursuant to FASB ASC Topic 715, *Compensation – Retirement Plans. See* the Adopting Release, *supra* note 1, at n.194. Except for the assumption concerning retirement age, a registrant is not permitted to deviate from these assumptions and take into consideration the individual circumstances of the NEO or the plan. *See* the Current Staff Guidance, *supra* note 24, at Q&A 124.01. A benefit specified in the plan document or the executive's contract itself is not an assumption. *See id.* at Q&A 124.04.

29. *See* the Current Staff Guidance, *supra* note 24, at Q&A 124.02. If the registrant wants to report the actuarial present value of the accumulated benefit using the older age as the retirement age, that information may be presented in an additional column to the table. *Id.*

30. *See* the Adopting Release, *supra* note 1, at n.297 and the accompanying text.

31. *See* the Current Staff Guidance, *supra* note 24, at Q&A 124.01.

it acknowledges and understands that the calculations based on the use of general plan assumptions will not necessarily result in as precise an estimate of the value of the accumulated benefit as using assumptions that reflect the specific characteristics and individual circumstances of the NEO subject to the disclosure or the subject plan.

Accordingly, assumptions regarding "preretirement decrements" should not be factored into the computation.[32] Instead, for purposes of calculating the actuarial present value amount, a registrant should assume that each NEO will live to and retire at the plans' normal retirement age (or the earlier retirement age if the NEO may retire with unreduced benefits) and ignore for purposes of the calculation any actuarially determined preretirement decrements.[33] Typically, the assumptions used for financial statement reporting purposes that should be used for computing the actuarial present value of the accumulated benefit are:

- the discount rate;
- the lump-sum interest rate (if applicable);
- postretirement mortality; and
- payment distribution assumptions.[34]

Any contingent benefits arising upon death, early retirement, or other events resulting in a termination of employment should be reported in the Potential Payments upon Termination or Change-in-Control disclosure.[35]

A registrant must disclose in the accompanying textual narrative the valuation method and all material assumptions applied in quantifying the present value of the current accrued benefit.[36] A benefit specified in the plan document or the executive's contract itself is not an assumption.[37] A registrant may satisfy all or part of this disclosure requirement by reference to a discussion of those assumptions in the registrant's financial statements, footnotes to the financial statements,

---

32. *See id.* at Q&A 124.04.
33. *Id.*
34. *Id.*
35. *Id. See* Chapter 12.
36. *See* Instruction 2 to Item 402(h)(2).
37. *Id.*

or discussion in the Management's Discussion and Analysis.[38] While the SEC Staff has not been formally asked, it is believed that, similar to the disclosure of assumptions in the Stock Awards and Options Awards columns of the Summary Compensation Table, it would be permissible to set out the assumptions in the accompanying narrative discussion itself.

Under some defined benefit plans, a participant will earn (accrue) a particular benefit at a specified age (for example, upon attaining age 55). In this situation, it is not apparent from the executive compensation disclosure rules how a registrant should measure the actuarial present value of the accumulated pension benefit. For example, if a NEO at age 40 is granted an award if he or she stays with the registrant until age 60, it is not clear how the registrant should measure the value of this benefit when the NEO is age 50 and the normal retirement age under the plan is age 65. The SEC Staff has indicated that, in this situation, the computation should be based on the accumulated benefit as of the pension measurement date, assuming that the NEO continues to live and will work for the registrant until retirement and, thus, will reach age 60 and receive the award.[39]

In the case of a "cash balance" pension plan,[40] the amount to be reported in the table as the present value of the accumulated benefit is the actuarial present value of a NEO's accumulated benefit under the plan, computed as of the same plan measurement date used for purposes of the registrant's audited financial statements for the last completed fiscal year, even though the amount of the accrued benefit that the participant will receive under the plan differs from this hypothetical accumulated benefit amount.[41]

---

38. *Id.* The sections so referenced are deemed part of the disclosure provided pursuant to this Item. *Id.*

39. *See* the Current Staff Guidance, *supra* note 24, at Q&A 124.03.

40. A cash balance pension plan is a defined benefit plan in which the participant's benefit may be determined by the amount represented in a hypothetical "account" notionally maintained for that participant. The "accrued benefit" is the amount credited to a participant's cash balance account as of any date, which the participant has the right to receive as a lump sum upon termination of employment.

41. *See* the Current Staff Guidance, *supra* note 24, at Q&A 124.05. A registrant may disclose the actual account balance for a NEO in a footnote to the column. *Id.*

Payments and Benefits

Column (e) of the table is to report the amount of any withdrawals by or distributions made to a NEO during the last completed fiscal year from each disclosed plan. Except where the receipt of benefits payable pursuant to a defined benefit or actuarial plan is accelerated pursuant to a change in control of the registrant, these amounts are reported exclusively in this table and are not reportable in the All Other Compensation column of the Summary Compensation Table.[42]

The reporting of a withdrawal or distribution in the table should not have an impact on the amount reported in the Change in Pension Value and Nonqualified Deferred Compensation Earnings column of the Summary Compensation Table. In other words, a withdrawal or distribution is not "netted" against a change in the value of a pension benefit in the year of the withdrawal or distribution. The change in value of the benefit is first reported in full in the Summary Compensation Table and, concurrently, the amount of the withdrawal or distribution is reported in this table.[43]

If there have been no withdrawals or distributions during the last completed fiscal year, this column may be omitted from the table.[44]

Accompanying Narrative Disclosure

The Pension Benefits Table is to be accompanied by a succinct narrative description of any material factors the disclosure of which would

---

42. See Instruction 2 to Item 402(c)(2)(ix). As proposed, the amount of pension benefits paid to a NEO during the last completed fiscal year would have been reported in the Summary Compensation Table. See Proposed Item 402(c)(2)(ix)(G). In adopting the rules, this amount was shifted to the Pension Benefits Table since the increase in the value of the pension benefit would have been previously disclosed in the Summary Compensation Table. This change eliminated the risk of "double counting" as pension benefits are now disclosed only once in the Summary Compensation Table. See also Instruction 1 to Item 402(c)(2)(viii).

43. This approach is essentially confirmed by the Current Staff Guidance, supra note 24, at Interpretation 219.04, which provides that if the actuarial present value of the accumulated pension benefit for a NEO on the pension measurement date of the prior fiscal year was $1 million, and the present value of the accumulated pension benefit on the pension measurement date of the most recently completed fiscal year is $1 million, but during the most recently completed fiscal year the NEO earned and received an in-service distribution of $200,000, then $200,000 should be reported as an increase in pension value in the Change in Pension Value and Nonqualified Deferred Compensation Earnings column of the Summary Compensation Table.

44. See Item 402(a)(5).

be necessary to an investor's understanding of each plan covered by the table.[45] While the material factors to be disclosed will vary from registrant to registrant depending on the facts, the rules give several examples of the type of factors that a registrant should consider addressing:

- the material terms and conditions of the payments and benefits available under the plan, including the plan's normal retirement payment, benefit formula, and eligibility standards, and the effect of the form of benefit elected on the amount of annual benefits;[46]
- if any NEO is currently eligible for early retirement under any plan, the identity of that NEO and the plan, and a description of the plan's early retirement payment and benefit formula and eligibility standards;[47]
- the specific elements of compensation (for example, salary, bonus, etc.) included in applying the payment and benefit formula, identifying each such element;[48]
- with respect to NEOs' participation in multiple plans, the different purposes for each plan;[49] and
- the registrant's policies with regard to such matters as granting extra years of credited service.[50]

Although the SEC Staff did not comment extensively on the Pension Benefits Table either in its focused review project or in the Staff Report, it has informally indicated that registrants should be sensitive to the length and complexity of the narrative descriptions accompanying the table. Accordingly, it is advisable for registrants to be mindful that these

---

45. Item 402(h)(3).

46. Item 402(h)(3)(i). For this purpose, "normal retirement" means retirement at the normal retirement age as defined in the plan, or, if not so defined, the earliest time at which a participant may retire under the plan without any benefit reduction due to age. *Id.*

47. Item 402(h)(3)(ii). For this purpose, "early retirement" means retirement at the early retirement age as defined in the plan, or otherwise available to the executive under the plan. *Id.*

48. Item 402(h)(3)(iii).

49. Item 402(h)(3)(iv).

50. Item 402(h)(3)(v).

descriptions are to be "succinct", and written for an audience that is probably not well-versed in the intricacies of actuarial science.[51]

Smaller Reporting Companies

While smaller reporting companies are not required to provide a Pension Benefits Table as part of their executive compensation disclosure, they are required to include a narrative description of the material terms of each plan that provides for the payment of retirement benefits, or benefits that will be paid primarily following retirement, including, but not limited to, tax-qualified defined benefit plans and supplemental executive retirement plans to the extent material to an understanding of their executive compensation program.[52]

---

51. For examples of the narrative disclosure accompanying the Pension Benefits Table, *see* the McKesson Corporation Definitive Proxy Statement (Form 14A) filed June 20, 2011 (file no. 001-13252) and the Pfizer, Inc. Definitive Proxy Statement (Form 14A) filed Mar. 22, 2011 (file no. 001-03619). For an example of narrative disclosure accompanying the Pension Benefits Table that provides an explanation of how defined benefit plans operate, see the Black Box Corporation Definitive Proxy Statement (Form 14A) filed June 23, 2011 (file no. 000-18706).

52. *See* Item 402(q)(1).

11

Nonqualified Deferred Compensation Table

General

The Nonqualified Deferred Compensation Table is the second of the two required postemployment disclosure tables.[1] It is intended to provide investors with a comprehensive overview of each named executive officer's (NEO's) participation in nonqualified defined contribution and other deferred compensation plans and arrangements that are maintained by the registrant.[2] Over the past decade, as the use of these

---

1. Item 402(i). A smaller reporting company is not required to provide a Nonqualified Deferred Compensation Table as part of its executive compensation disclosure. *See* Executive Compensation and Related Person Disclosure, Release Nos. 33-8732A, 34-54302A, IC-27444A (Aug. 29, 2006), 71 Fed. Reg. 53,158 (Sept. 8, 2006) [hereinafter Adopting Release], *available at* http://www.sec.gov/rules/final/2006/33-8732a.pdf, at Section II.D.1, and Smaller Reporting Company Regulatory Relief and Simplification, Release Nos. 33-8876, 34-56994, 39-2451 (Dec. 19, 2007), 73 Fed. Reg. 934 (Jan. 4, 2008), *available at* http://www.sec.gov/rules/final/2007/33-8876.pdf, at Section III.C.1. *But see* "Smaller Reporting Companies," *infra*.

2. Nonqualified deferred compensation plans and arrangements provide for the deferral of compensation that does not satisfy the minimum coverage, nondiscrimination, and other rules that qualify such broad-based plans and arrangements for favorable income tax treatment under the Internal Revenue Code. *See* Executive Compensation and Related Party Disclosure, Release Nos. 33-8655, 34-53185, IC-27218 (Jan. 27, 2006), 71 Fed. Reg. 6542 (Feb. 8, 2006), *available at* http://www.sec.gov/rules/proposed/33-8655.pdf, at n.150, and the Adopting Release, *supra* note 1, at n.143. Nonqualified defined contribution and other deferred compensation plans and

plans has increased, nonqualified deferred compensation has come to represent a sizable portion of many executives' retirement income. Since the payment of these amounts often represents a significant corporate liability, in recent years investors have sought to better understand how these plans operate, the amounts that executives have set aside for future receipt, the rate at which those amounts have been growing, and the corresponding cost to the registrant.[3]

The table presents, on a plan-by-plan basis[4] for each NEO, information about contributions, earnings, and withdrawals from each nonqualified defined contribution plan and nonqualified deferred compensation plan or arrangement that was maintained by the registrant during the last completed fiscal year. It also provides disclosure of the account balances that have accumulated under each plan and arrangement as of the end of the last completed fiscal year. Thus, investors are able to better understand the scope and magnitude of a registrant's nonqualified deferred compensation obligations to its NEOs, as well as see the full amount of the earnings generated on these accounts for the last fiscal year.

The Securities and Exchange Commission (SEC) envisions that investors be able to track the changes in each NEO's account balances from fiscal year to fiscal year through the table. Accordingly, an investor should be able to take the outstanding account balance as of the beginning of the last completed fiscal year (as reflected in the prior fiscal year's table), and by tracking contributions, earnings, withdrawals, and distributions during the covered fiscal year arrive at the account balance reported in the table as of the end of the fiscal year. In this respect, the table differs from the other disclosure tables, which do not contemplate

---

arrangements are generally unfunded, and their taxation is governed by Section 409A of the Internal Revenue Code (26 U.S.C. § 409A). *Id.*

3. Under the former rules, disclosure about nonqualified deferred compensation was limited to above-market or preferential earnings paid or payable during the fiscal year. *See* former Item 402(b)(2)(iii)(C)(2) and (v)(B). Amounts deferred at the election of a NEO were to be reported in the Salary or Bonus column, as appropriate, for the fiscal year in which earned. *See* Instruction 1 to former Item 402(b)(2)(iii)(A) and (B).

4. *See* Division of Corporation Finance, Compliance and Disclosure Interpretations – Regulation S-K (July 8, 2011) [hereinafter Current Staff Guidance], *available at* http://www. sec.gov/divisions/corpfin/guidance/regs-kinterp.htm, at Q&A 125.03. *See also* Questions and Answers, Technical Session Between the SEC Staff and the Joint Committee on Employee Benefits (May 6, 2008) [hereinafter 2008 JCEB Questions], *available at* http://www.americanbar. org/content/dam/aba/migrated/2011_build/employee_benefits/sec_2008.authcheckdam.pdf, at Question No. 7.

any type of reconciliation of the amounts reported from fiscal year to fiscal year.

The table covers only nonqualified plans and arrangements. Information about the NEOs' participation in a registrant's tax-qualified Section 401(k) plan or other tax-qualified defined contribution plans is not reported in this table.[5]

Tabular Format

The Nonqualified Deferred Compensation Table is to be presented in the following tabular format:

NONQUALIFIED DEFERRED COMPENSATION

Name (a)	Executive Contributions in Last FY ($) (b)	Registrant Contributions in Last FY ($) (c)	Aggregate Earnings in Last FY ($) (d)	Aggregate Withdrawals/Distributions ($) (e)	Aggregate Balance at Last FYE ($) (f)
Principal Executive Officer (PEO)					
Principal Financial Officer (PFO)					
A					
B					
C					

The table includes the following information for the last completed fiscal year:

- the name of the NEO (column (a));[6]

---

5. In fact, the only disclosure required about tax-qualified defined contribution plans consists of Summary Compensation Table disclosure of any registrant contributions to such plans during the last completed fiscal year (*see* Item 402(c)(2)(ix)(E)). This differentiates this disclosure from that required under the Pension Benefits Table. *See* Chapter 10.

6. Item 402(i)(2)(i).

- the aggregate dollar amount of executive contributions during the registrant's last fiscal year (column (b));[7]
- the aggregate dollar amount of registrant contributions during the registrant's last fiscal year (column (c));[8]
- the aggregate dollar amount of interest or other earnings accrued during the registrant's last fiscal year (column (d));[9]
- the aggregate dollar amount of all withdrawals by and distributions to the named executive officer during the registrant's last fiscal year (column (e));[10] and
- the dollar amount of the total balance of the NEO's account as of the end of the registrant's last fiscal year (column (f)).[11]

As with most of the disclosure tables, the applicable fiscal year is to be added to the title of the table.[12]

Identification of Named Executive Officers

Column (a) of the table is to list each of the registrant's NEOs for the last completed fiscal year. Unlike the Summary Compensation Table, it is not necessary to include the executive's principal position when he or she is being identified.

Executive Contributions

Column (b) of the table is to report the amount that a NEO contributed to each nonqualified defined contribution and nonqualified deferred compensation plan or arrangement during the last completed fiscal year. Following the adoption of the executive compensation disclosure rules, there was some uncertainty as to whether these contributions are to be reported on a cash or accrual basis. For example, if a NEO's contribution to a nonqualified deferred compensation plan consists of base salary earned in fiscal 2011 (which is reported as base salary earned in the fiscal

---

7. Item 402(i)(2)(ii).
8. Item 402(i)(2)(iii).
9. Item 402(i)(2)(iv).
10. Item 402(i)(2)(v).
11. Item 402(i)(2)(vi).
12. *See* the Instruction to Item 402.

2011 Summary Compensation Table), but this amount is not actually credited to the executive's plan account until fiscal 2012, should the registrant report the contribution when the right to the compensation accrued (for fiscal 2011) or when the payment to the plan account was actually made (for fiscal 2012)?

After a few proxy seasons where disclosures reflected both approaches, the staff of the SEC's Division of Corporation Finance (SEC Staff) appears to have indicated a preference for a "accrual" basis, rather than a "cash" basis, approach.[13] As explained in more detail in the next section, the Staff has indicated that the primary objective is to ensure that the information that is presented in the Nonqualified Deferred Compensation Table is consistent with the information presented in the Summary Compensation Table. Note that the use of a cash basis reporting approach may create an inconsistency between the amounts reported in the table and in the Summary Compensation Table (which is to be prepared on an accrual basis).

Typically, the source of a NEO's contributions to nonqualified defined contribution and nonqualified deferred compensation plans and arrangements will be his or her base salary and annual incentive award payments for the fiscal year. To minimize the risk that these amounts will be "double counted" (that is, that they will be inadvertently added to the compensation reported for the NEO in the Summary Compensation Table), the executive compensation disclosure rules require a registrant to provide a footnote to the table quantifying the extent to which the amounts reported in this column have been reported as compensation received or earned in the last completed fiscal year in the registrant's Summary Compensation Table.[14]

The amounts reportable in this column are not limited to amounts contributed to a formal nonqualified defined contribution or nonqualified deferred compensation plan, however. Other types of compensation, the receipt of which has been deferred, must also be included in column (b). For example, where an equity award has vested, and the plan under which it was granted provides for the deferral of its receipt, the deferred receipt of the vested equity award must be included

---

13. As discussed in the following section, in the context of the reporting of registrant contributions, the SEC Staff has indicated that the accrual approach should be used. *See* the Current Staff Guidance, *supra* note 4, at Q&A 125.04. *See* "Registrant Contributions," *infra*. *See also* the 2008 JCEB Questions, *supra* note 4, at Question No. 7.

14. *See* the Instruction to Item 402(i)(2).

in the table.[15] This is the case whether the deferral is at the election of the NEO or pursuant to the terms of the equity award or plan.[16]

Registrant Contributions

Column (c) of the table is to report the amount that the registrant contributed to each nonqualified defined contribution and nonqualified deferred compensation plan or arrangement for each NEO during the last completed fiscal year. The SEC Staff has taken the position that a registrant should report these contributions on an accrual basis.[17]

This guidance strongly suggests that the overall reporting in the Nonqualified Deferred Compensation Table is to be made on an "accrual" basis, rather than a "cash" basis. Subsequent discussions with the SEC Staff have underscored this position. Initially, practitioners raised two potential concerns in response to the Staff's interpretation on registrant contributions. First, these practitioners pointed out, some registrants do not credit their matching contributions to an executive deferral arrangement until the fiscal year following the fiscal year in which the deferral election is made. Accordingly, these matching contributions may not appear in the Summary Compensation Table until the fiscal year in which made. Requiring registrant, and, by extension, executive, contributions to be reported on an "accrual" basis would result in a potential inconsistency in the reporting results between information in the Summary Compensation Table and the Nonqualified Deferred Compensation Table.

In addition, the practitioners pointed out, the reporting of the dollar amount of a NEO's total account balance as of the end of the registrant's last completed fiscal year in column (f) of the table, the Aggregate Balance at Last Fiscal Year-End column, appears to contemplate a "cash" basis approach, again creating a potential internal inconsistency within the table between column (b), the dollar amount of aggregate executive

---

15. *See* the Current Staff Guidance, supra note 4, at Q&A 125.05.

16. *Id.*

17. *See* the Current Staff Guidance, *supra* note 4, at Q&A 125.04 ("Question: Item 402(i)(2)(iii) calls for disclosure of aggregate company contributions to each nonqualified deferred compensation plan during the company's last fiscal year. For an excess plan related to a qualified plan, the contributions earned in 2008, which are reportable in the All Other Compensation column of the 2008 Summary Compensation Table, are not credited to the executive's account until January 2009. Are those contributions considered company contributions "during" 2008? Answer: Yes.").

contributions during the registrant's last completed fiscal year (which would be reported on an "accrual" basis) and column (f).

In response, the SEC Staff has indicated informally that the information reported in the Nonqualified Deferred Compensation Table should be consistent with the information reported in the Summary Compensation Table for the last completed fiscal year. Consequently, since the "All Other Compensation" column (column (i)) of the Summary Compensation Table is to include registrant contributions or other allocations to vested and unvested defined contribution plans,[18] the Nonqualified Deferred Compensation Table should also include this information.[19] As a result, a registrant matching contribution or other allocation to a NEO's deferral account should be reflected in both the "Registrant Contributions in Last Fiscal Year" column (column (c)) and "Aggregate Balance at Last Fiscal Year-End" column (column (f)) of the table where the payment of the contribution or other allocation is ministerial in nature (that is, the registrant is obligated to make the contribution or other allocation).[20] In addition, a registrant should provide a footnote to the relevant columns of the table disclosing that the amounts reported include contributions or other allocations that will be made after the end of the last completed fiscal year.

Since, as noted, these registrant contributions will have also been reported in the All Other Compensation column of the Summary Compensation Table,[21] there is a risk that the disclosure of this information may lead to "double counting" (that is, these amounts may be inadvertently added to the compensation reported for the NEO in the Summary Compensation Table). To mitigate this possibility, the rules require a registrant to provide a footnote to the table quantifying the extent to which the amounts reported in this column have been

---

18. *See* Item 402(c)(2)(ix)(E). Note that the amounts required to be reported pursuant to this requirement will not necessarily correspond precisely with what is to be reported in column (c) since the Summary Compensation Table disclosure requirement covers registrant contributions or other allocations to *all* vested and unvested defined contribution plans (both tax-qualified and nonqualified), while column (c) covers only *nonqualified* plans and arrangements.

19. *See* Questions and Answers, Technical Session Between the SEC Staff and the Joint Committee on Employee Benefits (May 4, 2010), *available at* http://www.americanbar.org/content/dam/aba/events/employee_benefits/2010_sec_qa.authcheckdam.pdf, at Question No. 4.

20. *Id.*

21. *See* Item 402(c)(2)(ix)(E).

reported as compensation received or earned in the last completed fiscal year in the registrant's Summary Compensation Table.[22]

Interest and Other Earnings Disclosure

Column (d) of the table is to report the amount of interest and other earnings that accrued during the last completed fiscal year to a NEO's account under each nonqualified defined contribution and nonqualified deferred compensation plan or arrangement. As with contributions, a registrant will need to decide whether it is going to report these earnings on a cash or accrual basis.[23] The reporting requirement applies to both investment earnings on elective deferrals and investment earnings on registrant contributions.[24]

There is no symmetry between the information reported in this column for defined contribution plans and that required in the Pension Benefits Table for defined benefit plans. In the case of defined benefit pension plans, the rules require disclosure of the present value of the accumulated benefits for both tax-qualified and nonqualified plans, while here there is no requirement to report investment earnings attributable to tax-qualified defined contribution plans.[25]

For purposes of column (d), this disclosure is to encompass *all* earnings that accrued during the last completed fiscal year, not just the above-market or preferential portion of such earnings that must be reported in the Summary Compensation Table.[26] To the extent that a portion of the reported amounts constitute above-market or preferential earnings, there is a risk that the disclosure of this information may lead to

---

22. *See* the Instruction to Item 402(i)(2).

23. *See* "Executive Contributions," *supra.*

24. Arguably, there is a difference between these two amounts. A NEO could have received the compensation that has been electively deferred and invested it privately without incurring a disclosure obligation.

25. There is no requirement to report the amount of investment or other earnings accrued during the last completed fiscal year under a tax-qualified defined contribution plan, such as a Section 401(k) plan. *See* the Current Staff Guidance, *supra* note 4, at Q&A 119.10. *See also* W. Alan Kailer, Hunton & Williams, *The Securities and Exchange Commission's Executive Compensation Rules—Preparing the Executive Compensation Tables* (Jan. 2012) [hereinafter Kailer], at A-21 and B-22.

26. *See* Item 402(c)(2)(viii)(B). *See* also the Adopting Release, *supra* note 1, at n.186 and the accompanying text. For a discussion of above-market and preferential earnings, see "Pension Value Changes and Above-Market and Preferential Earnings—Above-Market and Preferential Earnings" in Chapter 4.

"double counting" (that is, these amounts may be inadvertently added to the compensation reported for the NEO in the Summary Compensation Table). To mitigate this possibility, the rules require a registrant to provide a footnote to the table quantifying the extent to which the amounts reported in this column have been reported as compensation received or earned in the last completed fiscal year in the registrant's Summary Compensation Table.[27] Essentially, a registrant must use a footnote to differentiate between the above-market or preferential portion of the reported earnings and the remainder of the earnings.

The amounts that are to be reported in column (d) are not explicitly described in the rules. While "interest" is self-explanatory, from the outset questions were raised as to what type of items constituted reportable "earnings." The SEC Staff has indicated that for purposes of column (d), "earnings" includes dividends, stock price appreciation (and depreciation),[28] and other similar items.[29] This position is consistent with the overall objective of the table, which, as previously described, is intended to show the annual change in the aggregate account balance for each NEO. Consequently, the amounts reportable in column (d) should encompass any increase or decrease in the balance of a nonqualified defined contribution or nonqualified deferred compensation plan account during the last completed fiscal year that is not attributable to contributions, withdrawals, or distributions during the year.[30]

Aggregate Withdrawals and Distributions

Column (e) of the table is to report the amount of any withdrawals by or distributions made to a NEO during the last completed fiscal year from each nonqualified defined contribution and nonqualified deferred compensation plan or arrangement. There is no requirement to report the amount of any withdrawals or distributions made to a NEO under any tax-qualified Section 401(k) plan.[31] Unlike the table's other columns,

---

27. *See* the Instruction to Item 402(i)(2).

28. Where, for example, the return on deferrals is tied to the performance of the registrant's stock.

29. *See* the Current Staff Guidance, *supra* note 4, at Q&A 125.02.

30. *Id.*

31. *Id.* at Q&A 119.10. *See also* Kailer, *supra* note 25, at A-23 and B-22.

there is no risk of "double-counting" here since benefits paid pursuant to defined contribution and similar plans are not reportable in the All Other Compensation column of the Summary Compensation Table.[32] Instead, those amounts are to be reported exclusively in this table.

Aggregate Account Balances

Column (f) of the table is to report the total balance of a NEO's account under each nonqualified defined contribution and nonqualified deferred compensation plan or arrangement as of the end of the last completed fiscal year. As with contributions and earnings, a registrant will need to decide whether it is going to report these account balances on a cash or accrual basis.[33]

Since, in most instances, these account balances will reflect amounts that have been previously reported in the current and prior Summary Compensation Tables, there is a risk that the disclosure of this information may lead to "double counting" (that is, these amounts may be inadvertently added to the compensation reported for the NEO in the Summary Compensation Table). To mitigate this possibility, the rules require a registrant to provide a footnote to the table quantifying the extent to which the amounts reported in this column previously were reported as compensation paid to or earned by the NEO in the registrant's Summary Compensation Table for the current and previous fiscal years.[34] This footnote is intended to help investors understand the extent to which amounts payable as deferred compensation represent compensation previously reported, rather than additional currently earned compensation.

---

32. *See* Instruction 2 to Item 402(c)(2)(ix). Even though the Instruction refers explicitly only to defined benefit and actuarial plans, the SEC Staff has indicated that it is intended to apply to defined contribution plans as well. *See* the Current Staff Guidance, *supra* note 4, at Q&A 119.10.

33. *See* "Executive Contributions," *supra*. An inconsistent application of this principle could result in column figures that cannot be reconciled to each other.

34. *See* the Instruction to Item 402(i)(2). This footnote should disclose the sum of the amounts included in the Summary Compensation Table for the last completed and prior fiscal years (including above-market and preferential earnings), but without reduction for withdrawals and distributions. This may lead to overreporting where a NEO's account balance has been reduced as a result of withdrawals and distributions that aren't included in the Summary Compensation Table. *See* Kailer, *supra* note 25, at A-23 and B-21.

Note that this requirement applies only to amounts that were actually previously reported in the Summary Compensation Table. If an amount that is otherwise reported in column (f) was not actually previously reported in the Summary Compensation Table (either as a result of the transition guidance in the Adopting Release or because a NEO is appearing in the table for the first time), it does not need to be disclosed in this footnote.[35] Thus, since the three-year transition period for implementing the Summary Compensation Table is now complete, the quantification need only cover the amounts that are reported in the three-year period covered by the Summary Compensation Table.[36] During this transition period, the quantification need not include amounts reported in Summary Compensation Tables prepared under the former rules.

Accompanying Narrative Disclosure

The Nonqualified Deferred Compensation Table is to be accompanied by a succinct narrative description of any material factors the disclosure of which would be necessary to an investor's understanding of each plan and arrangement covered by the table.[37] While the material factors to be disclosed will vary from registrant to registrant depending

---

35. *See* the Current Staff Guidance, *supra* note 4, at Q&A 125.01. Since the purpose of the Instruction is to facilitate an understanding that nonqualified deferred compensation is reported elsewhere in the compensation tables over time, the inclusion of this additional information is not required. Thus, it is not necessary to quantify the extent to which the amounts reported in column (f) were reported in Summary Compensation Tables prepared under the former rules.

36. While the quantification may cover a longer period (*see* Questions and Answers, Technical Session Between the SEC Staff and the Joint Committee on Employee Benefits (May 8, 2007), [hereinafter 2007 JCEB Questions] *available at* http://www.abanet.org/jceb/2007/SEC07Final.pdf, at Question No. 13), limiting the disclosure to the three-year period covered by the Summary Compensation Table serves the purpose of preventing investors from "double-counting" reported compensation. Some observers have noted that the reporting of amounts reported in previous year's Summary Compensation Tables beyond this three-year period does not provide investors with useful information because it only picks up a NEO's contributions to a plan or arrangement during the fiscal years in which he or she was a NEO after the effective date of the rules (and, thus, does not fully reflect the extent to which the fiscal year-end account balance is attributable to a NEO's contributions). To the extent that a registrant opts to quantify the full amount of a NEO's contributions (including contributions that were never reported in a Summary Compensation Table), the disclosure should make clear what is being reported. *See* the 2007 JCEB Questions at Question No. 13(a).

37. Item 402(i)(3).

on the facts, the rules give several examples of the type of factors that a registrant may consider addressing:[38]

- the type or types of compensation that may be deferred, and any limitations (by percentage of compensation or otherwise) on the extent to which deferral is permitted;[39]
- the measure or measures used for calculating interest or other plan earnings (including whether such measure or measures are selected by the NEO or the registrant, and the frequency and manner in which the selections may be changed), quantifying interest rates and other earnings measures applicable during the registrant's last fiscal year;[40] and
- the material terms of the plan or arrangement with respect to payouts, withdrawals, and other distributions.[41]

Where a plan's earnings are calculated by reference to the actual earnings of an investment medium, such as a mutual fund or other securities (for example, the registrant's stock), it is sufficient to identify the reference security and quantify its return.[42] In this instance, the disclosure may be aggregated to the extent the same measure applies to more than one NEO.[43]

While the Adopting Release suggests that this narrative disclosure should follow the table,[44] there does not appear to be any reason why this information cannot precede the table. In fact, several registrants provide the contemplated descriptions of their plans and arrangements before presenting the table as a way of making the information reported easier for investors to understand. The rules themselves do not appear to impose any ordering requirement for the presentation of this information.

---

38. Given the importance of Section 409A of the Internal Revenue Code Section (26 U.S.C. § 409A) in the design and operation of nonqualified deferred compensation arrangements, a registrant may want to consider addressing the income tax implications for both the participant and the registrant of such arrangements as part of the required narrative description.

39. Item 402(i)(3)(i).

40. Item 402(i)(3)(ii). *See also* the Adopting Release, *supra* note 1, at n.187 and the accompanying text.

41. Item 402(i)(3)(iii).

42. *See* the Adopting Release, *supra* note 1, at n.311 and the accompanying text.

43. *Id.*

44. *Id.*

Smaller Reporting Companies

While smaller reporting companies are not required to provide a Nonqualified Deferred Compensation Table as part of their executive compensation disclosure, they are required to include a narrative description of the material terms of each plan that provides for the payment of retirement benefits, or benefits that will be paid primarily following retirement, including, but not limited to, tax-qualified defined contribution plans and nonqualified defined contribution plans to the extent material to an understanding of their executive compensation program.[45]

---

45. *See* Item 402(q)(1).

12

Potential Payments upon Termination or Change-in-Control Disclosure

General

The final piece of the required postemployment disclosure focuses on the compensatory payments and benefits that a registrant has agreed to provide its named executive officers (NEOs) in the event of a termination of employment or following a change in control of the registrant.[1] As noted in the Adopting Release, the Securities and Exchange Commission (SEC) "has long recognized that 'termination provisions are distinct from other plans in both intent and scope and, moreover, are of particular

---

1. Item 402(j). A smaller reporting company is not required to provide information about potential payments upon termination of employment or a change in control of the company as part of its executive compensation disclosure. *See* Executive Compensation and Related Person Disclosure, Release Nos. 33-8732A, 34-54302A, IC-27444A (Aug. 29, 2006), 71 Fed. Reg. 53,158 (Sept. 8, 2006) [hereinafter Adopting Release], *available at* http://www.sec.gov/rules/final/2006/33-8732a.pdf, at Section II.D.1, and Smaller Reporting Company Regulatory Relief and Simplification, Release Nos. 33-8876, 34-56994, 39-2451 (Dec. 19, 2007), 73 Fed. Reg. 934 (Jan. 4, 2008), *available at* http://www.sec.gov/rules/final/2007/33-8876.pdf, at Section III.C.1. *But see* "Smaller Reporting Companies," *infra*.

interest to shareholders."[2] More importantly, in recent years investors were increasingly active in seeking more meaningful information about registrant severance policies and practices in an effort to better monitor the effectiveness of these arrangements.

The approach taken by the rules differs significantly from the prior disclosure requirements. Under the former rules, only a general description of severance and change-in-control plans and arrangements was required, and then only to the extent that the amount involved exceeded $100,000.[3] There was no requirement to quantify the potential amounts that were payable under these plans and arrangements. As a result, this disclosure did not give investors a sense of the magnitude of these payments or when the amounts would be payable. Perhaps even more importantly, board compensation committees were frequently unaware of the amount of the obligation to which a registrant had committed itself.

Consequently, the executive compensation disclosure rules, which largely cover the same situations as the former rules, require much more detailed information about the arrangements themselves, as well as an estimate of the amounts payable, in the event that a NEO leaves the registrant or receives payments or benefits as a result of a change in control of the registrant or a change in his or her responsibilities. This quantification requirement is intended to give investors an effective means of better understanding and evaluating the potentially significant amounts of compensation that may be involved in these arrangements.

While the quantified amounts are simply estimates, registrants should recognize that, given the potential inclusion of severance payments in the Summary Compensation Table, investors are likely compare the actual payments received against the previously disclosed estimates to identify any material discrepancies. Consequently, in preparing the required disclosure, registrants should be sensitive to this possibility and be prepared to defend their interpretation of the

2. *See* the Adopting Release, *supra* note 1, at n.312, quoting from Disclosure of Executive Compensation, Release No. 33-6486 (Sept. 23, 1983), 48 Fed. Reg. 44,467, at Section III.E.

3. *See* former Item 402(h)(2): "describe the terms and conditions of . . . the following contracts or arrangements: . . . Any compensatory plan or arrangement, including payments to be received from the registrant, with respect to a NEO, if such plan or arrangement results or will result from the resignation, retirement or any other termination of such executive officers' employment with the registrant and its subsidiaries or from a change in control of the registrant or a change in the NEO's responsibilities following a change in control and the amount involved, including all periodic payments or installments, exceeds $100,000."

operation of the relevant severance or change-in-control arrangements should questions subsequently arise.

Disclosure Format

Unlike the other required postemployment disclosures, the information about severance and change-in-control plans and arrangements does not have to be presented in a tabular format.[4] In fact, the Adopting Release indicates that the required information is to be presented in narrative form.[5] Nonetheless, consistent with its plain-English principles the SEC encourages registrants to develop their own tables to report post-employment compensation if such tabular presentation facilitates clearer, more concise disclosure. Given the rule's emphasis on quantifying the estimated payments and benefits that would be provided in each described termination or change-in-control scenario, since the 2007 proxy season most companies use a combination of narrative and tabular disclosure to present the required information.[6] Throughout its review of 2007 proxy filings and thereafter, the staff of the SEC's Division of Corporation Finance (SEC Staff) expressed a preference for tabular disclosure when practical and consistent with the purposes of the rules.[7]

---

4. While the SEC solicited comment on whether to require presentation of the required information in a tabular format, ultimately it chose not to do so. This decision was based, in part, on recognition of the difficulty in prescribing a single format that would accommodate the numerous variations in severance and change-in-control arrangements and the factors that determine payments under such arrangements. *See* the Adopting Release, *supra* note 1, at Section VI.

5. *See* the Adopting Release, *supra* note 1, at n.314 and the accompanying text.

6. *See, e.g.,* the Eli Lilly and Company Definitive Proxy Statement (Form 14A) filed Mar. 7, 2011 (file no. 001-06351).

7. *See* Division of Corporation Finance, *Staff Observations in the Review of Executive Compensation Disclosure* (Oct. 9, 2007) [hereinafter Staff Report], *available at* http://www. sec.gov/divisions/corpfin/guidance/execcompdisclosure.htm, under the heading "Format." The SEC Staff has also encouraged registrants to provide totals of the payments and benefits available to the NEOs under each termination and change-in-control scenario to facilitate investor understanding. *Id.*

Disclosure Requirements

Under the rules, a registrant must disclose, with respect to each contract, agreement, plan, or arrangement, whether written or unwritten, that provides for any payment or payments to a NEO at, following, or in connection with his or her termination of employment, including, without limitation, any resignation, severance, retirement, or a constructive termination of employment, or a change in control of the registrant, or a change in the NEO's responsibilities, with respect to each NEO:

- the specific circumstances that would trigger the payment or payments or the provision of other benefits, including perquisites and health care benefits;[8]
- the estimated payments and benefits that would be provided pursuant to each triggering event, whether they would or could be lump sum or annual, disclosing the duration and by whom they would be provided;[9]
- how the appropriate payment and benefit levels are determined under the various triggering events;[10]
- any material conditions or obligations applicable to the receipt of payments or benefits;[11] and
- any other material factors regarding each such contract, agreement, plan, or arrangement.[12]

Identification of Named Executive Officers

The required disclosure must separately address the potential payments and benefits for each of the registrant's NEOs.[13] While this clearly includes the registrant's principal executive officer (PEO), principal financial officer (PFO), and the registrant's three most highly compensated executive officers (other than the PEO and PFO) who were

8. Item 402(j)(1).
9. Item 402(j)(2).
10. Item 402(j)(3).
11. Item 402(j)(4).
12. Item 402(j)(5).
13. *See* the introductory language of Item 402(j).

serving as executive officers at the end of the last completed fiscal year,[14] it also includes any individual who served as the registrant's PEO or PFO (or acted in a similar capacity) at any time during the last completed fiscal year, as well as the two additional individuals for whom disclosure is required under Item 02(a)(3)(iv).[15] Although the rules do not appear to require that a registrant include a NEO's principal position when he or she is being discussed, either in the narrative text of any discussion or any tabular disclosure, it is advisable to do so to facilitate an investor's understanding of the disclosure.

Reportable Arrangements

The disclosure applies to any contract, agreement, plan, or arrangement, whether written or unwritten, that provides for payments to or benefits on behalf of a NEO. Thus, the severance provisions of an employment agreement would be covered by the disclosure.[16] Similarly, the terms and conditions of an employee equity plan providing for accelerated vesting of outstanding awards in the event of a change in control of the registrant would also be covered by the disclosure.

Given the broad scope of the type of arrangements covered, registrants must be conscious of any unwritten policies and practices for compensating their executives, particularly upon a termination of employment, which may trigger disclosure. For example, a registrant that has an unwritten "policy" of accelerating the vesting of outstanding equity awards upon an executive's retirement after 20 years of continuous service will need to describe this practice and quantify the value of this benefit even though it is not reflected in any formal plan or arrangement.

---

14. *See* "Persons Covered" in Chapter 2.

15. As provided in Item 402(a)(3)(iv), these are individuals who would have been among the registrant's three most highly compensated executive officers (other than the registrant's chief executive officer and chief financial officer) but for the fact that they were not serving as executive officers of the registrant at the end of the last completed fiscal year.

16. Note that Item 402(e) requires a registrant to provide a narrative description of any material factors necessary to an understanding of the information disclosed in the Summary Compensation Table and the Grants of Plan-Based Awards Table, such as the material terms of each NEO's employment agreement or arrangement. *See* Item 402(e)(1)(i). Presumably, the portion of any such agreement addressing compensatory payments and benefits upon a termination of employment or in connection with a change in control of the registrant may be covered under this disclosure item with an appropriate cross-reference.

Since the disclosure is intended to highlight payments and benefits that are being provided primarily to executives, a registrant need not provide information with respect to contracts, agreements, plans, or arrangements to the extent they do not discriminate in scope, terms, or operation in favor of executive officers of the registrant and as long as they are available generally to all salaried employees.[17] Consequently, registrants are not required to describe and quantify many organization-wide arrangements, such as health, disability, hospitalization, and medical reimbursement plans, which provide postemployment benefits to all of the registrant's employees, including its executives.

While the wording of this Instruction suggests that it is potentially applicable to a broad range of plans and arrangements, it is important to recognize that its reach is not unlimited. For example, the employee equity plans of some registrants provide for full and immediate vesting of all outstanding unvested awards upon a change in control of the registrant and include a provision to this effect in each recipient's award agreement (whether the recipient is an executive officer or an employee of the registrant). Nonetheless, the SEC Staff has indicated that a registrant may not rely on the Instruction to omit these awards from its change-in-control disclosure.[18] In this situation, the Instruction's standard that the "scope" of the arrangements not discriminate in favor of executive officers would not be satisfied where the awards to executives are in greater amounts than those provided to salaried employees.[19]

---

17. *See* Instruction 5 to Item 402(j). While the intended scope of the "available generally to all salaried employees" language is not entirely clear, it is believed that foreign (that is, non–United States) employees may be excluded from the analysis. In other words, if a plan or arrangement is available generally to all of a registrant's salaried U.S. employees, but not its foreign salaried employee, it still should qualify for the Instruction's exclusion. Similarly, if a plan was at one time available generally to all salaried employees, but eligibility for the plan has been closed such that new salaried employees (including executives) are not permitted to participate in the plan, it also should qualify for the Instruction's exclusion to the extent that it otherwise satisfies the conditions of the exclusion.

18. *See* Division of Corporation Finance, Compliance and Disclosure Interpretations – Regulation S-K (July 8, 2011) [hereinafter Current Staff Guidance], *available at* http://www.sec.gov/divisions/corpfin/guidance/regs-kinterp.htm, at Q&A 126.02.

19. *Id.*

Reportable Events

The disclosure should cover any payment to or the receipt of benefits by a NEO at, following, or in connection with any termination of his or her employment, a change in control of the registrant, or a change in the NEO's responsibilities. Unlike the former rule, there is no minimum dollar threshold for disclosure. Thus, even payments and benefits that total less than $100,000 must be disclosed. Given the absence of a minimum disclosure threshold, registrants need to be diligent in evaluating any and all potential payments and benefits that may result upon a termination of employment or a change in control since even a nominal amount will need to be described and quantified as part of this disclosure.

Registrants should also be thorough in describing the definitions that govern the occurrence of a triggering event, as well as the material assumptions and conditions that influence the operation of the relevant severance or change-in-control provisions. Registrants will need to balance their desire to provide the precise terms and conditions that govern these provisions with the SEC's mandate that the disclosure conform to its plain-English principles.[20]

Termination of Employment

The rules specify three events resulting in a termination of employment that trigger disclosure: resignation, retirement, and a constructive termination. As the rules further note, however, this list is not exhaustive. Accordingly, if a NEO's employment is terminated with cause, without cause, or as a result of a disability or a voluntary separation of service, and he or she receives or is to receive payments or benefits in connection with the applicable event, disclosure is required.[21] Similar disclosure is required if a NEO is eligible to receive payments or benefits on his or her death.

While the rules also expressly identify "severance" as a triggering event, it is not clear whether this is simply shorthand for the broad categories of voluntary and involuntary terminations of employment

---

20. See "Plain-English Requirement" in Chapter 2.

21. This disclosure is presumably broader than under former Item 402(h)(2), which covered compensatory plans or arrangements resulting from "the resignation, retirement or any other termination of such executive's employment" and did not contain the illustrative language of the current rules.

that result in severance payments, or whether a more limited set of circumstances was contemplated.

Further, the termination of employment does not necessarily have to involve the registrant. In the case of a NEO who is an employee of a subsidiary,[22] the relevant disclosure should cover payments made by, as well as benefits receivable from, both the subsidiary and, if applicable, the registrant.

Change in Control

Disclosure is required if a NEO receives or is to receive payments or benefits in connection with a change in control of the registrant. For example, if the registrant has an employee equity plan that provides for accelerated vesting of outstanding unvested awards upon a change in control, disclosure is required even though the registrant's NEOs will remain employed following the transaction.

Thus, in some situations, a registrant's compensation arrangements may provide for the vesting of equity awards upon the change in control (a "single trigger"[23] event) and the payment of cash severance and specified other benefits upon a termination of employment (either actual or constructive) within a specified period of time following the change in control (a "double trigger"[24] event). Each of these occurrences is considered to be a separate reportable event for purposes of the disclosure and will need to be separately explained and quantified.

A "change in control" is not defined in the rules. Instead, the precise scope of this triggering event will depend on the definition in the relevant contract, agreement, plan, or arrangement providing for the payment or benefit to be reported.

Change in Responsibilities

Even though a change in job responsibilities is customarily associated with a constructive termination of employment following a change of control of a registrant, it is not so limited for disclosure purposes. In the Adopting Release, the SEC confirmed that this aspect of the disclosure

---

22. *See* Instruction 2 to Item 402(a)(3).

23. A "single trigger" arrangement is one under which the stipulated amount is payable upon the change in control of the registrant.

24. A "double trigger" arrangement is one under which the stipulated amount is payable upon a specified termination of employment preceding or following a change in control of the registrant.

requirement is not limited to a change in responsibilities in connection with a change in control.[25] Thus, any payment that is or would be payable to, or benefit received or receivable by, a NEO due to a material change[26] in his or her role or responsibilities with the registrant would need to be described. For example, a registrant policy that provides executives with additional compensation (such as an additional equity award) in connection with a promotion could necessitate a discussion (and, possibly, quantification) of these potential amounts. As a practical matter, however, such arrangements are unlikely to arise very often.

Reportable Payments and Benefits

The disclosure should include any amount that is paid or payable, directly or indirectly, to a NEO as a result of a triggering event. It should also include any benefit received or receivable, directly or indirectly, by the NEO as a result of the triggering event. Thus, a registrant must both describe the nature of the payment or benefit, as well as quantify its amount.[27] While the intent of this disclosure requirement is to pick up any type of payment or benefit associated with a termination of employment or a change in control of a registrant, payments in the nature of perquisites and health care benefits[28] are expressly identified as two categories of benefits that must be described and quantified as part of the disclosure.[29]

It is also important to note that the disclosure applies only to payments and benefits that are payable as a result of the triggering event itself. In many instances, this amount will differ from the total amount of compensation that an executive will receive upon a termination of employment (the so-called "walk away" number) since it does not

---

25. *See* the Adopting Release, *supra* note 1, at n.313. This differs from former Item 402(h)(2), which limited this disclosure to situations involving "a change in a NEO's responsibilities following a change-in-control."

26. Although Item 402(j) does nor contain a materiality threshold for disclosure, presumably a minor or nonsubstantive change in a NEO's responsibilities would not trigger disclosure. Nonetheless, registrants should be cautious about compensating their executives in connection with promotions or other job changes that could potentially be disclosable under this provision.

27. Item 402(j)(2).

28. *But see* Item 402(a)(6)(ii), which excludes broad-based, nondiscriminatory group life, health, hospitalization, and medical reimbursement plans from disclosure.

29. Item 402(j)(1).

include previously earned and vested amounts that have accrued but that the executive has not actually received (for example, vested but unexercised in-the-money stock options and nonqualified deferred compensation account balances). While these amounts will have been previously reported (as part of the current fiscal year or prior fiscal years' disclosure), there is an emerging best practice either to include the earned and accrued compensation as part of this disclosure or to provide this information as an accompaniment to the required information. Nonetheless, most registrants continue to limit their termination and change-in-control disclosure to the payments and benefits that are triggered by the event itself, and did not include amounts that would otherwise be payable to their NEOs without regard to their employment status.

A registrant also must disclose the form of payment (annual or lump sum) and the duration of the payment or benefit.[30] Finally, the registrant must indicate by whom the payment will be provided.[31] While the proper application of these requirements is not readily apparent, most interpretive issues that arise in evaluating specific postemployment compensation arrangements can probably be answered through the lens of the "principles-based" disclosure doctrine that permeates the rules. For example, in the case of an executive retirement plan that provides payments for life in the event of a change in control of the registrant, it may not be clear whether the potential value of this benefit should be reported as an annual amount (with the accompanying disclosure of the NEO's actuarially determined remaining life) or on a lump sum basis. While the SEC Staff has not taken a position on this issue, the most appropriate way to present the required information is likely to involve reporting the present value of the annuity payment, as this approach is consistent with how pension benefits are reported in the Pension Benefits Table, and provides shareholders with the most complete picture of what the pension enhancement is worth.

Determining Payments and Benefits

The disclosure should include a discussion of how the appropriate payment and benefit levels are determined under each of the various

---

30. *Id.*
31. *Id.*

triggering events. The precise scope of this disclosure is somewhat elusive. At one level, the discussion should address the relevant provisions and formulas that are used to calculate the payments and benefits that would be payable to or received by each NEO, and not the methodologies that the registrant employed to quantify the amounts reported pursuant to this disclosure.[32] To the extent that the discussion covers design and policy considerations with respect to the structure and operation of the relevant provisions, however, this information is probably better suited for inclusion in the Compensation Discussion and Analysis (CD&A).

Most registrants satisfy this requirement by summarizing the specific terms and conditions of the relevant provisions that would result in the provision of payments and benefits upon the occurrence of a triggering event.

Quantifying Potential Payments and Benefits

The key aspect of the disclosure is the requirement to quantify the estimated payments and benefits that would be paid to or received by the NEOs as a result of a triggering event. In making these estimates, a registrant is to assume that

- each relevant triggering event took place on the last business day of the registrant's last completed fiscal year; and
- the price per share of the registrant's securities was the closing market price as of that date.[33]

Although this framework should cover most of the potential scenarios under which the estimated payments and benefits are to be calculated, there may be situations in which it is unclear whether a right to payment would exist or what amount would be payable.[34] Under the

32. This requirement differs from the proposed disclosure item, which called for a description and explanation of the specific factors used to determine the appropriate payment and benefit levels under the various triggering events. This language was revised in an attempt to avoid a mere repetition of the specific information about specific benefits, such as the pension payout formula and actuarial assumptions. See the Adopting Release, *supra* note 1, at n.316.

33. *See* Instruction 1 to Item 402(j).

34. One situation where this uncertainty may arise would involve an arrangement that provides for a "gross-up" or other tax reimbursement payment in connection with a termination of employment following a change in control of a registrant. See "Specific Disclosure Items— "Gross-Ups" and Other Tax Reimbursements," *infra*.

rules, a registrant is required to provide quantitative disclosure even where uncertainties exist as to amounts payable under its plans and arrangements. In the event of such uncertainties as to the provision of payments and benefits or the amounts involved, a registrant is required to make a reasonable estimate (or provide a reasonable estimated range of amounts) applicable to the payment or benefit and disclose the material assumptions underlying such estimates or estimated ranges in its disclosure.[35] In such event, the disclosure would require forward-looking information as appropriate.[36]

There is no requirement to disclose the assumptions underlying the calculations made to quantify the estimated payments and benefits and, not surprisingly, few registrants provide this information.

Material Conditions or Obligations Applicable to Receipt of Payments or Benefits

In the event that the receipt of a payment or benefit is conditioned upon satisfaction of or compliance with a material condition or obligation, a registrant must describe and explain the condition and/or obligation. Typically, this will involve compliance with noncompetition, nonsolicitation, or nondisparagement restrictions for a specified period of time and/or execution of a confidentiality agreement with the registrant. Note, however, that the disclosure requirement is not expressly limited to these types of agreements, but covers any material condition or obligation.

In the event that such a condition or obligation exists, the registrant must also indicate the duration of the agreement and disclose and describe any provision regarding the registrant's ability to waive a breach of the agreement.[37]

---

35. *See* Instruction 1 to Item 402(j).

36. *Id.* In this event, the disclosure will be considered forward-looking information as appropriate that falls within the safe harbors for disclosure of such information. *See, e.g.,* Securities Act Section 27A (15 U.S.C. § 77z-2) and Exchange Act Section 21E (15 U.S.C. § 78u-5).

37. Item 402(j)(4).

Other Material Factors

As with many of the other disclosure provisions, registrants must supplement the enumerated required disclosures with any other material factors about each disclosed contract, agreement, plan, or arrangement that are important to an investor's understanding of these arrangements. While the type of information that may be discussed here will vary from registrant to registrant, in the Adopting Release the SEC indicates, by way of illustration, that this disclosure would include whether an executive simultaneously receives both severance and retirement benefits.[38]

To the extent that an understanding of these arrangements involves an explanation of how these severance and change-in-control arrangements fit into the registrant's overall compensation objectives and strategy and affect the decisions that are made regarding other compensation elements, the SEC Staff has indicated that this discussion should be included in the CD&A.[39] Similarly, any description and related explanation of how the registrant has determined the appropriate payment and benefit levels under the various circumstances that trigger payments or the provision of benefits under termination of employment and change-in-control agreements should be part of the CD&A.[40]

Specific Disclosure Items

Equity Awards

Many severance and change-in-control provisions provide for accelerated vesting of outstanding and unvested equity awards. Initially, registrants used a variety of methodologies to quantify the economic effect of these acceleration provisions, including, among others, the following:

- the intrinsic value of the award (that is, the difference (or "spread") between the closing market price of the registrant's securities as of the last business day of the registrant's last

---

38. *See* the Adopting Release, *supra* note 1, at n.317. This practice is commonly known as a "double dip."

39. *See* the Staff Report, *supra* note 7, under the heading "Change-in-Control and Termination Arrangements."

40. *Id.*

completed fiscal year and the exercise or purchase price of the award);

- the incremental increase in the fair value of the award (calculated pursuant to then-effective Statement of Financial Accounting Standards (SFAS) 123(R)) based on the hypothetical amendment of the award to reflect the effects of the acceleration in vesting; and
- the portion of the original grant date fair value amount, if any (calculated pursuant to SFAS 123(R)) that remained unrecognized for financial statement reporting purposes as of the transaction date.

The SEC Staff has indicated that for purposes of this disclosure, a registrant should use the "spread" to calculate the estimated value of the award.[41]

In some situations, in addition or as an alternative to accelerated vesting, a severance or change-in-control arrangement provides for an extension of the term of an outstanding stock option (for example, one year from the date of termination of employment or until the expiration of the full contractual term). It is not necessary to quantify the economic effect of such an extension. A registrant should describe the extension as part of its discussion of the estimated payments and benefits that would be provided to the NEO.

Perquisites

For purposes of this disclosure, the same disclosure and itemization thresholds used for the Summary Compensation Table apply to the disclosure of perquisites and other personal benefits. Thus, the SEC's two-part analytical framework will be relevant to determining whether an item is a disclosable perquisite.[42] In addition, perquisites and other personal benefits may be excluded from the disclosure only if the

---

41. *See* the Current Staff Guidance, *supra* note 18, at Q&A 126.01. According to the SEC Staff, since Item 402(j) requires quantification of what a NEO would have received assuming the triggering event took place on the last business day of the registrant's last completed fiscal year, disclosure of the "spread" at that date is consistent with Instruction 1 to Item 402(j), which prescribes using the closing market price per share of the registrant's securities on the last business day of the registrant's last completed fiscal year.

42. *See* Executive Compensation and Related Party Disclosure, Release Nos. 33-8655, 34-53185, IC-27218 (Jan. 27, 2006), 71 Fed. Reg. 6542 (Feb. 8, 2006), *available at* http://www.sec.gov/rules/proposed/33-8655.pdf, at Section II.B.1.d.iii, and the Adopting Release, *supra* note 1, at Section II.C.1.e.i.

aggregate amount of such compensation will be less than $10,000.[43] Finally, individual perquisites and personal benefits are to be identified and quantified as required for purposes of the disclosure in the Summary Compensation Table.[44]

Health Care Benefits

The disclosure of health care benefits was added to the final rules[45] in response to the widespread practice of providing enhanced medical and health care benefits to executives upon their retirement or other termination of employment and in recognition of the significant cost of those benefits to the registrant.[46] This disclosure requirement applies only to "executive-only" arrangements or to the additional or enhanced benefits that are provided to a NEO beyond the registrant's normal postretirement health care program. To the extent that a NEO is merely eligible to participate in the registrant's broad-based, nondiscriminatory health care program when he or she terminates employment, disclosure is not required.[47]

While it is not expressly specified in the rules, it is believed that the reportable amount is the present value of the promised future benefit calculated as of the last business day of the registrant's last completed fiscal year. In quantifying health care benefits, the registrant must use the same assumptions that it used for financial statement reporting purposes under generally accepted accounting principles.[48]

---

43. *See* Instruction 2 to Item 402(j).

44. *See* Instruction 4 to Item 402(c)(2)(ix).

45. As proposed, the disclosure expressly referred only to perquisites. *See* Proposed Item 402(k)(1).

46. *See* Item 402(j)(1).

47. A registrant need not provide information with respect to contracts, agreements, plans, or arrangements to the extent they do not discriminate in scope, terms, or operation in favor of its executive officers and that are available generally to all salaried employees. *See* Instruction 5 to Item 402(j). In addition, the SEC Staff has indicated that this exclusion applies to broad-based nondiscriminatory disability plans that satisfy these nondiscrimination requirements. *See* the Current Staff Guidance, *supra* note 18, at Q&A 117.07. *See also* Questions and Answers, Technical Session between the SEC Staff and the Joint Committee on Employee Benefits (May 3, 2011), *available at* http://www.americanbar.org/content/dam/aba/events/employee_benefits/2010_sec_qas.final.110811.authcheckdam.pdf, at Question No. 1.

48. *See* Instruction 2 to Item 402(j). These would be the assumptions applied under FASB ASC Topic 715, *Compensation – Retirement Plans.*

Life Insurance Benefits

Life insurance benefits potentially payable to a NEO upon a termination of employment raise a difficult disclosure question. Presumably, where a NEO participates in a group life insurance plan that does not discriminate in scope, terms, or operation in favor of executive officers and is available generally to all salaried employees, there is no requirement to report the potential benefits payable under the plan as part of this disclosure.[49]

In the case of life insurance provided by the registrant to a NEO that does not qualify for this exclusion, it is problematic as to whether the potential benefits must be estimated as part of this disclosure. On the one hand, it is arguable that the rules are concerned only with the registrant's cost of providing life insurance for the benefit of its executives.[50] Under this approach, the amount of the benefits payable to a NEO (or the NEO's survivors) would not be relevant to investors. On the other hand, since the rules specifically call for the disclosure of potential "benefits" that would be provided in each covered circumstance, it is more likely that the SEC contemplated that, to the extent provided, these amounts are to be disclosed.[51] Disclosure practices in this area continue to vary.[52]

Ultimately, the decision to disclose this information will turn on its materiality to investors. At a minimum, the required disclosure should describe the life insurance coverage. In addition, where the benefit amounts are significant (determined under the registrant's particular facts and circumstances), it may be advisable to disclose this information as well.[53]

---

49. *See* Item 402(a)(6)(ii). The exclusion to the definition of the term "plan" clearly applies to the premiums payable by the registrant under the plan.

50. *See* Item 402(c)(2)(ix)(E).

51. *See also* Item 402(a)(2), which states that "[a]ll such compensation shall be reported pursuant to Item 402, even if also called for by another requirement, including transactions between the registrant and a third party where a purpose of the transaction is to furnish compensation to any such NEO or director." It is worth noting that the SEC Staff has informally indicated that the reporting concepts that apply under Item 402(j) differ from those governing the reporting of life insurance benefits in the Summary Compensation Table. *See* Questions and Answers, Technical Session between the SEC Staff and the Joint Committee on Employee Benefits (May 5, 2009), *available at* http://www.americanbar.org/content/dam/aba/migrated/2011_build/employee_benefits/sec_2009.authcheckdam.pdf, at Question No. 6.

52. *See, e.g.* the General Electric Company Definitive Proxy Statement (Form 14A) filed Mar. 14, 2011 (file no. 001-00035), which disclosed the amounts payable to its NEOs under its supplemental life insurance plans.

53. A similar analysis would appear to be appropriate in the case of supplemental disability insurance plans.

The SEC Staff has informally indicated that, where a registrant maintains a "death benefit only" plan (that is, a plan that provides for the payment of a death benefit to designated beneficiaries equal to a multiple of an executive officer's final base salary in the event of a termination of employment due to death),[54] the possible payment to a NEO from the registrant's general assets should be disclosed as a potential payment upon termination of employment.[55]

Retirement Benefits and Nonqualified Deferred Compensation

In recognition of the enhanced disclosure of retirement benefits in the Pension Benefits Table and nonqualified deferred compensation plans and arrangements in the Nonqualified Deferred Compensation Table, the rules do not require disclosure of these amounts in connection with any triggering event to the extent that the form and amount of any payment or benefit is fully disclosed in the applicable table and related narrative disclosure.[56] Instead, the registrant can simply refer to that disclosure.[57] To the extent that the form or amount of any such payment or benefit would be enhanced (that is, increased) or its vesting or other provisions accelerated in connection with any termination of employment or change in control of the registrant, however, the enhancement (increase) or acceleration must be described and the amounts involved quantified as part of this disclosure.[58]

Some registrants have been troubled by the implications of this Instruction as it applies to pension benefits, pointing out that the amounts

---

54. Unlike a non-equity split-dollar life insurance arrangement, in which the designated beneficiaries directly receive life insurance proceeds, the benefits under a "death benefits only" plan are paid directly by the registrant from its general assets. The registrant may, but is not required to, purchase a life insurance policy to hedge against this future liability.

55. *See* Questions and Answers, Technical Session Between the SEC Staff and the Joint Committee on Employee Benefits (May 4, 2010) [hereinafter 2010 JCEB Questions], *available at* http://www.americanbar.org/content/dam/aba/events/employee_benefits/2010_sec_qa.authcheckdam.pdf, at Question 1.

56. *See* Instruction 3 to Item 402(j).

57. *Id.* Further, there is no requirement to reconcile any difference between the actuarial present value of the accumulated pension benefits as reported in the Pension Benefits Table (which is determined as of the pension plan measurement date used for financial statement reporting purposes) and this present value amount calculated as of fiscal year-end (which is the measurement point under this disclosure). In the near future, this difference should disappear as registrants shift their pension plan measurement date to their fiscal year-end.

58. *Id.*

reported in the Pension Benefits Table represent the actuarial present value of the accumulated pension benefit, and not the amount that a NEO would actually receive if he or she were to terminate employment as of fiscal year-end. Notwithstanding this discrepancy, the SEC Staff does not require registrants to quantify pension benefits as part of the disclosure unless those benefits are enhanced or accelerated as a result of the triggering event.[59] Nonetheless, some registrants have elected to provide this additional information, either in their Pension Benefits Table[60] or as part of this disclosure.

"Gross-Ups" and Other Tax Reimbursements

Although not specifically identified in the rules, it is clear from both the Proposing and Adopting Releases that any "gross-up" or other amount reimbursed to a NEO for the payment of taxes in connection with his or her termination of employment or a change in control of the registrant is to be described and quantified as part of the disclosure. While there are a variety of situations in which such payments may arise, the most common arrangement involves a "gross-up" or reimbursement to cover the excise taxes imposed by the Internal Revenue Code in connection with a so-called "excess parachute payment."[61]

The calculations involved in determining whether an excise tax would result from a change-in-control payment are exceedingly complex and depend on the particular facts and circumstances that exist at the time of the underlying transaction. Consequently, it is not surprising that registrants have faced numerous challenges in determining whether a "gross-up" or tax reimbursement payment would even arise under the hypothetical circumstances contemplated by the disclosure and, if so, how to estimate this amount.[62] For example, the date used in quantifying

---

59. While the SEC Staff has not formally given a reason for its position, it may be based, in part, on the belief that the information in the Pension Benefits Table is sufficient to give investors an understanding of the amounts that would be potentially received by a NEO and to relieve registrants from the burden of having to make additional pension-related calculations as part of the severance and change-in-control disclosure.

60. *See, e.g.* the Pfizer Inc. Definitive Proxy Statement filed Mar. 22, 2011 (file no. 001-03619), which includes additional columns in the Pension Benefits Table disclosing the value of an annual annuity payable as of fiscal year-end (as well as the lump sum amount payable), and provides a cross-reference to that table in its termination and change-in-control disclosure.

61. *See* Sections 280G and 4999 of the Internal Revenue Code (26 U.S.C. §§ 280G and 4999).

62. For example, if a severance agreement contains a covenant not to compete and the arrangement assigns a specific value to the covenant (for example, one year's base salary), the

the estimated payments can affect the amount of a "gross-up" payment by suggesting that benefits would be accelerated or by changing the five-year "base period" for computing the average annual taxable amount to which the parachute payment is compared. The SEC Staff has indicated that where the last business day of the last completed fiscal year for a calendar-year registrant is not December 31, the registrant may calculate the excise tax and related "gross-up" amount assuming that the change-in-control transaction occurred on December 31, rather than the last business day of its last completed fiscal year, using the registrant's stock price as of the last business day of its last completed fiscal year.[63] The registrant may not substitute January 1 of the current fiscal year for the last business day of the registrant's last completed fiscal year, which would effectively change the five-year "base period" to include the registrant's last completed fiscal year.[64] While it is not required, given the complexity of the calculation, a registrant should consider describing the various assumptions (for example, income tax rates, stock option assumption or substitution arrangements, and discount rates) that have been used in the calculation to assist investors in analyzing the estimated payment.

If a registrant does not provide a "gross-up" or tax reimbursement payment to its NEOs, it is not required to perform an excise tax calculation as part of the required disclosure, even though the imposition of the tax would reduce the amount that its executive ultimately would receive. Instead, the registrant may simply indicate that the amounts payable to its NEOs in the event of a change in control may be subject to reduction under the Internal Revenue Code's "excess parachute payment" provisions.

Special Situations

Where a triggering event (for example, termination of employment) has actually occurred for a NEO and that individual was not serving as a

---

determination of whether an "excess parachute payment" exists will depend on an analysis of whether this amount is reasonable compensation or properly attributable to the covenant. This may be a difficult assessment to make in a hypothetical situation, and may limit the registrant's ability to take a contrary position for federal income tax purposes in an actual transaction setting. Some registrants have begun to indicate that the estimated "gross-up" amount has not been reduced by these factors and, instead, represents its maximum exposure under the reimbursement provision in the event of a change in control under the hypothetical facts.

    63. *See* the Current Staff Guidance, *supra* note 18, at Interpretation 226.01.

    64. *Id.*

NEO of the registrant at the end of the last completed fiscal year, only the disclosure for that specific triggering event need be provided for that NEO.[65] So, for example, if a NEO retires during the last completed fiscal year, a registrant need only provide disclosure concerning the payments and benefits that the executive actually received as a result of that triggering event. This relaxation of the general disclosure requirement makes compliance easier for registrants and ensures that investors receive meaningful disclosure.

The SEC Staff has appeared willing to extend the principle reflected in the Instruction to post-fiscal-year-end terminations under certain limited circumstances. For example, where a NEO leaves the registrant after the end of the last completed fiscal year, but before the registrant's proxy statement is filed, the Staff has indicated that it is permissible to provide disclosure only for the triggering event that actually occurred, rather than providing the disclosure for several additional scenarios that no longer can occur, as long as the following conditions are present:

- a current report on Form 8-K has been filed by the registrant disclosing the executive's departure;[66]
- the executive is not the registrant's PEO or PFO and will not be a NEO for the current fiscal year;[67] and
- the severance package applicable to the executive's termination of employment is not newly negotiated (but, instead, has the same terms that otherwise would apply).[68]

Another situation that has been presented to the SEC Staff involved a registrant that was preparing to file a proxy statement for its annual meeting of shareholders at which, among other things, the registrant was planning to solicit the approval of its shareholders of a transaction in which the registrant would be acquired. In this case, the registrant had postemployment compensation arrangements in place for its

---

65. *See* Instruction 4 to Item 402(j).

66. *See* Item 5.02(b) of Form 8-K (17 C.F.R. 249.308).

67. Based on the application of Item 402(a)(3)(iv).

68. *See* the Current Staff Guidance, *supra* note 18, at Interpretation 226.02. The SEC Staff's position is limited in scope to mitigate concerns that a registrant is attempting to avoid disclosure under Exchange Act Rule 12b-20 (17 C.F.R. 240.12b-20). In other words, the conditions that the Staff has imposed are intended to ensure that the circumstances giving rise to the termination of employment didn't occur until after the close of the last completed fiscal year and the registrant is simply seeking to truncate its required disclosure when, in fact, at fiscal year-end, all possible termination scenarios still existed.

employees. If the transaction were to be approved, however, each of the registrant's NEOs would be eligible to receive compensation pursuant to termination agreements that would be specific to the acquisition. In this instance, the SEC Staff indicated that the registrant could not satisfy this disclosure requirement by merely describing and quantifying the potential payments for the NEOs under the termination agreements that were specific to the pending acquisition, because, were the transaction not to be approved (either because shareholders failed to vote in favor of the transaction or any applicable regulatory authority declined to give its approval), the registrant's generally applicable postemployment compensation arrangements would continue to apply.[69] In addition, the Staff pointed out that a comparison of the compensation payable under the acquisition-specific agreements with the amounts payable under the generally applicable postemployment arrangements may be material to an investor's voting decision with respect to the pending acquisition and, therefore, should be provided.[70]

A third situation that has been presented to the SEC Staff involved a registrant-sponsored death benefit-only ("DBO") plan for the registrant's executive officers. The DBO plan resulted in payment of a death benefit to one or more designated beneficiaries equal to a multiple of an executive officer's final base salary in the event of his or her death. Unlike a non-equity split-dollar life insurance arrangement, in which the designated beneficiary or beneficiaries directly receives the life insurance proceeds, the benefits under the DBO plan are paid directly by the registrant from its general assets. The registrant may, but is not required to, purchase a life insurance policy to hedge against this future DBO liability. In this instance, the Staff indicated that the potential payment to a NEO under the DBO plan should be disclosed under Item 402(j) as a potential payment or benefit upon a termination of employment.[71]

---

69. *See* the Current Staff Guidance, *supra* note 18, at Interpretation 226.03.

70. *Id.*

71. *See* the 2010 JCEB Questions *supra* note 55, at Question No. 1. In addition, where there is no life insurance involved, in the event of an actual termination of employment due to death, any payment or accrual under the DBO plan is to be reported in the "All Other Compensation" column of the Summary Compensation Table pursuant to Item 402(c)(2)(ix)(D) for the fiscal year in which the NEO dies. *Id.*

Smaller Reporting Companies

While smaller reporting companies are not required to provide disclosure about payments and benefits in the event of a termination of employment or following a change in control of the registrant as part of their executive compensation disclosure, they are required to include a narrative description of the material terms of each contract, agreement, plan, or arrangement, whether written or unwritten, that provides for a payment or payments to a NEO at, following, or in connection with the resignation, retirement, or other termination of a NEO, or a change in control of the smaller reporting company, or a change in the NEO's responsibilities following a change in control, with respect to each NEO.[72]

---

72. *See* Item 402(q)(2).

13

Director Compensation Table

General

While the disclosure of director pay has long been part of the executive compensation reporting system,[1] the executive compensation disclosure rules employ a relatively new approach for presenting this information. Reflecting the growing size and sophistication of director compensation programs, the rules require that the amount of compensation for each director be quantified. In addition, they require that this information to be presented in a tabular format, accompanied by a narrative discussion of any additional material information necessary to an understanding of the information presented in the table.[2]

Under the rules, the disclosure of director compensation is similar to that of executive compensation, with the Director Compensation

---

1. *See, e.g.,* former Item 402(g).

2. The Securities and Exchange Commission (SEC) first proposed amending the format for the presentation of director compensation information in 1995. *See* Streamlining and Consolidation of Executive and Director Compensation Disclosure, Release Nos. 33-7184, 34-35894 (June 27, 1995), 60 Fed. Reg. 35,633 (July 10, 1995), *available at* http://www.sec.gov/rules/proposed/33-7184.txt. This proposal was coupled with a separate proposal to permit registrants to reduce the detailed executive compensation information provided in their proxy statement by instead furnishing that information in their annual reports on Form 10-K. The SEC did not act on either proposal.

Table resembling the Summary Compensation Table.[3] And, as a result, the same principles that govern the preparation of the Summary Compensation Table generally apply to the analogous provisions of this table.[4]

While the table is similar in form and content to the Summary Compensation Table, however, there is one critical distinction—the table is limited to only one year's compensation information (that of the last completed fiscal year), while the Summary Compensation Table contains three years' information.[5] In addition, none of the supplemental tables to the Summary Compensation Table are required for directors.

Although it is true that director compensation programs have gotten more complex over the years, programs continue to vary widely from registrant to registrant. While the programs of larger registrants may include a variety of elements, such as equity-based compensation, incentive plans, retirement plans, and other forms of compensation, some registrants continue to use relatively simple pay arrangements based primarily on cash fees. Thus, Director Compensation Tables vary significantly from registrant to registrant, reflecting the components of each particular program.[6]

Tabular Format

The Director Compensation Table is to be presented in the following tabular format:

---

3. The requirements for the Director Compensation Table are set forth in Item 402(k). For the requirements applicable to smaller reporting companies, see Item 402(r).

4. See, e.g., the Instruction to Item 402(k).

5. Although the SEC proposed disclosure comparable to that required by the Grants of Plan-Based Awards Table for directors (see the Instruction to Proposed Item 402(l)(2)(iv) and (v)), that proposal was not adopted. Nonetheless, certain information about directors' equity holdings at fiscal year-end is required under the current rules. See "Stock Awards" and "Option Awards," infra.

6. See Item 402(a)(5), which permits a registrant to omit a column from a required table if there has been no compensation awarded to, earned by, or paid to any of the directors required to be reported in that column in the fiscal year covered by that table.

DIRECTOR COMPENSATION

Name (a)	Fees Earned or Paid in Cash ($) (b)	Stock Awards ($) (c)	Option Awards ($) (d)	Nonequity Incentive Plan Compensation ($) (e)	Change in Pension Value and Nonqualified Deferred Compensation Earnings (f)	All Other Compensation ($) (g)	Total ($) (h)
A							
B							
C							
D							
E							

The table includes the following information for the last completed fiscal year:

- the name of the director (column (a));[7]
- the aggregate dollar amount of all fees earned or paid in cash for services as a director (column (b));[8]
- the dollar amount recognized for financial statement reporting purposes with respect to the fiscal year for all stock awards, as determined in accordance with Financial Accounting Standards Board Accounting Standards Codification Topic 718, *Compensation—Stock Compensation* (FASB ASC Topic 718) (column (c));[9]
- the dollar amount recognized for financial statement reporting purposes with respect to the fiscal year for all stock option awards, as determined in accordance with FASB ASC Topic 718 (column (d));[10]
- the dollar value of all earnings for services performed during the fiscal year pursuant to nonequity incentive plans, and all earnings on any outstanding awards (column (e));[11]
- the sum of the aggregate change in the actuarial present value of the director's accumulated benefit under all defined benefit and

---

7. Item 402(k)(2)(i).
8. Item 402(k)(2)(ii).
9. Item 402(k)(2)(iii).
10. Item 402(k)(2)(iv).
11. Item 402(k)(2)(v).

actuarial pension plans (including supplemental plans)[12] and above-market or preferential earnings on nonqualified deferred compensation, including any such earnings on nonqualified defined contribution plans (column (f));[13]

- all other compensation for the covered fiscal year that the registrant could not properly report in any other column of the table (column (g));[14] and
- the dollar value of total compensation for the covered fiscal year (column (h)).[15]

Generally, the rules for the disclosure of compensation information in the Summary Compensation Table also apply to the disclosure of comparable compensation items for directors.[16] As with most of the disclosure tables, the applicable fiscal year is to be added to the title of the table.[17]

The compensation values to be reported in the Director Compensation Table must be reported in dollars and rounded to the nearest dollar.[18] In addition, reported compensation values must be reported numerically, providing a single numerical value for each grid in the table.[19]

Where compensation was paid to or received by a director in a currency other than dollars, a footnote to the table must be provided to identify that currency and describe the rate and methodology used to convert the payment amounts to dollars.[20]

Any amounts that are deferred, whether pursuant to a Section 401(k) plan or otherwise, are to be included in the appropriate column of the table for the covered fiscal year.[21] While a registrant may find it advisable to include a footnote to the appropriate column indicating the amount that has been deferred, such disclosure is not required.

---

12. Item 402(k)(2)(vi)(A).
13. Item 402(k)(2)(vi)(B).
14. Item 402(k)(2)(vii).
15. Item 402(k)(2)(viii).
16. *See* the Instruction to Item 402(k).
17. *See* the Instruction to Item 402.
18. *See* the Instruction to Item 402(k) and Instruction 2 to Item 402(c).
19. *Id.*
20. *Id.*
21. *See* the Instruction to Item 402(k) and Instruction 4 to Item 402(c).

Compensation Subject to Reporting

As with the Summary Compensation Table, all compensation must be included in the table. As with the Summary Compensation Table, however, this general principle is not all-encompassing. Only compensation that has been actually paid, earned, or awarded for services performed as a director must be reported in the table.[22] Thus, in the case of a director who also is an executive officer (but not a named executive officer (NEO)) of the registrant, who does not receive any additional compensation for services provided as a director,[23] the compensation that this director receives for services as an executive officer does not need to be reported in the table.[24]

In the case of a director who also is an employee (but not an executive officer) of the registrant, Item 404(a) of Regulation S-K requires disclosure of the transaction pursuant to which the director is compensated for services provided as an employee.[25] Because disclosure of this employee compensation transaction in the table typically would result in a clearer, more concise presentation of the information, however, the staff of the SEC's Division of Corporation Finance (SEC Staff) has indicated that, in this situation, if the employee compensation

---

22. As with the Summary Compensation Table, there are three additional qualifications to this principle. Perquisites and other personal benefits received by a director do not need to be disclosed to the extent that their total value is less than $10,000. Further, the disclosure of earnings on nonqualified deferred compensation is limited to the above-market or preferential portion of such earnings. Finally, registrant payments regarding broad-based, nondiscriminatory group life, health, hospitalization, and medical reimbursement plans do not need to be disclosed. See Item 402(a)(6)(ii).

23. Assuming that the conditions in Instruction 5(a)(ii) to Item 404(a) of Regulation S-K (17 C.F.R. 229.404(a) Instruction 5) are satisfied (that is, the executive officer is not an immediate family member and such compensation would have been reported under Item 402 as compensation earned for services to the registrant if the executive officer was a NEO, and such compensation has been approved, or recommended to the board of directors of the registrant for approval, by the compensation committee of the registrant's board of directors).

24. See Division of Corporation Finance, Compliance and Disclosure Interpretations – Regulation S-K (July 8, 2011) [hereinafter Current Staff Guidance], available at http://www.sec.gov/divisions/corpfin/guidance/regs-kinterp.htm, at Interpretation 227.02. In fact, the director may be omitted from the table altogether, provided that the registrant provides a footnote or narrative disclosure explaining that the director is an executive officer, other than a NEO, who does not receive any additional compensation for services provided as a director. Id.

25. In the SEC Staff's view, Instruction 5 to Item 404(a) does not apply because the person is not an executive officer or is not receiving compensation other than as a director reported in the Director Compensation Table as required by Item 402(k).

transaction is reported in the Director Compensation Table, it need not be repeated with the other Item 404(a) disclosure.[26]

Occasionally, a current director previously will have been an employee of the registrant and will be receiving a pension that was earned for services rendered as an employee. The SEC Staff has indicated that if payment of the pension is not conditioned on his or her service as a director, the pension benefits do not need to be disclosed in the table, whether or not the director receives compensation for services provided as a director.[27] If service as a director generates new accruals to the pension, however, disclosure would be required in the All Other Compensation column (column (f)) of the table.[28] Presumably, this disclosure would involve only the accruals attributable to service as a director.

Identification of Directors

Column (a) of the table is to list each individual who served as a member of the registrant's board of directors *during any part* of the last completed fiscal year.[29] Thus, the table must include a person who served as a director for part of the fiscal year (for example, from the beginning of the last completed fiscal year until the registrant's annual meeting of shareholders), even if that person was no longer a director as of the end of the last completed fiscal year.[30] Similarly, disclosure is required for a person who served as a director during the last completed fiscal year, even if that person does not stand for reelection the next year.[31]

Where a director is also a NEO whose compensation is subject to disclosure in the Summary Compensation Table and his or her compensation for service as a director is fully reflected in the Summary Compensation Table, the supplemental disclosure tables, and the

---

26. *See* the Current Staff Guidance, *supra* note 24, at Interpretation 227.03. Footnote or narrative disclosure to the table should explain the allocation to services provided as an employee. *Id.*

27. *See id.* at Interpretation 227.04.

28. *Id.*

29. *See id.* at Q&A 127.01.

30. *Id.*

31. *See id.* at Q&A 127.02.

required postemployment disclosures, he or she does not need to be included in this table.[32]

If all of the individual compensation elements and amounts for two or more directors are identical, the directors may be grouped in a single row in the table.[33] In this case, the names of the directors for whom disclosure is presented on a group basis should be clear from the table.[34]

Fees Earned or Paid in Cash

Column (b) of the table is to report fees earned or paid in cash to an individual for service as a director. These amounts include, without limitation, annual retainer fees, committee and/or chairmanship fees, and meeting fees.[35] Fees paid in stock are to be reported separately as described below.

The use of the phrase "earned or paid" raises a question about the proper treatment of fees that are (1) paid in advance for services that will be rendered in the following fiscal year and (2) paid in arrears for services that were rendered during the last completed fiscal year. While the SEC Staff has not taken a formal position on this question, the better approach appears to be to report only fees earned or paid in respect of services that were rendered during the fiscal year to which the disclosure relates.[36]

So, for example, where a registrant pays its directors an annual retainer in quarterly installments in advance, so that the last installment paid during a fiscal year relates to services that will be rendered in the following fiscal year, these amounts should not be reported in the column for the last completed fiscal year.[37] Similarly, where a registrant pays its directors their cash fees following the end of the fiscal year

---

32. Item 402(k)(2)(i). As was the case under the former rules, these compensation amounts are to be disclosed in the Summary Compensation Table along with footnote disclosure indicating what amounts reflected in that table are compensation for services as a director. *See* Instruction 3 to Item 402(c).

33. *See* the Instruction to Item 402(k)(2).

34. *Id.*

35. Item 402(k)(2)(ii).

36. *See* Cleary Gottlieb Steen & Hamilton LLP, *Common Questions: Navigating the SEC's New Compensation Rules* (Jan. 19, 2007) [hereinafter Cleary Memorandum], at Q&A 44.

37. *Id.*

covered by the disclosure and during which the related services were rendered, these amounts should be reported in the column for the last completed fiscal year, not the fiscal year in which they are actually paid. Once a registrant has established an approach for reporting director fees, this approach should be consistently applied from fiscal year to fiscal year.

If the cash fees earned in a covered fiscal year are not calculable through the latest practicable date, a footnote is to be used (attached to column (b)) disclosing that the fees are not calculable through the latest practicable date and providing the date that the fees are expected to be determined.[38] Once the cash fees have been determined, such amount must then be disclosed in a current report on Form 8-K.[39]

A registrant is to include in column (b) any cash fees that are forgone at the election of a director under which stock, equity-based, or another form of noncash compensation instead has been received by the director.[40] The receipt of any such noncash compensation instead of cash fees must be disclosed in a footnote added to the column. Unlike the comparable provision in the Summary Compensation Table, since a Grants of Plan-Based Awards Table is not required for directors, there is no additional disclosure required beyond this footnote.

If the amount of cash fees forgone at the election of the director was less than the value of the equity-based compensation received, or if the agreement pursuant to which the director had the option to elect settlement in stock or equity-based compensation was within the scope of FASB ASC Topic 718,[41] then different reporting treatment results. In the former situation, the incremental value of an equity award is to be reported in the Stock Awards or Option Awards columns of the table, as the case may be, and, in the latter situation, the award is to be reported in total in the Stock Awards or Option Awards columns, as the case may be, instead of this column.[42]

In both of these special cases, the amounts reported in the Stock Awards or Option Awards columns would be the dollar amounts recognized for financial statement reporting purposes with respect to the award, and footnote disclosure would be provided reporting the

---

38. *See* the Instruction to Item 402(k) and Instruction 1 to Item 402(c)(2)(iii) and (iv).
39. *Id.* The filing is to be made under Item 5.02(e) of Form 8-K (17 C.F.R. 469.308).
40. *See* the Instruction to Item 402(k) and Instruction 2 to Item 402(c)(2)(iii) and (iv).
41. For example, the right to stock settlement is embedded in the terms of the award.
42. *See* the Current Staff Guidance, *supra* note 24, at Q&A 119.03.

circumstances of the award or awards.[43] Appropriate disclosure about the equity-based compensation received instead of cash fees also must be provided as part of the supplemental disclosure to the Stock Awards and Option Awards columns discussed below.[44]

Stock Awards

Column (c) of the table is to report the dollar amount of the aggregate grant date fair value for financial statement reporting purposes with respect to all stock[45] awards granted to each director during the last completed fiscal year. This amount is to be determined in accordance with FASB ASC Topic 718.[46] Thus, an award made during the last completed fiscal year is to be reported in this column whether it is fully vested on the grant date or whether it has a multiple-year vesting schedule.[47]

While the aggregate grant date fair value of all stock awards is reported in the table, a registrant must disclose in a footnote (attached to column (c)), on a director-by-director basis, the full grant date fair value of each stock award as determined in accordance with FASB ASC Topic 718.[48] The SEC Staff has indicated that this disclosure is to correspond

---

43. *Id.*

44. *See* "Stock Awards" and "Option Awards," *infra.*

45. For these purposes, the term "stock" means instruments such as common stock, restricted stock, restricted stock units, phantom stock, phantom stock units, common stock equivalent units, or any similar instruments that do not have option-like features. *See* Item 402(a)(6)(i).

46. As originally adopted, Item 402(k)(2)(iii) would have required disclosure of the aggregate grant date fair value of all stock awards granted to the director during the last completed fiscal year computed in accordance with FASB ASC Topic 718. This requirement was modified in December 2006. *See* Executive Compensation Disclosure, Release Nos. 33-8765, 34-55009 (Dec. 22, 2006), 71 Fed. Reg. 78,338 (Dec. 29, 2006) [hereinafter December 2006 Release], *available at* http://www.sec.gov/rules/final/2006/33-8765.pdf. Subsequently, the SEC reversed this decision in December 2009 to return to its original reporting position. *See* Proxy Disclosure Enhancements, Release Nos. 33-9089, 34-61175, IC-29092 (December 16, 2009), 74 Fed. Reg. 68,334 (December 23, 2009) [hereinafter 2009 Adopting Release], *available at* http://www.sec.gov/rules/final/33-9089.pdf. For a discussion of the implications of this disclosure requirement, see "Stock Awards—Amount to Be Reported" in Chapter 4.

47. *See* W. Alan Kailer, *The Securities and Exchange Commission's Executive Compensation Rules—Preparing the Executive Compensation Tables* (Jan. 2012), at B-29.

48. *See* the Instruction to Item 402(k)(2)(iii) and (iv). In the case of a smaller reporting company, the only information required in a footnote is the aggregate number of stock awards outstanding at fiscal year-end. *See* the Instruction to Item 402(r)(2)(iii) and (iv).

to the disclosure for executives in the Grants of Plan-Based Awards Table. Consequently, this requirement applies only to stock awards granted during the registrant's last completed fiscal year.[49]

If the stock award being reported is subject to service-based vesting conditions, the estimate of forfeitures related to those conditions is to be disregarded.[50] A footnote must be attached to the column describing all forfeitures during the year.[51]

A registrant must also disclose in a footnote (attached to column (c)) all assumptions made in the valuation of the stock awards reported in the column.[52] While the rules indicate that this disclosure should be made by reference to a discussion of those assumptions in the registrant's financial statements, footnotes to the financial statements, or discussion in the Management's Discussion and Analysis (MD&A),[53] the SEC Staff has informally indicated that it is also permissible to set out the assumptions in the footnote itself.

Depending on the nature of the stock awards being reported, the assumption disclosure may be minimal. Under FASB ASC Topic 718, the grant date fair value of many stock-based awards is based on the market price of the registrant's securities on the date of grant. In this instance, there may not be any assumptions to disclose.

Finally, a registrant must disclose in a footnote (also attached to column (c)) the aggregate number of stock awards outstanding at the end of the last completed fiscal year.[54] The SEC Staff has indicated that this disclosure is to correspond to the disclosure for executives in the Outstanding Equity Awards at Fiscal Year-End Table. Consequently, this requirement applies only to unvested stock awards (including unvested stock units).[55]

---

49. *See* the Current Staff Guidance, *supra* note 24, at Q&A 127.03.

50. *See* the Instruction to Item 402(k) and the Instruction to Item 402(c)(2)(v) and (vi).

51. *Id.*

52. *See* the Instruction to Item 402(k) and the Instruction to Item 402(c)(2)(v) and (vi).

53. *Id.* The sections so referenced are deemed part of the disclosure provided pursuant to Item 402.

54. *See* the Instruction to Item 402(k)(2)(iii) and (iv).

55. *See* the Current Staff Guidance, *supra* note 24, at Q&A 127.04.

Option Awards

Column (d) of the table is to report the dollar amount of the aggregate grant date fair value for financial statement reporting purposes with respect to all stock options[56] granted to each director during the last completed fiscal year. This amount is to be determined in accordance with FASB ASC Topic 718.[57] Options are reportable in this column whether or not they are accompanied by tandem stock appreciation rights (SARs).[58] Thus, an option granted during the last completed fiscal year is to be reported in this column whether it is fully vested on the grant date or whether it has a multiple-year vesting schedule.

While the aggregate grant date fair value of all option awards is reported in the table, a registrant must disclose in a footnote (attached to column (d)), on a director-by-director basis, the full grant date fair value of each stock option award as determined in accordance with FASB ASC Topic 718.[59] The SEC Staff has indicated that this disclosure is to correspond to the disclosure for executives in the Grants of Plan-Based Awards Table. Consequently, this requirement applies only to stock options granted during the registrant's last completed fiscal year.[60]

If the stock option being reported is subject to service-based vesting conditions, the estimate of forfeitures related to those conditions is to be disregarded.[61] A footnote must be attached to the column describing all forfeitures during the year.[62]

A registrant must also disclose in a footnote (attached to column (d)) all assumptions made in the valuation of the stock options reported

---

56. For these purposes, the term "option" means instruments such as stock options, SARs, and similar instruments with option-like features. *See* Item 402(a)(6)(i).

57. As originally adopted, Item 402(k)(2)(iii) would have required disclosure of the aggregate grant date fair value of all option awards granted to the director during the last completed fiscal year computed in accordance with FASB ASC Topic 718. Subsequently, the SEC reversed this decision in December 2009 to return to its original reporting position. *See* the 2009 Adopting Release *supra* note 46. For a discussion of the implications of this disclosure requirement, see "Option Awards—Amount to Be Reported" in Chapter 4.

58. *See* Item 402(k)(2)(iv).

59. *See* the Instruction to Item 402(k)(2)(iii) and (iv). In the case of a smaller reporting company, the only information required in a footnote is the aggregate number of option awards outstanding at fiscal year-end. *See* the Instruction to Item 402(r)(2)(iii) and (iv).

60. *See* the Current Staff Guidance, *supra* note 24, at Q&A 127.03.

61. *See* the Instruction to Item 402(k) and the Instruction to Item 402(c)(2)(v) and (vi).

62. *Id.*

in the column.[63] While the rules indicate that this disclosure should be made by reference to a discussion of those assumptions in the registrant's financial statements, footnotes to the financial statements, or discussion in the MD&A,[64] the SEC Staff has informally indicated that it is also permissible to set out the assumptions in the footnote itself.

Depending on the number of stock options being reported, a registrant may find it advisable to set forth the assumptions relating to its reported options as part of this disclosure.

In addition, a registrant must also disclose in a footnote (also attached to column (d)) the aggregate number of stock options outstanding at the end of the last completed fiscal year.[65] The SEC Staff has indicated that this disclosure is to correspond to the disclosure for executives in the Outstanding Equity Awards at Fiscal Year-End Table. Consequently, this requirement applies only to unexercised stock options (whether or not exercisable).[66] Note that because a Grants of Plan-Based Awards Table is not required for directors, where the exercise price of a stock option granted to a director is determined using a valuation methodology other than the closing market price of the registrant's common stock on the date of grant, it is not necessary to disclose the excess of the closing market price over the actual exercise price as it is for grants to NEOs. Where this difference is so large that the omission would make the disclosure misleading, it should be disclosed in a footnote to the table.[67]

While the SEC had initially required disclosure of the incremental fair value (as determined in accordance with FASB ASC Topic 718 resulting from the repricing of an option (or a SAR or other similar

---

63. *See* the Instruction to Item 402(k) and the Instruction to Item 402(c)(2)(v) and (vi).

64. *Id.* The sections so referenced are deemed part of the disclosure provided pursuant to Item 402.

65. *See* the Instruction to Item 402(k)(2)(iii) and (iv).

66. *See* the Current Staff Guidance, *supra* note 24, at Q&A 127.04. Originally, the SEC had proposed to require, by means of a footnote to the appropriate column, disclosure for each director of the outstanding equity awards at fiscal year-end as would be required if the Outstanding Equity Awards at Fiscal Year-End Table for NEOs was required for directors. *See* the Proposed Instruction to Item 402(l)(2)(iv) and (v). In the final rules, however, the SEC simplified the relevant instruction to require footnote disclosure only of the aggregate numbers of stock awards and option awards outstanding at fiscal year-end. The ambiguity of this instruction necessitated the SEC Staff's interpretive guidance.

67. *See* the Cleary Memorandum, *supra* note 36, at Q&A 40.

option-like instrument) during the last completed fiscal year,[68] that disclosure was rescinded as part of the December 2006 changes.[69]

Nonequity Incentive Plan Compensation

Column (e) of the table is to report the dollar value of all amounts earned by a director during the last completed fiscal year pursuant to nonequity incentive plan[70] awards for services performed. As is the case with the corresponding disclosure requirement in the Summary Compensation Table,[71] the amount to be reported is the amount earned during the last completed fiscal year regardless of when the related services were performed.

If the relevant performance measure is satisfied during the covered fiscal year (including for a single year in a plan with a multiyear performance measure), the earnings are reportable for that fiscal year, even if not payable until a later date, and are not reportable again in the fiscal year when amounts are paid to the director.[72]

In addition, any earnings earned or paid during the fiscal year on outstanding awards must also be reported in this column. To the extent that both award amounts and earnings are reportable, the earnings on nonequity incentive plan compensation must be identified and quantified in a footnote to column (e), whether the earnings were paid during the covered fiscal year, payable during the period but deferred at the election of the director, or payable by their terms at a later date.[73]

---

68. *See* Executive Compensation and Related Person Disclosure, Release Nos. 33-8732A, 34-54302A, IC-27444A (Aug. 29, 2006), 71 Fed. Reg. 53,158 (Sept. 8, 2006) [hereinafter Adopting Release], *available at* http://www.sec.gov/rules/final/2006/33-8732a.pdf, at nn.160 & 161 and the accompanying text.

69. *See* the December 2006 Release, *supra* note 46, at n.30 and the accompanying text.

70. A "nonequity incentive plan" is a plan providing compensation intended to serve as incentive for performance to occur over a specified period, whether such performance is measured by reference to financial performance of the registrant or an affiliate, the registrant's stock price, or any other performance measure (an "incentive plan"), or portion of an incentive plan, under which awards are granted that fall outside the scope of FASB ASC Topic 718. *See* Item 402(a)(6)(iii). Consequently, such a plan is most commonly a cash-based incentive plan.

71. *See* the Adopting Release, *supra* note 68, at Section II.C.1.c.ii. For a more detailed discussion of this disclosure requirement, *see* "Nonequity Incentive Plan Compensation" in Chapter 4.

72. *See* the Instruction to Item 402(k) and Instruction 1 to Item 402(c)(2)(vii).

73. *See* the Instruction to Item 402(k) and Instruction 2 to Item 402(c)(2)(vii).

Pension Value Changes and Above-Market and Preferential Earnings

Column (f) of the table is to report two distinct compensation items: the aggregate change in the actuarial present value of each director's accumulated benefit under the registrant's defined benefit and actuarial pension plans in which he or she is a participant,[74] and any above-market or preferential earnings on nonqualified deferred compensation, including any such earnings on nonqualified defined contribution plans.

The required disclosure about defined benefit pension plans applies to each plan that provides for the payment of retirement benefits, or benefits that will be paid primarily following retirement, including, but not limited to, tax-qualified defined benefit plans and supplemental executive retirement plans (SERPs).[75] It does not apply to tax-qualified defined contribution plans and nonqualified defined contribution plans.[76]

While a Pension Benefits Table is not required for directors, the amount to be reported in column (f) should be the difference between the amount that would have been required to be reported for the director for the covered fiscal year if such a table were required[77] and the amount that would have required to be reported for the director for the prior completed fiscal year.[78] Accordingly, this actuarial present value of the accumulated benefits is to be calculated from the pension plan measurement date used for financial statement reporting purposes with respect to the registrant's audited financial statements for the prior completed fiscal year to the pension plan measurement date used for

---

74. This item is not required in the case of smaller reporting companies. *See* Item 402(r) (2)(vi).

75. *See* the Instruction to Item 402(k) and Instruction 1 to Item 402(c)(2)(viii). As proposed, registrants would have been required to disclose the aggregate annual increase in the actuarial value of all defined benefit and actuarial pension plans in the All Other Compensation column of the Director Compensation Table. *See* Proposed Item 402(l)(2)(vii)(F). As described in the Adopting Release, *supra* note 68, that proposal was modified to create the current required disclosure.

76. *Id.*

77. This amount is to be calculated based on the amount required to be disclosed pursuant to Item 402(h)(2)(iv).

78. *See* the Instruction to Item 402(k) and Instruction 1 to Item 402(c)(2)(viii).

financial statement reporting purposes with respect to the registrant's audited financial statements for the covered fiscal year.[79]

The required disclosure of earnings on nonqualified deferred compensation and nonqualified defined contribution plans applies only to above-market and preferential earnings.[80] For this purpose, interest on nonqualified deferred compensation is "above market" only if the rate of interest exceeds 120 percent of the applicable federal long-term rate, with compounding (as prescribed under Section 1274(d) of the Internal Revenue Code), at the rate that corresponds most closely to the rate under the registrant's plan at the time the interest rate or formula is set.[81] Only the above-market portion of the interest must be included in the column. If the applicable interest rates vary depending on conditions such as a minimum period of continued service, the reported amount should be calculated assuming satisfaction of all conditions to receiving interest at the highest rate.[82] A registrant may, but is not required to, provide footnote or narrative explaining its criteria for determining any portion of the earnings considered to be above-market.[83]

Dividends (and dividend equivalents) on deferred compensation denominated in shares of the registrant's stock are "preferential" only if earned at a rate higher than dividends on the registrant's common stock.[84] Again, only the preferential portion of the dividends or equivalents need be included in the column.

Where a registrant is disclosing both a pension value change and above-market or preferential earnings in column (f), it must use a

---

79. Item 402(k)(2)(vii)(A). For a more detailed discussion of this disclosure requirement, see "Pension Value Changes and Above-Market and Preferential Earnings—Pension Plan Value Changes" in Chapter 4.

80. As proposed, registrants would have been required to disclose *all* earnings on nonqualified deferred compensation in the All Other Compensation column of the Director Compensation Table. *See* Proposed Item 402(l)(2)(vii)(B). That proposal was not adopted. Unlike the disclosure for NEOs, there is no requirement to provide a Nonqualified Deferred Compensation Table for directors. Consequently, the full amount of nonqualified deferred compensation earnings paid to or accrued on behalf of directors during a covered fiscal year need not be disclosed. For a more detailed discussion of this disclosure requirement, see "Pension Value Changes and Above-Market and Preferential Earnings—Above-Market and Preferential Earnings" in Chapter 4.

81. *See* the Instruction to Item 402(k) and Instruction 2 to Item 402(c)(2)(viii). In the event of a discretionary reset of the interest rate, the requisite calculation must be made on the basis of the interest rate at the time of such reset, rather than when originally established. *Id.*

82. *Id.*

83. *Id.*

84. *Id.*

footnote to identify and quantify the separate amounts attributable to each of the compensation items.[85] If the amount of the pension value change for a covered fiscal year is negative, it is to be disclosed using a footnote, but should not be reflected in the sum reported in the column itself.[86]

All Other Compensation

Column (g) of the table is to report each compensation item that is not otherwise properly reportable in columns (b)–(f) of the table. This requirement applies to all compensatory items, regardless of their amount.[87] In other words, there is generally no de minimis threshold below which disclosure is not required. All items of compensation are required to be included in the table without regard to whether such items are required to be identified other than as specifically required by the rules.[88]

Any compensation item reported in this column for a director that is not a perquisite or personal benefit and whose value exceeds $10,000 must be identified and quantified in a footnote to column (g).[89]

The rules provide a nonexclusive list of the type of compensation items that should be disclosed in column (g) for each director:

- perquisites and other personal benefits, or property, unless the aggregate amount of such items is less than $10,000;[90]
- "gross-ups" or other amounts reimbursed during the covered fiscal year for the payment of taxes;[91]
- securities of the registrant (or its subsidiaries) purchased at a discount to their market price;[92]
- amounts paid or accrued to any director pursuant to a plan or arrangement in connection with his or her resignation,

---

85. *See* the Instruction to Item 402(k) and Instruction 3 to Item 402(c)(2)(viii).

86. *Id.*

87. Item 402(k)(2)(vii).

88. *See* Instruction 2 to Item 402(k)(2)(vii).

89. *Id.* In the case of smaller reporting companies, this identification and quantification requirement applies only if it is deemed material in accordance with Item 402(o)(7). *See* Item 402(r)(2)(vii).

90. Item 402(k)(2)(vii)(A).

91. Item 402(k)(2)(vii)(B).

92. Item 402(k)(2)(vii)(C).

retirement, or any other termination of service, or a change in control of the registrant;[93]

- registrant contributions or other allocations to vested and unvested defined contribution plans;[94]
- consulting fees earned from, or paid or payable by the registrant (and/or its subsidiaries);[95]
- the annual costs of payments and promises of payments pursuant to director legacy programs and similar charitable award programs;[96]
- the dollar value of any insurance premiums paid by, or on behalf of, the registrant during the covered fiscal year with respect to life insurance for the benefit of a director;[97] and
- the dollar value of any dividends or other earnings paid on stock or option awards, when those amounts were not factored into the grant date fair value required to be reported for the stock or option award.[98]

While many of the disclosure requirements for the Director Compensation Table track those of the Summary Compensation Table, because this table is not supplemented with additional compensation tables (as is that disclosure), there may be instances when information will be required in this column that does not need to be provided in the All Other Compensation column of the Summary Compensation Table. For example, generally benefits paid pursuant to defined benefit and actuarial plans and nonqualified defined contribution plans are not reportable in the All Other Compensation column of the Summary Compensation Table.[99] Instead, those amounts are to be reported in the Pension Benefits Table[100] and Nonqualified Deferred Compensation Table,[101] as the case may be. Because there are no corresponding tables

---

93. Item 402(k)(2)(vii)(D).

94. Item 402(k)(2)(vii)(E).

95. Item 402(k)(2)(vii)(F).

96. Item 402(k)(2)(vii)(G).

97. Item 402(k)(2)(vii)(H).

98. Item 402(k)(2)(vii)(I).

99. *See* Instruction 2 to Item 402(c)(2)(ix) and the Current Staff Guidance, *supra* note 24, at Q&A 119.10. See also "All Other Compensation—Other Items—Retirement Plans and Arrangements" in Chapter 4.

100. *See* Chapter 10.

101. *See* Chapter 11.

for directors, however, benefits paid under comparable plans for directors would need to be reported in this column.[102]

Perquisites

The reporting of perquisites and other personal benefits received by directors is similar to the treatment of NEO perquisites.[103] Perquisites and other personal benefits may be excluded as long as the total value of all perquisites and personal benefits for an individual director is less than $10,000.[104] If the total value of all perquisites and personal benefits is $10,000 or more for any director, then each perquisite or personal benefit, regardless of its amount, must be identified by type.[105] The SEC Staff has indicated that in the case of any item for which the director has actually fully reimbursed the registrant for its total cost, such item does not need to be considered a perquisite or other personal benefit and, therefore, does not need to be separately identified by type.[106] Reliance on the Staff's position depends on compliance with two conditions.

First, there must be "actual" reimbursement. While the SEC Staff has not interpreted the meaning of this term, it is possible that it is intended to require an actual economic payment from the director to the registrant. Under this view, a credit or offset, or a notional entry representing the director's payment of the cost, may not be sufficient. Second, the reimbursement must be of the item's "total cost," rather than just its "incremental cost." While it is unclear what is meant by the term "total cost," the methodology involved in determining this amount is likely to vary depending on the item involved.

---

102. While the Instruction to Item 402(k) expressly incorporates Instructions 1 and 5 to Item 402(c)(2)(ix) into the Director Compensation Table, it does not do so with respect to Instruction 2. See the December 2006 Release, supra note 46, at n.30. Note, however, that this result does not apply with respect to pension benefits earned by a director as an executive officer. See the Current Staff Guidance, supra note 24, at Interpretation 227.04.

103. See Chapter 4. For a discussion of perquisites and their identification, see Chapter 5.

104. In one respect, the former rules were more stringent when it came to reporting perquisites and other personal benefits received by directors. Former Item 402(g) required the disclosure of any compensation arrangement for directors, without regard to the amount involved. Item 402(k)(2)(vii)(A) requires perquisites to be disclosed only if their aggregate value is $10,000 or more.

105. See Instruction 3 to Item 402(k)(2)(vii). If the $10,000 disclosure threshold is otherwise exceeded, a perquisite or other personal benefit must be separately identified by type even if the provision of the perquisite or personal benefits involved no aggregate incremental cost to the registrant. See the Current Staff Guidance, supra note 24, at Q&A 119.03.

106. See the Current Staff Guidance, supra note 24, at Q&A 119.03.

As with the concept of "aggregate incremental cost," the SEC Staff has declined to provide a specific definition of how this amount should be calculated. The Staff has indicated, by way of example, however, that a NEO would have "fully reimbursed" a registrant for a meal at a country club if he or she reimbursed not only the cost of the meal but also a proportional amount of the country club dues paid by the registrant.[107]

Where perquisites and personal benefits are required to be reported for a director, then each perquisite or personal benefit that exceeds the greater of $25,000 or 10 percent of the total amount of perquisites and personal benefits for that director must be separately quantified and disclosed in a footnote to column (g).[108]

As with executive perquisites, perquisites and other personal benefits received by directors are to be valued on the basis of the aggregate incremental cost to the registrant.[109] In the case of a perquisite or other personal benefit for which footnote quantification is required, a registrant must describe in the footnote its methodology for computing the aggregate incremental cost of the item.[110]

While reimbursements of taxes owed with respect to perquisites or other personal benefits must be reported in column (g), they are subject to separate quantification and identification as tax reimbursements[111] even if the associated perquisites or other personal benefits are not required to be reported because the total amount of all perquisites or personal benefits for an individual director is less than $10,000 or are required to be identified but are not required to be separately quantified.[112]

Tax Payments

Any tax payment made to or for a director during the last completed fiscal year, whether in the nature of a "gross-up" payment or other tax reimbursement, is reportable in column (g). The reporting of these payments is similar to the treatment of such payments made to a NEO.[113]

---

107. *Id.*

108. *Id.*

109. *Id.*

110. *Id.*

111. Item 402(k)(2)(vii)(B).

112. *See* Instruction 3 to Item 402(k)(2)(vii).

113. *See* "All Other Compensation—Tax Payments" in Chapter 4.

Discount Securities Purchases

If a director purchases any security of the registrant or any of its subsidiaries from the registrant or a subsidiary, as the case may be, whether through the deferral of fees[114] or otherwise, at a discount from the securities' market price at the date of purchase, the compensation cost of the security, computed in accordance with FASB ASC Topic 718, is reportable in column (g) unless that discount is available generally either to all security holders or to all salaried employees of the registrant.[115] The reporting of these payments is similar to the treatment of such payments made to a NEO.[116]

Severance and Change-in-Control Payments

To the extent that a director is paid an amount or has an amount accrued for his or her benefit pursuant to a plan or arrangement in connection with his or her resignation, retirement, or any other termination of service as a director, or in connection with a change in control of the registrant, the amount is reportable in column (g).[117] For this purpose, an "accrued" amount is an amount for which payment has become due.[118] The SEC Staff has indicated that for purposes of determining whether an amount is reportable because it is accrued, if a director's performance necessary to earn an amount is complete, it is an amount that should be reported.[119] In contrast, if an amount will be payable two years after a termination event if the director cooperates with (or complies with a covenant not to compete with) the registrant during that period, the amount is not reportable because the director's performance is still necessary for the payment to become due.[120]

---

114. While Item 402(k)(2)(vii)(C) refers to "salary or bonus," it is presumed that this reference is intended to mean fees earned or paid in cash for services as a director.

115. Item 402(k)(2)(vii)(C).

116. *See* "All Other Compensation—Discount Securities Purchases" in Chapter 4.

117. Item 402(k)(2)(vii)(D).

118. *See* the Instruction to Item 402(k) and Instruction 5 to Item 402(c)(2)(ix).

119. *See* the Current Staff Guidance, *supra* note 24, at Q&A 119.13. For example, if a director has completed all performance to earn an amount, but payment is subject to a six-month deferral in order to comply with Section 409A of the Internal Revenue Code (26 U.S.C. § 409A), the amount would be an accrued amount subject to disclosure.

120. *Id.*

Consulting Fees

Consulting arrangements between a registrant and a director are disclosable as director compensation in column (g), even where such arrangements cover services provided by the director to the registrant other than as a director (for example, as an economist).[121]

Legacy and Charitable Award Programs

The annual costs of payments and promises of payments pursuant to director legacy programs and similar charitable award programs are reportable in column (g). A program in which a registrant agrees to make a donation to one or more charitable institutions in a director's name, payable by the registrant currently or on a designated event, such as the retirement or death of the director, is considered a charitable award or director legacy program for purposes of this disclosure.[122] The amount to be disclosed in column (g) is the annual cost of such payments and promises of payments. Where such disclosure is required, a registrant must also provide footnote disclosure of the total dollar amount payable under the program and the other material terms of each such program.[123]

The SEC Staff has indicated that even where a charitable matching program is available to all employees of the registrant, the program must be included in column (g).[124] The reportable item in the Director Compensation Table applies to "the annual costs of payments and promises of payments pursuant to director legacy programs and similar charitable award programs." In the Staff's view, any registrant-sponsored charitable award program in which a director can participate would be a "similar charitable award program."[125]

---

121. See the Current Staff Guidance, *supra* note 24, at Interpretation 227.01.

122. See Instruction 1 to Item 402(k)(2)(vii).

123. *Id.*

124. See the Current Staff Guidance, *supra* note 24, at Q&A 127.05. See also Questions and Answers, Technical Session Between the SEC Staff and the Joint Committee on Employee Benefits (May 8, 2007), *available at* http://www.abanet.org/jceb/2007/SEC07Final.pdf, at Question No. 22.

125. *Id.* In the SEC Staff's view, the exclusion for "information regarding group life, health, hospitalization, or medical reimbursement plans that do not discriminate in scope, terms, or operation, in favor of executive officers or directors of the registrant and that are available generally to all salaried employees" in Item 402(a)(6)(ii) is not available here. *Id.*

Dividends and Earnings on Equity Awards

The reporting of the dollar value of any dividends or other earnings paid on stock or option awards is similar to the treatment of this item for NEOs.[126] Consequently, such amounts are reportable only when the dividend or earnings were not factored into the grant date fair value of the related equity award. Note that earnings on nonequity incentive plan awards are required to be reported elsewhere as provided in the rules and are not reportable in column (g).[127]

Total Compensation

Column (h) of the table is to report the dollar value of the total compensation of each director for the covered fiscal year. With respect to each person listed in the table, this total will be the sum of all of the amounts reported in columns (b) through (g) of the table.

Supplemental Narrative Disclosure

Consistent with the general approach of the rules, a registrant is to provide a narrative disclosure to accompany the table describing any material factors necessary to an understanding of the information reported in the table.[128] While a registrant must use its judgment to decide what information needs to be disclosed and material factors will vary among registrants depending on their particular compensation programs and the relevant facts, examples of such factors may include, among other things, a description of the standard fee arrangements (cash, equity, and other) that the registrant has in place for its directors, such as fees for retainer, committee service, service as chairman of the board or a committee, and meeting attendance.[129] In addition, to the extent that a director has a different compensation arrangement than his

---

126. *See* "All Other Compensation—Dividends and Earnings on Equity Awards" in Chapter 4.

127. *See* the Instruction to Item 402(k) and Instruction 1 to Item 402(c)(2)(ix).

128. Item 402(k)(3).

129. Item 402(k)(3)(i).

or her colleagues, it may also be necessary to identify that director and describe the terms of that arrangement.[130]

The SEC has also indicated that in view of investor interest in equity award grant practices, particularly following the revelation of widespread stock option backdating issues, this narrative disclosure may also need to address a registrant's equity award timing or dating practices when directors are eligible to receive stock options and other equity awards as part of their compensation packages.[131]

While the SEC does not require tabular presentation of the narrative disclosure, such as a breakdown of standard fee arrangements, consistent with its plain-English principles it encourages tabular presentation where such a presentation would facilitate an understanding of the disclosure.[132]

---

130. Item 402(k)(3)(ii).

131. *See* the Adopting Release, *supra* note 68, at n.64.

132. *See* the Adopting Release, *supra* note 68, at Section VI.

14

Other Compensation Disclosure Requirements

In addition to Item 402, there are several other Securities and Exchange Commission (SEC) rules that require the disclosure of executive compensation-related information.

Performance Graph

General

In view of the scope and purpose of the Compensation Discussion and Analysis (CD&A), the SEC proposed to eliminate the Performance Graph.[1] This disclosure, which was introduced in 1992,[2] required a registrant, as part of its executive compensation disclosure, to provide a line graph comparing its cumulative total shareholder return with a performance indicator of the overall stock market and either a published

---

1. *See* Executive Compensation and Related Party Disclosure, Release Nos. 33-8655, 34-53185, IC-27218 (Jan. 27, 2006), 71 Fed. Reg. 6542 (Feb. 8, 2006), *available at* http://www.sec.gov/rules/proposed/33-8655.pdf, at Section II.A.4.

2. *See* Executive Compensation Disclosure, Release Nos. 33-6962, 34-31327, IC-19032 (Oct. 16, 1992), 57 Fed. Reg. 48,126 (Oct. 21, 1992), *as modified,* Executive Compensation Disclosure: Correction, Release Nos. 33-6966, 34-31420, IC-19085 (Nov. 9, 1992), 57 Fed. Reg. 53,985 (Nov. 9, 1992), at Section II.I.

industry index or a registrant-determined peer comparison.[3] Given the widespread availability of stock performance information about registrants, industries, and indexes through the Internet and other sources and the more detailed requirements of the CD&A,[4] the SEC believed the Performance Graph to be unnecessary.

Many commenters objected to the Performance Graph's elimination, however, contending that the ready accessibility of this information, particularly for retail investors, made it a popular and useful tool for comparing a registrant's performance against the market and its peers.[5] In addition, as a standardized analytical measure, it promoted comparability between registrants in an easily understood and economical manner.[6]

In view of these comments, the SEC decided to retain the Performance Graph. To avoid undermining its expectations that the CD&A address corporate performance measures beyond those reflected by stock price, however, the SEC chose to move this information from the executive and director compensation disclosure to the Regulation S-K item requiring information about the market price of, and dividends on, a registrant's common equity.[7]

As under the former rules, the Performance Graph is considered to be furnished to, rather than filed with, the SEC.[8] Further, it is required only in a registrant's annual report to shareholders[9] that accompanies or precedes a proxy or information statement relating to an annual meeting of shareholders at which directors are to be elected (or special meeting or

---

3. *See* former Item 402(l). Together with the Board Compensation Committee Report (*see* former Item 402(k)), the Performance Graph was intended to depict the relationship, if any, between a registrant's executive compensation policies and corporate performance as measured by stock price.

4. *See* Items 402(b)(2)(v) and (vi).

5. *See* Executive Compensation and Related Person Disclosure, Release Nos. 33-8732A, 34-54302A, IC-27444A (Aug. 29, 2006), 71 Fed. Reg. 53,158 (Sept. 8, 2006) [hereinafter Adopting Release], *available at* http://www.sec.gov/rules/final/2006/33-8732a.pdf, at Section II.B.4.

6. *Id.*

7. *See* Item 201(e) of Regulation S-K (17 C.F.R. 229.201(e)). A smaller reporting company is not required to provide a Performance Graph. *See* Instruction 6 to Item 201(e).

8. *See* Instruction 8 to Item 201(e). Thus, it will not be deemed to be "soliciting material" or to be "filed" with the SEC or subject to Regulation 14A or 14C (17 C.F.R. 240.14a-1 to 240.14a-104 or 240.14c-1 to 240.14c-101), or incorporated by reference into any filing except to the extent that the registrant specifically incorporates it into a Securities Act or Exchange Act filing. *Id.*

9. *See* Exchange Act Rule 14a-3 (17 C.F.R. 240.14a-3) and Exchange Act Rule 14c-3 (17 C.F.R. 240.14c-3).

written consents in lieu of such meeting).[10] Nonetheless, some registrants continue to provide the Performance Graph in their definitive proxy statement, as well as in their annual report to shareholders.[11]

Disclosure Requirements

The Performance Graph is to consist of a line graph comparing the yearly percentage change in the registrant's cumulative total shareholder return on a class of common stock registered under Section 12 of the Exchange Act[12] with:

- the cumulative total return, assuming reinvestment of dividends, of a broad equity market index that includes companies whose equity securities are traded on the same exchange or are of comparable market capitalization; *provided, however,* that if the registrant is a company within the Standard & Poor's 500 Stock Index, the registrant must use that index; and

- the cumulative total return, assuming reinvestment of dividends, of

  - a published industry or line-of-business index;
  - peer issuer(s) selected in good faith;[13] or

---

10. *See* Instruction 7 to Item 201(e). This information will not be deemed to be incorporated by reference into any filing under the Securities Act or the Exchange Act, except to the extent that the registrant specifically incorporates it by reference. *Id.* The SEC Staff has confirmed that, even though Item 5 of Form 10-K indicates that a registrant is required to furnish the information required under Item 201 of Regulation S-K, the Performance Graph is not required to be included in an annual report on Form 10-K. *See* Division of Corporation Finance, Compliance and Disclosure Interpretations – Regulation S-K (July 8, 2011) [hereinafter Current Staff Guidance], *available at* http://www.sec.gov/divisions/corpfin/guidance/regs-kinterp.htm, at Q&A 106.10. While a registrant may include the Performance Graph in its annual report on Form 10-K, doing so will not satisfy the requirement to provide the graph in its annual report to shareholders pursuant to Exchange Act Rule 14a-3 (17 C.F.R. 240.14a-3) or Exchange Act Rule 14c-3 (17 C.F.R. 240.14c-3) unless it is using a "Form 10-K wrap" approach to satisfy the requirements of Exchange Act Rule 14a-3 or Rule 14c-3. *See* the Current Staff Guidance, at Q&A 106.11.

11. *See* the Current Staff Guidance, *supra* note 10, at Q&A 106.12.

12. 15 U.S.C. § 78l. This figure is to be measured by dividing the sum of the cumulative amount of dividends for the measurement period, assuming dividend reinvestment, and the difference between the registrant's share price at the end and the beginning of the measurement period, by the share price at the beginning of the measurement period. *See* Item 201(e)(1).

13. If the registrant does not select its peer issuer or issuers on an industry or line-of-business basis, it must disclose the basis for its selection. *See* Item 201(e)(1)(ii)(B).

- issuer(s) with similar market capitalization(s), but only if the registrant does not use a published industry or line-of-business index and does not believe it can reasonably identify a peer group.[14]

The Performance Graph is to cover a five-year period ending with the last completed fiscal year.[15] A registrant may choose to graph a longer period, but the measurement point must remain the same.[16] A registrant also may include comparisons using other performance measures, such as return on average common shareholders' equity, in addition to total shareholder return as long as the meaning of any such measure is clear from the Performance Graph and any related legend or other disclosure.[17] A merger or other acquisition involving a registrant, where the registrant remains in existence and its common stock remains outstanding, does not change the presentation of the registrant's Performance Graph.[18]

In preparing the graph, a registrant should use, to the extent feasible, comparable methods of presentation and assumptions for the total shareholder return calculations.[19] If a registrant constructs its own peer group index for purposes of the comparison, it must use the same methodology to calculate both its total shareholder return and that of the peer group index.[20] A registrant also should assume the reinvestment

---

14. If the registrant uses this alternative, the graph must be accompanied by a statement of the reasons for this selection. *See* Item 201(e)(1)(ii)(C).

15. The precise measurement period is to be the period beginning at the "measurement point" established by the market close on the last trading day before the beginning of the registrant's fifth preceding fiscal year, through and including the end of the registrant's last completed fiscal year. *See* Item 201(e)(2). If the class of securities being measured has been registered under Section 12 of the Exchange Act for a shorter period of time, the period covered by the Performance Graph may correspond to that time period. *Id.* In addition, a registrant created by a spin-off may begin its Performance Graph presentation on the effective date of the registration of its common stock under Section 12 of the Exchange Act. *See* the Current Staff Guidance, *supra* note 10, at Interpretation 206.08.

16. *See* Instruction 3 to Item 201(e). In addition, a registrant may plot monthly or quarterly returns in its performance graph provided that each return is plotted at the same interval, and the annual changes in cumulative total return are reflected clearly. *See* the Current Staff Guidance, *supra* note 10, at Q&A 106.06.

17. *See* Instruction 4 to Item 201(e). *See also* the Adopting Release, *supra* note 5, at n.115. This flexibility differs from the former rules, which conditioned the use of other performance measures in addition to total shareholder return on the board compensation committee including a description of the link between the measure and the level of compensation in the Board Compensation Committee Report. *See* Instruction 4 to former Item 402(l).

18. *See* the Current Staff Guidance, *supra* note 10, at Interpretation 206.10.

19. *See* Instruction 1(a) to Item 201(e).

20. *Id.*

of dividends into additional shares of the same class of equity securities at the frequency with which dividends are paid on such securities during the applicable fiscal year.[21] Further, in constructing the Performance Graph, the closing price at the measurement point[22] must be converted into a fixed investment, stated in dollars, in the registrant's stock (or in the stocks represented by a given index) with cumulative returns for each subsequent fiscal year measured as a change from that investment.[23] Each fiscal year is to be plotted with points showing the cumulative total return as of that point.[24]

For purposes of preparing the Performance Graph, the "published industry or line-of-business index" may be any index that is prepared by a party other than the registrant or an affiliate of the registrant[25] and that is accessible to the registrant's shareholders.[26] If prepared by the registrant or an affiliate of the registrant, the index must also be widely recognized and used.[27]

A registrant with several distinct lines of business may construct a composite peer group index composed of entities from different industry groups, representing each of the registrant's lines of business (with the lines of business weighted by revenues or assets). The basis and amount

---

21. *See* Instruction 1(b) to Item 201(e).

22. In the case of a newly public registrant, the registrant may not choose between using the price shown in the registration statement for its initial public offering of securities, the opening price on the first trading day, or the closing market price on the first trading day when preparing its initial Performance Graph. The registrant should use the closing market price at the end of the first trading day. *See* the Current Staff Guidance, *supra* note 10, at Q&A 106.09.

23. *See* Instruction 2(a) of Item 201(e). In lieu of data for the last trading day prior to the end of a given fiscal year, a registrant may use data for the last day in that year made available by a third-party index provider. *See* the Current Staff Guidance, *supra* note 10, at Interpretation 206.07.

24. *See* Instruction 2(b) of Item 201(e). The value of the investment as of each point plotted on a given return line is the number of shares held at that point multiplied by the then-prevailing share price. *Id.*

25. Note that a registrant may use a self-prepared index if it is widely recognized and used. *See* Item 201(e)(3).

26. For guidance concerning the use of trade group indices and of composite indices composed of more than one published index, *see* Executive Compensation Disclosure; Securityholder Lists and Mailing Requests, Release Nos. 33-7009, 34-32723 (Aug. 6, 1993), 58 Fed. Reg. 42,882 (Aug. 12, 1993) [hereinafter 1993 Release], at Section IV.B.2. Self-constructed indices (which include those prepared by a third party for the registrant and which are not "published") are not prohibited or discouraged by Item 201(e) of Regulation S-K. They just must be weighted by market capitalization (as are most published indices) and include identification of the component issuers. *See* the Current Staff Guidance, *supra* note 10, at Interpretation 206.15.

27. *Id.*

of the weighting should be disclosed. Alternatively, the registrant may plot a separate peer index line for each of its lines of business.[28]

If a registrant uses a peer issuer or issuers' comparison or a comparison with issuers with similar market capitalizations, it must disclose the identity of those issuers.[29] In addition, the returns of each component issuer of the group must be weighted according to the respective issuer's stock market capitalization at the beginning of each period for which a return is indicated.[30]

If a registrant changes indices from one fiscal year to the next, it must explain the reason or reasons for the change.[31] In addition, it also must compare its total shareholder return with that of both the newly selected index and the index used in the immediately preceding fiscal year.[32] These rules also apply where a registrant changes the entities comprising a self-constructed index from the index used in the prior fiscal year,[33] with two limited exceptions. Presentation on the old basis is not required:

- if an entity is omitted solely because it is no longer in the line of business or industry; or
- the changes in the composition of the index result from the application of preestablished objective criteria.[34]

In these two cases, a specific description of, and the bases for, the change must be disclosed, including the names of the companies deleted from the new index.[35]

Likewise, if a registrant becomes listed on a national securities exchange that is different from the exchange it was listed on in the prior fiscal year, the change needs to be reflected in the Performance Graph if the registrant also changes its broad equity market indices as a result.

---

28. *See* the Current Staff Guidance, *supra* note 10, at Interpretation 206.11.

29. *See* Instruction 5 to Item 201(e). A registrant-constructed peer issuer(s) comparison or a comparison with issuers with similar market capitalizations may exclude the registrant. *See* the Current Staff Guidance, *supra* note 10, at Q&A 106.08.

30. *Id. See also* the Current Staff Guidance, *supra* note 10, at Q&A 106.07.

31. *See* Item 201(e)(4).

32. *Id. See also* the Current Staff Guidance, *supra* note 10, at Interpretation 206.12 ("If a company selects its own peer group and subsequently changes the group, an additional line showing the newly selected index should be added to the performance graph.")

33. *See* the 1993 Release, supra note 26, at Section IV.B.1.

34. *See* the Current Staff Guidance, *supra* note 10, at Interpretation 206.05.

35. *Id.*

For example, if a registrant that had been listed on the American Stock Exchange (AMEX) becomes listed on a different national securities exchange and now plans to use the Standard & Poor's 500 as its broad equity market index rather than the AMEX Composite Index, the registrant must provide a narrative explanation of the change in indices and compare returns based on the old and new index on the graph.[36]

Special Situations

Over the years, the staff of the SEC's Division of Corporation Finance (SEC Staff) has addressed a number of special situations that have an impact on the preparation of the Performance Graph. For example, in the case of a registrant that spins off a portion of its business, the Staff has indicated that the registrant should treat that transaction as a special dividend, make the appropriate adjustments to its shareholder return data, and disclose the occurrence of the transaction and resultant adjustments in its Performance Graph.[37]

In a second situation, a registrant was preparing its first proxy statement following its emergence from bankruptcy. The new class of stock that was issued under the bankruptcy plan started trading in March 2006. Accordingly, the measurement period for the Performance Graph was from March 2006 through December 2006. The SEC Staff indicated that the registrant could plot the Performance Graph on a monthly basis and could continue the graph beyond December 2006 as long as the December 2006 plotting point was clearly shown. The Staff also indicated that this same principle applies to initial public offerings of securities and spin-off situations with a short fiscal year.[38]

---

36. *See* the Current Staff Guidance, *supra* note 10, at Interpretation 206.06.

37. *See* the Current Staff Guidance, *supra* note 10, at Interpretation 206.09.

38. *See* the Current Staff Guidance, *supra* note 10, at Interpretation 206.14. The SEC Staff has also stated that registrants that have a short fiscal year (for example, following an initial public offering of securities, as the result of a spin-off, or after emerging from bankruptcy) must prepare a Performance Graph for the short year unless the short year is 30 days or less. *See* the Current Staff Guidance, *supra* note 10, at Interpretation 206.13.

Equity Compensation Plan Information

General

To better enable investor understanding of how a registrant uses equity-based awards in its employee compensation programs, registrants must provide tabular disclosure of the number of outstanding stock options, warrants, and other rights granted to participants in equity compensation plans, as well as the number of securities remaining available for future issuance under these plans.[39] This information is to be presented on the basis of equity compensation plans that have been approved by shareholders and equity compensation plans that have not been approved by shareholders.[40] This information is to be included in a registrant's annual report on Form 10-K each year,[41] as well as in its proxy or information statement in years in which the registrant is submitting a compensation plan (whether an equity or a cash plan) for shareholder action.[42] To induce registrants to include the information in their proxy statements, even if a compensation plan is not being submitted for shareholder action at the annual meeting of shareholders, the SEC permits a registrant to incorporate the information into its annual report on Form 10-K from its proxy or information statement.[43]

This disclosure is to be comprehensive. Accordingly, it covers any compensation plan and individual compensation arrangement[44] of the registrant (or parent, subsidiary, or affiliate of the registrant) under which the registrant's equity securities may be issued to employees

---

39. Item 201(d) of Regulation S-K (17 C.F.R. 229.201(d)). In spite of the fact that Item 5 of Form 10-K indicates that a registrant is required to furnish the information required under Item 201 of Regulation S-K, the SEC Staff has indicated that the Item 201(d) disclosure is to be included (or incorporated by reference) in Part III, rather than Part II, of Form 10-K (given that Item 12 of Form 10-K expressly states that a registrant is required to furnish the information required under Item 201(d)). *See* the Current Staff Guidance, *supra* note 10, at Q&A 106.01.

40. Item 201(d)(1)(i) and (ii).

41. *See* Item 12 of Part III of Form 10-K (17 C.F.R. 249.310).

42. *See* Item 10(c) of Schedule 14A and Item 1 of Schedule 14C. Unless it is part of a document that is incorporated by reference into a prospectus, this information does not need to be provided in any Securities Act registration statement. *See* Instruction 9 to Item 201(d).

43. General Instruction G.3 to Form 10-K. *See* the Current Staff Guidance, *supra* note 10, at Q&A 106.01.

44. For purposes of this Item, an "individual compensation arrangement" includes, but is not limited to, a written compensation contract within the meaning of "employee benefit plan" under Rule 405 of Regulation C (17 C.F.R. 230.405) and a plan (whether or not set forth in any formal document) applicable to one person as provided under Item 402(a)(6). *See* Instruction 2 to Item 201(d).

or nonemployees (such as directors, consultants, advisors, vendors, customers, suppliers, or lenders) in exchange for consideration in the form of goods or services.[45] It does not include, however, plans, contracts, or arrangements involving the issuance of warrants or rights to all of a registrant's security holders as such on a pro rata basis (such as a stock rights offering) or any employee benefit plan that is intended to meet the qualification requirements of Section 401(a)[46] of the Internal Revenue Code.[47]

A compensation plan that permits awards to be settled in either cash or stock must be included in the tabular disclosure. A plan that permits awards to be settled in cash only, however, need not be included in the tabular disclosure since the purpose of the requirement is to enable investors to better understand the dilutive effect of a registrant's equity compensation program and cash-only plans are not dilutive.[48]

Disclosure Requirements

The Equity Compensation Plan Information Table is to be presented in the following tabular format:[49]

---

45. *See* Instruction 1 to Item 201(d). Essentially, the disclosure covers any compensation arrangement that is described in Financial Accounting Standards Board Accounting Standards Codification Topic 718, *Compensation—Stock Compensation* (FASB ASC Topic 718) and Financial Accounting Standards Board Accounting Standards Codification Subtopic 505-50, *Equity—Equity-Based Payments to Non-Employees*. If more than one class of equity security is issued under its equity compensation plans, a registrant should aggregate plan information for each class of security. *See* Instruction 3 to Item 201(d).

46. 26 U.S.C. § 401(a).

47. *See* Instruction 1 to Item 201(d). The same treatment applies to a foreign employee benefit plan that is similar in substance to a plan qualified under Section 401(a) of the Internal Revenue Code (26 U.S.C. § 401(a)) in terms of being broad-based, compensatory, and nondiscriminatory. The same analysis applies for purposes of determining whether a plan must be filed as an exhibit pursuant to Item 601(b)(10)(iii)(B) of Regulation S-K, based on the exclusion provided by Item 601(b)(10)(iii)(C)(4). *See* the Current Staff Guidance, *supra* note 10, at Interpretation 206.03.

48. *See* the Current Staff Guidance, *supra* note 10, at Interpretation 206.02 Note, however, that, pursuant to Item 10 of Schedule 14A (17 C.F.R. 240.14a-101), if a registrant is seeking shareholder approval of any plan pursuant to which cash (or noncash) compensation may be paid or distributed, the registrant must include the disclosure required by Item 201(d) in its definitive proxy statement with respect to its plans under which equity securities of the registrant are authorized for issuance. *Id.*

49. Item 201(d)(1).

EQUITY COMPENSATION PLAN INFORMATION

Plan Category	Number of Securities to Be Issued upon Exercise of Outstanding Options, Warrants, and Rights (a)	Weighted-Average Exercise Price of Outstanding Options, Warrants, and Rights (b)	Number of Securities Remaining Available for Future Issuance Under Equity Compensation Plans (Excluding Securities Reflected in Column (a)) (c)
Equity compensation plans approved by security holders			
Equity compensation plans not approved by security holders			
Total			

The table includes the following information as of the end of the registrant's most recently completed fiscal year with respect to compensation plans (including individual compensation arrangements) under which the registrant's equity securities are authorized for issuance, aggregated into two categories: (all compensation plans previously approved by shareholders and all compensation plans not previously approved by shareholders).[50]

- the number of securities to be issued upon the exercise of outstanding options, warrants, and rights (column (a));[51]
- the weighted-average exercise price of the outstanding options, warrants, and rights disclosed in column (a) (column (b));[52] and
- other than securities to be issued upon the exercise of the outstanding options, warrants, and rights disclosed in column

---

50. The securities that may be issued under an equity compensation plan that has received Bankruptcy Court approval, but not shareholder approval, should be reported in the category of compensation plans "not previously approved by shareholders" for purposes of the table. *See* the Current Staff Guidance, *supra* note 10, at Interpretation 206.01. A footnote may be added to disclose the Bankruptcy Court approval. *Id.*

51. Item 201(d)(2)(i). A registrant may aggregate the information regarding individual compensation arrangements with the plan information required by this paragraph. *See* Instruction 4 to Item 201(d).

52. Item 201(d)(2)(ii). A registrant may aggregate the information regarding individual compensation arrangements with the plan information required by this paragraph. *See* Instruction 4 to Item 201(d).

(a), the number of securities remaining available for future issuance under the plan (column (c)).[53]

To ensure full transparency about nonshareholder-approved plans, a registrant must describe briefly, in narrative form, the material features of any such plan.[54] In addition, if an equity compensation plan contains a formula for calculating the number of securities available for issuance under the plan, including, without limitation, a formula that automatically increases the number of securities available for issuance by a percentage of the number of outstanding securities of the registrant (an "evergreen" provision), this formula must be disclosed in a footnote to the table.[55]

A registrant may aggregate information regarding a compensation plan assumed in connection with a merger, consolidation, or other acquisition where the registrant may make subsequent grants or awards of its equity securities with the information disclosed in the table about its own plans.[56] However, the individual options, warrants, or rights assumed in connection with the transaction are to be disclosed on an aggregated basis in a footnote to the table.[57]

Application to Specific Types of Awards

The SEC Staff has taken the position that, once issued, shares of restricted stock that have been granted subject to forfeiture pursuant to an equity compensation plan are neither "to be issued upon exercise of outstanding options, warrants and rights" (column (a) of the table) nor "available for future issuance" (column (c) of the table) and, therefore, are not reportable in the Equity Compensation Plan Information Table.[58]

---

53. Item 201(d)(2)(iii). In the case of equity securities disclosed in this column that are not subject to the exercise of stock options, warrants, or rights, a registrant must disclose the number of such securities and the type of plan under which they may be issued separately for each such plan in a footnote to the table. *See* Instruction 6 to Item 201(d).

54. Item 201(d)(3). If the registrant's financial statements contain a description of the nonshareholder-approved plan that meets the requirements of this Item, a cross-reference to that description will be deemed to satisfy this requirement. *See* Instruction 7 to Item 201(d).

55. *See* Instruction 8 to Item 201(d).

56. *See* Instruction 5 to Item 201(d).

57. *Id.*

58. *See* the Current Staff Guidance, *supra* note 10, at Q&A 106.02. If the shares of restricted stock are later forfeited, they would be reportable in column (c) of the table until granted again. *Id.*

The SEC Staff also has indicated that shares that may be issued under performance share awards if specified performance targets are met (that is, an award denominated in shares has been made, but no shares will be issued until the performance targets are met), and shares that are credited as phantom shares under a deferred compensation plan that will be issued as actual shares upon termination of employment, must be reported in column (a) of the table as securities to be issued upon the exercise of outstanding options, warrants, and rights.[59] If the number of shares subject to these awards overstates expected dilution (such as where the award reflects the maximum number of shares to be awarded upon maximum performance at a target level that is unlikely to be achieved), this situation should be addressed in a footnote to the table.[60]

Further, the SEC Staff has taken the position that, where a registrant has granted stock appreciation rights (SARs) that may be settled solely in stock (that is, the rights are exercisable for an amount of the registrant's common stock with a value equal to the increase in the fair market value of the common stock from the date of grant until the date of exercise), the registrant may use the fair market value of its common stock at fiscal year-end for purposes of reporting the number of shares to be issued upon the exercise of the SARs.[61]

Finally, the SEC Staff has indicated that, where a registrant maintains an employee stock purchase plan covered by Section 423 of the Internal Revenue Code,[62] under which there are outstanding rights to purchase shares of the registrant's stock at a floating exercise price (that is, 85 percent of the lower of (a) the market price of the stock at the beginning of a purchase period or (b) the market price of the stock at the future closing of the purchase period), the shares subject to these outstanding rights should be reported in column (c) of the table, together with any shares remaining issuable under the plan.[63] Shares subject to

---

59. *See* the Current Staff Guidance, *supra* note 10, at Q&A 106.03. A footnote to the table should describe the nature of the awards and explain that the weighted-average exercise price information required in column (b) of the table does not take these awards into account. *Id.*

60. *Id.*

61. *See* the Current Staff Guidance, *supra* note 10, at Interpretation 206.04. The registrant should describe this assumption in a footnote to the table. *Id.*

62. 26 U.S.C. § 423.

63. *See* the Current Staff Guidance, *supra* note 10, at Q&A 106.04. A footnote should be added to the table disclosing the total number of shares remaining available for issuance, as well as the number of shares subject to purchase during any current purchase period.

the outstanding rights should *not* be reported in column (a) of the table as subject to outstanding options, warrants, or rights.[64]

Compensation Plan Disclosure

General

Where a registrant submits a compensation plan to its security holders for their consideration and action, it must include a brief description of the material terms and conditions of the plan, as well as other specified information, in its proxy statement.[65] This requirement applies to both cash and noncash (equity-based) compensation plans. In addition, as described above, the registrant must include the Equity Compensation Plan Information Table and related information as part of this disclosure.[66]

Disclosure Requirements

Item 10 consists of both narrative and tabular disclosure. In addition to summarizing the materials terms and conditions of the plan, this disclosure must identify the class of persons eligible to participate in the plan, the number of persons in each class, and the basis for their participation.[67]

In the case of the tabular disclosure, a New Plan Benefits Table is to be presented in the following tabular format disclosing the benefits or amounts that will be received by or allocated to (1) each of the

---

64. *Id.*

65. *See* Item 10 of Schedule 14A (17 C.F.R. 240.14a-101). If the action to be taken involves a material amendment or modification of an existing plan, the disclosure is to be presented with respect to the plan as proposed to be amended or modified and is to indicate any material differences from the existing plan. *See* Instruction 1 to Item 10.

66. *See* Item 10(c). See "Equity Compensation Plan Information," *supra*. If action is to be taken to approve a new compensation plan under which equity securities of the registrant may be issued, information about the plan is to be disclosed as required by Item 10 and is not to be included in the Item 201(d) disclosure. If action is to be taken to amend or modify an existing compensation plan under which equity securities of the registrant may be issued, the registrant must include information about securities previously authorized for issuance under the plan (including any outstanding options, warrants, and rights previously granted pursuant to the plan and any securities remaining available for future issuance under the plan) in the Item 201(d) disclosure. Any additional securities that are the subject of the plan amendment or modification must be disclosed as required by Item 10 and are not be included in the Item 201(d) disclosure. *See* the Instruction to Item 10(c).

67. *See* Item 10(a)(1).

registrant's named executive officers (NEOs),[68] (2) all current executive officers as a group, (3) all current directors who are not executive officers as a group, and (4) all employees, including all current officers who are not executive officers, as a group under the plan being acted upon, to the extent that such benefits or amounts are determinable:[69]

NEW PLAN BENEFITS

Plan Name

Name and Position	Dollar Value ($)	Number of Units
CEO		
A		
B		
C		
D		
Executive-Officer Group		
Non-Executive-Officer Director Group		
Non-Executive-Officer Employee Group		

If the benefits or amounts that are otherwise to be reported in the table are not determinable, a registrant should state the benefits or amounts that would have been received by or allocated to each of the enumerated persons and groups for the last completed fiscal year if the plan had been in effect, if such benefits or amounts may be determined.[70]

If the plan to be acted upon can be amended, other than by a vote of security holders, to increase the cost thereof to the registrant or to alter the allocation of the benefits as between the enumerated persons and groups, the registrant should state the nature of the amendments that can be made to effect that result.

---

68. *See* Item 402(a)(3). Additional columns should be added to the table for each plan for which shareholder action is being taken. *See* the Instruction to the New Plan Benefits Table.

69. *See* Item 10(a)(2).

70. *See* Item 10(a)(2)(iii).

Retirement Plans

In the case of a pension or retirement plan that is submitted for security holder action, in addition to the foregoing information,[71] a registrant also must disclose:

- the approximate total amount necessary to fund the plan with respect to past services, the period over which such amount is to be paid, and the estimated annual payments necessary to pay the total amount over such period; and
- the estimated annual payment to be made with respect to current services.

Stock Option Plans

In the case of a specific award or a plan that provides for the grant of stock options, warrants, or rights that is submitted for security holder action, in addition to the foregoing information, a registrant also must disclose:[72]

- the title and amount of securities underlying such options, warrants, or rights;
- the prices, expiration dates, and other material conditions upon which the options, warrants, or rights may be exercised;
- the consideration received or to be received by the registrant (or a subsidiary) for the granting or extension of the options, warrants, or rights;
- the market value of the securities underlying the options, warrants, or rights as of the latest practicable date; and
- in the case of stock options, the federal income tax consequences of the issuance and exercise of such options to the recipient and the registrant.[73]

Further, the registrant must disclose the number of stock options received or to be received by each of the enumerated persons and groups, as well as each director nominee, each associate of any such director,

---

71. A registrant may replace the New Plan Benefits Table with the Pension Benefits Table required by Item 402(h)(2). *See* Item 10(b)(1)(ii).

72. This requirement does not apply to warrants or rights to be issued to security holders as such on a pro rata basis. See Instruction 3 to Item 10.

73. *See* Item 10(b)(2)(i).

executive officer, or nominee, and any other person who received or is to receive 5 percent of the options, if such benefits or amounts are determinable.[74]

Finally, the SEC must be informed, as supplemental information when the proxy statement is first filed, as to when the options, warrants, or rights and the underlying shares will be registered under the Securities Act or, if they will not be registered, the section of the Securities Act or SEC rule under which exemption from such registration is claimed, and the facts relied on to make the exemption available.[75]

Filing Requirement

If the compensation plan is contained in a written document, three copies of the plan are to be filed with the SEC at the time copies of the proxy statement and form of proxy are first filed.[76] Electronic filers are to file with the SEC a copy of the written plan document in electronic format as an appendix to the proxy statement. It need not be provided to security holders unless it is a part of the proxy statement.[77]

Compensation Committee Disclosure

General

At the same time as the SEC adopted the current executive compensation disclosure rules, it also consolidated its disclosure requirements regarding director independence and related corporate governance disclosure requirements under a single disclosure item.[78] Among other things, the corporate governance provisions require new disclosures about the compensation committee of a registrant's board of directors that are similar to the disclosures required about audit and nominating committees of the board of directors. These requirements are set forth in Item 407(e) of Regulation S-K.[79]

In addition, the Dodd-Frank Wall Street Reform and Consumer Protection Act[80] includes a provision requiring enhanced

---

74. *See* Item 10(b)(2)(ii).
75. *See* Instruction 4 to Item 10.
76. *See* Instruction 2 to Item 10.
77. *Id.*
78. *See* the Adopting Release, *supra* note 5, at Section V.D.
79. 17 C.F.R 229.407(e).
80. Pub.L. No. 111-203, 124 Stat. 1376 (July 2010).

independence standards for members of the compensation committee of a board of directors and an assessment of the independence of any potential advisors to the compensation committee. The SEC has proposed a new disclosure rule concerning the use of compensation consultants and conflicts of interest. As of the date of this publication, this rule had not yet been adopted.

Disclosure Requirements

If a registrant does not have a standing compensation committee (or committee performing similar functions), it must state the basis for the view of the board of directors that it is appropriate for the registrant not to have such a committee.[81] It also must identify each director who participates in the consideration of executive officer and director compensation.[82] Further, a registrant must disclose whether its compensation committee has a charter,[83] and, if it does, make the charter available through its corporate website or in an appendix to its proxy materials.[84]

As part of the required disclosure, a registrant must provide a narrative description of its processes and procedures for considering and determining executive and director compensation, including

- the scope of authority of the compensation committee (or persons performing the equivalent functions);[85] and
- the extent to which the compensation committee (or persons performing the equivalent functions) may delegate this authority to other persons, specifying what authority may be so delegated and to whom.[86]

---

81. Item 407(e)(1).

82. *Id.*

83. Item 407(e)(2).

84. *See* Instruction 2 to Item 407. Where the charter is available on a registrant's Web site, the disclosure must provide the registrant's Web site address where it can be accessed. *Id.* Where the charter is provided in a registrant's proxy materials, it must be physically included in these materials at least once every three years or if the charter has been materially amended since the beginning of the registrant's last fiscal year. *Id.* In years where the charter is not included in the registrant's proxy materials (and it is not posted on the registrant's corporate Web site), the disclosure must identify in which of the prior fiscal years the charter was physically included in such materials. *Id.*

85. Item 407(3)(i)(A).

86. Item 407(e)(i)(B).

Role of Executive Officers

If any of a registrant's executive officers plays any role in determining or recommending the amount or form of executive and director compensation, the registrant must provide a narrative description of each individual's involvement in the decision-making process.[87] Although this information is to be provided as part of a registrant's corporate governance disclosure, comments raised by the SEC Staff as part of its 2007 focused review project indicate that the Staff does not view this disclosure as a substitute for the inclusion of comparable information in the registrant's CD&A that is material to an investor's understanding of the registrant's executive compensation program. Consequently, in preparing its disclosure, a registrant must be cognizant of the different purposes of this apparently overlapping disclosure requirement.[88] In the case of the corporate governance disclosure, the focus is on the registrant's corporate governance structure that is in place for considering and determining executive and director compensation, such as the scope of authority of the compensation committee and others in making pay decisions, as well as the resources used by the committee.[89] This suggests disclosure that is largely process-oriented. In the case of the CD&A, the focus of the disclosure is on material information about the registrant's compensation policies and objectives and providing a perspective on the quantitative disclosure of NEO compensation as reported in the compensation tables.[90] Thus, this disclosure should encompass an explanation of the executive officers' role in setting policy and making compensation decisions to the extent material to understanding those policies and decisions.

While the requirement covers any executive officer, for most registrants, this disclosure is likely to involve the registrant's chief executive officer. It is advisable that this discussion address, among other things, whether the executive has the ability to call or attend meetings of the compensation committee of the board of directors, whether

---

87. Item 407(e)(ii).

88. Another significant distinction involves potential liability considerations. Information about the role of any executive officer in determining or recommending the amount or form of executive compensation that is included in a registrant's CD&A is incorporated by reference into its annual report on Form 10-K, while similar information included in the registrant's corporate governance disclosure is not. *See* Item 11 of Form 10-K (17 C.F.R. 249.310).

89. *See* the Adopting Release, *supra* note 5, at Section V.B.

90. *Id.*

the executive met with the compensation consultant retained by the compensation committee, whether the executive retained or had access to any other compensation consultant who influenced the registrant's executive compensation, and the amount of input the executive had in developing compensation packages.

Role of Compensation Consultants

A registrant also must disclose the role of any compensation consultant or consultants in determining or recommending the amount or form of executive and director compensation.[91] This disclosure must:

- identify the consultant or consultants;
- state whether the consultant is engaged directly by the compensation committee (or the persons performing the equivalent functions) or any other person;
- describe the nature and scope of the consultant's assignment; and
- describe the material elements of the instructions or directions given to the consultant with respect to the performance of its duties under the engagement.[92]

This disclosure is to be made with respect to any compensation consultant with any role in determining or recommending the amount or form of executive or director compensation, not just those compensation consultants, if any, that have been retained by the registrant's board of directors or compensation committee.[93] Accordingly, this would necessarily include any compensation consultant engaged by the registrant itself.

In addition, the consent[94] of the compensation consultant is not required if a consultant is identified for purposes of this disclosure requirement in a filing that is incorporated by reference into a Securities

---

91. *See* Item 407(e)(iii).

92. *Id.* A proposal that would have required disclosure of the identity of any executive officers of the registrant that the compensation consultant contacted in carrying out its assignment was determined by the SEC to be unnecessary and, thus, was omitted from the new rules. *See* the Adopting Release, *supra* note 5, at n.496 and the accompanying text.

93. *See* the Current Staff Guidance, *supra* note 10, at Q&A 133.05. See also the Commentary to Section 308A.05 of the NYSE Listed Company Manual.

94. Securities Act Rule 436(a) (17 C.F.R. 230.436(a)) provides that if any portion of the report or opinion of an expert or counsel is quoted or summarized as such in a Securities Act registration statement or in a prospectus, the written consent of the expert or counsel must be filed as an exhibit to the registration statement and must expressly state that the expert or counsel consents to such quotation or summarization.

Act registration statement.[95] Identifying a compensation consultant and the role that the consultant had in determining or recommending the amount or form of executive and director compensation does not result in the compensation consultant being deemed an "expert" for the purposes of the Securities Act, or mean that the compensation consultant has expertized any portion of the disclosure regarding executive and director compensation or compensation committee processes.[96]

Although this information is to be provided as part of a registrant's corporate governance disclosure, comments raised by the SEC Staff as part of its 2007 focused review project indicate that the Staff does not view this disclosure as a substitute for the inclusion of comparable information in the registrant's CD&A that is material to an investor's understanding of the registrant's executive compensation program. Consequently, as in the case of the role of executive officers in determining or recommending executive and director compensation, a registrant must be cognizant of the different purposes of each disclosure requirement in addressing the role of compensation consultants.[97] Once again, while the corporate governance disclosure will be largely process-oriented, the CD&A covers the compensation consultant's role in setting policy and making compensation decisions to the extent material to understanding those policies and decisions.

Compensation Consultant Conflicts of Interest

There were investor concerns that the provision of services by a compensation consultant to both a registrant and the compensation committee of the registrant's board of directors may create the appearance, or risk, of a conflict of interest calling into question the objectivity of the compensation consultant's executive compensation recommendations. In response, the SEC amended its rules in December 2009[98] to require disclosure about the fees paid to

---

95. *See* the Current Staff Guidance, *supra* note 10, at Q&A 133.06.

96. *Id.*

97. Another significant distinction involves potential liability considerations. Information about the role of any compensation consultant in determining or recommending the amount or form of executive compensation that is included in a registrant's CD&A is incorporated by reference into its annual report on Form 10-K, while similar information included in the registrant's corporate governance disclosure is not. *See* Item 11 of Form 10-K (17 C.F.R. 249.310).

98. *See* Proxy Disclosure Enhancements, Release Nos. 33-9089, 34-61175, IC-29092 (December 16, 2009), 74 Fed. Reg. 68,334 (December 23, 2009) [hereinafter 2009 Adopting Release], *available at* http://www.sec.gov/rules/final/33-9089.pdf. *See also* Proxy Disclosure

compensation consultants and their affiliates when they have played a role in determining or recommending the amount or form of executive and director compensation, and they have also provided additional services to the registrant.[99]

As the SEC observed, many compensation consultants, or their affiliates, are retained by a registrant's management to provide a broad range of additional services, such as benefits administration, human resources consulting, and actuarial services. The fees generated by these additional services may be more significant than the fees earned by the consultants for their executive and director compensation services. As a result, the extent of the fees and provision of additional services by a compensation consultant or an affiliate may create the risk of a conflict of interest that may call into question the objectivity of the consultant's advice and recommendations on executive compensation. Consequently, the required information is provided to enable investors to better assess the potential conflicts a compensation consultant may have in recommending executive compensation, and the compensation decisions made by the board of directors.

Under the disclosure requirement, in addition to describing the role of the compensation consultant in determining or recommending the amount or form of executive and director compensation as summarized above, a registrant is also required to provide fee disclosure related to the retention of a compensation consultant in certain circumstances.

Specifically, if the board of directors, the compensation committee of the board of directors, or any other person or persons performing the equivalent functions has engaged its own consultant to provide advice or recommendations on the amount or form of executive and director compensation and this consultant, or an affiliate or affiliates of the consultant, provide other nonexecutive compensation consulting services to the registrant, fee and related disclosure is required, provided the fees for the nonexecutive compensation consulting services exceed $120,000 during the registrant's fiscal year.[100] Subject to this disclosure threshold, a registrant must disclose:

---

and Solicitation Enhancements, Release Nos. 33-9052, 34-60280, IC-28817 (July 10, 2009), 74 Fed. Reg. 35076 (July 17, 2009) [hereinafter 2009 Proposing Release], *available at* http://www. sec.gov/rules/proposed/2009/33-9052.pdf.

99. Item 407(e)(3)(iii). For these purposes, "additional services" are not limited to additional services for non-executive employees. *See* the Current Staff Guidance, *supra* note 10, at Q&A 133.10.

100. Item 407(e)(3)(iii)(A). In this situation, the SEC believes that the receipt of fees for nonexecutive compensation consulting services by the consultant presents the potential

- the aggregate fees paid for services provided to either the board of directors or the compensation committee (or person performing the equivalent functions) with respect to determining or recommending the amount or form of executive and director compensation;
- the aggregate fees paid for the nonexecutive compensation consulting services provided by the compensation consultant or its affiliates;
- whether the decision to engage the compensation consultant or its affiliates for the nonexecutive compensation consulting services was made or recommended by management; and
- whether the board of directors or the compensation committee approved these nonexecutive compensation consulting services provided by the compensation consultant or its affiliate.[101]

There is no limitation on the types of services that are included in "additional services" for purposes of the disclosure requirement.[102] Accordingly, if the compensation consultant also sells products to the registrant, then the revenues generated from such sales should be included in the "aggregate fees for any additional services provided by the compensation consultant or its affiliates."[103]

While there is no requirement to disclose the nature and extent of the additional services provided by the compensation consultant and its affiliates to the registrant, some registrants have included this information as part of their disclosure to facilitate investor understanding of the existence or nature of any potential conflict of interest.

Where the board of directors or the compensation committee (or person performing the equivalent functions) has not engaged its own compensation consultant, fee disclosure is required if a compensation consultant, or an affiliate, provides executive compensation consulting services and nonexecutive compensation consulting services to the registrant, provided the fees for the nonexecutive compensation consulting services exceed $120,000 during the registrant's fiscal year.[104]

---

conflict of interest intended to be highlighted for investors.

101. *Id.*

102. *See* the Current Staff Guidance, *supra* note 10, at Q&A 133.12.

103. *Id.*

104. Item 407(e)(3)(iii)(B). While the SEC recognized that, in this situation, the board of directors (or the compensation committee), which typically is primarily responsible for determining the compensation paid to senior executives, may not be relying on the

On the other hand, this disclosure (that is, fee and related disclosure) for compensation consultants that work with management (whether for executive compensation consulting services only, or for both executive compensation consulting and other nonexecutive compensation consulting services) is not required if the board of directors or the compensation committee (or person performing the equivalent functions) has its own separate consultant. In the SEC's view, when the board of directors (or compensation committee) engages its own compensation consultant, it mitigates concerns about potential conflicts of interest involving compensation consultants engaged by the registrant.[105]

In addition, for purposes of this disclosure requirement, services involving only broad-based nondiscriminatory plans or the provision of information, such as surveys, that are not customized for the registrant, or are customized based on parameters that are not developed by the consultant, are not treated as "executive compensation consulting services." Note that in the case of the exception for compensation surveys, the exception is not available if the compensation consultant provides advice or recommendations in connection with the information provided in the survey.

Where a compensation consultant's activities include consulting on broad-based, non-discriminatory plans and/or providing information that either is not customized for a particular registrant or is customized based on parameters that are not developed by the compensation consultant, as well as determining or recommending the amount or form of executive and director compensation, whether the fees for the former activities are to be considered fees for "determining or recommending the amount or form of executive and director compensation" or fees for "additional services" will depend on the facts and circumstances of each activity.[106] Fees for consulting on broad-based, non-discriminatory plans in which executive officers or directors participate and for providing

---

compensation consultant used by the registrant and, therefore, conflicts of interest may be less of a concern, it believed that when the registrant has a compensation consultant and the board of directors (or compensation committee) does not have its own compensation consultant to help filter any advice provided by the registrant's compensation consultant, the concerns about board reliance on consultants that may have a conflict are sufficiently present to require this approach.

105. This exception is available without regard to whether the registrant's compensation consultant participates in meetings of the board of directors or compensation committee.

106. *See* the Current Staff Guidance, supra note 10, at Q&A 133.11.

information relating to executive and director compensation, such as survey data (in each case, that would otherwise qualify for the exclusion from disclosure if they were the only services provided), are considered to be fees for "determining or recommending the amount or form of executive and director compensation" for purposes of reporting fees under the rule.[107] "Consulting" on broad-based, non-discriminatory plans does not also include any related services, however, such as benefits administration, human resources services, actuarial services, and merger integration services, all of which are "additional services" for purposes of the disclosure requirement.[108] Finally, if the non-customized information relates to matters other than executive or director compensation, the fees for such information would be considered fees for "additional services."[109]

Additional Conflict of Interest Disclosure Requirements

New Section 10C(c)(2) of the Exchange Act requires each registrant to disclose in any proxy or consent solicitation material for an annual meeting of shareholders (or a special meeting in lieu of the annual meeting) whether the registrant's compensation committee has retained or obtained the advice of a compensation consultant; whether the work of the compensation consultant has raised any conflict of interest; and, if so, the nature of the conflict and how the conflict (was) or is being addressed. The Dodd-Frank Act contemplates that the SEC will adopt rules to implement this disclosure requirement.

On March 30, 2011, the SEC proposed rules to implement the requirements of Section 10C(c)(2) of the Exchange Act. As proposed, the new disclosure would be integrated into the existing disclosure requirements of Item 407 of Regulation S-K. The highlights of the proposed rules are:

- The disclosure would be required only in a proxy or information statement for an annual meeting of shareholders (or a special meeting in lieu of an annual meeting) at which directors are to be elected.[110]

---

107. *Id.*

108. *Id.*

109. *Id.*

110. While Section 10C(c)(2) states that the disclosure is to be included in *any* proxy or consent solicitation material for an annual meeting of shareholders (or a special meeting in lieu of the annual meeting), based on the statute's provision that the compensation consultant

- The disclosure would be required to be made by all registrants subject to the Exchange Act, whether listed or unlisted, and whether or not a controlled company.[111]
- The disclosure requirement would be triggered whenever a compensation committee "retained or obtained the advice of a compensation consultant" during the registrant's last completed fiscal year.[112]
- Disclosure would be required even if the consultant provides only advice on broad-based plans or provides only noncustomized benchmark data.

Citing the "open-ended" nature of the statutory provision, the SEC is not proposing to define the term "conflict of interest." Nonetheless, the SEC is proposing that registrants use the independence factors that must be considered by the compensation committee of a listed issuer when retaining a compensation advisor[113] as among the factors that registrants should consider in determining whether there is a conflict of interest that may need to be disclosed.[114]

Where a compensation committee determines that there is a conflict of interest with the compensation consultant based on the relevant facts and circumstances, the registrant would be required to provide a clear, concise, and understandable description of the specific conflict and how the registrant has addressed it. A general description of the registrant's policies and procedures to address conflicts of interest or

---

disclosure be made "in accordance with the regulations of the Commission," the SEC is proposing to limit the disclosure to meetings where directors will be elected—the meetings at which it views this information to be most relevant.

111. While Section 10C(g) specifically exempts controlled companies, as defined in Section 10C(g), from all of the requirements of Section 10C, based on the statute's provision that the compensation consultant disclosure be made "in accordance with the regulations of the Commission," the SEC is proposing to extend the disclosure to controlled companies, which are already subject to the disclosure requirements of Item 407(e)(3).

112. As proposed, the phrase "obtained the advice" would relate to whether a compensation committee or management has requested or received advice from a compensation consultant, regardless of whether there is a formal engagement of the consultant or a client relationship between the compensation consultant and the compensation committee or management or any payment of fees to the consultant for its advice.

113. *See* Section 10C(b)(2) of the Exchange Act. See also proposed Exchange Act Rule 10C-1(b)(4)(i) – (v).

114. In addition, a registrant would be expected to consider the specific facts and circumstances relating to a consultant's engagement to determine whether there may be a conflict of interest that would be required to be disclosed.

the appearance of conflicts of interest would not be sufficient to satisfy this disclosure requirement.[115]

Compensation Committee Interlocks and Insider Participation

Under the heading "Compensation Committee Interlocks and Insider Participation," a registrant must:

- Identify each person who served as a member of the compensation committee of the registrant's board of directors (or board committee performing equivalent functions) during the last completed fiscal year.[116] As part of this disclosure, the registrant must indicate each committee member who
  - was, during the fiscal year, an officer or employee of the registrant;[117]
  - was formerly an officer of the registrant;[118] or
  - had any relationship requiring disclosure by the registrant under the SEC's related person disclosure rules.[119]

- If the registrant does not have a compensation committee (or other board committee performing equivalent functions), it must identify each officer and employee and any former officer who, during the last completed fiscal year, participated in deliberations of the registrant's board of directors concerning executive officer compensation.[120]

- Describe any of the following relationships that existed during the last completed fiscal year:
  - An executive officer of the registrant served as a member of the compensation committee (or other board committee performing equivalent functions or, in the absence of any such committee, the entire board

---

115. *See* Proposed Item 407(e)(3)(iii)

116. Item 407(e)(4)(i).

117. Item 407(e)(4)(i)(A).

118. Item 407(e)(4)(i)(B).

119. Item 407(e)(4)(i)(C). See also "Related Person Transactions," *infra*. In this event, the related person disclosure is to accompany the Item 407(e)(4)(i) information. *Id.*

120. Item 407(e)(4)(ii).

of directors) of another entity,[121] one of whose executive officers served on the compensation committee (or other board committee performing equivalent functions or, in the absence of any such committee, the entire board of directors) of the registrant.[122]

- An executive officer of the registrant served as a director of another entity, one of whose executive officers served on the compensation committee (or other board committee performing equivalent functions or, in the absence of any such committee, the entire board of directors) of the registrant.[123]

- An executive officer of the registrant served as a member of the compensation committee (or other board committee performing equivalent functions or, in the absence of any such committee, the entire board of directors) of another entity, one of whose executive officers served as a director of the registrant.[124]

The disclosure required under this provision about a compensation committee member or other director of the registrant who also served as an executive officer of another entity is to be accompanied by the disclosure required under the SEC's related person disclosure rules with respect to that person.[125]

Compensation Committee Report

The consolidated corporate governance disclosure requirements also include the requirements for the new Compensation Committee Report that is to accompany a registrant's CD&A.[126] For a discussion of these requirements, see "Compensation Committee Report" in Chapter 3.

---

121. For purposes of this provision, the term "entity" does not include an entity that is exempt from tax under Section 501(c)(3) of the Internal Revenue Code (26 U.S.C. § 501(c)(3)). *See* the Instruction to Item 407(e)(4).

122. Item 407(e)(4)(iii)(A).

123. Item 407(e)(4)(iii)(B).

124. Item 407(e)(4)(iii)(C).

125. Item 407(e)(4)(iv).

126. Item 407(e)(5).

Compensation-Related Risk Disclosure

Among its many impacts, the global economic crisis of 2008 and 2009 focused investor attention on corporate risk, including the risks associated with a registrant's incentive compensation arrangements. In particular, many investors became concerned that, in some cases, the design, structure, and particular application of incentive compensation policies and practices could create inadvertent incentives that significantly, and inappropriately, increased the registrant's risk profile, without adequate recognition of these risks. Most alarmingly, these risks were not limited to executive compensation arrangements.

In addition to the compensation policies and practices covering a registrant's executive officers, a registrant's broader compensation policies and arrangements for other its employees could also have significant consequences for the organization. This concern, combined with a growing belief that compensation policies were becoming increasingly disconnected from long-term corporate performance because the interests of management and some employees, in the form of incentive compensation, and the long-term well-being of the registrant are not sufficiently aligned, prompted a response from the SEC in 2009.

Acknowledging that registrants, and in turn investors, may be negatively impacted where the design or operation of a compensation program creates incentives that encourage behavior inconsistent with the overall interests of the registrant, the SEC proposed,[127] and subsequently adopted,[128] rules requiring registrants to evaluate their overall employee compensation policies and practices that create incentives that can affect a registrant's risk profile and, in certain situations, provide disclosure about the management and mitigation of those risks.

Disclosure Requirement

If a registrant determines that its compensation policies and practices for all employees, including nonexecutive officers, create risks that are reasonably likely to have a material adverse effect on the registrant, it must discuss these policies and practices as they relate to its risk

---

127. *See* the 2009 Proposing Release, supra note 98, at Section II.A.
128. *See* the 2009 Adopting Release, *supra* note 98, at Section II.A.1.

management practices and its incentive compensation arrangements that give rise to such risks.[129]

As reflected in the rule itself, disclosure is required only if the risks associated with the registrant's compensation policies and practices are:

- reasonably likely
- to have a material and
- adverse effect on the registrant.[130]

This framework is intended to balance the expectation that a registrant's compensation policies can enhance its business interests by encouraging innovation and appropriate levels of risk-taking with the need for disclosure. By focusing on risks that are "reasonably likely to have a material adverse effect" on a registrant, the rule is intended to elicit disclosure about incentives in the registrant's compensation policies and practices that would be most relevant to investors.[131] Thus, if a registrant maintains compensation policies and practices for different groups that mitigate or balance incentives, these may be considered in deciding whether the risks arising from the registrant's compensation policies and practices for employees are reasonably likely to have a material adverse effect on the registrant as a whole.

In addition, disclosure is only required if the compensation policies and practices are reasonably likely to have a material "adverse" effect on the registrant.[132] By focusing the disclosure on material adverse effects, the rule limits the possibility of voluminous and unnecessary

---

129. *See* Item 402(s) of Regulation S-K (17 C.F.R. 229.402(s)). The disclosure requirement does not apply to smaller reporting companies. *See* the 2009 Adopting Release, *supra* note 98, at Section II.A.1.c. In this regard, the SEC concluded that, at this time, these companies are less likely to have the types of compensation policies and practices that are intended to be addressed by the rule.

130. As proposed, the rule would have required a discussion and analysis of a registrant's compensation policies if the risks arising from those policies "may have a material effect on the company" as part of its CD&A. The change to the "reasonably likely" standard was intended to parallel the requirement of the Management Discussion and Analysis (Item 303 of Regulation S-K (17 C.F.R. 229.303)), which requires risk-oriented disclosure of known trends and uncertainties that are material to the business, as well as concerns of some commenters that the proposed rule might have caused registrants attempting compliance to burden shareholders and investors with voluminous disclosure of potentially insignificant and unnecessarily speculative information about their compensation policies.

131. This change from the proposed rule was intended to address concerns that the proposal did not allow registrants to consider compensating or offsetting steps or controls designed to limit risks of certain compensation arrangements.

132. As proposed, the rule would have required disclosure if the registrant's policies or practices that would have "any effect" on the registrant. *See* Proposed Item 402(b)(2).

discussions of compensation arrangements that may effectively mitigate inappropriate risk-taking incentives.

The effect of the compensation policies and practices is to be measured by reference to the registrant as a whole, rather than a policy or practice's impact on a particular business unit, division, or function. Finally, in making its determination, a registrant is permitted to take into consideration compensation policies and plan features that are intended to mitigate risk in assessing the overall impact of its risk-encouraging incentives.

Scope of Disclosure

The disclosure requirement covers a registrant's compensation policies and practices for all employees, not just those policies and practices affecting its executive officers.[133] Thus, in determining whether disclosure is required, a registrant must review both its executive compensation program and its compensation plans and arrangements for its general workforce as well.

Where a registrant concludes that its compensation policies and practices are not reasonably likely to have a material adverse effect on its business as a whole, no disclosure is required. Nor is a registrant required to provide "negative" disclosure; that is, a statement indicating that it has concluded that its compensation policies and practices are not reasonably likely to have a material adverse effect. Nonetheless, as discussed further below, many registrants provide some disclosure about their compensation-related risk profile, often describing the process used to reach the conclusion that no disclosure is required and discussing their policies and practices for managing and mitigating their compensation-related risks.

During the 2010 proxy season, the initial year of compliance under the rule, the SEC Staff issued comments to registrants that omitted any reference to their compensation-related risk review in their proxy statements requesting supplemental information about the process undertaken to reach the conclusion that no disclosure was necessary in response to Item 402(s). Subsequently, the Staff explained that these requests had been made to ensure that registrants had, in fact,

---

133. The broad scope of this rule is underscored by its inclusion in a separate paragraph of Item 402, rather than, as originally proposed, as part of the requirements governing the content of the CD&A. This modification in the final rule preserved the scope of the CD&A to compensation matters involving the registrant's NEOs.

conducted an assessment of their compensation-related risks and to better understand what constitutes a thorough risk assessment process. The Staff also confirmed that there is no requirement under Item 402(s) to provide disclosure in the proxy statement if there is nothing to report with respect to a risk having a material adverse effect on a registrant.[134]

Situations Where Material Risks May Exist

The rule contains a nonexclusive list of situations where compensation programs may have the potential to raise material risks to registrants, and the examples of the types of issues that would be appropriate for a registrant to address.[135] While the actual situations requiring disclosure will vary depending on the particular registrant and its compensation program, there are a number of situations that potentially could trigger discussion, including, among others, compensation policies and practices:

- at a business unit of the registrant that carries a significant portion of the registrant's risk profile;
- at a business unit with compensation structured significantly differently than other units within the registrant;
- at a business unit that is significantly more profitable than others within the registrant;
- at a business unit where the compensation expense is a significant percentage of the unit's revenues; and
- that vary significantly from the overall risk and reward structure of the registrant, such as when bonuses are awarded upon accomplishment of a task, while the income and risk to the registrant from the task extend over a significantly longer period of time.[136]

---

134. *See* Questions and Answers, Technical Session Between the SEC Staff and the Joint Committee on Employee Benefits (May 4, 2010) [hereinafter 2010 JCEB Questions] *available at* http://www.americanbar.org/content/dam/aba/events/employee_benefits/2010_sec_qa.authcheckdam.pdf, at Question No. 9.

135. *See* Item 402(s).

136. As previously noted, the SEC indicated that this list is not intended to be exclusive. In fact, there may be other features of a registrant's compensation policies and practices that have the potential to incentivize its employees to create risks that are reasonably likely to have a material adverse effect on the registrant. At the same time, in the case of the situations listed in the rule, a registrant may, under appropriate circumstances, conclude that its compensation policies and practices are not reasonably likely to have a material adverse effect on the registrant.

Issues That May Need to Be Addressed in Disclosure

As in the case of the CD&A, a registrant is to employ a "principles-based" approach when drafting its disclosure. The rule contains a nonexclusive list of the range of issues that may need to be addressed in situations where a registrant determines that its compensation policies and practices examples are reasonably likely to have a material adverse effect on its business. If disclosure is required, these examples should be tailored to the specific facts and circumstances of the registrant. In other words, a registrant must assess the information that is identified by the example in light of the registrant's particular situation.[137]

The issues that a registrant may need to address regarding its compensation policies or practices include the following:

- the general design philosophy of the registrant's compensation policies and practices for employees whose behavior would be most affected by the incentives established by the policies and practices, as such policies and practices relate to or affect risk-taking by those employees on behalf of the registrant, and the manner of their implementation;[138]
- the registrant's risk assessment or incentive considerations, if any, in structuring its compensation policies and practices or in awarding and paying compensation;[139]
- how the registrant's compensation policies and practices relate to the realization of risks resulting from the actions of employees in both the short term and the long term, such as through policies requiring clawbacks or imposing holding periods;[140]
- the registrant's policies regarding adjustments to its compensation policies and practices to address changes in its risk profile;[141]

---

137. Thus, a generic or boilerplate disclosure that the incentives are designed to have a positive effect, or that compensation levels may not be sufficient to attract or retain employees with appropriate skills in order to enable the registrant to maintain or expand operations, would not be appropriate to satisfy the disclosure requirement.

138. Item 402(s)(1).

139. Item 402(s)(2).

140. Item 402(s)(3).

141. Item 402(s)(4).

- material adjustments the registrant has made to its compensation policies and practices as a result of changes in its risk profile;[142] and
- the extent to which the registrant monitors its compensation policies and practices to determine whether its risk management objectives are being met with respect to incentivizing its employees.[143]

Relationship to CD&A Disclosure

While the rule encompasses compensation policies and practices for all employees, it is not intended to preempt the existing requirement that registrants address risk issues if they represent a material aspect of a registrant's compensation policies and practices for its NEOs. The SEC Staff has underscored this point in a speech by John White, the then-director of the Division of Corporation Finance:

Would it be prudent for compensation committees, when establishing targets and creating incentives, not only to discuss how hard or how easy it is to meet the incentives, but also to consider the particular risks an executive might be incentivized to take to meet the target—with risk, in this case, being viewed in the context of the enterprise as a whole? I'll let you think about what Congress might want. We know what our rules require. That is, to the extent that such considerations are or become a material part of a company's compensation policies or decisions, a company would be required to discuss them as part of its CD&A.[144]

Compliance Trends

To date, almost no registrants have concluded that disclosure of their policies and practices of compensating their employees, including nonexecutive officers, as they relate to risk management practices and risk-taking incentives has been required. Consequently, there have been almost no examples of such disclosures in registrant proxy statements.

---

142. Item 402(s)(5).

143. Item 402(s)(6).

144. *See* John W. White, Director, Division of Corporation of Finance, U.S. Securities and Exchange Comm'n, *Executive Compensation Disclosure: Observations on Year Two and a Look Forward to the Changing Landscape for 2009,* Remarks Before The 3rd Annual Proxy Disclosure Conference (Oct. 21, 2008), available at http://www.sec.gov/news/speech/2008/spch102108jww.htm.

While the SEC solicited comment on whether a registrant should be required to affirmatively state that it has determined that the risks arising from its compensation policies are not reasonably expected to have a material effect on its business if it has concluded that disclosure was not required, ultimately it decided not to adopt such a requirement because it would not provide investors with useful information and would create potential liability for registrants. Thus, there is no requirement that a registrant affirmatively state that it has determined that the risks arising from or associated with its compensation policies and practices are not reasonably likely to have a material adverse effect on the registrant.

Nonetheless, because of the high degree of investor interest in the issue of compensation-related risk and registrants' desire to reassure their shareholders that they have appropriate safeguards in place to minimize excessive and unreasonable risk-taking, most companies have opted to provide some level of voluntary disclosure about their compensation-related risk analysis. This analysis is conducted to determine if the mandatory disclosure is required, as well as if the registrants have appropriate policies and practices for managing and mitigating their compensation-related risks as part of their executive compensation disclosure.[145]

The SEC Staff has indicated that, although the rule does not specify where the required disclosure should be presented, to ease investor understanding, it recommends that the disclosure be presented together with a registrant's other Item 402 disclosure.[146] The Staff would have concerns if this disclosure is difficult to locate or is presented in a way that obscures it. While most registrants have followed this guidance, typically presenting the disclosure immediately following the CD&A and immediately preceding the Summary Compensation Table, others have included it as part of their discussion of the risk oversight responsibilities of their board of directors.

---

145. *See, for example,* the Western Digital Corporation Definitive Proxy Statement (Form 14A) filed September 27, 2011 (file no. 001-08703).

146. *See* the Current Staff Guidance, *supra* note 10, at Q&A 128A.01. While this guidance is directed toward any required disclosure, its underlying rationale would appear to apply equally to voluntary disclosure about a registrant's compensation policies and practices as they relate to the registrant's risk management.

Related Person Transactions

General

To provide investors with a materially complete picture of all existing financial relationships, a registrant must disclose, in addition to executive and director compensation information, information about related person transactions. These requirements, which address transactions and relationships, including indebtedness involving the registrant and related persons, the independence of directors and director nominees, and the interests of management, are set out in Item 404 of Regulation S-K.[147]

The disclosure requirements are expansive and largely principles-based. As a practical matter, this means that the determination of whether a transaction must be disclosed depends on a materiality analysis of the transaction and the parties involved, rather than a "bright-line" standard as under the former rules. Also, since a registrant need only be a "participant" in, rather than a "party" to, the transaction, more transactions are potentially subject to disclosure.[148]

Disclosure Requirements

A registrant must provide specific detailed information about any transaction[149] since the beginning of its last fiscal year, or any currently proposed transaction, in which the registrant was or is to be a participant

---

147. 17 C.F.R. 229.404. Item 404 was substantially revised in 2006 as part of the revisions to the executive and director compensation disclosure requirements. *See* the Adopting Release, *supra* note 5, at Section V.A. In addition, the separate related party transaction rules for small business issuers contained in Regulation S-B (17 C.F.R. 228.10 et seq.) were repealed and replaced by a new set of provisions incorporated into Regulation S-K. *See* Smaller Reporting Company Regulatory Relief and Simplification, Release Nos. 33-8876, 34-56994, 39-2451 (Dec.19, 2007), 73 Fed. Reg. 934 (Jan. 4, 2008), *available at* http://www.sec.gov/rules/final/2007/33-8876.pdf.

148. This change more accurately connotes the registrant's involvement in the transaction since, as a participant, it encompasses situations where the registrant benefits from the transaction but is not technically a contractual party to the transaction (for example, when a NEO receives compensation from a third party). *See* the Adopting Release, *supra* note 5, at n.418 and the accompanying text.

149. For purposes of Item 404(a), a "transaction" includes, but is not limited to, any financial transaction, arrangement, or relationship (including any indebtedness or guarantee of indebtedness), or any series of similar transactions, arrangements, or relationships. *See* Instruction 2 to Item 404(a). The term is not to be interpreted narrowly. *See* the Adopting Release, *supra* note 5, at Section V.A.1.b.

where the amount involved exceeds $120,000[150] and any related person had or will have a direct or indirect material interest.[151] For purposes of this disclosure, a "related person" includes any individuals who were in the following categories at any time during the period covered by the disclosure:

- any director or executive officer;
- any director nominee; and
- any immediate family member[152] of the director, executive officer, or director nominee.[153]

For purposes of the related person disclosure rules, when determining the compensation of an immediate family member who shares the same household of a director, executive officer, or director nominee for purposes of calculating whether the amount involved in a potentially disclosable transaction exceeds $120,000, the SEC Staff has informally indicated that the $120,000 amount should be calculated on the basis of the compensation paid from the start of the registrant's last completed fiscal year through the time of filing of the proxy statement in which the disclosure will be made.[154]

A related person also includes the following persons who had a direct or indirect material interest in a transaction when it occurred or existed:

---

150. This amount represented an increase from the prior $60,000 disclosure threshold. *See* former Item 404(a). In the case of a smaller reporting company, the threshold is the lesser of $120,000 or 1 percent of the average of the smaller reporting company's total assets at year-end for the last two completed fiscal years. *See* Item 404(d)(i). The $120,000 threshold is not to be construed as a "bright-line" materiality standard. *See* the Adopting Release, *supra* note 5, at Section V.A.1. When the amount involved in a transaction exceeds the prescribed threshold, a registrant should evaluate whether the related person has a direct or indirect material interest in the transaction to determine if disclosure is required. *Id.*

151. Item 404(a).

152. The term "immediate family member" means any child, stepchild, parent, stepparent, spouse, sibling, mother-in-law, father-in-law, son-in-law, daughter-in-law, brother-in-law, or sister-in-law of such director, executive officer, or director nominee, and any person (other than a tenant or employee) sharing the same household of such director, executive officer, or director nominee. *See* Instruction 1a.iii to Item 404(a). The SEC Staff has informally noted that, for purposes of Item 404(a), an "immediate family member" is not limited to individual's who live in the director, executive officer, or director nominee's household. *See* the 2010 JCEB Questions, *supra* note 134, at Question No. 7.

153. *See* Instruction 1.a to Item 404(a).

154. *See* the 2010 JCEB Questions, *supra* note 152, at Question No. 7.

- a security holder with a 5 percent or greater beneficial interest in any class of the registrant's voting securities; and
- any immediate family member[155] of any such security holder.[156]

The materiality standard to be applied when evaluating the need for disclosure is the same as under the former rules.[157] Thus, materiality is based on the significance of the information to investors in light of all the circumstances.[158]

Where a transaction must be reported, the following information must be disclosed:

- the name of the "related" person and his or her relationship to the registrant;
- the person's interest in the transaction with the registrant, including the related person's position or relationship with, or ownership in, a firm, corporation, or other entity that is a party to or has an interest in the transaction; and
- the approximate dollar value of the amount involved in the transaction and of the related person's interest in the transaction.[159]

Executive and Director Compensation

While the disclosure objectives of Item 404(a) are broad enough to encompass all compensation-related arrangements between a registrant and its executive officers and directors, the rules provide an exclusion for most of these situations. Disclosure of compensation to an executive officer is not required if:

- the compensation is reported pursuant to Item 402; or
- the executive officer is not an immediate family member[160] and the compensation would have been reported under Item 402 as compensation earned for services to the registrant if

155. See supra note 152.

156. See Instruction 1.b to Item 404(a).

157. See the Adopting Release, supra note 5, at Section V.A.1.

158. See Basic v. Levinson, 485 U.S. 224 (1988), and TSC Industries v. Northway, 426 U.S. 438 (1976).

159. See Item 404(a)(1)–(4).

160. See supra note 152. Presumably, this reference is to an immediate family member of an executive officer, director, or a 5 percent or greater beneficial owner of a registrant voting security.

the executive officer was a NEO, and the compensation had been approved, or recommended to the registrant's board of directors for approval, by the compensation committee[161] of the registrant's board of directors.[162]

Similarly, director compensation does not have to be disclosed if it is reported pursuant to the current executive compensation disclosure rules.[163]

This treatment is not as generous as under the former rules, which permitted information about compensatory transactions that was required under both Item 402 and Item 404 to be excluded from disclosure under one item if it was disclosed under the other item.[164] As set forth above, the Item 404(a) exclusions are fairly narrow. As a result, there may be situations where compensation information will be required to be disclosed under the rules, while the related person transaction giving rise to the compensation also will be disclosable under Item 404(a).[165]

Further, since the compensation of executive officers who are not NEOs may be excluded from Item 404(a) disclosure only if it has been approved, or recommended to the registrant's board of directors for approval, by the compensation committee, registrants will need to ensure that their compensation policies require committee approval of all elements of executive officer compensation or face reporting this information as part of their related person disclosure.

---

161. Or the group of independent directors performing a similar function.

162. *See* Instruction 5.a to Item 404(a).

163. *See* Instruction 5.b to Item 404(a).

164. *See* former Items 402(a)(2) and 402(a)(5).

165. *See* the Adopting Release, *supra* note 5, at Section II.C.7. For example, where a NEO receives an amount from a third party that is intended to serve as compensation, the transaction may be reportable under both Item 402 (as compensation of a NEO) and Item 404 (as a related person transaction between the registrant and the third party).

15

Shareholder Advisory Votes on Executive Compensation

Of all the measures that have been considered or implemented to address investor concerns about executive compensation, none has the potential to have a long-term impact on compensation policies and practices as the shareholder advisory vote on executive compensation; which is known colloquially as a "say-on-pay" vote. The introduction of a mandatory advisory vote on the compensation of a registrant's named executive officers (NEOs) compensation in the 2011 proxy season has already had a dramatic impact on registrants' executive compensation disclosure, which is quickly reorienting proxy statements as "communication," rather than simply "compliance," materials. How these votes will ultimately change the executive compensation landscape remains to be seen, but if the first 15 months of mandatory say-on-pay votes is any indication, the increased level of shareholder engagement should produce executive pay programs that are better aligned with investor interests and a greater level of transparent disclosure.

How the Rules Came About

A shareholder vote on a registrant's executive compensation is relatively new in the United States. Nonetheless, it is an idea that has taken hold and, in less than five years, grown from a policy proposal being advanced by shareholders at individual companies to a statutory requirement that, by 2013, will apply to virtually all publicly traded companies. While, as of yet, say-on-pay has not been effective in reversing the upward trend of executive compensation, it has led to greater engagement between registrants and institutional investors over compensation and governance issues.

The concept of a nonbinding shareholder advisory vote on executive compensation originated in the United Kingdom in the late 1990s, and eventually became a requirement in 2002 when the U.K. introduced rules for an annual advisory vote on the directors' remuneration report.[1] In subsequent years, half a dozen companies saw their remuneration reports rejected by investors, including a precedent-setting vote in 2003 involving GlaxoSmithKline PLC.[2] In the U.K., companies began to work more closely with their major investors prior to their annual general meetings to ensure their support on executive compensation matters. Other jurisdictions, including Australia, the Netherlands, Norway, and Sweden, soon adopted their own legislation providing shareholders with a vote on executive pay.[3]

Shareholder proposals seeking a policy for an annual advisory vote on the compensation of a registrant's top executives first appeared in the United States in 2006. The American Federation of State, County and Municipal Employees (AFSCME) filed such proposals at a handful of well-known publicly traded companies[4] and, while none of the proposals

---

1. *See* the 2002 Directors' Remuneration Report Regulations. *See also* Sections 420 and 439 of the Companies Act 2006.

2. Approximately 51% of the votes cast on the company's directors' remuneration report objected to the employment agreement of its chief executive officer, Dr. Jean-Pierre Garnier, which provided for a £22 million salary and bonus severance package. Subsequently, the global pharmaceutical company revised the terms of the agreement and agreed to review and revise its executive compensation policies and practices.

3. The Australian legislation called for an annual advisory vote, while the Norwegian and Swedish legislation provided for an annual binding vote. The Netherlands legislation provided for a binding vote to adopt a remuneration policy for executives and thereafter upon any major changes to the policy.

4. Proposals seeking an annual advisory vote on executive compensation were included in the 2006 proxy materials of Countrywide Financial Corporation, The Home Depot, Inc., Merrill Lynch, Sara Lee Corporation, Sun Microsystems, Inc., and U.S. Bancorp. While a

were successful, they averaged approximately 42 percent support, an unusually high level for a first-time initiative.

2007 Developments

During 2007, with other investor advocates[5] following AFSCME's lead and spurred on by the then-exploding options backdating scandal, more than 60 registrants received proposals from shareholders seeking an advisory vote on executive compensation,[6] with more than 40 of the proposals coming to a vote. Ultimately, eight of these proposals received majority support.[7] Once again, the proposal received approximately 41 percent support at the companies where an actual vote was conducted, indicating a high degree of broad support for the concept. Following its vote, Verizon Communications, Inc., adopted a formal policy for an annual shareholder advisory vote on executive compensation beginning with its 2009 annual meeting of stockholders.[8] In addition, one registrant, Aflac Inc., became the first U.S. company to voluntarily

---

proposal was also filed with the Bank of America, subsequently it was withdrawn when the registrant agreed to increase its executive compensation disclosure and conduct further discussions on the subject.

5. The investors pursuing the advisory vote on executive compensation proposals included, among others, public pension funds (such as the New York City Employees' Retirement System), asset managers (such as Hermes Asset Management), foundations, and members of the Interfaith Center on Corporate Responsibility.

6. Generally, these shareholder proposals took one of four forms: a proposal for a vote on the Compensation Committee Report, a proposal for a vote on the registrant's Compensation Discussion and Analysis, a proposal for a vote on the Summary Compensation Table, or a proposal for a vote on whether the current level of compensation was appropriate.

7. Shareholder proposals seeking a registrant policy for an annual shareholder advisory vote on executive compensation received majority support at Activision, Inc., Blockbuster, Inc., Clear Channel Communication, Inc., Ingersoll-Rand Company, Ltd., Motorola, Inc., Par Pharmaceutical Companies, Inc., Valero Energy Corporation, and Verizon Communications, Inc. In addition, in early 2007, a "Working Group on the Advisory Vote on Executive Compensation Disclosure" was formed to study shareholder advisory votes on executive pay. This group included nearly a dozen publicly-traded companies, including Pfizer, Inc., Intel Corporation, Bristol-Myers Squibb Co., Schering-Plough Corporation, American International Group, Inc., JP Morgan Chase & Co., and Colgate-Palmolive Co. as well as four United States state pension funds, including AFSCME and the California Public Employees' Retirement System, two large United Kingdom funds, and Walden Asset Management.

8. This decision followed a shareholder vote in which 50.8% of the votes were cast in favor of a proposal calling on the registrant to hold an annual advisory vote on executive compensation. See "Verizon Board Adopts Policy on Advisory Shareholder Vote Related to Executive Compensation," available at http://www22.verizon.com/investor/verizon_board_adopts_policy_on_advisory_shareholder.htm.

agree to conduct an actual advisory vote on its executive compensation program, beginning with its 2009 annual meeting of shareholders.[9]

At the same time, the then-Chairman of the Financial Services Committee of the House of Representatives, Barney Frank, introduced legislation in the 110th Congress that would allow shareholders to cast a nonbinding vote on a registrant's executive compensation program.[10] While the bill was easily approved by the House of Representatives, by a largely party-line vote of 269-134, a companion measure stalled in the Senate.[11]

2008 Developments

During 2008, approximately 90 registrants received shareholder proposals seeking a policy implementing an annual advisory vote on executive compensation. Average support for the proposals that actually went to a shareholder vote was approximately 42 percent. Nearly one-quarter of these proposals received majority support.[12]

In addition, several of the companies that had seen their shareholders approve a resolution seeking an advisory vote announced their decision to adopt a formal policy giving shareholders a nonbinding advisory vote on executive compensation, typically beginning in 2009.[13]

---

9. The decision to adopt the policy was sparked by a shareholder proposal submitted by Boston Common Asset Management seeking an advisory vote policy. The registrant's initial decision to hold the vote in 2009 was based on the consideration that this would be the first year in which shareholders would have access to three years' data on executive compensation in the Summary Compensation Table. See "Aflac Adopts Non-Binding 'Say On Pay' Shareholder Vote," *available at* http://www.aflac.com/aboutaflac/pressroom/pressreleasestory.aspx?rid=962932. Subsequently, Aflac moved up the date of its first shareholder advisory vote on executive compensation to its 2008 annual meeting of shareholders. See "Aflac Moves Up 'Say-on-Pay' Shareholder Vote to 2008," *available at* http://www.aflac.com/aboutaflac/pressroom/pressreleasestory.aspx?rid=1078006.

10. *See* H.R. 1257, the *Shareholder Vote on Executive Compensation Act,* which also would have given shareholders a nonbinding vote on "golden parachute" compensation arrangements. Previously, Representative Frank had introduced H.R. 4291, the *Protection Against Executive Compensation Abuse Act,* in the 109th Congress, which, similarly, would have mandated an annual advisory vote on executive compensation.

11. *See* S. 1181, the *Shareholder Vote on Executive Compensation Act* (Obama D.-IL).

12. Shareholder proposals seeking a registrant policy for an annual shareholder advisory vote on executive compensation received majority support at Apple, Inc., Alaska Air Group, Inc., Ingersoll-Rand Company, Ltd., Lexmark International Group, Inc., PG&E Corporation, Motorola, Inc., Rackable Systems, Inc., South Financial Group, Inc., Sun Microsystems,Inc., Tech Data Corporation, and Valero Energy Corporation.

13. *See, e.g.,* Blockbuster, Inc., "Blockbuster Board Adopts Non-Binding 'Say on Pay' Shareholder Vote," *available at* http://blockbuster.mwnewsroom.com/manual-releases/Blockbuster-Board-Adopts-Non-Binding--Say-on-Pay--.

Finally, RiskMetrics Group, Inc. joined Aflac as the only registrants to voluntarily hold advisory votes on their executive compensation programs.[14] Both companies registered strong support from shareholders on their pay programs.

2009 Developments

During 2009, approximately 100 registrants received shareholder proposals seeking a policy implementing an annual vote on executive compensation. Seventy of these proposals were voted on and received an average support of 46.5 percent of votes cast. The proposals at 24 different registrants received votes of over 50 percent.[15]

In March 2009, the enactment of the American Recovery and Reinvestment Act of 2009 (ARRA)[16] amended the executive compensation provisions of the Emergency Economic Stabilization Act of 2008 (EESA) to require all registrants receiving financial assistance under the Troubled Asset Relief Program (TARP) to conduct an annual advisory vote on executive compensation as long as they were a TARP participant.[17] This resulted in approximately 350 registrants, almost

---

14. The RiskMetrics proposal actually involved three separate votes: the first addressing its executive compensation philosophy, the second its 2007 executive compensation decisions, and the third its 2008 performance objectives. See the RiskMetrics Group, Inc. Definitive Proxy Statement filed April 23, 2008 (file no. 001-33928). Additional registrants that conducted shareholder advisory votes on executive compensation in 2008 included H&R Block, Inc. (advisory vote on executive "pay-for-performance" compensation policies and procedures), Jackson Hewitt Tax Service, Inc. (advisory vote on executive compensation), Littlefield Corporation (advisory vote on compensation of President and CEO and directors), and Zale Corporation (advisory vote on executive "pay-for-performance" policies and procedures).

15. Shareholder proposals seeking a registrant policy for an annual shareholder advisory vote on executive compensation received majority support at Apple, Inc., Applied Micro Circuits Corporation, Cisco Systems, Inc., ConocoPhillips, CVS Caremark Corporation, The Dow Chemical Company, Edison International, Inc., General Mills, Inc., Hain Celestial Group, Inc., Honeywell International, Inc., Jones Apparel Group, Inc., KB Home, Lexmark International, Inc., Marathon Oil Corporation, Pfizer, Inc., Plum Creek Timber Company, Inc., Prudential Financial, Inc., Pulte Homes, Inc., Supervalu, Inc., Tecumseh Products Company, Tupperware Brands Corporation, Valero Energy Corporation, XTO Energy, Inc., and YUM! Brands, Inc.

16. Pub. L. No. 111-5, Title II, 110 Stat. (2009). Section 7001 of ARRA amended the executive compensation and corporate governance provisions of Section 111 of EESA. See 12 U.S.C. § 5221.

17. See Section 111(e) of the EESA, which requires any entity that has received or will receive financial assistance under the TARP to "permit a separate shareholder vote to approve the compensation of executives, as disclosed pursuant to the compensation disclosure rules of the Commission (which disclosure shall include the compensation discussion and analysis, the compensation tables, and any related material)."

entirely financial institutions, conducting a vote during the 2009 proxy season.

In addition, approximately 15 other registrants, including Motorola, Inc., and Verizon Communications, Inc., conducted votes as a result of previous proposals supported by a majority of their shareholders or on their own initiative. By the end of the year, 65 registrants announced that they had voluntarily adopted a policy to conduct an annual advisory vote on their executive compensation program. Support for a shareholder advisory vote on executive compensation continued to maintain traction in Congress. On July 31, 2009, H.R. 3269, the *Corporate and Financial Institution Compensation Fairness Act of 2009*, passed the House of Representatives. The House bill included a section that required a say-on-pay vote for all publicly-traded registrants in the United States. Additionally, it contained a provision for a shareholder advisory vote on "golden parachutes." In the Senate, S. 1074, the *Shareholder Bill of Rights*, was introduced on May 19, 2009. The House and Senate bills were eventually folded into H.R. 4173 and became part of the Dodd–Frank Wall Street Reform and Consumer Protection Act, which was signed by President Obama on July 21, 2010.[18]

In addition, the Obama Administration expressed support for legislation mandating a say-on-pay requirement, and said it would authorize the Securities and Exchange Commission (SEC) to implement say-on-pay requirements for all registrants, not only those that were TARP participants, contingent on Congressional approval. Additionally, the Department of the Treasury reconciled its proposals from February 4, 2009, with Congressional amendments to the EESA in the Final Interim Rule on TARP Standards for Compensation and Corporate Governance.[19]

2010 Developments

Section 951 of the Dodd-Frank Act added Section 14A(a)(1) to the Exchange Act, thereby requiring registrants, at least once every three years, to include a resolution in their proxy materials for their annual meetings of shareholders soliciting shareholder approval, on a

18. *See* H.R. 4173, which passed the House of Representatives on Dec. 11, 2009. The Senate version of the bill, S. 3217, was subsequently redesignated H.R. 4173 to simplify reconciliation of the two bills. *See also* Section 14A of the Exchange Act as added by Section 951 of the Dodd-Frank Wall Street Reform and Consumer Protection Act (Pub. L. No. 111-203, 124 Stat. 1376 (July 21, 2010)).

19. (June 6, 2009). 74 Fed. Reg. 28,394 (June 15, 2009).

nonbinding basis, of the compensation paid to their senior executive officers. But this provision went farther than this primary vote, also requiring registrants, at least once every six years, to solicit the views of their shareholders on the frequency with which these advisory votes on executive compensation should be held. In the context of a merger or other extraordinary transaction, the provision also requires registrants to conduct a shareholder advisory vote on any golden parachute compensation arrangements that will be payable to certain executive officers of the parties to the transaction.

Advisory Vote on Named Executive Officer Compensation

The central provision in Section 14A of the Exchange Act is the shareholder advisory vote on NEO compensation.[20] Generally, Section 14A(a)(1) provision requires registrants to include a separate resolution in the proxy materials for their annual or other meeting of securityholders at which directors will be elected and for which the SEC's rules require executive compensation disclosure pursuant to Item 402 of Regulation S–K. This resolution is to ask shareholders to approve, in a nonbinding vote, the compensation of their executive officers, as disclosed under Item 402 (Say-on-Pay Vote).[21] While this reference to Item 402 expressly limits the vote to the compensation of the registrant's NEOs, as a practical matter, the vote is considered to be a referendum on the registrant's executive compensation program and the policies and practices implementing the program.

Under Section 14A, this requirement became effective for a registrant's first annual or other meeting of securityholders occurring on or after January 21, 2011.[22] Thereafter, subsequent Say-on-Pay Votes

---

20. Section 14A (a)(1) of the Exchange Act (15 U.S.C. § 78n-1(a)(1)). *See also* Section 951 of the Dodd-Frank Act.

21. *Id. See also* Exchange Act Rule 14a-21(a) (17 C.F.R. 240.14a-21(a)).

22. In its rules fleshing out the framework for this new requirement, the SEC delayed effectiveness until April 4, 2011. *See* Shareholder Approval of Executive Compensation and Golden Parachute Compensation, Release Nos. 33-9178, 34-63768 (Jan. 25, 2011), 76 Fed. Reg. 6010 (Feb. 2, 2011) [hereinafter Say-on-Pay Adopting Release], *available at* http://www.sec.gov/rules/final/2011/33-9178.pdf. *See also* Shareholder Approval of Executive Compensation and Golden Parachute Compensation, Release Nos. 33-9153, 34-63124 (Oct. 10, 2010), 75 Fed. Reg. 66590 (Oct. 28, 2010) [hereinafter Say-on-Pay Proposing Release], *available at* http://www.sec.gov/rules/proposed/2010/33-9153.pdf.

are to be held as each registrant chooses, subject only to its decision whether to abide by the results of its Frequency Vote and the overall requirement that a vote be held at least once every three years.[23]

As the provision makes clear, the Say-on-Pay Vote is nonbinding on a registrant and its board of directors, and specifically may not be construed as:

- overruling a decision by the registrant or its board of directors;
- creating or implying any change in or additional fiduciary duty for the registrant or the board; or
- restricting or limiting the ability of shareholders to make proposals for inclusion in proxy materials relating to executive compensation.[24]

While the Say-on-Pay Vote requirement itself is fairly straightforward, the SEC has addressed several technical matters relating to Section 14A(a)(1) in its rules providing guidance on the operation of the requirement, including the following:

- The inclusion of a separate resolution providing for a Say-on-Pay Vote in a registrant's proxy materials does not require the filing of a preliminary proxy statement.[25]
- A registrant is not required to use any specific language or form of resolution in conducting a Say-on-Pay Vote.[26] Nonetheless, while registrants should retain flexibility to craft the resolution

---

23. *See* Exchange Act Rule 14a-21(a) (17 C.F.R. 240.14a-21(a)), which specifies that the Say-on-Pay Vote is required only when proxies are being solicited for an annual meeting of security holders at which directors will be elected, or a special meeting in lieu of such annual meeting, which is when disclosure of executive compensation pursuant to Item 402 is required.

24. *See* Section 14A(c) of the Exchange Act (15 U.S.C. § 78n-1(c)).

25. *See* Exchange Act Rule 14a-6(a)(7) (17 C.F.R. 240.14a-6(a)(7)). This exemption from filing of a preliminary proxy statement also extends to an advisory vote on executive compensation in the case of a TARP recipient.

26. *See* the Say-on-Pay Adopting Release, *supra* note 25, at Section II.A.1.c. As the SEC noted, this is consistent with the approach taken by the SEC in adopting Exchange Act Rule 14a-20 to implement the shareholder advisory vote on executive compensation for TARP recipients. *Id.* The SEC Staff has indicated that it is permissible for the Say-on-Pay Vote proposal to omit the words, "pursuant to Item 402 of Regulation S-K," and to replace such words with a plain English equivalent, such as "pursuant to the compensation disclosure rules of the Securities and Exchange Commission, including the compensation discussion and analysis, the compensation tables and any related material disclosed in this proxy statement." *See* Division of Corporation Finance, Exchange Act Rules (Feb. 13, 2012) [hereinafter Current Staff Exchange Act Rules Guidance], *available at* http://www.sec.gov/divisions/corpfin/guidance/exchangeactrules-interp.htm, at Q&A 169.05.

language, a Say-on-Pay Vote resolution must relate to all of the executive compensation disclosure set forth pursuant to Item 402, that is, the Compensation Discussion and Analysis (CD&A), the compensation tables, and the other narrative disclosure accompanying the compensation tables.[27]

- The Say-on-Pay Vote relates to the executive compensation disclosure required to be included in the proxy statement, which generally includes the CD&A, the compensation tables, and the narrative disclosure on executive compensation that accompanies the compensation tables.

- Disclosure relating to the compensation of directors is not subject to the Say-on-Pay Vote.[28]

- Disclosure related to a registrant's compensation policies and practices as they relate to risk management and risk-taking incentives are not subject to the Say-on-Pay Vote,[29] except to the extent that risk considerations are a material aspect of a registrant's compensation policies or decisions for NEOs (where such information would be included as part of the CD&A). Such disclosure would be considered by shareholders when voting on executive compensation.

- If a registrant includes disclosure of golden parachute compensation arrangements pursuant to Item 402(t) of Regulation S-K[30] in its proxy materials for an annual meeting of shareholders, this disclosure is subject to the Say-on-Pay Vote.[31]

- A registrant is required to disclose in its proxy statement for an annual meeting (or other meeting of shareholders for which executive compensation disclosure pursuant to Item 402 of Regulation S-K is required) the fact that a separate shareholder

---

27. *See* the Instruction to Exchange Act Rule 14a-21(a) (17 C.F.R. 240.14a-21(a)). The registrant's resolution must indicate that the shareholder advisory vote is to approve the compensation of the registrant's NEOs as disclosed pursuant to Item 402 of Regulation S–K The following is a nonexclusive example of a resolution that would satisfy the requirements of this subsection: "RESOLVED, that the compensation paid to the company's named executive officers, as disclosed pursuant to Item 402 of Regulation S–K, including the Compensation Discussion and Analysis, compensation tables and narrative discussion is hereby APPROVED." *Id.* Subsequently, the SEC Staff has addressed the resolution's wording on the proxy card.

28. *See* Instruction 1 to Exchange Act Rule 14a-21 (17 C.F.R. 240.14a-21).

29. *Id.*

30. 17 C.F.R. 229.402(t).

31. *See* Instruction 2 to Exchange Act Rule 14a-21 (17 C.F.R. 240.14a-21).

vote on executive compensation is being held and a brief explanation of the general effect of the vote, such as whether the vote is nonbinding.[32]

Recently, the staff of the SEC's Division of Corporation Finance (SEC Staff) has indicated that, with respect to the proxy card and voting instruction form, the following are examples of advisory vote descriptions that would be consistent with Exchange Act Rule 14a-21's requirement for shareholders to be given an advisory vote to approve the compensation paid to a registrant's NEOs, as disclosed pursuant to Item 402.

- "to approve the company's executive compensation";
- "advisory approval of the company's executive compensation";
- "advisory resolution to approve executive compensation"; or
- "advisory vote to approve named executive officer compensation."[33]

Results of Say-on-Pay Vote in 2011

While there were numerous predictions that, once unleashed, the availability of a shareholder advisory vote on executive compensation would result in the disapproval of a large number of executive compensation programs, this did not turn out to be the case in 2011. Of the approximately 3,100 registrants that reported the results of their initial Say-on-Pay Vote as required by the Dodd-Frank Act, only 42 registrants disclosed that their proposal had received more "against" than "for" votes.[34] On average, registrants received approximately 92 percent support for the compensation of their named executive officers.

---

32. *See* Item 24 to Schedule 14A (17 C.F.R. 240.14a-101). This should also disclose the current frequency of the Say-on-Pay Vote and when the next such vote will occur.

33. *See* the Current Staff Exchange Act Rules Guidance, *supra* note 26, at Q&A 169.07. In addition, the SEC Staff indicated that the following is an example of an advisory vote description that would not be consistent with Exchange Act Rule 14a-21 because it is not clear from the description as to what shareholders are being asked to vote on: "To hold an advisory vote on executive compensation." In the Staff's view, shareholders could interpret this example as asking them to vote on whether or not the registrant should hold an advisory vote on executive compensation in the future, rather than asking shareholders to actually approve, on an advisory basis, the compensation paid to the registrant's NEOs. *Id.*

34. An additional three registrants, Cooper Industries, Hemispherex Biopharma, and IsoRay, reported results strongly suggesting that the Say-on-Pay Vote had failed, although, because of inconsistencies in the way votes were counted, a definitive conclusion could not be made.

Notably, approximately 300 other registrants reported "significant opposition" (that is, an "against" vote in excess of 25 percent of the votes cast on the proposal) to their Say-on-Pay proposal. While technically not a failed vote, these results clearly indicated that shareholders had concerns about the registrants' executive compensation programs.

It is clear that the prohibition on broker voting of uninstructed shares in executive compensation matters mandated by Section 957 of the Dodd-Frank Act[35] had an impact on the outcome of numerous Say-on-Pay Votes.[36] It was common to see the number of "broker nonvotes" exceed the difference between the votes "for" and "against" the Say-on-Pay proposal. In a few instances, the broker nonvotes even exceeded the aggregate number of votes cast on the proposal.

Today, most registrants are taking affirmative steps to minimize the risk of an unfavorable vote result, including some or all of the following:

- addressing any problematic features of their executive compensation program, to the extent that an existing pay policy or practice is objectionable to one or more of the major proxy advisory firms or an institutional investor or where the compensation committee in considering installing a new "best practice";
- reviewing their current executive compensation disclosure to see whether it can be improved, such as by adding an executive summary or making greater use of graphics to convey their key compensation messages;
- ensuring that their executive compensation disclosure effectively communicates the alignment between corporate performance and executive compensation, including, in some instances, conducting a simulation of the probable analysis to be performed by the major proxy advisory firms; and
- analyzing their shareholder base to determine whether the absence of broker voting of uninstructed shares will have any impact on the outcome of the vote.

---

35. *See* the discussion of Section 957 of the Dodd-Frank Act in Chapter 1.

36. In Section II.C.2 of the Say-on-Pay Proposing Release, *supra* note 22, the SEC confirmed that Section 957, and the related rule changes of the national securities exchanges, apply to the shareholder advisory votes on executive compensation.

Frequency of Advisory Votes on Named Executive Officer Compensation

In an eleventh-hour surprise, the House-Senate conferees on the Dodd-Frank Act scrapped the proposal that would have mandated an annual Say-on-Pay Vote and, instead, agreed that each registrant's shareholders be given the opportunity to decide for themselves how often to hold a Say-on-Pay Vote. Perhaps influenced by the decisions of several large registrants to conduct shareholder advisory votes on their executive compensation programs every two or three years,[37] Congress opted to let registrants and their shareholders decide for themselves how often to hold a Say on Pay Vote, subject only to the requirement that the vote be held at least once every three years.

Accordingly, Section 14A(a)(2) of the Exchange Act requires that, not less frequently than once every six years, registrants must include a resolution in their proxy materials for their annual meetings of securityholders asking shareholders whether the Say-on-Pay Vote should take place every one, two, or three years (Frequency Vote).[38]

Under Section 14A, this requirement became effective for a registrant's first annual or other meeting of securityholders occurring on or after January 21, 2011.[39] Thereafter, subsequent Frequency Votes are to be held as each registrant chooses, subject only to the overall requirement that a vote be held at least once every six years.[40]

Like the Say-on-Pay Vote, the results of the Frequency Vote are nonbinding on a registrant and its board of directors and specifically may not be construed as:

---

37. *See*, for example, General Mills, Inc. (biennial shareholder advisory vote on executive compensation), Microsoft Corporation (triennial shareholder advisory vote on executive compensation), Pfizer, Inc. (biennial shareholder advisory vote on executive compensation), and Prudential Financial, Inc. (biennial shareholder advisory vote on executive compensation).

38. *See also* Exchange Act Rule 14a-21(b) (17 C.F.R. 14a-21(b)), which specifies that the Frequency Vote is required only when proxies are solicited for an annual meeting of security holders at which directors will be elected, or a special meeting in lieu of such annual meeting, which is when disclosure of executive compensation pursuant to Item 402 of Regulation S-K is required.

39. In its rules fleshing out the framework for this new requirement, the SEC delayed effectiveness until April 4, 2011. *See* the Say-on-Pay Adopting Release, *supra* note 22.

40. *See* Exchange Act Rule 14a-21(b) (17 C.F.R. 240.14a-21(b)).

- overruling a decision by the registrant or its board of directors;
- creating or implying any change in or additional fiduciary duty for the registrant or the board; or
- restricting or limiting the ability of shareholders to make proposals for inclusion in proxy materials relating to executive compensation.[41]

The SEC has addressed several technical matters relating to Section 14A(a)(2) in its rules providing guidance on the operation of the requirement, including the following:

- The inclusion of a separate resolution providing for a Frequency Vote in a registrant's proxy materials does not require the filing of a preliminary proxy statement.[42]
- A registrant is not required to use any specific language or form of resolution in conducting a Frequency Vote.[43]
- A registrant must structure the Frequency Vote to give shareholders four choices: whether the Say-on-Pay Vote will occur every year, every two years, or every three years, or to abstain on voting on the matter.[44]

---

41. *See* Section 14A(c) of the Exchange Act (15 U.S.C. § 78n-1(c)). *See also* Item 24 to Schedule 14A (17 C.F.R 240.14a-101), which requires disclosure in a registrant's proxy statement for an annual meeting (or other meeting of securityholders for which executive compensation disclosure pursuant to Item 402 of Regulation S-K is required) of the fact that a separate shareholder vote on executive compensation is being held and a brief explanation of the general effect of the vote, such as whether the vote is nonbinding, and, when applicable, disclose the current frequency of the Say-on-Pay Votes and when the next such vote will occur.

42. *See* Exchange Act Rule 14a-6(a)(7) (17 C.F.R. 240.14a-6(a)(7)).

43. In fact, the Frequency Vote need not be in the form of a "resolution." *See* the Current Staff Exchange Act Rules Guidance, *supra* note 26, at Q&A 169.04. Nonetheless, the SEC Staff has informally cautioned that the Frequency Vote resolution must be clearly stated. In other words, it must be clear that shareholders can vote on the options of every one, two, or three years (or abstain from voting), rather than solely following management's recommendation (if one is provided). As was seen during the 2011 proxy season, most registrants relied on the Staff's guidance to provide their Frequency Votes in a "proposal" format, such as by simply referencing the four choices that are available on the proxy card. The Staff has also indicated that it is permissible for the Frequency Vote to include the words "every year, every other year, or every three years, or abstain" in lieu of "every 1, 2, or 3 years, or abstain." Id. at Q&A 169.06.

44. *See* Exchange Act Rule 14a-4(b)(3) (17 C.F.R. 240.14a-4(b)(3)). This rule solved a dilemma raised by Section 14A(a)(2) itself which did not indicate whether the Frequency Vote was to be a choice between the three alternatives set forth in the provision or whether a registrant could recommend a specific approach (for example, every three years) for approval or rejection by shareholders. This dilemma was further complicated by the proxy rules themselves which provided that, in the case of a matter being submitted for shareholder action, the person

- While a registrant is permitted to include a recommendation as to how shareholders should vote on the frequency of future Say-on-Pay Votes,[45] they must make clear in these circumstances that the proxy card provides for four choices (every one, two, or three years, or abstain) and that shareholders are not voting to approve or disapprove the registrant's recommendation.[46]

- A registrant may exclude a shareholder proposal that would provide an advisory vote or seek future advisory votes to approve the compensation of executives as disclosed pursuant to Item 402 or that relates to the frequency of future advisory votes on executive compensation, provided that in the most recent Frequency Vote a single year (that is, one, two, or three years) received approval of a majority of the votes cast on the matter and the registrant has adopted a policy on the frequency of Say-on-Pay Votes that is consistent with the choice of the majority of votes cast in the such a Frequency Vote.[47]

Reporting the Results of the Vote

Following any annual meeting of securityholders at which a matter was submitted to a vote of shareholders, and the meeting involved the election of directors, a registrant must file a current report on Form 8-K disclosing, among other things, a brief description of each matter voted on at the meeting (such as a Say-on-Pay Vote and/or a Frequency Vote); and stating the number of votes cast for, against, or withheld, as well as the number of abstentions and broker nonvotes as to each such

---

being solicited is to be afforded an opportunity to specify by boxes a choice between approval or disapproval of, or abstention with respect to, each separate matter referred to therein as intended to be acted upon (other than with respect to director elections). *See* Exchange Act Rule 14a-4(b)(1) (17 C.F.R. 240.14a-4(b)(1)).

45. In fact, if a registrant wishes to exercise discretionary authority with respect to the Frequency Vote in the case of a form of proxy in which a choice is not specified by the security holder, it must specify in the form of proxy how it intends to vote the shares represented by the proxy, which, typically, will conform to its recommendation. *See* Exchange Act Rule 14a-4(b)(1) (17 C.F.R. 240.14a-4(b)(1)).

46. *See* the Say-on-Pay Adopting Release, *supra* note 22, at Section II.B.3.a. In addition, because the Frequency Vote is merely advisory, the SEC did not prescribe a standard for determining which frequency has been "adopted" by shareholders. *Id.* at footnote 121.

47. *See* the Note to Exchange Act Rule 14a-8(i)(10) (17 C.F.R. 240.14a-8(i)(10)). The SEC Staff has informally indicated that this Note also applies to shareholder proposals seeking votes on matters that are already "subsumed" within the Say-on-Pay Vote or Frequency Vote.

matter.[48] In the case of the Frequency Vote, this disclosure must state the number of votes cast for each of one year, two years, and three years, as well as the number of abstentions.[49]

With respect to the effect of the Frequency Vote, a registrant is not precluded from conducting the required Say-on-Pay Vote on a frequency which differs from the preference of its shareholders as reflected in the most recent Frequency Vote.[50] The registrant is required, however, to publicly disclose its decision as to how frequently it will conduct Say-on-Pay Votes following each Frequency Vote.[51] Specifically, a registrant must file an amendment to its prior current report on Form 8-K that discloses the preliminary and final results of the votes conducted at its annual meeting of shareholders. Thus, a registrant must disclose whether it intends to follow the results of its most recent Frequency Vote or intends to conduct its Say-on-Pay Votes on a different schedule.

Results of Frequency Vote in 2011

Although Congress gave registrants and their shareholders the opportunity to hold Say-on-Pay Votes on a periodic, rather than an annual, basis, in 2011 shareholders overwhelmingly expressed a preference for annual advisory votes, which preferences resulted in most registrants deciding to conduct future Say-on-Pay Votes each year.

Of the approximately 3,100 registrants that reported the results of their initial Frequency Vote as required by the Dodd-Frank Act:

---

48. *See* Item 5.07(b) of Form 8-K (17 C.F.R. 249.308). *See also* Proxy Disclosure Enhancements, Release Nos. 33-9089, 34-61175, IC-29092 (Dec. 16, 2009), 74 Fed. Reg. 68,334 (Dec. 23, 2009), *available at* http://www.sec.gov/Archives/edgar/data/rules/final/2009/33-9089.pdf, at Section II.E.

49. *Id.*

50. *See* the Say-on-Pay Adopting Release, *supra* note 22, at Section II.B.6.

51. *See* Item 5.07(d) of Form 8-K (17 C.F.R. 249.308). As adopted, no later than 150 calendar days after the end of the annual or other meeting of securityholders at which the Frequency Vote was conducted, but in no event later than 60 calendar days prior to the deadline for submission of shareholder proposals under Exchange Act Rule 14a-8 (17 C.F.R. 240.14a-8), as disclosed in the registrant's most recent proxy statement for an annual or other meeting of securityholders relating to the election of directors at which the Frequency Vote was conducted, a registrant must amend the most recent current report on Form 8-K filed pursuant to Item 5.07(b) to disclose the registrant's decision in light of such vote as to how frequently the registrant will include a Say-on-Pay Vote proposal in its proxy materials until the next required Frequency Vote. This information may be reported on the Form 8-K filed pursuant to Item 5.07(b) to report the results of the annual meeting. In addition, the SEC Staff has informally indicated that disclosure of the information required by either Item 5.07(b) or (d) of Form 8-K may be included in a timely-filed quarterly report on Form 10-Q or annual report on Form 10-K.

- 1,630 registrants saw their board of directors recommend an annual Say-on-Pay Vote and in all but four instances (99.6 percent) the registrants' shareholders concurred with this recommendation.[52]
- 81 registrants saw their board of directors recommend a biennial Say-on-Pay Vote. Sixty-seven percent of these registrants (54 companies) saw their shareholders express a preference for an annual vote.
- 1,293 registrants saw their board of directors recommend a triennial Say-on-Pay Vote. Approximately 49 percent of these registrants (632 companies) saw their shareholders express a preference for an annual vote.
- 78 registrants saw their board of directors make no recommendation at all with respect to the Frequency Vote. In this situation, 78 percent of these registrants (61 companies) saw their shareholders express a preference for an annual vote, 14 express a preference for a triennial vote, and three for a biennial vote.

While Section 14A(c) of the Exchange Act expressly states that the Frequency Vote is not binding on a registrant or its board of directors and, among other things, is not to be construed as overruling a decision of the registrant or the board, in all but a handful of instances registrants have disclosed that they intend to abide by the preference of their shareholders as indicated by the Frequency Vote in conducting Say-on-Pay Votes going forward. Whether seeking to minimize shareholder (and public) criticism or genuinely interested in maintaining a regular channel of communication on executive pay matters, approximately 85 percent of the registrants that conducted a Say-on-Pay Vote in 2011 intend to conduct annual votes going forward, at least until their next Frequency Vote (which must be held no later than 2017).

While the SEC's rule contemplates that the decision on the frequency of future Say-on-Pay Votes would take place well after the annual meeting of shareholders at which the Frequency Vote was held, numerous registrants, in filing their current report on Form 8-K to report the results of their annual meeting, also used this report to disclose this decision.

---

52. Of the four registrants that saw their shareholders express a preference for something other than an annual Say-on-Pay Vote, in three instances shareholders expressed a preference for a triennial vote and in one instance shareholders expressed a preference for a biennial vote. As of the date of this publication, two registrants had disclosed that, in accordance with the preference of their shareholders, future Say-on-Pay Votes would be held every three years.

Advisory Vote on "Golden-Parachute" Compensation

Finally, Section 14A of the Exchange Act addresses the use of golden parachutes or similar compensation arrangements in connection with an acquisition, merger, consolidation, or proposed sale or other disposition of all or substantially all of the assets of a registrant through a pair of requirements. First, Section 14A(b)(1) of the Exchange Act imposes a mandatory disclosure requirement for all proxy or consent solicitation materials pursuant to which shareholders are being asked to approve a merger or other extraordinary corporate transaction. Under this requirement, any person making a proxy or consent solicitation seeking shareholder approval of a merger or other extraordinary corporate transaction must disclose in a clear and simple form:

- any agreements or understandings that such person has with any NEO of the registrant (or that it has with the NEOs of the acquiring issuer) concerning any type of compensation (whether present, deferred, or contingent) that is based on or otherwise relates to the merger or other extraordinary corporate transaction; and
- the aggregate total of all such compensation that may (and the conditions upon which it may) be paid or become payable to or on behalf of such executive officer.[53]

Second, Section 14A(b)(2) of the Exchange Act requires that these disclosed agreements or understandings with the registrant's NEOs must be approved by shareholders pursuant to a separate nonbinding vote at the meeting where shareholders are asked to approve the merger or other extraordinary corporate transaction that would trigger the payment of the compensation (Say-on-Golden-Parachutes Vote), unless such agreements or understandings have previously been subject to a Say-on-Pay Vote.[54]

---

53. In addition, similar disclosure would be required by an acquiring registrant of any agreements or understandings that it has with its NEOs and that it has with the NEOs of the target company in transactions in which the acquiring registrant is seeking shareholder approval of a merger or other transaction. See Items 5(a)(5) and 5(b)(3) of Schedule 14A.

54. See also Exchange Act Rule 14a-21(c) (17 C.F.R 240.14a-21(c)), which specifies that the Say-on-Golden-Parachutes Vote is required in proxy statements for meetings at which shareholders are asked to approve an acquisition, merger, consolidation, or proposed sale or other disposition of all or substantially all of a registrant's assets.

As with the other shareholder advisory votes, the Say-on-Golden-Parachutes Vote is nonbinding on a registrant and its board of directors, and specifically may not be construed as:

- overruling a decision by the registrant or its board of directors;
- creating or implying any change in or additional fiduciary duty for the registrant or the board; or
- restricting or limiting the ability of shareholders to make proposals for inclusion in proxy materials relating to executive compensation.[55]

These requirements became effective for proxy statements and other acquisition-related filings initially filed on or after April 25, 2011.[56]

One objective of this vote appears to be aimed at discouraging registrants from installing overly generous golden parachute compensation arrangements on the eve of a merger or other extraordinary corporate transaction. While the Say-on-Golden-Parachutes Vote won't affect the outcome of the transaction—or even impact the form and amount of the compensation arrangements—it will allow shareholders to at least register their displeasure with this maneuver. Thus, the advisory vote may place a greater premium on registrants having their golden parachute compensation arrangements in place well before a proposed transaction and, potentially, subject to the general Say-on-Pay Vote to take advantage of the exception to the Say-on-Golden-Parachutes Vote requirement.

Disclosure Requirements

In connection with any proxy or consent solicitation seeking shareholder approval of a merger or other extraordinary corporate transaction, the person making the solicitation must disclose in the proxy or consent solicitation materials, in a clear and simple form, any

---

55. *See* Section 14A(c) of the Exchange Act (15 U.S.C. § 78n-1(c)).

56. Notwithstanding the statutory language indicating that the Say-on-Golden Parachutes Vote was effective on or after January 21, 2011, the SEC took the position that, because the statute required the disclosure prescribed by Section 14A(b)(1) of the Exchange Act (15 U.S.C. § 78n-1(b)(1)) to be made "in accordance with regulations to be promulgated by the Commission," the Say-on-Golden-Parachutes Vote and related disclosure would not be required for merger proxy statements relating to a meeting of securityholders until the final rules were adopted. The final rules were adopted by the SEC on January 25, 2011, and became effective on April 4, 2011. The Say-on-Golden-Parachutes Vote provision became effective on April 25, 2011. *See* the Say-on-Pay Adopting Release, *supra* note 22.

agreements or understandings that such person has with any NEOs of such issuer (or of the acquiring issuer, if such issuer is not the acquiring issuer) concerning any type of compensation (whether present, deferred, or contingent) that is based on or otherwise relates to the merger or other extraordinary corporate transaction and the aggregate total of all such compensation that may (and the conditions upon which it may) be paid or become payable to or on behalf of such executive officer.

This disclosure requirement also applies to several additional forms and schedules under the federal securities laws, even though not specifically required under the Dodd-Frank Act. These include:

- information statements filed pursuant to Regulation 14C;
- proxy or consent solicitations that do not contain merger proposals, but require disclosure of information under Item 14 of Schedule 14A pursuant to Note A of Schedule 14A;
- registration statements on Forms S-4 and F-4 containing disclosure relating to mergers and similar transactions;
- "going private" transactions on Schedule 13E-3; and
- third-party tender offers on Schedule TO and Schedule 14D-9 solicitation/recommendation statements.

Further, Schedule TO has been amended to clarify that this disclosure is not required in a third-party bidders' tender offer statement, so long as the subject transaction is not also an Exchange Act Rule 13e-3 "going private" transaction. Registrants filing solicitation/recommendation statements on Schedule 14D-9 in connection with third-party tender offers will be obligated to provide the requested compensation disclosure.

It is important to note that the disclosure requirements of Section 14A(b)(1) are not dependent on the Say-on-Golden-Parachutes Vote itself. In other words, although the requirement for a Say-on-Golden-Parachutes Vote does not arise where an agreement or understanding has been previously subject to a Say-on-Pay Vote, the disclosure requirement applies to all change-in-control-related compensation agreements and understandings, regardless of whether (or when) they have been subject to a shareholder advisory vote.

Tabular Disclosure

To satisfy this disclosure requirement, the SEC adopted new narrative and tabular disclosure of NEOs' golden parachute arrangements.[57] To reflect the realities of many merger and other extraordinary corporate transactions, this disclosure is intended to cover any golden parachute compensation arrangements among the target and acquiring companies and the NEOs of each.

The centerpiece of the disclosure is the Golden Parachute Compensation Table that requires the presentation of quantitative disclosure of the individual elements of compensation that a NEO would receive that are based on or otherwise relate to the merger or other extraordinary corporate transaction, and the total amount that would be received by each NEO. The Golden Parachute Compensation Table is to be presented in the following tabular format:[58]

Golden Parachute Compensation

GOLDEN PARACHUTE COMPENSATION

Name	Cash ($)	Equity ($)	Pension/ NQDC ($)	Per-quisites/ Benefits ($)	Tax Reim- burse-ment ($)	Other ($)	Total ($)
(a)	(b)	(c)	(d)	(e)	(f)	(g)	(h)
PEO							
PFO							
A							
B							
C							

---

57. Item 402(t) of Regulation S-K (17 C.F.R. 229.402(t)). For this purpose, the NEOs subject to disclosure include a registrant's principal executive officer, principal financial officer, and the three most highly compensated executive officers (other than the PEO and PFO) who were serving as executive officers at the end of the last completed fiscal year (*see* Item 402(a)(3) (i), (ii), and (iii)). In the case of a smaller reporting company, the NEOs subject to disclosure include the registrant's principal executive officer and the two most highly compensated executive officers (other than the PEO) who were serving as executive officers at the end of the last completed fiscal year (*see* Item 402(m)(2)(i) and (ii)). Disclosure is not required with respect to individuals who would have been among the most highly compensated executive officers but for the fact that they were not serving as executive officers at the end of the last completed fiscal year. *See* Instruction 1 to Item 402(t). *See also* the Say-on-Pay Adopting Release, *supra* note 22, at footnote 252.

58. Item 402(t)(1).

The table includes the following information:

- the name of the NEO (column (a));[59]
- the aggregate dollar value of any cash severance payments, including but not limited to payments of base salary, bonus, and prorated nonequity incentive compensation plan payments (column (b));[60]
- the aggregate dollar value of:
    - stock awards for which vesting would be accelerated;[61]
    - in-the-money option awards for which vesting would be accelerated;[62]
    - payments in cancellation of stock and option awards (column (c));[63]
- the aggregate dollar value of pension and nonqualified deferred compensation benefit enhancements (column (d));[64]
- the aggregate dollar value of perquisites and other personal benefits or property, and health care and welfare benefits (column (e));[65]
- the aggregate dollar value of any tax reimbursements (column (f));[66]
- the aggregate dollar value of any other compensation that is based on or otherwise relates to the transaction not properly reported in columns (b) through (f) (column (g));[67] and
- the aggregate dollar value of the sum of all amounts reported in columns (b) through (g) (column (h)).[68]

If the disclosure is being included in a proxy or consent solicitation seeking shareholder approval of a merger or other extraordinary

---

59. Item 402(t)(2)(i).

60. Item 402(t)(2)(ii).

61. Item 402(t)(2)(iii)(A).

62. Item 402(t)(2)(iii)(B).

63. Item 402(t)(2)(iii)(C). The quantification of dollar amounts based on a registrant's stock price is required to be based on the closing market price per share as of the latest practicable date. *See* Instruction 1 to Item 402(t)(2).

64. Item 402(t)(2)(iv).

65. Item 402(t)(2)(v).

66. Item 402(t)(2)(vi).

67. Item 402(t)(2)(vii).

68. Item 402(t)(2)(viii).

corporate transaction,[69] the amounts to be disclosed in the Golden Parachute Compensation Table are to be calculated assuming that:

- the triggering event took place on the latest practicable date; and
- the price per share of the registrant's securities is to be determined as follows:
    - if the shareholders are to receive a fixed dollar amount, the price per share will be that amount, and
    - if the value is not a fixed dollar amount, the price per share will be the average closing market price of the registrant's securities over the first five business days following the first public announcement of the transaction.[70]

For each of the columns in the table requiring the presentation of a separate category of compensation, a registrant must include a footnote quantifying each separate form of compensation included in the aggregate total reported in the column.[71] In addition, the registrant also must include the value of all perquisites and other personal benefits or property.[72] Finally, for purposes of quantifying health care benefits, the registrant must use the assumptions used for financial reporting purposes under generally accepted accounting principles.[73]

Relationship to Item 402(j) Disclosure

While the items in the Golden Parachute Compensation Table resemble the disclosure that is required under Item 402(j) of Regulation S-K with respect to a registrant's compensatory arrangements for its NEOs in the event of a termination of employment or a change in control of the registrant, the disclosure required in the Golden Parachute Compensation

---

69. Or if the disclosure is included in a proxy or consent solicitation that includes disclosure under Item 14 of Schedule 14A (240.14a-101) pursuant to Note A of Schedule 14A.

70. *See* Instruction 1 to Item 402(t)(2). In the case of in-the-money stock options, the dollar value of option awards for which vesting will be accelerated is to be calculated by determining the difference between the price as previously-described and the exercise or base price of the options. *Id.*

71. *See* Instruction 4 to Item 402(t)(2).

72. *Id.* Individual perquisites and personal benefits are to be identified and quantified as required by Instruction 4 to Item 402(c)(2)(ix).

73. *Id.*

Table differs in two notable respects.[74] First, the disclosure requirements under Item 402(j) do not require disclosure about arrangements such as group life, health, hospitalization, or medical reimbursement plans that do not discriminate in scope, terms, or operation in favor of executive officers or directors of the registrant and that are available generally to all salaried employees.[75] No such exclusion is provided under Item 402(t).[76] Similarly, the disclosure requirements under Item 402(j) permit the exclusion of de minimis perquisites and other personal benefits (that is, with a value of less than $10,000).[77] Once again, no such exclusion is provided under Item 402(t).[78] Finally, the SEC determined that meeting the dictate of Section 14A(b)(1) that the information be presented in a "clear and simple form" is most appropriately satisfied by tabular disclosure, which is not required under Item 402(j).

Executives Covered

For purposes of the disclosure requirement, the NEOs subject to disclosure include a registrant's principal executive officer, principal financial officer, and the three most highly compensated executive officers (other than the PEO and PFO) for whom disclosure was required in the registrant's most recent filing with the SEC under either the Securities Act or the Exchange Act that required the inclusion of a Summary Compensation Table.[79] In the case of a smaller reporting company, the NEOs subject to disclosure include the registrant's principal executive officer and the two most highly compensated executive officers (other than the PEO) who were serving as executive officers at the end of the last completed fiscal year.[80] In either of these cases, disclosure is not required with respect to individuals who would have been among the most highly compensated executive officers but for the fact that they

---

74. While the SEC considered making its disclosure requirements under Item 402(j) applicable to merger proxy statements, ultimately it concluded that certain compensation elements required by Section 14A(b)(1) of the Exchange Act were not covered by this existing disclosure.

75. *See* Instruction 5 to Item 402(j).

76. *See* Item 402(a)(6)(ii) and Item 402(m)(5)(ii).

77. *See* Instruction 2 to Item 402(j).

78. *See* Instruction 4 to Item 402(t)(2).

79. *See* Instruction 1 to Item 402(t). *See also* Item 402(a)(3)(i), (ii), and (iii)).

80. *See* Instruction 1 to Item 40(t). *See also* Item 402(m)(2)(i) and (ii).

were not serving as executive officers at the end of the last completed fiscal year.[81]

The SEC Staff has indicated that, where a registrant files an annual meeting proxy statement in March 2011 (including the 2010 Summary Compensation Table), hires a new principal executive officer in May 2011, and prepares a merger proxy in September 2011, the registrant may not exclude the new principal executive officer from either the Golden Parachute Compensation Table or the Say-on-Golden Parachutes Vote included in the proxy materials for the merger.[82] In other words, the Summary Compensation Table is instructive only with respect to the most highly compensated executive officers who must be included in the Golden Parachute Compensation Table and not the principal executive officer and the principal financial officer, who are NEOs regardless of compensation level.[83]

Arrangements Covered

The amounts to be quantified in the Golden Parachute Compensation Table are to be based on the relevant agreement or understanding, whether written or unwritten, between each NEO and the acquiring company or target company, concerning any type of compensation, whether present, deferred, or contingent, that is based on or otherwise relates to a merger or other extraordinary corporate transaction.[84] The disclosable amounts are limited, however, only to compensation that is

---

81. *See* Instruction 1 to Item 402(t). *See also* the Say-on-Pay Adopting Release, *supra* note 22, at footnote 252.

82. *See* Division of Corporation Finance, Compliance and Disclosure Interpretations – Regulation S-K (July 8, 2011) [hereinafter Current Staff Guidance], *available at* http://www.sec.gov/divisions/corpfin/guidance/regs-kinterp.htm, at Q&A 128B.01.

83. As the SEC Staff notes, Instruction 1 to Item 402(t) specifies that Item 402(t) information must be provided for the individuals covered by Items 402(a)(3)(i), (ii), and (iii) of Regulation S-K. Instruction 1 to Item 402(t)(2) applies only to those executive officers who are included in the Summary Compensation Table under Item 402(a)(3)(iii), because they are the three most highly compensated executive officers other than the principal executive officer and the principal financial officer. Under Items 402(a)(3)(i) and (ii), the principal executive officer and the principal financial officer are, per se, NEOs, regardless of compensation level. Consequently, Instruction 1 to Item 402(t)(2) is not instructive as to whether the principal executive officer or principal financial officer is a NEO. The Staff goes on to state that this position also applies to Instruction 2 to Item 1011(b), which is the corresponding instruction in Regulation M-A. *See* the Current Staff Guidance, *supra* note 82, at Q&A 288.01.

84. The obligation to provide information in the Golden Parachute Compensation Table does not apply to agreements and understandings providing for the payment of compensation based on or relating to a merger or other extraordinary transaction with senior managers of foreign private issuers. *See* Instruction 2 to Item 402(t).

based on or otherwise relates to the subject transaction.[85] In other words, the Golden Parachute Compensation Table does not require the inclusion of so-called "walk-away" numbers (that is, amounts accumulated under retirement plans or in nonqualified deferred compensation accounts or previously vested equity awards).[86]

In addition, the disclosure requirements are slightly broader than the Say-on-Golden-Parachutes Vote required by Section 14A(b)(2). That is, they cover more agreements and understanding than are required to be subject to the advisory vote. To ensure disclosure of the full scope of the golden parachute compensation arrangements applicable to a merger or other extraordinary corporate transaction, the SEC requires disclosure of the arrangements between a target company and any of its NEOs and any NEOs of the acquiring company, as well as the arrangements between an acquiring company and any of its NEOs and any NEOs of the target company. When a target company seeks shareholder approval of a merger or other extraordinary corporate transaction, however, the golden parachute compensation arrangements between the acquiring company and the NEOs of the target company are beyond the scope of the required vote.[87]

In the event that uncertainties exist as to the provision of payments and benefits or the amounts involved, a registrant is required to make a reasonable estimate applicable to the payment or benefit and disclose the material assumptions underlying these estimates in its disclosure.[88]

Finally, with respect to each column in the table requiring the presentation of a separate category of compensation (other than the All Other Compensation column), a registrant is required to identify and quantify, by means of separate footnotes, amounts attributable to "single-trigger" arrangements (that is, amounts triggered by a change-

---

85. *See* Instruction 1 to Item 402(t)(2).

86. Nor would disclosure or quantification be required with respect to bona fide post-transaction employment agreements to be entered into in connection with the merger or other extraordinary corporate transaction.

87. *See* Instruction 7 to Item 402(t)(2). In cases where disclosure of arrangements between an acquiring company and the NEOs of the soliciting target company are required, the registrant must clarify whether these agreements are included in the Say-on-Golden Parachutes Vote by providing a separate table of all agreements and understandings subject to the shareholder advisory vote required by Section 14A(b)(2) of the Exchange Act (15 U.S.C. § 78n-1(b)(2)), if different from the full scope of the golden parachute compensation arrangements subject to disclosure. *Id.*

88. In such event, the disclosure would require forward-looking information as appropriate.

in-control for which payment is not conditioned upon the executive officer's termination of employment without cause or resignation for good reason) and amounts attributable to "double-trigger" arrangements (that is, amounts triggered by a change-in-control for which payment is conditioned upon the executive officer's termination of employment without cause or resignation for good reason within a limited time period following the change-in-control).[89]

Where certain golden parachute compensation arrangements have previously been subject to a Say-on-Pay Vote (whether or not such vote was approved by shareholders), a registrant conducting a Say-on-Golden Parachutes Vote to cover new golden parachute compensation arrangements and understandings, and/or the revised terms of arrangements and understandings that were previously subject to a Say-on-Pay Vote, must provide two separate Golden Parachute Compensation Tables—one table to disclose all golden parachute compensation arrangements, including both the arrangements and amounts previously disclosed and subject to a Say-on-Pay Vote and the new arrangements and understandings and/or the revised arrangements and understandings.[90] The second table is to disclose only the new arrangements and understandings and/or revised arrangements and understandings subject to the Say-on-Golden-Parachutes Vote.[91]

Narrative Disclosure

In addition to the Golden Parachute Compensation Table, registrants are required to provide a succinct narrative description of any material factors necessary to understand each such contract, agreement, plan, or arrangement and the payments quantified in the table.[92] Such factors are to include, but are not limited to, a description of:

- the specific circumstances that would trigger the payment or payments;[93]
- whether the payment or payments would or could be lump sum, or annual, disclosing the duration, and by whom they would be provided;[94] and

---

89. *See* Instruction 5 to Item 402(t)(2).
90. *See* Instruction 6 to Item 40(t)(2).
91. *See* Instruction 6 to Item 402(t)(2).
92. Item 402(t)(3).
93. Item 402(t)(3)(i).
94. Item 402(t)(3)(ii).

- any material conditions or obligations applicable to the receipt of the payment or benefits, including, but not limited to, noncompete, nonsolicitation, nondisparagement, or confidentiality agreements, including the duration of such agreements and provisions regarding waiver or breach of such agreements.[95]

Advisory Vote Requirements

Compared to the disclosure requirement, the Say-on-Golden-Parachutes Vote itself is straightforward. As previously described, this provision requires that any proxy or consent or authorization relating to the proxy or consent solicitation material containing the Golden Parachute Compensation Table include a separate resolution asking shareholders to approve, in a nonbinding vote, such agreements or understandings and compensation as disclosed, unless such agreements or understandings previously have been subject to a Say-on-Pay Vote.[96]

As with the other shareholder advisory votes, the SEC Staff is addressing technical matters relating to Section 14A(b)(2) as they arise. To date, the Staff has provided the following guidance on the operation of the vote requirement:

- A registrant is not required to use any specific language or form of resolution in conducting a Say-on-Golden Parachutes Vote.[97]

---

95. Item 402(t)(3)(iii).

96. Section 14A(b)(2) of the Exchange Act (15 U.S.C. § 78n-1(b)(2)) . *See also* Exchange Act Rule 14a-21(c) (17 C.F.R. 240-14a-21(c)).

97. Note that, as adopted by the SEC, the disclosure requirements of Proposed Item 402(t) of Regulation S-K are slightly broader than the Say-on-Golden-Parachutes Vote required by Section 14A(b)(2). To ensure disclosure of the full scope of the golden parachute compensation arrangements applicable to a merger or other extraordinary corporate transaction, the adopted rules require disclosure of the arrangements between a target company and any of its NEOs and any NEOs of the acquiring company, as well as the arrangements between an acquiring company and any of its NEOs and any NEOs of the target company. When a target company seeks shareholder approval of a merger or other extraordinary corporate transaction, however, the golden parachute compensation arrangements between the acquiring company and the NEOs of the target company are beyond the scope of the required vote. See Instruction 7 to Proposed Item 402(t)(2) of Regulation S-K for the special disclosure requirements in this situation.

Exception to Advisory Vote Requirement

Section 14A(b)(2) of the Exchange Act provides that a Say-on-Golden Parachutes Vote is not required with respect to any agreements or understanding that previously have been subject to a Say-on-Pay Vote.[98] This provision requires only that the golden parachute compensation arrangements have been subject to a prior Say-on-Pay Vote. It does not require that these arrangements have been approved by shareholders in such vote. Once a golden parachute compensation arrangement has satisfied the conditions of the exception, it is not subject to a Say-on-Golden-Parachutes Vote, but only to the extent that it is still in effect and its terms have not subsequently been modified. New golden parachute compensation arrangements and any revisions to previously-approved golden parachute compensation arrangements are subject to a separate shareholder advisory vote as required by Section 14A(b)(2).[99]

Where a registrant seeks to satisfy the exception to the Say-on-Golden Parachutes Vote requirement, it must include the disclosure required by Item 402(t), including the Golden Parachute Compensation Table, in its annual meeting proxy statement soliciting the Say-on-Pay Vote.[100] In this instance, the amounts to be disclosed in the Golden Parachute Compensation Table are to be calculated assuming that:

- the triggering event took place on the last business day of the registrant's last completed fiscal year; and
- the price per share of the registrant's securities is to be the closing market price of the registrant's securities as of that date.[101]

---

98. *See also* Exchange Act Rule 14a-21(c) (17 C.F.R. 240-14a-21(c)).

99. *See* note 90 *supra* and its accompanying text.

100. The amounts to be disclosed in the Golden Parachute Compensation Table are to be calculated based on the closing market price per share of the registrant's securities on the last business day of the registrant's last completed fiscal year, consistent with the quantification standards used in Item 402(j) of Regulation S-K. *See* Instruction 2 to Item 402(t)(2).

101. *See* Instruction 2 to Item 402(t)(2). In the case of in-the-money stock options, the dollar value of option awards for which vesting will be accelerated is to be calculated by determining the difference between the previously described price and the exercise or base price of the options. *Id.*

As contemplated, this disclosure must satisfy the current disclosure requirement in annual meeting proxy statements with respect to the change-in-control arrangements of the registrant's NEOs. The registrant would still be obligated to include in the annual meeting proxy statement, however, the disclosure required by Item 402(j) about payments that may be made to the NEOs upon termination of employment not made in connection with a change-in-control of the registrant.

Results of Say-on-Golden-Parachutes Vote in 2011

In 2011, for the most part, registrants engaging in a merger or other extraordinary corporate transaction faithfully complied with the requirements of the Golden Parachute Compensation Table. Most the variations in the disclosure between registrants were based on the complexity of the golden parachute compensation arrangements themselves, which were most frequently reflected through the length and number of footnotes accompanying the table.

The advisory votes themselves were largely a nonevent. Every vote was approved, although, in most instances, at a level somewhat lower than the vote approving the related transaction. To date, with one exception in early 2012, every vote has been approved, although at a level somewhat lower than the vote approving the underlying transaction. In addition, registrants generally also took pains to make clear that the golden parachute compensation arrangements were contractual in nature and that the outcome of the vote would not impact the registrant's obligation to honor the arrangements.

As for the exception to the Say-on-Golden-Parachutes Vote, while, initially, it was expected that many registrants would seek to take advantage of the exception by including their golden parachute compensation arrangements under their Say-on-Pay Vote, this did not materialize in 2011.Only a few dozen registrants voluntarily included the Item 402(t) golden parachute compensation disclosure in their annual meeting proxy statements.

There were at least four significant reasons for this development. First, many registrants were concerned that the addition of the Golden Parachute Compensation Table to the executive compensation disclosure in their annual proxy materials would unduly confuse shareholders, thereby requiring a lengthy explanation of the differences between their post-employment compensation disclosure pursuant to Item 402(j) and their change-in-control disclosure under new Item 402(t).

Second, registrants quickly determined that the principal benefit of satisfying the exception would be, at best, incremental since any new agreements or understandings involving golden parachute compensation arrangements or changes to existing agreements or understandings would trigger the requirement for a separate Say-on-Golden-Parachutes Vote, notwithstanding the status of the prior arrangements. Thus, the exception did not offer any assurance that an advisory vote wouldn't be required in the event of a merger or other extraordinary transaction.

Third, the major proxy advisory firms announced that they would more closely scrutinize the post-employment compensation arrangements of a registrant seeking to take advantage of the exception. This heightened scrutiny discouraged many registrants from changing their disclosure, particularly in situations where they were already concerned about the firms' potential evaluation of their executive compensation program.

Finally, some registrants expressed concern that providing such disclosure voluntarily could be misinterpreted as a signal to the market that the registrant could be engaged in a significant transaction in the coming months.

Treatment of Specific Types of Issuers

Smaller Reporting Companies

Section 14A of the Exchange Act confers upon the SEC the authority to exempt certain issuers or classes of issuers from the Say-on-Pay Vote and the Frequency Vote requirements.[102] Pursuant to this authority, the SEC decided to defer compliance with these requirements for smaller

---

102. *See* Section 14A(e) of the Exchange Act. While Section 951 of the Dodd-Frank Act gives the SEC the authority, by rule or order, to exempt an issuer or class of issuers from the advisory vote requirements of Section 14A(a), expressly stating that, in determining whether to grant an exemption, the SEC is to take into account whether the advisory vote "disproportionately burdens small issuers," the SEC has decided that, because the shareholder advisory votes and additional disclosure required by Section 14A would be significant for investors in all companies, including smaller reporting companies, it does not intend to exercise this authority. *See* the Say-on-Pay Proposing Release, *supra* note 22, at Section II.E.

reporting companies[103] until such company's first annual or other meeting of shareholders occurring on or after January 21, 2013.[104]

Note that this exemption did not extend to the Say-on-Golden-Parachutes Vote, which became effective for smaller reporting companies with respect to proxy and information statements, as well as other enumerated schedules and forms, on or after April 25, 2011, the same date as applicable to all other categories of registrants.

When the Say-on-Pay Vote and Frequency Vote become applicable to smaller reporting companies in 2013, these votes will not alter the executive compensation disclosure requirements for the companies that elect to rely on the scaled disclosure system for smaller reporting companies. In other words, since a CD&A is not required under Item 402 of Regulation S-K for smaller reporting companies, the SEC has confirmed that the Say-on-Pay Vote requirement does not alter this position.[105]

Emerging Growth Companies

The recently-enacted "Jumpstart Our Business Startups Act,"[106] among other things, amends the federal securities laws to create a new category of issuer, the emerging growth company.[107] To facilitate the initial offering of securities to the public, the JOBS Act streamlines the registration process under the Securities Act and relaxes the regulatory burden under the Exchange Act on emerging growth companies.

Among other things, Section 102 of the JOBS Act amends Section 14A of the Exchange Act to exempt emerging growth companies from all of the shareholder advisory vote requirements of the statute (which includes the Say-on-Pay Vote, the Frequency Vote, and the Say-on-Golden-Parachutes Vote) until the registrant is no longer an emerging growth company. Specifically, a registrant that is no longer an emerging growth company must include a separate resolution providing for a Say-on-Pay Vote in its proxy materials not later than the end of:

---

103. A "smaller reporting company" is defined in Item 10(f)(1) of Regulation S-K.

104. *See* Exchange Act Rule 14a-21(a) and (b).

105. *See* Instruction 3 to Exchange Act Rule 14a-21.

106. Pub. L. No. 112-106, 126 Stat. 306 (April 16, 2012).

107. *See* Section 101 of the JOBS Act, amending Section 2(a) of the Securities Act of 1933 (15 U.S.C. § 77b(a)) and Section 3(a) of the Exchange Act (15 U.S.C. § 78c(a)). As adopted, an "emerging growth company" means an issuer that had total annual gross revenues of less than $1 billion (indexed for inflation every five years by the SEC) during its most recently completed fiscal year.

- in the case of a registrant that was an emerging growth company for less than two years after the date of the effectiveness of its initial public offering of common equity securities under the Securities Act, the three-year period beginning on such date; and

- in the case of any other registrant, the one-year period beginning on the date the registrant is no longer an emerging growth company.[108]

TARP Recipients

Registrants that are recipients of financial assistance under TARP, which was created by the EESA,[109] are required to conduct a separate shareholder vote to approve the compensation of their executives, as disclosed pursuant to Item 402 of Regulation S–K, including the CD&A, the compensation tables, and any related material,[110] when soliciting proxies in connection with an annual or other meeting of shareholders at which directors will be elected. As in the case of the Say-on-Pay Vote required by the Dodd-Frank Act, the reference to Item 402 expressly limits the vote to the compensation of the registrant's NEOs.

This requirement applies throughout the period in which any obligation arising from the financial assistance provided under TARP remains outstanding. Because the vote required of TARP recipients is effectively the same vote that is required under Section 14A(a)(1) of the Exchange Act, the SEC has indicated that a shareholder vote to approve executive compensation under Exchange Act Rule 14a-20 for registrants with outstanding indebtedness under TARP will satisfy Exchange Act Rule 14a-21(a). Consequently, a registrant that conducts an annual

---

108. A registrant that is an emerging growth company as of the first day of a fiscal year continues to qualify as an emerging growth company until the earliest of: (a) the last day of the fiscal year in which its annual gross revenues exceed $1 billion; (b) the last day of the fiscal year following the fifth anniversary of its initial public offering of common equity securities; (c) the date on which it has issued more than $1 billion in nonconvertible debt during the previous three-year period; or (d) the date on which it is considered to be a "large accelerated filer" for purposes of the federal securities laws. *See* Section 2(a)(19) of the Securities Act (15 U.S.C. § 77b(a)(19)) and Section 3(a)(80) of the Exchange Act (15 U.S.C. § 78c(a)(80)).

109. Division A of Pub. L. No. 110-343 (2008). A "TARP recipient" is any entity that has received or will receive financial assistance under TARP. *See* Section 111(a)(3) of the EESA (12 U.S.C. § 5221(a)(3)).

110. Section 111(e) of the EESA (12 U.S.C. § 5221(e)). *See also* Exchange Act Rule 14a-20 (17 C.F.R. 240.14a-20).

shareholder advisory vote to approve executive compensation pursuant to EESA is not required to conduct a separate shareholder advisory vote on executive compensation under Section 14A(a)(1) until it has repaid all indebtedness under TARP.[111]

In addition, since TARP participants are required to conduct an annual shareholder advisory vote on executive compensation so long as they are indebted under TARP, the SEC has determined that it was neither necessary nor appropriate in the public interest or consistent with the protection of investors to require a registrant to conduct a Frequency Vote when it already is required to conduct advisory votes on executive compensation annually regardless of the outcome of such a vote and has exempted TARP recipients from this requirement.[112]

In the case of a TARP recipient that is a smaller reporting company, this requirement to conduct a separate shareholder vote to approve executive compensation is not intended to require the registrant to include a CD&A in its proxy statements in order to comply with this rule.[113] In addition, in the case of a smaller reporting company, the required vote must be to approve the compensation of the NEOs as disclosed pursuant to the scaled disclosure requirements for such registrants.[114]

---

111. In this instance, the registrant is required to include a separate shareholder advisory vote on executive compensation pursuant to Section 14A(a)(1) of the Exchange Act and Exchange Act Rule 14a-21(a) for the first annual meeting of shareholders after it has repaid all outstanding indebtedness under TARP. *See* the Say-on-Pay Adopting Release, *supra* note 22, at Section 2.C.3.

112. Exchange Act Rule 14a-21(b) (17 C.F.R. 240.14a-21(b)). This rule exempts a registrant with outstanding indebtedness under TARP from the Say-on-Pay Vote and the Frequency Vote until it has repaid all outstanding indebtedness under TARP. Similar to the approach for the Say-on-Pay Vote under Exchange Act Rule 14a-21(a), such a registrant is required to conduct a Frequency Vote for the first annual meeting of shareholders after it has repaid all outstanding indebtedness under TARP. *See* the Say-on-Pay Adopting Release, *supra* note 22, at Section II. C.3.

113. *See* the Note to Exchange Act Rule 14a-20.

114. These disclosure requirements are set forth in Item 402(m) through (q) of Regulation S-K.

Related Matters

Effect of Say-on-Pay Vote

As part of its rulemaking, the SEC amended Item 402(b) of Regulation S-K to require registrants to address in their CD&A whether and, if so how, their compensation policies and decisions have taken into account the results of their most recent Say-on-Pay Vote.[115] While initially framed as a discussion of responses to prior Say-on-Pay Votes on a cumulative basis,[116] the SEC revised the disclosure requirement in its final rules to solely cover the registrant's immediately preceding shareholder advisory vote.[117]

Disclosure by Institutional Investment Managers

To promote greater transparency about how institutional investors have cast their votes on the shareholder advisory votes, Section 14A of the Exchange Act requires each institutional investment manager subject to Section 13(f) of the Exchange Act[118] to report each year how it voted on any shareholder advisory vote conducted by one of its portfolio companies, unless such vote is otherwise required to be reported publicly by SEC rule.[119] It is believed that this requirement will have the effect of compelling fund managers, who may otherwise have been inclined to cast their votes routinely with the registrant, to take a closer look at the executive compensation program before reaching a voting decision.

---

115. Item 402(b)(2)(vii).
116. *See* the Say-on-Pay Proposing Release, *supra* note 22, at Section II.A.3.
117. *See* the Say-on-Pay Adopting Release, *supra* note 22, at Section II.A.3.
118. 15 U.S.C. § 78m(f).
119. Section 14A(d) of the Exchange Act (15 U.S.C. § 78n-1(d)).

Appendix

A

Item 402 of Regulation S-K (17 C.F.R. 229.402)

Effective: 9 April 2012

§ 229.402 (Item 402) Executive compensation.

(a) *General—*

(1) *Treatment of foreign private issuers.* A foreign private issuer will be deemed to comply with this Item if it provides the information required by Items 6.B and 6.E.2 of Form 20–F (17 CFR 249.220f), with more detailed information provided if otherwise made publicly available or required to be disclosed by the issuer's home jurisdiction or a market in which its securities are listed or traded.

(2) *All compensation covered.* This Item requires clear, concise and understandable disclosure of all plan and non-plan compensation awarded to, earned by, or paid to the named executive officers designated under paragraph (a)(3) of this Item, and directors covered by paragraph (k) of this Item, by any person for all services rendered in all capacities to the registrant and its subsidiaries, unless otherwise specifically excluded from disclosure in this Item. All such compensation shall be reported pursuant to this Item, even if also called for by another requirement, including transactions between the registrant and a third party where a purpose of the transaction is to furnish compensation to any such named executive

officer or director. No amount reported as compensation for one fiscal year need be reported in the same manner as compensation for a subsequent fiscal year; amounts reported as compensation for one fiscal year may be required to be reported in a different manner pursuant to this Item.

(3) *Persons covered.* Disclosure shall be provided pursuant to this Item for each of the following (the "named executive officers"):

(i) All individuals serving as the registrant's principal executive officer or acting in a similar capacity during the last completed fiscal year ("PEO"), regardless of compensation level;

(ii) All individuals serving as the registrant's principal financial officer or acting in a similar capacity during the last completed fiscal year ("PFO"), regardless of compensation level;

(iii) The registrant's three most highly compensated executive officers other than the PEO and PFO who were serving as executive officers at the end of the last completed fiscal year; and

(iv) Up to two additional individuals for whom disclosure would have been provided pursuant to paragraph (a)(3)(iii) of this Item but for the fact that the individual was not serving as an executive officer of the registrant at the end of the last completed fiscal year.

Instructions to Item 402(a)(3). 1. *Determination of most highly compensated executive officers.* The determination as to which executive officers are most highly compensated shall be made by reference to total compensation for the last completed fiscal year (as required to be disclosed pursuant to paragraph (c)(2)(x) of this Item) reduced by the amount required to be disclosed pursuant to paragraph (c)(2)(viii) of this Item, *provided, however,* that no disclosure need be provided for any executive officer, other than the PEO and PFO, whose total compensation, as so reduced, does not exceed $100,000.

2. *Inclusion of executive officer of subsidiary.* It may be appropriate for a registrant to include as named executive officers one or more executive officers or other employees of subsidiaries in the disclosure required by this Item. See Rule 3b–7 under the Exchange Act (17 CFR 240.3b–7).

3. *Exclusion of executive officer due to overseas compensation.* It may be appropriate in limited circumstances for a registrant not to include in the disclosure required by this Item an individual, other than its PEO or PFO, who is one of the registrant's most highly compensated executive officers

due to the payment of amounts of cash compensation relating to overseas assignments attributed predominantly to such assignments.

(4) *Information for full fiscal year.* If the PEO or PFO served in that capacity during any part of a fiscal year with respect to which information is required, information should be provided as to all of his or her compensation for the full fiscal year. If a named executive officer (other than the PEO or PFO) served as an executive officer of the registrant (whether or not in the same position) during any part of the fiscal year with respect to which information is required, information shall be provided as to all compensation of that individual for the full fiscal year.

(5) *Omission of table or column.* A table or column may be omitted if there has been no compensation awarded to, earned by, or paid to any of the named executive officers or directors required to be reported in that table or column in any fiscal year covered by that table.

(6) *Definitions.* For purposes of this Item:

(i) The term *stock* means instruments such as common stock, restricted stock, restricted stock units, phantom stock, phantom stock units, common stock equivalent units or any similar instruments that do not have option-like features, and the term *option* means instruments such as stock options, stock appreciation rights and similar instruments with option-like features. The term *stock appreciation rights* ("*SARs*") refers to SARs payable in cash or stock, including SARs payable in cash or stock at the election of the registrant or a named executive officer. The term *equity* is used to refer generally to stock and/or options.

(ii) The term *plan* includes, but is not limited to, the following: Any plan, contract, authorization or arrangement, whether or not set forth in any formal document, pursuant to which cash, securities, similar instruments, or any other property may be received. A plan may be applicable to one person. Except with respect to the disclosure required by paragraph (t) of this Item, registrants may omit information regarding group life, health, hospitalization, or medical reimbursement plans that do not discriminate in scope, terms or operation, in favor of executive officers or directors of the registrant and that are available generally to all salaried employees.

(iii) The term *incentive plan* means any plan providing compensation intended to serve as incentive for performance to occur over a specified period, whether such performance is measured by reference to financial performance of the registrant or an affiliate, the registrant's stock price, or any other performance measure. An *equity incentive plan* is an incentive plan or portion of an incentive plan under which awards are granted that fall within the scope of FASB ASC Topic 718, *Compensation—Stock Compensation*. A *non-equity incentive plan* is an incentive plan or portion of an incentive plan that is not an equity incentive plan. The term *incentive plan award* means an award provided under an incentive plan.

(iv) The terms *date of grant* or *grant date* refer to the grant date determined for financial statement reporting purposes pursuant to FASB ASC Topic 718.

(v) *Closing market price* is defined as the price at which the registrant's security was last sold in the principal United States market for such security as of the date for which the closing market price is determined.

(b) *Compensation discussion and analysis.*

(1) Discuss the compensation awarded to, earned by, or paid to the named executive officers. The discussion shall explain all material elements of the registrant's compensation of the named executive officers. The discussion shall describe the following:

(i) The objectives of the registrant's compensation programs;

(ii) What the compensation program is designed to reward;

(iii) Each element of compensation;

(iv) Why the registrant chooses to pay each element;

(v) How the registrant determines the amount (and, where applicable, the formula) for each element to pay;

(vi) How each compensation element and the registrant's decisions regarding that element fit into the registrant's overall compensation objectives and affect decisions regarding other elements; and

(vii) Whether and, if so, how the registrant has considered the results of the most recent shareholder advisory vote on executive compensation required by section 14A of the Exchange Act (15 U.S.C. 78n–1) or § 240.14a–20 of this chapter in determining compensation policies and decisions and, if so, how that consideration has affected the registrant's executive compensation decisions and policies.

(2) While the material information to be disclosed under Compensation Discussion and Analysis will vary depending upon the facts and circumstances, examples of such information may include, in a given case, among other things, the following:

(i) The policies for allocating between long-term and currently paid out compensation;

(ii) The policies for allocating between cash and non-cash compensation, and among different forms of non-cash compensation;

(iii) For long-term compensation, the basis for allocating compensation to each different form of award (such as relationship of the award to the achievement of the registrant's long-term goals, management's exposure to downside equity performance risk, correlation between cost to registrant and expected benefits to the registrant);

(iv) How the determination is made as to when awards are granted, including awards of equity-based compensation such as options;

(v) What specific items of corporate performance are taken into account in setting compensation policies and making compensation decisions;

(vi) How specific forms of compensation are structured and implemented to reflect these items of the registrant's performance, including whether discretion can be or has been exercised (either to award compensation absent attainment of the relevant performance goal(s) or to reduce or increase the size of any award or payout), identifying any particular exercise of discretion, and stating whether it applied to one or more specified named executive officers or to all compensation subject to the relevant performance goal(s);

(vii) How specific forms of compensation are structured and implemented to reflect the named executive officer's individual performance and/or individual contribution to these items of the registrant's performance, describing the elements of individual performance and/or contribution that are taken into account;

(viii) Registrant policies and decisions regarding the adjustment or recovery of awards or payments if the relevant registrant performance measures upon which they are based are restated or otherwise adjusted in a manner that would reduce the size of an award or payment;

(ix) The factors considered in decisions to increase or decrease compensation materially;

(x) How compensation or amounts realizable from prior compensation are considered in setting other elements of compensation (e.g., how gains from prior option or stock awards are considered in setting retirement benefits);

(xi) With respect to any contract, agreement, plan or arrangement, whether written or unwritten, that provides for payment(s) at, following, or in connection with any termination or change-in-control, the basis for selecting particular events as triggering payment (e.g., the rationale for providing a single trigger for payment in the event of a change-in-control);

(xii) The impact of the accounting and tax treatments of the particular form of compensation;

(xiii) The registrant's equity or other security ownership requirements or guidelines (specifying applicable amounts and forms of ownership), and any registrant policies regarding hedging the economic risk of such ownership;

(xiv) Whether the registrant engaged in any benchmarking of total compensation, or any material element of compensation, identifying the benchmark and, if applicable, its components (including component companies); and

(xv) The role of executive officers in determining executive compensation.

Instructions to Item 402(b). 1. The purpose of the Compensation Discussion and Analysis is to provide to investors material information that is necessary to an understanding of the registrant's compensation policies and decisions regarding the named executive officers.

2. The Compensation Discussion and Analysis should be of the information contained in the tables and otherwise disclosed pursuant to this Item. The Compensation Discussion and Analysis should also cover actions regarding executive compensation that were taken after the

registrant's last fiscal year's end. Actions that should be addressed might include, as examples only, the adoption or implementation of new or modified programs and policies or specific decisions that were made or steps that were taken that could affect a fair understanding of the named executive officer's compensation for the last fiscal year. Moreover, in some situations it may be necessary to discuss prior years in order to give context to the disclosure provided.

3. The Compensation Discussion and Analysis should focus on the material principles underlying the registrant's executive compensation policies and decisions and the most important factors relevant to analysis of those policies and decisions. The Compensation Discussion and Analysis shall reflect the individual circumstances of the registrant and shall avoid boilerplate language and repetition of the more detailed information set forth in the tables and narrative disclosures that follow.

4. Registrants are not required to disclose target levels with respect to specific quantitative or qualitative performance-related factors considered by the compensation committee or the board of directors, or any other factors or criteria involving confidential trade secrets or confidential commercial or financial information, the disclosure of which would result in competitive harm for the registrant. The standard to use when determining whether disclosure would cause competitive harm for the registrant is the same standard that would apply when a registrant requests confidential treatment of confidential trade secrets or confidential commercial or financial information pursuant to Securities Act Rule 406 (17 CFR 230.406) and Exchange Act Rule 24b–2 (17 CFR 240.24b–2), each of which incorporates the criteria for non-disclosure when relying upon Exemption 4 of the Freedom of Information Act (5 U.S.C. 552(b)(4)) and Rule 80(b) (4) (17 CFR 200.80(b)(4)) thereunder. A registrant is not required to seek confidential treatment under the procedures in Securities Act Rule 406 and Exchange Act Rule 24b–2 if it determines that the disclosure would cause competitive harm in reliance on this instruction; however, in that case, the registrant must discuss how difficult it will be for the executive or how likely it will be for the registrant to achieve the undisclosed target levels or other factors.

5. Disclosure of target levels that are non-GAAP financial measures will not be subject to Regulation G (17 CFR 244.100—102) and Item 10(e) (§229.10(e)); however, disclosure must be provided as to how the number is calculated from the registrant's audited financial statements.

(c) *Summary compensation table—*

> (1) *General.* Provide the information specified in paragraph (c)(2) of this Item, concerning the compensation of the named executive officers for each of the registrant's last three completed fiscal years, in a Summary Compensation Table in the tabular format specified below.

Summary Compensation Table

Name and principal position	Year	Salary ($)	Bonus ($)	Stock awards ($)	Option awards ($)	Non-equity incentive plan compensation ($)	Change in pension value and non-qualified deferred compensation earnings ($)	All other compensation ($)	Total ($)
(a)	(b)	(c)	(d)	(e)	(f)	(g)	(h)	(i)	(j)
PEO									
PFO									
A									
B									
C									

> (2) The Table shall include:

>> (i) The name and principal position of the named executive officer (column (a));

>> (ii) The fiscal year covered (column (b));

>> (iii) The dollar value of base salary (cash and non-cash) earned by the named executive officer during the fiscal year covered (column (c));

>> (iv) The dollar value of bonus (cash and non-cash) earned by the named executive officer during the fiscal year covered (column (d));

> *Instructions to Item 402(c)(2)(iii) and (iv).*

1. If the amount of salary or bonus earned in a given fiscal year is not calculable through the latest practicable date, a footnote shall be included disclosing that the amount of salary or bonus is not calculable through the latest practicable date and providing the date that the amount of salary or bonus is expected to be determined, and such amount must then be disclosed in a filing under Item 5.02(f) of Form 8–K (17 CFR 249.308).

2. Registrants shall include in the salary column (column (c)) or bonus column (column (d)) any amount of salary or bonus forgone at the

election of a named executive officer under which stock, equity-based or other forms of non-cash compensation instead have been received by the named executive officer. However, the receipt of any such form of non-cash compensation instead of salary or bonus must be disclosed in a footnote added to the salary or bonus column and, where applicable, referring to the Grants of Plan-Based Awards Table (required by paragraph (d) of this Item) where the stock, option or non-equity incentive plan award elected by the named executive officer is reported.

> (v) For awards of stock, the aggregate grant date fair value computed in accordance with FASB ASC Topic 718 (column (e));
>
> (vi) For awards of options, with or without tandem SARs (including awards that subsequently have been transferred), the aggregate grant date fair value computed in accordance with FASB ASC Topic 718 (column (f));

Instruction 1 to Item 402(c)(2)(v) and (vi). For awards reported in columns (e) and (f), include a footnote disclosing all assumptions made in the valuation by reference to a discussion of those assumptions in the registrant's financial statements, footnotes to the financial statements, or discussion in the Management's Discussion and Analysis. The sections so referenced are deemed part of the disclosure provided pursuant to this Item.

Instruction 2 to Item 402(c)(2)(v) and (vi). If at any time during the last completed fiscal year, the registrant has adjusted or amended the exercise price of options or SARs previously awarded to a named executive officer, whether through amendment, cancellation or replacement grants, or any other means ("repriced"), or otherwise has materially modified such awards, the registrant shall include, as awards required to be reported in column (f), the incremental fair value, computed as of the repricing or modification date in accordance with FASB ASC Topic 718, with respect to that repriced or modified award.

Instruction 3 to Item 402(c)(2)(v) and (vi). For any awards that are subject to performance conditions, report the value at the grant date based upon the probable outcome of such conditions. This amount should be consistent with the estimate of aggregate compensation cost to be recognized over the service period determined as of the grant date under FASB ASC Topic 718, excluding the effect of estimated forfeitures. In a footnote to the table, disclose the value of the award at the grant date assuming that the highest level of performance conditions will be achieved if an amount less than the maximum was included in the table.

(vii) The dollar value of all earnings for services performed during the fiscal year pursuant to awards under non-equity incentive plans as defined in paragraph (a)(6)(iii) of this Item, and all earnings on any outstanding awards (column (g));

Instructions to Item 402(c)(2)(vii). 1. If the relevant performance measure is satisfied during the fiscal year (including for a single year in a plan with a multi-year performance measure), the earnings are reportable for that fiscal year, even if not payable until a later date, and are not reportable again in the fiscal year when amounts are paid to the named executive officer.

2. All earnings on non-equity incentive plan compensation must be identified and quantified in a footnote to column (g), whether the earnings were paid during the fiscal year, payable during the period but deferred at the election of the named executive officer, or payable by their terms at a later date.

(viii) The sum of the amounts specified in paragraphs (c)(2)(viii) (A) and (B) of this Item (column (h)) as follows:

(A) The aggregate change in the actuarial present value of the named executive officer's accumulated benefit under all defined benefit and actuarial pension plans (including supplemental plans) from the pension plan measurement date used for financial statement reporting purposes with respect to the registrant's audited financial statements for the prior completed fiscal year to the pension plan measurement date used for financial statement reporting purposes with respect to the registrant's audited financial statements for the covered fiscal year; and

(B) Above-market or preferential earnings on compensation that is deferred on a basis that is not tax-qualified, including such earnings on nonqualified defined contribution plans;

Instructions to Item 402(c)(2)(viii). 1. The disclosure required pursuant to paragraph (c)(2)(viii)(A) of this Item applies to each plan that provides for the payment of retirement benefits, or benefits that will be paid primarily following retirement, including but not limited to tax-qualified defined benefit plans and supplemental executive retirement plans, but excluding tax-qualified defined contribution plans and nonqualified defined contribution plans. For purposes of this disclosure, the registrant should use the same amounts required to be disclosed pursuant to paragraph (h)(2)(iv) of this Item for the covered fiscal year and the amounts that were or would have been required to be reported for the executive officer pursuant to paragraph (h)(2)(iv) of this Item for the prior completed fiscal year.

2. Regarding paragraph (c)(2)(viii)(B) of this Item, interest on deferred compensation is above-market only if the rate of interest exceeds 120% of the applicable federal long-term rate, with compounding (as prescribed under section 1274(d) of the Internal Revenue Code, (26 U.S.C. 1274(d))) at the rate that corresponds most closely to the rate under the registrant's plan at the time the interest rate or formula is set. In the event of a discretionary reset of the interest rate, the requisite calculation must be made on the basis of the interest rate at the time of such reset, rather than when originally established. Only the above-market portion of the interest must be included. If the applicable interest rates vary depending upon conditions such as a minimum period of continued service, the reported amount should be calculated assuming satisfaction of all conditions to receiving interest at the highest rate. Dividends (and dividend equivalents) on deferred compensation denominated in the registrant's stock ("deferred stock") are preferential only if earned at a rate higher than dividends on the registrant's common stock. Only the preferential portion of the dividends or equivalents must be included. Footnote or narrative disclosure may be provided explaining the registrant's criteria for determining any portion considered to be above-market.

3. The registrant shall identify and quantify by footnote the separate amounts attributable to each of paragraphs (c)(2)(viii)(A) and (B) of this Item. Where such amount pursuant to paragraph (c)(2)(viii)(A) is negative, it should be disclosed by footnote but should not be reflected in the sum reported in column (h).

> (ix) All other compensation for the covered fiscal year that the registrant could not properly report in any other column of the Summary Compensation Table (column (i)). Each compensation item that is not properly reportable in columns (c)–(h), regardless of the amount of the compensation item, must be included in column (i). Such compensation must include, but is not limited to:
>
> > (A) Perquisites and other personal benefits, or property, unless the aggregate amount of such compensation is less than $10,000;
> >
> > (B) All "gross-ups" or other amounts reimbursed during the fiscal year for the payment of taxes;

(C) For any security of the registrant or its subsidiaries purchased from the registrant or its subsidiaries (through deferral of salary or bonus, or otherwise) at a discount from the market price of such security at the date of purchase, unless that discount is available generally, either to all security holders or to all salaried employees of the registrant, the compensation cost, if any, computed in accordance with FASB ASC Topic 718;

(D) The amount paid or accrued to any named executive officer pursuant to a plan or arrangement in connection with:

(1) Any termination, including without limitation through retirement, resignation, severance or constructive termination (including a change in responsibilities) of such executive officer's employment with the registrant and its subsidiaries; or

(2) A change in control of the registrant;

(E) Registrant contributions or other allocations to vested and unvested defined contribution plans;

(F) The dollar value of any insurance premiums paid by, or on behalf of, the registrant during the covered fiscal year with respect to life insurance for the benefit of a named executive officer; and

(G) The dollar value of any dividends or other earnings paid on stock or option awards, when those amounts were not factored into the grant date fair value required to be reported for the stock or option award in column (e) or (f); and

Instructions to Item 402(c)(2)(ix). 1. Non-equity incentive plan awards and earnings and earnings on stock and options, except as specified in paragraph (c)(2)(ix)(G) of this Item, are required to be reported elsewhere as provided in this Item and are not reportable as All Other Compensation in column (i).

2. Benefits paid pursuant to defined benefit and actuarial plans are not reportable as All Other Compensation in column (i) unless accelerated pursuant to a change in control; information concerning these plans is reportable pursuant to paragraphs (c)(2)(viii)(A) and (h) of this Item.

3. Any item reported for a named executive officer pursuant to paragraph (c)(2)(ix) of this Item that is not a perquisite or personal benefit and whose value exceeds $10,000 must be identified and quantified in a footnote to column (i). This requirement applies only to compensation for the last fiscal year. All items of compensation are required to be included in the Summary Compensation Table without regard to whether such items are required to be identified other than as specifically noted in this Item.

4. Perquisites and personal benefits may be excluded as long as the total value of all perquisites and personal benefits for a named executive officer is less than $10,000. If the total value of all perquisites and personal benefits is $10,000 or more for any named executive officer, then each perquisite or personal benefit, regardless of its amount, must be identified by type. If perquisites and personal benefits are required to be reported for a named executive officer pursuant to this rule, then each perquisite or personal benefit that exceeds the greater of $25,000 or 10% of the total amount of perquisites and personal benefits for that officer must be quantified and disclosed in a footnote. The requirements for identification and quantification apply only to compensation for the last fiscal year. Perquisites and other personal benefits shall be valued on the basis of the aggregate incremental cost to the registrant. With respect to the perquisite or other personal benefit for which footnote quantification is required, the registrant shall describe in the footnote its methodology for computing the aggregate incremental cost. Reimbursements of taxes owed with respect to perquisites or other personal benefits must be included in column (i) and are subject to separate quantification and identification as tax reimbursements (paragraph (c)(2)(ix)(B) of this Item) even if the associated perquisites or other personal benefits are not required to be included because the total amount of all perquisites or personal benefits for an individual named executive officer is less than $10,000 or are required to be identified but are not required to be separately quantified.

5. For purposes of paragraph (c)(2)(ix)(D) of this Item, an accrued amount is an amount for which payment has become due.

> (x) The dollar value of total compensation for the covered fiscal year (column (j)). With respect to each named executive officer, disclose the sum of all amounts reported in columns (c) through (i).

Instructions to Item 402(c). 1. Information with respect to fiscal years prior to the last completed fiscal year will not be required if the registrant was not a reporting company pursuant to section 13(a) or 15(d) of the Exchange Act (15 U.S.C. 78m(a) or 78o(d)) at any time during that year, except that the registrant will be required to provide information for any such year if that information previously was required to be provided in response to a Commission filing requirement.

2. All compensation values reported in the Summary Compensation Table must be reported in dollars and rounded to the nearest dollar. Reported compensation values must be reported numerically, providing a single numerical value for each grid in the table. Where compensation was paid to or received by a named executive officer in a different currency, a footnote must be provided to identify that currency and describe the rate and methodology used to convert the payment amounts to dollars.

3. If a named executive officer is also a director who receives compensation for his or her services as a director, reflect that compensation in the Summary Compensation Table and provide a footnote identifying and itemizing such compensation and amounts. Use the categories in the Director Compensation Table required pursuant to paragraph (k) of this Item.

4. Any amounts deferred, whether pursuant to a plan established under section 401(k) of the Internal Revenue Code (26 U.S.C. 401(k)), or otherwise, shall be included in the appropriate column for the fiscal year in which earned.

(d) *Grants of plan-based awards table.*

(1) Provide the information specified in paragraph (d)(2) of this Item, concerning each grant of an award made to a named executive officer in the last completed fiscal year under any plan, including awards that subsequently have been transferred, in the following tabular format:

Grants of Plan-Based Awards

Name	Grant date	Estimated future payouts under non-equity incentive plan awards			Estimated future payouts under equity incentive plan awards			All other stock awards: Number of shares of stock or units (#)	All other option awards: Number of securities underlying options (#)	Exercise or base price of option awards ($/ Sh)	Grant date fair value of stock and option awards
		Threshold ($)	Target ($)	Maximum ($)	Threshold (#)	Target (#)	Maximum (#)				
(a)	(b)	(c)	(d)	(e)	(f)	(g)	(h)	(i)	(j)	(k)	(l)
PEO											
PFO											
A											
B											
C											

(2) The Table shall include:

(i) The name of the named executive officer (column (a));

(ii) The grant date for equity-based awards reported in the table (column (b)). If such grant date is different than the date on which the compensation committee (or a committee of the board of directors performing a similar function or the full board of directors) takes action or is deemed to take action to grant such awards, a separate, adjoining column shall be added between columns (b) and (c) showing such date;

(iii) The dollar value of the estimated future payout upon satisfaction of the conditions in question under non-equity incentive plan awards granted in the fiscal year, or the applicable range of estimated payouts denominated in dollars (threshold, target and maximum amount) (columns (c) through (e));

(iv) The number of shares of stock, or the number of shares underlying options to be paid out or vested upon satisfaction of the conditions in question under equity incentive plan awards granted in the fiscal year, or the applicable range of estimated payouts denominated in the number of shares of stock, or the number of shares underlying options under the award (threshold, target and maximum amount) (columns (f) through (h));

(v) The number of shares of stock granted in the fiscal year that are not required to be disclosed in columns (f) through (h) (column (i));

(vi) The number of securities underlying options granted in the fiscal year that are not required to be disclosed in columns (f) through (h) (column (j));

(vii) The per-share exercise or base price of the options granted in the fiscal year (column (k)). If such exercise or base price is less than the closing market price of the underlying security on the date of the grant, a separate, adjoining column showing the closing market price on the date of the grant shall be added after column (k) and

(viii) The grant date fair value of each equity award computed in accordance with FASB ASC Topic 718 (column (l)). If at any time during the last completed fiscal year, the registrant has adjusted or amended the exercise or base price of options, SARs or similar option-like instruments previously awarded to a named executive officer, whether through amendment, cancellation or replacement grants, or any other means ("repriced"), or otherwise has materially modified such awards, the incremental fair value, computed as of the repricing or modification date in accordance with FASB ASC Topic 718, with respect to that repriced or modified award, shall be reported.

Instructions to Item 402(d). 1. Disclosure on a separate line shall be provided in the Table for each grant of an award made to a named executive officer during the fiscal year. If grants of awards were made to a named executive officer during the fiscal year under more than one plan, identify the particular plan under which each such grant was made.

2. For grants of incentive plan awards, provide the information called for by columns (c), (d) and (e), or (f), (g) and (h), as applicable. For columns (c) and (f), *threshold* refers to the minimum amount payable for a certain level of performance under the plan. For columns (d) and (g), *target* refers to the amount payable if the specified performance target(s) are reached. For columns (e) and (h), *maximum* refers to the maximum payout possible under the plan. If the award provides only for a single estimated payout, that amount must be reported as the *target* in columns (d) and (g). In columns (d) and (g), registrants must provide a representative amount based on the previous fiscal year's performance if the target amount is not determinable.

3. In determining if the exercise or base price of an option is less than the closing market price of the underlying security on the date of the grant, the registrant may use either the closing market price as specified in paragraph (a)(6)(v) of this Item, or if no market exists, any other formula prescribed for the security. Whenever the exercise or base price reported in column (k) is not the closing market price, describe the methodology for determining the exercise or base price either by a footnote or accompanying textual narrative.

4. A tandem grant of two instruments, only one of which is granted under an incentive plan, such as an option granted in tandem with a performance share, need be reported only in column (i) or (j), as applicable. For example, an option granted in tandem with a performance share would be reported only as an option grant in column (j), with the tandem feature noted either by a footnote or accompanying textual narrative.

5. Disclose the dollar amount of consideration, if any, paid by the executive officer for the award in a footnote to the appropriate column.

6. If non-equity incentive plan awards are denominated in units or other rights, a separate, adjoining column between columns (b) and (c) shall be added quantifying the units or other rights awarded.

7. Options, SARs and similar option-like instruments granted in connection with a repricing transaction or other material modification shall be reported in this Table. However, the disclosure required by this Table does not apply to any repricing that occurs through a pre-existing formula or mechanism in the plan or award that results in the periodic adjustment of the option or SAR exercise or base price, an antidilution provision in a plan or award, or a recapitalization or similar transaction equally affecting all holders of the class of securities underlying the options or SARs.

8. For any equity awards that are subject to performance conditions, report in column (l) the value at the grant date based upon the probable outcome of such conditions. This amount should be consistent with the estimate of aggregate compensation cost to be recognized over the service period determined as of the grant date under FASB ASC Topic 718, excluding the effect of estimated forfeitures.

(e) *Narrative disclosure to summary compensation table and grants of plan-based awards table.*

(1) Provide a narrative description of any material factors necessary to an understanding of the information disclosed in the tables required by paragraphs (c) and (d) of this Item. Examples of such factors may include, in given cases, among other things:

(i) The material terms of each named executive officer's employment agreement or arrangement, whether written or unwritten;

(ii) If at any time during the last fiscal year, any outstanding option or other equity-based award was repriced or otherwise materially modified (such as by extension of exercise periods, the change of vesting or forfeiture conditions, the change or elimination of applicable performance criteria, or the change of the bases upon which returns are determined), a description of each such repricing or other material modification;

(iii) The material terms of any award reported in response to paragraph (d) of this Item, including a general description of the formula or criteria to be applied in determining the amounts payable, and the vesting schedule. For example, state where applicable that dividends will be paid on stock, and if so, the applicable dividend rate and whether that rate is preferential. Describe any performance-based conditions, and any other material conditions, that are applicable to the award. For purposes of the Table required by paragraph (d) of this Item and the narrative disclosure required by paragraph (e) of this Item, performance-based conditions include both performance conditions and market conditions, as those terms are defined in FASB ASC Topic 718; and

(iv) An explanation of the amount of salary and bonus in proportion to total compensation.

Instructions to Item 402(e)(1). 1. The disclosure required by paragraph (e)(1)(ii) of this Item would not apply to any repricing that occurs through a pre-existing formula or mechanism in the plan or award that results in the periodic adjustment of the option or SAR exercise or base price, an antidilution provision in a plan or award, or a recapitalization or similar transaction equally affecting all holders of the class of securities underlying the options or SARs.

2. Instructions 4 and 5 to Item 402(b) apply regarding disclosure pursuant to paragraph (e)(1) of this Item of target levels with respect to specific quantitative or qualitative performance-related factors considered by the compensation committee or the board of directors, or any other factors or criteria involving confidential trade secrets or confidential commercial or financial information, the disclosure of which would result in competitive harm for the registrant.

(2) [Reserved]

(f) *Outstanding equity awards at fiscal year-end table.*

(1) Provide the information specified in paragraph (f)(2) of this Item, concerning unexercised options; stock that has not vested; and equity incentive plan awards for each named executive officer outstanding as of the end of the registrant's last completed fiscal year in the following tabular format:

Outstanding Equity Awards at Fiscal Year-End

Name	Option awards					Stock Awards			
	Number of securities underlying unexercised options (#) exercisable	Number of securities underlying unexercised options (#) unexercise-able	Equity incentive plan awards: Number of securities underlying unexercised unearned options (#)	Option exercise price ($)	Option expiration date	Number of shares or units of stock that have not vested (#)	Market value of shares of units of stock that have not vested (#)	Equity incentive plan awards: Number of unearned shares, units or other rights that have not vested (#)	Equity incentive plan awards: Market or payout value of unearned shares, units, or other rights have not vested ($)
(a)	(b)	(c)	(d)	(e)	(f)	(g)	(h)	(i)	(j)
PEO									
PFO									
A									
B									
C									

(2) The Table shall include:

(i) The name of the named executive officer (column (a));

(ii) On an award-by-award basis, the number of securities underlying unexercised options, including awards that have been transferred other than for value, that are exercisable and that are not reported in column (d) (column (b));

(iii) On an award-by-award basis, the number of securities underlying unexercised options, including awards that have been transferred other than for value, that are unexercisable and that are not reported in column (d) (column (c));

(iv) On an award-by-award basis, the total number of shares underlying unexercised options awarded under any equity incentive plan that have not been earned (column (d));

(v) For each instrument reported in columns (b), (c) and (d), as applicable, the exercise or base price (column (e));

(vi) For each instrument reported in columns (b), (c) and (d), as applicable, the expiration date (column (f));

(vii) The total number of shares of stock that have not vested and that are not reported in column (i) (column (g));

(viii) The aggregate market value of shares of stock that have not vested and that are not reported in column (j) (column (h));

(ix) The total number of shares of stock, units or other rights awarded under any equity incentive plan that have not vested and that have not been earned, and, if applicable the number of shares underlying any such unit or right (column (i)); and

(x) The aggregate market or payout value of shares of stock, units or other rights awarded under any equity incentive plan that have not vested and that have not been earned (column (j)).

Instructions to Item 402(f)(2). 1. Identify by footnote any award that has been transferred other than for value, disclosing the nature of the transfer.

2. The vesting dates of options, shares of stock and equity incentive plan awards held at fiscal-year end must be disclosed by footnote to the applicable column where the outstanding award is reported.

3. Compute the market value of stock reported in column (h) and equity incentive plan awards of stock reported in column (j) by multiplying the closing market price of the registrant's stock at the end of the last completed fiscal year by the number of shares or units of stock or the amount of equity incentive plan awards, respectively. The number of shares or units reported in columns (d) or (i), and the payout value reported in column (j), shall be based on achieving threshold performance goals, except that if the previous fiscal year's performance has exceeded the threshold, the disclosure shall be based on the next higher performance measure (target or maximum) that exceeds the previous fiscal year's performance. If the award provides only for a single estimated payout, that amount should be reported. If the target amount is not determinable, registrants must provide a representative amount based on the previous fiscal year's performance.

4. Multiple awards may be aggregated where the expiration date and the exercise and/or base price of the instruments is identical. A single award consisting of a combination of options, SARs and/or similar option-like instruments shall be reported as separate awards with respect to each tranche with a different exercise and/or base price or expiration date.

5. Options or stock awarded under an equity incentive plan are reported in columns (d) or (i) and (j), respectively, until the relevant performance condition has been satisfied. Once the relevant performance condition has been satisfied, even if the option or stock award is subject to forfeiture conditions, options are reported in column (b) or (c), as appropriate, until they are exercised or expire, or stock is reported in columns (g) and (h) until it vests.

(g) *Option exercises and stock vested table.*

(1) Provide the information specified in paragraph (g)(2) of this Item, concerning each exercise of stock options, SARs and similar instruments, and each vesting of stock, including restricted stock, restricted stock units and similar instruments, during the last completed fiscal year for each of the named executive officers on an aggregated basis in the following tabular format:

Option Exercises and Stock Vested

Name	Option awards			Stock awards	
	Number of shares acquired on exercise (#)	Value realized on exercise ($)		Number of shares acquired on vesting (#)	Value realized on vesting ($)
(a)	(b)	(c)		(d)	(e)
PEO					
PFO					
A					
B					
C					

(2) The Table shall include:

(i) The name of the executive officer (column (a));

(ii) The number of securities for which the options were exercised (column (b));

(iii) The aggregate dollar value realized upon exercise of options, or upon the transfer of an award for value (column (c));

(iv) The number of shares of stock that have vested (column (d)); and

(v) The aggregate dollar value realized upon vesting of stock, or upon the transfer of an award for value (column (e)).

Instruction to Item 402(g)(2). Report in column (c) the aggregate dollar amount realized by the named executive officer upon exercise of the options or upon the transfer of such instruments for value. Compute the dollar amount realized upon exercise by determining the difference between the market price of the underlying securities at exercise and the exercise or base price of the options. Do not include the value of any related payment or other consideration provided (or to be provided) by the registrant to or on behalf of a named executive officer, whether in payment of the exercise price or related taxes. (Any such payment or other consideration provided by the registrant is required to be disclosed in accordance with paragraph (c)(2)(ix) of this Item.) Report in column (e) the aggregate dollar amount realized by the named executive officer upon the vesting of stock or the transfer of such instruments for value. Compute the aggregate dollar amount realized upon vesting by multiplying the number of shares of stock or units by the market value of the underlying shares on the vesting date. For any amount realized upon exercise or vesting for which receipt has been deferred, provide a footnote quantifying the amount and disclosing the terms of the deferral.

(h) *Pension benefits.*

(1) Provide the information specified in paragraph (h)(2) of this Item with respect to each plan that provides for payments or other benefits at, following, or in connection with retirement, in the following tabular format:

Pension Benefits

Name (a)	Plan name (b)	Number of years credited service (#) (c)	Present value of accumulated benefit ($) (d)	Payments during last fiscal year ($) (e)
PEO				
PFO				
A				
B				
C				

(2) The Table shall include:

(i) The name of the executive officer (column (a));

(ii) The name of the plan (column (b));

(iii) The number of years of service credited to the named executive officer under the plan, computed as of the same pension plan measurement date used for financial statement reporting purposes with respect to the registrant's audited financial statements for the last completed fiscal year (column (c));

(iv) The actuarial present value of the named executive officer's accumulated benefit under the plan, computed as of the same pension plan measurement date used for financial statement reporting purposes with respect to the registrant's audited financial statements for the last completed fiscal year (column (d)); and

(v) The dollar amount of any payments and benefits paid to the named executive officer during the registrant's last completed fiscal year (column (e)).

Instructions to Item 402(h)(2). 1. The disclosure required pursuant to this Table applies to each plan that provides for specified retirement payments and benefits, or payments and benefits that will be provided primarily following retirement, including but not limited to tax-qualified defined benefit plans and supplemental executive retirement plans, but excluding tax-qualified defined contribution plans and nonqualified defined contribution plans. Provide a separate row for each such plan in which the named executive officer participates.

2. For purposes of the amount(s) reported in column (d), the registrant must use the same assumptions used for financial reporting purposes under generally accepted accounting principles, except that retirement age shall be assumed to be the normal retirement age as defined in the plan, or if not so defined, the earliest time at which a participant may retire under the plan without any benefit reduction due to age. The registrant must disclose in the accompanying textual narrative the valuation method and all material assumptions applied in quantifying the present value of the current accrued benefit. A benefit specified in the plan document or the executive's contract itself is not an assumption. Registrants may satisfy all or part of this disclosure by reference to a discussion of those assumptions in the registrant's financial statements, footnotes to the financial statements, or discussion in the Management's Discussion and Analysis. The sections so referenced are deemed part of the disclosure provided pursuant to this Item.

3. For purposes of allocating the current accrued benefit between tax qualified defined benefit plans and related supplemental plans, apply the limitations applicable to tax qualified defined benefit plans established by the Internal Revenue Code and the regulations thereunder that applied as of the pension plan measurement date.

4. If a named executive officer's number of years of credited service with respect to any plan is different from the named executive officer's number of actual years of service with the registrant, provide footnote disclosure quantifying the difference and any resulting benefit augmentation.

(3) Provide a succinct narrative description of any material factors necessary to an understanding of each plan covered by the tabular disclosure required by this paragraph. While material factors will vary depending upon the facts, examples of such factors may include, in given cases, among other things:

(i) The material terms and conditions of payments and benefits available under the plan, including the plan's normal retirement payment and benefit formula and eligibility standards, and the effect of the form of benefit elected on the amount of annual benefits. For this purpose, normal retirement means retirement at the normal retirement age as defined in the plan, or if not so defined, the earliest time at which a participant may retire under the plan without any benefit reduction due to age;

(ii) If any named executive officer is currently eligible for early retirement under any plan, identify that named executive officer and the plan, and describe the plan's early retirement payment and benefit formula and eligibility standards. For this purpose, early retirement means retirement at the early retirement age as defined in the plan, or otherwise available to the executive under the plan;

(iii) The specific elements of compensation (e.g., salary, bonus, etc.) included in applying the payment and benefit formula, identifying each such element;

(iv) With respect to named executive officers' participation in multiple plans, the different purposes for each plan; and

(v) Registrant policies with regard to such matters as granting extra years of credited service.

(i) *Nonqualified defined contribution and other nonqualified deferred compensation plans.*

(1) Provide the information specified in paragraph (i)(2) of this Item with respect to each defined contribution or other plan that provides for the deferral of compensation on a basis that is not tax-qualified in the following tabular format:

Nonqualified Deferred Compensation

Name (a)	Executive contributions in last FY ($) (b)	Registrant contributions in last FY ($) (c)	Aggregate earnings in last FY ($) (d)	Aggregate withdrawals/ distributions ($) (e)	Aggregate balance at last FYE ($) (f)
PEO					
PFO					
A					
B					
C					

(2) The Table shall include:

(i) The name of the executive officer (column (a));

(ii) The dollar amount of aggregate executive contributions during the registrant's last fiscal year (column (b));

(iii) The dollar amount of aggregate registrant contributions during the registrant's last fiscal year (column (c));

(iv) The dollar amount of aggregate interest or other earnings accrued during the registrant's last fiscal year (column (d));

(v) The aggregate dollar amount of all withdrawals by and distributions to the executive during the registrant's last fiscal year (column (e)); and

(vi) The dollar amount of total balance of the executive's account as of the end of the registrant's last fiscal year (column (f)).

Instruction to Item 402(i)(2). Provide a footnote quantifying the extent to which amounts reported in the contributions and earnings columns are reported as compensation in the last completed fiscal year in the registrant's Summary Compensation Table and amounts reported in the aggregate balance at last fiscal year end (column (f)) previously were reported as compensation to the named executive officer in the registrant's Summary Compensation Table for previous years.

(3) Provide a succinct narrative description of any material factors necessary to an understanding of each plan covered by tabular disclosure required by this paragraph. While material factors will vary depending upon the facts, examples of such factors may include, in given cases, among other things:

(i) The type(s) of compensation permitted to be deferred, and any limitations (by percentage of compensation or otherwise) on the extent to which deferral is permitted;

(ii) The measures for calculating interest or other plan earnings (including whether such measure(s) are selected by the executive or the registrant and the frequency and manner in which selections may be changed), quantifying interest rates and other earnings measures applicable during the registrant's last fiscal year; and

(iii) Material terms with respect to payouts, withdrawals and other distributions.

(j) *Potential payments upon termination or change-in-control.* Regarding each contract, agreement, plan or arrangement, whether written or unwritten, that provides for payment(s) to a named executive officer at, following, or in connection with any termination, including without limitation resignation, severance, retirement or a constructive termination of a named executive officer, or a change in control of the registrant or a change in the named executive officer's responsibilities, with respect to each named executive officer:

(1) Describe and explain the specific circumstances that would trigger payment(s) or the provision of other benefits, including perquisites and health care benefits;

(2) Describe and quantify the estimated payments and benefits that would be provided in each covered circumstance, whether they would or could be lump sum, or annual, disclosing the duration, and by whom they would be provided;

(3) Describe and explain how the appropriate payment and benefit levels are determined under the various circumstances that trigger payments or provision of benefits;

(4) Describe and explain any material conditions or obligations applicable to the receipt of payments or benefits, including but not limited to non-compete, non-solicitation, non-disparagement or confidentiality agreements, including the duration of such agreements and provisions regarding waiver of breach of such agreements; and

(5) Describe any other material factors regarding each such contract, agreement, plan or arrangement.

Instructions to Item 402(j). 1. The registrant must provide quantitative disclosure under these requirements, applying the assumptions that the triggering event took place on the last business day of the registrant's last completed fiscal year, and the price per share of the registrant's securities is the closing market price as of that date. In the event that uncertainties exist as to the provision of payments and benefits or the amounts involved, the registrant is required to make a reasonable estimate (or a reasonable estimated range of amounts) applicable to the payment or benefit and disclose material assumptions underlying such estimates or estimated ranges in its disclosure. In such event, the disclosure would require forward-looking information as appropriate.

2. Perquisites and other personal benefits or property may be excluded only if the aggregate amount of such compensation will be less than $10,000. Individual perquisites and personal benefits shall be identified and quantified as required by Instruction 4 to paragraph (c)(2)(ix) of this Item. For purposes of quantifying health care benefits, the registrant must use the assumptions used for financial reporting purposes under generally accepted accounting principles.

3. To the extent that the form and amount of any payment or benefit that would be provided in connection with any triggering event is fully disclosed pursuant to paragraph (h) or (i) of this Item, reference may be made to that disclosure. However, to the extent that the form or amount of any such payment or benefit would be enhanced or its vesting or other provisions accelerated in connection with any triggering event, such enhancement or acceleration must be disclosed pursuant to this paragraph.

4. Where a triggering event has actually occurred for a named executive officer and that individual was not serving as a named executive officer of the registrant at the end of the last completed fiscal year, the disclosure required by this paragraph for that named executive officer shall apply only to that triggering event.

5. The registrant need not provide information with respect to contracts, agreements, plans or arrangements to the extent they do not discriminate in scope, terms or operation, in favor of executive officers of the registrant and that are available generally to all salaried employees.

(k) *Compensation of directors.*

(1) Provide the information specified in paragraph (k)(2) of this Item, concerning the compensation of the directors for the registrant's last completed fiscal year, in the following tabular format:

Director Compensation

Name	Fees earned or paid in cash ($)	Stock awards ($)	Option awards ($)	Non-equity incentive plan compensation ($)	Change in pension value and non-qualified deferred compensation earnings ($)	All other compensation ($)	Total ($)
(a)	(b)	(c)	(d)	(e)	(f)	(g)	(h)
A							
B							
C							
D							
E							

(2) The Table shall include:

(i) The name of each director unless such director is also a named executive officer under paragraph (a) of this Item and his or her compensation for service as a director is fully reflected in the Summary Compensation Table pursuant to paragraph (c) of this Item and otherwise as required pursuant to paragraphs (d) through (j) of this Item (column (a));

(ii) The aggregate dollar amount of all fees earned or paid in cash for services as a director, including annual retainer fees, committee and/or chairmanship fees, and meeting fees (column (b));

(iii) For awards of stock, the aggregate grant date fair value computed in accordance with FASB ASC Topic 718 (column (c));

(iv) For awards of options, with or without tandem SARs (including awards that subsequently have been transferred), the aggregate grant date fair value computed in accordance with FASB ASC Topic 718 (column (d));

Instruction to Item 402(k)(2)(iii) and (iv). For each director, disclose by footnote to the appropriate column: the grant date fair value of each equity award computed in accordance with FASB ASC Topic 718; for each option, SAR or similar option like instrument for which the registrant has adjusted or amended the exercise or base price during the last completed fiscal year, whether through amendment, cancellation or replacement grants, or any other means ("repriced"), or otherwise has materially modified such awards, the incremental fair value, computed as of the repricing or modification date in accordance with FASB ASC Topic 718; and the aggregate number of stock awards and the aggregate number of option awards outstanding at fiscal year end. However, the disclosure required by this Instruction does not apply to any repricing that occurs through a pre-existing formula or mechanism in the plan or award that results in the periodic adjustment of the option or SAR exercise or base price, an antidilution provision in a plan or award, or a recapitalization or similar transaction equally affecting all holders of the class of securities underlying the options or SARs.

> (v) The dollar value of all earnings for services performed during the fiscal year pursuant to non-equity incentive plans as defined in paragraph (a)(6)(iii) of this Item, and all earnings on any outstanding awards (column (e));
>
> (vi) The sum of the amounts specified in paragraphs (k)(2)(vi)(A) and (B) of this Item (column (f)) as follows:
>
>> (A) The aggregate change in the actuarial present value of the director's accumulated benefit under all defined benefit and actuarial pension plans (including supplemental plans) from the pension plan measurement date used for financial statement reporting purposes with respect to the registrant's audited financial statements for the prior completed fiscal year to the pension plan measurement date used for financial statement reporting purposes with respect to the registrant's audited financial statements for the covered fiscal year; and
>>
>> (B) Above-market or preferential earnings on compensation that is deferred on a basis that is not tax-qualified, including such earnings on nonqualified defined contribution plans;
>
> (vii) All other compensation for the covered fiscal year that the registrant could not properly report in any other column of the Director Compensation Table (column (g)). Each compensation item that is not properly reportable in columns (b)–(f), regardless of the amount of the compensation item, must be included in column (g). Such compensation must include, but is not limited to:
>
>> (A) Perquisites and other personal benefits, or property, unless the aggregate amount of such compensation is less than $10,000;
>>
>> (B) All "gross-ups" or other amounts reimbursed during the fiscal year for the payment of taxes;

(C) For any security of the registrant or its subsidiaries purchased from the registrant or its subsidiaries (through deferral of salary or bonus, or otherwise) at a discount from the market price of such security at the date of purchase, unless that discount is available generally, either to all security holders or to all salaried employees of the registrant, the compensation cost, if any, computed in accordance with FASB ASC Topic 718;

(D) The amount paid or accrued to any director pursuant to a plan or arrangement in connection with:

(1) The resignation, retirement or any other termination of such director; or

(2) A change in control of the registrant;

(E) Registrant contributions or other allocations to vested and unvested defined contribution plans;

(F) Consulting fees earned from, or paid or payable by the registrant and/or its subsidiaries (including joint ventures);

(G) The annual costs of payments and promises of payments pursuant to director legacy programs and similar charitable award programs;

(H) The dollar value of any insurance premiums paid by, or on behalf of, the registrant during the covered fiscal year with respect to life insurance for the benefit of a director; and

(I) The dollar value of any dividends or other earnings paid on stock or option awards, when those amounts were not factored into the grant date fair value required to be reported for the stock or option award in column (c) or (d); and

Instructions to Item 402(k)(2)(vii). 1. Programs in which registrants agree to make donations to one or more charitable institutions in a director's name, payable by the registrant currently or upon a designated event, such as the retirement or death of the director, are charitable awards programs or director legacy programs for purposes of the disclosure required by paragraph (k)(2)(vii)(G) of this Item. Provide footnote disclosure of the total dollar amount payable under the program and other material terms of each such program for which tabular disclosure is provided.

2. Any item reported for a director pursuant to paragraph (k)(2)(vii) of this Item that is not a perquisite or personal benefit and whose value

exceeds $10,000 must be identified and quantified in a footnote to column (g). All items of compensation are required to be included in the Director Compensation Table without regard to whether such items are required to be identified other than as specifically noted in this Item.

3. Perquisites and personal benefits may be excluded as long as the total value of all perquisites and personal benefits for a director is less than $10,000. If the total value of all perquisites and personal benefits is $10,000 or more for any director, then each perquisite or personal benefit, regardless of its amount, must be identified by type. If perquisites and personal benefits are required to be reported for a director pursuant to this rule, then each perquisite or personal benefit that exceeds the greater of $25,000 or 10% of the total amount of perquisites and personal benefits for that director must be quantified and disclosed in a footnote. Perquisites and other personal benefits shall be valued on the basis of the aggregate incremental cost to the registrant. With respect to the perquisite or other personal benefit for which footnote quantification is required, the registrant shall describe in the footnote its methodology for computing the aggregate incremental cost. Reimbursements of taxes owed with respect to perquisites or other personal benefits must be included in column (g) and are subject to separate quantification and identification as tax reimbursements (paragraph (k)(2) (vii)(B) of this Item) even if the associated perquisites or other personal benefits are not required to be included because the total amount of all perquisites or personal benefits for an individual director is less than $10,000 or are required to be identified but are not required to be separately quantified.

> (viii) The dollar value of total compensation for the covered fiscal year (column (h)). With respect to each director, disclose the sum of all amounts reported in columns (b) through (g).

Instruction to Item 402(k)(2). Two or more directors may be grouped in a single row in the Table if all elements of their compensation are identical. The names of the directors for whom disclosure is presented on a group basis should be clear from the Table.

(3) *Narrative to director compensation table.* Provide a narrative description of any material factors necessary to an understanding of the director compensation disclosed in this Table. While material factors will vary depending upon the facts, examples of such factors may include, in given cases, among other things:

(i) A description of standard compensation arrangements (such as fees for retainer, committee service, service as chairman of the board or a committee, and meeting attendance); and

(ii) Whether any director has a different compensation arrangement, identifying that director and describing the terms of that arrangement.

Instruction to Item 402(k). In addition to the Instruction to paragraphs (k)(2)(iii) and (iv) and the Instructions to paragraph (k)(2)(vii) of this Item, the following apply equally to paragraph (k) of this Item: Instructions 2 and 4 to paragraph (c) of this Item; Instructions to paragraphs (c)(2)(iii) and (iv) of this Item; Instructions to paragraphs (c)(2)(v) and (vi) of this Item; Instructions to paragraph (c)(2)(vii) of this Item; Instructions to paragraph (c)(2)(viii) of this Item; and Instructions 1 and 5 to paragraph (c)(2)(ix) of this Item. These Instructions apply to the columns in the Director Compensation Table that are analogous to the columns in the Summary Compensation Table to which they refer and to disclosures under paragraph (k) of this Item that correspond to analogous disclosures provided for in paragraph (c) of this Item to which they refer.

(l) *Smaller reporting companies.* A registrant that qualifies as a "smaller reporting company," as defined by Item 10(f) (§229.10(f)(1)), may provide the scaled disclosure in paragraphs (m) through (r) instead of paragraphs (a) through (k) and (s) of this Item.

(m) *Smaller reporting companies—General—*

(1) *All compensation covered.* This Item requires clear, concise and understandable disclosure of all plan and non-plan compensation awarded to, earned by, or paid to the named executive officers designated under paragraph (m)(2) of this Item, and directors covered by paragraph (r) of this Item, by any person for all services rendered in all capacities to the smaller reporting company and its subsidiaries, unless otherwise specifically excluded from disclosure in this Item. All such compensation shall be reported pursuant to this Item, even if also called for by another requirement, including transactions between the smaller reporting company and a third party where a purpose of the transaction is to furnish compensation to any such named executive officer or director. No amount reported as compensation for one fiscal year need be reported in the same manner as compensation for a subsequent fiscal year; amounts reported as compensation for one fiscal year may be required to be reported in a different manner pursuant to this Item.

(2) *Persons covered.* Disclosure shall be provided pursuant to this Item for each of the following (the "named executive officers"):

> (i) All individuals serving as the smaller reporting company's principal executive officer or acting in a similar capacity during the last completed fiscal year ("PEO"), regardless of compensation level;
>
> (ii) The smaller reporting company's two most highly compensated executive officers other than the PEO who were serving as executive officers at the end of the last completed fiscal year; and
>
> (iii) Up to two additional individuals for whom disclosure would have been provided pursuant to paragraph (m)(2)(ii) of this Item but for the fact that the individual was not serving as an executive officer of the smaller reporting company at the end of the last completed fiscal year.

Instructions to Item 402(m)(2).

1. *Determination of most highly compensated executive officers.* The determination as to which executive officers are most highly compensated shall be made by reference to total compensation for the last completed fiscal year (as required to be disclosed pursuant to paragraph (n)(2)(x) of this Item) reduced by the amount required to be disclosed pursuant to paragraph (n)(2)(viii) of this Item, *provided, however,* that no disclosure need be provided for any executive officer, other than the PEO, whose total compensation, as so reduced, does not exceed $100,000.

2. *Inclusion of executive officer of a subsidiary.* It may be appropriate for a smaller reporting company to include as named executive officers one or more executive officers or other employees of subsidiaries in the disclosure required by this Item. See Rule 3b–7 under the Exchange Act (17 CFR 240.3b–7).

3. *Exclusion of executive officer due to overseas compensation.* It may be appropriate in limited circumstances for a smaller reporting company not to include in the disclosure required by this Item an individual, other than its PEO, who is one of the smaller reporting company's most highly compensated executive officers due to the payment of amounts of cash compensation relating to overseas assignments attributed predominantly to such assignments.

(3) *Information for full fiscal year.* If the PEO served in that capacity during any part of a fiscal year with respect to which information is required, information should be provided as to all of his or her

compensation for the full fiscal year. If a named executive officer (other than the PEO) served as an executive officer of the smaller reporting company (whether or not in the same position) during any part of the fiscal year with respect to which information is required, information shall be provided as to all compensation of that individual for the full fiscal year.

(4) *Omission of table or column.* A table or column may be omitted if there has been no compensation awarded to, earned by, or paid to any of the named executive officers or directors required to be reported in that table or column in any fiscal year covered by that table.

(5) *Definitions.* For purposes of this Item:

(i) The term *stock* means instruments such as common stock, restricted stock, restricted stock units, phantom stock, phantom stock units, common stock equivalent units or any similar instruments that do not have option-like features, and the term *option* means instruments such as stock options, stock appreciation rights and similar instruments with option-like features. The term *stock appreciation rights* ("*SARs*") refers to SARs payable in cash or stock, including SARs payable in cash or stock at the election of the smaller reporting company or a named executive officer. The term *equity* is used to refer generally to stock and/or options.

(ii) The term *plan* includes, but is not limited to, the following: Any plan, contract, authorization or arrangement, whether or not set forth in any formal document, pursuant to which cash, securities, similar instruments, or any other property may be received. A plan may be applicable to one person. Except with respect to disclosure required by paragraph (t) of this Item, smaller reporting companies may omit information regarding group life, health, hospitalization, or medical reimbursement plans that do not discriminate in scope, terms or operation, in favor of executive officers or directors of the smaller reporting company and that are available generally to all salaried employees.

(iii) The term *incentive plan* means any plan providing compensation intended to serve as incentive for performance to occur over a specified period, whether such performance is measured by reference to financial performance of the smaller reporting company or an affiliate, the smaller reporting company's stock price, or any other performance measure. An equity incentive plan is an incentive plan or portion of an incentive plan under which awards are granted that fall within the scope of FASB ASC Topic 718. A *non-equity incentive plan* is an incentive plan or portion of an incentive plan that is not an equity incentive plan. The term *incentive plan award* means an award provided under an incentive plan.

(iv) The terms *date of grant* or *grant date* refer to the grant date determined for financial statement reporting purposes pursuant to FASB ASC Topic 718.

(v) *Closing market price* is defined as the price at which the smaller reporting company's security was last sold in the principal United States market for such security as of the date for which the closing market price is determined.

(n) *Smaller reporting companies—Summary compensation table—*

(1) *General.* Provide the information specified in paragraph (n)(2) of this Item, concerning the compensation of the named executive officers for each of the smaller reporting company's last two completed fiscal years, in a Summary Compensation Table in the tabular format specified below.

Summary Compensation Table

Name and principal position	Year	Salary ($)	Bonus ($)	Stock awards ($)	Option awards ($)	Nonequity incentive plan compensation ($)	Nonqualified deferred compensation earnings ($)	All other compensation ($)	Total ($)
(a)	(b)	(c)	(d)	(e)	(f)	(g)	(h)	(i)	(j)
PEO									
A									
B									

(2) The Table shall include:

(i) The name and principal position of the named executive officer (column (a));

(ii) The fiscal year covered (column (b));

(iii) The dollar value of base salary (cash and non-cash) earned by the named executive officer during the fiscal year covered (column (c));

(iv) The dollar value of bonus (cash and non-cash) earned by the named executive officer during the fiscal year covered (column (d));

Instructions to Item 402(n)(2)(iii) and (iv).

1. If the amount of salary or bonus earned in a given fiscal year is not calculable through the latest practicable date, a footnote shall be included disclosing that the amount of salary or bonus is not calculable through the latest practicable date and providing the date that the amount of salary or bonus is expected to be determined, and such amount must then be disclosed in a filing under Item 5.02(f) of Form 8–K (17 CFR 249.308).

2. Smaller reporting companies shall include in the salary column (column (c)) or bonus column (column (d)) any amount of salary or bonus forgone at the election of a named executive officer under which stock, equity-based or other forms of non-cash compensation instead have been received by the named executive officer. However, the receipt of any such form of non-cash compensation instead of salary or bonus must be disclosed in a footnote added to the salary or bonus column and, where applicable, referring to the narrative disclosure to the Summary Compensation Table (required by paragraph (o) of this Item) where the material terms of the stock, option or non-equity incentive plan award elected by the named executive officer are reported.

(v) For awards of stock, the aggregate grant date fair value computed in accordance with FASB ASC Topic 718 (column (e));

(vi) For awards of options, with or without tandem SARs (including awards that subsequently have been transferred), the aggregate grant date fair value computed in accordance with FASB ASC Topic 718 (column (f));

Instruction 1 to Item 402(n)(2)(v) and (n)(2)(vi). For awards reported in columns (e) and (f), include a footnote disclosing all assumptions made in the valuation by reference to a discussion of those assumptions in the smaller reporting company's financial statements, footnotes to the financial statements, or discussion in the Management's Discussion and Analysis. The sections so referenced are deemed part of the disclosure provided pursuant to this Item.

Instruction 2 to Item 402(n)(2)(v) and (n)(2)(vi). If at any time during the last completed fiscal year, the smaller reporting company has adjusted or amended the exercise price of options or SARs previously awarded to a named executive officer, whether through amendment, cancellation or replacement grants, or any other means ("repriced"), or otherwise has materially modified such awards, the smaller reporting company shall include, as awards required to be reported in column (f), the incremental fair value, computed as of the repricing or modification date in accordance with FASB ASC Topic 718, with respect to that repriced or modified award.

Instruction 3 to Item 402(n)(2)(v) and (vi). For any awards that are subject to performance conditions, report the value at the grant date based upon the probable outcome of such conditions. This amount should be consistent with the estimate of aggregate compensation cost to be recognized over the service period determined as of the grant date under FASB ASC Topic 718, excluding the effect of estimated forfeitures. In a footnote to the table, disclose the value of the award at the grant date assuming that the highest level of performance conditions will be achieved if an amount less than the maximum was included in the table.

> (vii) The dollar value of all earnings for services performed during the fiscal year pursuant to awards under non-equity incentive plans as defined in paragraph (m)(5)(iii) of this Item, and all earnings on any outstanding awards (column (g));

Instructions to Item 402(n)(2)(vii).

1. If the relevant performance measure is satisfied during the fiscal year (including for a single year in a plan with a multi-year performance measure), the earnings are reportable for that fiscal year, even if not payable until a later date, and are not reportable again in the fiscal year when amounts are paid to the named executive officer.

2. All earnings on non-equity incentive plan compensation must be identified and quantified in a footnote to column (g), whether the earnings were paid during the fiscal year, payable during the period but deferred at the election of the named executive officer, or payable by their terms at a later date.

> (viii) Above-market or preferential earnings on compensation that is deferred on a basis that is not tax-qualified, including such earnings on nonqualified defined contribution plans (column (h));

Instruction to Item 402(n)(2)(viii). Interest on deferred compensation is above-market only if the rate of interest exceeds 120% of the applicable federal long-term rate, with compounding (as prescribed under section 1274(d) of the Internal Revenue Code, (26 U.S.C. 1274(d))) at the rate that corresponds most closely to the rate under the smaller reporting company's plan at the time the interest rate or formula is set. In the event of a discretionary reset of the interest rate, the requisite calculation must be made on the basis of the interest rate at the time of such reset, rather than when originally established. Only the above-market portion of the interest must be included. If the applicable interest rates vary depending upon conditions such as a minimum period of continued service, the reported amount should be calculated assuming satisfaction of all conditions to receiving interest at the highest rate. Dividends (and dividend equivalents) on deferred compensation denominated in the smaller reporting company's stock ("deferred stock") are preferential only if earned at a rate higher than dividends on the smaller reporting company's common stock. Only the preferential portion of the dividends or equivalents must be included. Footnote or narrative disclosure may be provided explaining the smaller reporting company's criteria for determining any portion considered to be above-market.

(ix) All other compensation for the covered fiscal year that the smaller reporting company could not properly report in any other column of the Summary Compensation Table (column (i)). Each compensation item that is not properly reportable in columns (c) through (h), regardless of the amount of the compensation item, must be included in column (i). Such compensation must include, but is not limited to:

(A) Perquisites and other personal benefits, or property, unless the aggregate amount of such compensation is less than $10,000;

(B) All "gross-ups" or other amounts reimbursed during the fiscal year for the payment of taxes;

(C) For any security of the smaller reporting company or its subsidiaries purchased from the smaller reporting company or its subsidiaries (through deferral of salary or bonus, or otherwise) at a discount from the market price of such security at the date of purchase, unless that discount is available generally, either to all security holders or to all salaried employees of the smaller reporting company, the compensation cost, if any, computed in accordance with FASB ASC Topic 718;

(D) The amount paid or accrued to any named executive officer pursuant to a plan or arrangement in connection with:

(1) Any termination, including without limitation through retirement, resignation, severance or constructive termination (including a change in responsibilities) of such executive officer's employment with the smaller reporting company and its subsidiaries; or

(2) A change in control of the smaller reporting company;

(E) Smaller reporting company contributions or other allocations to vested and unvested defined contribution plans;

(F) The dollar value of any insurance premiums paid by, or on behalf of, the smaller reporting company during the covered fiscal year with respect to life insurance for the benefit of a named executive officer; and

(G) The dollar value of any dividends or other earnings paid on stock or option awards, when those amounts were not factored into the grant date fair value required to be reported for the stock or option award in column (e) or (f); and

Instructions to Item 402(n)(2)(ix).

1. Non-equity incentive plan awards and earnings and earnings on stock or options, except as specified in paragraph (n)(2)(ix)(G) of this Item, are required to be reported elsewhere as provided in this Item and are not reportable as All Other Compensation in column (i).

2. Benefits paid pursuant to defined benefit and actuarial plans are not reportable as All Other Compensation in column (i) unless accelerated pursuant to a change in control; information concerning these plans is reportable pursuant to paragraph (q)(1) of this Item.

3. Reimbursements of taxes owed with respect to perquisites or other personal benefits must be included in the columns as tax reimbursements (paragraph (n)(2)(ix)(B) of this Item) even if the associated perquisites or other personal benefits are not required to be included because the aggregate amount of such compensation is less than $10,000.

4. Perquisites and other personal benefits shall be valued on the basis of the aggregate incremental cost to the smaller reporting company.

5. For purposes of paragraph (n)(2)(ix)(D) of this Item, an accrued amount is an amount for which payment has become due.

(x) The dollar value of total compensation for the covered fiscal year (column (j)). With respect to each named executive officer, disclose the sum of all amounts reported in columns (c) through (i).

Instructions to Item 402(n).

1. Information with respect to the fiscal year prior to the last completed fiscal year will not be required if the smaller reporting company was not a reporting company pursuant to section 13(a) or 15(d) of the Exchange Act (15 U.S.C. 78m(a) or 78o(d)) at any time during that year, except that the smaller reporting company will be required to provide information for any such year if that information previously was required to be provided in response to a Commission filing requirement.

2. All compensation values reported in the Summary Compensation Table must be reported in dollars and rounded to the nearest dollar. Reported compensation values must be reported numerically, providing a single numerical value for each grid in the table. Where compensation was paid to or received by a named executive officer in a different currency, a footnote must be provided to identify that currency and describe the rate and methodology used to convert the payment amounts to dollars.

3. If a named executive officer is also a director who receives compensation for his or her services as a director, reflect that compensation in the Summary Compensation Table and provide a footnote identifying and itemizing such compensation and amounts. Use the categories in the Director Compensation Table required pursuant to paragraph (r) of this Item.

4. Any amounts deferred, whether pursuant to a plan established under section 401(k) of the Internal Revenue Code (26 U.S.C. 401(k)), or otherwise, shall be included in the appropriate column for the fiscal year in which earned.

(o) *Smaller reporting companies—Narrative disclosure to summary compensation table.* Provide a narrative description of any material factors necessary to an understanding of the information disclosed in the Table required by paragraph (n) of this Item. Examples of such factors may include, in given cases, among other things:

(1) The material terms of each named executive officer's employment agreement or arrangement, whether written or unwritten;

(2) If at any time during the last fiscal year, any outstanding option or other equity-based award was repriced or otherwise materially

modified (such as by extension of exercise periods, the change of vesting or forfeiture conditions, the change or elimination of applicable performance criteria, or the change of the bases upon which returns are determined), a description of each such repricing or other material modification;

(3) The waiver or modification of any specified performance target, goal or condition to payout with respect to any amount included in non-stock incentive plan compensation or payouts reported in column (g) to the Summary Compensation Table required by paragraph (n) of this Item, stating whether the waiver or modification applied to one or more specified named executive officers or to all compensation subject to the target, goal or condition;

(4) The material terms of each grant, including but not limited to the date of exercisability, any conditions to exercisability, any tandem feature, any reload feature, any tax-reimbursement feature, and any provision that could cause the exercise price to be lowered;

(5) The material terms of any non-equity incentive plan award made to a named executive officer during the last completed fiscal year, including a general description of the formula or criteria to be applied in determining the amounts payable and vesting schedule;

(6) The method of calculating earnings on nonqualified deferred compensation plans including nonqualified defined contribution plans; and

(7) An identification to the extent material of any item included under All Other Compensation (column (i)) in the Summary Compensation Table. Identification of an item shall not be considered material if it does not exceed the greater of $25,000 or 10% of all items included in the specified category in question set forth in paragraph (n)(2)(ix) of this Item. All items of compensation are required to be included in the Summary Compensation Table without regard to whether such items are required to be identified.

Instruction to Item 402(o). The disclosure required by paragraph (o) (2) of this Item would not apply to any repricing that occurs through a pre-existing formula or mechanism in the plan or award that results in the periodic adjustment of the option or SAR exercise or base price, an antidilution provision in a plan or award, or a recapitalization or similar transaction equally affecting all holders of the class of securities underlying the options or SARs.

(p) *Smaller reporting companies—Outstanding equity awards at fiscal year-end table.*

(1) Provide the information specified in paragraph (p)(2) of this Item, concerning unexercised options; stock that has not vested; and equity incentive plan awards for each named executive officer outstanding as of the end of the smaller reporting company's last completed fiscal year in the following tabular format:

Outstanding Equity Awards at Fiscal Year-End

	Option awards					Stock Awards			
Name	Number of securities underlying unexercised options (#) exercisable	Number of securities underlying unexercised options (#) unexerciseable	Equity incentive plan awards: Number of securities underlying unexercised unearned options (#)	Option exercise price ($)	Option expiration date	Number of shares or units of stock that have not vested (#)	Market value of shares of units of stock that have not vested ($)	Equity incentive plan awards: Number of unearned shares, units or other rights that have not vested (#)	Equity incentive plan awards: Market or payout value of unearned shares, units, or other rights that have not vested ($)
(a)	(b)	(c)	(d)	(e)	(f)	(g)	(h)	(i)	(j)
PEO									
A									
B									

(2) The Table shall include:

(i) The name of the named executive officer (column (a));

(ii) On an award-by-award basis, the number of securities underlying unexercised options, including awards that have been transferred other than for value, that are exercisable and that are not reported in column (d) (column (b));

(iii) On an award-by-award basis, the number of securities underlying unexercised options, including awards that have been transferred other than for value, that are unexercisable and that are not reported in column (d) (column (c));

(iv) On an award-by-award basis, the total number of shares underlying unexercised options awarded under any equity incentive plan that have not been earned (column (d));

(v) For each instrument reported in columns (b), (c) and (d), as applicable, the exercise or base price (column (e));

(vi) For each instrument reported in columns (b), (c) and (d), as applicable, the expiration date (column (f));

(vii) The total number of shares of stock that have not vested and that are not reported in column (i) (column (g));

(viii) The aggregate market value of shares of stock that have not vested and that are not reported in column (j) (column (h));

(ix) The total number of shares of stock, units or other rights awarded under any equity incentive plan that have not vested and that have not been earned, and, if applicable the number of shares underlying any such unit or right (column (i)); and

(x) The aggregate market or payout value of shares of stock, units or other rights awarded under any equity incentive plan that have not vested and that have not been earned (column (j)).

Instructions to Item 402(p)(2).

1. Identify by footnote any award that has been transferred other than for value, disclosing the nature of the transfer.

2. The vesting dates of options, shares of stock and equity incentive plan awards held at fiscal-year end must be disclosed by footnote to the applicable column where the outstanding award is reported.

3. Compute the market value of stock reported in column (h) and equity incentive plan awards of stock reported in column (j) by multiplying the closing market price of the smaller reporting company's stock at the end of the last completed fiscal year by the number of shares or units of stock or the amount of equity incentive plan awards, respectively. The number of shares or units reported in column (d) or (i), and the payout value reported in column (j), shall be based on achieving threshold performance goals, except that if the previous fiscal year's performance has exceeded the threshold, the disclosure shall be based on the next higher performance measure (target or maximum) that exceeds the previous fiscal year's performance. If the award provides only for a single estimated payout, that amount should be reported. If the target amount is not determinable, smaller reporting companies must provide a representative amount based on the previous fiscal year's performance.

4. Multiple awards may be aggregated where the expiration date and the exercise and/or base price of the instruments is identical. A single

award consisting of a combination of options, SARs and/or similar option-like instruments shall be reported as separate awards with respect to each tranche with a different exercise and/or base price or expiration date.

5. Options or stock awarded under an equity incentive plan are reported in columns (d) or (i) and (j), respectively, until the relevant performance condition has been satisfied. Once the relevant performance condition has been satisfied, even if the option or stock award is subject to forfeiture conditions, options are reported in column (b) or (c), as appropriate, until they are exercised or expire, or stock is reported in columns (g) and (h) until it vests.

(q) *Smaller reporting companies—Additional narrative disclosure.* Provide a narrative description of the following to the extent material:

(1) The material terms of each plan that provides for the payment of retirement benefits, or benefits that will be paid primarily following retirement, including but not limited to tax-qualified defined benefit plans, supplemental executive retirement plans, tax-qualified defined contribution plans and nonqualified defined contribution plans.

(2) The material terms of each contract, agreement, plan or arrangement, whether written or unwritten, that provides for payment(s) to a named executive officer at, following, or in connection with the resignation, retirement or other termination of a named executive officer, or a change in control of the smaller reporting company or a change in the named executive officer's responsibilities following a change in control, with respect to each named executive officer.

(r) *Smaller reporting companies—Compensation of directors.*

(1) Provide the information specified in paragraph (r)(2) of this Item, concerning the compensation of the directors for the smaller reporting company's last completed fiscal year, in the following tabular format:

Director Compensation

Name	Fees earned or paid in cash ($)	Stock awards ($)	Option awards ($)	Non-equity incentive plan compensation ($)	Nonqualified deferred compensation earnings ($)	All other compensation ($)	Total ($)
(a)	(b)	(c)	(d)	(e)	(f)	(g)	(h)
A							
B							
C							
D							
E							

(2) The Table shall include:

(i) The name of each director unless such director is also a named executive officer under paragraph (m) of this Item and his or her compensation for service as a director is fully reflected in the Summary Compensation Table pursuant to paragraph (n) of this Item and otherwise as required pursuant to paragraphs (o) through (q) of this Item (column (a));

(ii) The aggregate dollar amount of all fees earned or paid in cash for services as a director, including annual retainer fees, committee and/or chairmanship fees, and meeting fees (column (b));

(iii) For awards of stock, the aggregate grant date fair value computed in accordance with FASB ASC Topic 718 (column (c));

(iv) For awards of options, with or without tandem SARs (including awards that subsequently have been transferred), the aggregate grant date fair value computed in accordance with FASB ASC Topic 718 (column (d));

Instruction to Item 402(r)(2)(iii) and (iv). For each director, disclose by footnote to the appropriate column, the aggregate number of stock awards and the aggregate number of option awards outstanding at fiscal year end.

(v) The dollar value of all earnings for services performed during the fiscal year pursuant to non-equity incentive plans as defined in paragraph (m)(5)(iii) of this Item, and all earnings on any outstanding awards (column (e));

(vi) Above-market or preferential earnings on compensation that is deferred on a basis that is not tax-qualified, including such earnings on nonqualified defined contribution plans (column (f));

(vii) All other compensation for the covered fiscal year that the smaller reporting company could not properly report in any other column of the Director Compensation Table (column (g)). Each compensation item that is not properly reportable in columns (b) through (f), regardless of the amount of the compensation item, must be included in column (g) and must be identified and quantified in a footnote if it is deemed material in accordance with paragraph (o)(7) of this Item. Such compensation must include, but is not limited to:

(A) Perquisites and other personal benefits, or property, unless the aggregate amount of such compensation is less than $10,000;

(B) All "gross-ups" or other amounts reimbursed during the fiscal year for the payment of taxes;

(C) For any security of the smaller reporting company or its subsidiaries purchased from the smaller reporting company or its subsidiaries (through deferral of salary or bonus, or otherwise) at a discount from the market price of such security at the date of purchase, unless that discount is available generally, either to all security holders or to all salaried employees of the smaller reporting company, the compensation cost, if any, computed in accordance with FASB ASC Topic 718;

(D) The amount paid or accrued to any director pursuant to a plan or arrangement in connection with:

(1) The resignation, retirement or any other termination of such director; or

(2) A change in control of the smaller reporting company;

(E) Smaller reporting company contributions or other allocations to vested and unvested defined contribution plans;

(F) Consulting fees earned from, or paid or payable by the smaller reporting company and/or its subsidiaries (including joint ventures);

(G) The annual costs of payments and promises of payments pursuant to director legacy programs and similar charitable award programs;

(H) The dollar value of any insurance premiums paid by, or on behalf of, the smaller reporting company during the covered fiscal year with respect to life insurance for the benefit of a director; and

(I) The dollar value of any dividends or other earnings paid on stock or option awards, when those amounts were not factored into the grant date fair value required to be reported for the stock or option award in column (c) or (d); and

Instruction to Item 402(r)(2)(vii). Programs in which smaller reporting companies agree to make donations to one or more charitable institutions in a director's name, payable by the smaller reporting company currently or upon a designated event, such as the retirement or death of the director, are charitable awards programs or director legacy programs for purposes of the disclosure required by paragraph (r)(2)(vii)(G) of this Item. Provide footnote disclosure of the total dollar amount payable under the program and other material terms of each such program for which tabular disclosure is provided.

> (viii) The dollar value of total compensation for the covered fiscal year (column (h)). With respect to each director, disclose the sum of all amounts reported in columns (b) through (g).

Instruction to Item 402(r)(2). Two or more directors may be grouped in a single row in the Table if all elements of their compensation are identical. The names of the directors for whom disclosure is presented on a group basis should be clear from the Table.

> (3) *Narrative to director compensation table.* Provide a narrative description of any material factors necessary to an understanding of the director compensation disclosed in this Table. While material factors will vary depending upon the facts, examples of such factors may include, in given cases, among other things:
>
> (i) A description of standard compensation arrangements (such as fees for retainer, committee service, service as chairman of the board or a committee, and meeting attendance); and
>
> (ii) Whether any director has a different compensation arrangement, identifying that director and describing the terms of that arrangement.

Instruction to Item 402(r). In addition to the Instruction to paragraph (r)(2)(vii) of this Item, the following apply equally to paragraph (r) of this Item: Instructions 2 and 4 to paragraph (n) of this Item; the Instructions to paragraphs (n)(2)(iii) and (iv) of this Item; the Instructions to paragraphs (n)(2)(v) and (vi) of this Item; the Instructions to paragraph (n)(2)(vii) of this Item; the Instruction to paragraph (n)(2)(viii) of this Item; the Instructions to paragraph (n)(2)(ix) of this Item; and paragraph (o)(7) of this Item. These Instructions apply to the columns in the Director Compensation Table that are analogous to the columns in the Summary Compensation Table to which they refer and to disclosures under paragraph (r) of this Item that correspond to analogous disclosures provided for in paragraph (n) of this Item to which they refer.

(s) *Narrative disclosure of the registrant's compensation policies and practices as they relate to the registrant's risk management.* To the extent that risks arising from the registrant's compensation policies and practices for its employees are reasonably likely to have a material adverse effect on the registrant, discuss the registrant's policies and practices of compensating its employees, including non-executive officers, as they relate to risk management practices and risk-taking incentives. While the situations requiring disclosure will vary depending on the particular registrant and compensation policies and practices, situations that may trigger disclosure include, among others, compensation policies and practices: at a business unit of the company that carries a significant portion of the registrant's risk profile; at a business unit with compensation structured significantly differently than other units within the registrant; at a business unit that is significantly more profitable than others within the registrant; at a business unit where compensation expense is a significant percentage of the unit's revenues; and that vary significantly from the overall risk and reward structure of the registrant, such as when bonuses are awarded upon accomplishment of a task, while the income and risk to the registrant from the task extend over a significantly longer period of time. The purpose of this paragraph(s) is to provide investors material information concerning how the registrant compensates and incentivizes its employees that may create risks that are reasonably likely to have a material adverse effect on the registrant. While the information to be disclosed pursuant to this paragraph(s) will vary depending upon the nature of the registrant's business and the compensa-tion approach, the following are examples of the issues that the registrant may need to address for the business units or employees discussed:

(1) The general design philosophy of the registrant's compensation policies and practices for employees whose behavior would be most affected by the incentives established by the policies and practices, as such policies and practices relate to or affect risk taking by employees on behalf of the registrant, and the manner of their implementation;

(2) The registrant's risk assessment or incentive considerations, if any, in structuring its compensation policies and practices or in awarding and paying compensation;

(3) How the registrant's compensation policies and practices relate to the realization of risks resulting from the actions of employees in both the short term and the long term, such as through policies requiring claw backs or imposing holding periods;

(4) The registrant's policies regarding adjustments to its compensation policies and practices to address changes in its risk profile;

(5) Material adjustments the registrant has made to its compensation policies and practices as a result of changes in its risk profile; and

(6) The extent to which the registrant monitors its compensation policies and practices to determine whether its risk management objectives are being met with respect to incentivizing its employees.

(t) *Golden parachute compensation.*

(1) In connection with any proxy or consent solicitation material providing the disclosure required by section 14A(b)(1) of the Exchange Act (15 U.S.C. 78n–1(b)(1)) or any proxy or consent solicitation that includes disclosure under Item 14 of Schedule 14A (§240.14a–101) pursuant to Note A of Schedule 14A, with respect to each named executive officer of the acquiring company and the target company, provide the information specified in paragraphs (t)(2) and (3) of this section regarding any agreement or understanding, whether written or unwritten, between such named executive officer and the acquiring company or target company, concerning any type of compensation, whether present, deferred or contingent, that is based on or otherwise relates to an acquisition, merger, consolidation, sale or other disposition of all or substantially all assets of the issuer, as follows:

Golden Parachute Compensation

Name	Cash ($)	Equity ($)	Pension/ NQDC ($)	Perquisites/ benefits ($)	Tax reimburse-ment ($)	Other ($)	Total ($)
(a)	(b)	(c)	(d)	(e)	(f)	(g)	(h)
PEO							
PFO							
A							
B							
C							

(2) The table shall include, for each named executive officer:

(i) The name of the named executive officer (column (a));

(ii) The aggregate dollar value of any cash severance payments, including but not limited to payments of base salary, bonus, and pro-rated non-equity incentive compensation plan payments (column (b));

(iii) The aggregate dollar value of:

(A) Stock awards for which vesting would be accelerated;

(B) In-the-money option awards for which vesting would be accelerated; and

(C) Payments in cancellation of stock and option awards (column (c));

(iv) The aggregate dollar value of pension and nonqualified deferred compensation benefit enhancements (column (d));

(v) The aggregate dollar value of perquisites and other personal benefits or property, and health care and welfare benefits (column (e));

(vi) The aggregate dollar value of any tax reimbursements (column (f));

(vii) The aggregate dollar value of any other compensation that is based on or otherwise relates to the transaction not properly reported in columns (b) through (f) (column (g)); and

(viii) The aggregate dollar value of the sum of all amounts reported in columns (b) through (g) (column (h)).

Instructions to Item 402(t)(2).

1. If this disclosure is included in a proxy or consent solicitation seeking approval of an acquisition, merger, consolidation, or proposed sale or other disposition of all or substantially all the assets of the registrant, or in a proxy or consent solicitation that includes disclosure under Item 14 of Schedule 14A (§240.14a–101) pursuant to Note A of Schedule 14A, the disclosure provided by this table shall be quantified assuming that the triggering event took place on the latest practicable date, and that the price per share of the registrant's securities shall be determined as follows: If the shareholders are to receive a fixed dollar amount, the price per share shall be that fixed dollar amount, and if such value is not a fixed dollar amount, the price per share shall be the average closing market price of the registrant's securities over the first five business days following the first public announcement of the transaction. Compute the dollar value of in-the-money option awards for which vesting would be accelerated by determining the difference between this price and the exercise or base price of the options. Include only compensation that is based on or otherwise relates to the subject transaction. Apply Instruction 1 to Item 402(t) with respect to those executive officers for whom disclosure was required in the issuer's most recent filing with the Commission under the Securities Act (15 U.S.C. 77a *et seq.*) or Exchange Act (15 U.S.C. 78a *et seq.*) that required disclosure pursuant to Item 402(c).

2. If this disclosure is included in a proxy solicitation for the annual meeting at which directors are elected for purposes of subjecting the disclosed agreements or understandings to a shareholder vote under section 14A(a)(1) of the Exchange Act (15 U.S.C. 78n–1(a)(1)), the disclosure provided by this table shall be quantified assuming that the triggering event took place on the last business day of the registrant's last completed fiscal year, and the price per share of the registrant's securities is the closing market price as of that date. Compute the dollar value of in-the-money option awards for which vesting would be accelerated by determining the difference between this price and the exercise or base price of the options.

3. In the event that uncertainties exist as to the provision of payments and benefits or the amounts involved, the registrant is required to make a reasonable estimate applicable to the payment or benefit and disclose material assumptions underlying such estimates in its disclosure. In such event, the disclosure would require forward-looking information as appropriate.

4. For each of columns (b) through (g), include a footnote quantifying each separate form of compensation included in the aggregate total reported. Include the value of all perquisites and other personal benefits or property. Individual perquisites and personal benefits shall be identified and quantified as required by Instruction 4 to Item 402(c)(2)(ix) of this section. For purposes of quantifying health care benefits, the registrant must use the assumptions used for financial reporting purposes under generally accepted accounting principles.

5. For each of columns (b) through (h), include a footnote quantifying the amount payable attributable to a double-trigger arrangement (*i.e.*, amounts triggered by a change-in-control for which payment is conditioned upon the executive officer's termination without cause or resignation for good reason within a limited time period following the change-in-control), specifying the time-frame in which such termination or resignation must occur in order for the amount to become payable, and the amount payable attributable to a single-trigger arrangement (*i.e.*, amounts triggered by a change-in-control for which payment is not conditioned upon such a termination or resignation of the executive officer).

6. A registrant conducting a shareholder advisory vote pursuant to §240.14a–21(c) of this chapter to cover new arrangements and understandings, and/or revised terms of agreements and understandings that were previously subject to a shareholder advisory vote pursuant to §240.14a–21(a) of this chapter, shall provide two separate tables. One table shall disclose all golden parachute compensation, including both the arrangements and amounts previously disclosed and subject to a shareholder

advisory vote under section 14A(a)(1) of the Exchange Act (15 U.S.C. 78n–1(a)(1)) and §240.14a–21(a) of this chapter and the new arrangements and understandings and/or revised terms of agreements and understandings that were previously subject to a shareholder advisory vote. The second table shall disclose only the new arrangements and/or revised terms subject to the separate shareholder vote under section 14A(b)(2) of the Exchange Act and §240.14a–21(c) of this chapter.

7. In cases where this Item 402(t)(2) requires disclosure of arrangements between an acquiring company and the named executive officers of the soliciting target company, the registrant shall clarify whether these agreements are included in the separate shareholder advisory vote pursuant to §240.14a–21(c) of this chapter by providing a separate table of all agreements and understandings subject to the shareholder advisory vote required by section 14A(b)(2) of the Exchange Act (15 U.S.C. 78n–1(b)(2)) and §240.14a–21(c) of this chapter, if different from the full scope of golden parachute compensation subject to Item 402(t) disclosure.

(3) Provide a succinct narrative description of any material factors necessary to an understanding of each such contract, agreement, plan or arrangement and the payments quantified in the tabular disclosure required by this paragraph. Such factors shall include, but not be limited to a description of:

(i) The specific circumstances that would trigger payment(s);

(ii) Whether the payments would or could be lump sum, or annual, disclosing the duration, and by whom they would be provided; and

(iii) Any material conditions or obligations applicable to the receipt of payment or benefits, including but not limited to non-compete, non-solicitation, non-disparagement or confidentiality agreements, including the duration of such agreements and provisions regarding waiver or breach of such agreements.

Instructions to Item 402(t).

1. A registrant that does not qualify as a "smaller reporting company," as defined by §229.10(f)(1) of this chapter, must provide the information required by this Item 402(t) with respect to the individuals covered by Items 402(a)(3)(i), (ii) and (iii) of this section. A registrant that qualifies as a "smaller reporting company," as defined by §229.10(f)(1) of this chapter, must provide the information required by this Item 402(t) with respect to the individuals covered by Items 402(m)(2)(i) and (ii) of this section.

2. The obligation to provide the information in this Item 402(t) shall not apply to agreements and understandings described in paragraph (t)(1) of this section with senior management of foreign private issuers, as defined in §240.3b–4 of this chapter.

Instruction to Item 402. Specify the applicable fiscal year in the title to each table required under this Item which calls for disclosure as of or for a completed fiscal year.

[71 FR 53241, Sept. 8, 2006; 71 FR 56225, Sept. 26, 2006, as amended at 71 FR 78350, Dec. 29, 2006; 73 FR 958, Jan. 4, 2008; 74 FR 68362, Dec. 23, 2009; 76 FR 6043, Feb. 2, 2011; 76 FR 50121, Aug. 12, 2011]

Principles Matter
John W. White

Director, Division of Corporation Finance
U.S. Securities and Exchange Commission

Practising Law Institute Conference
New York, NY
September 6, 2006

Thank you, Scott. It is truly a pleasure to be here at PLI today, at what I believe is the first comprehensive program that's been put together to address the new executive compensation disclosure rules that the Commission approved a little over a month ago.

I realize that there will be many conferences, as well as countless training programs by executive compensation specialists, and by law firms, as the fall progresses. And there will be countless more presentations to boards of directors and officers of public companies about the new rules. Obviously, members of the SEC staff will not be able to be present at most of these.

But I do hope there is a theme that will permeate all of them—which is what I would like to talk about this morning. That theme is what I consider to be the most important thread that runs throughout this rulemaking—the meaning and significance of principles-based disclosure. Before I turn to that, however, I must first give the standard disclaimer that you have heard so many times before, that the views I'm going to express today are solely my own and do not necessarily reflect the views of the Securities and Exchange Commission or of any members of its staff other than myself.

I realize this may sound like a broken record to those of you who have heard me talk in the past, but I place an incredibly high premium on conferences such as this one and on continuing education programs in general. Simply put, none of us can know everything, and none of us can go it alone. And we really shouldn't try to. PLI should be commended on having assembled such an impressive cast for today's program, and I'm sure you're looking forward as much as I am to learning from our stellar faculty today. But please note—your participation today is no less important than theirs. I believe that disclosure counsel and advisors have a critical role to play as the new rules become the norm. And that's precisely because these rules are so principles-based—there are far fewer bright line rules than some may have wanted, there are no cookie cutters that can be used to produce good disclosure, there are no computer programs that can generate the right words on the page.

As the SEC Commissioners and various staff members (including myself) have noted repeatedly, executive compensation has changed dramatically in the past decade—in its amount, in its form, in its complexity—while our related disclosure rules had remained stagnant. I believe that part of what motivated the Commission to update its rules was a recognition of this fact and that our rules need to reflect and respond to the changes in American business and our capital markets. But in the same vein as what I said a moment ago, the Commission cannot do it alone. We relied tremendously on the overwhelming, and very constructive, feedback we received from all quarters during the comment period on the rule proposal. And now that the rules have been finalized, we are relying on all of you to help make them work right in practice.

Companies will greatly benefit from the advice and counsel of intelligent people with sound judgment who understand the significance of principles-based disclosure—how to ask the right questions, how to get the right answers and how to translate those answers into disclosure that is clear, understandable and useful to investors. I sincerely hope and anticipate that each of you can be leaders in this considerable effort. I've learned over the years that a key early step in successfully rolling out an important new project—and executive compensation disclosure for the 2007 proxy season is such a project—is finding your partners and training the guides. If you'll accept the challenge of standing with the Commission on this one, I'd like you to start with a two-word message: *principles matter*.

The Principle of a Principles-Based System

There are a wide variety of views on how to explain the term "principles-based" although everyone seems to have the same general idea. I personally like the description Robert Herz, chairman of the FASB, gave in 2002:

> Under a principles-based approach, one starts with laying out the key objectives of good reporting in the subject area and then provides guidance explaining the objective and relating it to some common examples. While rules are sometimes unavoidable, the intent is not to try to provide specific guidance or rules for every possible situation. Rather, if in doubt, the reader is directed back to the principles.[1]

Bob was talking about accounting and financial reporting, of course, and that's often where we hear the phrase "principles-based." But it applies equally well to other types of disclosure, and the Commission has embraced it in the recent executive compensation disclosure rulemaking, among other places.

In their study on principles-based accounting a few years ago,[2] my predecessors on the SEC staff noted the difficulties of a pure principles-based—or "principles-only"—system and concluded that some structure is useful. Similarly, in the new rules, the Commission requires some level of tabular presentation both to provide comparability as well as to serve as a framework for an effective principles-based approach. There are a variety of new tables, and the often focused-on Summary Compensation Table has been modified to present all compensation components in dollar amounts and then to add across to a single, aggregate dollar amount for each named executive officer. But even for these tables to work, principles must be followed to determine, and describe, the right entries.

Principles-based disclosure is not a new concept at the Commission. And as you help companies understand how to meet their new principles-based compensation disclosure obligations, you are not at a loss for past learning. Former Commissioner Cyndi Glassman noted in a speech last March (which I would commend to everyone), that "[o]f all of our disclosure rules, MD&A may be the most principles-based."[3] As such, companies have already been challenged, especially in the past several years, to tell a compelling story with their MD&A's, to make that story relevant, qualitative and contextual, and to avoid mere quantitative disclosure that just repeats the data that is already in the financial statements. Commissioner Glassman referred to an "elevator analysis"—that is, "x" went up and "y" went down—which is, as she said, "descriptive, but not very informative." If you've been doing your MD&A right, you have not ended your drafting when the elevator doors open and you already have a good idea what principles-based disclosure means and what it should look like. As the Commission noted in the Adopting Release, MD&A is an especially good starting point for the new, equally principles-based, Compensation Discussion & Analysis, or CD&A. I'll return to this important subject in just a moment.

I have referred to the principles-based theme as a thread that runs throughout the executive compensation disclosure rulemaking, and if you study the Release carefully, you will see that the phrase appears in multiple places. As a concept, I believe it runs even deeper than just the places that are expressly labeled as such. But calling something principles-based is only a start. For it to have the meaning and impact that it should requires that those who are making the necessary disclosures embrace the concept as much as the regulators who have promulgated the standards.

So what does it mean that key components of executive compensation disclosure are principles-based, and how does that intersect with the role of disclosure counsel and advisors who are charged with the important job of shepherding a company through these new requirements? Going back to Bob Herz's description, what are the key objectives of good reporting in these areas? And I would add to that: how does ascribing to a principles-based approach both help answer the hard disclosure questions and also produce a better end-product for investors?

I'd like to try to answer these questions by looking at a couple of specific examples in our new rules. And in each case, I hope you will see that the principles do matter.

Compensation Discussion & Analysis

Descriptions of the new Compensation Discussion & Analysis section may be the current, favorite home of the term "principles-based." And I believe that is telling and appropriate. Just as CD&A is at the heart of the Commission's recent rulemaking, its principles-based foundation is at the heart of what quality disclosure in this area should be. CD&A is what gives context to the required tables and the numbers in them. As Chairman Cox explained at the Open Meeting at which the Commission adopted the new disclosure rules, CD&A "will give companies an opportunity to explain their compensation policies, and to share with investors how they arrived at the particular levels and forms of compensation for their highest paid executives."[4]

The Commission went on to explain in its Adopting Release:

> The purpose of the Compensation Discussion and Analysis disclosure is to provide material information about the compensation objectives and policies for named executive officers without resorting to boilerplate

disclosure. The [CD&A] is intended to put into perspective for investors the numbers and narrative that follow it.[5]

The rules do provide six questions that CD&A *must* answer, and I'm sure we'll be hearing more about those in the panel that follows. The rules also provide 15 examples of topics a company *might* consider addressing in its CD&A. Those examples are neither exhaustive nor mandatory. It is the company, and those drafting its disclosure, that must determine what is material to the company and those making investment and voting decisions. They must then craft the appropriate disclosure that is responsive to those questions and is tailored to the company's particular facts and circumstances.

As I have said, CD&A is at the heart of principles-based compensation disclosure, and we could probably spend hours talking about how that might work, how it should work. But I'd like to look at CD&A from one specific, narrow (but important) vantage point and to think about how its principles-based design should make the right questions easier to identify and the answers easier to develop.

In the Release, the Commission describes the time period CD&A must cover—the last fiscal year. But then the Commission explains that

> [CD&A] may also require discussion of post-termination compensation arrangements, on-going compensation arrangements, and policies that the company will apply on a going-forward basis. [CD&A] should also cover actions regarding executive compensation that were taken after the last fiscal year's end. Actions that should be addressed might include, as examples only, the adoption or implementation of new or modified programs and policies or specific decisions that were made or steps that were taken that could affect a fair understanding of the named executive officer's compensation for the last fiscal year. Moreover, in some situations it may be necessary to discuss prior years in order to give context to the disclosure provided.[6]

What does that mean? Well, going back again to Bob Herz's description, we know that one disclosure objective with the CD&A is to provide perspective and context for investors in understanding the rest of the company's executive compensation disclosure. So what additional disclosure, talking about other years, might be necessary or helpful to give that perspective and context, given the general requirement to cover the last fiscal year? That's where *principles matter*.

We all know that the end of a year may be a fairly arbitrary date that is no different than any other day. Or it may not be. But the point is that I can't answer that for your company. Only you can. There's no bright line in CD&A that says if something happens on January 1, after year-end, then it doesn't matter. Same if it happens on February 1. Or if it happened two years ago.

Imagine a hypothetical where five years ago, a company was going through a particularly difficult time, and an executive agreed to work at minimum wage until the company turned itself around. That turn-around happened last year, and the company's Board rewarded her with a handsome compensation package. The compensation might even seem disproportionate to what this executive did last year, or to the company's peers. I believe most companies in that situation would be happy, perhaps even eager, to explain in their CD&A the context for last year's apparently oversized compensation. The principle would be the same, though, if the numbers and the story went another way. Perhaps this executive endured her pay cut throughout all of last year, but the company turned around in February and the Board just awarded her a substantial bonus or pay raise. It happened after the year end, but it might be invaluable context to understanding the executive's compensation for the year in question. However the facts play out, the disclosure outcome, in principle, should be the same—tell investors the story, completely and fairly, in the context of understanding what was going on with your compensation programs. Let your investors know why the company did what it did, and what effect you expect that to have.

So applying this principle, if something that happened five years ago, or two years ago, is not material to an understanding of your compensation last year, then you do not need to talk about those prior years, or agonize over the excerpt I read a few minutes ago, that CD&A is not limited to the past fiscal year. On the other hand, if something that happened several years ago, or something that happened early this year, before your proxy is prepared, is relevant or necessary to a fair understanding of the year in question, then you do need to talk about it. The same could be true with regard to something that everyone expects to happen next year. The principle that must be applied demands this, and it should in turn guide your analysis and make the requisite disclosures more obvious.

Perquisites

To move on to another example, how do the principles help us understand perquisites disclosure? After all, the phrase "principles-based" does not roll off the tongue quite as often with talk of perks as it does with CD&A, but I believe it should. In the recent Release, the Commission once again declined to provide any bright-line rules as to what constitutes a perquisite or personal benefit. As the Commission said,

> "We continue to believe that it is not appropriate for Item 402 to define perquisites or personal benefits, given that different forms of these items continue to develop, and thus a definition would become outdated."[7]

The principle, however, will not become outdated.

Perquisites are an important piece of executive compensation. Subject to a de minimis exception provided in the rules, companies need to disclose to investors the perquisites they provide executives, and their value. For clarity, the Commission has retained its position that the value of a perquisite is its aggregate incremental cost to the company. But it's up to you to figure out what that is.

As to what is a perquisite, the Commission has provided interpretive guidance for analyzing and answering this question. In this regard, as I am sure you have read, a company should engage in a two-step analysis:

1.   An item is not a perquisite or personal benefit if it is integrally and directly related to the performance of the executive's duties.
2.   Otherwise, an item is a perquisite or personal benefit if it confers a direct or indirect benefit that has a personal aspect, without regard to whether it may be provided for some business reason or for the convenience of the company, unless it is generally available on a non-discriminatory basis to all employees.

Key phrases in this analysis include "integrally and directly related to the performance of the executive's duties", "direct or indirect benefit that has a personal aspect", and "generally available on a non-discriminatory basis to all employees." You may lament the fact that I cannot give you a hard and fast definition of any of those phrases, but if you let the principles guide you, you will not run astray.

One area of perks analysis that has received considerable attention in recent years is that of executives' personal usage of corporate aircraft. Within that area is a fairly narrow question of whether the costs of a "deadhead" flight leg must be included in the calculation of the perk's value. A deadhead flight leg is when a plane flies essentially empty—typically in order to return to its home base, such as the corporate headquarters.

So the corporate aircraft may take an executive and her family out to Colorado for a ski vacation and then return to corporate headquarters in Virginia. As far as I know, everyone would agree that the flight from Virginia to Colorado was a perquisite for the executive. And it should be valued and disclosed in keeping with the Commission's rules.

With regard to the deadhead leg, I assume that flight from Colorado to Virginia is not cost-free. Perhaps your pilot and flight crew are on salary and the cost of employing them does not change at all based on flight legs. Or alternatively, perhaps they're paid by the hour, or by the mile, and so the flight from Colorado to Virginia does cause the company to incur additional costs. Every company probably has added fuel costs to fly the plane back home, even empty. There might also be added landing fees, or weather report fees, and so on. Many of these incremental costs could easily vary from company to company, depending on the facts and circumstances.

And it could be more complicated. What if instead of flying back home empty, the plane flew on to Texas to pick up another executive from a business trip? Colorado is closer to Texas than Virginia is, so presumably that might change the company's calculation of its aggregate incremental costs. What if the plane had to fly empty to France to pick up another executive from a business meeting? It would have flown empty from Virginia to pick up the other executive in France in any event, but Virginia is closer to France than Colorado is. Again, the costs might change.

To my mind, most companies will typically need to engage in a facts and circumstances analysis to determine the aggregate, incremental cost of a corporate aircraft perk, including any deadhead legs. But countless well-educated and intelligent people have debated this one and come to different answers as to whether the cost of the deadhead leg even needs to be considered at all. I think that stops too short. In my view, if a deadhead flight leg causes a company to incur incremental costs, those must be included in the calculation of the perk's value.

Aside from aggregate incremental cost, there is no firm rule in the Commission Release, or from the staff, on valuing corporate aircraft usage, let alone deadhead flight legs. There are, however, principles, and companies should not play games with these questions or their answers to them and the disclosures that go with them. I would encourage someone faced with this issue to think through the analysis above carefully, and remember the goals of a principles-based system. What is the disclosure objective? Provide your investors with the value of the perquisites your company accords its executives, based on their aggregate incremental costs. And provide your investors with the material information they need in order to understand that valuation, its context, and the particular facts and circumstances of those perquisites. Remember, *principles matter*.

I have tried to use a couple of different examples to illustrate the importance of principles-based disclosure. There are, of course, many other examples that arise from the recent rulemaking that we could look at—disclosure of option grant practices and disclosure of related party transactions are two that I particularly like and which I hope I will have the chance to address in future forums like this one. I would certainly encourage everyone to think about those two topics carefully in the context of principles-based disclosure.

But, as we all learn to be guides in this principles-based world, let's go back, for a moment, to the fundamentals of principles-based disclosure. Remember the Bob Herz quote. He explained that there is not a specific rule for every possible situation, but there is a principle. As we've seen with perks, there's no bright line rule about deadhead flight legs and what to do with them in calculating a perk's value. But there is a principle.

You may all recall a speech about executive compensation disclosure that my predecessor, Alan Beller, gave two years ago—often referred to as the "all means all" speech even though it never actually uses those words. In his remarks, Alan noted, and I quote, "in the area of executive compensation, management's retort to advice to make additional disclosure may too often be 'Where does it say we have to disclose that?' "[8] Well, depending on the item, there still may not be express words in the rules requiring specific disclosure. But now you will have something to point to, and something to say if asked Alan's question: you will explain that *it's the principles that matter*. To the extent that management is still looking for a flashing sign, the Commission has made it clear that, at least in some regards, they must now look to the principles. I hope that executives at America's public companies will heed and appreciate this, as you, as their advisors and counsel, help them craft the disclosure that their investors have long deserved, and which the Commission now demands.

Plain English

I do have one final disclosure thought to leave with you. I believe it's equally useful (and important) to apply a basic principle of good disclosure to everything you draft. In any of these areas, the disclosure should be clear and concise and provide meaningful information to investors that is easy to understand. The substance and content of your disclosure need to be principles-based; the presentation does as well. It needs to be in Plain English.

Plain English is a phrase, like "principles-based", that may get thrown around a lot. It's important to remember what it really means though. It does not mean "dumbing down". It does not require stripping your disclosure of depth or context. It does mean presenting complex information in a clear and concise manner that is understandable to a broad audience. It takes time to write well, to write disclosure that is understandable and useful to investors. Take that time. Use the active voice, and speak directly. Write for investors, not lawyers.

Conclusion

I started my remarks today by talking about the new Compensation Discussion & Analysis section. Obviously, no one has drafted one of these before. There's no boilerplate out there, no precedents to mark up and reuse. If you're used to getting pressure to "match up" your disclosure to the disclosure of your company's peers or competitors, that won't exist this first year. You have a chance to start with a clean slate in that sense. Take it, and make a difference. And as you're working on those CD&A's for the first time, I hope you will remember my remarks this morning and what I've said about principles-based disclosure.

As we all look ahead to the upcoming proxy season, I am sincerely heartened and enthusiastic about the chances of witnessing a sea change in the quality, and usefulness, of executive compensation disclosure. I believe that the groundwork the Commission has laid in adopting its new principles-based disclosure standards has considerably advanced the interests of investors. That vision will not reach fruition, however, without the partnership of America's companies in stepping up and providing the public with their own principles-based disclosures. That's where we need your help, and I hope we have given you a standard, and examples, to cite to your skeptical clients. Remember the message that should be conveyed: *the principles matter.*

Thank you.

Endnotes

1.   "Remarks before the Financial Executives International Current Financial Reporting Issues Conference," Robert H. Herz, November 4, 2002.

2.   "Study Pursuant to Section 108(d) of the Sarbanes-Oxley Act of 2002 on the Adoption by the United States Financial Reporting System of a Principles-Based Accounting System," by the Office of the Chief Accountant and the Office of Economic Analysis, U.S. Securities and Exchange Commission, July 25, 2003, available at http://www.sec.gov/news/studies/principlesbasedstand.htm.

3.   "Remarks before the Tenth Annual Corporate Counsel Institute: Priorities and Concerns at the SEC," Cynthia A. Glassman, Commissioner, U.S. Securities and Exchange Commission, March 9, 2006, available at http://www.sec.gov/news/speech/spch030906cag.htm.

4.   "Introductory Remarks at the SEC Open Meeting," Christopher Cox, Chairman, U.S. Securities and Exchange Commission, July 26, 2006, available at http://www.sec.gov/news/speech/2006/spch072606cc.htm.

5.   SEC Release No. 33-8732A, "Executive Compensation and Related Party Disclosures," August 29, 2006, (the "Release"), at p. 29, available at http://www.sec.gov/rules/final/2006/33-8732a.pdf.

6.   Release at pp 34-35.

7.   Release at p.73.

8.   "Remarks Before Conference of the NASPP, The Corporate Counsel and the Corporate Executive," Alan L. Beller, Director, Division of Corporation Finance, October 20, 2004, available at http://www.sec.gov/news/speech/spch102004alb.htm.

The Principles Matter: Options Disclosure
John W. White

Director, Division of Corporation Finance
U.S. Securities and Exchange Commission

Corporate Counsel Conference
Washington, DC
September 11, 2006

Thank you, Jesse (wherever you are) and Alan. A double introduction is a first for me—I am very appreciative.

I am very happy to be here this morning, as you start your two-day conference on the new executive compensation disclosure rules. You have assembled an impressive faculty and have set out an ambitious agenda for yourselves for the next two days.

Tomorrow, the Chief Counsel of my Division, David Lynn, will be joining you, and offering his insights as well. Dave and I, and other representatives of the Commission's staff, are signed up for quite a number of these programs, but we obviously will not be able to be at all the conferences about the new rules. And we will not be physically present at any of the countless presentations that lawyers and compensation specialists will be making to boards of directors and executive officers in the coming months.

Nor will we participate in the ensuing disclosure discussions. Nonetheless, there is at least one theme that I hope will permeate all of the conferences, presentations and discussions. And that theme is where I would like to start my own remarks this morning—the meaning and significance of principles-based disclosure.

Before I turn to that, however, I must first remind you that the views I'm going to express today are solely my own, and do not necessarily reflect the views of the Securities and Exchange Commission, or of any members of its staff, other than myself.

In thinking about today's program, I have assumed that many in the audience are lawyers and other compensation and disclosure specialists who will be working diligently this upcoming proxy season to help companies comply with the new rules and to get their disclosures right. The Commission relied tremendously on the overwhelming and very constructive feedback we received from all quarters during the comment period on the rule proposal. And now that the rules have been finalized, we are relying on all of you to help make them work right in practice. Fortunately, in my opinion, the Commission's new rules are rather uniquely structured so that advisors, like you, will be able to make that critical difference. The key to remember—as I articulated in a speech by the same name that I gave last week in New York—is two simple words: *principles matter*.

Principles, in my view, are an important thread running throughout the Commission's recent rulemaking. And I believe that looking at principles as they apply to various specific areas of the rulemaking is a useful learning tool. In last week's "Principles Matter" speech (which has been posted on the Commission website),[1] I looked at two different areas of the new rules— Compensation Discussion & Analysis and perquisites—each through the lens of principles. I also used those two examples in helping to show the critical role that disclosure counsel and advisors can play in a principles-based disclosure world. When you have a chance, I urge you to take a look at those remarks as they are very intertwined with my theme this morning.

This morning, I'd like to look specifically at how principles work in a third area in the recent rulemaking: that is, the disclosure of option grant practices. When I was studying the program that Jesse and his team have put together for this conference, it struck me that no separate panel seemed directly focused on the stock option angle of our new disclosure guidance. So hopefully if I spend a few minutes on that area this morning, I won't be stepping on anyone's toes later in the day. As you may know, this area was extremely important to the Commission, and I actually called it "a release within a release" when we were working on the final rulemaking.[2]

Principles-Based Disclosure and the New CD&A

There are a wide variety of views on how to explain the term "principles-based". Although everyone seems to have the same general idea of what they're talking about, I think it's important, before we put the term into action, that we have a mutual understanding of what it means. For my part, I find the description that Robert Herz, chairman of the FASB, gave in 2002 to be very useful:

> Under a principles-based approach, one starts with laying out the key objectives of good reporting in the subject area, and then provides guidance explaining the objective and relating it to some common examples. While rules are sometimes unavoidable, the intent is not to try to provide specific guidance, or rules, for every possible situation. Rather, if in doubt, the reader is directed back to the principles.[3]

Now, Bob was talking about accounting and financial reporting, of course, and that's often where we hear the phrase "principles-based". The Commission, however, has embraced it in numerous other places, including the recent executive compensation disclosure rulemaking.

Within this rulemaking, the new CD&A section is probably the place that most often gets tagged with the term "principles-based". Clearly, a solid understanding of principles-based disclosure is vital to preparing and providing investors with a high quality CD&A. If you have read the recent Release, you have been directed by the Commission to look to the existing MD&A (Management's Discussion & Analysis) as a model for understanding the function and operation of the new CD&A. I believe this analogy is very apt. Not only do they share similar acronyms, but more importantly MD&A and CD&A share a commitment to and provide a place for principles-based disclosure.

Last week, I referred to a speech that our former Commissioner Cyndi Glassman gave in March.[4] Commissioner Glassman was absolutely right in noting that "[o]f all of our disclosure rules, MD&A may be the most principles-based." So, when approaching the challenge of drafting your company's first CD&A, please don't forget the body of learning that companies already have from their experiences of drafting MD&A. The description of the term "principles-based" that I borrowed from Bob Herz, talks about starting with the "key objectives" of good reporting in a particular area. So what are the key objectives of good reporting (or more specifically, good disclosure) for executive compensation, and especially for the CD&A? CD&A is what gives context to the required tables and the numbers in them.

As the Commission stated in the Adopting Release:

> The purpose of the Compensation Discussion and Analysis disclosure is to provide material information about the compensation objectives and policies for named executive officers without resorting to boilerplate disclosure. The Compensation Discussion and Analysis is intended to put into perspective for investors the numbers and narrative that follow it.[5]

The rules do provide six questions that CD&A *must* answer, as well as 15 examples of topics a company *might* consider addressing. Those examples are neither exhaustive nor mandatory. A company (and those drafting its disclosure) must determine what is material to the company. What do the company's investors need to know? They must then craft the appropriate disclosure that is responsive to those questions and is tailored to the company's particular facts and circumstances.

Disclosure of Options Practices

So how does that broad description of the objectives of CD&A apply to options disclosure? Within the Release, right up front, the Commission took special care to talk about the application of its new rules for CD&A to option grant practices.[6] Principles clearly play a critical role here. In addition to detailed, new tabular disclosure requirements about option grants and their value (which you will be hearing more about in the panels later today that deal with the tables), the Commission is now requiring clear, principles-based narrative disclosure in the CD&A about a company's programs, plans and practices pertaining to option grants to executives.

As you all know, there has been a lot of media and other attention paid recently to various option grant practices, using labels like "backdating," "spring loading" and "bullet dodging". Those terms mean different things to different people. The Commission did not use any of them in the Release, and I will not be using them today. Rather, the Commission talked about two separate, general categories of options practices—(1) those relating to the timing of option grants and (2) those related to the pricing of option grants (or setting exercise prices).

Before looking at these practices, I believe it is important to note upfront that the Commission's new rules (and the guidance in the Release) are *prospective*. The Commission did not comment on past practices in the Release. I also believe it is important to remember that the Commission was very careful to highlight that it was not speaking to the substance of executive compensation, in either form or amount, in any way. As our

Chairman, Chris Cox, stated at the Open Meeting when the new rules were adopted, "It is not the job of the SEC to judge what constitutes the "right" level of compensation for an executive or to place limits on what executives are paid."[7] Our concern is with disclosure.

So let's turn now to the option practices and disclosure guidance in the Release. With regard to the first category of practices I mentioned a moment ago—timing practices—the Commission explained that these involve the granting of options in coordination with the release of material non-public information. Timing may be in coordination with the release of positive or negative material information, and it might take place by delaying or accelerating the information release, or by delaying or accelerating the option grant. There are a lot of different permutations and combinations there, but they all boil down to option grant "programs, plans or practices" that require appropriate disclosure and discussion under the new rules and the guidance in the Release.

The second general category of option grant practices relates to "pricing." Pricing practices involve establishing a strike price for an option grant that is different from the stock's closing market price on the date of grant. Generally speaking, the exercise price of an option grant is the closing market price of the underlying stock on the grant date. Companies may, however, establish different exercise prices provided they comply with the applicable disclosure requirements and follow the correct accounting. The Release provides guidance about two methods for establishing a different exercise price—by setting the exercise price based on (1) the stock's price on a date prior to the grant date, or (2) a formula, often using some combination of the stock's price at various times on the grant date or during a time window before (and sometimes after) the grant. As long as the option grants are properly disclosed and the company accounts for them correctly, there is nothing per se wrong with following one of those practices.

What does proper disclosure look like, then, if a company chooses to engage in either timing or pricing practices with regard to its option grants to its executives? As I said before, there are some fairly detailed new tabular disclosures that companies must provide. Moreover (and this is what I want to focus on today), in keeping with a principles-based system, the Commission provided in the Release several questions and examples in order to help companies craft the right disclosure in their CD&A specifically about option grants.

The very first question for special consideration that the Commission poses in the Release is, "Does a company have any program, plan or practice to time option grants to its executives in coordination with the release of material non-public information?"[8] This question is only a suggestion, and as I alluded to earlier, it should not be considered either mandatory or exhaustive. It does, however, deserve careful consideration. Think in principle about what it means to "time an option grant in coordination with the release of material non-public information."

The most obvious example of a timing practice might involve a company that times its options grants to precede the release of a positive earnings or new product announcement, with the expectation that the company's stock price will enjoy a boost when that announcement comes out and the option recipient will likewise benefit from his options being quickly, or more substantially, "in the money".

The principle also applies, though, to a company that delays an option grant, or accelerates a news release, to ensure that negative information is fully absorbed by the market before an option grant is awarded. People may assert that delaying an option grant until after all information is in the market (even if that means the stock price goes down) somehow "smells different" than accelerating an option grant to precede a positive news announcement (which would be anticipated to then boost the stock's price). But for the Commission's new disclosure rules and guidance, those two situations are really two sides of the same coin. If they exist, they both are "programs, plans or practices" related to option grants, and they both may need to be disclosed and discussed appropriately.

As another variant, the principle applies equally to a company that times its options grants to either precede or follow, as appropriate, a known (or anticipated) upcoming, material announcement from a third party— such as an FDA announcement that it has either approved or denied a critical drug application on which the company has pinned its hopes. In all these situations, remember the principle and don't let your analysis, or your disclosure, end with the most obvious example or overly simplistic answers.

Let's look at another question. The second illustrative question that the Commission posed in the Release is, "How does any program, plan or practice to time option grants to executives fit in the context of the company's program, plan or practice, if any, with regard to option grants to employees more generally?"[9] Our newest Commissioner, Kathy Casey, first raised the excellent point that the requisite context for understanding option grants to executives may go beyond the executive suite itself. While it's true that the Commission's disclosure rules pertain to *executive* compensation, it's not good enough to ask only the simple questions, to keep your blinders on, to not think outside the box. Does your company have a program, plan or practice for option grants which it follows with regard to all of its employees generally? Or is this a special situation that applies only to executives, or only to select executives? The answers to those questions may well inform or shine extra light on how a company follows such a practice, what benefits the company receives from it, or what effect it has on the executive recipients. Or, it may not. But the point of principles-based disclosure is that companies, and their advisors, need to figure that out, and to make sure they're disclosing the relevant, material information about their companies' particular facts and circumstances. Again, remember the key message here— *principles matter*. And give your investors the material disclosure they want, need and deserve.

The Release talks at length about timing and pricing practices with regard to options specifically. Those are two critical analytic elements, but please don't lose sight of the overarching principles in this sense either. If other practices relating to option grants are developed in the future—as they undoubtedly will be—they will also be covered by these principles-based disclosure requirements, even though the Release doesn't name them, and we may not (any of us) yet know what they are.

Similarly, the Release has an entire section that speaks about "options", but you should understand that the principles the Commission has promulgated undoubtedly apply to other equity awards, such as stock appreciation rights (SARs) and restricted stock that operate in the same field. Leaning again on my friend Mr. Herz, think about the key objectives of good reporting in this area, and the principles will guide your disclosure. As the Release expressly states, companies should consider their own facts and circumstances, and include all relevant material information in their corresponding disclosures. The questions and guidance in the Release are only a start. Use your disclosure to provide the necessary context and perspective about your company, for your investors.

Conclusion

Obviously we stand at a fairly unique juncture at which tremendous media and law enforcement attention is being paid to companies' option grant practices. It's not clear to me how the public, or history, will end up judging past practices. At the same time, the Commission has outlined a clear path for how these issues should be addressed going forward. No one has drafted a CD&A before, or crafted disclosure in light of the Commission's recent guidance on disclosure of option grant practices. I, at least, am not aware of any company that has otherwise used its proxy disclosure to provide its investors with a clear understanding of what the company is doing, and what it's achieving, with its option grants. I hope you will see your company's next proxy statement, therefore, as an opportunity "to get it right the first time." And I hope you will help America's public companies seize that opportunity. Each of you has an invaluable role to play in guiding and assisting your clients and your companies in answering that call. Remember, the two-word message of this morning: *principles matter.*

Thank you very much for giving me the opportunity today to share a few of my thoughts with you on the new rules. I hope you find the next two days to be both enjoyable and rewarding.

Endnotes

1.   "Principles Matter," John W. White, Director, Division of Corporation Finance, U.S. Securities and Exchange Commission, September 6, 2006, available at http://www.sec.gov/news/speech/2006/spch090606jww.htm.

2.   SEC Release No. 33-8732A, "Executive Compensation and Related Party Disclosures," August 29, 2006, (the "Release"), available at http://www.sec.gov/rules/final/2006/33-8732a.pdf.

3.   "Remarks before the Financial Executives International Current Financial Reporting Issues Conference," Robert H. Herz, November 4, 2002.

4.   "Remarks before the Tenth Annual Corporate Counsel Institute: Priorities and Concerns at the SEC," Cynthia A. Glassman, Commissioner, U.S. Securities and Exchange Commission, March 9, 2006, available at http://www.sec.gov/news/speech/spch030906cag.htm.

5.   Release at p. 29.

6.   Release at pp. 18-27.

7.   "Introductory Remarks at the SEC Open Meeting," Christopher Cox, Chairman, U.S. Securities and Exchange Commission, July 26, 2006, available at http://www.sec.gov/news/speech/2006/spch072606cc.htm.

8.   Release at p. 26.

9.   Id.

An Expansive View of Teamwork: Directors, Management, and the SEC
John W. White

Director, Division of Corporation Finance
U.S. Securities and Exchange Commission

Practising Law Institute Fourth Annual Directors' Institute
    on Corporate Governance
New York, NY
September 25, 2006

Thank you, Betsy, for that gracious introduction. As you may recall, although wearing a different hat then, I, like you, had the pleasure of participating in PLI's first Directors' Institute three years ago. It's an honor to be invited back. Since I joined the staff of the SEC last March, I have spoken with groups representing corporate executives and management, disclosure counsel, auditors and others. But this is the first chance I've had in my relatively new role to speak at a program that is dedicated to directors and their unique, and uniquely important, role in corporate America. I am delighted to be here.

The SEC of course takes very seriously its commitment to being "the investor's advocate" in the public sphere. That charge is no less true for all of you who, as directors, directly represent those investors who are the stockholders of your companies. We share common, important interests in that regard, and I think a common understanding of our roles and objectives can be mutually beneficial. In my time during your lunch today, I would like then to talk specifically about the importance of the SEC staff's review of public company disclosures and how understanding that process may be a resource for you as directors. I'd then like to look briefly at several features of the recent executive compensation disclosure rulemaking that are intertwined with your role as directors. Before I do that, though, I need to remind you that the views I'm going to express today are solely my own and do not necessarily reflect the views of the Securities and Exchange Commission or of any members of its staff other than myself. Since I will mention him later, I should perhaps also extend that same so-called "standard disclaimer" on behalf of the Commission's new Chief Accountant and my colleague, Conrad Hewitt, and underscore that the disclaimer makes clear that even if I quote him, Conrad is not on the hook for anything I say.

Understanding Corporation Finance

As Betsy said, I am currently serving as the director of the SEC's Division of Corporation Finance. The SEC of course has four divisions: Investment Management, Market Regulation, Corporation Finance and Enforcement, as well as numerous, no less important, offices. The first two divisions I named—Investment Management and Market Regulation—attend specifically to the vast worlds of mutual funds and investments companies, of broker-dealers, the stock exchanges, clearing agencies and our capital markets. I realize some of you represent or have experience with companies that move in those special regulatory circles, but my perspective today is that of publicly-held companies more generally, in all industries—some 12,000 public companies in total. The Division of Corporation Finance reviews, and oversees to some extent, the public disclosures that those companies must craft and file with the SEC. The Division of Enforcement for its part cuts across all those distinctions and ferrets out and pursues wrong-doers in all areas covered by the SEC's jurisdiction. So individuals and companies that would routinely deal with one of the other three divisions could have Enforcement knock on their doors at any time. For today, I will just hope that your own companies and their executives never warrant the attention of my 1,000-plus colleagues in Enforcement.

So if you're a director of a publicly-traded company, or an advisor to those directors—I believe most of you fit in one of those categories or the other—what should you understand about the Division of Corporation Finance? To help answer that question, I'd like to talk with you for a few minutes about our disclosure review process, how it works and how you can work with it.

The Structure and Objectives of Corporation Finance

The Division of Corporation Finance is divided into two halves—unequal perhaps in size, but certainly not in importance. One half, which we refer to as "disclosure operations", handles our reviews of the filings and disclosures made by public companies; the other half provides interpretive and rulemaking advice and basically does everything else. Disclosure operations, which is my focus today, has 11 different review offices, organized principally according to trade or industry type—for example, Telecommunications, Financial Services, Healthcare and Insurance, Natural Resources and Food, and so on. There are teams of 30 to 35 accountants and lawyers in each review office, and each public company is assigned to a particular office. Presumably, many of you are familiar with the disclosure reviews that your companies have undergone with Corporation Finance in the past; these groups are where those reviews happen. There are close to 400 people who work in disclosure operations and approximately another 100 in the interpretive and rulemaking offices, all based at the SEC's headquarters in Washington, DC.

At various points in the Commission's history, Corporation Finance's disclosure reviews have focused on companies issuing, or selling, public securities, such as IPO's or secondary offerings. These remain an important area of review for us, but we do not stop there. The Division has a long history of also reviewing the regular, periodic filings that public companies are required to provide for their current and would-be investors—the 10-K, 10-Q, proxy statement, etc. And after the passage of the Sarbanes-Oxley Act in 2002, this process of reviewing the periodic filings of established public companies became an express charge. Sarbanes-Oxley requires (which is new) that the SEC must review the filings, including specifically the annual report on Form 10 K, of every listed company "on a regular and systematic basis for the protection of investors," and that, for all reporting companies, these reviews take place no less often that once every three years. This means that you can no longer regard the SEC's review of your company as haphazard—the luck of the draw—it is instead a routine event. I am proud to say that the Division successfully completed its first three-year review cycle last fall, covering all 12,000 public companies. Please understand that I can take no credit for this, given that I was still with all of you in the private sector at that time. But I can say that we are now well into the second round at Corporation Finance and will review close to 4500 companies in the first year of that round which ends this week. One other thought: I said at least every three years. We review hundreds of companies more often than every three years—so this is not like jury duty here in New York where you get a pass for a few years after your name comes up and you serve one time.

The Nature of Disclosure Review

But what exactly does "disclosure review" mean and why should all of you, as directors, care? After all, you presumably (hopefully) have competent and well-qualified executives and staff, perhaps even outside counsel or other advisors, who help your company provide disclosure that is useful to investors and complies with all the relevant legal and regulatory requirements. You also all have independent auditors who take a second look at your financial statements after your management has prepared them. All the same, in my opinion there are several reasons why our disclosure review can be helpful to you, as directors, and why you should pay attention to it. I also think it's important for you to understand what that review *isn't* as much as what it *is*.

I mentioned the 11 offices that make up our disclosure operations group. And I mentioned our Sarbanes-Oxley charge to review the filings of every public company at least once every three years. As a general matter, you can expect that your companies' recurring reviews will be handled by the same office each time, and you may even have the same staff person or persons processing your filings on a repeat basis. Your financial statements will be reviewed by our accountants; your narrative and other non-financial disclosures may be reviewed by lawyers and other staff as well. At any given point in time, a company's filings may be undergoing review and the company itself may or may not know about that.

When the staff of Corporation Finance decides to comment on a company's public filings (and it does not necessarily do so for every company whose disclosure it reviews), it will typically issue a "comment letter" which will provide you with the staff's thoughts on where your filings could be improved or where the staff feels it needs more information. The company typically will then in turn respond in writing to the staff's points. Often, supplemental conversations between the company and the Division's staff will also take place. Some of our comments may require revising and resubmitting past filings; in other cases, it may be possible to address our comments in future reports. These specifics, and what the staff expects, will come out through the comment process. This process, although private when occurring, will at its conclusion become public, as I will explain shortly.

I imagine some of you may have heard about SEC comments on your company's disclosure in the past. When I was still wearing my private sector hat, I listened to, and sometimes participated in, presentations about SEC comments at corporate board meetings. Notice that I didn't use the word "discussion" but rather "presentation". Unfortunately, I believe the process is often *presented* to the board—assuming it reaches the board at all. And it is presented as an almost adversarial exercise. Almost as a "win or lose," zero-sum situation. The company exalts if it prevailed over the staff's disclosure requests and comments. On some occasions, management may seek to minimize the burden the process places on the directors by minimizing the information conveyed to the board about it. But is that attitude actually helpful to your company, or appropriate for you? Think about the Commission's role and your role, as directors, with regard to investors. How different are they? If you do think about it, you may not want management to "shield" you from the SEC comment process. You may care especially about understanding those areas that have attracted the SEC staff's attention.

I was having lunch last week with the Commission's recently appointed Chief Accountant, Conrad Hewitt, and we were talking about today's program and the remarks I planned to make. I should perhaps let you know that Conrad has served on more corporate boards, and more audit committees, than anyone else I know—at least ten at my last count, although not all at the same time of course. Conrad agreed that I could share with you the high premium that he always placed on Corporation Finance's disclosure review comments when he was sitting in your seat and that he shares my belief that directors—and not just management or disclosure counsel—should be familiar with those comments and should see them as a valuable resource.

A the same time, Corporation Finance's reviews of public company filings are not represented as comprehensive, nor should they be understood as such. If the staff either issues no comments or concludes its review process (after issuing and resolving comments), no one should think that the SEC or the staff is in any way ensuring the health of the company or even blessing the thoroughness or quality of its disclosures. That responsibility remains distinctly with the company and in that sense, with all of you. Corporation Finance's reviews are, however, substantive and frequently substantial. The staff takes time and care to provide thoughtful and meaningful comments. A knee jerk reaction to be dismissive of those comments, or to "fight" them, is seldom, in my opinion, the right response.

I mentioned earlier that the Division's disclosure review offices are organized according to broad industry and commercial categories. As such, the staff members in those offices become very familiar with a cross-section of companies that often have similar businesses and similar disclosure issues. The insight and perspective that come from reviewing the disclosures of multiple companies—in many cases over a number of years—is another unique value that the staff's comments can offer you and one which I would urge you not to dismiss out of hand. I fully recognize that sometimes a comment may seem off base, or to miss the point, and I've heard counsel relish pointing those out. But in my experience, staff comments often go directly to the heart of key issues (particularly on the accounting side) that warrant the attention of a careful and conscientious board member. Sometimes, even just asking a question (even if not directly on point) reveals a great deal and can lead to improved disclosure. I would urge you to keep an open mind and think about how the staff's comments might advance the needs and interests of your team to the benefit of your investors. I would encourage you (and Conrad would encourage you) to think of the comment letters that we send out as not only being inquiries directed at your company, but also as being a resource for you as a director.

As you all know, you generally must sign your company's annual report on Form 10-K. And if that report is incorporated into a subsequent offering document for a public issuance of securities by your company, then you will have liability for the disclosures in that document with regard to that offering. The Corporation Finance review process and the comment letters we issue are there for you to look at and understand. I would urge you not to overlook them. If I were a director, I would want to make sure I received a copy of each of my company's comment letters and, equally important, the responses my company submitted. Understand the questions the staff has asked, the answers the company has provided and the revisions it has made to its filings. Use that understanding, then, to help set the benchmarks for your company's future disclosures. I do not mean to suggest that directors need to be at the front lines of preparing their companies' public filings. You do need to understand your company's disclosures, however, and this can be one more tool in your toolbox to do that. It will not do the whole job for you, but it can help.

Finally, you should also understand that this same tool is now freely available to your investors, your competitors and any other interested person. This is a relatively new phenomenon. But after a particular review is completed, the staff of the Division of Corporation Finance posts its comment letters, and the responses it received from the company, on the SEC's website where they are searchable and retrievable by the public at no cost. I am sure your management and their advisors understand this, but it's one more thing to keep in mind when crafting responses to my staff's comment letters. One day, your neighbor may read them. And more importantly, your own bosses, your shareholders, may as well.

The Interpretive and Rulemaking Offices

I referred earlier to the other "half" of Corporation Finance—the interpretive and rulemaking offices. And although my focus this morning has been on disclosure operations and their review of your companies' filings, I would be remiss if I did not at least mention the important work done by these other offices in my Division. These are the people who support disclosure operations and provide interpretive and other specialized guidance and services to the Commission, to investors and to America's public companies. You will find our Office of Rulemaking here, for example. The Office of Chief Counsel, for its part, is the entry point—whether by phone or letter—for questions that public companies and their advisors, or other interested parties, may have about the applicable securities laws and regulations. Our Office of the Chief Accountant, which is distinct from the Commission's Office of the Chief Accountant, operates in this "half" of Corporation Finance and provides accounting and financial reporting expertise when complex disclosure situations present themselves in those areas. We have an Office of International Corporate Finance which deals exclusively with the special circumstances and needs of the foreign registrant community. We also have an office devoted solely to Mergers and Acquisitions and the related disclosures and filings that go with those transactions. Another office deals with Small Business Policy, and so on. For all of you, your company may at any point in time find one of our specialized interpretive offices to be a resource for you or they all may operate relatively silently in the background from your perspective. Unlike disclosure operations, there is no required recurring interaction between any of them and any of you.

In the past 20 minutes or so, I have talked with you about how Corporation Finance and the work we do can overlap with your own interests. Each of you, by virtue simply of being a director of a public company, has a responsibility for understanding your company and its disclosures. (Obviously, you have a number of other responsibilities as well.) I hope I have also given you a sense of the many important responsibilities that the staff of Corporation Finance shoulders, and I hope what I have said has given you some insight into how the staff approaches those responsibilities and how our work might in turn be a help to you. Although I have only had the pleasure of working in the Division for six months myself, it's important to me to take a moment of your time to emphasize how proud I am of each and every member of Corporation Finance for the contributions they make each and every day. They truly give meaning to the concept of being "the investor's advocate."

In the next few minutes, I'd like to talk briefly about a few pieces of the Commission's recent executive compensation disclosure rulemaking and what I see as some of the more significant intersections that this rulemaking has with all of you as directors.

Executive Compensation

As we heard from the panel that preceded me—and as I'm fairly confident you all already knew—the Commission adopted significant revisions to our rules for executive compensation disclosure two months ago tomorrow, on July 26. I recognize that all of you, and especially those of you who serve on compensation committees, have a keen interest in, and responsibility for, the *substance*—that is, the amount and form and nature—of your executives' compensation. Overseeing and compensating those executives are some of the most important things you do as a board. The Commission's interest in executive compensation, however, is all about *disclosure*. The Commission takes very seriously its often repeated pronouncement that it is not in the business of setting executive compensation—not even in subtle ways—nor is it in the business of judging companies or boards about the decisions they make in this area. Our purpose and our role at the SEC do obviously intersect with your own, however, in this sense: we have crafted our rules and we will monitor their implementation with the goal in mind of helping investors obtain the information—need about the compensation decisions that *you* make. Investors can then judge those decisions how ever they choose—they are, after all, the owners of the company and the ones ultimately paying those bills.

The details and meanings of our recent rulemaking, and the disclosures that we expect to see, have been receiving a great deal of attention at various programs, including this one, and I'm sure that this will continue to be true in the coming months. I do not have the time today to review our rules in any depth, and you have already heard from an excellent panel on the topic. I believe that everyone should understand and remember, though, that the SEC's rulemaking was substantial and comprehensive. The structure and requirements of the Summary Compensation Table have been meaningfully revised, and companies will now be required to present one number reflecting *total* compensation for each named executive. As Chairman Cox pointed out at our open meeting in July, "among the most important features of these new rules is that there will now be one bottom-line number, including all options, for an executive's total compensation. And that number will be comparable from company to company."[1] I would, of course, echo the Chairman and I personally anticipate that this will be a critical piece of the disclosure that investors will start receiving in the next proxy season. The Commission also adopted rules requiring disclosure of *director* compensation (including a requirement to provide one *total* number), significantly revising our rules for disclosure of related party transactions and revising our rules and providing more interpretive guidance for perquisites disclosure (including perquisites provided to directors). The SEC also provided substantial guidance on disclosure of practices pertaining to stock option grants to executives (and, again, to directors). Obviously, I cannot go over all of these changes today, but I would like to zero in on a few of the ways in which I see our recent rulemaking as particularly affecting directors.

Compensation Discussion & Analysis

I imagine you are all familiar with the old "Board Compensation Committee Report on Executive Compensation" that used to appear in the proxy statement. As its name suggests, it was a report by the compensation committee—not the company or management. As the Commission had proposed last January and you heard this morning, that report has been eliminated and a new, principles-based Compensation Discussion & Analysis (or CD&A) section is now required in your company's proxy statement and annual report on Form 10 K. In addition, a new and very different Compensation Committee Report will also be required going forward.

The new CD&A section is at the heart of the new rules. In the most summary terms, it is designed to be a principles-based overview explaining the policies and decisions related to executive compensation. That principles-based theme is critical to our recent rulemaking and one which I have been stressing in other forums when speaking about the new rules. If you are interested in this quite important topic and its intended impact on your company's disclosure, I would refer you to a speech that I gave three weeks ago at another PLI program devoted almost entirely to the new rules[2]. In those remarks, I tried to lay out the meaning and significance of a principles-based approach and how embracing it can aid both investors and companies. Among other things, that speech, entitled "Principles Matter", takes a look at what "principles-based" means specifically with regard to the new CD&A. Those remarks are available on the SEC website, and I also saw copies out at the registration desk this morning. Today, however, I'd like to focus on another facet of CD&A—how does it fit in the scheme of your company's public disclosures overall?

As the phrasing of that question subtly acknowledges, CD&A is your *company's* disclosure, not your board's or your compensation committee's. And, as company disclosure, it will be covered by those famous certifications that your CEO and CFO must make for your company's annual report on Form 10-K. So, as you can imagine, management at your company and those charged with crafting and signing off on your company's disclosures may now have a heightened interest in the CD&A, at least compared to the interest they had in the old board compensation committee report that has been eliminated (and which was not subject to the certifications). At the same time, executives who are personally covered by the disclosure rules can be expected to have a continuing and still heightened interest in what exactly the company discloses about their individual compensation. Investors seem to have a heightened interest in all of the above. In crafting the final rule, we at the Commission heard investors when they told us in their comment letters that they continue to have a heightened interest in what all of you, as directors, are doing, and that they still wanted to hear from compensation committees directly. Investors did not want the board to be divorced from the company's disclosure about executive compensation just because of the new format. Which takes me to the new Compensation Committee Report.

The new Compensation Committee Report was modeled on the Audit Committee Report, which has already been required (in a totally different context of course) by the Commission's rules for several years. In form, the Compensation Committee Report is very simple. It needs to contain only two thoughts. First, it must contain a statement as to whether the compensation committee has reviewed and discussed the Compensation Discussion and Analysis with management. Second, it must say whether, based on such a review and discussion, the committee has recommended that the CD&A be included in the company's annual report on Form 10-K and proxy statement. Unlike the CD&A itself, the new Compensation Committee Report will appear over the names of the compensation committee members and will be furnished, not filed. Now that may seem to some a technical, legal distinction but its importance for what we're discussing today is that your CEO and CFO will not have to certify your compensation committee's report. Nor will your company have the same liability with regard to the report as it does for company disclosures that are filed. I would suggest, however, that as board members, and particularly if you are compensation committee members, you should not take that report any less seriously.

I tried to suggest in the first part of my remarks today how you might look to SEC staff comments in the review process to better do your job as directors. Strengthen your team how ever you can. I would similarly encourage you to have an expansive approach to how you, as directors—and here

I am speaking especially to compensation committee members—can work with management to enhance both the substance of your company's executive compensation disclosures and the procedures you follow for generating them.

I mentioned very briefly that your CEO and CFO will now be called upon to certify your company's Compensation Discussion and Analysis. As I also said earlier, that section of your company's disclosure must address the policies and decisions related to executive compensation. One objection that we heard to having that section be company disclosure is that it unfairly makes the CEO and CFO responsible for board and compensation committee actions that are outside the officers' "jurisdiction", for lack of a better word. Your compensation committee report, as well as any consultations and discussions you may have about your CD&A section, can help provide your officers with the necessary insights and understanding they need in making their certifications. And this, in fact, is a two-way street. Your own comfort and your own knowledge can be equally fortified and improved through this process. And if you become more involved and more adept with these issues, that will inure to the benefit of your shareholders and investors more generally, which of course comes full circle to your overlap with the SEC. The Commission has carefully structured a disclosure system in this area designed to further the interests and address the needs of investors. I hope you can see it in many ways as also offering the potential of furthering your interests and addressing your needs as directors. One important footnote—I would encourage you again to take a look at my remarks on principles based disclosure. They highlight and explain this crucial concept and, I believe, may help you and your company in drafting and evaluating your CD&A sections in the future.

Compensation and Other Disclosures about Directors

Finally, I just wanted to quickly point out one other area of our recent rule-making that undoubtedly intersects with all of you—the company will now be required to tell its investors significantly more information about you, as directors, including your total compensation. Director compensation for the last fiscal year will now be required to be disclosed in a new Director Compensation Table (along with related narrative), which will be similar in format to the Summary Compensation Table that is the primary vehicle for disclosing the amounts of your executives' compensation. As with executives, companies will be required to disclose one *total* number for a director's compensation, which will include the dollar value of option grants to directors and perquisites, among other compensation. And don't forget what I was saying earlier about the CD&A and principles-based disclosure. As appropriate, companies will need to consider providing narrative disclosure about director compensation that is analogous to that found in the new CD&A. Our new rules for director compensation disclosure (and some exceptions) are comprehensive and fairly detailed. I would encourage you to get more advice about them if you don't feel in command of the subject today. I spoke a few moments ago about various flash points of heightened interest that we might anticipate for persons in various positions; here is another possible one for all of you, individually, as directors.

There are also multiple other ways in which your company's disclosure may be required to talk about you. Our rules require disclosures about director independence and how the board made its determinations in that area. You should all also understand, whether you are on the compensation committee or not, that the company will now be required to provide disclosure about that committee's processes and procedures for the consideration of executive and director compensation. Our rules for disclosure of related person transactions, which also apply to you, have changed. Again, if you have not yet been well-briefed about these (and other) aspects of the recent rulemaking, I would strongly encourage you to get that information, ask any questions you have, and make sure you understand the various ways in which your company's disclosure going forward will be expected to speak about you. The better you understand it, in my opinion, the more you can do to help ensure that your company will provide your investors with the high quality, clear and useful disclosures they deserve.

Conclusion

More than ever before, you are today doing your jobs as directors very much in the public eye. And the investors who elected you to your important positions are relying on you and your leadership. Investors and the Commission may have great expectations for you, and may place great demands on you, but I hope I have shown you today a couple of ways in which you are not alone as you take up the important tasks before you. I hope you will embrace an expansive view of who and what may contribute to your team and its efforts, and how the SEC, its staff and even its rules may facilitate your success rather than standing as obstacles in your path.

Thank you for sharing your time with me today. I wish each of you much future success on behalf of America's investors.

Endnotes

1.   "Introductory Remarks at the SEC Open Meeting", Christopher Cox, Chairman, U.S. Securities and Exchange Commission, July 26, 2006, available at http://www.sec.gov/news/speech/2006/spch072606cc.htm.

2.   "Principles Matter," John W. White, Director, Division of Corporation Finance, U.S. Securities and Exchange Commission, September 6, 2006, available at http://www.sec.gov/news/speech/2006/spch090606jww.htm.

Executive Compensation Disclosure and the Important Role of CFOs

John W. White

Director, Division of Corporation Finance
U.S. Securities and Exchange Commission

CFO Executive Board
New York, NY
October 3, 2006

Thank you, Silvio. I am very pleased to be here today at this dinner meeting of members from the CFO Executive Board. I very much appreciate your giving me a bit of your time to talk with you about an area of considerable current interest at the SEC—executive compensation disclosure. As I will explain in a moment, I am particularly focused this evening on the fact that each of you is the principal financial officer (as our rules at the SEC refer to you)[1] of a major public company, and I am hoping executive compensation disclosure is an area of interest for each of you. I certainly think it should be—perhaps even more so than you've realized thus far. CFOs play a very important role in America's businesses and in fact to our economy as a whole, as I have no doubt you all appreciate. The Commission's executive compensation disclosure rules also acknowledge this fact in multiple ways, as I will try to explain.

Before I go any further into my remarks, however, I need to share with you all the so-called "standard disclaimer" that applies to SEC staff remarks. As a matter of policy the SEC disclaims responsibility for any private comments or speeches from its staff. You should understand that my remarks this evening represent only my own views and not necessarily those of the Commission or of other members of the staff.

So my topic this evening is the Commission's recently adopted and significantly revised rules for executive compensation disclosure. The Commission adopted these final rules at an open meeting on July 26, 2006, and in the intervening two months, I have already had the opportunity to spend many hours addressing various groups of lawyers, compensation specialists, management, and last week even directors about what they should expect from the new rules and what the rules will be expecting of them. It is very important to me, and to the Commission, that all the necessary players are on board and on the team as these new rules go into effect for the next proxy season. All of you—as chief or principal financial officers—have a special place in that mix. Tonight, I would like to lay out briefly for you where I see some of the key intersections between the new rules and your own positions as CFOs.

First, however, I need to make one thing very clear and to delineate the SEC's role and place from various other voices that are being heard increasingly loudly about executive compensation. I have already used the word "disclosure" a couple of times this evening, and I really want to emphasize that the Commission's new rules are all about disclosure. I believe the Commission and its staff take very seriously the charge—as our Chairman, Chris Cox, has made clear[2]—that the Commission is not in the business of setting executive compensation. Not even in subtle ways. Nor is the Commission in the business of judging companies or boards about the decisions they make in this area. The Commission is, however, strongly committed to helping investors get the information they need (through required disclosures for public companies) about executive compensation so that shareholders and investors can judge that, how ever they choose and react how ever they like.

I also believe that the Commission is quite genuinely not trying to judge, change or affect the compensation of anyone in this room. That does not mean, of course, that our new rules will not have a substantial effect on all of you and on your colleagues in your companies' executive suites. I believe they will. I would like to look at three specific ways in which you can (and should, in my view) be involved in all of this:

1.   Your involvement in the substance of your company's disclosure, particularly the new Compensation Discussion & Analysis;
2.   Your involvement in refining and adjusting your company's disclosure controls and procedures; and
3.   Your involvement with your board's compensation committee and its new Compensation Committee Report.

CFOs and the Substance of Executive Compensation Disclosure

So first of all, the substance of the new rules. I have no intention of getting into the weeds and taking you through the details of required disclosure going forward. I know you all have many others to help you on that score and who will be at the front lines for your companies in compiling the necessary information and preparing the company's disclosure. But there is one key point that you all should know—under the new rules, companies will be required to include disclosure in their proxy statements about their CFO's compensation. This is new, and it is irrelevant how much or how little any of you might make.

The old rules required compensation disclosure about the CEO (as a category) and the four other most highly compensated executives, calculated based on salary and bonus. The new rules, which become effective in December and for most of you will apply to your next proxy statement—will require disclosure about the compensation of the CEO and the CFO (by titles, or categories) as well as the next three most highly compensated executives. Under the new rules, the amount of compensation used to calculate the three highest is based on *everything* with a few limited exceptions. Importantly it is not just salary and bonus. So this figure includes the dollar value of option grants, the value of perquisites, and numerous other types of awards.

And if this thought horrifies you, please understand you won't be spared even by giving up your title or quitting your job. Disclosure will be required about anyone who served as the CFO, or CEO, during any part of the year. And if you should leave, any severance you receive will be included in your compensation disclosure.

The release the SEC put out with its new rules is entitled "Executive Compensation and Related Person Disclosure" and covers substantially more than proxy disclosures of executive compensation (although that's critically important and is the central topic of the rulemaking). Just as a quick overview and summary, the final adopted rules cover:

- executive compensation disclosure, including, among other things, new tabular disclosure (with a single compensation total)
  - a new Compensation Discussion & Analysis section, which I will turn to in just a minute
  - perquisites guidance
  - disclosure about post-termination (retirement or otherwise) or change-in-control payments
- disclosure of related party transactions
- disclosures about the compensation committee, about director independence determinations and other related corporate governance matters
- director compensation disclosure
- disclosure about security ownership of management and directors, including shares pledged by management
- new rules and guidance about disclosures of stock option grants and option grant programs, plans and practices

I'd be happy at the end of my remarks to talk about any of this in more detail if you have any questions. I also hope that perhaps some of you will be newly motivated after I stop talking to make sure someone at your company or on your team keeps talking and fills you in on what you should know and what you want to know.

Compensation Discussion & Analysis (CD&A)

I do want to make one other last point under this broad "substance" umbrella. You may have heard that proxy statements under the new rules will be required to include a new "Compensation Discussion & Analysis", or CD&A, section. That section will also be deemed "filed" and will be incorporated into your company's annual reports on Form 10-K (more on the significance of that in a moment).

The new CD&A section is at the heart of the Commission's new rules. Given your CFO perspective, I know you are already very familiar with MD&A, or Management's Discussion & Analysis. CD&A will bear many similarities to MD&A, albeit covering a different subject matter. In the most summary terms, CD&A is designed to be a principles-based overview explaining—that is, "discussing and analyzing", or the "D&A" part—the policies and decisions related to executive compensation. And as CFOs, you should particularly appreciate the meaning of principles-based disclosure, as it is not only central to MD&A but is also a close relative of the principles-based standards that are so much in focus lately in the accounting and financial reporting worlds.

The principles-based theme is critical to our recent rulemaking and one which I have been stressing in other forums when speaking on this topic and trying to explain how it works in the disclosure arena. When trying to explain how it works, I personally have found it useful to look at a 2002 speech on principles-based accounting that FASB Chairman Bob Herz gave.[3] If you are interested in this important element of the new rules and its intended impact on your company's disclosure, I would also refer you to a speech that I gave three weeks ago here in New York. In those remarks, I tried to lay out the meaning and significance of a principles-based approach and how embracing it can aid both investors and companies. Among other things, that speech, entitled "Principles Matter", takes a look at what "principles-based" means specifically with regard to the new CD&A. Those remarks are available on the SEC website.[4]

And, more importantly, in this compensation world which is often dominated by lawyers and compensation specialists of all types, you as CFOs bring a different perspective. As I have said, you are presumably familiar both with MD&A (and how it works) and with the principles-based theme from the accounting world. I hope you become involved and take a leadership role in this new and critically important disclosure that your company will be preparing and giving its investors for the first time in the coming months.

Disclosure Controls and Procedures

I'd like to put the content of the new rules aside now and talk for a moment about process. I have to assume you all have spent much time in the world of internal control over financial reporting (the famous SOX 404). I also assume you are familiar with the related requirement that public companies maintain disclosure controls and procedures which apply to all information filed or submitted to the SEC. Among other things, I assume you're very familiar with these controls because they should be feeding into and contributing to your ability to make the certifications that are required of each of you, as a CFO, under Section 302 of the Sarbanes-Oxley Act.

I alluded earlier to the new and expanded types of compensation information required by the new rules. To my mind, a company needs to be reviewing and, where necessary, revamping its disclosure controls and procedures to make sure that those are up to this task. I imagine many of you already have done so, or hopefully have at least substantially started that process, since information from this year (all the way back to the start of the year) will be required to be disclosed in the next proxy. And remember there are two separate and distinct reasons, both related to your certifications, that you should especially care about disclosure controls and procedures.

- As I said earlier, your company's disclosure controls and procedures provide much of the support you need in making your required certifications (and don't forget your 906 certifications for that matter, on which you have personal criminal liability); but also
- Your Section 302 certification specifically speaks to your responsibility for disclosure controls and procedures and to you, as CFO and a certifying officer, having evaluated those and disclosed your conclusions about them in your company's public filing—you cannot hide your head in the sand on this one.

So what kind of updating might your disclosure controls and procedures need? I cannot answer that question for you. For one thing, it's not my place—the answer depends on your company's specific facts and circumstances. For another thing, we don't possibly have enough time this evening to even scratch the surface. I would urge you all, however, to be actively involved in those updates and make sure you're satisfied with how they've been planned and how they're progressing. And make sure your team is thinking outside the box. Because of the new requirements in the executive compensation arena, you may need to include more people, different people who have never been involved in your public company disclosures in the past. You may need to set up new processes and circuits for gathering, compiling and analyzing information even before making disclosure determinations. Remember that the universe of people at the company for whom disclosures may be required has been expanded in many cases.

I am sorry I cannot provide you any definite or detailed answers but I would strongly urge each of you to make sure someone else does or, arguably even better, that you yourself are actively involved in coming up with these answers for your company. And please don't leave this task for another day. If it waits until the 11th hour, it is unlikely to get done right and it is unlikely to work effectively. You have a personal obligation under the securities laws as well as to your investors. Please plan ahead and if there is to be one take away for you from tonight, let this one be it. Get the processes and procedures going to your satisfaction—any compensation specialists, disclosure lawyers or other advisors you have should be on top of this— make sure they are and that you are as well.

Role of the Compensation Committee

I am sure that countless compensation consultants and other specialists have a wealth of advice about how our new rules will be changing the landscape for the compensation committee. I believe that's true in at least some respects, and I think it's an important topic. But speaking with all of you tonight, I would just like to look at one narrow slice of the compensation committee pie—specifically, how does the Compensation Committee's changing role under the new rules relate to all of you and more specifically to your certifications and to those disclosure controls and procedures we were just discussing.

I imagine many, if not all, of you are familiar with the old "Board Compensation Committee Report on Executive Compensation" that used to appear in the proxy statement. As its name suggests, that one was a report by the compensation committee—not the company or management, and you did not certify to it. That report, however, has now been eliminated and replaced in some measure by the new CD&A section. In addition, a new and very different Compensation Committee Report will also be required going forward which I will describe shortly.

Perhaps we should step back just for a moment and return to a point I alluded to when talking about the new CD&A—it is filed company disclosure. Among other things, that means that it will be covered by your required SOX 302 certification. In some ways, the CD&A covers the same ground the old board compensation committee report covered. To my mind, it also covers much more. It's also company disclosure, and you each are personally on the hook (through your certifications) for what it says. I can hear some of you saying, "How can that be fair?"

In response, I would make a couple of points. First of all, the CD&A really is company—not compensation committee—disclosure. Remember the analogy to MD&A—in this sense too, the two are in the same camp and they are part of your company's total disclosure. But to the extent the CD&A speaks to anything that you might feel you really can't assess the accuracy of, the Commission has mandated that the Compensation Committee supply a new report, which you will be able to look to as an important part of your process (your controls) of getting comfortable with the whole of your company's disclosure.

So if you'll allow me just a couple more minutes of your time, I would like to talk briefly about the new compensation committee report and how it relates to you. The Compensation Committee Report was modeled on the existing Audit Committee Report, and it must contain just two statements:

1. whether the compensation committee has reviewed and discussed the Compensation Discussion and Analysis with management; and

2. based on this review and discussions, whether the compensation committee recommended to the Board of Directors that the CD&A be included in the company's annual report on Form 10-K and proxy statement.

The Compensation Committee Report will appear over the names of the compensation committee members and will be *furnished*, not filed—so even though it will be incorporated into your company's 10-K, your certification will not cover this report.

But this report, assuming your committee does recommend inclusion of the CD&A in your company's filings, should help you with the background and comfort you need in making your certifications. Similarly, if your company and your compensation committee do choose to engage in the review and discussions that the CD&A contemplates, I would think that should also help you as part of your disclosure controls and procedures. I should note that the SEC does not require those reviews and discussions (note the use of the word "whether" in the compensation committee report) but I imagine many companies will do so. I would also encourage all of you, individually, to think about what you feel you need and then to make sure you get it. Do you need the chairman of your compensation committee to be more involved, at an earlier stage? If you do, then I personally would urge you to try to get that started. In another speech I gave last week at the Practising Law Institute's Directors' Institute here in New York, I similarly urged directors, especially those serving on compensation committees, to have the same attitude and to understand what their companies, and their management, might need from them in light of the new rules.[5] Don't sit idly by between now and the date your proxy (or even your 10-K) gets filed. Do whatever you need to be prepared.

Conclusion

In conclusion, I hope you are all convinced (if you weren't already) that the Commission's new executive compensation disclosure rules should be of fundamental interest to each of you individually. I acknowledged earlier the critical role you play to American business. And as I hope you know, you also play a critical role under the securities laws—for your shareholders and for investors more generally. The certifications you sign are one reason for this but those certifications are, to my mind, even more importantly a reflection of all the other, more fundamental reasons that you are so key to your investors. In other words, your certifications are important because of your substantive contributions and your importance to your company and because of all the insights and understandings you have that investors will never be able to fully share. You can, however—precisely because of your critical role and your authority at your company—help investors get a little closer to your insights and your understanding. Do what you can— what you and your colleagues in the executive suite are probably uniquely qualified to do—to make sure your company's disclosures are the best they can be. I know each of you is an incredibly busy person, but I think you will find that the rewards of doing this are more than worth the time and effort.

Understanding and pursuing the principles of the new executive compensation disclosure rules is one way you can do that. If you appreciate and embrace the importance of this disclosure (and after all, it includes disclosure about your compensation), I imagine that attitude might go a long way toward inspiring and enlisting the others around you to share your sincerity and your commitment to the cause. You can also advance the needs and interests of your shareholders by structuring your company's disclosure controls and procedures so that they are aligned with these new disclosure tasks. And I hope you also understand how doing so is in your own best interest and can help serve your own needs. It truly is a complete circle, and I am convinced that if all the players on the team share the same understandings and the same commitment to the same goals, then you, your company and your investors will all reap the benefits. Thank you again for your time this evening.

Endnotes

1. The Sarbanes-Oxley Act of 2002 and the Commission's rules that have followed the passage of that Act, including the new executive compensation disclosure rules, use the term "principal financial officer". For purposes of these remarks, "CFO" refers to exactly the same person or title as "principal financial officer".

2. See, e.g., "Introductory Remarks at the SEC Open Meeting," Christopher Cox, Chairman, U.S. Securities and Exchange Commission, July 26, 2006, available at http://www.sec.gov/news/speech/2006/spch072606cc.htm.

3. "Remarks before the Financial Executives International Current Financial Reporting Issues Conference," Robert H. Herz, November 4, 2002.

4. "Principles Matter," John W. White, Director, Division of Corporation Finance, U.S. Securities and Exchange Commission, September 6, 2006, available at http://www.sec.gov/news/speech/2006/spch090606jww.htm.

5. "An Expansive View of Teamwork: Directors, Management and the SEC," John W. White, Director, Division of Corporation Finance, U.S. Securities and Exchange Commission, September 25, 2006, available at http://www.sec.gov/news/speech/2006/spch092506jww.htm.

Appendix
F

Where's the Analysis?
John W. White

Director, Division of Corporation Finance
U.S. Securities and Exchange Commission

The 2nd Annual Proxy Disclosure Conference: Tackling Your 2008
   Compensation Disclosures
San Francisco, CA
October 9, 2007

Good afternoon. Thank you, Jesse [Brill]. I am excited to return to San Francisco to talk about executive compensation disclosure in the 2007 proxy season—the first season under the new requirements the Commission adopted just over a year ago. The staff's observations on the first year disclosures were published this morning, and what a great forum this is to reflect on where we are in our pursuit of the "clearer and more complete picture of compensation" that the Commission sought in adopting the new rules.

In the next half hour, I plan to share with you some of my views on where the first-year disclosures have realized this goal and where they have not. The positives are substantial—and there is a wealth of new information available to investors for the first time. Investors have been provided with the most comprehensive disclosure ever regarding how much public companies pay their executives and directors. There are some very important areas, however, where work remains for next year.

As I noted, these are my views—so let me go ahead and provide you the required disclaimer—the views that I'm going to express today are solely my own and do not necessarily reflect the views of the Securities and Exchange Commission or of any members of the Commission or its staff, other than myself.

It was in this city, at this series of conferences, three years ago in 2004, that my predecessor Alan Beller started it all off with his memorable "all means all" speech.[1] We have come a long way since then—382 pages of proposals,[2] almost 30,000 comment letters,[3] 489 pages of adopting releases,[4] 112 interpretations,[5] a first full season of disclosures and, most recently, a staff report on the first year disclosures after 350 reviews.[6] On Alan's "all means all" point, we have made great progress—the rules are pretty clear on what compensation companies need to disclose, and what they need to quantify. The new tables and footnotes, and what companies are required to put in them, take us a long way toward our disclosure goals in this area.

The Commission made clear in adopting the new rules, however, that it is looking for more than just the value of the components of compensation and a total value of compensation. What is that "more" it is looking for? In order to provide investors with more than just tables of numbers, the Commission created the new Compensation Discussion & Analysis requirement to "put into perspective for investors the numbers and narrative that follow it." This "overview" is very much a principles-based requirement, like the MD&A section with which we are all so familiar. In an instruction to the CD&A requirement, the Commission made clear that CD&A "should focus on the material principles underlying the registrant's executive compensation policies and decisions and the most important factors relevant to the *analysis* of those policies and decisions." My emphasis on the word "analysis" should provide you with a pretty good idea of the principal place where I believe many companies came up short—where disclosure can be improved. More on that in just a moment.

Let's turn to the Division's report, which was published this morning. Our report largely provides an overview of our principal areas of comment. Rather than waiting to reflect the give and take of the individual company comment process, we have published our observations as soon as initial comments were issued to all the companies. One observation: these comments reflect places where we believe companies may need to provide additional or clearer disclosure in future filings. That's the very nature of the comment process. But we should not lose sight of the fact that implementing the new disclosure requirements, gathering the new information, and crafting the new disclosures for investors, often writing on a clean slate, was a substantial task in the first year. As a whole, company efforts were quite admirable, and investors are well-served by the new disclosures.

Principles-Based Disclosure and Materiality

For context, let me briefly go back to the principles-based regime of CD&A, to the role of examples, and to materiality. Last year as we headed into the first season, I made a series of remarks based on the idea that, in drafting first-year CD&As, companies needed to focus on using the principles-based regime outlined in the adopting release—because, "principles matter."[7] That certainly remains the case, and "principles still matter."

Recall how principles-based disclosure works. There are overarching disclosure principles—and the Commission laid those out in the release and the rules. You've heard them and read them. And then there are examples—and the Commission provided 15 of them. These examples are just that. They neither encompass the universe of possible required disclosures, nor are they mandatory. Companies need not discuss each example, as disclosure is required only where material. The instructions to the CD&A provide a pretty clear mandate in this regard. Let me repeat what I just said. Disclosure is required only where material.

Analysis

Now, back to our comments. Several key themes recur in our comments, one of which I want to lay out a bit more bluntly than in the report. And these are my views of course.

Far too often, meaningful analysis is missing—this is the biggest shortcoming of the first-year disclosures. Stated simply—Where's the analysis?

I know no better way to emphasize this than to go to the very examples that the staff highlighted in the report. A good starting point, and a representative example, is disclosure of compensation philosophies and decision-making processes. We saw a great deal of detail this year, but what was missing was a discussion of *how* and *why* those philosophies and processes resulted in the numbers the company presented in its tabular disclosure. There also was a great deal of detail on individual compensation components, but little discussion of how the amounts paid or awarded under each compensation element—and how the total compensation delivered from all these elements (what some refer to as wealth accumulation)—affected the decisions that companies made regarding amounts paid or awarded under other compensation elements. That's missing analysis.

A few more examples where analysis was missing include disclosures with respect to benchmarks, differences in compensation policies and decisions among executive officers, and change-in-control arrangements. I don't plan to go through these today—they are discussed in the report if you'd like more detail. I will instead take you through one additional example—performance targets. I'm spending a bit of extra time on this area for a couple reasons. It was one of the most commented on areas in the first-year disclosures and it also brings together not only the missing analysis theme, but also the concepts of principles and materiality as the foundation for your disclosure decisions.

As we all know, and as I just noted, the new rules include 15 examples of items that may be material elements of a company's compensation policies and decisions, and therefore require CD&A disclosure. Two of these examples go to what items of corporate performance are used in setting compensation and how they are used. Discussion of performance targets comes up in the context of these examples.

In reviewing the first-year disclosures on performance targets, we were disappointed to find that, though a significant number of companies apparently use performance goals or targets, far too often an analysis of *how* the targets were used in setting compensation was missing. In our comment process, we approached these disclosures from the starting point of materiality—as we all know, the CD&A rules require disclosure with respect to an example only where material. So, just to say it another way, depending on whether the CD&A examples that relate to corporate performance are material for your company, performance targets are a disclosure point that may or may not need to be addressed.

What did we ask for? You guessed it—for more analysis. We often found it difficult to understand how companies used targets or considered qualitative individual performance to set compensation and make decisions. Our comments were not intended to suggest that every CD&A must necessarily address disclosure regarding targets for the year in question, or any other year. In the first instance, a company needs to determine whether use of corporate performance items is material, and for which years, and to address disclosure and confidentiality accordingly. Where targets appeared to be material based on what was disclosed, but the company did not disclose specific targets, we asked that the company either disclose the targets or demonstrate why doing so would cause competitive harm. In those instances where a target is properly omitted based on the competitive harm standard, the company must discuss, in a meaningful way, how difficult it will be for the executive or how likely it will be for the company to achieve that target.

Just to expand briefly on one last related point—my references to the years for which disclosure must be addressed. This takes us back to principles (as well as to an instruction in the rules).[8] As we know, CD&A must cover the last fiscal year, but depending on materiality, there are a number of situations where a company may also find it necessary to discuss targets for either prior years, the current year, or later years, to place their disclosure in context or "affect a fair understanding" of a named executive officer's compensation. This might occur with a multi-year compensation plan or where targets varied materially from year-to-year.

So, I hope that gives perspective on where many of our comments fell regarding analysis. In looking at disclosures and staff comment letters on those disclosures, you certainly can come up with more. But I think that if you look at the areas I've mentioned, you will understand where the Division feels companies can improve their analysis in the coming proxy season.

Presentation

With that, I'm going to take you briefly through a second key area of our comments on the first-year disclosures—manner of presentation. Put simply, "presentation matters." The revised rules require companies to disclose a great deal of information—and that information goes to the heart of how it compensates its executive officers. How a company provides that information is, in many ways, as important as its content.

Manner of presentation is not limited to plain English principles, although our requests for clearer and more understandable disclosure constitute a significant portion of our comments in this area. The Commission specifically affirmed its support for plain English principles in the adopting release for the new rules, noting that "[c]learer, more concise presentation of executive and director compensation . . . can facilitate more informed investing and voting decisions in the face of complex information about these important areas." And I think that we can all agree that with executive compensation we often are dealing with complex information.

Chairman Cox, who is particularly focused on the importance of clear, concise, and understandable disclosure in all Commission initiatives, will be speaking later this week on plain English principles at a symposium on plain language in Washington DC,[9] so I am going to leave the real message on manner of presentation for him. But I will mention a couple things I'd like you to focus on.

Disclosure can fail in either of two different ways—it can be presented clearly and understandably without being meaningful or responsive to disclosure requirements or, conversely, it can be responsive in content without being clear and understandable. The first of these failures takes us back to analysis. Although companies generally appear to have made a good faith effort to provide clear and understandable disclosure, we found that many omitted critical information—largely the "how" and "why" of their executive compensation decisions. This is where we asked for enhanced disclosure most often. Where we ask companies to add or enhance their analysis, this does not mean that we are trying to undermine efforts at plain English-compliant disclosure. Our requests for improved analysis need not lengthen disclosure. Rather, with careful drafting, I believe companies can achieve a succinct and effective discussion that provides the required disclosure *and* embraces plain English principles.

In this regard, I refer you to the Division's report, where we have described a few of the ways we have suggested companies can improve the content of their disclosure without compromising plain English principles. Where companies include boilerplate discussions of individual performance, they should instead provide specific analysis of how they considered and used individual performance to determine each individual's compensation. Where a company has simply repeated in its CD&A information that it also presents in the required compensation tables, it should replace the redundant disclosure with a clear and concise analysis of that information. Where disclosure has been (or appears to have been) lifted directly from the technical language of a compensation plan or employment agreement, the company should redraft that disclosure in a more clear, concise, and understandable manner.

I think that if companies and their disclosure counsel embrace this guidance, and make changes consistent with the spirit of the guidance, it will quickly become apparent that you can be responsive to both staff requests for additional analysis and the plain English requirements.

One final thought in this area, one that intersects both the topics of presentation and analysis, and that appears in the report in our discussion of performance targets. We have heard concerns expressed by company executives and disclosure counsel that the staff, in its comment process, may be asking for quantitative explanations of decisions that may in fact be subjective assessments of individual performance. Let me assure you— that is not our intent. We are simply asking these companies to present how these decisions were made—as the report phrases it, "to clearly lay out the way that qualitative inputs are ultimately translated into objective pay determinations." In talking to company executives and disclosure counsel in the past couple of months, we frequently have been provided with very clear, straightforward explanations of this. That is exactly what we are looking for—*in* the filing.

Second-Year Disclosure

After all that, I know that many will now say, "Show us the good examples." However, even with my disclaimer, I feel constrained from highlighting individual company disclosures—good or bad. I also don't want to see everyone coming back with identical boilerplate disclosure next year. But I will say, there are good disclosures out there—they will be discussed at this and other conferences I'm sure—and I would challenge you all to consider those examples as you draft disclosure tailored to reflect the individual circumstances of your company, and next year to aspire to become one of those examples—if you are not one already. Don't let this coming year's disclosures be just a mark-up of the first year. Instead step back and ask some very important questions.

- What is material to my shareholders, to my investors, as they examine the compensation of our executives and make their voting decisions for our board of directors and investment decisions with respect to our company?
- What are the material elements of individual executive and corporate performance that are considered in setting executive compensation?
- What is the relationship between the objectives of our compensation program and the different elements of compensation?
- What are the material factors that relate to our compensation decision-making process?

Then, sit down and focus on two very important aspects of your disclosure:

Analysis. Focus on how and why you reached the compensation decisions you made in your CD&A. Don't provide a laundry list of facts. Discuss and analyze the elements of your decision-making. Some have suggested that the way to ensure proper emphasis of analysis is to require companies to provide a separate section titled "Analysis" in the CD&A. This suggestion is one of many good ideas. I will leave it to you, however, to determine how best to highlight the analysis.

Presentation matters. Focus on being clear, concise and understandable. Our rules require you to provide substantial amounts of
information. Consider ways to present your information in a manner
that helps people understand it. Consider presenting layered disclosure.
Consider using tables and charts to present complex information.
Continue your innovative efforts to use these tools to illustrate the
relationship between compensation objectives and different forms
of pay.

So, going forward, the question becomes—where do you, and we at the SEC,
fit into this process?

Disclosure Counsel. Let's start with you—disclosure counsel and other
advisors. What is your role in improving second-year disclosures? Alan
Beller said it in 2004, I've said it in the past, and I will keep saying it.
You must not lose sight of who your client is—the company. Not the
CEO. Not the CFO. Not any other member of management. And, not
the board. It is troublesome, to say the least, when I hear the suggestion
that some have lost sight of their role in this very sensitive area. Executive compensation disclosure must be guided by counsel acting for the
company. The information the company's shareholders seek and need
should guide your disclosure advice, and the company's disclosure
decisions. A company's shareholders want to see what executive compensation decisions a company makes and how it makes them. That is
your audience. That is your client.

SEC Staff. Those of us on the SEC staff, where do we fit in? In our
future reviews of executive compensation disclosures, we will have the
benefit of what we learned and continue to learn in the first year. We
will certainly expect to see the results of our call for more and better
analysis and clearer, more concise disclosure. In issuing comments this
year, we realized that each company was faced with an entirely new
disclosure regime for executive compensation. We took into account
each company's learning curve. We issued a lot of comments in which
we asked companies to revise their future disclosure, not their current
disclosure. We asked a lot of questions so we could better understand
why companies made the disclosure they did.

As we enter the second season, we will expect companies to have taken our
guidance to heart, and I anticipate that you will see that heightened expectation
reflected in the type and focus of our comments and reactions next year.

With that, I want to close with one thought, which is really quite simple,
and you have no doubt heard it before—step back next year and start with a

clean slate, a blank sheet of paper. Now when I listen to that, it sounds like pretty dull jargon—a nice platitude. You'll no doubt nod, and then go on.

So let me try a simple, more practical suggestion. One that perhaps will show up in those lists of practice points many of you develop.

This fall. Before anyone starts drafting your CD&A. Ask every key participant (from the compensation committee chair on down) to turn in one page—no more than a page—perhaps even with the caption "Analysis." Hand them a copy of our just-issued staff report so that they see our concerns about missing analysis. Then ask for bullets. Those bullets should reflect what he or she sees, from their perspective, as the key "hows" and "whys," including, as appropriate

- the key analytic tools used by the compensation committee,
- the findings that emerged from the analysis, and
- the resulting actions taken impacting executive compensation in the last year.

In short, the key points of analysis. The next step for the drafting team is obvious. Call this process collecting the "clean slate" lists. Consider building it into your procedures. Follow up on getting the lists.

So, that's it. Thank you for inviting me, and I look forward to seeing your disclosures next year.

Endnotes

1. "Remarks Before Conference of the NASPP, the Corporate Counsel and the Corporate Executive," Alan L. Beller, Director, Division of Corporation Finance, October 20, 2004, available at /news/speech/spch102004alb.htm.

2. SEC Release No. 33-8655, "Executive Compensation and Related Party Disclosure," January 27, 2006, available at http://www.sec.gov/rules/proposed/33-8655.pdf; SEC Release No. 33-8735, "Executive Compensation Disclosure," August 29, 2006, available at http://www.sec.gov/rules/proposed/2006/33-8735.pdf.

3. Comment File No. S7-03-06, available at http://www.sec.gov/rules/proposed/s70306.shtml.

4. SEC Release No. 33-8732A, "Executive Compensation and Related Person Disclosure (conforming amendments)," August 29, 2006, available at http://www.sec.gov/rules/final/2006/33-8732a.pdf; SEC Release No. 33-8765, "Executive Compensation Disclosure," December 22, 2006, available at http://www.sec.gov/rules/final/2006/33-8765.pdf.

5. Division of Corporation Finance Disclosure and Compliance Interpretations, available at http://www.sec.gov/divisions/corpfin/cfguidance.shtml#regs-k.

6.   "Staff Observations in the Review of Executive Compensation Disclosure, Division of Corporation Finance," available at http://www.sec.gov/divisions/corpfin/guidance/execcompdisclosure.htm.

7.   "Principles Matter," John W. White, Director, Division of Corporation Finance, September 6, 2006, available at http://www.sec.gov/news/speech/2006/spch090606jww.htm; "The Principles Matter: Options Disclosure," John W. White, Director, Division of Corporation Finance, September 11, 2006, available at http://www.sec.gov/news/speech/2006/spch091106jww.htm; "Principles Matter: Related Person Transactions Disclosure and Disclosure Controls and Procedures," John W. White, Director, Division of Corporation Finance, October 12, 2006, available at http://www.sec.gov/news/speech/2006/spch101206jww.htm.

8.   Instruction 2 to Item 402(b) of Regulation S-K states:

The Compensation Discussion and Analysis should be of the information contained in the tables and otherwise disclosed pursuant to this Item. The Compensation Discussion and Analysis should also cover actions regarding executive compensation that were taken after the registrant's last fiscal year's end. Actions that should be addressed might include, as examples only, the adoption or implementation of new or modified programs and policies or specific decisions that were made or steps that were taken that could affect a fair understanding of the named executive officer's compensation for the last fiscal year. Moreover, in some situations it may be necessary to discuss prior years in order to give context to the disclosure provided.

See also, SEC Release No. 8732A, "Executive Compensation and Related Person Disclosure (conforming amendments)," August 29, 2006 ("Commenters also requested clarification as to whether Compensation Discussion and Analysis is limited to compensation for the last fiscal year, like the former Board Compensation Committee Report on Executive Compensation that was required prior to these amendments. While the Compensation Discussion and Analysis must cover this subject, the Compensation Discussion and Analysis may also require discussion of post-termination compensation arrangements, on-going compensation arrangements, and policies that the company will apply on a going-forward basis. Compensation Discussion and Analysis should also cover actions regarding executive compensation that were taken after the last fiscal year's end. Actions that should be addressed might include, as examples only, the adoption or implementation of new or modified programs and policies or specific decisions that were made or steps that were taken that could affect a fair understanding of the named executive officer's compensation for the last fiscal year. Moreover, in some situations it may be necessary to discuss prior years in order to give context to the disclosure provided.").

9.   Symposium on Plain Language: Public Policy and Good Business, Center for Plain Language, October 12, 2007.

Executive Compensation Disclosure: Observations on the 2009 Proxy Season and Expectations for 2010
Shelley Parratt

Deputy Director, Division of Corporation Finance
U.S. Securities and Exchange Commission

The 4th Annual Proxy Disclosure Conference: Tackling Your 2010
Compensation Disclosures
San Francisco, California
November 9, 2009

Thank you, Jesse, for that kind introduction, and good morning. I'm very glad to be here with you today to share my thoughts on the current state of executive compensation disclosure under the Commission's rules and to talk about what we expect to see in the 2010 proxy season.

First, though, I need to remind you that the views I express today are my own, and do not necessarily represent the views of the Commission or other members of the staff.

Over the last several years, executive compensation has been subject to much debate. It seems that people from Main Street to Wall Street—and everywhere in between—have an intense interest in the topic. And with the ongoing challenges in the economy, there seems to be even more focus on executive compensation and its link to corporate accountability. Nearly every day there is a headline claiming that underperforming companies are overpaying their executives.

There is no reason to believe that the scrutiny of executive compensation practices at public companies will subside anytime soon. It is in a company's best interest to communicate clearly and effectively about its executive compensation and the Commission's disclosure requirements are designed to help you do that. While I'm not sure clear and transparent disclosure can trump emotion when it comes to money, it can't hurt.

The SEC's role in this area is not to regulate *how* companies compensate their executives, but rather to see that investors have the critical disclosure they need to make informed investment and voting decisions. The Compensation Discussion and Analysis is essential to providing investors with meaningful insight into the compensation policies and decisions of the companies in which they choose to invest. The CD&A is where a company tells its story about why it made the decisions it made.

The Division's Disclosure Program

As a starting point, I thought it might be helpful to mention briefly the role of the Division's disclosure review program.

The Sarbanes-Oxley Act of 2002 requires that we review each reporting company at least once every three years.[1] It's a well-known fact that we review a substantial number of companies more frequently—and a large number of them every year. To place the scope of this program in context, in each of the last three fiscal years, we have reviewed the disclosure of more than 5,000 companies.

While many of our reviews are focused on a company's financial statements and related disclosure, we also remain focused on a company's non-financial disclosure, including its executive compensation disclosure. Our review of executive compensation disclosure is part of our normal review process and we continue to allocate significant resources to reviewing these disclosures. I'm sure many of you have received comments from us on your executive compensation disclosure during the past two years. If we have not reviewed your filings in either of the last two years, the chances are very good that we're planning to do so this year.

Observations on 2009 Executive Compensation Disclosure

The Division has provided you with a report on the state of executive compensation disclosure at this conference over the past few years. When John White spoke to you in October 2007, he encouraged companies to start with a "clean slate" in drafting their CD&As[2] and take to heart the guidance the staff provided on executive compensation disclosure.[3] A year later, he reported that our comments on executive compensation disclosure mirrored those of the first year—companies needed to provide enhanced disclosure of their analyses and enhance their disclosure of performance targets and benchmarking.[4] Throughout this time, the Division has continued to provide companies with specific comments on their disclosure, reports on comment themes, and disclosure guidance in the form of Compliance and Disclosure Interpretations.

So, following what seems to have become a tradition, here I am in 2009 providing observations about executive compensation disclosure.

Following the end of the 2009 proxy season, we decided to take a look back at our comments and the state of issuers' disclosure. We wanted to identify common comment areas, understand how companies were responding to our comments, and evaluate whether we could improve the consistency of our comments and review of responses to those comments.

In looking back over the comments we issued, we noticed a couple of things. First, we found that we're pretty consistent in the comments we issued on executive compensation disclosure. Second, we noticed a pattern: companies we had previously reviewed continued to provide enhanced executive compensation disclosure and address the primary themes of comments as we identified in our 2007 report. Since 2007, these companies have enhanced their analyses and disclosure about performance targets and benchmarking, and as a result, we did not issue many comments to them. This doesn't mean that these companies couldn't improve their disclosure, but, for the most part, it appears that they have been paying attention to the disclosure requirements and our comment themes.

As for the companies we had not previously reviewed, we found that we issued a substantial number of comments addressing our common comment themes, even though we have made those themes public since October 2007.

Based on this review, we're left with one simple conclusion. The reason for ongoing comments in these areas is not because companies do not understand the disclosure requirements—to the contrary, we believe that there is a general understanding of the rules. Rather, it seems that many are reluctant to address these comment themes until we provide specific comments requesting enhanced disclosure. Anecdotal evidence suggests the same—that companies may be disinclined to disclose detailed compensation information and prepare a rigorous analytical discussion of compensation practices until we ask them to do so in a review.

So where does that leave us? I hate to sound like a broken record, but once again, I must remind you to take a proactive approach to improving your CD&A disclosure. There's no need to wait for us to comment on your disclosure—after all, it is *your* disclosure. More importantly, your obligation to comply with our requirements is the same whether or not we review and comment on your disclosure. And even if we do not review your disclosure, your shareholders are reading it and are making voting and investment decisions based on it. That should be reason enough to motivate you to make your disclosure as good as it can possibly be.

That said, I'd like to mention two topics where companies should focus their attention in the coming year—analysis and performance targets.

Analysis

In 2007, John White asked "Where's the Analysis?" and two years later, we often still can't find it. While many companies have improved their discussions of how and why they made the decisions they did, far too many companies continue to describe—in exhaustive detail—the framework in which they made the compensation decision, rather than the decision itself. The result is that the "how" and the "why" get lost in all the detail.

I'm not saying that you shouldn't provide a discussion of the framework. Our rules require a company to discuss how it determined compensation amounts for each material element of executive compensation, and the framework can be a useful tool to provide context for that disclosure. While the framework may provide context to investors, the CD&A should not be so technical and process-oriented that it obscures the explanation of what the compensation is designed to reward. A company's analysis of its compensation decisions should present shareholders with meaningful insight into its compensation policies and decisions, including the reasons behind them. Where analysis is lacking, shareholders are often left with a pages-long discussion that is heavy on process but does not explain the reasons why the named executive officers were compensated as they were.

I can't stress the "analysis" part of the Compensation Discussion and Analysis enough. Factual statements about what the company or compensation committee did or did not do are not enough. It isn't sufficient for a company to state that its compensation committee used tally sheets, wealth accumulation analyses, or internal pay equity analyses in making compensation decisions. The company should discuss how the committee used these tools to determine compensation amounts and structures, and explain why it reached its decisions. If a committee's pay determinations were simply subjective decisions, the company should say that. Otherwise, it isn't sufficient for a company to state simply that the committee made compensation decisions based on unspecified qualitative factors. A company should discuss the specific qualitative factors the committee considered and, as we put it back in 2007, "clearly lay out the way that qualitative inputs are ultimately translated into objective pay determinations."[5] Remember, your disclosure should tell your story and the story isn't complete without the analysis.

I don't want to leave you with the impression that the state of analysis in CD&A disclosure is abysmal. I do want to leave you with the impression that we think there are areas in which companies can and should improve. In the current economic environment, with the increased scrutiny on executive compensation, there is no better time to take a hard look at how you could improve your company's disclosure. This may be as simple as improving communications between the company's compensation decision-makers and the drafters of CD&A. Or it could be as simple as starting over with a blank sheet of paper.

We've heard that investors are becoming more and more frustrated by the increase in boilerplate language and CD&A length. We hear repeatedly that there is too much unnecessary bulk and we encourage you to see where you can shorten your disclosure by deleting unnecessary background and process-oriented information. The quality of your analysis is not measured by its length. We urge you to step back and make sure the real story is coming through loud and clear.

Performance Targets

Those of you who have attended this program in the past know that a speech about executive compensation disclosure isn't complete without a discussion of performance targets. We issue more comments on performance targets than any other executive compensation disclosure item. When you say you pay for performance, we look for disclosure that will help your shareholders understand how your pay programs achieve that goal.

Investors feel strongly that companies should disclose performance targets and we want to make sure that companies understand our disclosure requirements on this critical topic. Let's start with the basics. When it comes to performance targets and disclosure, a company must first determine whether corporate or individual performance targets are material to its compensation policies and decisions. Making this determination often involves difficult judgment calls and, depending on the circumstances, we may question your conclusions.

In this regard, 2009 presented a host of public company compensation challenges. We saw instances where boards set performance targets that ultimately were not met, and as a result, bonuses were not awarded. We also saw instances where a board abandoned or ignored performance targets—the board awarded bonuses in an exercise of discretion rather than based on the established performance targets. These situations raised the question of whether the targets in question were material to the company's compensation policies and decisions.

The fact that a performance target was not met or was otherwise disregarded may be a factor to consider in the materiality determination, but it is not a dispositive one. Even where it does not result in an actual payout, a performance target may be material if, based on the company's specific facts and circumstances, it plays an important role in the way the company incentivizes its management.[6] Moreover, where a company pays its executives incentive compensation even though the relevant targets were not met, it can suggest that the targets, and compensation, are not sensitive to risk since the compensation is paid without regard to the risk outcome. In the absence of disclosure about those targets, we question whether shareholders are presented with the complete picture with which they can judge whether the board is acting in their best interests. Accordingly, in most cases, we would expect to see companies disclose and discuss such targets in their CD&A.

Where a company determines that certain performance targets are material, then it must specifically—and if applicable, quantitatively—disclose the targets, unless such disclosure would cause it substantial competitive harm.

Many companies use commercially-sensitive metrics in determining incentive compensation for their executive officers, and they are reluctant to disclose specific performance targets. They are concerned that competitors could use the information to harm the company's business. We do not want our rules to drive compensation committees to tie pay to the wrong measure simply to avoid competitive harm that would come from disclosure of the measure. To address these concerns, our rules seek to balance full disclosure with commercial realities. Companies may omit specific quantitative or qualitative performance-related targets, even where they are material to compensation policies and decisions, if disclosing them would likely cause competitive harm to the company.[7]

The standard that applies in this context is the same standard that would apply if a company were to file a formal request for confidential treatment of trade secrets or commercial or financial information contained in a material contract exhibit to a Securities Act or Exchange Act filing.[8] The touchstone of this standard is that the information must be confidential and disclosure of it would likely "cause substantial harm to the competitive position of the person from whom the information was obtained."[9] However, we've heard there is some confusion about the application of this standard to justify omitting a performance target. I'd like to try to clear up that confusion.

To justify omission of material performance targets based on the likelihood of competitive harm, a company must engage in the same analysis as it would in the context of a formal confidential treatment request. In our filing reviews, if a company's disclosure indicates that it uses performance targets in its compensation programs and it does not disclose those targets, we will likely ask it to explain its basis for omitting the targets. In a surprising number of instances, we find that companies failed to develop a thorough legal analysis prior to filing.

We understand that there's concern that we have applied a more rigorous competitive harm standard to compensatory arrangements than we have to material contracts. We have not intended for this to be the case. I'm not sure why people have the impression that the staff "goes easier" on confidential treatment requests relating to material contracts than on competitive harm arguments relating to performance targets. We apply the same standard to each analysis—even if we may review one kind of request more frequently than another. If you believe we are inappropriately concluding that your situation does not qualify for the exclusion, you should not hesitate to request reconsideration of your facts and circumstances. We include detailed instructions on how to seek this reconsideration on the SEC website.[10]

In our review of our comments on 2009 disclosure and the responses to those comments, we paid particular attention to competitive harm comments and responses. In a number of cases, the staff engaged in a thorough evaluation of competitive harm arguments in the comment and response process. When we reviewed those comments and responses, we found that where companies adequately explained the nexus between disclosure of the subject performance target and the potential for resulting competitive harm, we accepted the response and agreed with the omission of the specific target.

That said, it is often more difficult for companies to persuade us that disclosure of performance targets will result in competitive harm *after* the company has disclosed the amounts. This is especially true for targets that are tied to company-wide financial results that are publicly reported—such as targets tied to company-wide earnings per share. In this regard, we have yet to see any persuasive analyses explaining how competitors could pull together sufficiently-specific information about a company's future operations and strategy from the disclosure of these types of targets to cause the company competitive harm. Accordingly, absent highly unusual circumstances, companies should plan to disclose these kinds of performance targets if material to their compensation policies and decisions.

A final point I'd like to make on this topic is that when a company concludes that it may omit a performance target because disclosure would cause it competitive harm, it must disclose with meaningful specificity how difficult or likely it would be for the company or executive to achieve the undisclosed target.[11] A statement that the target is intended to be "challenging" is insufficient absent more detailed information. A company should provide support for the level of difficulty it asserts, which could include, for example, a discussion of the correlation between historical and future achievement of the relevant performance metric.

What to Expect from the Comment Process in 2010

Now that I've told you what we found in our review of staff comments on 2009 executive compensation disclosures, let me turn to our expectations for 2010 disclosures.

To begin with, the Division is currently reviewing the comment letters submitted on the Commission's recent proposal to enhance proxy disclosure, including that related to compensation.[12] In the proposal, the Commission focuses on the current requirement to discuss how compensation relates to risk and proposes to expand CD&A to address how a company's overall compensation policies for its employees may create incentives that can affect the company's overall risk.[13] You should start thinking about how you would gather the additional information necessary to make the proposed disclosures because the proposed risk disclosure enhancements may well be in place for the coming proxy season. If this proposal is adopted, you can expect the new disclosure to be of interest to us in our reviews. Of course, the staff and Commission will carefully review the comment letters before the Commission decides on final rules.

In our first several years of reviewing disclosures under the existing rules, we wanted to encourage compliance generally by issuing futures comments[14] to give companies and their advisors time to understand and apply the new requirements to their circumstances and compensation practices. As companies have been digesting and applying the rules, we too have been enhancing our understanding of how they apply to various facts and circumstances. As we enter our fourth year of disclosure, our expectations for quality disclosure are heightened and we will reflect this in our comments.

What does that mean for you? It means that after three years of futures comments, we expect companies and their advisors to understand our rules and apply them thoroughly. So, any company that waits until it receives staff comments to comply with the disclosure requirements should be prepared to amend its filings if it does not materially comply with the rules.

What should you focus on this year? Well, it's no secret where we think companies can improve disclosure—I think we've been pretty clear about it in our comments, reports and speeches—but let me remind you one more time. First, please focus on making your disclosure more meaningful and understandable. When a company explains its compensation decision-making processes but does not explain why it made the compensation decisions it made, we will ask for enhanced disclosure of the analysis. When a company states that it determined a material element of compensation based on the achievement of performance targets, we will ask for specific disclosure of the targets and the actual achievement level against the targets, or for the company to provide us with an explanation of how such disclosure would cause it competitive harm. And if disclosure of material performance targets is not required, we will insist on meaningful degree of difficulty disclosure. When a company refers to a peer group used for benchmarking purposes, we'll ask for the names of the peer group companies and how you selected them, and where actual awards fell relative to the benchmark. Companies and their advisors should take care to address these themes as they draft next year's executive compensation disclosure. Now is the time to undertake an earnest attempt to prepare the best possible executive compensation disclosure consistent with the principles set forth in the rules.

As a principles-based disclosure requirement, the CD&A provides companies with wide discretion on how to address those principles. As such, companies should think broadly and not limit their disclosure to the non-exclusive examples the Commission provided in Item 402(b) of Regulation S-K. Where additional disclosure would be material to an understanding of a company's compensation policies or decisions, a company should provide that disclosure. While our principles-based disclosure requirement doesn't specifically require companies to disclose all aspects of their compensation programs, in these economic times with the attention shareholders are paying to executive compensation, a company should evaluate evolving materiality concerns with a view towards complete and transparent executive compensation disclosure.

Closing

In closing, our goal in our review process is to help public companies provide investors with high-quality executive compensation disclosure that complies with both the letter and the spirit of the Commission's disclosure requirements. Don't wait for us to prod you into undertaking a good-faith effort to comply with the principles set forth in our disclosure requirements. Any company that waits until it receives staff comments to comply with the disclosure requirements should be prepared to amend its filings if we raise material comments. Now is the time to engage in a rigorous analysis to develop meaningful, coherent and comprehensive executive compensation disclosure.

While the SEC staff may appear to serve as your editor from time to time, the CD&A is your story to tell, not ours. Read our guidance. Read the publicly-available comment letters. Take a fresh look at the disclosure requirements. Pay attention to what the market is looking for. Your disclosure will be better if you do.

Thank you again for inviting me to join you today.

Endnotes

1.   See Sarbanes-Oxley Act of 2002, Pub. L. 107-204, Title IV, § 408, 116 Stat. 790 (July 30, 2002).

2.   See "Where's the Analysis?," John W. White, Director, Division of Corporation Finance, October 9, 2007, available at http://www.sec.gov/news/speech/2007/spch100907jww.htm.

3.   See, e.g., "Staff Observations in the Review of Executive Compensation Disclosure, Division of Corporation Finance," available at http://www.sec.gov/divisions/corpfin/guidance/execcompdisclosure.htm.

4.   See "Executive Compensation Disclosure: Observations on Year Two and a Look Forward to the Changing Landscape for 2009," John W. White, Director, Division of Corporation Finance, October 21, 2008, available at http://www.sec.gov/news/speech/2008/spch102108jww.htm.

5.   "Staff Observations in the Review of Executive Compensation Disclosure, Division of Corporation Finance," *supra* note 3.

6.   See Item 402(b)(2)(vi) of Regulation S-K.

7.   See Instruction 4 to Item 402(b) of Regulation S-K.

8.   Formal confidential treatment requests can be made pursuant to Securities Act Rule 406 (17 C.F.R. § 230.406) or Exchange Act Rule 24b-2 (17 C.F.R. § 240.24b-2). Each of these rules incorporates the criteria for non-disclosure set forth in Exemption 4 of the Freedom of Information Act (5 U.S.C. § 552(b)(4)).

9.   Nat'l Parks & Conservation Ass'n v. Morton, 498 F.2d 765, 770 (D.C. Cir. 1974).

10.   See http://www.sec.gov/divisions/corpfin/cffilingreview.htm.

11.   See Instruction 4 to Item 402(b) of Regulation S-K.

12.   See Proxy Disclosure and Solicitation Enhancements, Release No. 33-9052 (July 10, 2009) ("Proxy Disclosure Enhancements Proposing Release"), available at http://www.sec.gov/rules/proposed/2009/33-9052.pdf.

13.   See Proxy Disclosure Enhancements Proposing Release, footnote 31.

14.   "Futures comments" are comments issued by the staff that ask companies to provide information or required disclosures in their response letters and/or in future filings, as opposed to in an amendment to the filing under review.

http://www.sec.gov/news/speech/2009/spch110909sp.htm

U.S. Securities and Exchange Commission, Division of Corporation Finance, Interpretive Guidance: Regulation S-K

Last Update: July 8, 2011

These Compliance & Disclosure Interpretations ("C&DIs") comprise the Division's interpretations of Regulation S-K. They replace the interpretations of Regulation S-K and Regulation S-B published in:

- the July 1997 Manual of Publicly Available Telephone Interpretations;
- the March 1999 Interim Supplement to the Manual of Publicly Available Telephone Interpretations;
- the November 2000 Current Issues and Rulemaking Projects Outline;
- the 2007 C&DIs on Items 201, 402, 403, 404 and 407; and
- the March 2008 C&DIs on smaller reporting companies.

The bracketed date following each C&DI is the latest date of publication or revision. A number of new C&DIs have been added. For C&DIs relating to Items 201, 402, 403, 404 and 407, as well as to smaller reporting companies, unless the C&DI has been revised or is a new C&DI, the bracketed date is the date on which the C&DI was last published in the sources noted above. All other C&DIs have been reviewed and, if necessary, updated, and are now republished as of July 3, 2008.

Questions and Answers of General Applicability

Section 117. Item 402(a)—Executive Compensation; General

Question 117.01

Question: When a company that is in the process of restating its financial statements has not filed its Form 10-K for the fiscal year ended December 31, 2005, must the company comply with the 2006 Executive Compensation Rules when it ultimately files the Form 10-K for the fiscal year ended December 31, 2005?

Answer: The company is not required to comply with the 2006 Executive Compensation rules in the Form 10-K for the fiscal year ended December 31, 2005. [Jan. 24, 2007]

Question 117.02

Question: If a company files a preliminary proxy statement under Exchange Act Rule 14a-6 which omits the executive and director compensation disclosure required by Item 402 of Regulation S-K, would the staff request a revised preliminary proxy statement and deem that the 10-calendar-day waiting period specified in Rule 14a-6 does not begin to run until the required information is filed?

Answer: Yes. However, given that the executive and director compensation rules were substantially revised in 2006, in a situation where a company that is complying with the 2006 rules for the first time files a preliminary proxy statement excluding the required executive and director compensation disclosure, the staff will not request a revised preliminary proxy statement nor deem the 10-calendar-day waiting period specified in Rule 14a-6 to be tolled, so long as: (1) the omitted executive and director compensation disclosure is included in the definitive proxy statement; (2) the omitted disclosure does not relate to the matter or matters that caused the company to have to file preliminary proxy materials; and (3) the omitted disclosure is not otherwise made available to the public prior to the filing of the definitive proxy statement. [Feb. 12, 2007]

Question 117.03

Question: During 2009, a company recovers (or "claws-back") a portion of an executive officer's 2008 bonus. How does this affect the company's 2009 Item 402 disclosure for that executive officer?

Answer: The portion of the 2008 bonus recovered in 2009 should not be deducted from 2009 bonus or total compensation for purposes of determining, pursuant to Items 402(a)(3)(iii) and (iv), whether the executive is a named executive officer for 2009. If the executive is a named executive officer for 2009, the Summary Compensation Table should report for the 2008 year, in the Bonus column (column (d)) and Total column (column (j)), amounts that are adjusted to reflect the "clawback," with footnote disclosure of the amount recovered. As the instruction to Item 402(b) provides, if "necessary to an understanding of the registrant's compensation policies and decisions regarding the named executive officers," the Compensation Discussion and Analysis should discuss the reasons for the "claw-back" and how the amount recovered was determined. [Aug. 14, 2009]

Question 117.04

Question: During 2009, a company grants an equity award to an executive officer. The same award is forfeited during 2009 because the executive officer leaves the company. Should the grant date fair value of this award be included for purposes of determining 2009 total compensation and identifying 2009 named executive officers?

Answer: Yes. [Jan. 20, 2010]

Question 117.05

Question: A registrant with a calendar fiscal year end has filed a Securities Act registration statement (or post-effective amendment) for which it seeks effectiveness after December 31, 2009, but before its 2009 Form 10-K is due. Must it include Item 402 disclosure for 2009 in the registration statement before it can be declared effective?

Answer: If the registration statement is on Form S-1, then it must include Item 402 disclosure for 2009 before it can be declared effective. This is because 2009 is the last completed fiscal year. Part I, Item 11(l) of Form S-1 specifically requires Item 402 information in the registration statement, which includes Summary Compensation Table disclosure for each of the registrant's last three completed fiscal years and other disclosures for the last completed fiscal year. General Instruction VII of Form S-1, which permits a registrant meeting certain requirements to incorporate by reference the Item 11 information, does not change this result because the registrant has not yet filed its Form 10-K for the most recently completed fiscal year.

On the other hand, Form S-3's information requirements are satisfied by incorporating by reference filed and subsequently filed Exchange Act documents; for example, there is no specific line item requirement in Form S-3 for Item 402 information. Accordingly, a non-automatic shelf registration statement on Form S-3 can be declared effective before the Form 10-K is due. Securities Act Forms C&DI 123.01 addresses the situation in which a company requests effectiveness for a non-automatic shelf registration statement on Form S-3 during the period between the filing of the Form 10-K and the definitive proxy statement. [Feb. 16, 2010]

Question 117.06

Question: An individual who was the company's principal financial officer for part of the last completed fiscal year was serving the company as an executive officer in a different capacity at the end of that year, and was among the company's three most highly compensated executive officers. Does the company include this individual as a named executive officer pursuant to Item 402(a)(3)(iii), as one of its three most highly compensated executive officers other than the principal executive officer and principal financial officer who were serving as executive officers at the end of the last completed fiscal year?

Answer: No. The company includes this individual as a named executive officer pursuant to Item 402(a)(3)(ii), as an individual who served as principal financial officer during the fiscal year. The company identifies its three most highly compensated executive officers pursuant to Item 402(a)(3)(iii) from among individuals serving as executive officers at the end of the last completed fiscal year who did not serve as its principal executive officer or principal financial officer at any time during that year. [June 4, 2010]

Question 117.07

Question: Item 402(a)(6)(ii) provides that "registrants may omit information regarding group life, health, hospitalization, or medical reimbursement plans that do not discriminate in scope, terms or operation, in favor of executive officers or directors of the registrant and that are available generally to all salaried employees." Does this provision also apply to a disability plan that satisfies these nondiscrimination conditions?

Answer: Yes. To the extent that the disability plan provides benefits not related to termination of employment, a registrant may rely on Item 402(a)(6)(ii) to omit information regarding the disability plan. To the extent that the disability plan provides benefits related to termination of employment, a registrant may rely on Instruction 5 to Item 402(j) to omit information regarding the disability plan. [July 8, 2011]

Section 118. Item 402(b)—Executive Compensation; Compensation Discussion and Analysis

Question 118.01

Question: Is the guidance regarding Compensation Discussion and Analysis disclosure concerning option grants that is provided in Section II.A.2 of Securities Act Release No. 8732A applicable to other forms of equity compensation?

Answer: The same disclosure provisions governing required disclosure about option grants also govern disclosure about restricted stock and other non-option equity awards. This includes the example of potential material information identified in Item 402(b)(2)(iv) of Regulation S-K, which indicates that it may be appropriate to discuss how the determination is made as to when awards are granted, including awards of equity-based compensation such as options. [Jan. 24, 2007]

Question 118.02

Question: In presenting Compensation Discussion and Analysis disclosure about prior option grant programs, plans or practices, are companies required to provide disclosures about programs, plans or practices that occurred outside the scope of the information contained in the tables and otherwise disclosed pursuant to Item 402 (including periods before and after the information contained in the tables and otherwise disclosed pursuant to Item 402)?

Answer: Yes, in certain cases, depending on a company's particular circumstances, disclosure may be required as contemplated by Instruction 2 to Item 402(b) of Regulation S-K. [Jan. 24, 2007]

Question 118.03

Question: Are companies required to include disclosure about programs, plans or practices relating to option grants in the Compensation Discussion and Analysis disclosure for their first fiscal year ending on or after December 15, 2006, or is this disclosure only required for future fiscal periods?

Answer: Companies are required to include disclosure about programs, plans or practices relating to option grants in the Compensation Discussion and Analysis disclosure for fiscal years ending on or after December 15, 2006, as well as any other periods where necessary as contemplated by Instruction 2 to Item 402(b) of Regulation S-K. [Jan. 24, 2007]

Question 118.04

Question: How does a company determine if it may omit disclosure of performance target levels or other factors or criteria under Instruction 4 to Item 402(b)?

Answer: A company should begin its analysis of whether it is required to disclose performance targets by addressing the threshold question of materiality in the context of the company's executive compensation policies or decisions. If performance targets are not material in this context, the company is not required to disclose the performance targets. Whether performance targets are material is a facts and circumstances issue, which a company must evaluate in good faith.

A company may distinguish between *qualitative/subjective* individual performance goals (e.g., effective leadership and communication) and *quantitative/objective* performance goals (e.g., specific revenue or earnings targets). There is no requirement that a company provide quantitative targets for what are inherently subjective or qualitative assessments—for example, how effectively the CEO demonstrated leadership.

When performance targets are a material element of a company's executive compensation policies or decisions, a company may omit targets involving confidential trade secrets or confidential commercial or financial information *only if* their disclosure would result in competitive harm.

A company should use the same standard for evaluating whether target levels (and other factors or criteria) may be omitted as it would use when making a confidential treatment request under Securities Act Rule 406 or Exchange Act Rule 24b-2; however, no confidential treatment request is required to be submitted in connection with the omission of a performance target level or other factors or criteria.

To reach a conclusion that disclosure would result in competitive harm, a company must undertake a competitive harm analysis taking into account its specific facts and circumstances and the nature of the performance targets. In the context of the company's industry and competitive environment, the company must analyze whether a competitor or contractual counterparty could extract from the targets information regarding the company's business or business strategy that the competitor or counterparty could use to the company's detriment. A company must have a reasoned basis for concluding, after consideration of its specific facts and circumstances, that the disclosure of the targets would cause it competitive harm. The company must make its determination based on the established standards for what constitutes confidential commercial or financial information, the disclosure of which would cause competitive harm. These standards have largely been addressed in case law, including *National Parks and Conservation Association v. Morton*, 498 F.2d 765 (D.C. Cir. 1974); *National Parks and Conservation Association v. Kleppe*, 547 F.2d 673 (D.C. Cir. 1976); and *Critical Mass Energy Project v. NRC*, 931 F.2d 939 (D.C. Cir. 1991), *vacated & reh'g en banc granted*, 942 F.2d 799 (D.C. Cir. 1991), *grant of summary judgment to agency aff'd en banc*, 975 F.2d 871 (D.C. Cir. 1992). To the extent that a performance target level or other factor or criteria otherwise has been disclosed publicly, a company cannot rely on Instruction 4 to withhold the information.

The competitive harm standard is the only basis for omitting performance targets if they are a material element of the registrant's executive compensation policies or decisions.

Because Compensation Discussion and Analysis will be subject to staff review, a company may be required to demonstrate that withholding target information meets the confidential treatment standard, and will be required to disclose the information if that standard is not met. Finally, a company that relies on Instruction 4 to omit performance targets is required by the instruction to discuss how difficult it will be for the executive or how likely it will be for the company to achieve the undisclosed target level or other factor or criteria. [July 3, 2008]

Question 118.05

Question: Item 402(b)(2)(xiv) provides, as an example of material information to be disclosed in the Compensation Discussion and Analysis, depending on the facts and circumstances, "[w]hether the registrant engaged in any benchmarking of total compensation, or any material element of compensation, identifying the benchmark and, if applicable, its components (including component companies)." What does "benchmarking" mean in this context?

Answer: In this context, benchmarking generally entails using compensation data about other companies as a reference point on which—either wholly or in part—to base, justify or provide a framework for a compensation decision. It would not include a situation in which a company reviews or considers a broad-based third-party survey for a more general purpose, such as to obtain a general understanding of current compensation practices. [July 3, 2008]

Question 118.06 *[same as Question 133.08]*

Question: Regarding the role of compensation consultants in determining or recommending the amount or form of executive and director compensation, on what basis should a company differentiate between the requirements of Item 407(e)(3)(iii) and Item 402(b)'s Compensation Discussion and Analysis disclosure?

Answer: The information regarding "any role of compensation consultants in determining or recommending the amount or form of executive and director compensation" required by Item 407(e)(3)(iii) is to be provided as part of the company's Item 407(e)(3) compensation committee disclosure. See Release 33-8732A at Section V.D, Corporate Governance Disclosure. If a compensation consultant plays a material role in the company's compensation-setting practices and decisions, then the company should discuss that role in the Compensation Discussion and Analysis section. [July 3, 2008]

Question 118.07

Question: In Compensation Discussion and Analysis (CD&A), is a company required to discuss executive compensation, including performance target levels, to be paid in the current year or in future years?

Answer: No. The CD&A covers only compensation "awarded to, earned by, or paid to the named executive officers." Although Instruction 2 to Item 402(b) provides that the CD&A should also cover actions regarding executive compensation that were taken after the registrant's last fiscal year's end, such disclosure requirement is limited to those actions or steps that could "affect a fair understanding of the named executive officer's compensation for the last fiscal year." [Mar. 4, 2011]

Question 118.08

Question: Instruction 5 to Item 402(b) provides that "[d]isclosure of target levels that are non-GAAP financial measures will not be subject to Regulation G and Item 10(e); however, disclosure must be provided as to how the number is calculated from the registrant's audited financial statements." Does this instruction extend to non-GAAP financial information that does not relate to the disclosure of target levels, but is nevertheless included in Compensation Discussion & Analysis ("CD&A") or other parts of the proxy statement—for example, to explain the relationship between pay and performance?

Answer: No. Instruction 5 to Item 402(b) is limited to CD&A disclosure of target levels that are non-GAAP financial measures. If non-GAAP financial measures are presented in CD&A or in any other part of the proxy statement for any other purpose, such as to explain the relationship between pay and performance or to justify certain levels or amounts of pay, then those non-GAAP financial measures are subject to the requirements of Regulation G and Item 10(e) of Regulation S-K.

In these pay-related circumstances only, the staff will not object if a registrant includes the required GAAP reconciliation and other information in an annex to the proxy statement, provided the registrant includes a prominent cross-reference to such annex. Or, if the non-GAAP financial measures are the same as those included in the Form 10-K that is incorporating by reference the proxy statement's Item 402 disclosure as part of its Part III information, the staff will not object if the registrant complies with Regulation G and Item 10(e) by providing a prominent cross-reference to the pages in the Form 10-K containing the required GAAP reconciliation and other information. [July 8, 2011]

Section 119. Item 402(c)—Executive Compensation; Summary Compensation Table

Question 119.01

Question: If a person that was not a named executive officer in fiscal years 1 and 2 became a named executive officer in fiscal year 3, must compensation information be disclosed in the Summary Compensation Table for that person for all three fiscal years?

Answer: No, the compensation information only for fiscal year 3 need be provided in the Summary Compensation Table. [Jan. 24, 2007]

Question 119.02

Question: Should a discretionary cash bonus that was not based on any performance criteria be reported in the Bonus column (column (d)) of the Summary Compensation Table pursuant to Item 402(c)(2)(iv) or in the Non-equity Incentive Plan Compensation column (column (g)) pursuant to Item 402(c)(2)(vii)?

Answer: The bonus should be reported in the Bonus column (column (d)). In order to be reported in the Non-equity Incentive Plan Compensation column (column (g)) pursuant to Item 402(c)(2)(vii), the bonus would have to be pursuant to a plan providing for compensation intended to serve as incentive for performance to occur over a specified period that does not fall within the scope of Financial Accounting Standards Board Statement of Financial Accounting Standards No. 123 (revised 2004), *Share-Based Payment* ("FAS 123R"). The outcome with respect to the relevant performance target must be substantially uncertain at the time the performance target is established and the target is communicated to the executives. The length of the performance period is not relevant to this analysis, so that a plan serving as an incentive for a period less than a year would be considered an incentive plan under Item 402(a)(6)(iii). Further, amounts earned under a plan that meets the definition of a non-equity incentive plan, but that permits the exercise of negative discretion in determining the amounts of bonuses, generally would still be reportable in the Non-equity Incentive Plan Compensation column (column (g)). The basis for the use of various targets and negative discretion may be material information to be disclosed in the Compensation Discussion and Analysis. If, in the exercise of discretion, an amount is paid over and above the amounts earned by meeting the performance measure in the non-equity incentive plan, that amount should be reported in the Bonus column (column (d)). [Jan. 24, 2007]

Question 119.03

Question: Instruction 2 to Item 402(c)(2)(iii) and (iv) provides that companies are to include in the Salary column (column (c)) or the Bonus column (column (d) € any amount of salary or bonus forgone at the election of a named executive officer under which stock, equity-based, or other forms of non-cash compensation have been received instead by the named executive officer. In a situation where the value of the stock, equity-based or other form of non-cash compensation is the same as the amount of salary or bonus foregone at the election of the named executive officer, does this mean the amounts are only reported in the Salary or Bonus column and not in any other column of the Summary Compensation Table?

Answer: Yes, under Instruction 2 to Item 402(c)(2)(iii) and (iv) the amounts should be disclosed in the Salary or Bonus column, as applicable. The result would be different if the amount of salary or bonus foregone at the election of the named executive officer was less than the value of the equity-based compensation received instead of the salary or bonus, or if the agreement pursuant to which the named executive officer had the option to elect settlement in stock or equity-based compensation was within the scope of FAS123R (e.g., the right to stock settlement is embedded in the terms of the award). In the former case, the incremental value of an equity award would be reported in the Stock Awards or Option Awards columns, and in the latter case the award would be reported in the Stock Awards or Option Awards columns. In both of these special cases, the amounts reported in the Stock Awards and Option Awards columns would be the dollar amounts recognized for financial statement reporting purposes with respect to the applicable fiscal year, and footnote disclosure should be provided regarding the circumstances of the awards. Appropriate disclosure about equity-based compensation received instead of salary or bonus must be provided in the Grants of Plan-Based Awards Table, the Outstanding Equity Awards at Fiscal Year End Table and the Option Exercises and Stock Vested Table. [Aug. 8, 2007]

Question 119.04

Withdrawn Mar. 1, 2010

Question 119.05

Withdrawn Mar. 1, 2010

Question 119.06

Question: Instruction 3 to Item 402(c)(2)(viii) provides that where the amount of the change in the actuarial present value of the accumulated pension benefit computed pursuant to Item 402(c)(2)(viii)(A) is negative, the amount should be disclosed by footnote but should not be reflected in the sum reported in the Change in Pension Value and Nonqualified Deferred Compensation Earnings column (column (h)). When a company aggregates all of the decreases and increases in the value of a named executive officer's individual pension plans, should the company subtract negative values from positive values or should any individual plan decreases be treated as a zero?

Answer: In applying this instruction, a company may subtract negative values when aggregating the changes in the actuarial present values of the accumulated benefits under the plans, and apply the "no negative number" position of the instruction for the final number after aggregating all plans. Under this approach, if one plan had a $500 increase and another plan had a $200 decrease, then the net change in the actuarial present value of the accumulated pension benefits would be $300. [Jan. 24, 2007]

Question 119.07

Question: Item 402(c)(2)(ix)(A) and Instruction 4 to that item require a company to report as "All Other Compensation" perquisites and personal benefits if the total amount exceeds $10,000, and to identify each such item by type, regardless of the amount. If the $10,000 threshold is otherwise exceeded, must a company list by type those perquisites and personal benefits as to which there was no aggregate incremental cost to the company, or as to which the executive officer fully reimbursed the company for such cost?

Answer: If a perquisite or other personal benefit has no aggregate incremental cost, it must still be separately identified by type. Any item for which an executive officer has actually fully reimbursed the company should not be considered a perquisite or other personal benefit and therefore need not be separately identified by type. In this regard, for example, if a company pays for country club annual dues as well as for meals and incidentals and an executive officer reimburses the cost of meals and incidentals, then the company need not report meals and incidentals as perquisites, although it would continue to report the country club annual dues. If there was no such reimbursement, then the company would need to also report the meals and incidentals as perquisites. [July 3, 2008]

Question 119.08

Question: Item 402(c)(2)(ix)(C) indicates that stock purchased at a discount needs to be disclosed unless that discount is available generally to all security holders or to all salaried employees. The compensation cost, if any, is computed in accordance with FAS 123R. Footnote 221 to Securities Act Release No. 8732A seems to indicate that sometimes under FAS 123R there is no compensation cost. Does the footnote indicate that 423 plans must be disclosed?

Answer: No. Typically 423 plans need to be broad based and non-discriminatory to qualify for preferential tax treatment, which would be within the exception, even if they require some minimum of work hours—such as 10 hours a week—in order to be in the plan or the discount is larger than the 5% example in the footnote. The footnote explains that even if there is some discount, there may not be compensation cost under the accounting standard. [Jan. 24, 2007]

Question 119.09

Question: Item 402(c)(2)(ix)(G) requires disclosure of the dollar value of any dividends when those amounts were not factored into the grant date fair value required to be reported in the Grants of Plan-Based Awards Table. With regard to the treatment of dividends, dividend equivalents or other earnings on equity awards, is disclosure required in the All Other Compensation column (column (i)) if disclosure was not previously provided in the Grants of Plan-Based Awards Table for that named executive officer?

Answer: The company should analyze whether the dividends, dividend equivalents or other earnings would have been factored into the grant date fair value in accordance with FAS 123R. In this regard, the disclosure turns on how the rights to the dividends are structured and whether or not that brings them within the scope of FAS 123R for the purpose of the grant date fair value calculation. [Jan. 24, 2007]

Question 119.10

Question: Are deferred compensation payouts, lump sum distributions under Section 401(k) plans and earnings on 401(k) plans required to be disclosed in the Summary Compensation Table?

Answer: Non-qualified deferred compensation payouts are not disclosed in the Summary Compensation Table, but are rather disclosed in the Aggregate Withdrawals/ Distributions column (column (e)) of the Nonqualified Deferred Compensation Table. Lump sum distributions from 401(k) plans are not disclosed in the Summary Compensation Table, because the compensation that was deferred into the 401(k) plan was already disclosed in the Summary Compensation Table, as would be any company matching contributions. Earnings on 401(k) plans are not disclosed in the Summary Compensation Table because the disclosure requirement only extends to above-market or preferential earnings on non-qualified deferred compensation. [Jan. 24, 2007]

Question 119.11

Withdrawn Mar. 1, 2010

Question 119.12

Withdrawn Mar. 1, 2010

Question 119.13

Question: Item 402(c)(2)(ix)(D) requires disclosure in the "All Other Compensation" column of the amount paid or accrued to any named executive officer pursuant to any plan or arrangement in connection with any termination of such executive officer's employment with the company or its subsidiaries, or a change in control of the company. For this purpose, what standard applies for determining whether such an amount is reportable because it is accrued?

Answer: Instruction 5 to Item 402(c)(2)(ix) states that for purposes of Item 402(c)(2)(ix)(D) an accrued amount is an amount for which payment has become due. If the named executive officer's performance necessary to earn an amount is complete, it is an amount that should be disclosed. For example, if the named executive officer has completed all performance to earn an amount, but payment is subject to a six-month deferral in order to comply with Internal Revenue Code Section 409A, the amount would be an accrued amount subject to Item 402(c)(2)(ix)(D) disclosure. In contrast, if an amount will be payable two years after a termination event if the named executive officer cooperates with (or complies with a covenant not to compete with) the company during that period, the amount is not reportable under Item 402(c)(2)(ix)(D) because the executive officer's performance is still necessary for the payment to become due. As noted in Footnote 217 to Securities Act Release No. 8732A, such amounts that are payable in the future, as well as amounts reportable under Item 402(c)(2)(ix)(D), are reportable under Item 402(j). [Aug. 8, 2007]

Question 119.14

Question: Where the instructions to the Summary Compensation Table requiring footnote disclosure do not specifically limit the footnote disclosure to compensation for the company's last fiscal year, as do Instructions 3 and 4 to Item 402(c)(2)(ix), must the footnote disclosure cover the other years reported in the Summary Compensation Table?

Answer: If the instruction does not specifically limit footnote disclosure to compensation for the company's last fiscal year, footnote disclosure for the other years reported in the Summary Compensation Table would be required only if it is material to an investor's understanding of the compensation reported in the Summary Compensation Table for the company's last fiscal year. [July 3, 2008]

Question 119.15

Withdrawn Mar. 1, 2010

Question 119.16

Question: May a company provide the assumption information required by Instruction 1 to Item 402(c)(2)(v) and (vi) for equity awards granted in the company's most recent fiscal year by reference to the Grants of Plan-Based Awards Table if the company chooses to report that assumption information in that table?

Answer: Yes. [Mar. 1, 2010]

Question 119.17

Question: In 2008, a company enters into a retention agreement in which it agrees to pay the CEO a cash retention bonus, conditioned on the CEO remaining employed by the company through December 31, 2010. The cash retention bonus is not a non-equity incentive plan award, as defined in Item 402(a)(6)(iii). When is the cash retention bonus reportable in the company's Summary Compensation Table? When should it be discussed in Compensation Discussion and Analysis?

Answer: The cash retention bonus is reportable in the Summary Compensation Table for the year in which the performance condition has been satisfied. The same analysis applies to any interest the company is obligated to pay on the cash retention bonus, assuming the interest is not payable unless and until the performance condition has been satisfied. Before the performance condition has been satisfied, Instruction 4 to Item 402(c) would not require it to be reported in the Summary Compensation Table as a bonus that has been earned but deferred, and the bonus would not be reportable in the Nonqualified Deferred Compensation Table. However, the company should discuss the cash retention bonus in its Compensation Discussion and Analysis for 2008 and subsequent years through completion of the performance necessary to earn it. [July 3, 2008]

Question 119.18

Question: A person who was a named executive officer in year 1, but not in year 2, will again be a named executive officer in year 3. Must compensation information for this person be disclosed in the Summary Compensation Table for all three fiscal years?

Answer: Yes. [May 29, 2009]

Question 119.19

Question: A person who is a named executive officer for year 1 is entitled to a "gross-up" payment in respect of taxes on perquisites or other compensation provided during the year. The tax "gross-up" payment is not payable by the company until year 2. Is the tax "gross-up" payment reportable in the Summary Compensation Table in year 1?

Answer: Yes. To provide investors with a clearer view of all costs to the company associated with providing the perquisites or other compensation for which tax "gross-up" payments are being made, Item 402(c)(2)(ix)(B) disclosure of the tax "gross-up" payment should be included in the Summary Compensation Table for the same year as the related perquisites or other compensation. [May 29, 2009]

Question 119.20

Question: Instruction 3 to the Stock Awards and Option Awards columns specifies that the value reported for awards subject to performance conditions excludes the effect of estimated forfeitures. Does the grant date fair value reported for awards subject to time-based vesting also exclude the effect of estimated forfeitures?

Answer: Yes. The amount to be reported is the grant date fair value. FASB ASC Paragraph 718-10-30-27 provides, in relevant part, that "service conditions that affect vesting are not reflected in estimating the fair value of an award at the grant date because those conditions are restrictions that stem from the forfeitability of instruments to which employees have not yet earned the right." [Jan. 20, 2010]

Question 119.21

Question: In April 2010, a company grants an equity award to an executive officer, and the terms of the award do not provide for acceleration of vesting if the executive officer leaves the company. The grant date fair value of the award is $1,000. In November 2010, the executive officer will leave the company, and the company modifies the officer's same equity award to provide for acceleration of vesting upon departure. The fair value of the modified award, computed under FASB ASC Topic 718, is $800, reflecting a decline in the company's stock price. What dollar amount is included in 2010 total compensation for purposes of identifying 2010 named executive officers and reported in the executive officer's 2010 stock column with respect to this award if he will be a named executive officer? How would the company report the equity award if the award modification and executive's departure occur in 2011?

Answer: Consistent with Instruction 2 to Item 402(c)(2)(v) and (vi), the incremental fair value of the modified award, computed as of the modification date in accordance with FASB ASC Topic 718, as well as the grant date fair value of the original award must be reported in the 2010 stock column. Applying the guidance in paragraph 55-116 of FASB ASC Section 718-20-55, incremental fair value is computed as follows: the fair value of the modified award at the date of modification minus the fair value of the original award at the date of modification equals the incremental fair value of the modified award. In this fact pattern, the fair value of the original award at the date of modification is zero, because the executive officer left the company in November and the original award would not have vested. Therefore, the incremental fair value of the modified award is $800. As a result, the total amount reported is $1,800, which reflects the two compensation decisions the company made for this award in 2010. The same amount is included in 2010 total compensation for purposes of identifying the company's 2010 named executive officers pursuant to Items 402(a)(3)(iii) and (iv).

If the award modification and executive's departure occur in 2011, the company would report $1,000 in the 2010 stock column for the grant date fair value of the original award. In the 2011 stock column, the company would report $800 for the incremental fair value of the modified award. [Feb. 16, 2010]

Question 119.22

Question: During 2010, a company grants an annual incentive plan award to a named executive officer. Because no right to stock settlement is embedded in the terms of the award, the award is not within the scope of FASB ASC Topic 718. Therefore, it is a non-equity incentive plan award as defined in Rule 402(a)(6)(iii). The named executive officer elects to receive the award in stock. Instruction 2 to Item 402(c)(2)(iii) and (iv) does not apply because the award is an incentive plan award rather than a bonus. Should the company report the award in the stock awards column (column (e)) or in the non-equity incentive plan award column (column (g)) in its 2010 Summary Compensation Table? How should the award be reported in the Grants of Plan-Based Awards Table?

Answer: The company should report the award in the non-equity incentive plan award column (column (g)) of the Summary Compensation

Table, reflecting the compensation the company awarded, with footnote disclosure of the stock settlement. Similarly, in the Grants of Plan-Based Awards Table, the company should report the award in the estimated future payouts under non-equity incentive plan awards columns (columns (c)-(e)). The stock received upon settlement should not also be reported in the Grants of Plan-Based Awards Table because that would double count the award. [Feb. 16, 2010]

Question 119.23

Question: During 2010, a company grants annual incentive plan awards to its named executive officers. The awards permit the named executive officers to elect payment of the award for 2010 performance in company stock rather than cash, with the election to be made during the first 90 days of 2010. Such company stock will have a grant date fair value equal to 110% of the award that would be paid in cash. One named executive officer elects stock payment, and the others do not. How is the award reported for the named executive officer who elects stock payment? How is the award reported for the named executive officers who receive cash payment?

Answer: For the named executive officer who elects stock payment, the award is reported in the 2010 Summary Compensation Table and Grants of Plan-Based Awards Table as an equity incentive award. This is the case even if the amount of the award is not determined until early 2011 because all company decisions necessary to determine the value of the award are made in 2010. For the named executive officers who receive cash payment, the award is reported in the 2010 Summary Compensation Table and Grants of Plan-Based Awards Table as a non-equity incentive plan award. [Feb. 16, 2010]

Question 119.24

Question: In 2010, a company grants an executive officer an equity incentive plan award with a three-year performance period that begins in 2010. The equity incentive plan allows the compensation committee to exercise its discretion to reduce the amount earned pursuant to the award, consistent with Section 162(m) of the Internal Revenue Code. Under FASB ASC Topic 718, the fact that the compensation committee has the right to exercise "negative" discretion may cause, in certain circumstances, the grant date of the award to be deferred until the end of the three-year performance period, after the compensation committee has determined whether to exercise its negative discretion. If so, when and how should this award be reported in the Summary Compensation Table and Grants of Plan-Based Awards Table? In what year should this award be included in total compensation for purposes of determining if the executive officer is a named executive officer?

Answer: Use of grant date fair value reporting in Item 402 generally assumes that, as stated in FASB ASC Topic 718, "[t]he service inception date usually is the grant date." The service inception date may precede the grant date, however, if the equity incentive plan award is authorized but service begins before a mutual understanding of the key terms and conditions is reached. In a situation in which the compensation committee's right to exercise "negative" discretion may preclude, in certain circumstances, a grant date for the award during the year in which the compensation committee communicated the terms of the award and performance targets to the executive officer and in which the service inception date begins, the award should be reported in the Summary Compensation Table and Grants of Plan-Based Awards Table as compensation for the year in which the service inception date begins. Notwithstanding the accounting treatment for the award, reporting the award in this manner better reflects the compensation committee's decisions with respect to the award. The amount reported in both tables should be the fair value of the award at the service inception date, based upon the then-probable outcome of the performance conditions. This same amount should be included in total compensation for purposes of determining whether the executive officer is a named executive officer for the year in which the service inception date occurs. [Mar. 1, 2010]

Question 119.25

Question: A company grants annual nonequity incentive plan awards to its executive officers in January 2010. The awards' performance criteria are communicated to the executives at that time and are based on the company's financial performance for the year. Executives will not know the total amount earned pursuant to the award until the end of the year, when the compensation committee can determine whether or to what extent the performance criteria have been satisfied.

After the end of the year, the amounts earned pursuant to the awards are determined and communicated to the executive officers. One executive decides not to receive any payment of earnings pursuant to the award. For that executive, should the award be included in total compensation for purposes of determining if the executive is a named executive officer for 2010? Should the award be reported in the Grants of Plan-Based Awards Table and the Summary Compensation Table for 2010?

Answer: Yes. The executive officer's decision not to accept payment of the award does not change the fact that award was granted in and earned for services performed during 2010. Accordingly, the grant of the award should be included in the Grants of Plan-Based Awards Table, which will reflect the compensation committee's decision to grant the award in 2010. The earnings pursuant to the award, even though declined, should be included in total compensation for purposes of determining if the executive is a named executive officer for 2010 and reported in the Summary Compensation Table. The company should disclose the executive's decision not to accept payment of the award, which it can do either by adding a column to the Summary Compensation Table next to column (g), "Nonequity Incentive Plan Compensation," reporting the amount of nonequity incentive plan compensation declined, or by providing footnote disclosure to the Summary Compensation Table. Moreover, in Compensation Discussion and Analysis, the company should consider discussing the effect, if any, of the executive's decision on how the company structures and implements compensation to reflect performance. [Mar. 12, 2010]

Question 119.26

Question: A company has a practice of granting discretionary bonuses to its executive officers. Before the board of directors takes action to grant such bonuses for 2010, an executive officer advises the board that she will not accept a bonus for 2010. Should the company report in column (d) of the Summary Compensation Table the bonus award it would have granted her and include that amount in total compensation for purposes of determining if she is a named executive officer for 2010?

Answer: No, because the executive declined the bonus before it was granted, and therefore, no bonus was granted. [Mar. 12, 2010]

Question 119.27

Question: In 2010, Company A acquires Company B and, as part of the merger consideration, agrees to assume all outstanding Company B options. The Company B options have not been modified other than to adjust the exercise price to reflect the merger exchange ratio. For Company B executives who are now Company A executives: Should the Company B options that were granted in 2010 be included in total compensation for purposes of determining if an executive is a named executive officer of Company A for 2010 and reported in the Summary Compensation Table and Grants of Plan-Based Awards Table for 2010? Should Company A report the Company B options in its Outstanding Equity Awards at Fiscal Year-End

Table and Options Exercised and Stock Vested Table, as applicable, for 2010 and in subsequent years?

Answer: Because the assumed Company B options are part of the merger consideration, they do not reflect any 2010 executive compensation decisions by Company A. Therefore, Company A should not include Company B options granted in 2010 in total compensation for purposes of determining its 2010 named executive officers, and should not report the Company B options in its 2010 Summary Compensation Table and Grants of Plan-Based Awards Table. Because the Company B options are now Company A options, Company A should report them in its Outstanding Equity Awards at Fiscal Year-End Table and Options Exercised and Stock Vested Table, as applicable, for 2010 and subsequent years, with footnote disclosure describing the assumption of Company B options. [June 4, 2010]

Question 119.28

Question: At the beginning of Year 1, the compensation committee sets the threshold, target and maximum levels for the number of shares that may be earned for Year 1 under the company's performance-based equity incentive plan. Incentive awards are paid in the form of restricted shares, which are issued early in Year 2 after the compensation committee has certified the company's Year 1 performance results. Can the amount reported in the Stock Awards column reflect the grant date fair value of the number of restricted shares actually issued for Year 1, rather than the amount that reflects the probable outcome of the performance conditions as of the grant date, as prescribed by Instruction 3 to Item 402(c)(2)(v) and (vi)?

Answer: No. The grant date fair value for stock and option awards subject to performance conditions must be reported based on the probable outcome of the performance conditions as of the grant date, even if the actual outcome of the performance conditions—and therefore, the number of restricted shares actually awarded for Year 1—is known by the time of the filing of the proxy statement. [July 8, 2011]

Section 120. Item 402(d)—Executive Compensation; Grants of Plan-Based Awards Table

Question 120.01

Question: If an equity incentive plan award is denominated in dollars, but payable in stock, how is it disclosed in the Grants of Plan-Based Awards

Table since the headings for equity-based awards (columns (f), (g) and (h)) only refer to numbers and not dollars?

Answer: The award should be disclosed in the Grants of Plan-Based Awards Table by including the dollar value and a footnote to explain that it will be paid out in stock in the form of whatever number of shares that amount translates into at the time of the payout. In this limited circumstance, and if all the awards in this column are structured in this manner, it is acceptable to change the captions for columns (f) through (h) to show "($)" instead of "(#)." [Aug. 8, 2007]

Question 120.02

Question: If all of the non-equity incentive plan awards were made for annual plans, where the awards have already been earned, may the company change the heading over columns (c), (d) and (e) of the Grants of Plan-Based Awards Table that refers to "Estimated future payouts under non-equity incentive plan awards?"

Answer: Yes, if the awards were made in the same year they were earned and the earned amounts are therefore disclosed in the Summary Compensation Table, the heading over columns (c), (d) and (e) may be changed to "Estimated possible payouts under non-equity incentive plan awards." [Jan. 24, 2007]

Question 120.03

Renumbered as Question 122.04

Question 120.04

Renumbered as Question 122.05

Question 120.05

Withdrawn Mar. 1, 2010

Question 120.06

Question: Under a long-term incentive plan, a named executive officer receives an award for a target number of shares at the start of a three-year period, with one-third of this amount allocated to each of three single-year performance periods. How is grant date fair value determined for purposes of the disclosure required in column (l) of the table?

Answer: The grant date and grant date fair value are determined as provided in FAS 123R. Under paragraph A. 67 of FAS 123R, if all of the annual performance targets are set at the start of the three-year period, that is the grant date for the entire award. The grant date fair value for all three tranches of the award would be measured at that time, and would be reported in column (l). If each annual performance target is set at the start of each respective single-year performance period, however, paragraph A.68 of FAS 123R provides that each of those dates is a separate grant date for purposes of measuring the grant date fair value of the respective tranche. In this circumstance, only the grant date fair value for the first year's performance period would be measured and reported in column (l). [May 29, 2009]

Question 120.07

Question: During the fiscal year, an outstanding equity incentive plan award held by a named executive officer is amended or otherwise modified, resulting in incremental fair value under FAS 123R. Must the incremental fair value be reported in column (l) of the table?

Answer: Yes. This is required by Item 402(d)(2)(viii) and Instruction 7 to Item 402(d). [May 29, 2009]

Section 121. Item 402(e)—Executive Compensation; Narrative Disclosure to Summary Compensation Table and Grants of Plan-Based Awards Table

None

Section 122. Item 402(f)—Executive Compensation; Outstanding Equity Awards at Fiscal Year-End Table

Question 122.01

Question: A company has an equity incentive plan pursuant to which it grants awards that will vest, if at all, based on total shareholder return over a 3-year period. Awards were granted in 2005 ("2005 Awards") and will vest based on the company's total shareholder return from 1/1/05 through 12/31/07. 2006 was the second year of the 3-year performance period. Performance during 2005 was well above the maximum level. Performance during 2006 was below the threshold level. The combined performance for 2005 and 2006 would result in a payout at target if the performance period had ended on 12/31/06. Is it permissible to base disclosure on the actual multi-year performance to date (through the end of the last completed fiscal year)?

Answer: Yes. The number of shares or units reported in columns (d) or (i), and the payout value reported in column (j), should be based on achieving threshold performance goals, except that if performance during the last completed fiscal year (or, if the payout is based on performance to occur over more than one year, the last completed fiscal years over which performance is measured) has exceeded the threshold, the disclosure shall be based on the next higher performance measure (target or maximum) that exceeds the last completed fiscal year's performance (or, if the payout is based on performance to occur over more than one year, the last completed fiscal years over which performance is measured). [Aug. 8, 2007]

Question 122.02

Question: Instruction 2 to Item 402(f)(2) requires footnote disclosure of the vesting dates of the awards reported in the Outstanding Equity Awards at Fiscal Year-End Table. Can a company comply with this instruction by including a column in this table showing the grant date of each award reported and including a statement of the standard vesting schedule that applies to the reported awards?

Answer: Yes, provided, however, that if there is any different vesting schedule applicable to any of the awards, then the table would also need to include disclosure about any such vesting schedule. [July 3, 2008]

Question 122.03

Question: A company's performance-based restricted stock unit ("RSU") plan measures performance over a three-year period. After the end of the three-year performance period (2007-2009), the compensation committee will evaluate performance to determine the number of RSUs earned by the named executive officers. The named executive officers must remain employed by the company for a subsequent two-year service-based vesting period (2010-2011). Upon completion of service-based vesting, the company will pay the named executive officers the shares underlying the RSUs. In the Outstanding Equity Awards at Fiscal Year-End Table for fiscal year 2009, how should information about the shares underlying the RSUs be reported?

Answer: The number of shares reported should be based on the actual number of shares underlying the RSUs that were earned at the end of the three-year performance period. This is the case even if this number will be determined after the 2009 fiscal year end. The shares should not be reported in columns (i) and (j) because they are no longer subject to performance-based conditions. Instead, the shares should be reported in columns (g) and (h) because they are subject to service-based vesting. [May 29, 2009]

Question 122.04

Question: Should a company include in the Outstanding Equity Awards at Fiscal Year-End Table in-kind earnings on restricted stock awards that have earned share dividends or share dividend equivalents?

Answer: Yes. Outstanding in-kind earnings at the end of the fiscal year should be included in the table. However, in-kind earnings that vested during the fiscal year, or in-kind earnings that are already vested when the dividends are declared, instead should be reported in the Option Exercises and Stock Vested Table under Item 402(g) of Regulation S-K. [Jan. 24, 2007]

Question 122.05

Question: Instruction 3 to Item 402(f)(2) states that the issuer should report the market value of equity incentive plan awards using the closing market price at the end of the last completed fiscal year. The next sentence, however, states that the number of shares or units reported should be based on achieving threshold performance goals, "except that if the previous fiscal year's performance" has exceeded the threshold, disclosure is based on the next higher measure. Is the "previous fiscal year" the same year as the last completed fiscal year, or the year that preceded the last completed fiscal year?

Answer: For this purpose, the "previous fiscal year" means the same year as the "last completed fiscal year." [Aug. 8, 2007]

Section 123. Item 402(g)—Executive Compensation; Option Exercises and Stock Vested Table

Question 123.01

Question: When reporting on the exercise or settlement of a stock appreciation right in the Number of Shares Acquired on Exercise column (column (b)) of the Option Exercises and Stock Vested Table, should a company report the net number of shares received upon exercise, or the gross number of shares underlying the exercised stock appreciation right?

Answer: As would be the case with the cashless exercise of options, the total number of shares underlying the exercised stock appreciation right should be reported in column (b), rather than just the amount representing the increase of the stock price since the grant of the award. A footnote or narrative accompanying the table could explain and quantify the net number of shares received. [Jan. 24, 2007]

Section 124. Item 402(h)—Executive Compensation; Pension Benefits

Question 124.01

Question: Instruction 2 to Item 402(h)(2) indicates that the company must use the same assumptions used for financial reporting purposes under generally accepted accounting principles, except for the retirement age assumption, when computing the actuarial present value of a named executive officer's accumulated benefit under each pension plan. May the company deviate from the assumptions used for accounting purposes given the individual circumstances of the named executive officer or the plan?

Answer: No. [Jan. 24, 2007]

Question 124.02

Question: Instruction 2 to Item 402(h)(2) specifies that in calculating the actuarial present value of a named executive officer's accumulated pension benefits, the assumed retirement age is to be the normal retirement age as defined in the plan, or, if not defined, the earliest time at which the named executive officer may retire without any benefit reduction. While many plans have a specifically defined retirement age, some plans also have a provision that allows participants to retire at an earlier age without any benefit reduction. In this case, which age should the company use in making its calculation?

Answer: When a plan has a stated "normal" retirement age and also a younger age at which retirement benefits may be received without any reduction in benefits, the younger age should be used for determining pension benefits. The older age may be included as an additional column. [Jan. 24, 2007]

Question 124.03

Question: How do you measure the actuarial present value of the accumulated benefit of a pension plan in the situation where a particular benefit is earned at a specified age? For instance, if a named executive officer at age 40 is granted an award if he stays with his company until age 60, how should the company measure this benefit when the executive is age 50 and the normal retirement age under the plan is age 65?

Answer: The computation should be based on the accumulated benefit as of the pension measurement date, assuming that the named executive continues to live and will work at the company until retirement and thus will reach age 60 and receive the award. [Jan. 24, 2007]

Question 124.04

Question: Should assumptions regarding pre-retirement decrements be factored into the calculation of the actuarial present value of a named executive officer's accumulated benefit under a pension plan?

Answer: For purposes of calculating the actuarial present value for the Pension Benefits Table, the registrant should assume that each named executive officer will live to and retire at the plan's normal retirement age (or the earlier retirement age if the named executive officer may retire with unreduced benefits) and ignore for the purposes of the calculations what actuaries refer to as pre-retirement decrements. Therefore, the assumptions used for financial statement reporting purposes that should be used for calculating the actuarial present value are the discount rate, the lump sum interest rate (if applicable), post-retirement mortality, and payment distribution assumptions. Any contingent benefits arising upon death, early retirement or other termination of employment events should be disclosed in the post-employment narrative disclosure required under Item 402(j) of Regulation S-K. [Jan. 24, 2007]

Question 124.05

Question: A cash balance pension plan is a defined benefit plan in which the retiree's benefits may be determined by the amount represented in a hypothetical "account" for that participant. The "accrued benefit" is the amount credited to a participant's cash balance account as of any date, which the participant has the right to receive as a lump sum upon termination of employment. Can a company report, as the present value of the accumulated benefit for a cash balance plan, the "accrued benefit"?

Answer: No. The same as for other defined benefit plans, the amount disclosable in the Pension Benefits Table as the present value of accumulated benefit for a cash balance plan is the actuarial present value of the named executive officer's accumulated benefit under the plan, computed as of the same plan measurement date used for purposes of the company's audited financial statements for the last completed fiscal year. [Aug. 8, 2007]

Section 125. Item 402(i)—Executive Compensation; Nonqualified Defined Contribution and Other Nonqualified Deferred Compensation Plans

Question 125.01

Question: The instruction to Item 402(i)(2) of Regulation S-K requires footnote disclosure quantifying the extent to which amounts reported in the table were reported as compensation in the Summary Compensation Table in the last completed fiscal year and in previous fiscal years. What should be noted by footnote when amounts were not previously reported (either because of the transition guidance in <u>Securities Act Release No. 8732A</u> or when a named executive officer appears in the table for the first time)?

Answer: The purpose of the instruction is to facilitate an understanding that non-qualified deferred compensation is reported elsewhere within the executive compensation disclosure over time. Amounts only need to be disclosed by footnote if they were actually previously reported in the Summary Compensation Table. [Jan. 24, 2007]

Question 125.02

Question: Item 402(i)(2)(iv) requires disclosure of the dollar amount of aggregate interest or other earnings accrued during the registrant's last fiscal year. What items, other than interest, are "earnings" for this purpose?

Answer: "Earnings" include dividends, stock price appreciation (or depreciation), and other similar items. The purpose of the table is to show changes in the aggregate account balance at fiscal year end for each named executive officer. Thus, "earnings" should encompass any increase or decrease in the account balance during the last completed fiscal year that is not attributable to contributions, withdrawals or distributions during the year. [Aug. 8, 2007]

Question 125.03

Question: Item 402(i)(1) calls for the Nonqualified Deferred Compensation Plan Table to provide the specified information "with respect to each defined contribution or other plan that provides for the deferral of compensation on a basis that is not tax-qualified." Does this item mean that this information should be provided on a plan-by-plan basis?

Answer: Yes. [July 3, 2008]

Question 125.04

Question: Item 402(i)(2)(iii) calls for disclosure of aggregate company contributions to each nonqualified deferred compensation plan during the company's last fiscal year. For an excess plan related to a qualified plan, the contributions earned in 2008, which are reportable in the All Other Compensation column of the 2008 Summary Compensation Table, are not credited to the executive's account until January 2009. Are those contributions considered company contributions "during" 2008?

Answer: Yes. [July 3, 2008]

Question 125.05

Question: An equity award has vested, and the plan under which it was granted provides for the deferral of its receipt. Item 402(i)(1) calls for the Nonqualified Deferred Compensation Plan Table to provide the specified information "with respect to each defined contribution or other plan that provides for the deferral of compensation on a basis that is not tax-qualified." Does this item require the deferred receipt of the vested equity award to be included in the Nonqualified Deferred Compensation Plan Table?

Answer: Yes. This is the case whether the deferral is at the election of the named executive officer or pursuant to the terms of the equity award or plan. [Aug. 14, 2009]

Section 126. Item 402(j)—Executive Compensation; Potential Payments Upon Termination or Change-in-Control

Question 126.01

Question: In the event that options are accelerated upon a termination or change-in- control, for purposes of Item 402(j) disclosure should the value of the accelerated options be calculated using the "spread" between exercise and market price (as of fiscal year end) or the FAS 123R value recognized in connection with the acceleration?

Answer: For purposes of Item 402(j), the company should use the "spread" to calculate the value of the award. Since Item 402(j) requires quantification of what a named executive officer would have received assuming the event took place on the last business day of the registrant's last completed fiscal year, disclosure of the "spread" at that date is consistent with Instruction 1 to 402(j), which prescribes using the closing market price per share of the registrant's securities on last business day of the registrant's last completed fiscal year. [Aug. 8, 2007]

Question 126.02

Question: A company's employee stock option plan provides for full and immediate vesting of all outstanding unvested awards upon a change-in-control of the company and this provision is included in each option recipient's award agreement (whether the recipient is an executive officer or an employee). Instruction 5 to Item 402(j) provides that a company need not provide information with respect to contracts, agreements, plans, or arrangements to the extent they are available generally to all salaried employees and do not discriminate in scope, terms, or operation, in favor of executive officers of the company. Can the company rely on Instruction 5 to omit disclosure of these awards when quantifying the estimated payments and benefits that would be provided to named executive officers upon a change-in-control?

Answer: No. The Instruction 5 standard that the "scope" of arrangements not discriminate in favor of executive officers would not be satisfied where the option awards to executives are in amounts greater than those provided to all salaried employees. [Aug. 8, 2007]

Section 127. Item 402(k)—Executive Compensation; Compensation of Directors

Question 127.01

Question: Is director compensation disclosure required under Item 402(k) of Regulation S-K for a person who served as a director for part of the last completed fiscal year, even if the person was no longer a director at the end of the last completed fiscal year?

Answer: Yes. If a person served as a director during any part of the last completed fiscal year the person must be included in the Director Compensation Table. [Jan. 24, 2007]

Question 127.02

Question: Is director compensation disclosure required under Item 402(k) of Regulation S-K for a person who served as a director during the last completed fiscal year but will not stand for re-election the next year?

Answer: Yes. If a person served as a director during any part of the last completed fiscal year the person must be included in the Director Compensation Table. [Jan. 24, 2007]

Question 127.03

Question: Does the Instruction to Item 402(k)(2)(iii) and (iv) require footnote disclosure, for each director, of the grant date fair value of each equity award outstanding or only of the awards granted during the company's last completed fiscal year?

Answer: Like the corresponding disclosure for named executive officers in the Grants of Plan-Based Awards Table, this Director Compensation Table requirement applies only to stock and option awards granted during the company's last completed fiscal year. [Aug. 8, 2007]

Question 127.04

Question: Does the Instruction to Item 402(k)(2)(iii) and (iv) requirement to provide footnote disclosure, for each director, of the aggregate number of stock awards and the aggregate number of option awards outstanding at fiscal year end include exercised options or vested stock awards?

Answer: No. Like the corresponding disclosure for named executive officers in the Outstanding Equity Awards at Fiscal Year-End Table, this Director Compensation Table requirement applies only to unexercised option awards (whether or not exercisable) and unvested stock awards (including unvested stock units). [Aug. 8, 2007]

Question 127.05

Question: Can a charitable matching program that is available to all employees be excluded from the disclosure required of "director legacy or charitable awards programs" under Item 402(k)(2)(vii)(G) based on the exclusion for "information regarding group life, health, hospitalization, or medical reimbursement plans that do not discriminate in scope, terms or operation, in favor of executive officers or directors of the registrant and that are available generally to all salaried employees" in the Item 402(a)(6)(ii) definition of "plan"?

Answer: No. A charitable matching program available to all employees must be included in the Director Compensation Table. The Director Compensation Table disclosure applies to "the annual costs of payments and promises of payments pursuant to director legacy programs and similar charitable award programs." Any company-sponsored charitable award program in which a director can participate would be a "similar charitable award program." [Aug. 8, 2007]

Section 128. Items 402(l) to (r)—Executive Compensation; Smaller Reporting Companies

None

Section 128A—Item 402(s) Narrative disclosure of the registrant's compensation policies and practices as they relate to the registrant's risk management

Question 128A.01

Question: The requirement to provide narrative disclosure of the registrant's compensation policies and practices as they relate to the registrant's risk management is in Item 402(s), rather than included as part of Compensation Discussion and Analysis in Item 402(b). Where should a registrant present Item 402(s) disclosure in its filings?

Answer: The new rules do not specify where the disclosure should be presented. However, to ease investor understanding, the staff recommends that Item 402(s) disclosure be presented together with the registrant's other Item 402 disclosure. The staff would have concerns if the Item 402(s) disclosure is difficult to locate or is presented in a fashion that obscures it. [Jan. 20, 2010]

Section 128B—Item 402(t) Golden Parachute Compensation

Question 128B.01

Question: Instruction 1 to Item 402(t)(2) provides that Item 402(t) disclosure will be required for those executive officers who were included in the most recently filed Summary Compensation Table. If a company files its annual meeting proxy statement in March 2011 (including the 2010 Summary Compensation Table), hires a new principal executive officer in May 2011 and prepares a merger proxy in September 2011, may the company rely on this instruction to exclude the new principal executive officer from the merger proxy's say on golden parachute vote and Item 402(t) disclosure?

Answer: No. Instruction 1 to Item 402(t) specifies that Item 402(t) information must be provided for the individuals covered by Items 402(a)(3)(i), (ii) and (iii) of Regulation S-K. Instruction 1 to Item 402(t)(2) applies only to those executive officers who are included in the Summary Compensation Table under Item 402(a)(3)(iii), because they are the three most highly compensated executive officers other than the principal executive officer and the principal financial officer. Under Items 402(a)(3)(i) and (ii), the principal executive officer and the principal financial officer are, per se, named executive officers, regardless of compensation level. Consequently, Instruction 1 to Item 402(t)(2) is not instructive as to whether the principal executive officer or principal financial officer is a named executive officer. This position also applies to Instruction 2 to Item 1011(b), which is the corresponding instruction in Regulation M-A. [Feb. 11, 2011]

Interpretive Responses Regarding Particular Situations

Section 217. Item 402(a)—Executive Compensation; General

217.01 Whether a spin-off is treated like the IPO of a new "spun-off" registrant for purposes of Item 402 disclosure depends on the particular facts and circumstances. When determining whether disclosure of compensation before the spin-off is necessary, the "spun-off" registrant should consider whether it was a reporting company or a separate division before the spin-off, as well as its continuity of management. For example, if a parent company spun off a subsidiary which conducted one line of the parent company's business, and before and after the spin-off the executive officers of the subsidiary: (1) were the same; (2) provided the same type of services to the subsidiary; and (3) provided no services to the parent, historical compensation disclosure likely would be required. In contrast, if a parent company spun off a newly formed subsidiary consisting of portions of several different parts of the parent's business and having new management, it is more likely that the spin-off could be treated as the IPO of a new "spun-off" registrant. [Jan. 24, 2007]

217.02 Following a merger among operating companies, there is no concept of "successor" compensation. Therefore, the surviving company in the merger need not report on compensation paid by predecessor corporations that disappeared in the merger. Similarly, a parent corporation would not pick up compensation paid to an employee of its subsidiary prior to the time the subsidiary became a subsidiary (i.e., when it was a target). Moreover, income paid by such predecessor companies need not be counted in computing whether an individual is a named executive officer of the surviving corporation. A different result may apply, however, in situations involving an amalgamation or combination of companies. A different result also applies where an operating company combines with a shell company, as defined in Securities Act Rule 405, as provided in Interpretive Response 217.12, below. [Aug. 8, 2007]

217.03 A subsidiary of a public company is going public. The officers of the subsidiary previously were officers of the parent, and in some cases all of the work that they did for the parent related to the subsidiary. The registration statement of the subsidiary would not be required to include compensation previously awarded by the parent corporation. The subsidiary would start reporting as of the IPO date. [Jan. 24, 2007]

217.04 Instruction 1 to Item 402(a)(3) states that the generally required compensation disclosure regarding highly compensated executive officers need not be set forth for an executive officer (other than the principal executive officer or principal financial officer) whose total compensation for the last fiscal year, reduced by the amount required to be disclosed by Item 402(c)(2)(viii), did not exceed $100,000. A reporting company that recently changed its fiscal year end from December 31st to June 30th is preparing its transition report for the 6-month period ended June 30th, having filed its Form 10-K for the fiscal year ended 6 months earlier on December 31st. The reporting company generally has a group of executive officers that earn in excess of $100,000 each year. In addition, during the 6-month period, the company made an acquisition that resulted in new executive officers that, on an annual basis, will earn more than $100,000. During the 6-month period, however, none of these existing or new officers earned more than $100,000 in total compensation. The company asked whether disclosure under Item 402 regarding these officers therefore would not be required in the report being prepared for the 6-month period. The Division staff advised that no disclosure need be provided with respect to executive officers that started employment with the company during the 6-month period and did not, during that period of employment, earn more than $100,000. With respect to executive officers that were employed by the company both during and before the 6-month period, however, Item 402 disclosure would have to be provided for those who earned in excess of $100,000 during the one-year period ending June 30th (the same ending date as the six-month period, but extending back over 6 months of the preceding fiscal year). [Jan. 24, 2007]

217.05 If a company changes its fiscal year, report compensation for the "stub period," and do not annualize or restate compensation. In addition, report compensation for the last three full fiscal years, in accordance with Item 402 of Regulation S-K. For example, in late 1997 a company changed its fiscal year end from June 30 to December 31. In the Summary Compensation Table, provide disclosure for each of the following four periods: July 1, 1997 to December 31, 1997; July 1, 1996 to June 30, 1997; July 1, 1995 to June 30,

1996; and July 1, 1994 to June 30, 1995. Continue providing such disclosure for four periods (three full fiscal years and the stub period) until there is disclosure for three full fiscal years after the stub period (December 31, 2000 in the example). If the company was not a reporting company and was to do an IPO in February 1998, it would furnish disclosure for both of the following periods in the Summary Compensation Table: July 1, 1997 to December 31, 1997; and July 1, 1996 to June 30, 1997. [Jan. 24, 2007]

217.06 Compensation of both incoming and departing executives should not be annualized. [Jan. 24, 2007]

217.07 A caller asked whether an executive officer, other than the principal executive officer or principal financial officer, could be considered a "named executive officer" if the executive officer became a non-executive employee during the last completed fiscal year and did not depart from the registrant. If an executive officer becomes a non-executive employee of a registrant during the preceding fiscal year, consider the compensation the person received during the entire fiscal year for purposes of determining whether the person is a named executive officer for that fiscal year. If the person thus would qualify as a named executive officer, disclose all of the person's compensation for the full fiscal year, i.e. compensation for when the person was an executive officer and for when the person was a non-executive employee. [Jan. 24, 2007]

217.08 A parent and its subsidiary are both Exchange Act reporting companies. Some of the executive officers of the parent may receive a portion of their compensation from the subsidiary corporation. The Division staff advised that if an executive spends 100% (or near 100%) of the executive's time for the subsidiary but is paid by the parent, then the compensation paid by the parent has to be reported in the executive compensation table of the subsidiary. However, if an allocation of the monies paid by the parent would be necessary because the executive officer splits time between the parent and the subsidiary, the payments allocable to services to the parent need not be included in the subsidiary's executive compensation table. In addition, in the event that the subsidiary pays a management fee to the parent for use of the executives, disclosure of the structure of the management agreement and fees would have to be reported under Item 404. Compensation paid by the subsidiary to executives of the parent company must be included in the parent's executive compensation table if such payments are paid directly by the subsidiary. If the payments are part of a management contract, disclosure of the structure of the management agreement and fees would have to be reported under Item 404. [July 3, 2008] *[same as C&DI 230.11]*

217.09 Parent and its consolidated subsidiary are public companies. X was CEO of parent for all of 2007, and was CEO of subsidiary for part of 2007. Y was an executive officer of the parent for 2007, and was CFO of the subsidiary for 2007. Even though parent made all salary and bonus payments to X and to Y, pursuant to intercompany accounting: 60% of X's 2007 salary and bonus was allocated to the subsidiary; and 85% of Y's 2007 salary and bonus was allocated to the subsidiary. If 100% of Y's salary and bonus are included, Y would be one of parent's three most highly compensated executive officers for 2007, but if the 85% allocable to subsidiary is excluded, Y would not be a parent NEO.

On these facts, the staff takes the view that 100% of the salary and bonus of each of X and Y should be counted in determining the parent's three most highly compensated executive officers and disclosed in the parent's Summary Compensation Table. Parent's NEO determinations and compensation disclosures should not be affected by whether its subsidiary is public or private. The staff also takes the view that subsidiary's Summary Compensation Table should report the respective percentages (60% for X and 85% for Y) of salary and bonus allocated to the subsidiary's books. Each Summary Compensation Table should include footnote disclosure noting the extent to which the same compensation is reported in both tables. [July 3, 2008]

217.10 A company's reimbursement to an officer of legal expenses with respect to a lawsuit in which the officer was named as a defendant, in her capacity as an officer, is not disclosable pursuant to Item 402 of Regulation S-K. [Jan. 24, 2007]

217.11 A caller inquired whether a filing that is made on January 2 must include compensation for the previous year ended December 31 when compensation information may not be incorporated by reference into the filing. The Division staff's position is that compensation must be included for such year because registrants should have those numbers available. However, if bonus or other amounts for the prior year have not yet been determined, this should be noted in a footnote together with disclosure regarding the date the bonus will be determined, any formula or criteria that will be used and any other pertinent information. When determined, the bonus or other amount must be disclosed in a filing under Item 5.02(f) of Form 8-K. Further, where the compensation disclosure depends upon assumptions used in the financial statements and those financial statements have not yet been audited, it is permissible for the company to note this fact in the compensation disclosure. [Jan. 24, 2007]

217.12 Shareholders of a shell company, as defined in Securities Act Rule 405, will vote on combining the shell company with an operating company. The combination will have the effect of making the operating company subject to the reporting requirements of Section 13(a) or 15(d) of the Exchange Act. The disclosure document soliciting shareholder approval of the combination (whether a proxy statement, Form S-4, or Form F-4) needs to disclose: (1) Item 402 disclosure for the shell company before the combination; (2) Item 402 disclosure regarding the operating company that the operating company would be required to make if filing a 1934 Act registration statement, including Compensation Discussion and Analysis disclosure; and (3) Item 402 disclosure regarding each person who will serve as a director or an executive officer of the surviving company required by Item 18(a)(7)(ii) or 19(a)(7)(ii) of Form S-4, including Compensation Discussion and Analysis disclosure that may emphasize new plans or policies (as provided in the Release 33-8732A text at n. 97). The Form 10-K of the combined entity for the fiscal year in which the combination occurs would provide Item 402 disclosure for the named executive officers and directors of the combined entity, complying with Item 402(a)(4) of Regulation S-K and Instruction 1 to Item 402(c) of Regulation S-K. [Aug. 8, 2007]

217.13 Options or other rights to purchase securities of the parent or a subsidiary of the registrant should be reported in the same manner as compensatory options to purchase registrant securities. [Jan. 24, 2007]

217.14 Item 402(c)(2)(ix)(G) requires Summary Compensation Table disclosure of the dollar value of any insurance premiums paid by, or on behalf of, the registrant during the covered fiscal year with respect to life insurance for the benefit of a named executive officer. Item 402(j) requires description and quantification of the estimated payments and benefits that would be provided in each covered termination circumstance, including the proceeds of such life insurance payable upon a named executive officer's death. However, if an executive officer dies during the last completed fiscal year, the proceeds of a life insurance policy funded by the registrant and paid to the deceased executive officer's estate need not be taken into consideration in determining the compensation to be reported in the Summary Compensation Table, or in determining whether the executive is among the registrant's up to two additional individuals for whom disclosure would be required under Item 402(a)(3)(iv). [May 29, 2009]

Section 218. Item 402(b)—Executive Compensation; Compensation Discussion and Analysis

None

Section 219. Item 402(c)—Executive Compensation; Summary Compensation Table

219.01 A registrant need not report earnings on compensation that is deferred on a basis that is not tax qualified as above-market or preferential earnings within the meaning of Item 402(c)(2)(viii)(B) where the return on such earnings is calculated in the same manner and at the same rate as earnings on externally managed investments to employees participating in a tax-qualified plan providing for broad-based employee participation. See n. 43 to Release No. 34-31327 (Oct. 16, 1992); American Society of Corporate Secretaries (Jan. 6, 1993). For example, many issuers provide for deferral of salary or bonus amounts not covered by tax-qualified plans where the return on such amounts is the same as the return paid on amounts invested in an externally managed investment fund, such as an equity mutual fund, available to all employees participating in a non-discriminatory, tax-qualified plan (e.g., 401(k) plan). Although this position generally will be available for so-called "excess benefit plans" (as defined for Rule 16b-3(b)(2) purposes), it may not be appropriately applied in the case of a pure "top-hat" plan or SERP (Supplemental Employee Retirement Plan) that bears no relationship to a tax-qualified plan of the issuer. When in doubt, consult the staff. For a deferred compensation plan with a cash-based, interest-only return, earnings would not be reportable as "above-market" unless the rate of interest exceeded 120% of the applicable federal long-term rate, as stated in Instruction 2 to Item 402(c)(2)(viii). Non-qualified deferred compensation plan earnings that are "above-market or preferential" are reportable even if the deferred compensation plan is unfunded and thus subject to risk of loss of principal. [Jan. 24, 2007]

219.02 Item 402(c)(2)(ix)(G) requires disclosure in the "All Other Compensation" column of the dollar value of any dividends or other earnings paid on stock or option awards, when those amounts were not factored into the grant date fair value required to be reported for the stock or option award. If a company credits stock dividends on unvested restricted stock units, but does not actually pay them out until the restricted stock units vest, those dividends should be reported in the year credited, rather than the year vested (and actually paid). [Aug. 8, 2007]

219.03 Item 402(c)(2)(viii) of Regulation S-K and Item 402(h)(2)(iii) and (iv) of Regulation S-K require amounts that are computed as of the same pension plan measurement date used for financial reporting purposes with respect to the company's audited financial statements for the last completed fiscal year. The rules reference the same pension plan measurement date as is used for financial statement reporting purposes so that the company would not have to use different assumptions when computing the present value for executive compensation disclosure and financial reporting purposes. The pension plan measurement date for most pension plans is September 30, which, in the case of calendar-year companies, does not correspond with the company's fiscal year. This means that the pension benefit information will be presented for a period that differs from the fiscal year period covered by the disclosure. Under recent changes in pension accounting standards, the pension measurement date will be changed to be the same as the end of the company's fiscal year. In the year in which companies change their pension measurement date, they may use an annualized approach for the disclosure of the change in the value of the accumulated pension benefits in the Summary Compensation Table (thereby adjusting the 15 month period to a 12 month period) when the transition in pension plan measurement date occurs, so long as the company includes disclosure explaining it has followed this approach. The actuarial present value computed on the new measurement date should be reported in the Pension Benefits Table. [Jan. 24, 2007]

219.04 If the actuarial present value of the accumulated pension benefit for a named executive officer on the pension measurement date of the prior fiscal year was $1,000,000, and the present value of the accumulated pension benefit on the pension measurement date of the most recently completed fiscal year is $1,000,000, but during the most recently completed fiscal year the named executive officer earned and received an in-service distribution of $200,000, then $200,000 should be reported as the increase in pension value in the Change in Pension Value and Nonqualified Deferred Compensation Earnings column (column (h)) of the Summary Compensation Table. [Jan. 24, 2007]

Section 220. Item 402(d)—Executive Compensation; Grants of Plan-Based Awards Table

220.01 Where a named executive officer exercises "reload" options and receives additional options upon such exercise, the registrant is required to report the additional options as an option grant in the Grants of Plan-Based Awards Table. In the Summary Compensation Table, the registrant would include the grant date fair value of the additional options in the aggregate amount reported. [Mar. 1, 2010]

220.02 If plans do not include thresholds or maximums (or equivalent items), the registrant need not include arbitrary sample threshold and maximum amounts. For example, for a non-equity incentive plan that does not specify threshold or maximum payout amounts (for example, a plan in which each unit entitles the executive to $1.00 of payment for each $.01 increase in earnings per share during the performance period), threshold and maximum levels need not be shown as "0" and "N/A" because the payouts theoretically may range from nothing to infinity. Rather, an appropriate footnote should state that there are no thresholds or maximums (or equivalent items). [Jan. 24, 2007]

Section 221. Item 402(e)—Executive Compensation; Narrative Disclosure to Summary Compensation Table and Grants of Plan-Based Awards Table

None

Section 222. Item 402(f)—Executive Compensation; Outstanding Equity Awards at Fiscal Year-End Table

222.01 A company grants stock options that provide for immediate exercise in full as of the grant date, subject to the company's right to repurchase (at the exercise price) if the executive terminates employment with the company before a specified date. If the executive officer exercises the option before the repurchase restriction lapses, he or she effectively receives restricted stock subject to forfeiture until the repurchase restriction lapses. In this circumstance, the Outstanding Equity Awards table should show the shares received as stock awards that have not vested (columns (g) and (h)) until the repurchase restriction lapses, and the exercise should not be reported in the Option Exercises and Stock Vested Table. Instead, as the shares acquired by the executive officer cease to be subject to the repurchase provision, those shares should be reported as stock awards (columns (d) and (e)) in the Option Exercises and Stock Vested Table. If the executive officer exercises the option after the repurchase restriction lapses, it is reported in the same manner as a regular stock option. [Aug. 8, 2007]

Section 223. Item 402(g)—Executive Compensation; Option Exercises and Stock Vested Table

None

Section 224. Item 402(h)—Executive Compensation; Pension Benefits

None

Section 225. Item 402(i)—Executive Compensation; Nonqualified Defined Contribution and Other Nonqualified Deferred Compensation Plans

None

Section 226. Item 402(j)—Executive Compensation; Potential Payments Upon Termination or Change-in-Control

226.01 Item 402(j) requires quantitative disclosure of estimated payments and benefits, applying the assumptions that the triggering event took place on the last business day of the company's last completed fiscal year and the price per share of the company's securities is the closing market price as of that date. The date used for Item 402(j) quantification disclosure can affect the quantification of tax "gross-ups" with respect to the Internal Revenue Code Section 280G excise tax on excess parachute payments, such as by suggesting that benefits would be accelerated or by changing the five-year "base period" for computing the average annual taxable amount to which the parachute payment is compared. Where the last business day of the last completed fiscal year for a calendar year company is not December 31, the company may calculate the excise tax and related "gross-up" on the assumption that the change-in-control occurred on December 31, rather than the last business day of its last completed fiscal year, using the company stock price as of the last business day of its last completed fiscal year. The company may not substitute January 1 of the current year for the last business day of the company's last completed fiscal year, which would change the five-year "base period" to include the company's last completed fiscal year. [Aug. 8, 2007]

226.02 Following the end of the last completed fiscal year (2006), but before the proxy statement is filed, a named executive officer leaves the company (in early 2007). A Form 8-K disclosing this termination is filed, as required by Item 5.02(b) of Form 8-K. This named executive officer is not the principal executive officer or the principal financial officer and will not be a named executive officer for the current fiscal year (2007) based on Item 402(a)(3)(iv). The severance package that applied to the named executive officer's termination is not newly negotiated but instead has the same terms that otherwise would apply. In these limited circumstances, it is permissible to provide Item 402(j) disclosure for the named executive officer only for the triggering event that actually occurred (even though beyond the scope of Instruction 4 to Item 402(j) because it took place after the end of the last completed fiscal year), rather than providing the disclosure for several additional scenarios that no longer can occur. [Aug. 8, 2007]

226.03 A company will file a proxy statement for its regular annual meeting that also will solicit shareholder approval of a transaction in which the company would be acquired. The company has post-termination compensation arrangements that apply generally. Assuming that the acquisition is approved, however, all the named executive officers will be covered by termination agreements that that will be specific to the acquisition. The company cannot satisfy Item 402(j) by disclosing *only* the termination agreements that are specific to the pending acquisition for the following reasons: If the company's shareholders and/or any applicable regulatory authority do not approve the acquisition, the company's generally applicable post-termination arrangements will continue to apply. In addition, comparison of the acquisition-specific agreements with the generally applicable post-termination arrangements may be material. [Aug. 8, 2007]

Section 227. Item 402(k)—Executive Compensation; Compensation of Directors

227.01 Consulting arrangements between the registrant and a director are disclosable as director compensation under Item 402(k)(2)(vii), even where such arrangements cover services provided by the director to the issuer other than as director (e.g., as an economist). [Jan. 24, 2007]

227.02 A company has an executive officer (who is not a named executive officer) who is also a director. This executive officer does not receive any additional compensation for services provided as a director, and the conditions in Instruction 5.a.ii to Item 404(a) of Regulation S-K are satisfied. The compensation that this director receives for services as an executive officer does not need to be reported in the Director Compensation Table under Item 402(k) of Regulation S-K. The director may be omitted from the table, provided that footnote or narrative disclosure explains that the director is an executive officer, other than a named executive officer, who does not receive any additional compensation for services provided as a director. [Aug. 8, 2007]

227.03 A company has a director who also is an employee (but not an executive officer). Item 404(a) requires disclosure of the transaction pursuant to which the director is compensated for services provided as an employee. (Instruction 5 to Item 404(a) does not apply because the person is not an executive officer or does not have compensation reported for services as a director in the Director Compensation Table required by Item 402(k).) However, disclosure of this employee compensation transaction in the Director Compensation Table typically would result in a clearer, more concise presentation of the information. In this situation, if the employee compensation transaction is reported in the Director Compensation Table, it need not be repeated with the other Item 404(a) disclosure. Footnote or narrative disclosure to the Director Compensation Table should explain the allocation to services provided as an employee. [Aug. 8, 2007]

227.04 A current director previously was an employee of the company and receives a pension that was earned for services rendered as a company employee. If payment of the pension is not conditioned on his or her service as a director, the pension benefits do not need to be disclosed in the Director Compensation Table, whether or not the director receives compensation for services provided as a director. If service as a director generates new accruals to the pension, disclosure would be required in column (f) of the Director Compensation Table. [Aug. 8, 2007]

Section 228. Items 402(l) to (r)—Executive Compensation; Smaller Reporting Companies

None

U.S. Securities and Exchange Commission, Division of Corporation Finance: Staff Observations in the Review of Executive Compensation Disclosure

October 9, 2007

Executive Summary

The Division of Corporation Finance has completed its initial review of the executive compensation and related disclosure of 350 public companies under the Securities and Exchange Commission's new and revised rules relating to executive compensation disclosure. Two principal themes emerge from our reviews and our individualized comments to these companies.

First, the Compensation Discussion and Analysis needs to be focused on *how* and *why* a company arrives at specific executive compensation decisions and policies. This does not mean that disclosure needs to be longer or more technical; indeed shorter, crisper, and clearer would often be better. The focus should be on helping the reader understand the basis and the context for granting different types and amounts of executive compensation.

Second, the manner of presentation matters—in particular, using plain English and organizing tabular and graphical information in a way that helps the reader understand a company's disclosure. The executive compensation rules require companies to disclose a great deal of information. Techniques such as providing an executive summary, or creating tables or charts tailored to a company's particular executive compensation program, can make the disclosure more useful and meaningful. We encourage companies to continue thinking about how executive compensation information—from the big picture to the details—can be better organized and presented for both the lay reader and the professional.

Introduction

The Securities and Exchange Commission's new and revised rules relating to executive compensation disclosure became effective on November 7, 2006. These rules have significantly changed the disclosure a public company provides about how it compensates its most highly paid executive officers, including its principal executive officer and its principal financial officer, and its directors. On December 22, 2006, the Commission further amended the disclosure requirements for executive and director compensation with respect to how a public company discloses stock and option award compensation. The revised rules also update and clarify the related person transaction disclosure requirements and consolidate and add corporate governance disclosure requirements.

In the Division of Corporation Finance's regular review of public company current and periodic reports, we routinely provide comments to companies in which we seek clarification of current disclosure or additional information so we may better understand why a company made a particular disclosure. In some instances, we may ask a company to revise or enhance its disclosure by amending the document in which it has provided it. In other instances, we may ask a company to revise or enhance its disclosure in future filings.

In 2007, we undertook a project to review the executive compensation and other related disclosure of 350 public companies to evaluate compliance with the revised rules and provide guidance on how those companies could improve their disclosure. In identifying 350 companies for review, we sought to cover a broad range of industries. No one should interpret our selection of any company for review as part of this project as any indication of our views regarding the quality of that company's disclosure.

We have provided comments to companies based on a company's individual facts and circumstances and the nature and extent of its disclosure. Our goal in providing comments to companies is to assist them in enhancing the overall disclosure in their filings. These reviews are ongoing. Not less than 45 days after we complete our review of a company's filing, we will post the correspondence containing our comments and company responses to our comments on the SEC's EDGAR system.

In this report, we discuss the principal comments we provided to companies. Because our reviews are ongoing, our discussion is limited to our initial comments and does not reflect how companies may propose to revise their disclosure in response to them. We encourage companies to review their disclosure and prepare future disclosure consistent with the principles and themes of our comments. In our comments, we seek, where applicable, more direct, specific, clear and understandable disclosure. We believe this will foster enhanced and more informative executive compensation disclosure.

Manner of Presentation

Item 402 of Regulation S-K requires a company to provide "clear, concise, and understandable disclosure of all plan and non-plan compensation awarded to, earned by, or paid to the named executive officers . . . and directors . . . by any person for all services, rendered in all capacities . . . ."

In a number of instances, we suggested ways we thought companies could improve the manner in which they presented their executive compensation disclosure. For example, in a significant percentage of the filings we reviewed, we suggested that companies should consider making some items of their disclosure more prominent. Throughout our long history of reviewing company disclosure, we have often found that where a company emphasizes material information and de-emphasizes less important information, investor understanding of the company's disclosure is improved. As another example of our comments in this area, we suggested that companies could improve their presentation by emphasizing in their Compensation Discussion and Analysis how and why they established compensation levels, and de-emphasizing and shortening lengthy discussions of compensation program mechanics.

Format

For the most part, we found the format of executive compensation and other related disclosure to be relatively consistent across the 350 company filings. We commented on the format or manner of presentation where we found it adversely affected the overall readability of the company's disclosure. In adopting the revised rules, the Commission stated that the Compensation Discussion and Analysis is meant to be a narrative overview at the beginning of the compensation disclosure, putting into perspective the numbers in the tables that follow it. Where a company placed its required compensation tables before the Compensation Discussion and Analysis, we asked it to relocate those tables so that they would follow the Compensation Discussion and Analysis.

Approximately two-thirds of the companies we reviewed included charts, tables and graphs not specifically required by the revised rules. In almost every instance, we found these additional presentations to be helpful. For example, we found that a number of companies voluntarily included a table in which they presented information regarding potential payments upon termination or change-in-control. To enhance investor understanding of these tables, we suggested to some companies that they disclose the total amounts they would be required to pay their named executive officers upon termination or a change-in-control.

We encourage methods of presentation that are tailored to a particular company's circumstances, which we believe can be useful to investor understanding. Of the 350 companies we reviewed, a few companies included alternative summary compensation tables. Where a company presented an alternative summary compensation table that we found to be confusing or one which included compensation amounts calculated in a manner inconsistent with the revised rules, we asked the company to de-emphasize the alternative table and ensure that it was not presented more prominently than the required table. To the extent that a company's discussion or presentation of an alternative summary compensation table did not overshadow or detract from the required tables, we generally did not comment. Where the title of an alternative summary compensation table could lead a reader to assume that the alternative table was part of the required compensation tables, we asked the company to change the title. Where necessary, we asked companies to state that an alternative summary compensation table is not a substitute for the information the revised rules require. Finally, we asked those companies that presented alternative summary compensation tables to explain differences between compensation amounts presented in those tables and compensation amounts presented in the required tables.

Clarity

When the Commission adopted the revised rules it affirmed its support of plain English principles by stating that "[c]learer, more concise presentation of executive and director compensation, related person transactions, beneficial ownership and corporate governance matters can facilitate more informed investing and voting decisions in the face of complex information about these important areas." Companies are required to follow the drafting principles presented in Exchange Act Rules 13a-20 and 15d-20 when presenting their executive and director compensation, related person transactions, beneficial ownership and corporate governance disclosures in reports they are required to file under Exchange Act Section 13(a) or 15(d). These rules contain the plain English requirements.

It is important to recognize that disclosure can be clear and under-standable yet not meaningful or responsive to disclosure requirements. Conversely, disclosure can be responsive in content, but not clear and understandable. As we discuss below, we found that, in several instances, companies made a good faith effort to provide clear and understandable disclosure, but fell short of full compliance with the underlying disclosure requirements. For example, we found that a significant number of companies could improve their analyses of how and why they made certain executive compensation decisions. Where we ask a company to add analysis, or enhance its analysis, we do not necessarily think that it should lengthen its disclosure. Rather, careful drafting consistent with plain English principles could result in a shorter, more concise and effective discussion that complies with our rules.

In adopting the revised rules, the Commission stated that "[t]he purpose of the Compensation Discussion and Analysis disclosure is to provide material information about the compensation objectives and policies for named executive officers without resorting to boilerplate disclosure." Where we found that a company presented boilerplate disclosure, we asked it to provide a clear and concise discussion of its own facts and circumstances. For example, we asked a significant number of companies to replace boilerplate discussions of individual performance with more specific analysis of how the compensation committee considered and used individual performance to determine executive compensation. Where a company repeated information from the required compensation tables, we asked it to replace that disclosure with a clear and concise analysis of the information in the required compensation tables or to relocate the discussion to the narrative following the appropriate tables or the footnotes to those tables. Where a company's disclosure appeared identical to language in a compensation plan or employment agreement, we asked it to present the information in a clear and understandable manner.

Although we recognize that several of the required tables require companies to present a number of columns, we asked some companies to be mindful of font size in their tables and related footnote presentations and to increase, where practicable, font size to enhance readability.

Compensation Discussion and Analysis

When the Commission adopted the revised rules, it stated that they "are intended to provide investors with a clearer and more complete picture of compensation to principal executive officers, principal financial officers, the other highest paid executive officers and directors." To bring this picture into focus, the Commission adopted a new principles-based requirement for a company to provide material information about compensation objectives and policies for its named executive officers, the Compensation Discussion and Analysis.

In adopting the Compensation Discussion and Analysis, the Commission presented a disclosure concept and provided both principles and examples to help companies identify disclosure applicable to their own facts and circumstances. The Commission expressly stated that the Compensation Discussion and Analysis "strikes an appropriate balance that will effectively elicit meaningful disclosure, even as new compensation vehicles develop over time." The principles-based disclosure concept allows each company to assess its own facts and circumstances and determine what elements of the company's compensation policies and decisions are material and warrant disclosure.

The Commission explained that the primary focus of the Compensation Discussion and Analysis should be "[m]uch like the overview that we have encouraged companies to provide with their Management's Discussion and Analysis of Financial Condition and Results of Operations. . . ." The Commission stated that "the new Compensation Discussion and Analysis calls for a discussion and analysis of the material factors underlying compensation policies and decisions reflected in the data presented in the tables." Further, the Commission advised companies that "the Compensation Discussion and Analysis requirement is principles-based, in that it identifies the disclosure concept and provides several illustrative examples." The Commission also made clear that, in addition to discussing its compensation policies and decisions, a company responding to the principles-based disclosure requirement must analyze the material factors underlying those policies and decisions.

In many of our comment letters, we asked companies to enhance their analyses of compensation policies and discussions, including how they determined the amounts of specific compensation elements. In providing these comments to companies, our goal is to help companies enhance their discussions of *how* they arrived at the particular levels and forms of compensation that they chose to award to their named executive officers and *why* they pay that compensation, giving investors an *analysis* of the results of their compensation decisions. We discuss a number of these comment areas below.

Compensation Philosophies and Decision Mechanics

We found that a number of companies discussed their compensation philosophies and decision mechanics in great detail. We asked a substantial number of companies to refocus their Compensation Discussion and Analysis presentations on the substance of their compensation decisions and to disclose how they analyzed information and why their analyses resulted in the compensation they paid. For example, where a company provided a lengthy discussion about its compensation philosophies, we suggested that it improve its Compensation Discussion and Analysis by explaining how and why those philosophies resulted in the numbers they presented in the required tables. Similarly, where a company provided a lengthy discussion about its decision-making process, we suggested that, rather than explaining the process, it explain how its analysis of relevant information resulted in the decisions it made.

We asked a significant number of companies to discuss the extent to which the amounts paid or awarded under each compensation element affected the decisions they made regarding amounts they paid or awarded under other compensation elements. Consistent with Item 402(b)(1)(vi), we asked these companies to place in context how and why the determinations they made with regard to one compensation element may or may not have influenced decisions they made with respect to other compensation elements they contemplated or awarded. Where a company disclosed that its compensation committee analyzed "tally sheet" information, for example, we asked the company to explain what "tally sheet" information was and discuss how it impacted the committee's decision on compensation awards.

Differences in Compensation Policies and Decisions

Item 402(b) requires companies to discuss their compensation policies and their decisions regarding compensation of their named executive officers. When adopting this requirement, the Commission stated that "[t]he Compensation Discussion and Analysis should be sufficiently precise to identify material differences in compensation policies and decisions for individual named executive officers where appropriate. Where policies or decisions are materially similar, officers can be grouped together. Where, however, the policy or decisions for a named executive officer are materially different, for example in the case of a principal executive officer, his or her compensation should be discussed separately." Where a company's disclosure, including that in the Summary Compensation Table, led us to believe that its policies and decisions for individual named executive officers may be materially different, we reminded the company of the Commission's statement.

Performance Targets

Item 402(b)(2) provides fifteen examples of items that may be material elements of a company's compensation policies and decisions. Among the elements of a company's compensation policies and decisions that may be material and warrant disclosure is the company's use of corporate and individual performance targets. Evaluating whether corporate and individual performance targets warrant disclosure is not a new concept for public companies in preparing their executive compensation disclosure. Prior to 2006, the Commission's executive compensation disclosure rules required a company's compensation committee to describe each measure of company performance on which it based the Chief Executive Officer's compensation. Companies were not required to disclose target levels involving confidential commercial or business information where disclosure would have had an adverse effect on the company.

In adopting the revised rules, the Commission carefully considered public company disclosure practices and the differing views of a wide variety of commenters. Rather than presenting a specific requirement to disclose corporate and individual performance targets, the Commission adopted a principles-based disclosure model in which a company determines whether performance targets are a material element of its compensation policies and decisions. If a company determines they are material, Item 402 provides the disclosure framework for the company to follow.

We found that a substantial number of companies alluded to using, or disclosed that they used, corporate and individual performance targets to set compensation policies and make compensation decisions. We found that corporate performance targets ranged from financial targets such as earnings per share, EBITDA, and growth in net sales, to operational or strategic goals such as increases in market share or targets specific to a particular division or business unit. Most companies we reviewed disclosed that their compensation committees considered individual performance in making executive compensation decisions, although few companies disclosed how they analyzed individual performance or whether they focused on specific individual performance goals as part of that analysis.

We issued more comments regarding performance targets than any other disclosure topic in our review of the executive compensation and other related disclosure of the 350 companies. We often found it difficult to understand how companies used these performance targets or considered qualitative individual performance to set compensation policies and make compensation decisions. In making these comments, we do not seek to require companies to defend what may properly be subjective assessments in terms of purely objective or quantitative criteria, but rather only to clearly lay out the way that qualitative inputs are ultimately translated into objective pay determinations.

Where it appeared that performance targets were material to a company's policy and decision-making processes and the company did not disclose those targets, we asked it to disclose the targets or demonstrate to us that disclosure of the particular targets could cause it competitive harm.[1] We reminded companies of Instruction 4 to Item 402(b) which requires them to discuss how difficult it will be for the executive or how likely it will be for the company to achieve undisclosed target levels or other factors. Where a company omitted a performance target amount but discussed how difficult or likely it would be for the company or individual to achieve that target, we often sought more specific disclosure that would enhance investor understanding of the difficulty or likelihood.

Where a company presented a non-GAAP financial figure as a performance target and the company did not disclose how it would calculate that figure, consistent with Instruction 5 to Item 402(b)(2), we asked it to disclose how it would do so. For example, where a company disclosed total shareholder return as a performance target, we asked the company to disclose how it would calculate total shareholder return and describe how it would influence compensation decisions.

In adopting the revised rules and addressing commenters' requests for clarification about whether the Compensation Discussion and Analysis is limited to compensation for the last fiscal year or should also address prior or current year matters, the Commission stated:

> While the Compensation Discussion and Analysis may also require discussion of post-termination compensation arrangements, on-going compensation arrangements, and policies that the company will apply on a going-forward basis, Compensation Discussion and Analysis should also cover actions regarding executive compensation that were taken after the last fiscal year's end. Actions that should be addressed might include, as examples only, the adoption or implementation of new or modified programs and policies or specific decisions that were made or steps that were taken that could affect a fair understanding of the named executive officer's compensation for the last fiscal year. Moreover, in some situations it may be necessary to discuss prior years in order to give context to the disclosure provided.

While disclosure will always depend upon each company's particular facts and circumstances, there are a number of situations where a company may find it necessary to discuss prior and current year performance targets to place its disclosure in context or affect a fair understanding of a named executive officer's compensation. It also may be material for a company to disclose whether the company or the named executive officer achieved or failed to achieve targets in prior years. Those situations may include, for example, where a company has a multiple year compensation plan or where target levels vary materially between years. Where a company's disclosure implied that its current or prior year targets were material to an understanding of a named executive officer's compensation for the last fiscal year or were otherwise material in the context of that company's Compensation Discussion and Analysis, consistent with Instruction 2 to Item 402(b) of Regulation S-K, we asked it to disclose prior year and current year targets.

Benchmarks

When a company discloses that it has used compensation information from other companies to determine its own compensation levels, the company may be engaging in benchmarking its total compensation or other material elements of compensation. Benchmarking is presented in Item 402(b)(2) as an example of information that may be material to an individual company's compensation policies and decisions. If a company uses benchmarking, and it is material to its compensation policies and decisions, Item 402 requires it "to identify the benchmark and, if applicable, its components (including component companies)."

In a substantial number of comments, we asked companies to provide a more detailed explanation of how they used comparative compensation information and how that comparison affected compensation decisions.

Where a company stated that it used comparative compensation information, but retained discretion on how to use it, we asked it to provide appropriate disclosure. For example, if a company stated that it benchmarked its compensation, but it retained discretion to benchmark to a different point or range, or to not benchmark at all, we asked it to disclose the nature and extent of that discretion and whether or how it exercised that discretion.

Where a company indicated that it benchmarked compensation to its peers, but did not identify the peers or provide sufficient details concerning the benchmarking it used, we asked it to identify the companies to which it compared itself as well as the compensation components it used in that comparison. In addition, where a company indicated that it benchmarked compensation to a vague or broad range of data regarding those companies, we asked it to explain more specifically where its compensation fell within that range.

Change-in-Control and Termination Arrangements

We found that a significant number of companies could enhance their Compensation Discussion and Analysis by discussing and analyzing their decisions regarding change-in-control and termination arrangements with the named executive officers. Item 402(b)(1)(v) requires a company to disclose how it determines the amount and formula, where applicable, to pay for each compensation element. Item 402(b)(1)(vi) requires a company to discuss how each compensation element, and the company's decisions regarding that element, fit into the company's overall compensation objectives and affect decisions regarding other compensation elements. We asked a number of companies to disclose why they structured the material terms and payment provisions in their change-in-control and termination arrangements as they did. We also asked companies to discuss how potential payments and benefits under these arrangements may have influenced their decisions regarding other compensation elements.

Executive and Director Compensation Tables

We did not detect any common themes in our reviews of the required named executive officer and director compensation tables, the footnotes to the tables, or the narratives that followed them. Overall, we issued relatively few comments to companies on this area of their disclosure. Our comments regarding the required tables generally related to specific disclosure requirements or other information concerning a particular company's individual facts and circumstances. For example, if it appeared that a company made undisclosed assumptions in valuing option awards, we asked it to disclose those assumptions in the footnotes to the required table or provide an appropriate cross-reference to the discussion of the assumptions elsewhere in the company's filing. As another example, in the Grants of Plan-Based Awards table, where it appeared that a company did not disclose each grant of an award made to a named executive officer in the last completed fiscal year under any plan, we asked it to do so. Finally, where a company did not disclose the vesting dates of options, shares of stock, and equity incentive plan awards held at fiscal-year end by footnote to the applicable column in its Outstanding Equity Awards at Fiscal Year-End table, we asked it to do so.

Compensation Committee Report

A number of companies furnished compensation committee reports that did not include all of the information our rules require. For example, some companies did not indicate whether the compensation committee reviewed and discussed the Compensation Discussion and Analysis with management. We asked these companies to revise their future reports to include all required information.

Related Person Transaction Disclosure

We issued relatively few comments on related person transaction disclosure. We did, however, ask a number of companies to provide a statement that their policies and procedures for review, approval, or ratification of related person transactions are in writing and, if not, to explain how they evidence their policies and procedures. Furthermore, as the Commission stated when adopting the revised rules, disclosure regarding related person transactions is integral to "a materially complete picture of financial relationships with a company," and we will continue to review company disclosures with this standard in mind.

Corporate Governance

Our comments on corporate governance matters primarily focused on who was involved in making compensation decisions. We identified a number of areas where a company could provide a more complete picture of which individuals and which procedures it relied upon to consider and determine executive and director compensation, consistent with the requirements of Item 407(e)(3). Where a company's disclosure was unclear about exactly who made the compensation decisions, we asked for clarification. Item 407(e)(3)(ii) requires a company to describe the role of executive officers in determining or recommending the amount or form of executive and director compensation. Where a company indicated that its principal executive officer had a role in the compensation decision-making process, we asked it to describe his or her role. Item 407(e)(3)(iii) requires companies to disclose the role compensation consultants played in the decision-making process, and we asked a number of companies to do so. In particular, we asked companies to more specifically disclose the nature and scope of a consultant's assignment and material instructions the company gave it.

Endnote

1. Those companies that believe their explanation to us should receive confidential treatment should determine whether requesting confidential treatment of that explanation pursuant to Rule 83 is appropriate. SEC Rule 200.83 governs the procedures under which a company may request confidential treatment for information contained in a response letter or for supplemental information it provides to us. Rule 83 requires the company to submit a written request for confidential treatment at the time it provides the information to us.

Index

W

About the Author

Mark A. Borges is a principal with Compensia, Inc., a national management consulting firm providing executive compensation advisory services to compensation committees and senior management of knowledge-based and other companies. He is a frequent writer and speaker on SEC executive compensation disclosure issues.

Prior to joining Compensia, Borges was a principal with Mercer in Washington, D.C., where he provided assistance and advice to the firm's consultants and clients regarding legislative, regulatory, and judicial developments affecting executive compensation. Prior to Mercer, he was a Special Counsel in the Office of Rulemaking, Division of Corporation Finance with the SEC. Previously, Borges was General Counsel for ShareData, Inc., the leading provider of soft ware for employee stock plan administration, prior to its acquisition by E*TRADE Group, Inc. in 1998.

Borges practiced law with the firms of Ware & Friedenrich (now DLA Piper) and Pillsbury, Madison & Sutro (now Pillsbury Winthrop Shaw Pittman LLP), specializing in equity compensation and insider trading matters as well as venture capital finance.

A California native, Borges graduated from Humboldt State University and went on to receive his J.D. from Santa Clara University and an L.L.M. in Taxation from New York University. He is a member of the American Bar Association.